INTERNATIONAL
ECONOMICS

GRID SERIES IN ECONOMICS

INTERNATIONAL ECONOMICS

Theory and Practice

by

Alan Batchelder

Kenyon College

Gambier, Ohio

Kanji Haitani

State University of New York

College at Fredonia

Printed in the United States

1   2   3   4 ☒ 4   3   2   1

Library of Congress Cataloging in Publication Data

Batchelder, Alan B.   Aug. 25, 1980
  International Economics: Theory and Practice.

  (Grid Series in Economics)
  International Economic Relations.   I.   Haitani,
Kanji, joint author.   II.   Title.
HF1411.B323   337   70-21770
ISBN 0-88244-231-7

To Joan

To Masako

Contents

Preface

This book is designed to provide a full and clear exposition of the central theories of international economics and to relate them directly to the international economic problems and issues of the 1980s.

SALIENT FEATURES

The two salient features of this text are:

1. *Its thorough and careful exposition of the basic analytical tools of international economics.* This oldest branch of economics contains some of the discipline's most complex and difficult theoretical constructs. Yet some of these theories are indispensable for a full and complete understanding of the problems and issues that plague the international economic community today. We believe that the most effective way in which the essentials of international economic theory can be fully mastered with confidence by concerned students is to induce them to work with us, in a logical step-by-step progression, that builds up a few carefully selected theoretical constructs. We invite readers to join us in the exciting undertaking of working through selections from the treasury of international economic theory and to learn while doing so. To achieve maximum efficiency in this use of student time, many beautiful but esoteric intellectual exercises – e.g., the Rybczynski Theorem and the algebraic proof of the Marshall-Lerner Condition – have been left out of the text.

Our guiding rule has been this; if a theory is worth mentioning, it is worth the space required for a clear explanation of its character. Our object is not to expose students to terms and theories. Our object is to help students to master theories. Most of the book's exposition is conducted verbally, often with simple numerical examples and carefully developed diagrams. There are virtually no algebraic manipulations.

2. *Its emphasis on realism and relevance in dealing with the problems and issues of international economic relations.* The book contains ample quantities of discussion about the historical and institutional factors that shape the character of contemporary international economic relations and problems. This text is set apart from others, however, not

because it deals with real problems, but because it makes a determined and studious effort to connect reality with theory. Many texts, in our opinion, treat theory and reality as though they existed in separate universes. In contrast, much of this volume is devoted to the task of linking the two in meaningful and operational ways. Here is an example: The theory of comparative costs suggests that nations gain by specializing and trading in those goods in which each has comparative advantage. The reality of the matter, however, is that most nations try to export everything they *can* produce at home. Most businesspeople, workers and government officials do not think in terms of comparative costs, but debate the issue of rising imports in terms of national "interests" and international competitive strength. In this book, the gap between comparative cost theory and the lobbyists' arguments for protection is filled by extensive discussions of theories of trade patterns, export competitiveness, exchange-rate biases, and the political theory of trade restrictions.

Another example of realism: Most texts approach the issue of international monetary arrangements from the viewpoint of the theoretical dichotomy of fixed versus flexible exchange rates. Since the present system of managed floating does not fall neatly under either category, most texts treat it as something of an anomaly. Discussion, then, tends to center upon the relative merits and demerits of the two theoretical models. This book, in contrast, accepts the present system as completely legitimate, and discusses in depth the practical difficulties and the theoretical issues involved in its management.

AUDIENCE AND LEVEL

This book is designed as a text for an upper-division undergraduate course in international economics. We assume that each student has been exposed to the basic economic theory (both micro and macro) covered in the typical introductory course. For the benefit of the average student, some of the more advanced concepts — e.g., isoquants, production possibility frontiers, and consumer surplus — are explained fully before they are applied to particular problems. Simple numerical examples and diagrams are used extensively; no mathematics beyond the most elementary algebra is required.

LENGTH

The entire content of this volume, either with or without the appendixes, can be completed comfortably in a one-semester course. Some chapters may be omitted for a one-quarter course. For two-semester or two-quarter courses, other books and articles can be added. The Instructor's Manual suggests alternative outlines for courses of different length.

PEDAGOGICAL DEVICES

Each chapter is divided into *sections,* each preceded by a centered heading printed in capital letters. The appendixes that are included in some chapters can be omitted without loss of continuity. The end-of-chapter questions are directly related to the specific discussions, tables, or figures contained in that chapter.

Most international economics texts introduce their readers to all the basic theories. This book is different because every model is presented step by step so beginners can move forward earning growing confidence. We have tried to be kind to instructors by including all the basic theories, institutions, and history. We have also tried to be kind to students. When explaining difficult and involved theoretical concepts, we have preferred to err on the side of using too many, rather than too few, words. In many cases, we explain a particular concept in more than one way. In every case, we have paid special attention to logical progression of exposition.

Throughout, our stress is on helping students learn to *do,* to become able to take pen and paper and reason out each theory independently. In addition, we have applied the theories to current events. We want to convince students that "economic theory" means "useful." Therefore, we have concentrated on, among other subjects, real gains to individuals from trade, the bogey of cheap foreign labor, the depredations of the Organization of Petroleum Exporting Countries, the determinants of international competitiveness, and the present system of floating exchange rates. In each descriptive section, we have tied the description of institutions and events to the relevant theories. For example, we have made extensive use of the theory of comparative advantage when explaining international exchange rates, the role of cheap foreign labor, and the history of American tariffs.

Students who read carefully and who work the end-of-chapter problems will come to know how each theoretical model works, why it works, and how they can apply it. We hope that, as students read this book, they will become missionaries able and eager to explain much of international economics to people who have not completed a well taught course in this most useful subject.

ACKNOWLEDGEMENTS

James M. Wilson of Grid Publishing is largely responsible for the completion of this book. His unwavering support and confidence kept the authors going when other attractions tended to distract them.

H. Steward Fitzgibbon, III, Anderson L. Hartzell, Andrew M. Johnston, Kenneth J. Patsey, Steven O. Russell, and Eric R. Stahlfeld were the first — very able — students to use the first draft of the text. Their comments were very useful to us when we were preparing revisions. Professor Donald A. Wells, of the University of Arizona, read most of the manuscript and made numerous suggestions. We were pleased to be able to incorporate almost all of those suggestions in the final text.

Kathy Brissey Crowe, a most excellent typist, translated the manuscript into text copy. We are grateful for her able help.

We hope to prepare a second edition of this book. We, therefore, invite suggestions from our readers. We will most gratefully acknowledge all suggestions that we follow.

Alan B. Batchelder
Gambier, Ohio

Kanji Haitani
Fredonia, New York

August 1980.

PART I

INTRODUCTION

The Gains from Trade Versus Our Fear of Goods

More is better than less. Not always. Not everywhere. "One more for the road" would be an exception to the rule. More rattlesnakes would also be an exception. But for most people most of the time, more life, more time, and more production are better than less.

The primary objective of most economic analysis is to identify practical ways to get more output per person. And more output per person is expected to lead to longer lives, more leisure time, and an expanding range of choices for individuals. Microeconomics concentrates on efficiency in the use of fully employed resources. Macroeconomics concentrates on getting full employment of fixed quantities of resources. Growth economics concentrates on getting more resources. All of this to get a bigger output per person. In general, the public applauds all of these goals of economists. And then there is international economics. Again, economists work to raise output per person. But in this area, many among the public are doubtful and many are opposed. Consider this analysis by radio's "Midnight Economist," William R. Allen:

TRADE IF YOU MUST — BUT STAY AWAY FROM FOREIGNERS

Despite romantic notions of the shrewd but honest "Yankee trader," many have doubts about international trade — at least, about imports. Whatever may be the attractiveness of domestic trade, we best beware trade with foreigners, who are wily rather than shrewd, devious rather than honest, and who commonly have beady, little eyes, set too close together.

The misgivings seem to be supported by the recent United States balance of trade. Beginning in the 1870s — a century ago — Americans consistently sold more goods and services to the rest of the world than they bought. We have had an "export surplus" — until the last few years. [In recent years, we have imported more than we have exported] and this "import balance" has been substantial. The goods-and-services import balance is commonly, but misleadingly, called an "unfavorable" balance or a "deficit."

Who gains and who loses in a trade? It *is* true — isn't it? — that what is gained by one trader has to be lost by the other? From where else could the gain have come?

No, the gain of the one trader does *not* come out of the hide of the other. If that *were* the case, why would the loser have participated in this uncoerced exchange?

But *how* can Charlie and Linus swap assets so that *both* are made better off? There are *mutual* gains when *each* trader prefers to have the things he buys than the things he must sell. Charlie prefers, or puts a greater value on, the goods he imports than the goods he exports in order to pay for what he buys. But the same is true of Linus. Charlie and Linus are not twins in their preferences. With different tastes and different inventories, they attach different values to goods. And *each* considers *himself* to be better off, on balance, by obtaining his imports for the export price he is required to pay.

But wait. Are we saying that a person is made better off by what he *imports* (that is, by what he *acquires*) and that exports are a *price* to be paid, a *cost* to be borne? Precisely. The gains from trade emanate from *imports*; exports are a *drain* of wealth; and the more we get per unit of exports, the better.

So we currently have an import balance of goods and services, as we did throughout our first century, a period of great economic growth. When we have an import balance, we obtain, for our own consumption and investment, more of the output of the rest of the world than they get from us. Faced with scarcity, how nice it is to have the rest of the world contribute, on balance, to *our* standard of living.

Normally, it seems obvious that a buyer gains from what he *gets,* not from what he gives up — and the *lower* the price he must pay for what he gets, the greater is his gain. But in the realm of international economics, in which we deal with those wily, devious, beady-eyed foreigners, some oddly prefer less to more of good things and to pay higher prices than lower.[1]

Though odd, it is true that many Americans want to export more goods and services than they import. They want an export surplus in order to provide jobs for American workers. That opinion begs the question, "Why should Americans work and produce so more products can be given to foreigners than foreigners give to Americans in exchange?" The same question can be asked using William Allen's terminology, "Why should Americans pay foreigners a *price* which is higher than the value of Americans' *acquisitions* from foreigners?" The answer to both these questions is "Unless some Americans want to make a gift

to foreigners, there is no reason." (An export surplus can be an investment in the future, but that is not why many Americans want a
surplus.)

THE FEAR OF GOODS

Yet many Americans — and many Germans, Japanese, and French —
retain, from past centuries, a "fear of goods." They fear too much will be
produced, and fear even more will be imported. As individuals, they
never have enough. But when influencing government policy, they
want to get rid of goods and prevent more from coming into the country.
They favor putting people to work, and then exporting their products.
And they hope more goods will be sent out as exports than will be
permitted into the country as imports.

As individuals, most Americans — and most Germans, Japanese, and
French — would not like the idea of working longer hours merely so
foreigners can have more. They would rather work fewer hours and
enjoy consuming better and cheaper goods made by foreigners. Yet more
work and less consumption are in fact what the advocates of restrictions
on imports are suggesting when they urge, "Restrict imports and save
our jobs!" This is indeed odd; it defies common sense.

Common sense can be — and often is — a powerful weapon in our
battles against specious reasoning. Yet it can go only so far. Too often,
common sense becomes a stumbling block to true understanding. Common sense tells us we should restrict imports and protect our jobs. But
common sense also tells us that cheaper imports help raise our living
standards. So what are we to do? Common sense can no longer be relied
upon since it gives us conflicting answers.

WHEN COMMON SENSE FAILS

When common sense fails, we must resort to reasoning. We must
analyze the problem rationally and come to a reasoned conclusion.
Unlike common sense, reasoning is often abstruse, tedious, and laborious. Yet reason we must, if we want to be liberated from ignorance,
prejudice, and sophistry.

This book provides reasoned analysis of the problems and issues of
international economic relations. The ultimate objective of this text
remains one with that of microeconomics, macroeconomics, and growth
economics — all three of which provide relevant theories and are used
extensively here. It seeks to identify practical measures to raise output
per person in order to permit longer lives, more leisure time, and an
expanding range of choices for individuals. To this end, our analysis
starts with the issue of free trade versus protectionism. Much of this

book is devoted to an analysis of the ongoing struggle between advocates of fewer restrictions on international trade and advocates of restrictions to limit imports. The struggle is an old one. The advocates of government restrictions on trade are members of the world's oldest professional political lobby. This book will yield them little comfort. Most of the analysis in this book will produce arguments in support of fewer restrictions, more exports, *and* more imports.

A basic question is, "Why should freer trade lead to greater output?" That question and others can be answered in real terms without mentioning money or exchange rates between the moneys of different nations. Much of the analysis of this book is in real terms.

But most foreign trade involves money. Money obscures the nature of real factors. Money confuses and misleads common sense. Money thus complicates international trade and adds to the need for reasoned economic analysis. Therefore, much of this book is devoted to an explanation of the role of money in foreign trade. Through real analysis and through monetary analysis, the ultimate objective remains to explain the means whereby international exchanges of goods and services raise the well-being of the residents of participating nations.

ENDNOTE

1. William R. Allen, *Midnight Economist: Radio Essays* (Los Angeles: International Institute for Economic Research, 1980), pp. 59-60. William R. Allen is professor of economics at U.C.L.A. and president of the International Institute for Economic Research. His nightly series of three-minute economics commentaries is heard on nearly 200 radio stations around the country. This particular commentary was aired in July 1979.

2

The Facts of International Economic Life

The subject matter of this book is *international economic relations*. They are sufficiently different from domestic (or *intra*national) economic relations to warrant a separate field of study. International economics addresses itself to the task of explaining and analyzing international economic relations and their attendant problems.

FACTORS MAKING INTERNATIONAL RELATIONS UNIQUE

What factors make *international* economic transactions different or uniquely separated from *intranational* transactions? In what basic way does a movement of goods from California to Mexico, for example, differ from that between California and New York? Although various reasons may be readily cited, a little reflection will convince us that the fundamental source of the difference between international and intranational economic relations is found in the political divisions of the world into sovereign nation-states.

POLITICAL DIVISIONS

The basic fact of global economic life is that the world consists of sovereign nation-states each with its own sets of laws, regulations, and policies. While residents of the State of New York, for example, can engage in commercial transactions with residents of the State of California with virtually no restriction, United States residents may not so readily enter similar relations with residents of other nations. Different countries may have different laws and regulations governing the importing and exporting of products. International exchanges of goods are often subject to such barriers as tariff duties and import quotas. In extreme cases, as in the Centrally Planned Economies — such as Russia and China — external economic transactions are conducted solely by government agencies. Even in the market-oriented economies, the extent to which trade and payments relations are subject to governmental control varies from country to country.

Government intervention with international flows of goods, services, and capital is but one of the several ways in which political divisions affect the character of international economic relations. Political divisions also mean the existence of different national monetary systems, the relative immobility of factors of production across national boundaries, and differences in domestic economic policies.

National Monetary Systems

One important corollary of political divisions is the existence of different national currencies. In order to pay for goods and services traded internationally, one national currency must be exchanged for another. Such an exchange requires foreign exchange markets in which owners of one national currency can purchase another currency. In foreign exchange markets — as in all other markets — changes in supply and in demand bring frequent changes in the market price of each currency. These changes in the values of national currencies affect, and are affected by, the volume and composition of the flows of goods, services, and capital among nations. Furthermore, these changes in the rates of exchange between national currencies expose international traders and investors to exchange losses (or gains), which present no problem to those who trade and invest domestically.

Governments frequently intervene in foreign exchange markets to keep the exchange rates of currencies from moving freely in response to supply and demand forces. Governments also may impose restrictions on transactions in foreign exchange, thereby affecting the international flows of goods, services, and capital.

International Factor Immobility

Another significant corollary of political divisions is the relative immobility of the factors of production across national boundaries. Partly because of political restrictions (e.g., immigration laws) and in part because of the differences in languages and other sociocultural factors, labor is relatively immobile internationally. While it is relatively easy for a New Yorker to move to California seeking a better employment opportunity, movements between, say, Argentina and India, are much more difficult and costly. Similar inhibitions exist, though to a lesser degree, against international movements of capital and management.

International factor immobility tends to perpetuate the substantial differences in real wages that now exist among nations. These real wage differences reflect differences among nations in output per capita. Table 2-1 shows Gross National Product (GNP) and GNP per capita for selected nations for 1977. These figures show that, in 1977, the United States, with a GNP of nearly $2 trillion, was the world's foremost industrial power, followed by the Soviet Union, Japan, and West Germany.

TABLE 2-1   GNP AND GNP PER CAPITA OF SELECTED COUNTRIES, 1977

	GNP (billions of U.S. dollars)[a]	GNP per capita (U.S. dollars)[a]
Low Income Countries		
Bangladesh	7.3	90
Ethiopia	3.3	110
Zaire	3.3	130
Burma	4.4	140
India	94.8	150
Viet Nam	8.1	160
Pakistan	14.2	190
Indonesia	40.1	300
Egypt	12.1	320
Nigeria	33.2	420
Thailand	18.4	420
Philippines	20.0	450
Colombia	17.7	720
Middle Income Countries		
Korea, Republic of	29.5	820
Turkey	46.5	1,110
Mexico	70.9	1,120
China, Republic of (Taiwan)	19.7	1,170
South Africa	36.2	1,340
Brazil	157.9	1,360
Argentina	46.4	1,730
Iran	75.2	2,160
Spain	115.8	3,190
Industrialized Countries		
Italy	194.4	3,440
United Kingdom	247.1	4,420
Japan	641.8	5,670
France	387.1	7,290
Germany, Federal Republic of	501.0	8,160
Canada	197.1	8,460
United States	1,874.4	8,520
Sweden	76.8	9,250
Centrally Planned Economies		
China, People's Republic of	345.4	390
U.S.S.R.	781.9	3,020
Poland	109.3	3,150
Germany, Democratic Republic of	79.1	4,680

[a]Based on conversion at average rates of exchange for the 1975-77 period.

Source: International Bank for Reconstruction and Development, *World Development Report, 1979* (New York: Oxford University Press, 1979), pp. 126-127.

Excluding the so-called Centrally Planned Economies, we may divide the nations of the world into three categories by their 1977 GNP per capita: industrially developed nations and oil-rich countries with per capita output in 1977 of $3,200 or more, semideveloped countries with per capita GNP of between $800 and $3,200, and less developed countries with per capita output of $800 or less. Subsequent chapters will show that these wide international disparities in per capita output and income are due to international differences in technological sophistication and in endowments of factors of production. Those later chapters will also show that these international differences in applied technology and in factor endowments constitute the basic causes of international trade.

Domestic Economic Policies

Yet a third corollary of the existence of different political units is the great variety among nations in their domestic economic policies. We have already noted that nations may have different foreign trade and exchange-rate policies. Additionally, there is a host of domestic economic policies that are pursued with different objectives, mechanisms, and degrees of vigor: monetary policy, fiscal policy, incomes policy, development policy, environmental policy, energy policy, and antitrust policy, to name a few. Economic relations between nations pursuing different economic policies or pursuing similar policies with different emphases are bound to generate problems that are uniquely international in nature.

NATIONALISM

The preceding paragraphs of this chapter have enumerated various factors that derive from the sovereignty of nations and that characterize international trade. One other factor — nationalism — distinguishes domestic from international economic relations. As subsequent chapters will show, international trade is fundamentally no different from trade between regions within a country (or, for that matter, trade between persons). Nations, as well as regions within a nation, gain from specialization and exchange made possible by the differences in the distribution of productive factors and in the level of technology. Why is it, then, that the residents of a nation often exhibit strong negative feelings towards imports from other nations, while being indifferent to "imports" from other regions within the same country? The answer must be found in the emotional and chauvinistic content of nationalism which often drives people to see the world as divided into "us versus foreigners." This mentality tends to cloud the basic economic logic behind international trade, namely, that all trading nations gain from specialization and exchange. Thus, to the extent that nationalism is a powerful force in a nation, it will distinguish the nation's international economic relations from its domestic relations.

SOME STATISTICS ON INTERNATIONAL TRADE AND PAYMENTS

It may be instructive to examine the magnitudes of some key aspects of international economic relations. Table 2-1 showed the great disparity that exists among nations in GNP per capita. This section presents additional statistics concerning international merchandise trade (volume, composition, and direction), balances of payments, and exchange rates of national currencies.

WORLD TRADE STATISTICS

Table 2-2 shows the volume of exports and imports of major trading nations and economic blocks during 1978. An examination of the table

TABLE 2-2   WORLD EXPORTS AND IMPORTS, 1978

Country	Exports		Imports	
	Value[a]	Percent	Value[a]	Percent
World[b]	1,188[c]	100.0	1,232[c]	100.0
Industrial countries	814	68.5	837	68.0
United States	144	12.2	183	14.9
West Germany	142	12.0	122	9.9
Japan	98	8.2	80	6.5
France	79	6.6	82	6.7
United Kingdom	72	6.1	79	6.4
Italy	56	4.7	56	4.5
Netherlands	50	4.2	54	4.4
Belgium	45	3.8	49	4.0
Canada	48	4.0	46	3.7
Others[d]	80	6.7	86	7.0
Other Europe, Oceania, and South Africa	80	6.7	97	7.9
Oil Exporting Countries	141	11.9	102	8.3
Less Developed Countries	153	12.9	194	15.7

[a]Billions of U.S. dollars.
[b]Excluding Centrally Planned Economies.
[c]The value of world imports exceeds the value of exports because most nations report import values c.i.f. (cost, insurance, freight) and export values f.o.b. (free on board).
[d]Austria, Denmark, Norway, Sweden, and Switzerland.
Source: International Monetary Fund, *International Financial Statistics*, September 1979, pp. 46-47.

reveals some interesting facts. Note, for example, that the three largst exporting nations in the world were the United States, West Germany, and Japan, with the export value of the United States being only slightly larger than that of West Germany and about 50 percent larger than that of Japan.

A nation's share in world trade can be measured by the average of its export and import volumes expressed as a percent of world trade volume. Using this measure, we observe that the United States' share of world trade was 13.5 percent in 1978, while the industrially developed nations accounted for about two-thirds of world trade. Oil-exporting nations accounted for about one-tenth of world trade, while all other LDCs combined accounted for only 14 percent. The large trade surplus (i.e., exports less imports) of the oil-exporting nations was offset largely by the equally large trade deficit of the oil-importing developing nations.

The relative importance of international trade for each country may be indicated by the "trade ratio," or the volume of trade (the mean average of its exports and imports) divided by the country's GNP. Trade ratios of twelve nations are shown in Table 2-3. These ratios indicate the relative "openness" or "closedness" of the national economies. The United States and Brazil, with their vast size and great diversity of resources, are relatively independent of foreign trade, as indicated by their low trade ratios of 7.7 and 7.4 percent, respectively, for 1978. The larger West European nations, on the other hand, are more dependent on foreign trade, with trade ratios ranging roughly from 15 to 25 percent. Smaller trading nations, in contrast, are much more dependent on foreign trade. Japan's trade ratio, 9.1 percent, is surprisingly low in view of the nation's dependence on imported raw materials and its visibility in world export markets.

TABLE 2-3   FOREIGN TRADE[a] AS A PERCENTAGE OF GNP, SELECTED COUNTRIES, 1978

Country	Percentage	Country	Percentage
Taiwan	49.6	Italy	21.5
Belgium	48.0	West Germany	20.7
Netherlands	39.8	France	17.0
South Korea	30.1	Japan	9.1
United Kingdom	24.4	United States	7.7
Canada	23.3	Brazil	7.4

[a]Foreign trade equals average of merchandise exports and imports.
Source: International Monetary Fund, *International Financial Statistics,* September 1979.

U.S. TRADE STATISTICS

Table 2-4 shows the U.S. trade balances in major product categories in 1970, in 1974, and in 1978, as well as export and import values for 1978.

TABLE 2-4   U. S. TRADE BALANCE BY CATEGORY, SELECTED YEARS, AND U. S.
EXPORTS AND IMPORTS, 1978
(billions of U. S. dollars)

| Product | Trade Balance[a] | | | Exports 1978 | Imports 1978 |
	1970	1974	1978		
Merchandise, total	2.64	− 3.11	− 30.88	141.15	172.03
Agricultural products	1.48	11.62	14.45	29.41	14.96
Crude materials, excl. fuels	1.29	4.86	6.25	15.55	9.30
Mineral fuels and lubricants	− 1.48	− 22.01	− 38.23	3.88	42.11
Manufactured products	1.35	2.42	− 13.35	92.31	105.66
Chemicals	2.38	4.80	6.19	12.62	6.43
Iron and steel	− 0.76	− 2.59	− 5.55	1.71	7.26
Machinery, total	6.09	12.08	12.62	37.02	24.40
Electrical	0.03	1.68	1.80	6.97	5.17
Transport equipment, total	0.62	2.05	− 0.97	22.25	23.22
Motor vehicles and parts	− 1.52	− 2.38	− 7.39	13.24	20.63
Textiles	− 0.53	0.19	0.03	2.23	2.20

[a]Exports minus imports.

Source: U. S. Department of Commerce, *Survey of Current Business,* various issues.

Of the $141 billion in exports in 1978, a little over one-third (34.6 percent) were primary products (largely agricultural commodities) and the rest were manufactured goods. Of manufactured exports, 64 percent were machinery and transport equipment, and 14 percent were chemicals. Of the $172 billion in imports, 25 percent were mineral fuels (predominantly petroleum) and 61 percent were manufactured goods. Of manufactured imports, machinery and transport equipment constituted 45 percent, and iron and steel accounted for 7 percent. The overall trade pattern of the United States in 1978 can thus be described as one of exporting primarily manufactured products (mainly machinery and equipment) and secondarily agricultural products, and importing primarily manufactured goods (fairly well distributed among various product categories) and secondarily petroleum.

Table 2-4 shows that the overall trade balance of the country declined drastically in the 1970s, but there were marked differences in the trends among the major product categories. The most conspicuous development was the sharp rise in the importation of petroleum, starting in 1974. Undoubtedly the $38-billion net petroleum imports of 1978 contributed significantly to the $31-billion deficit in the merchandise trade account of that year. Other deficit areas were iron and steel and motor vehicles. The table also shows that the United States had large surpluses in agricultural products, crude materials, chemicals, and machinery in general.

The absence of a definite surplus-deficit pattern in the United States trade in manufactures merits a brief note. In view of the often-heard clamor for protection by both management and labor in such distressed industries as textiles and clothing, color television, steel, and automobiles, the ordinary American citizen cannot be faulted for being under the impression that imports of foreign manufactured goods are larger, even much larger, than exports of American manufactured goods. It is true that in some manufacturing industries, American imports exceed exports. Table 2-5 shows this to be the case in the automobile, steel, textile, clothing, footwear, and consumer electronics industries. But a very different picture emerges when we compare imports and exports in other major manufacturing industries, also shown in Table 2-5. The excess of imports over exports in the six industries listed above was offset more than twice over by the surplus of exports over imports in just four industries: aircraft, computers, general machinery, and chemicals. An inevitable conclusion is that the United States still enjoys eminent competitive strength in many manufactured products, particularly in machinery and chemicals. Subsequent chapters will examine the theory of comparative advantage (why a nation is competitive in some products and not in others), but suffice it to say at this point that (1) a nation cannot as a rule have superior competitiveness in *all* products, (2) those who are hurt by imports, in any country, are naturally vociferous in their demand for protection, and (3) those who benefit from imports and those who do well in exporting tend to remain quiet respecting their own nation's foreign trade policies.

TABLE 2-5   UNITED STATES TRADE BALANCES IN SELECTED
COMMODITIES, 1974-75 AVERAGE[a]
(millions of U. S. dollars)

Aircraft and parts[b]	5,437
Computers and parts	2,094
Other nonelectric machinery[c]	10,645
Basic chemicals and compounds	1,474
Motor vehicles and parts	− 1,824
Steel products	− 1,956
Textile, clothing, and footwear	− 2,925
Consumer electronics	− 1,763

[a]Free alongside ship (f.a.s.) values.
[b]Excludes engines.
[c]Excludes aircraft, automobile engines and parts, and office machines.
Source: *International Economic Report of the President, 1977*, p. 152.

Table 2-6 shows the geographical distribution of United States exports and imports for 1977-78. Canada was the largest trading partner of the United States, followed by Japan. About 61 percent of American exports went to the developed countries in 1977-78, while America received from them about 56 percent of its imports. Imports from the OPEC countries constituted about one fifth of total U. S. imports. The trade volume between the United States and the Centrally Planned Economies was surprisingly small; U. S. purchases from them were insignificant, having been roughly one percent of total U. S. imports.

TABLE 2-6   UNITED STATES TRADE BY GEOGRAPHICAL REGIONS,
1977-78 AVERAGE
(billions of U.S. dollars)

	Exports to	Imports from	Balance
Canada	27.1	31.6	− 4.5
Japan	11.7	21.5	− 9.8
Western Europe	37.3	32.1	5.2
(Of which European Community)	(29.6)	(25.6)	(4.0)
Other developed countries[a]	4.1	3.6	0.5
Less developed countries[b]	33.1	37.0	− 3.9
OPEC members[c]	15.5	32.4	−16.9
Centrally planned economies	3.6	1.6	2.0
Total	132.4	159.8	−27.4

[a]Australia, New Zealand, and Republic of South Africa.
[b]Excluding OPEC members.
[c]Organization of Petroleum Exporting Countries. Figures for Qatar and United Arab Emirates are estimated by the authors.
Source: U.S. Bureau of the Census, *Statistical Abstracts of the United States: 1979*, pp. 862-865.

WORLD PAYMENTS STATISTICS

Table 2-7 shows the current-account balances of payments of selected countries for the 1972-78 period. (A nation's current-account balance lists all its external receipts and payments which arise from flows of goods and services and of grants. Capital movements are not included.

TABLE 2-7   CURRENT ACCOUNT BALANCES OF PAYMENTS OF SELECTED
COUNTRIES, 1972-78
(billions of U.S. dollars)

Country	1972-78 Average	1977	1978
Canada	− 2.8	− 4.0	− 4.6
France	− 1.7	− 3.2	3.8
West Germany	5.1	3.8	8.9
Italy	− 0.4	2.3	6.3
Japan	4.8	11.0	17.5
United Kingdom	− 2.2	0.7	0.8
United States	− 0.5	− 13.9	− 13.9
Developed nations, total	−	− 25.7[a]	5[a]
OPEC nations	−	37.9[a]	14[a]
Non-oil developing nations	−	− 14.6[a]	− 23[a]
Centrally planned economies	−	2.4[a]	4[a]

[a]Estimate by *Encyclopaedia Britannica*.
Source: International Monetary Fund, *International Financial Statistics*, July 1978 and September 1979; *Encyclopaedia Britannica, 1979 Book of the Year*, p. 333.

See Chapter 14.) West Germany, Japan, and the oil-exporting nations as a group ran large surpluses during the period, while the United States, Canada, and the less developed nations as a group ran deficits. One striking fact of international payments during the 1970s was the huge current-account surpluses of the oil-exporting countries. This means the oil-importing nations must have had huge deficits, since one nation's surplus is necessarily another nation's deficit. During the 1970s, the deficits were shared by developed and developing nations alike, except that some developed nations — notably West Germany and Japan — managed to run surpluses in spite of sharply rising prices of petroleum.

WORLD EXCHANGE RATE STATISTICS

Since 1973, most of the currencies of the developed, market-oriented countries have been "floating;" that is, their values are determined by the forces of supply and demand in foreign exchange markets with varying degrees of intervention by national governments. To the extent that governments intervene more or less to influence exchange rates, the float is said to be more or less "dirty." During the 1970s, most floats were very dirty. Table 2-8 shows the changing values of some representative currencies between 1970 and 1980. (Curious readers will find that each issue of the *Wall Street Journal* reports on the exchange rates of the preceding business day.)

TABLE 2-8   EXCHANGE RATES OF SELECTED MAJOR CURRENCIES, SELECTED YEARS

(Units of national currencies per U.S. dollar)

Currency	1970[a]	1974[a]	1978[a]	1980[b]
Australian dollar	0.8929	0.7536	0.8692	0.8635
Belgian franc	50.000	36.123	28.800	28.190
Canadian dollar	1.0112	0.9912	1.1860	1.1506
Deutsche mark	3.6600	2.4095	1.8280	1.7628
French franc	5.5542	4.4445	4.1800	4.0955
Italian lira	625.00	649.43	829.75	837.60
Japanese yen	360.00	300.95	194.60	219.50
Netherlands guilder	3.6200	2.5065	1.9690	1.9300
Pound sterling	0.4167	0.4258	0.4915	0.4237
South African rand	0.7143	0.6896	0.8696	0.7722
Spanish peseta	70.000	56.112	70.110	70.000
Swedish krona	5.1732	4.0805	4.2955	4.1580
Swiss franc	4.3730	2.5400	1.6200	1.6265

[a]Year-end figures.
[b]As of 30 June 1980.
Source: [a]International Monetary Fund, *International Financial Statistics Yearbook 1979*. [b]*Wall Street Journal*, 1 July 1980, p. 29.

It may be noted that the figures shown in Table 2-8 are the number of units of national currencies per U.S. dollar. Thus, a *decrease* in the figures represents an *increase* in the value of the national currency (an appreciation or upward revaluation), and simultaneously a corresponding *decrease* in the value of the dollar (a depreciation or devaluation of the dollar). For example, the Deutsche mark appreciated from DM3.66 to a dollar in 1970 to DM1.7628 to a dollar in 1980. The U.S. dollar, during the same period, depreciated from $0.2733 (= 1 ÷ 3.66) to a Deutsche mark to $0.5673 (= 1 ÷ 1.7628) to a Deutsche mark.

Some currencies appreciated considerably against the dollar during the 1970s, while many others depreciated vis-à-vis the dollar. These changes have a very important bearing on the changes in each country's national output and income, trade, and balance of payments. Exchange rates affect, and in turn are affected by, these variables, as will be shown in subsequent chapters.

STUDY QUESTIONS

1. In what basic ways are *international* economic relations different from *intranational* (or domestic) economic relations?
2. Give some concrete examples of international economic relations which you have found reported in the media in recent months. Be sure to include some examples that do not involve any merchandise (goods) movements and some other examples that involve neither goods nor services (e.g., insurance, transportation, royalties, tourism).
3. Classify the examples in Question 2 above as being primarily concerned with the movements of goods and services (trade relations), movements of financial claims (payments relations), or movements in factors of production.
4. Identify and describe the *political* aspects of the international economic relations you observed in Question 2 above.
5. What do you think would happen to the U.S. economy if the United States cut off all of its international economic relations today?
6. How do you think the international disparities in per capita income and output affect international economic relations? As best you can at this early stage, write *why* you believe these effects follow.
7. If you have not already done so in answer to Question 6, tell what you think are the effects of cheap foreign labor upon American working men and women.
8. Do you think imports are hurting the American economy and American workers? Do you think imports are hurting the economies and workers of America's trading partners (say Canada, Japan, or Germany)? If your answers are yes, why do you think nations choose to engage in activities that hurt themselves? If your answers are no, why do you think many people believe otherwise?
9. How do you characterize the United States as a trading nation? (Consider its trade ratio, the commodity composition of its imports and exports, and the geographical distribution of its imports and exports.)

10. Find the most recent values of the currencies given in Table 2-8. Do you notice any significant changes in values since the mid-1980 figures? If so, what do you think have caused the changes?

11. Do you think a deficit in America's current-account balance is favorable or unfavorable to the nation? Why?

PART II

SOCIAL WELFARE: THEORIES OF THE GAINS FROM TRADE

3

Gains from Comparative Advantage Specialization

WHY IMPORT IF WE CAN MAKE IT?

After the Korean War ended in 1953, America became a pretty quiet place; so quiet that one of the Senate's most heated debates during 1955 was over President Eisenhower's foreign trade program. The Administration bill (H.R. 1) called for an extension of the President's powers to cut tariffs — without prior approval of Congress — in exchange for comparable trade concessions from other nations. There was passionate opposition. Senator George W. Malone, Republican of Nevada and the bill's sharpest critic, charged that the bill was "an economic Yalta[1], a sellout of American working men and investors."[2] On the day the Senate voted approval, the *New York Times* published a satirical letter from an individual who argued, ostensibly, that Americans should not import any products that can be produced in America by Americans. Said the author:

> This letter is intended to bring to your attention reasons underlying the argument of some of us opposing the [proposed foreign trade program]. To this end, I present the case of several gentlemen, including myself, who wish to grow bananas in New York State. To do so, we need tariff protection, which [the proposed legislation] undoubtedly would deny us. Reasons follow why we believe tariff protection for our proposed American Banana Company is justified.

> First, we are all aware of the low wages paid foreign labor...

> Our capital costs [which] will be very high for climatic disadvantages will force us to build gigantic greenhouses...A tariff is needed to raise the

prices Americans pay for bananas so we can afford to operate and hire American labor...Otherwise, due to expensive greenhouses, cheap foreign labor will prevent our operating...A tariff raising prices consumers pay for bananas will permit us to build acres of greenhouses...

By increasing tariffs, competition can be diminished, domestic prices can be raised, efficiency lowered and employment increased; and we will have bananas growing in New York State in case of war. For these reasons, my colleagues and I feel H.R. 1 does not merit approval.[3]

But H.R. 1 was approved. Tariffs were not imposed on bananas, and the American Banana Company has never gotten off the ground in New York or anywhere else in the United States.

But the political issues will be the same in the 1980s as in the 1950s, and the proponents of an American Banana Company raise the right question to begin this chapter: Why should we import a product which we are capable of producing in the United States? There is no question as to why we import foreign chrome and molybdenum. None has been found in the United States. But why should we import foreign bananas (which we could grow more easily in Florida than in New York), or foreign automobiles, or foreign textiles, or radios, or steel? We *could* produce them in the United States.

We all know the immediate answer to "Why import?" Americans import when the foreign product is cheaper than the American alternative, after all allowances are made for perceived quality differences. That is a sufficient reason for individual buyers but not for us as students of international economics. Serious students must look for an explanation as to *why* the prices of some foreign products are lower, while the prices of other foreign products are higher, than the prices of the same or directly comparable products of the United States. One thing we do know: "cheap foreign labor" is *not* the answer. This is because where foreign labor is cheap, it is cheap to all foreign producers; yet, in many cases, Americans can produce some products more cheaply than foreigners in spite of high American wages.

Instead, the answer to "Why cheaper?" or "Why more expensive?" is to be found — as everyone acquainted with microeconomic theory will anticipate — in the differences in *opportunity costs*. Recall the definition given in your introductory economics textbook. It went something like this:

The opportunity cost of doing something is the loss of the opportunity of doing the next best thing instead with the same time or resources.[4]

Or, in the words of another author:

What is the opportunity cost of sitting in an economics lecture? Since you are not working at some income-producing job, you do not have the opportunity to spend one more hour on the job and get one more hour's worth of pay. However, you have available other opportunities, such as playing tennis, or swimming, or reading a book for another class, or drinking coffee in the student union, or listening to records. The fact is you have numerous alternatives available to you, and you can measure the opportunity cost of an economics lecture by figuring out the value you place on the highest alternative among your available choices. Thus, the opportunity cost of your time is equal to its highest alternative use value. Hence, opportunity cost is sometimes called alternative cost.[5]

These quotations provide a reminder that the opportunity cost concept has very wide application. Now, back to bananas for a specific application.

Suppose that economic resources (land, capital, and labor) in Honduras are well suited for banana production, and American resources are better suited for the production of product X. If a ton of bananas is *not* grown in America, some land, capital, and labor is released from banana production and can be put to some best alternative use, say, to the production of 10 units of X. Conversely, if a ton of bananas is not grown in Honduras, the Honduran land, capital, and labor not producing bananas could also be used to produce X there. How much X? Less than the 10X which the Americans could produce with the resources required to produce a ton of bananas in America.

In other words, the opportunity cost of a ton of American bananas is higher than the opportunity cost of a ton of Honduran bananas. And the opportunity cost of X is higher in Honduras than in America. So America imports bananas from Honduras, and Honduras imports product X from America, in spite of the fact that bananas *could* be produced in America, and X in Honduras.

That, in brief, is the "real theory"[6] of international trade. Next, the details of this theory of comparative advantage and of specialization.

THE THEORY OF COMPARATIVE ADVANTAGE

International trade does enable us to enjoy better living conditions. This section will provide an explanation of the circumstances that, in general, assure participants that international trade can improve their living standards.

The central idea of the theory of comparative advantage is that nations cannot produce as much in isolation as they can produce by specializing and trading with one another. Put positively, the idea is that nations producing with full and efficient use of resources but in isolation can produce more and can raise real incomes by abandoning isolation and by specializing and trading. This sounds like something for nothing. In a way it is.

TWO COUNTRIES IN ISOLATION

We begin with a simple case: a world of only two nations, North and South, each producing only two products, wheat and cotton. Simplifying assumptions are made about production in each nation: consumer sovereignty, perfect competition, full employment, and maximum efficiency characterize wheat and cotton production in North and in South. Technology, population, and capital stock are assumed to remain constant during the time period considered. Factors (inputs) do not move between North and South. Money is not used in North or in South; so barter trade is the customary practice.

Next, some arithmetic assumptions are made about production in each country. These numbers will then be used to show how specialization and trade raise wheat output *and* cotton output above pretrade levels. In the absence of North-South trade, total production of wheat and cotton is:

	Wheat	Cotton
North:	10,000 tons	4,000 tons
South:	15,000 tons	2,000 tons
Total	25,000 tons	6,000 tons

North grows less wheat but more cotton than South, *not* necessarily because North is a better cotton-growing area (in fact, North is a little cool for cotton). Rather, Northerners grow less wheat and more cotton than Southerners because North is so much cooler than South that Northerners have a taste for much heavier clothing than Southerners care to wear. (In Chapters 7 and 8, we will consider other reasons why nations' production patterns may differ.) Here, the preliminary point is that an isolated nation that produces a lot of a particular product — because the people have a taste for it — may or may not be especially good at producing that product. And the reverse would also be true: even if an isolated Israel were, for whatever reasons of climate and resources, the best pig growing nation in the world, not many pigs would be raised there.

But tastes do change. What follows in North and in South if tastes within each nation shift away from cotton toward wheat? To answer, we must know the numbers that define the opportunity costs of producing more wheat.

Within each nation, all land is in use; all other resources are fully employed with maximum efficiency. Consequently, no more wheat can be grown in either country *unless* some cotton production is sacrificed. Suppose each country decides to grow 100 more tons of wheat than called for by the table above. How much cotton production would each country have to give up? If you say that Northerners, for example, must give up 40 tons of cotton to gain additional 100 tons of wheat — because an isolated North produces 10,000 tons of wheat and 4,000 tons of cotton — you are wrong. These figures merely indicate the results of Northerners' preferences as between cotton and wheat; they reveal nothing about the relative costs of producing the two products. (This difference will be made clearer in Chapter 5. See Figure 5-1.)

Opportunity Costs (Transformation Ratios)

Obviously some more assumptions about the relative production costs are needed. What *is* the cost of producing those additional 100 tons of wheat? Obviously we cannot say the cost is so many Northern dollars or Southern pesos; remember there is no money! Fortunately, there is an easy way out — the economist's technique of expressing the cost of something by its foregone alternative. We will express the cost of an additional 100 tons of wheat by the number of tons of cotton that must be sacrificed. This involves the use of the concept of opportunity cost.

In the two-product world, the opportunity cost of growing a ton of wheat in North is the tonnage of cotton that could be produced if cotton instead of 1 ton of wheat were grown. Let us now make the following arithmetic assumptions concerning the opportunity costs of wheat and of cotton in each country:

In North: 20 tons of wheat *or* 4 tons of cotton.
In South: 6 tons of wheat *or* 2 tons of cotton.

These figures should be interpreted in the following manner. If a typical Southern farm grows nothing but wheat during a year of normal weather, it produces 6 tons of wheat; whereas if it grows nothing but cotton during a year, it produces 2 tons of cotton. The same goes for North; in that country, 20 tons of wheat can be transformed, so to speak, into 4 tons of cotton by a typical farm switching production from wheat to cotton.[7]

What would be the opportunity cost of 100 tons of wheat? Before answering that question, let us first find the opportunity cost of *one* ton of wheat, that is, the *unit opportunity cost* of wheat. The figures given above can be simplified as follows:

In North: $20W = 4C$, or $1W = \frac{1}{5}C$
In South: $6W = 2C$, or $1W = \frac{1}{3}C$

In other words, 1 ton of wheat "costs" or "transforms into" $\frac{1}{5}$ ton of cotton in North; while in South, 1 ton of wheat is worth $\frac{1}{3}$ ton of cotton. These unit opportunity costs are also called (marginal) *transformation ratios* because they show the rate at which cotton transforms into wheat, and vice versa, at the margin of production. Note that the unit opportunity costs (or the transformation ratios) can also be shown with cotton as the base (or unit): In North, $1C = 5W$; in South, $1C = 3W$.

More of One, Less of the Other

Back to our original question: What is the cost of an additional 100 tons of wheat in each country? The answers can now be simply obtained by using the unit opportunity costs. In North, since $1W = \frac{1}{5} C$, the cost of 100 tons of wheat is 20 tons of cotton. In South, 100 tons of wheat is worth $33\frac{1}{3}$ tons of cotton since $1W = \frac{1}{3} C$.

If, in each country, wheat production is increased by 100 tons at the expense of cotton production (a loss of 20 tons of cotton production in North and $33\frac{1}{3}$ tons of cotton in South), our total production table will now look like this:

	Wheat	Cotton
North:	10,100 tons	3,980 tons
South:	15,100 tons	$1,966\frac{2}{3}$ tons
Total	25,200 tons	$5,946\frac{2}{3}$ tons

What is obvious here is that given the assumption of unchanged resources fully employed with full efficiency, an increase in production of one product necessarily involves lower production of the other product *as long as the two countries remain unspecialized and in isolation*.

More of one, less of the other. Obvious.

But so far, Northern and Southern production totals have come from maximum efficiency of resource use within each nation. Their production has not involved maximum efficiency in the two nations, *working together*.

But, if one of the two nations will shift its fully employed fixed quantity of resources from wheat to cotton while the other shifts resources from cotton to wheat, then production of wheat *and* of cotton can be increased simultaneously.

More of one *and* more of the other.

More of both because of a move toward worldwide maximum efficiency with each country specializing in the product in which it has "comparative advantage."

SPECIALIZATION WITH TRADE

In understanding how both nations can gain in both products simultaneously under conditions of international trade, the concept of *comparative advantage* is fundamental.

Comparative Advantage

Comparative advantage is a relative concept: Which of the two countries is *relatively* (or *comparatively*) better at producing which of the two goods? Since "better production" is synonymous with "lower-cost production," we can restate the question as: Which of the two countries has a relatively lower opportunity cost of producing which good? Let us first locate comparative advantage in wheat: the nation in which wheat's opportunity cost is least is said to have comparative advantage in wheat production. Thus, since

1W = ⅕ C in North, while
1W = ⅓ C in South,

North has comparative advantage in wheat production. The advantage is clear: South must forego production of ⅓ ton of cotton to grow a ton of wheat, whereas North need forego production of only ⅕ ton of cotton to grow a ton of wheat. In short, wheat "costs" less in North. Each ton of Southern wheat costs ⅓ ton of cotton, whereas a ton of Northern wheat costs only ⅕ ton of cotton. Therefore, North has comparative advantage in wheat production.

Which country has comparative advantage in cotton production? Since

1C = 5W in North, while
1C = 3W in South,

South has comparative advantage in cotton production. A ton of Northern cotton costs 5 tons of wheat; a ton of Southern cotton costs only 3 tons of wheat.

Let us return for a moment to the production figures of single farms:

Northerners can produce either 20W or 4C, while
Southerners can produce only 6W or 2C.

These contrasting numbers suggest that Northern farms may be, in some sense, superior to Southern farms. Superior machinery, smarter farmers, more fertilizer, better climate, or combinations of these could make Northern farms superior. Alternatively, Northern farms may simply be bigger than Southern farms. Whatever the reason, a Northern farm can grow more wheat and more cotton than can a Southern farm. But the Northern farm's superiority is *relatively greater in wheat* than in cotton. That is why North has *comparative* advantage in wheat production.

Since each Northern farm can also grow more cotton than a Southern farm, does North also have comparative advantage in cotton production? A comparison of the opportunity costs of cotton has already shown the answer to be "No." A North-South comparison of cotton output per farm, *by itself,* is insufficient for the identification of comparative advantage. But such a comparison of absolute figures *can* prove a red herring, so should be recognized as such and studiously ignored when working to locate comparative advantage.[8]

Now look back at the little table showing possible total initial production of wheat and cotton in each country. The table shows that, in isolation, Northerners grow less wheat — 10,000 tons — than Southerners grow — 15,000 tons; yet Northerners have comparative advantage in wheat production. Southerners grow less cotton — 2,000 tons — than Northerners — 4,000 tons; yet Southerners have comparative advantage in cotton production. The figures of this no-trade production table derive from the interaction of each nation's production possibilities *and* its citizens' tastes. These figures tell nothing about comparative advantage (just as the North-South comparison of wheat output per farm, or cotton output per farm, *considered separately,* told nothing about comparative advantage). Opportunity costs (or, what is the same thing, transformation ratios) alone identify comparative advantage. So, in this case:

North has comparative advantage in wheat production because ⅕ C is less than ⅓ C, and

South has comparative advantage in cotton production because 3W is less than 5W.

Opportunity cost is a *sacrifice* concept. Comparative advantage is found by identifying the country where production of the good involves minimum sacrifice.

The "Magic" of Specialization and Trade

Even with fully efficient use of fully employed resources, an isolated North or an isolated South can raise wheat output only by sacrificing cotton output. But, if each of the two countries increases production of the good in which it has comparative advantage, then production of both products can be increased simultaneously. Arithmetic can prove the latter point.

Given these opportunity costs for the products in which each country has comparative advantage:

South (in cotton): 1C = 3W
North (in wheat): 1W = ⅕ C

South can increase cotton production by 100 tons (a quite arbitrary round number) at an opportunity cost of 300 tons of wheat (= 100 × 3). North can offset South's wheat cut by raising Northern wheat production by 300 tons at an opportunity cost of 60 tons of cotton (= 300 × ⅕). The net result is:

	Cotton	Wheat
South:	+ 100 tons	− 300 tons
North:	− 60 tons	+ 300 tons
Total	+ 40 tons	No change

This example shows both nations with increased production of the product in which they have comparative advantage. The net effect is *more* cotton for the "world" (South and North combined), but *no* decrease in wheat production. Something for nothing.

Why would nations be interested in switching their production decisions like this? After all, the initial production patterns in both nations were supposed to have been optimal. Southerners were getting just the right combination of wheat and cotton. So were the Northerners. Why would Northerners now want to increase wheat production at the expense of cotton? Similarly, what incentives would lead Southerners to raise cotton production and reduce wheat production? The answer is simple: each country, by participating in a game of production-switching *and* trading, can get a share of specialization's beneficence, the 40 tons of extra cotton in this case.

Alternatively, the net effect could be more wheat and no decrease in cotton production. If, given South's +100 cotton and −300 wheat, North were to produce 100 fewer tons of cotton, North's wheat production could be increased by 500 tons. Thus:

	Cotton	Wheat
South:	+ 100 tons	− 300 tons
North:	− 100 tons	+ 500 tons
Total	No change	+ 200 tons

In the first example, North raised wheat production by 300 tons (net, no change in wheat, cotton up 40 tons). In the second example, North raised wheat production by 500 tons (net, no change in cotton, wheat up 200 tons). If North would raise wheat production by more than 300 tons but by less than 500 tons, for example:

	Cotton	Wheat
South:	+ 100 tons	− 300 tons
North:	− 70 tons	+ 350 tons
Total	+ 30 tons	+ 50 tons

then both cotton and wheat production could be increased. Something for nothing. If, in this case, South exports its additional 100 tons of cotton to North, and North exports its additional 350 tons of wheat to South, then the blizzard beleaguered Northerners would have 30 tons more cotton and the hungry Southerners would have 50 tons more wheat than before specialization and trading. *These are the gains from international trade.* (How the trading countries actually divide these gains will be studied in Chapter 5.)

EVERY COUNTRY HAS COMPARATIVE ADVANTAGE

The reciprocal of 6 is ⅙; the reciprocal of ³⁄₁₇ is ¹⁷⁄₃. Opportunity costs always involve reciprocals.

If 1 bangle costs ⅙ bead,
   1 bead costs 6 bangles.
If 1 elixer costs ¾ theriaca,
   1 theriaca costs ⁴⁄₃ elixers.

It follows from this that, if one of the two countries has comparative advantage in any one product, the other country *must* have comparative advantage in some other product. Why? Because whenever one number is greater than a second, the reciprocal of the first number must be smaller than the reciprocal of the second. For example:

if $3 < 5$,
$\frac{1}{3} > \frac{1}{5}$, and
if $\frac{3}{7} < \frac{6}{7}$, then
$\frac{7}{3} > \frac{7}{6}$.

If the opportunity costs of 1 wheat are 2 cotton in Erehwon and 3 cotton in Utopia, Erehwon has comparative advantage in wheat production since 2C is less than 3C. Then, the reciprocal arithmetic must follow so that the opportunity costs of 1 cotton are $\frac{1}{2}$ wheat in Erehwon and $\frac{1}{3}$ wheat in Utopia, and Utopia has comparative advantage in cotton since $\frac{1}{3}$ is less than $\frac{1}{2}$. Because 2C is less than 3C, $\frac{1}{2}$ W must be more than $\frac{1}{3}$ W. Every area has comparative advantage in something. Your comparative advantage is somebody else's comparative disadvantage; your comparative disadvantage is somebody else's relative advantage.

A conceivable esoteric exception would be a case in which typical farm production possibilities would be:

Area Alpha	Area Beta
3 tons wheat or 12 tons cotton	2 tons wheat or 8 tons cotton

in which case unit opportunity costs would be:

1W = 4C	1W = 4C
1C = ¼ W	1C = ¼ W

and neither area would have comparative advantage in either product. One can conceive of such a case, but it does not happen in reality. The real world is too diverse from place to place to permit any two areas to have the same transformation ratios in all goods.

This example is another reminder that absolute numbers are unimportant. The 3 wheat and 12 cotton are bigger respectively than the 2 wheat and the 8 cotton, but the transformation ratios are identical. Again, the moral: comparative advantage derives from relative, not absolute, differences in production costs.

Many of America's electronic, computer, and aeronautical exports represent a special kind of comparative advantage. This is the rather common case in which one area can produce a product and other areas cannot produce it at all. Then the production possibilities are:

U. S. Area	Other Area
6 tons bangles or 4 tons transitons	4 tons bangles or 0 ton transitons

in which case unit opportunity costs would be:

1B = 4T	1B = 0T
1T = ¼ B	1T = undefined

In this case, the U.S. Area must have comparative advantage in transiton production because the Other Area's opportunity cost of transitons is impossibly high. The Other Area must have comparative advantage in bangle production because the opportunity cost of bangles in that area is zero.

INTERNATIONAL, INTERREGIONAL, INTERPERSONAL COMPARATIVE ADVANTAGE

In the foregoing discussion we referred to specialization and trading between areas (Alpha, Beta) and countries (North, South). To which does comparative advantage best apply? To both, equally. Output can be greatest — i.e., resources can be used most efficiently — only when comparative advantage is allowed to determine production —

among nations,
among states and provinces,
among counties,
among townships, and, even
among individuals.

The classical economists (Adam Smith, David Ricardo, John Stuart Mill) defined "nation" as a region *within* which factors of production moved with perfect freedom but *between* which factors moved not at all. Where immigration and customs agents stand guard, "national" boundaries in this classical sense correspond to the national boundaries of politics. But factor movements are impeded by many obstacles other than political boundaries, and the theory of comparative advantage applies to every situation — from international through intercounty to interpersonal — where productive factors are immobile *and* where factors are available in proportions, one to another, different in one "nation" than in another "nation."

If all factors of production — including climate and other natural resources — were distributed in equal proportions in every area of the world (and if there were no economies of scale, and if technology were the same everywhere), then, as in the "esoteric exception" cited in the preceding subsection, opportunity costs would be everywhere the same. In such an extreme science-fiction case, no area would have comparative advantage in anything; so no gains from comparative advantage specialization would be possible.

In the future, factors of production may become much more evenly distributed around the world, in which case international and interregional trade might decline. But unless genetic engineering is permitted to make people much more alike, individuals will continue to represent the most extreme form of "nations" in that classical sense. We are born with unequal productive potentials and through education, occupational training, and experience, we increase those differences. Individuals are, therefore, like the classical "nations," possessed of productive resources in unequal proportions. These resources cannot be taken away from one person to be given to another (though, of course, one *can* teach another), but individuals can specialize and trade the products of their specialization.

Consider some examples of comparative advantage theory applied to individuals. An attorney may hire a man to type for her, and the typist may in turn buy legal services from the attorney. They make this interpersonal (or in that classical sense, international) exchange to obtain the benefits of comparative advantage specialization.

If, however, their production possibilities from a day's labor were:

	Legal service units	Typing units
For the woman:	18	54
For the man:	9	27

there would be no comparative advantage, so there would be no potential gains from specialization. If they were the only people in the world, each could as well do his or her own legalizing and typing as to buy either from the other. But if their production possibilities were:

	Legal service units	Typing units
For the woman:	18	54
For the man:	9	36

the woman would remain both a superior attorney and a superior typist. Nevertheless, the man would hold comparative advantage in typing, and both could gain from comparative advantage specialization while working for each other. So it happens in the real world that some professional women and men could be better typists than their secretaries, but when the professional people show comparative advantage in the activities of law or accounting, resources are used more efficiently when people with comparative advantage in professional work do professional work while people with comparative advantage in typing type. Conversely, some inferior attorneys practice law by default because they are even more inferior as typists; they suffer comparative disadvantages in typing — and in other work — which give them relative advantage in law.

In sum, whether the parties — or areas — compared are persons, townships, counties, or nations, almost every one will have comparative advantage in something. Resources that cannot move freely from one area — or person — to another can be used with maximum efficiency where they are located only if comparative advantage specialization is permitted everywhere. In the real world, comparative advantage specialization is not permitted everywhere. Subsequent chapters will consider the consequences when government intervention restricts world output — at least in the short run — by restricting such specialization.

ABSOLUTE ADVANTAGE

The concept of comparative advantage and the practicality of specialization and trade based on it may appear today to be mere common sense. This has not always been the case.

In 1776, in *An Inquiry into the Nature and Causes of the Wealth of Nations,* Adam Smith (1723-1790) wrote:

> It is the maxim of every prudent master of a family, never to attempt to make at home what it will cost him more to make than to buy...

> What is prudent in the conduct of every private family, can scarce be folly in that of a great kingdom. If a foreign country can supply us with a commodity cheaper than we ourselves can make it, better buy it of them with some part of the produce of our own industry, employed in a way in which we have some advantage.[9]

The larger context clearly showed that he did not think in terms of *comparative* advantage. Rather, he believed international trade followed from what we now call "absolute advantage." We can examine that concept here with an illustration based upon Adam Smith's scornful denunciation of the advocates of prohibitions against imports of lower-cost foreign products:

> By means of glasses, hotbeds, and hotwells, very good grapes can be raised in Scotland, and very good wine too can be made of them at about thirty times the expense for which at least equally good can be brought from foreign countries. Would it be a reasonable law to prohibit the importation of all foreign wines, merely to encourage the making of claret and burgundy in Scotland?[10]

He answered "No." with the example in mind looking something like this:

| | Labor required to produce one unit of | |
	Cloth	Wine
In Scotland:	50 hours	150 hours
In Portugal:	100 hours	5 hours

in which example all the hours of labor would be identical in effort and quality for cloth and for wine, and in Portugal and in England. Smith, like all other classical economists, assumed that the value of a commodity derived solely from the quantity of labor used to make it.[11] Therefore, in this example, Scotch wine was 30 times as costly as Portuguese wine, and Portuguese cloth was twice as costly as Scotch cloth. Clearly, in all such cases, both parties would benefit from absolute advantage specialization, and both would be hurt if British law were to prohibit the importation of claret and burgundy.

In Adam Smith's model, products would be imported only when, on this absolute labor cost scale, they could be produced at lower costs by foreigners. Smith saw only absolute advantage, but we can now see that his case of absolute advantage involved comparative advantage as well. By reworking Smith's example into the paradigm of this chapter, we can see how relative advantage governs production and trade in Smith's case. Smith's example showed hours of labor per output unit. We rework that example by calculating output per fixed quantity of labor. Arbitrarily, we choose to calculate output per 300 hours of labor. Given Smith's labor cost per unit of wine and per unit of cloth, we get:

	Output to be obtained at a cost of 300 hours of labor	
	Cloth	Wine
In Scotland:	6 units	2 units
In Portugal:	3 units	60 units

So, in the terms of our paradigm, the Scots have comparative advantage in cloth production (since ⅓ wine is less than 20 wine), and the Portuguese have comparative advantage in wine production.

In the foregoing example of Adam Smith, absolute and comparative advantages coincided. Can we generally state, then, that every case of absolute advantage is also an example of comparative advantage? The answer is "No." As we saw in the preceding subsection, an attorney who has absolute disadvantage in "legalizing" may, or may not, have comparative advantage in it. The converse is also true: relative advantage may or may not be accompanied by absolute advantage. It is only when one country has an absolute advantage in one product, and the other country in another product, that absolute and comparative advantages coincide. When one country has an absolute advantage (or disadvantage) in *both* products, we must locate its comparative advantage by finding in which product the country's advantage (or disadvantage) is *relatively greater*.

DAVID RICARDO'S GIANT STEP

That the direction of trade is established by, and the gains from trade derived from, specialization based on comparative, not absolute, advantage was discovered — or at least popularized — by another great classical economist David Ricardo (1772-1823).[12]

Following Smith's use of labor units as a standard of value, Ricardo's original example was this:

	Labor required to produce one unit of	
	Cloth	Wine
In England:	100 hours	120 hours
In Portugal:	90 hours	80 hours

Portugal can produce both items at lower labor cost than can England. Portugal has an absolute advantage, and England has an absolute disadvantage, in the production of *both* cloth and wine. Why, in such a case, should Portugal import something that could be produced for less at home? Common sense everywhere before Ricardo — and in many quarters in the twentieth century — replies: "Portugal should *not* import anything from the higher cost nation." Ricardo's answer was:

> Though she [Portugal] could make the cloth with the labour of 90 men, she would import it from a country where it required the labour of 100 men to produce it, because it would be advantageous to her rather to employ her capital in the production of wine, for which she would obtain more cloth from England, than she could produce by diverting a portion of her capital from the cultivation of vines to the manufacture of cloth.[13]

This is entirely true but not very clear. As in the Adam Smith example cited earlier, Ricardo's example is more easily utilized when reworked into this chapter's paradigm. A common multiplicand for 100, 120, 90, and 80 is 7,200. We can get output units in whole numbers by calculating cloth output and wine output per 7,200 hours of labor in each country given Ricardo's labor-cost assumptions. Therefore:

	Output to be obtained from the application of 7,200 hours of labor	
	Cloth	Wine
In England:	72 units	60 units
In Portugal:	80 units	90 units

England has comparative advantage in cloth production ($\frac{5}{6}$ wine is less than $\frac{9}{8}$ wine). Portugal has comparative advantage in wine production. David Ricardo had discovered and applied a new concept.

From that giant step in the progress of positive economics, Ricardo reached a normative conclusion:

> Under a system of perfectly free commerce, each country naturally devotes its capital and labour to such employments as are most beneficial to each. This pursuit of individual advantage is admirably connected with the universal good of the whole. By stimulating industry, by rewarding ingenuity, and by using most efficaciously the peculiar powers bestowed by nature, it distributes labour most effectively and most economically; while, by increasing the general mass of productions, it diffuses general benefit, and binds together by one common tie of interest and intercourse, the universal society of nations throughout the civilized world. It is this principle which determines that wine shall be made in France and Portugal, that corn shall be grown in America and Poland, and that hardware and other goods shall be manufactured in England.[14]

Ricardo discovered a formula for "increasing the general mass of productions," but would it be ever true that that action formula "diffuses general benefit, and binds together by one common tie of interest and intercourse, the universal society of nations"? The answer must entertain some reservations.

STUDY QUESTIONS

1. What, in a nutshell, are the gains from international trade? Give a brief answer without getting into numerical details.
2. What U.S. industries, do you think, are export industries? How can this be, when U.S. producers must pay the world's highest (or just about highest) wages?
3. If the dollar prices of some American products must be lower, while the dollar prices of other American products must be higher, than the dollar prices of comparable foreign products, what determines to which category of products a given product belongs?
4. Earlier in the chapter it was assumed that North's initial total production, without foreign trade, was 10,000 tons of wheat and 4,000 tons of cotton, with the opportunity costs of $20W = 4C$.
   (a) Draw a graph plotting quantity of cotton on the vertical axis and quantity of wheat on the horizontal axis. Then, locate a coordinate (a point) in the graph indicating the initial combination of the output quantities of wheat and cotton.
   (b) If the country decides to produce 1,000 additional tons of wheat, how many tons of wheat and cotton can now be produced?
   (c) Plot the new combination of the output quantities of wheat and cotton in the same graph.
   (d) Draw a straight line linking the two coordinates. What does the slope of this line indicate?
5. What is meant by the statement that the production cost of a given good is comparatively (or relatively) cheap in a country? Relative to what?
6. What is the minimum number of countries and of products needed to determine a pattern of comparative costs? Specifically, can we determine comparative costs in each of the following cases?
   (a) In America, the unit cost of bread is 50 cents and that of butter is $2.
   (b) In Germany, steel costs 300 marks per ton, while in France it costs 700 francs.
   (c) In Brazil, a pound of sugar costs twice as much as a pound of coffee beans; in Italy, they are equally priced.
7. If a given quantity of resources produces the following quantities of bananas and coffee beans in Guatemala and in Honduras:

	Bananas	Coffee beans
Guatemala:	18 tons	6 tons
Honduras:	16 tons	4 tons

   (a) What are the opportunity costs of the two products?
   (b) Which country has absolute advantage in which good?
   (c) Which country has comparative advantage in which good?
8. Production costs per bushel of apples and of pears in France and in Germany are shown below:

	Apples	Pears
France:	20 francs	10 francs
Germany:	12 marks	4 marks

   (a) Find the opportunity costs of the two goods in the two countries.
   (b) Which country has comparative advantage in which good?

9. Assume full employment and maximum efficiency within each country with initial total output (in millions of tons):

	Yazes	Xerks
Malaysia:	3	4
Nigeria:	5	2

and with opportunity costs of:

Malaysia: $2Y = 3X$
Nigeria: $6Y = 18X$

(a) Which country has comparative advantage in Yazes?
(b) What numbers must be compared to give that answer?
(c) Which country has comparative advantage in Xerks?
(d) What numbers must be compared to give that answer?
(e) Show that, *ceteribus paribus*, comparative advantage specialization would permit the two nations *combined* to raise Yazes production above 8 million tons while simultaneously raising Xerks production above 6 million tons. (Arbitrarily increase the output of comparative advantage production in each country by a few thousand tons.)

10. Repeat the preceding problem, except using opportunity costs of:

Malaysia: $6Y = 9X$
Nigeria: $2Y = 8X$

11. Make up a numerical example for two countries producing two products where there can be no comparative advantage specialization, hence no gains from trade. Do this, using:
(a) output quantities from a given amount of resources.
(b) unit production costs expressed in local currencies.

ENDNOTES

1. For ten years, Republicans — and some Democrats — had been charging that at the 1945 meeting of Roosevelt, Stalin, Churchill, and Chiang, at Yalta — a resort city on the Black Sea — Roosevelt had "given away" far too much to the Russians. "Yalta" was, therefore, in those years, an ultimate in pejoratives.
2. Allen Drury, "Senate Cuts Tariff Debate: Passage Tonight Is Possible," *New York Times,* 4 May 1955, p. 1.
3. Alan B. Batchelder, "Woes of Entrepreneurs: Increased Tariffs Asked to Lower Efficiency and Raise Prices," *New York Times,* 4 May 1955, p. 23.
4. Edwin G. Dolan, *Basic Economics* (Hinsdale, Ill.: The Dryden Press, 1977), p. 4.
5. Roger Leroy Miller, *Economics Today,* 2nd ed. (San Francisco: Canfield Press, 1976), pp. 13-14.
6. "Real" in a sense that no money is involved.
7. These output figures may suggest that Northern farms are larger than Southern farms or have superior soil, more favorable climate, or better tools; however, the reason(s) for North's greater output per farm need not be identified, for the relevant analysis is independent of these reason(s).
8. Because the Northern farm can outproduce (20W to 4C) the Southern farm (6W to 2C) in both wheat *and* cotton, one may easily be tempted to attribute comparative advantage to North for both products. The falsity of that conclusion may be seen more clearly after comparing a single Northern farm with a block of five Southern farms

whose production possibilities would be 30W or 10C. The Southern block-farm could outproduce the Northern farm in either wheat *or* cotton, but this rearrangement of Southern farms would not affect the location of comparative advantage. The Southern block-farm would still have unit opportunity costs of $1W = \frac{1}{3} C$ and $1C = 3W$; so comparative advantage would continue to reside with North for wheat (with $\frac{1}{5} C$ being less than $\frac{1}{3} C$), and with South for cotton (with 3W being less than 5W).

9. Adam Smith, *The Wealth of Nations,* The Modern Library (New York: Random House, 1937), p. 424.
10. *Ibid.,* p. 425.
11. Adam Smith undertook to identify some one thing that would have an intrinsic constant value that could be used to measure the exchange value of all other things. He suggested both "corn, the staple food of labour" ("corn" meaning grain in American English) and labor as a "real measure of the exchangeable value of all commodities," *Ibid.,* p. 38.
12. In 1701, an anonymous Englishman, writing in a pamphlet, at least implied the principle of comparative advantage. He did not, however, elaborate enough to convince a reader that he had discovered the principle. "Considerations on the East-India Trade," anonymous, reproduced in J. R. McCulloch, ed., *A Select Collection of Early English Tracts on Commerce* (Cambridge: Cambridge University Press, 1954), pp. 541-629, especially Chapter IV, pp. 568-570. Sir Robert Torrens, British army officer and, later, Member of Parliament, did identify the principle of comparative advantage in 1808, and did present it more clearly in 1815. He suggested that, though English costs might be lower in agriculture, England should produce manufactures if English manufacturing costs are even lower relative to foreign. Robert Torrens, *An Essay on the External Corn Trade* (London: J. Harchard, both the 1815 and 1820 editions), pp. 263-265. But having stated the principle, Torrens made no further use of it until after Ricardo had led the way.
13. David Ricardo, *On the Principles of Political Economy and Taxation* in Pierro Sraffa, ed., *The Works and Correspondence of David Ricardo* (Cambridge: Cambridge University Press, 1951), 1: 135.
14. *Ibid.,* pp. 133-34.

4

Comparative Costs and Exchange Rates

The preceding chapter showed that mutually beneficial trade can take place whenever pretrade opportunity costs differ between countries. Opportunity costs were expressed as transformation ratios — the cost of producing a ton of wheat was defined as the number of tons of cotton that had to be sacrificed. However, in actual trade relations among nations, barter deals are rare. Decisions to import or export are almost invariably made on the basis of a direct comparison of money prices expressed in a common currency unit. But if traders are to compare prices in terms of a single currency, they must know the relationship existing between the currencies of the nations involved. This relationship is defined by the *rate of exchange*. Once an exchange rate is established between two currencies, traders can easily tell whether a given good is cheaper or dearer at home than abroad, since they can compare the two prices of the good in units of either of the two currencies. Although exchange rates are sometimes determined by government fiat, in this and in the next chapter we will show that, in a free market, equilibrium exchange rates depend on both production possibilities and the wishes of the whole buying public in the nations involved.

DOMESTIC PRICES AND THE EXCHANGE RATE

THE RATE OF EXCHANGE

An *exchange rate* is the rate at which the money of one country can be exchanged for the money of another country. It is expressed as either the price of a foreign currency unit in terms of domestic currency units, or vice versa. For example, the exchange rate between the U.S. dollar and the French franc has recently been 1Fr = \$0.25, or, if stated as the price of the domestic currency in terms of the foreign, \$1 = 4Fr. The exchange rate between the dollar and the Brazilian cruzeiro has been about 1 Cr = \$0.02 or, stated the other way, \$1 = 50Cr.

When more than two currencies are involved, one can usually expect consistency among their exchange rates. Thus, one can easily reason from two foreign currency prices of the dollar to the exchange rate between the two foreign currencies; e.g., when \$1 = 50Cr and \$1 = 4Fr, then 50Cr = 4 Fr so 1CR = 0.08Fr and 1Fr = 12.5Cr.

When beginning the study of international economics, students are often distressed to find that every transformation ratio can be stated in two ways: either 1 ton of wheat = $3/7$ ton of cotton, or 1 ton of cotton = $7/3$ tons of wheat. An additional reason for distress is the circumstance that exchange rates also lend themselves to statements in reciprocal ways; thus, $\pounds 1$ = \$2.36 has the same meaning as \$1 = $\pounds 0.424$. International economics is characterized by such interchangeable statements. Nothing can be done to avoid them because they are inherent in the reciprocal nature of the arithmetic of international economic relations.

PRICE RATIO THE RECIPROCAL OF THE TRANSFORMATION RATIO

Exchange rates between currencies derive in part from domestic prices within the nations using those currencies and trading. In turn, domestic prices do not just happen randomly; they derive from and, in free markets, must be consistent with domestic transformation ratios.

The Chapter 3 example assumed that any Northern farm could produce either 4 tons of cotton or 20 tons of wheat. This assumption led to North's cotton-to-wheat transformation ratio of 4C/20W = 1C/5W = $1/5$. Money was not involved. Now, assume North to be a market economy using money called "dollars." In "market equilibrium" (meaning all profit and utility maximizers have done their best), the ratio of the cotton price to the wheat price must be $1/5$, the reciprocal of their transformation ratio, already given as $1/5$. Whether cotton is \$50 a ton and wheat \$10 or cotton \$2.50 a ton and wheat \$0.50, the price ratio must be $5/1$.

This price ratio must obtain because of the assumptions that North's transformation ratio is 1C = 5W, that North's farmers are profit maximizers, and that, in the absence of trade, some Northern farmers grow cotton while some others grow wheat. From those assumptions it follows that Northern farmers growing wheat must be as well off as Northern farmers growing cotton; otherwise those in one activity would give it up for the other. That some farmers continue growing cotton while other farmers continue growing wheat must mean that the income return from corn growing equals the income return from wheat growing. It follows that, since the wheat grower produces, on each acre, five times the units of physical output of the cotton farmer, the cotton farmer must receive a price per unit five times that received by the wheat grower.

South's transformation ratio is 2C/6W = 1C/3W = ⅓. The Southern cotton-to-wheat price ratio, therefore, must be ³⁄₁, the reciprocal of the transformation ratio. Southerners use money called "pesos" in their market economy. Their cotton-price/wheat-price ratio can be 9 pesos for C and 3 for W, or 21 pesos for C and 7 for W, or any other pair of numbers in the ratio of 3 to 1. This chapter will assume that in pretrade isolation, the domestic prices of cotton and wheat in North and South are:

| | Price per Ton | |
	North	South
Cotton:	$5	9 pesos
Wheat:	$1	3 pesos

THE EQUILIBRIUM INTERNATIONAL REAL TERMS OF TRADE

Suppose Northerners begin to trade with Southerners. Without foreign trade, North's *internal terms of trade* are the same as North's transformation ratio, 1C = 5W, meaning Northerners can get 1 cotton unit for 5 wheat units, however "unit" is defined. Similarly, South's internal terms of trade are 1C = 3W; Southerners can get one cotton unit for three wheat units. When international trade becomes possible, trade will begin only if participants can maintain their initial positions or better themselves through foreign trade. If international trade begins and if the traders do not use money but engage in barter deals, the international terms of trade *must* lie between the internal terms of trade of the two nations, i.e., between 1C = 5W and 1C = 3W inclusive.

For example, to repeat the argument of Chapter 3, an equilibrium barter terms of trade of 1C = 4W (or ¼C = 1W) might be established. Then Southerners could trade 1C for 4W, a better deal than the pretrade 1C for 3W; and Northerners could trade 1W for ¼C, a better deal than the pretrade 1W for ⅕C.

This chapter will not present the model that yields an equilibrium barter terms of trade. The next chapter will do that. Such an equilibrium is established through the interaction of international supply and demand — which, in technical language, is called the workings of "reciprocal" demand or the interaction of "offer" curves. The next chapter will fully describe the model that produces an equilibrium in barter — or real — trade. This chapter is limited to an examination of the monetary dimensions of the exchange of goods.

THE LIMITS OF SUSTAINABLE EXCHANGE RATES

Given the constraints of real opportunity costs and of equilibrium domestic prices, look for the range of exchange rates that will permit some trade to occur. Then, call these rates *"sustainable" exchange rates* because they will sustain at least some trade while all other exchange rates will prevent any trade.

In this chapter's simple two-nation two-product model, sustainable exchange rates are all those between the ratio derived by setting North's cotton price equal to South's cotton price and the ratio derived by setting North's wheat price equal to South's wheat price. This means that

if North's cotton @ $5 = South's @ 9 pesos and
if North's wheat @ $1 = South's @ 3 pesos,

we know in advance of detailed analysis that any equilibrium exchange rate must lie within the range of sustainable exchange rates that fall between

$1 = ⁹⁄₅ pesos (i.e., $5 = 9 pesos)

and

$1 = 3 pesos.

The point is that an equilibrium exchange rate must lie within constraints set by domestic money prices which are, in their turn, based on real opportunity costs.

Given the domestic prices assumed in this example:

	North	South
Cotton:	$5	9 pesos
Wheat:	$1	3 pesos

which good is cheaper in which country? The answers depend on the rate of exchange between the dollar and the peso. With different exchange rates, the answers differ. We will now set up five kinds of cases involving five distinctively different kinds of exchange rate. Experience with these five will prove the generalization stressed in this section respecting the range of sustainable exchange rates.

One unrealistic but quite convenient simplification will be made here — and in most of the models in this book — that transportation is costless between nations. There is no such thing as free locomotion of course, but the assumption of costless shipping greatly simplifies the analysis and does not distort any of the principal conclusions. Now, the five cases.

Case A: $1 = 1 Peso.

First, a rate arbitrarily chosen for its simplicity, $1 = 1 peso. Given this rate, the prices of the two products can be expressed in each country's currency units, as follows, dollar prices on the left, peso prices on the right:

	Dollar Price per Ton		Peso Price per Ton	
	of North's output	of South's output	of North's output	of South's output
Cotton:	$5	$9	5 pesos	9 pesos
Wheat:	$1	$3	1 peso	3 pesos

Whether the prices of the two goods are expressed in dollars or in pesos, the result is the same: both cotton and wheat are more expensive in South than in North. Under such a circumstance, there can be no trade. For mutually beneficial trade relations to exist between two nations, there must be two-way trade: one good must flow in one direction, and the other in the opposite direction. The reason for this may be obvious; the producer-exporter must be paid. Imports are the payments that compensate exporters.

When money, in the form of two national currencies, is involved, each country must be able to pay for its imports with the foreign currencies (foreign exchange) it earns by exporting its own products. Thus, there can be no viable, long-run trade relations unless residents of each nation want to buy something from the other nation. In this example, at the $1 = 1 peso exchange rate, it is clear that there can be no trade since everyone in South will want to buy *both* products from North, while no one in North will want to import products from South. We therefore must conclude that the exchange rate of $1 = 1 peso is not sustainable; it cannot generate two-way trade. It cannot because, at this rate, South's products are priced too high and North's goods are priced too low in terms of foreign currencies. Southerners want Northern goods, but no Northerner will accept any Southern pesos. Pesos are useless to Northerners. To elicit trade, the peso price of the dollar must be increased (or, what is the same thing, the dollar price of the peso must be cut). That change will raise the prices of North's products and lower the prices of South's products so Northerners will want to buy something from South.

Case B: $1 = 1.8 Pesos (or 1 Peso = $0.555)

The rate $1 = 1.8 pesos is deliberately chosen because it will prove to be what we will call a *"benchmark" rate*. Can you see why this particular rate is picked, given the initial domestic prices — in particular, given the domestic prices of cotton? If you have immediately grasped its significance, you are doing very well indeed in this very complex subject. Yes, it is the rate that equates the price of cotton in both nations.

	Dollar Price per Ton		Peso Price per Ton	
	of North's output	of South's output	of North's output	of South's output
Cotton:	$5	$5	9 pesos	9 pesos
Wheat:	$1	$1.67	1.8 pesos	3 pesos

If cotton is equally priced in both nations, there will be no cotton trade. But Southerners will want to buy Northern wheat. Wheat, however, will not be imported by South because Southerners will have no dollars to pay for any wheat imports from North. Northerners will have no use for pesos, and therefore will insist on payment in dollars, while Southerners will be unable to obtain any dollars because no Northerner wants to buy anything from South. The problem is that the peso price of the dollar is still low. What if it is raised a little further to $1 = 2 pesos?

Case C: $1 = 2 Pesos (or 1 Peso = $0.5)

At this rate, there can finally be two-way trade, as the following schedule shows:

	Dollar Price per Ton		Peso Price per Ton	
	of North's output	of South's output	of North's output	of South's output
Cotton:	$5	$4.5	10 pesos	9 pesos
Wheat:	$1	$1.5	2 pesos	3 pesos

Cotton is now cheaper in South; wheat is cheaper in North. The exchange rate is sustainable; it will permit some trade.

To endure, this exchange rate would have to be both sustainable and at equilibrium. An equilibrium rate of exchange is one that equates the monetary values of each country's exports and imports. In other words, if by exporting each country earns just enough foreign exchange to pay for its imports, then the rate of exchange is an equilibrium rate.(The exchange rate, after all, is a price. Like all other prices, it will tend to move to equilibrium, and it will tend to change in response to changes in supply and demand. See Chapter 13.)

Is the $1 = 2 pesos rate an equilibrium rate? Without more information, this question cannot be answered. (What South earns by exporting its cotton to North depends not only on cotton's *price* — $4.5 or 9 pesos per ton — but also on the *quantity* of cotton exported and in this chapter, no information is available about quantity.)

For the sake of symmetry, consider some even higher peso/dollar exchange rates. At $1 = 3 pesos, wheat prices are equalized between the two nations, and there will therefore be no trade (Case D). At $1 = 4 pesos, both products are more expensive in North than in South; and, again, there will be no trade (Case E). With Case E and with Case D, no one in South will want to buy anything from North.

Case D: $1 = 3 Pesos (or 1 Peso = $0.333)

	Dollar Price per Ton		Peso Price per Ton	
	of North's output	of South's output	of North's output	of South's output
Cotton:	$5	$3	15 pesos	9 pesos
Wheat:	$1	$1	3 pesos	3 pesos

Case E: $1 = 4 Pesos (or 1 Peso = $0.25)

	Dollar Price per Ton		Peso Price per Ton	
	of North's output	of South's output	of North's output	of South's output
Cotton:	$5	$2.25	20 pesos	9 pesos
Wheat:	$1	$0.75	4 pesos	3 pesos

Of the four categories of exchange rate that prevent trade, two (Cases B and D) are *"benchmark" rates*. They are so called because they define the benchmark limits between which an exchange rate must lie if it is to permit two-way trade. In the above example, an exchange rate, to be sustainable, must lie between $1 = 1.8 pesos and $1 = 3 pesos. The benchmark rates are easily calculated in a two-product, two-nation model. One benchmark rate is the rate that equalizes the prices of one product in both countries; the other benchmark rate equalizes the other product's prices in both nations.

This section has shown that opportunity costs (transformation ratios) translate into product prices that must be the reciprocals of the transformation ratios. But the price of one nation's product X, expressed in that nation's currency, cannot be compared with the price of the other nation's product X, expressed in that other nation's currency, *unless the exchange rate is known*. The rate of exchange, however, cannot be arbitrarily determined. It must lie between the two benchmark limits if it is to sustain any trade. The benchmark rates, in turn, are fundamentally determined by the transformation ratios (or their reciprocals, relative domestic prices).

WHAT ABOUT CHEAP FOREIGN LABOR?

Chapter 6 will ask about the relationship between cheap (foreign) labor and international trade. Readers can begin to prepare themselves for that question by asking themselves, "In the preceding example involving North, South, and each of the five kinds of exchange rates, what difference would it make — if any — if South were a very cheap labor country?" Try to be precise.

MONETARY GAINS FROM TRADE

In the last chapter, *real* gains from comparative advantage specialization were shown as the simultaneous increases in production of *both* products that can occur when each nation increases production in its comparative advantage product. Both nations can benefit from this increase in output.

Another way of viewing these gains from specialization is to look at the monetary benefits to people who buy the two products. This can be done in this case by comparing the prices Northern (or Southern) consumers pay for cotton and wheat before and after trade.

In no-trade isolation, a Northern consumer buying one ton of cotton and one ton of wheat per year pays $5 + $1 = $6. But if she can buy Southern cotton at a sustainable exchange rate of $1 = 2 pesos (Case C), then one ton of each costs: $4.5 + $1 = $5.5. There is a monetary gain of $0.5 to the Northern consumer. Savings also accrue to the Southern consumer. In no-trade isolation, a Southern consumer buying one ton of cotton and one ton of wheat would have paid 9 pesos + 3 pesos = 12 pesos. But if she can buy Northern wheat at an exchange rate of $1 = 2 pesos, then one ton of each costs 9 pesos + 2 pesos = 11 pesos. The saving of one peso is her monetary gain from comparative-advantage specialization and trade.

THE FOREIGN EXCHANGE MARKET
AND THE EXCHANGE RATE

Foreign exchange refers to various means of effecting international payments and is represented by a wide variety of highly liquid credit instruments such as foreign currencies, deposits in foreign banks denominated in foreign currencies, and bills of exchange drawn on foreign residents. These means of making international payments are bought and sold in *foreign exchange markets*. The institutions and operations of these markets will be discussed fully in Chapter 13. Because, in the absence of government intervention, the foreign exchange market determines exchange rates, this section previews the determinants of supply and demand in foreign exchange markets.

SUPPLY OF ONE CURRENCY EQUALS DEMAND FOR THE OTHER

There is one foreign exchange market for each pair of national currencies. In the example used in this chapter, that market is the dollar/peso market or, what is the same thing, the peso/dollar market.

Note that this market has no physical location; it is present wherever pesos are used to buy dollars or — again the same thing — dollars are used to buy pesos. In this market, the demand for one currency is the supply of the other, and vice versa. For example, when two pesos exchange for one dollar the party who provides the two pesos both (1) supplies two pesos (quantity) @ one dollar (price) and (2) demands one dollar (quantity) @ two pesos (price). Conversely, the party who provides the one dollar both (1) supplies the dollar (quantity) @ two pesos (price) and (2) demands two pesos (quantity) @ one dollar (price). Supply and demand can be shown in a sketch with pesos on the quantity axis and price, in dollars, on the y axis or in a sketch with dollars on the quantity axis and price, in pesos, on the y axis. This complex situation is inherent in foreign exchange transactions in which one currency is exchanged for another; it appears to be odd because money is being used to buy money. Such an exchange contrasts with the more familiar situation in which money is used to buy other things.

In the North-South wheat-cotton example, Northern exports (= Southern imports) of wheat simultaneously generate a supply of pesos and a demand for dollars. If the exports are paid for in dollars, Southern importers must obtain (demand) dollars in the foreign exchange market by providing (supplying) pesos. If, on the other hand, the exports are paid for in pesos, then the Northern exporters (who, after all, have no use for pesos per se since they must pay for materials, utilities, and labor with dollars) must convert pesos into dollars in the foreign exchange market. Either way, someone must supply pesos and — simultaneously — demand dollars. Whether wheat exports are paid for in dollars or pesos, the result is the same. Pesos are supplied and dollars are demanded in an amount equal to the value of Northern exports (= Southern imports). Similarly, Southern exports (= Northern imports) of cotton generate simultaneously a supply of dollars and a demand for pesos.

Figure 4-1 shows, in two panels, the two dimensions of the same foreign exchange market between the Northern dollar and the Southern peso. Panel A shows the dollar market where quantities of dollars are traded at prices expressed in pesos. Panel B, the mirror image of Panel A, shows the peso market where the "good" traded is the peso and the price is expressed in dollars. The demand-for-dollars curve, $D_\$$, in Panel A, and the supply-of-pesos curve, S_p, in Panel B are equivalent; that is, they are two faces of the same coin. This equivalence is indicated by the solid arrow linking the two curves. Similarly, the supply-of-dollars curve, $S_\$$, and the demand-for-pesos curve, D_p, connected by a broken arrow, present the identical information, only viewed from opposite sides.

It is important to understand clearly that Panels A and B of Figure 4-1 do not represent two different markets; they are merely two expressions of a single market, a market that knows no national boundaries, and in which all nationalities can play. Northerners may supply *or* demand pesos *or* dollars; similarly, Southerners may supply *or* demand pesos *or*

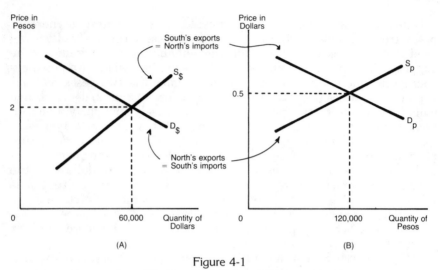

Figure 4-1
Markets for Dollars and Pesos

dollars. Therefore, neither a whole panel nor a single line of Figure 4-1 can be identified with a single nation or nationality.

The shapes of the supply and demand curves in Figure 4-1 are quite conventional. Against the peso price of dollars, the demand curve for dollars, $D_\$$, is drawn as downward sloping in Panel A. This slope can be explained in the following manner: The demand for dollars arises from North's exports (= South's imports). As the peso price of the dollar goes up, say from 2 pesos per dollar to 3 pesos per dollar, North's exports become increasingly more expensive in South. (A good that costs $1 in North costs 2 pesos in South if the exchange rate is 2 pesos per dollar; but it costs 3 pesos in South if the exchange rate is 3 pesos per dollar.) Consequently, the dollar value of North's exports (= South's imports) is lower at higher peso prices.[1] Hence the decrease in the quantity of dollars demanded. Conversely, the supply of dollars is a positive (upward sloping) function of the peso price of dollars. The slopes of the supply and demand curves of pesos in Panel B can be similarly explained. In fact, these demand-and-supply relationships are similar to the demand-and-supply relationships of any commodity; the quantity demanded will be smaller, and the quantity supplied will be greater, the higher the price — usually.

THE EQUILIBRIUM EXCHANGE RATE

Given an equilibrium price for eggs (or iron ore, or plywood), the quantity brought to market during a particular time period is exactly equal to the quantity buyers take away during that time period. Similarly, for foreign exchange, the equilibrium exchange rate is in effect if the quantity brought to market is exactly equal to the quantity buyers want to and do take away. In the example being used in this section, the equilibrium exchange rate is in effect when the quantity of dollars being offered for pesos is exactly equal to the quantity of dollars being demanded. Panel A of Figure 4-1 shows that such a rate exists when 2 pesos equal 1 dollar and when, as confirmed by Panel B, $0.5 equals 1 peso. If at this rate $60,000 are traded in the dollar market, then in the peso market 120,000 pesos are traded during the same time period. Again, we stress that one must not think that $60,000 *and* 120,000 pesos are traded in two separate transactions. What happens is that $60,000 are exchanged for 120,000 pesos, at the rate of 2 pesos per dollar (or $0.5 per peso).

The equality of supply and demand quantities also signifies the equality of export and import values, in each country and between the two countries. The value of North's exports = the value of North's imports = the value of South's exports = the value of South's imports = $60,000 = 120,000 pesos. It is important to remember that an equilibrium rate of exchange not only equates the quantities of currencies supplied and demanded in foreign exchange markets, but also equates each country's export and import values.[2]

This chapter has concentrated on a very simple two-product two-nation example. But the principles observed here do generalize to the complexity of the real world. For every national currency, there are exchange rates so extreme that no trade would occur either because no one would want to buy anything from that nation or because no one in that nation would want to buy anything from any other nation. In between those extremes are exchange rates that will sustain some trade, and somewhere among the sustainable rates is an equilibrium rate at which supply equals demand.

DISEQUILIBRIUM EXCHANGE RATES

Whenever a rate of exchange generates a disparity between a given currency's quantities demanded and supplied — or, what is the same thing, whenever a rate fails to equate a nation's imports and exports — we have a *disequilibrium rate*. Figure 4-2, Panel A, shows a situation where the actual peso/dollar rate, OA', is higher than the equilibrium rate, OA. At OA', the quantity of dollars supplied, OF, exceeds the quantity of dollars demanded, OC. The excess supply of dollars, CF, is unwanted by private demanders of dollars. Normally, such an excess supply would put a downward pressure on the peso price of dollars, and the price would move toward OA — unless a government (or governments) chooses to set the exchange rate at OA'. In such a case, the disequilibrium rate would persist; and the excess supply of dollars, CF, would equal South's trade *surplus* and North's trade *deficit* expressed in dollars.

The mirror image of the above situation is portrayed in Panel B of Figure 4-2. The actual dollar/peso rate, OB', is lower than the equilib-

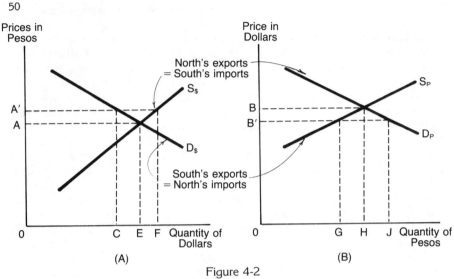

Figure 4-2
A Disequilibrium Rate of Exchange

rium rate, OB. The quantity of pesos demanded, OJ, exceeds the quantity supplied, OG. This excess demand for pesos, GJ, is the mirror image of the excess supply of dollars, CF. If government intervention permitted the excess supply to persist, then CF would equal North's trade deficit and South's trade surplus expressed in pesos.

Disequilibrium exchange rates prevail when a government intervenes in foreign exchange markets and artificially supports the value of a currency at above or below equilibrium levels. In the Figure 4-2 example, the artificially high peso/dollar rate (i.e., the artificially low dollar/peso rate) may be a result of the government of North artificially jacking up the peso price of its national currency, the dollar, for whatever reasons. In that case, the government of North must own foreign exchange *"reserves"* of pesos, and it must be using part of those peso reserves to buy the excess supply of dollars. Conversely, it could be that the government of South is artificially maintaining the low dollar price for its national currency, the peso. In this case, the government of South must be using pesos to buy dollars to be added to its dollar "reserves." Subsequent chapters will survey the reasons why governments may want to establish a disequilibrium exchange rate.

A government may establish a disequilibrium exchange rate either by drawing down or building up reserves or by simple fiat. If the disequilibrium rate is maintained through the use of reserves, the market continues to operate in the sense that all who voluntarily wish to buy or sell are able to do so at the rate being maintained by reductions in or additions to government foreign exchange reserves. If the disequilibrium rate is established by a government decree, it must be supported by a system of exchange control forbidding foreign exchange transactions at any other rate. In such a case, the appearance of a black market in foreign exchange is almost inevitable.

Disequilibrium rates of exchange represent *overvaluation* or *undervaluation* of the currencies. In the example portrayed in Figure 4-2, the dollar is overvalued relative to its true (equilibrium) value. The dollar whose equilibrium rate is OA pesos is artificially supported at the higher peso price of OA'. The overvaluation of the dollar necessarily means the undervaluation of the peso. In Panel B, the extent of the peso's undervaluation is the difference between OB and OB'. An overvaluation of the currency of a country generates a trade (or payments) deficit ("too many" imports) for the country, and an undervaluation is accompanied by a trade (or payments) surplus ("too many" exports). The size of the surplus or deficit will be known precisely if governments maintain the disequilibrium exclusively through the use of reserves. If decrees and controls are used to maintain the disequilibrium, no one will know the size of the potential surplus or deficit; and the accuracy of estimates will depend on the skills of the estimators.

Over- and undervaluations of currencies distort the commodity composition of a nation's trade as determined by comparative advantage. For example, under an overvalued currency, a nation's imports exceed its exports. This means that the nation has lost competitiveness in some goods in which it has comparative advantage. Specialization and trade based on comparative opportunity costs no longer lead to an equality of imports and exports. For nations to specialize and trade according to comparative advantage, therefore, it is important that an equilibrium exchange rate be maintained. The effects of an exchange-rate bias on a nation's commodity composition of trade will be discussed in Chapter 9. In the intervening chapters, unless otherwise noted, all the discussions of gains from, and patterns of, international trade will assume that equilibrium exchange rates prevail.

STUDY QUESTIONS

1. Suppose a given combination of resources produces either 5X or 20Y in a country called Alegra, and 5X or 30Y in a country called Bianca. In Alegra, one Y costs one dollar; in Bianca, one X costs 24 pesos.
    (a) Calculate the domestic transformation ratios between X and Y in Alegra and in Bianca.
    (b) Assuming market equilibrium in each country, what will be the price of X in Alegra? of Y in Bianca?
    (c) What would be happening within Alegra if the price of one X were (I) higher than you have suggested? or (II) lower than you have suggested?
    (d) On the basis of (a) and (b) above, which country has comparative advantage in which good?
    (e) Suppose Alegrans begin to *barter* trade with Biancans.
        (I) For the trading to be beneficial to Alegrans, a minimum of how many units of Biancan product must Alegrans have for one unit of their export?
        (II) For trading to be worthwhile to Biancans, a maximum of how many units of their product are Biancans willing to give for one unit of Alegran export?

(f) What, then, would be the limits of mutually beneficial barter terms of trade?

(g) Suppose that the two countries now begin to trade using money. Assume that there are no flows between the two countries other than those of goods X and Y. What would happen if the exchange rate between the dollar and the peso were $1 = 3 pesos?

(h) Calculate the two benchmark rates of exchange.

(i) Calculate the prices of the two goods, in each of the two countries, expressed in each of the two currencies, using a rate of exchange which is exactly at the midpoint between the two benchmark rates.

(j) Is the rate used in (i) above a sustainable rate? an equilibrium rate?

(k) Given the exchange rate used in (i) above, compute the monetary gain for an Alegran consumer and for a Biancan consumer, each buying one X *and* one Y.

2. What forces are at work to prevent *all* American products from becoming cheaper (or dearer) than *all* foreign products?

3. In what important sense does a foreign exchange market (say, between the dollar and the German mark) differ from a commodity market (say, of cotton)?

4. In the dollar-mark market, where do demands for dollars come from? Where do supplies of dollars come from?

5. Explain the relationships between (1) the over- or undervaluation of a currency, (2) the country's trade (or payments) balance, (3) the changes in the nation's foreign exchange reserves, and (4) the international competitiveness of the nation's products.

ENDNOTES

1. This is true provided that certain elasticity conditions are met. See Chapter 15.

2. In the greater complexity of the real world, an equilibrium rate of exchange is defined as the rate that equates a nation's balance of payments (merchandise, services, gifts, shares, bonds, and other IOUs) rather than its balance of trade (merchandise alone). See Chapter 14.

5

The International Division
of the Real Gains from Trade

Why should anyone gain from comparative advantage specialization and trade? How big will the gains be? How will the gains be divided? Chapter 3 established the engineering-arithmetic fact that answers the first question: If two nations have comparative advantage in particular products, comparative advantage specialization will bring an increase in total output of each of those products. That chapter, however, did not consider any way to determine the size of the potential ouput increases (the gains from specialization) or any way to tell how the gains would be divided between specializing trading partners.

Having brought money into the analysis, Chapter 4 established the arithmetic proposition that with perfectly competitive markets (so money price ratios will be inversely proportional to opportunity costs), international trade will bring domestic buyers lower money prices on newly imported products in which the importing nation has comparative disadvantage. But both Chapters 3 and 4 left unanswered the question of size of total gains from specialization and the question of division of specialization's gains between the trading partners.

This chapter will show:

1. How production possibility frontiers can be used to identify the exact size of the potential gains from comparative advantage specialization,
2. How two nations' demands for their comparative *dis*advantage products will interact to determine equilibrium terms of trade between two specializing trading partners, and
3. How the equilibrium terms of trade will determine the division of specialization's gains between trading partners.

The first step will be to show the exact size of the potential gains from comparative advantage specialization, using straight-line production possibility frontiers in each nation.

CALCULATING TOTAL GAINS FROM SPECIALIZATION

Because we need to consider total output possibilities, we must use production possibility frontiers, which in turn means we must begin to use geometry. In international economics, geometry is frequently used to portray the relationships characterizing a number of standard trade and payments models. For some readers, this geometry may be all new. For the sake of those who have no prior knowledge of any of these models, each will be explained in elementary detail.

Nevertheless, every person studying economics must occasionally despair when confronted by "another geometric sketch!" But do take heart with each one, for each is worth the effort required to master it. Here, we will soon begin to lean heavily upon the geometric models of Alfred Marshall, an English economist born in 1842, who kept copies of Aristotle and Plato at his right hand so he could turn from heavier reading and writing to *The Republic* for recreational reading. Despite this peculiar idea of fun, Marshall could give good advice. In regard to geometry, here are several paragraphs of avuncular Marshallian encouragement that may, when remembered, lift a reader's spirits in anticipation whenever a new geometric model of the economy is encountered:

The only apparatus which Ricardo and Mill brought to bear on the problems of pure economic theory was that of arithmetical illustration. But this is inadequate to the work. The use of numerical examples will perhaps enable the investigator to ascertain some of the consequences which may arise from the causes into whose operation he is inquiring: but it affords no security that he will discover all of these consequences or even the most important of them...

The pure theory of economic science requires the aid of an apparatus which can grasp and handle the general quantitative relations on the assumption of which the theory is based. The most powerful engines for such a purpose are supplied by the various branches of mathematical calculus. But diagrams are of great service...

Diagrams present simultaneously to the eye the chief forces which are at work, laid out, as it were, in a map; and thereby suggest results to which attention has not been directed by the use of the methods of mathematical analysis. The method of diagrams can be freely used by every one who is capable of exact reasoning, even though he have no knowledge of Mathematics. The reader, who will take the trouble to assure himself that he thoroughly understands the account of the curves given in the following paragraphs, will not find difficulty in following the reasoning to which they are afterwards applied.[1]

THE STRAIGHT LINE PRODUCTION POSSIBILITIES FRONTIER

The production possibilities frontier (PPF) is the first model we need. It shows, for two products, the maximum outputs that can be produced in a nation (or in any particular area), given its stock of resources, its technology, and its working habits (e.g., labor force participation ratios; length of work day and week; frequency of holidays, coffee breaks, etc.).

In Chapter 3 we assumed that a Northern farm could produce either 4 tons of cotton or 20 tons of wheat. If we now assume this farm to be one of 1,500 identical Northern farms, each producing only one of the two products, then North's production possibilities will be of the kind shown in Table 5-1. The top and bottom rows are included to show the output consequences of the extremes in which either all farms produce only wheat or all farms produce only cotton. The fourth row represents the initial production equilibrium assumed for North in Chapter 3. The other rows represent arbitrary divisions of the 1,500 farms into wheat and cotton production. Each reader should check the arithmetic of several rows to be sure that the cotton output shown is the maximum possible, given the number of farms devoted to wheat production.

The data of Table 5-1 are plotted as six points in Figure 5-1. Point N represents the initial production equilibrium assumed for North. The straight line connecting those six points is North's production possibilities frontier (PPF).

With full employment and maximum efficiency, North can produce any output combination represented by a point on the PPF. With some

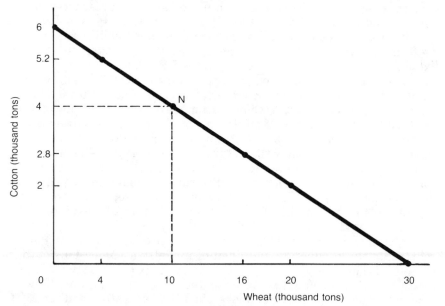

Figure 5-1
North's Production Possibilities Frontier for 1,500 Farms, Each Capable of Producing Either 20 Tons of Wheat or 4 Tons of Cotton

farms unused or with some used inefficiently, North can produce any output combination represented by a point below the PPF. But, unless North's productive resources are increased, North cannot reach an output combination represented by a point above the PPF of Figure 5-1.

TABLE 5-1 NORTH'S PRODUCTION POSSIBILITIES WITH 1,500 FARMS, EACH CAPABLE OF PRODUCING EITHER 20 TONS OF WHEAT OR 4 TONS OF COTTON

Numbers of Farms Producing		Total Output of	
Wheat	Cotton	Wheat (tons)	Cotton (tons)
1,500	0	30,000	0
1,000	500	20,000	2,000
800	700	16,000	2,800
500[a]	1,000[a]	10,000[a]	4,000[a]
200	1,300	4,000	5,200
0	1,500	0	6,000

[a]Represents the initial production situation assumed for North in Chapter 3.

The slope of North's PPF is $\frac{1}{5}$, or 1C/5W, the opportunity cost of wheat in terms of cotton on every Northern farm.[2] In the absence of foreign trade, the slope of North's PPF is the rate at which cotton and wheat will be exchanged in North. Call this North's *internal terms of trade.*

In the modern world, each nation's PPF moves out from year to year as technology improves and as each nation's stock of resources grows. Thus the location of North's 1982 PPF is sure to be farther from the origin than North's 1981 PPF, and probably somewhat different in slope as technological innovation changes opportunity costs. But, all the examples of this chapter will assume the PPF does *not* move.

South's PPF can be derived after some more information is added to the data base of Chapter 3. A Southern farm can produce either 2 tons of cotton or 6 tons of wheat. If we now assume this farm to be one of 3,500 identical Southern farms, then South's production possibilities will be of the kind shown in Table 5-2. Again, the top and bottom rows of the table are included to show the output consequences of the extremes in which either all farms produce only wheat or all farms produce only cotton. The third row represents the initial production equilibrium assumed for South in Chapter 3. The other rows represent only three among the many ways in which 3,500 farms can be divided into wheat and cotton producers.

The data of Table 5-2 are plotted as six points in Figure 5-2. Point S represents the production equilibrium initially assumed for South in Chapter 3. The straight line connecting those six points is South's PPF. South can attain the output represented by any point on or below its PPF but can reach a point above its PPF only after adding to its productive resources, or — as will be shown below — by comparative

TABLE 5-2   SOUTH'S PRODUCTION POSSIBILITIES WITH 3,500 FARMS,
EACH CAPABLE OF PRODUCING EITHER 6 TONS
OF WHEAT OR 2 TONS OF COTTON

Number of Farms Producing		Total Output of	
Wheat	Cotton	Wheat (tons)	Cotton (tons)
3,500	0	21,000	0
3,000	500	18,000	1,000
2,500[a]	1,000[a]	15,000[a]	2,000[a]
1,500	2,000	9,000	4,000
1,000	2,500	6,000	5,000
0	3,500	0	7,000

[a]Represents the initial production situation assumed for North in Chapter 3.

advantage specialization and trade. The slope of South's PPF is ⅓, the opportunity cost of wheat in terms of cotton on every Southern farm.[3] This is South's internal terms of trade; i.e., one ton of wheat trades for one-third ton of cotton.

THE TOTAL OUTPUT RECTANGLE

We are on our way to showing, given the resource and technology constraints of the PPFs, the exact size of the gain from comparative advantage specialization and trade. We will do this by showing (1) total output in the absence of specialization (Figure 5-3), (2) total output with complete specialization (Figure 5-4), and (3) the gain from specialization, which is the difference between (1) and (2).

In Figure 5-3, the PPFs of South and North are drawn within a single set of coordinates. North's PPF is the triangle UOY. South's PPF (triangle XQP) has been rotated 180° and drawn over North's PPF so that the pretrade production equilibrium, S, of South coincides with North's pretrade production equilibrium, N. In this admittedly awkward arrangement, total output of the two countries is represented by the dimensions of the edges of the total output rectangle, UOZQ. Total cotton output of both countries is 6,000 tons (OU), of which 4,000 tons (VN) are from Northern farms and 2,000 tons (WS) are from Southern farms. Total wheat output is 25,000 tons (OZ), of which 10,000 tons (TN) are produced by North and 15,000 tons (RS) are contributed by South. The dimensions of the edges of the rectangle UOZQ, therefore, show total output of cotton (6,000 tons) *and* total output of wheat (25,000 tons).

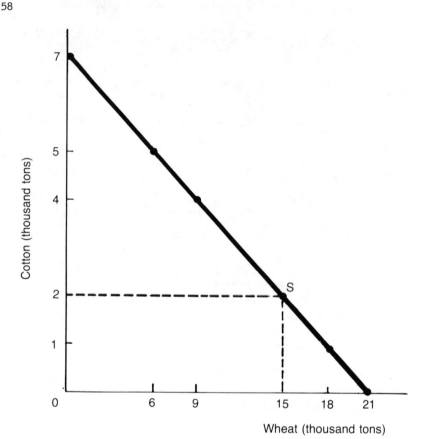

Figure 5-2
South's Production Possibilities Frontier for 3,500 Farms, Each Capable of Producing Either 6 Tons of Wheat of 2 Tons of Cotton

TOTAL GAINS FROM SPECIALIZATION

In Chapter 3 we demonstrated, by way of numerical examples, that North and South, by working together — that is, by engaging in comparative advantage specialization and trading — could increase total output of both cotton and wheat. We are now going to show this gain geometrically.

North has comparative advantage in wheat because the opportunity cost of wheat in terms of cotton is lower in North (⅕ ton of cotton) than in South (⅓ ton of cotton). Since North's comparative advantage lies in wheat, let it produce all wheat and no cotton, at point Y on its PPF. Similarly, let South specialize completely in cotton, at point X on its PPF. In Figure 5-4, North's complete-specialization-in-wheat production point Y is drawn to be coincident with South's complete-specialization-in-cotton-production point X. That point, in this case, is in the lower right hand corner of the new output rectangle. Call this

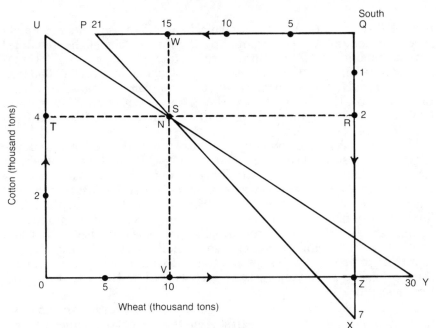

Figure 5-3
Total Wheat and Total Cotton Production When North and South Each
Produces in Isolated Equilibrium

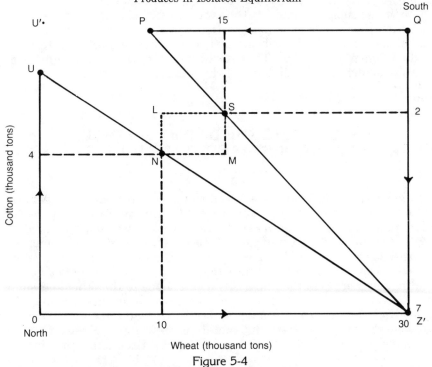

Figure 5-4
Total Wheat and Total Cotton Production with Complete Specialization, North Producing Wheat and South Producing Cotton

point Z' (= X = Y). Total production of wheat and cotton, under complete specialization, is now represented by the dimensions of the new total output rectangle, U'OZ'Q. Total cotton output of 7,000 tons (QZ') comes exclusively from Southern farms, and all of wheat output of 30,000 tons (OZ') is from Northern farms. The total *gain* from comparative advantage specialization is the increase in cotton ouput of 1,000 tons (from 6,000 to 7,000 tons) *and* the increase in wheat output of 5,000 tons (from 25,000 to 30,000 tons).

The gain is shown graphically in Figure 5-4 by the dimensions of the edges of the inscribed rectangle NMSL (NM = LS = 5,000 tons of wheat; LN = SM = 1,000 tons of cotton). The gain would be even greater if the pre-specialization production points N and S had been less in accord with each country's comparative advantage — that is, if they had been farther away from Z'. Conversely, if the pre-specialization production points had been closer to Z', the dimensions of the inscribed area would be smaller. From this the generalization follows that the less the two countries' pre-specialization production patterns are in agreement with their comparative advantage, the greater will be the potential gains from specialization.

This section's discussion has now gone two steps beyond the analysis presented in Chapter 3. In the first step, the arithmetic demonstration of the gains from trade has been converted to a geometric portrayal. In the second step, PPFs have been used to show the exact size of the potential gains available from complete specialization. Still missing, however, is a means to identify the exact division of these gains between the trading partners. The next section will require two steps to reach that end. First, it will describe a way to identify the equilibrium terms of trade between two nations. Then it will show how the equilibrium terms of trade determine the division of the gains from trade.

CALCULATING THE DIVISION BETWEEN TRADING NATIONS OF SPECIALIZATION'S GAINS

David Ricardo had discovered the formula for "increasing the general mass of productions" of nations that move from autarchy to comparative advantage specialization and trade. However, he was not able to identify a technique for determining the necessary or likely division of the "increased productions" between or among the specializing and trading nations. How would an increase in output be divided between two trading partners? Half to each? All to one, none to the other? Or some other division between those extremes? In the numerical example he used, Ricardo showed the gain to be divided approximately evenly between the two countries.[4] But that division was entirely arbitrary; it was simply a matter of elaborating the theme, "Each could have more."

JOHN STUART MILL'S CONTRIBUTION

Ricardo's good friend, James Mill (1773-1836), provided the son who scored the next conceptual breakthrough. John Stuart Mill (1806-1873) was a genius. At eight, he began to study Latin, Euclidean geometry, and algebra. His father took him, at age thirteen, through "a complete course in political economy" including a reading and rewriting of all the works of Ricardo. At age twenty-three, John Stuart Mill discovered and reported the general principle of what he called "reciprocal demand" equilibrium — the basis for generalizing about the traders' division of the gains from comparative advantage specialization.[5]

Mill reached two conclusions. First:

> ...when two countries trade together in two commodities, the exchangeable value of these commodities relatively to each other will adjust itself to the inclinations and circumstances of the consumers on both sides, in such manner that the quantities required by each country, of the article which it imports from its neighbour, shall be exactly sufficient to pay for one another.[6]

We will return to this generalization later and will expand it to explain the determination of the balance-of-payments equilibrium.

Mill's second conclusion was about the terms of trade:

> As the inclinations and circumstances of consumers cannot be reduced to any rule, so neither can the proportions in which the two commodities will be interchanged. We know that the limits within which the variation is confined are the ratio between their costs of production in the one country, and the ratio between their costs of production in the other.[7]

Mill's next sentence — paraphrased into the context of North, South, wheat, and cotton — generalized:

> One ton of wheat cannot exchange for more than one-third ton of cotton, nor for less than one-fifth. But they may exchange for any intermediate number. The ratios, therefore, in which the advantage of the trade may be divided between the two nations, are various;[8]

and finally,

> ...the country will gain, not in proportion to its own need of foreign articles, but to the need which foreigners have of the articles which itself produces.[9]

THE GEOMETRY OF MUTUALLY GAINFUL TERMS OF TRADE

Mill's description is about as clear as one can be without geometry. But this analysis is easier to follow when pursued through geometry. In our particular case, the essential facts are each nation's opportunity costs:

in North: 1 W = ⅕ C, 5 W = 1 C,
in South: 1 W = ⅓ C, and 3 W = 1 C.

What Mill observed was that the equilibrium terms of trade will be somewhere in the interval of 3 to 5 W per C; or, what is the same thing, of ⅕ to ⅓ C per W. Figure 5-5 portrays this interval.

In isolation, Northerners pay 5 tons of wheat per ton of cotton; in other words, they receive only ⅕ ton of cotton per ton of wheat sacrificed — that is, not produced. These are North's opportunity costs, and are represented in Figure 5-5 by line UZ', with a slope of 1C/5W. If Northerners could specialize in wheat and import more than ⅕ ton of cotton per ton of wheat exported, they would be better off. Thus, Northerners would gain from specializing in wheat and trading for cotton along any line steeper than UZ'.

In isolation, Southerners pay ⅓ ton of cotton per ton of wheat. In other words, they receive only 3 tons of wheat per ton of cotton sacrificed, that is, not produced. These are South's opportunity costs. In Figure 5-5, line PZ', with slope 1C/3W, represents South's opportunity costs. If Southerners could specialize in cotton and import more than 3 tons of wheat per ton of cotton exported, they would be better off. Southerners would

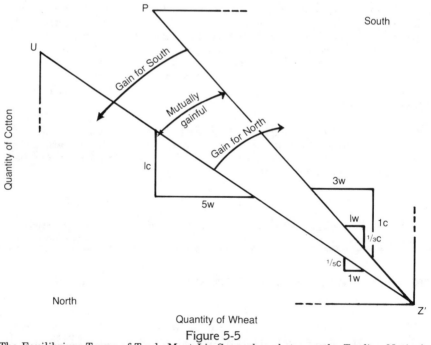

Figure 5-5
The Equilibrium Terms of Trade Must Lie Somewhere between the Trading Nation's Opportunity Costs

gain from specializing in cotton and trading for wheat along any line flatter than PZ'.

Figure 5-5 shows, in Mill's language, that North would not take less than ⅕ C per ton of wheat while South would not pay more than ⅓ C per ton of wheat. But any terms of trade between the slopes of UZ' and of PZ' would permit North to buy 1 ton of cotton for less than 5 tons of wheat (bringing more than ⅕ C per W) and would permit South to buy wheat for less than ⅓ ton of cotton per ton of wheat. Any terms of trade between UZ' and PZ', therefore, would make *both* nations better off.

MARSHALLIAN OFFER CURVES

To be able to determine the equilibrium terms of trade within a single geometric sketch, two Englishmen — Francis Y. Edgeworth (1845-1926) and Alfred Marshall — invented "offer curves." Here is the problem they solved: With comparative advantage specialization, North wants to spend wheat to buy cotton; South wants to spend cotton to buy wheat. This is *reciprocal demand*. But the usual demand sketch measures commodity quantity on one axis and money price on the other. To be able to use a single two-dimensional sketch to show the interaction between North's demand for cotton and South's demand for wheat, a "demand" sketch is needed that will measure wheat on one axis and cotton on the other. The Marshall-Edgeworth trick is to replace money price with units of the other commodity. They solved the problem by measuring opportunity cost on each axis. This is, after all, the essence of the pure theory of international trade: that cost — the real price — of one product is measurable in terms of units of the other product. Chapter 3 dealt only with such real costs.

The sections following this will develop Marshall-Edgeworth offer curves based on the North-South wheat-cotton example of previous chapters. The very next section will begin with demand curves that are quite ordinary, except that the price axis will show opportunity-cost units of the other product. Offer curves will be derived from these demand curves. Then North's offer curve and South's offer curve will be put together in a single sketch where they will define the North-South equilibrium terms of trade.

Demand with Price in Commodity Units

What does North's demand curve for cotton look like? Northerners' demand for cotton involves Northerners' willingness to give up wheat in exchange for cotton. So far, only one fact is known about Northerners' tastes for cotton and wheat.

Figure 5-4 shows that Northerners chose the pretrade production point, N, 4,000 tons of cotton and 10,000 tons of wheat produced and consumed in North. This is important information because it tells something about Northerners' relative preferences for cotton and wheat. Before trade, they could have produced — and consumed — 30,000 tons of wheat and no cotton. They did not. Instead, they chose to forego growing 20,000 tons of wheat in order to have 4,000 tons of cotton. In effect, they paid 20,000 tons of wheat to obtain 4,000 tons of cotton.

If Northerners were willing to pay 20,000W for 4,000C before trade, surely they would be willing to do likewise with trade. With complete specialization, Northerners grow 30,000 tons of wheat. By exporting 20,000 tons of wheat in exchange for 4,000 tons of Southern cotton, they could return to their pretrade consumption point, point N in Figure 5-4. This information identifies one point on North's demand curve for cotton. Northerners would pay, in exports, 20,000W to obtain 4,000C, in imports. That works out to 5W per C. In conventional language, this

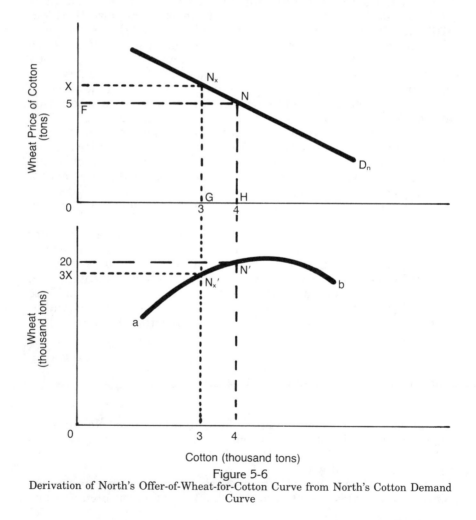

Figure 5-6
Derivation of North's Offer-of-Wheat-for-Cotton Curve from North's Cotton Demand Curve

means that at a real price of 5W per C, Northerners demand 4,000 tons of cotton.

This demand point is plotted in the upper half of Figure 5-6. At a real price of 5W per C, Northerners demand FN, 4,000 tons, of cotton; this is point N in Figure 5-6. Here, as on any demand curve, total expenditure is represented by the area of the rectangle inscribed between the axes and a point on the demand curve. The inscribed rectangle's height equals price; its width equals quantity demanded. With the price of 5W and quantity demanded of 4,000, the area of the rectangle OFNH is 20,000 tons of wheat. What is the significance of this quantity, 20,000 tons of wheat? It means that at a price of 5 tons of wheat per ton of cotton, Northerners are willing to pay 20,000 tons of wheat to obtain 4,000 tons of cotton. In other words, at this price of 5W per C, Northerners are willing to exchange (they will supply, they will offer) 20,000 tons of their wheat to get 4,000 tons of cotton.

In the upper graph of Figure 5-6, a demand line has been drawn through point N. This point N derived from the point N of Figure 5-1, but the rest of the demand curve drawn in Figure 5-6 is arbitrary. It has been given a conventional shape and has been introduced as the basis for derivation of North's wheat-for-cotton offer curve.

Converting a Demand Curve into an Offer Curve

North's demand for cotton implies North's supply of wheat. The upper graph of Figure 5-6 represents two measures: (1) horizontal distances represent cotton quantity *demanded* by North at each wheat price of cotton, and (2) inscribed rectangular areas represent wheat quantity *supplied* by North at each wheat price of cotton. This diagram is unsatisfactory because the amount of wheat offered (supplied) can be found only through multiplication. It cannot be read directly on either the vertical or the horizontal axis.

The Marshall-Edgeworth solution remedies this deficiency by providing for derivation of another curve in a graph in which the quantity of cotton demanded is measured along the horizontal axis as before, but in which the quantity of wheat supplied is read directly from the vertical axis. The lower graph of Figure 5-6 shows such a derivation. The information represented by point N in the upper graph is represented by point N' in the lower graph. Point N' is plotted to show the quantity of wheat supplied, measured along the vertical axis, is 20,000 tons, and to show the quantity of cotton demanded, measured as before on the horizontal axis, is 4,000 tons. The relevant price of 5W per C is represented in the lower graph by the slope of a line, ON', drawn from the origin. Against every value of quantity of cotton demanded read on the horizontal scale of Figure 5-6, corresponding values of quantity of wheat supplied (found by measuring the inscribed areas under the demand curve D_n) are plotted on the vertical scale. For example, against the quantity of cotton demanded of 3,000 tons at the price of X tons of wheat, point N'_x shows that the quantity of wheat supplied, measured along the vertical scale, is 3,000X tons (equal to the area OXN_xG). The curve ab that is traced out in the lower graph of Figure 5-6 is North's wheat-supply-&-cotton-demand curve, or simply North's offer curve. At any point on ab, quantity of cotton demanded is read horizontally, quantity of wheat supplied (offered) is measured vertically, and price is the slope of the line drawn from the origin.

In elementary economics courses, students are often asked to derive a total revenue (or expenditure) curve from a demand curve. That is essentially what the Marshall-Edgeworth solution does. The offer curve is a total expenditure curve. But here, total dollar revenue (or expenditure) is replaced by total wheat expenditure. In the elementary economics course, dollars are offered for cotton; in this exercise, real goods — here, tons of wheat — are offered for cotton. The relationship between the demand curve and the offer curve is thus a simple mechanical one. In the demand sketch of Figure 5-6, the vertical axis shows, for each cotton quantity, the maximum wheat price Northerners will pay. In the offer curve sketch of Figure 5-6, the vertical axis shows, for each cotton quantity, the maximum total wheat quantity Northerners will pay.

Mechanically, D_n and the offer curve, ab, of Figure 5-6 move up or down together. For example, if Northerners' demand for Southern cotton increases, D_n will shift up, and the offer curve, ab, will also shift up. For each cotton quantity, Northerners will have become willing to pay a higher unit price and a larger total quantity of wheat.

Figure 5-7 shows the derivation of South's cotton-supply-&-wheat-demand curve from the Southern demand curve for wheat. Again, as in Figure 5-6, one point, here, S, is based on information provided in Figure 5-4. Before specialization, South could have produced 7,000 tons of cotton. Instead, Southerners chose to forego 5,000 tons of cotton to obtain 15,000 tons of wheat. This was their choice at an opportunity cost of $1/3$ C per W. That choice is shown as point S in the upper graph of Figure 5-7. It is translated into point S' in the lower graph of Figure 5-7. Point S' shows Southerners' willingness to pay — to offer — up to a maximum of 5,000 tons of cotton to obtain 15,000 tons of wheat.

D_s is drawn through S and is given an arbitrarily chosen slope. Given D_s and its inscribed rectangles, the Southern offer curve, cd, is derived to show, for each wheat quantity, the maximum quantity of cotton Southerners are willing to pay.

Plotting Both Nations' Offer Curves in One Figure

Figure 5-8 puts it all together. In fact it puts so much together that one must make an extra effort to get it right the first time through.

First, the two PPFs of Figure 5-4 are reproduced in Figure 5-8. Both North and South are assumed to be completely specialized; so each produces at point Z' on its PPF. As in Figure 5-4, N and S are the pre-specialization consumption points.

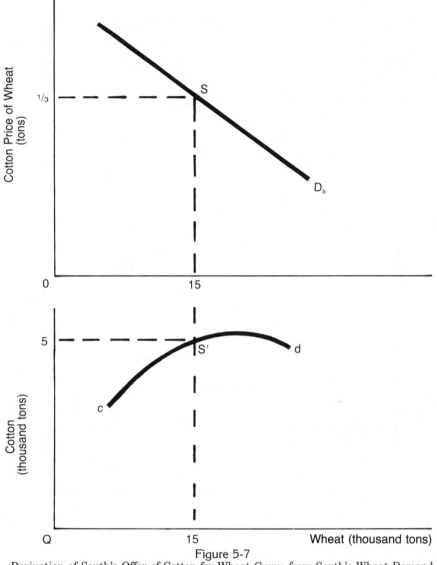

Figure 5-7

Derivation of South's Offer-of-Cotton-for-Wheat Curve from South's Wheat Demand
Curve

In Figure 5-8, atop Figure 5-4, the Northern and the Southern offer curves are drawn. In effect, the bottom graph of Figure 5-6 is placed atop Figure 5-8 with the origin of Figure 5-6 coincident with the Z' of Figure 5-8 and with the vertical wheat axis of Figure 5-6 rotated 90° to become the horizontal wheat axis of Figure 5-8.

Finally, through a most awkward adjustment, the bottom graph of Figure 5-7 is placed atop Figure 5-8 with the origin of Figure 5-7

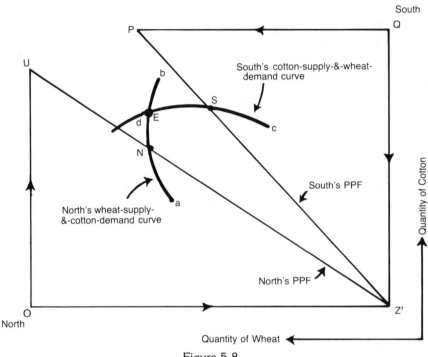

Figure 5-8
Determination of the Equilibrium Terms of Trade

coincident with the Z' of Figure 5-8 and with the horizontal wheat axis of Figure 5-7 rotated out from the page and over 180° to match the horizontal wheat axis of Figure 5-8 — except that, for both offer curves, the wheat axis is read from right to left. With that construction completed, both offer curves appear in a single graph in which the offer curves' origin is at the lower right-hand corner. If the same scale is used throughout this construction, points N' and S' of the offer curves will be coincident with points N and S on the PPFs from Figure 5-6.

Note that each axis represents two scales. For production and consumption of wheat and of cotton, use the inner PPF scales. Measure wheat quantity and cotton quantity from point O for North and from point Q for South.

For the two offer curves, which is to say, for exports and imports, use the outer scale. Measure wheat quantity and cotton quantity from point Z' for both North and South.

The result is that the inner (PPF) and the outer (offer-curve) scales read in opposite directions. For example, while the quantity of wheat offered by North is read on the outer horizontal scale from right to left (Z' to O), North's production and consumption of wheat are measured on the inner (PPF) scale from left to right (O to Z'). This makes sense since North's supply (offer) of wheat and its consumption of wheat are complementary and add up to its production. As more wheat is offered (to South) out of North's given output of wheat (OZ'), less is available for domestic consumption. As one increases, the other decreases. Thus, the quantity of wheat supplied and the quantity consumed must necessarily be read in opposite directions. The same holds true with South's export supply (read bottom up, from Z') and consumption (read top down from Q) of cotton.

The Terms-of-Trade Equilibrium

Now, at last, the Marshall-Edgeworth solution — how to use the offer curves to identify the equilibrium international terms of trade.

At any particular price, represented by a ray from Z' in Figure 5-8, the point on ab intersected by the ray will show the quantity of wheat North will offer, and the intersected point on cd will show the quantity of wheat South will demand. Those two quantities are unequal at every price except the price represented by the ray Z'E. So, the terms-of-trade equilibrium between North and South is determined by the intersection of the two offer curves at point E. At this point, North's demand for South's cotton is exactly matched by South's supply of cotton; and South's demand for North's wheat is matched by North's supply of wheat. The equilibrium terms of trade are expressed by the slope of the imaginary price line, Z'E; and, as argued in connection with Figure 5-5, such terms of trade must lie between the domestic opportunity costs (the internal terms of trade) in the two countries, expressed respectively by the slopes of Z'U and Z'P.[10]

Consider events if the terms of trade are not at the equilibrium. For example, what happens if the international terms of trade are those of Z'N in Figure 5-8 (the same as North's internal terms of trade)? North would offer less wheat than South would demand. So Southerners would bid up the cotton price of wheat. Alternatively, if the international terms of trade were those at or near Z'S, North would offer more wheat than South would demand, and the cotton price of wheat would be bid down. With offer curves as with ordinary supply and demand curves, if quantity demanded exceeds quantity supplied, price is bid up. If quantity supplied exceeds quantity demanded, price is forced down.

The greater North's demand for cotton becomes, the closer will be the equilibrium terms to $\frac{1}{5}$ C = 1W (the slope of Z'U) and the smaller will be North's share of the gain from trade (see below for more on share of gains). Similarly, the greater South's demand for wheat, the closer will be the equilibrium rate to $\frac{1}{3}$ C = 1W (the slope of Z'P) and the smaller will be South's gain. As Mill observed, gain will be "in proportion to...the need which foreigners have of the articles" the nation exports. The greater their need, the more the nation gains, and vice versa. This proposition can easily be shown geometrically. Suppose that North's demand for cotton increases. In Figure 5-6, both demand curve D_n and offer curve ab shift upward. This means that, in Figure 5-8, North's offer curve ab shifts to the left to intersect South's offer curve cd at a point closer to Z'U than at E. The conclusion may be obvious: An increase in a country's demand for another's product will result in a deterioration of the buyer's, and an improvement in the seller's, terms of trade.

DISTRIBUTION OF THE GAINS FROM SPECIALIZATION AND TRADE

Suppose that the terms-of-trade equilibrium is established by intersecting offer curves (not shown) at point E in Figure 5-9. Since under complete specialization both North and South are producing at point Z', equilibrium at point E means that North exports Z'V' of wheat to South, and South exports V'E (= Z'R') of cotton to North. The terms of trade in this transaction are V'E/Z'V', the slope of the broken line Z'E.

Point E thus becomes North's *consumption* point, after specialization and trade. Remember that before specialization and trade, point N was North's *production-and-consumption* point. By consuming at point E, North is beyond its production possibilities frontier Z'U. A comparison of the points N and E clearly shows that, after specialization and trade, North consumes VV' more of wheat and TT' more of cotton. This is North's share of the gains from comparative-advantage specialization and trade.

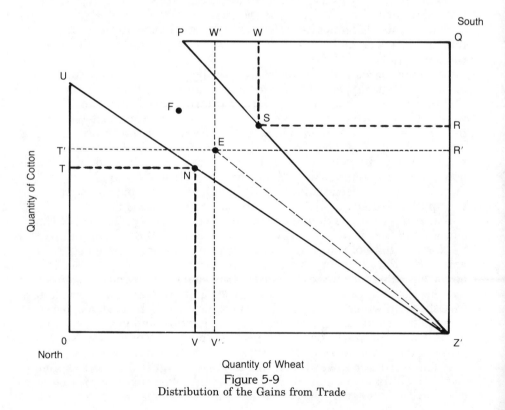

Figure 5-9
Distribution of the Gains from Trade

Similarly, South consumes at E with Z'R' of cotton exported to, and R'E of wheat imported from, North. Compared with the isolation equilibrium at S, South consumes WW' more wheat and RR' more cotton, at point E, which is beyond South's production possibilities frontier Z'P. This is South's share of the gains from specialization and trade. Comparative-advantage specialization and trade enables both countries to expand their consumption possibilities beyond their production possibilities frontiers.[11] Given the demand curve of each nation for the product it imports, the Marshall-Edgeworth solution permits exact identification of the equilibrium division of the gains that flow from comparative-advantage specialization and trade.

IDENTIFYING GAINS FROM TRADE WHERE PPFs ARE CONCAVE

The preceding section assumed that opportunity costs were constant throughout the production range in both North and South; so their production possibilities were expressed as straight lines. This is the classical Ricardian case, which leads to complete specialization in at least one nation once trade opens up between the two nations.

This next section makes the alternative assumption that the opportunity costs of each product increase as more of it is produced. This means that each nation's PPF is concave when viewed from the origin. It also means that free trade will not bring complete specialization in each nation. This section will use offer curves to identify, given concave PPFs, equilibrium terms of trade and the division of the gains from comparative-advantage specialization. First, however, several geometric tools must be developed.

THE CONCAVE PRODUCTION POSSIBILITIES FRONTIER

Earlier in this chapter, each of the 1,500 Northern farms was assumed to be capable of producing either 20 tons of wheat or 4 tons of cotton. This assumption led to the constant slope of North's production possibilities frontier (Figure 5-1), representing the constant opportunity cost of 5W:1C.

What happens when this rigid assumption is dropped and replaced by the more realistic assumption that some farms are more suited to wheat production and others are relatively more efficient in cotton production? This difference in productive efficiency might be attributable to the difference in the quality of the soil on each farm.

For simplicity, assume that North consists of just four farms with the following production possibilities:

Farm A: 30 tons of wheat or 2 tons of cotton,
Farm B: 20 tons of wheat or 4 tons of cotton,
Farm C: 15 tons of wheat or 6 tons of cotton, and
Farm D: 10 tons of wheat or 8 tons of cotton.

The four are listed here in order according to — what? Calculate opportunity costs on each farm to see that they are arrayed according to opportunity cost of wheat. Farm A has the lowest and Farm D has the highest opportunity cost of wheat.

If only Farm A produces wheat and the other three farms produce cotton, North would produce 30 tons of wheat and 18 tons of cotton. This combination, 30W and 18C, is one point on North's PPF. If each farm is required to plant either all wheat or all cotton, there are five possible maximum-efficiency output combinations of W and C, as shown below:

Farm(s) producing W	Farm(s) producing C	Total production	PPF point
None	A, B, C, D	0W, 20C	E
A	B, C, D	30W, 18C	F
A, B	C, D	50W, 14C	G
A, B, C	D	65W, 8C	H
A, B, C, D	None	75W, 0C	J

Given production possibilities data for n farms (here 4), and given an array of the farms by opportunity costs of one product, PPF points are easily calculated for n + 1 (here 5) output possibilities. The five points are plotted in Figure 5-10, and the points are connected by straight lines. Any point on a straight-line segment but away from the end of the segment shows a production possibility with some one farm planted partly to wheat, and partly to cotton, while all other farms specialize completely in one or the other product. The EFGHJ of Figure 5-10 is North's PPF. (Take a moment here to calculate total output if Farm D produces all wheat while all other farms produce all cotton. Why does that output combination not yield a point on the nation's PPF?)

With four farms, the PPF consists of five line segments. With 1,500 farms, the PPF would consist of 1,501 line segments. In the real world of many producers, the PPF consists of so many line segments that it would appear to be a smooth curve concave to the origin. That concavity represents the real-world situation of increasing opportunity cost. In Figure 5-10, as we move from point E toward point J, the opportunity cost of one ton of wheat measured in terms of the tonnage of cotton increases as follows: from E to F, $\frac{1}{15}$ ton; from F to G, $\frac{1}{5}$ ton; from G to H, $\frac{2}{5}$ ton; and from H to J, $\frac{4}{5}$ ton.[12] This means that as more wheat and less cotton is produced, wheat becomes increasingly more expensive in terms of cotton that must be foregone. This, surely, is the way the real world works. Similarly, as we move from point J toward point E, producing more cotton and less wheat, the opportunity cost of cotton increases.

Figure 5-11 portrays a smooth and concave production frontier, NN, for North. The slope of the curve at a given point on the curve represents

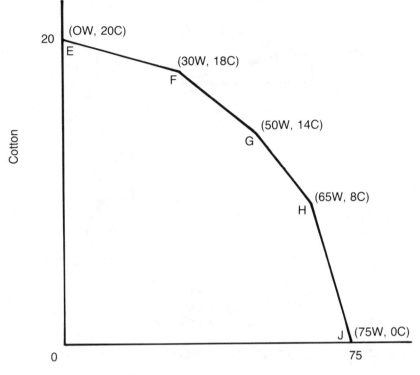

Figure 5-10
North's PPF with Four Dissimilar Farms

the (marginal) opportunity cost of wheat in terms of cotton, or $\Delta C/\Delta W$ ("Δ" means "a change in"). This ratio, $\Delta C/\Delta W$, is known as the *marginal rate of substitution in production,* or MRS_p; it is a synonym, in this example, for the opportunity cost of wheat. At point A, $MRS_p = \Delta C/\Delta W =$ ab/bc, where the line ac is tangent to NN at point A. At point B, MRS_p is much higher, namely, de/ef>ab/bc. The marginal rate of substitution in production increases as more wheat (and less cotton) is produced. This increase would be readily apparent if, in America, wheat production were extended from Kansas into Mississippi and Florida.

Exactly where on the concave PPF does a country produce in pretrade isolation? The answer depends on the relative taste or preference of the people for the two goods. If the people in North like to consume a large quantity of cotton but do not care for much wheat, they might settle at a point like A rather than B, and vice versa. In order to identify the exact point of optimum production on the PPF, we need to develop another economic concept portrayed as a geometric device — the indifference curve.

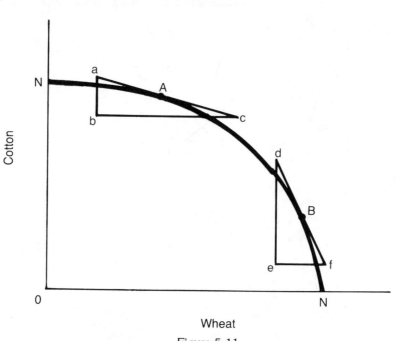

Figure 5-11
The Concave PPF and the Increasing MRS$_P$

THE COMMUNITY INDIFFERENCE CURVE

You may recall from your economics principles course that a consumer's relative preference for two products, say wheat and cotton, may be expressed by a convex curve called the *indifference curve*. In Figure 5-12, the individual is consuming OC of cotton and OW of wheat at point A on the indifference curve U. At this point, the consumer enjoys a certain level of satisfaction or "total utility," call it "U." The consumer, however, need not have that particular combination of cotton and wheat to experience the satisfaction level U. Normally, there exist possibilities for substitution between any two goods. In the present illustration, the individual could lose some cotton but would feel exactly the same level of satisfaction if enough more wheat were obtained. Suppose such an alternative combination of the two goods is represented by point B, at which OC' of cotton and OW' of wheat are consumed. The individual experiences the same level of satisfaction at points A and B; in other words, the consumer is *indifferent* between points A and B. All the points among which the consumer is indifferent can be found and connected by a curve such as U. The result is an *indifference curve*, U, representing a given level of satisfaction, U. Another curve (not shown) located farther away from the origin represents a higher level of consumer satisfaction or welfare. A series of such curves, each representing a successively higher level of consumer satisfaction, constitutes the *indifference map* of a given consumer.

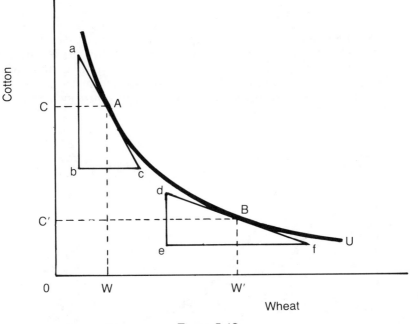

Figure 5-12
The Indifference Curve and the Decreasing MRS$_C$

Moving from A to B, the consumer would lose C'C of cotton and gain WW' of wheat. The consumer is willing to give up C'C of cotton for WW' of wheat. The ratio of the two quantities, C'C/WW' — or $\triangle$C/$\triangle$W — is known as the *marginal rate of substitution in consumption,* or MRS$_c$. To find the value of MRS$_c$ at a point, such as A, the slope of the line tangent to the indifference curve at that point must be found. The MRS$_c$ between cotton and wheat at point A, thus, is found by the slope of the line ac (ignoring the negative sign), or by the ratio ab/bc, in Figure 5-12. At point B, the MRS$_c$ is similarly found by the slope of the line df, the ratio de/ef. Unlike the MRS$_p$, which *increases* as more wheat is *produced,* MRS$_c$ *decreases* as more wheat is *consumed.* This can be seen by the fact that the slope of the indifference curve becomes flatter, or the corresponding ratio becomes smaller, as we move down along the curve. The diminishing marginal rate of substitution in consumption is attributable to the law of diminishing marginal utility of each good. As more wheat is consumed, for example, the consumer's marginal utility of wheat decreases, so that he or she is willing to give up increasingly less cotton for a given quantity of wheat.

   To conceive of an individual's indifference map is relatively easy. But the indifference curves required here are *community indifference curves,* the curves of an entire nation. These are more difficult to envision. Nevertheless, in the discussion that follows, community indifference maps will be assumed to exist for North and for South. The indifference map of each nation is assumed to represent accurately the combined preferences of everyone in the country.

EQUILIBRIUM IN ISOLATION

Back to the question raised earlier: At what point on its PPF will a country produce — and consume — in pretrade isolation? Figure 5-13 portrays a country's production frontier, NN, and a pair of community indifference curves, U and U'. This PPF represents the country's maximum production possibilities; it shows the country's resource constraint.

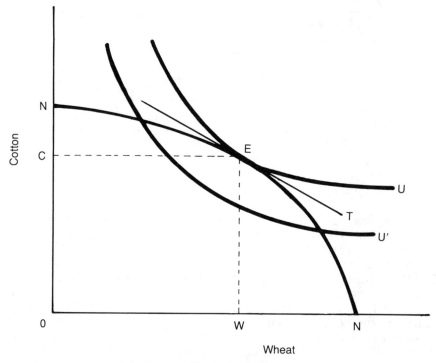

Figure 5-13
Equilibrium in Isolation

If the country makes full use of its available resources, it will produce at a point somewhere on its PPF. If the community chooses this point so it reaches its highest attainable level of satisfaction, it will choose the point on the highest attainable indifference curve. The indifference curve U' does not satisfy this requirement, since the community can reach other indifference curves that give the community higher levels of economic welfare. An indifference curve (not shown) that lies outside of NN, however, will not do either since such a level of welfare is unattainable because of the resource constraint. Thus, the highest attainable indifference curve is necessarily the one that is tangent to the PPF. In isolated equilibrium, this country produces, and consumes, at point E.

OC of cotton is produced *and* consumed, and OW of wheat is produced *and* consumed domestically. The line T, the common tangent to the indifference curve and the PPF, represents the equilibrium price ratio of the two goods prevailing in the domestic market; it is the internal terms of trade. The slope of the line T is equal (ignoring the minus sign) to the price ratio, P_w/P_c. At point E, the slopes of NN, T, and U are all equal; that is, $MRS_p = P_w/P_c = MRS_c$. The meaning of this equality is this: If, under market equilibrium, 3C transforms into 1W in production, then consumers must value 3C as equivalent to 1W, and the price of W must be three times the price of C.[13]

Take a moment now to turn back to Figure 5-1. To keep the initial presentation simple, no community indifference curves were drawn in Figure 5-1. If some of North's community indifference curves were to be drawn in Figure 5-1, which one would be most significant? The text asserted that in isolation, Northerners chose the production-consumption combination represented by point N. Presumably, therefore, N provided the Northern community with more satisfaction than would have come from any other output combination. Therefore, one of North's community indifference curves must be tangent to North's PPF at point N. Similarly, in Figure 5-2, one of South's community indifference curves must be tangent to South's PPF at point S. In every case, in no-trade isolation, a nation is in maximum-satisfaction equilibrium if it is at the point of tangency between its PPF and one of its community indifference curves.

EQUILIBRIUM WITH TRADE

Figure 5-14 portrays the equilibria, both before and after trade, of North and South. Note that South's production frontier, SS, is relatively taller than North's, NN. This difference in shape is attributable to the difference in the relative resource endowments of the two countries; South is better suited to produce cotton, and North is relatively more efficient in production of wheat.

Pretrade equilibria are identified by the tangency of indifference curves and PPFs, and are found at P_n and P_s, where North and South each produces both cotton and wheat and where each consumes all it produces. U_n and U_s represent the initial, pretrade levels of economic welfare in each nation. The pretrade real cost and price of cotton are higher in North. The cost and price of wheat are higher in South. This difference in relative costs and prices is indicated by the difference in the slope of the two domestic price lines, T_n and T_s.

Posttrade Production Equilibria

Previous sections of this chapter have shown that the posttrade equilibrium terms of trade will be determined by reciprocal demand

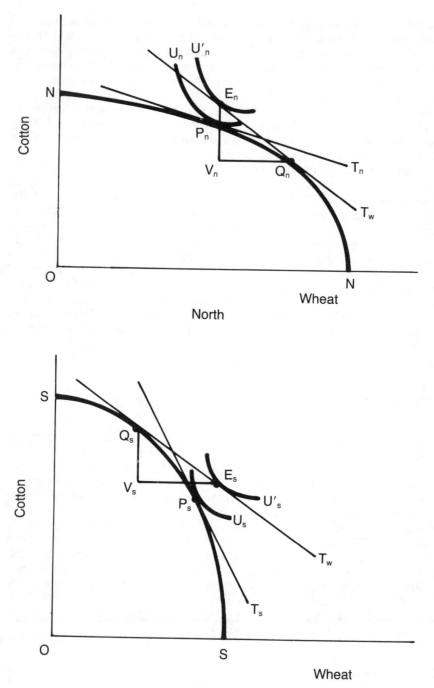

Figure 5-14
Equilibrium with Trade

manifested in national offer curves and will lie between the pretrade price ratios (internal terms of trade) of the two nations. Having established the principles of offer curves, the mechanics can be skipped in this more complex example. Assume that when North and South trade freely, the equilibrium international terms of trade are represented by the slope of the line T_w, drawn in both the upper and lower graphs of Figure 5-14.

With the change to the free-trade prices of cotton and wheat, South produces more cotton, and North produces more wheat. North reaches equilibrium at Q_n. South reaches equilibrium at Q_s. At these *posttrade* production points, Q_n and Q_s, the MRS_p in North is the same as in South and is equal to the slope of T_w, the equilibrium international terms of trade. Therefore, tangents to the two PPFs at points Q_n and Q_s both have the slope of the line T_w.

Posttrade Consumption Equilibria

Where then are the posttrade *consumption* points? Before trade, both nations' consumption possibilities were constrained by their production possibilities; in other words, their pretrade consumption combinations (then equal to their output combinations) could not lie outside their PPFs. In the adjustment to international-trade equilibrium, a delicate accommodation occurs among North's supply of export wheat (constrained by North's PPF), South's demand for import wheat (determined by South's indifference curve system), South's supply of export cotton (constrained by South's PPF), and North's demand for import cotton (determined by North's indifference curves). Equilibrium requires international terms of trade at which the total quantity of wheat North will offer just equals the quantity of wheat South demands for the cotton Southerners are induced to export to attract North's wheat offer. There will ordinarily be, as in Figure 5-14, a unique terms of trade, here T_w, at which what Northerners want to export, V_nQ_n, equals what Southerners want to import, V_sE_s, and what Southerners want to export, Q_sV_s, equals what Northerners want to import, V_nE_n. In equilibrium, North's consumption point is at E_n, on the highest indifference curve attainable by trade along T_w. South's consumption point is at E_s, on the highest indifference curve attainable by trade along T_w. There will be no other terms of trade under which each nation's exports will just equal the other nation's imports (where, in terms of geometry, the right triangle between North's production and consumption points will exactly equal the right triangle between South's production and consumption points).

In the posttrade, worldwide equilibrium, the opportunity costs are equal, and the price ratios of the two goods are equal in both nations; in fact, there exists only one product price ratio in the world, and it is equal to the slope of T_w. Since, in this worldwide equilibrium, the slopes of North's PPF and its indifference curve, and the slopes of South's PPF and its indifference curve, are all equal to the slope of T_w, the situation is one where MRS_c, MRS_p, and P_w/P_c in both nations are all equal.

Both countries' gains from trade are demonstrated by the fact that they are on higher indifference curves after trade than before. Both consume more wheat and more cotton than before trade. Comparative advantage specialization and trade have made it possible for them to expand their consumption possibilities beyond their production possibilities.[14]

Under conditions of increasing opportunity costs, specialization is less than complete. The difference in the pretrade domestic price ratios (opportunity costs) gives rise to gainful trade, and each country specializes in the production of the good for which it is better suited. However, as specialization progresses, the relative price (opportunity cost) of the specialized product rises in each country because of the increasing cost conditions. Further specialization ceases when opportunity costs are equalized in both countries. In this equilibrium, each country continues to produce a quantity of the good that it imports. Thus, for example, if free trade were permitted in sugar, America would import most of its sugar. But a few cane growers in Louisiana and a few beet growers in Colorado might have such low opportunity costs that they would continue to grow sugar cane and sugar beets.

STUDY QUESTIONS

1. Suppose there are two countries, Nepal and Senegal, producing two goods, Yazes and Xerks. Domestic transformation ratios between the two products are $5Y = 3X$ in Nepal and $2Y = 3X$ in Senegal. Using all of its available resources, Nepal can produce 5,000 tons of Yazes *or* 3,000 tons of Xerks. Similarly, Senegal can produce 4,000 tons of Yazes *or* 6,000 tons of Xerks. With full employment and maximum efficiency, but without trade, both countries actually produce, each, 2,000 tons of Yazes. Now, trade opens up between the two countries, and each specializes completely in the production of its comparative advantage product.
   (a) Identify comparative advantage in the two goods in the two countries by calculating opportunity costs.
   (b) Calculate the two nations' combined gains from trade by comparing the actual output quantities of the two countries before and after the comparative advantage specialization.
   (c) Sketch a graph (see Figure 5-4) showing equilibrium with complete specialization in production.
   (d) Suppose the intersection of offer curves establishes an equilibrium terms of trade at $1Y = 1X$, and at this rate Nepal exports 2,500 Yazes. Enter this equilibrium point in the graph you sketched in (c) above, and mark off export and import quantities of both countries.
   (e) Calculate the quantities of the two products consumed in each country after specialization, and show how the gains from trade are distributed between the two nations in terms of the increases in the quantities of the two goods consumed.
   (f) Check and make sure that the results of (e) agree with the results of (b) above.

2. In the text discussion of the determination of the equilibrium terms of trading using offer curves (Figures 5-6 through 5-8), we did not use concrete numerical examples. Let us do so in this study question.

The point N in Figure 5-1 gives one point on North's demand for cotton. As explained in the text, North wanted to consume, before specialization, 10,000 tons of wheat and 4,000 tons of cotton. After complete specialization, North produces 30,000 tons of wheat and 0 ton of cotton. Thus, in order to consume 4,000 tons of cotton, it must export (supply or offer) 20,000 tons of wheat. North thus demands 4,000 tons of cotton at an expenditure of 20,000 tons of wheat, or at a price of 5 tons of wheat per ton of cotton. We now have one point on North's demand curve for cotton: 4,000 tons of cotton is demanded at the price of 5W/1C (circled in the table below). Suppose other points on North's demand curve for cotton are as follows:

Wheat Price of Cotton (in tons of wheat)	Quantity of Cotton Demanded by North (tons)	North's Wheat Outlay for Cotton = Quantity of Wheat Supplied by North (tons)
2.6	6,000	
3.8	5,000	
5	4,000	20,000
$6\frac{1}{3}$	3,000	

(a) Complete the last column, which shows the quantities of wheat North is willing to supply (offer) to South in order to obtain the quantities of cotton shown in the second column.

Similarly, we know that one point on South's demand curve for North's wheat is 15,000 tons of wheat demanded at a total outlay of 5,000 tons of cotton, or at a price of $\frac{1}{3}$ ton of cotton per ton of wheat (circled in the table below). Suppose the rest of South's demand for wheat is as follows:

Cotton Price of Wheat (in tons of cotton)	Quantity of Wheat Demanded by South (tons)	South's Cotton Outlay for Wheat = Quantity of Cotton Supplied by South (tons)
0.4	12,000	
$\frac{1}{3}$	15,000	5,000
0.2$\overline{66}$	18,000	
0.2	21,000	
0.175	22,000	

(b) Complete the last column.

(c) On graph paper, locate an origin at the lower right-hand corner. On the right-side vertical axis, mark off Quantity of Cotton, bottom to top, from 0 to 7,000 tons. On the horizontal axis, mark off Quantity of Wheat, from right to left, from 0 to 30,000 tons. Referring to Figure 5-8, draw in the two countries' domestic transformation-ratio lines (Z'U and Z'P in Figure 5-8). Locate points N and S on these lines.

Now, draw in the two countries' offer curves using the figures in the last two columns of the two tables above. Then, draw in the equilibrium terms-of-trade line (like the line Z'E in Figure 5-9). You should find the slope of this line to be approximately equal to 0.23C/1W. Finally, observe the division of the gains from trade between the two countries in terms of the increases in the quantities of the two products consumed.

3. Refer to Figure 5-14.
   (a) Must the two triangles — $E_nV_nQ_n$ and $Q_sV_sP_s$ — be equal triangles? Why or why not?
   (b) How are the gains from trade shown graphically?
   (c) Is specialization complete or incomplete? Why is this so?

ENDNOTES

1. Alfred Marshall, *The Pure Theory of Foreign Trade* (London: The London School of Economics and Political Science, 1930), pp.4-5.
2. More precisely, the slope is *minus* ⅕. The minus sign is omitted to simplify the discussion. When drawing Figure 5-1, one might assume that a ton of cotton should be represented by the same distance interval as a ton of wheat. Figure 5-1 is not drawn this way; 6,000 tons of cotton are represented by a much longer distance than is used to represent 6,000 tons of wheat. But this *is* reasonable since a ton of cotton obviously is not a ton of wheat, and each ton of cotton has a different value than a ton of wheat. So this first diagram deliberately calls attention to the inherent inequality of the units measured on each axis.
3. If wheat output were measured on the vertical axis and cotton on the horizontal, South's PPF would have a slope of (minus) 3, the opportunity cost of cotton in terms of wheat on every Southern farm.
4. Ricardo's measure of the share of "gain" was in terms of the fall in real prices and could differ, depending upon elasticities of demand, from the share of "gain" measured in terms of units of increased production. See David Ricardo, *On the Principles of Political Economy and Taxation* in Pierro Sraffa, ed., *The Works and Correspondence of David Ricardo* (Cambridge: Cambridge University Press, 1951)1:135.
5. John Stuart Mill, *Essays on Some Unsettled Questions of Political Economy* in reprint No. 7, *Series of Reprints of Scarce Works of Political Economy* (London: The London School of Economics and Political Science, 1948), pp. 1-46. The argument is repeated in John Stuart Mill, *Principles of Political Economy,* Vol. II (Boston: Charles C. Little and James Brown, 1848), pp. 123-144.
6. Mill, *Essays,* p. 12.
7. *Ibid.*
8. *Ibid.*
9. *Ibid.,* p. 44.
10. Since the internal terms of trade (represented by the slopes of Z'U in North and Z'P in South) are the worst terms of trade each nation will have to accept in international trade, the portions of the offer curves showing terms of trade less favorable than the internal terms of trade (the aN portion of ab and the cS portion of cd) are not practical possibilities. Neither nation will buy abroad at terms inferior to those available at home.
11. Depending on the shapes and positions of the two offer curves, the terms-of-trade equilibrium may be established at a much different location, say, at point F in Figure 5-9. In such a case, both countries may not gain more of *both* commodities. With F, for example, North would have more cotton, but less wheat, than before trade. Even in such a case the gain from specialization and trade is clearly demonstrated by the fact that point F lies beyond both countries' production possibilities frontiers.
12. These incremental opportunity costs are found by dividing the changes, between points, in the quantity of C by the changes in the quantity of W, or by $\triangle C / \triangle W$. For example, between E and F, $\triangle C = 2$ (ignoring the minus sign) and $\triangle W = 30$; therefore, $\triangle C / \triangle W = \frac{2}{30}$ or $\frac{1}{15}$.
13. Notice again that the numerical scale on the wheat axis need not be the same as the numerical scale on the cotton axis.
14. Figure 5-14 shows that after specializing more in production, each country consumes more of both products than before trade. This, however, need not always be the case. Depending on the shape of the indifference curve maps of the two nations, North and/or South could choose to consume more of one product but less of the other after trade than before trade.

6

International Trade and the Real Incomes of Labor and of Capital

How does international trade affect labor's wages? If a nation as a whole gains from international trade, must that nation's labor force gain? Will a relatively well-to-do labor force be injured by imports from a nation with cheap labor? Finally, how do the wage effects of free trade compare with the wage effects that would follow from the free international mobility of labor? In this chapter, attention shifts from the welfare of the nation as a whole to the welfare of particular subgroups — labor and capital — and, at least by implication, to particular categories of labor.

The preceding five chapters implied that nations are composed of homogenous groups of individuals all affected in exactly the same way by foreign trade. The term, "gains to a nation," was used as though the gains accrued equally to every individual in the nation. This chapter will distinguish among particular groups of factor suppliers within each nation. In particular, it will distinguish between labor and owners of capital and will show how some individuals will lose while others are benefitting from international trade.

In the chapter's first section, the point will be: Despite the large numbers of Americans who fear the general "damage" to the country threatened by "cheap foreign labor," such fears are groundless. Cheap foreign labor is not a threat; unrestricted trade with cheap-labor nations is the means by which America obtains the gains of comparative advantage specialization and trade.

The second section of this chapter will consider again, briefly, a world where factors of production cannot move freely across national boundaries. It will distinguish between the production possibilities frontier

(PPF) of a two-nation world and the PPFs of the individual nations in that world. The idea of the real gain from trade was first developed in Chapter 3 using separate national PPFs. This chapter will show gain as a move from a production point *inside* the world PPF to a point *on* the world PPF. This use of the world PPF to show gains from trade draws on the familiar technique used in introductory economics textbooks to distinguish between efficient and inefficient production. This use of PPFs will also be helpful in the next section of this chapter where factors of production are assumed to move freely between non-trading nations.

This chapter's third section switches from a world of free trade and resource immobility to a world in which inputs move freely but trade is prohibited across national boundaries. The point will be that such labor migration (we will assume labor to be the input that moves) will bring equal wages to labor in both nations and equal returns to capital in both nations. This will mean that labor's real wage will rise in the area from which labor emigrates while falling in the area to which labor immigrates, while returns to capital will fall where labor emigrates and will rise where labor immigrates.

This chapter's final section will assert (leaving the details for an appendix) that immobile factors and free trade will have the same effects on wages and returns to capital as will no trade and freely mobile capital and labor. That is to say, free trade will tend to bring equal wages in all trading areas (for example, Italy, America, and Algeria) and equal returns to capital in all trading areas. This assertion, derived from the "standard" trade theory known as the Heckscher-Ohlin model (of which, much more in the next chapter) was originally developed by Eli Heckscher and was fully developed by Abba Lerner and Paul Samuelson. The assertion may be difficult to accept at its face value since real world examples do not seem to support it. Yet this theory remains useful if it is, as we believe it to be, accurate in describing *tendencies* that in fact do characterize the world.

THE "THREAT" OF CHEAP FOREIGN LABOR

The general public is easily convinced by the argument that high tariffs or low quotas are required if America's producers are to compete with Asian and Latin American producers who pay much lower wages. This argument has it that America's high living standards can be maintained only if the products of cheap foreign labor are kept out of America.

This same argument has even been advanced by supposedly knowledgeable politicians. Ray Marshall, President Carter's Secretary of Labor, was an economist before he became a politician. Nevertheless, in the spring of 1980, he expressed these views about foreign trade:

My philosophy on trade is rather simple. Where foreign imports represent fair and equitable competition, then I believe that American manufacturers must take their chances in the free market. But there are serious problems with following a rigid "free trader" philosophy. Trade is not really "free" unless all the elements of competition are equal. When foreign goods are produced by workers being paid depressed wages, or under unsafe and unhealthy conditions, or products are subsidized by governments, or where economic systems differ, then the conditions are not equal and I believe that we must take steps to protect domestic manufacturers from such unfair competition.[1]

If America were to take "steps to protect domestic manufacturers" from all "foreign goods...produced by workers being paid depressed wages," America would have to take steps against almost *all* foreign goods. Almost all foreign goods come from workers paid wages depressed below American workers' wages.

But the theory of comparative advantage is entirely independent of wage levels. This point deserves elaboration.

Most foreign wages *are* depressed below American wages. True! But that is, in terms of comparative advantage specialization and trade, irrelevant. Much of the evidence is obvious. Many American firms pay very high wages and continue to export. Yet news articles continue to imply that cheap foreign labor is a problem for Americans. For example, the *Wall Street Journal* reported in 1977:

> Last year, textile and clothing imports rose by 3% to $5.3 billion, accounting for about $2.8 billion of the nation's $9.2 billion merchandise trade deficit...Apparel workers in the Far East and Latin America often get paid a tenth of the average $3.55 an hour made by Americans in the industry.[2]

In 1977, United States firms did import $3.5 billion more in *clothing* than they exported. However, American firms exported a larger dollar value of *textiles* than they imported. Furthermore, American firms in 1977 sold $29.5 billion of manufactures to the developing countries (low-wage countries every one) while importing only $18.0 billion in manufactures from them. In contrast, five years earlier, America's manufacturing export surplus in 1972 was only $3.5 billion ($9.5 billion exports minus $6.0 billion imports).[3] These numbers show that more and more high wage Americans are being employed to produce goods to be sold *to* countries with very cheap foreign labor. In 1978, one out of every eight manufacturing jobs in the United States produced for export.[4] Total U.S. manufacturing exports rose in value from $95 billion in 1978 (17.0 percent of the world's total) to $117 billion in 1979 (17.4 percent of the world's total).[5] How can this be?

THE DETERMINANTS OF WAGE LEVELS

The immediate and most direct answer is that international trade is based upon comparative advantage, and comparative advantage is not affected by the general cheapness or dearness of labor in a given country. Subsequent chapters will show that relative cheapness of labor (or capital) results from differences among nations in national capital-labor endowment ratios, and that relative cheapness of labor (or capital) affects the comparative advantage of only those goods that tend to use relatively large quantities of labor (or capital) in production.

The absolute level of real wages of a given country, however, cannot affect the pattern of comparative advantage. In Chapters 3 and 5 the "real" theory of gains from international trade was presented without any mention of wage levels in the trading nations. Wage levels were not mentioned because neither wage levels nor changes in wage levels have any effect upon a nation's comparative advantage so long as opportunity costs remain unchanged. In Chapter 4, money was introduced into the analysis. Nevertheless, wage levels were not mentioned because they remained irrelevant to comparative advantages and gains from trade. However, the issue of cheap foreign labor comes immediately to a reader's mind when money is introduced, when foreign exchange rates are determined, and when the *Wall Street Journal* reports that American apparel workers are paid $3.55 an hour while some Latin Americans and Asians are paid only $0.35 an hour. Why the confusion?

Money must be discussed again below, but first a review of the two-nation two-product example introduced in Chapter 3, where the production possibilities on typical farms are:

	North	South
Cotton:	4 tons	2 tons
Wheat:	20 tons	6 tons

What determines the "cheapness" or "dearness" of labor — or the average real wage — in a nation? Based on general economic theory and assuming that wages are determined in large part by markets, a nation's real wages are higher,

1. the greater the amount of physical and human capital per worker, and
2. the more "advanced" the technology of the nation.

Thus, in the North-South example, if South has more physical capital per worker than has North and if Southern labor is on the average more educated than is Northern labor, then, even if technology is the same in both nations, Southern labor will, in a market economy, receive higher real wages than will Northern labor. Consequently, Southern labor will be "dear" and Northern labor will be "cheap."

Alternatively, North might use more advanced technology than South. Then, even if the amounts of physical and human capital per worker are the same in both countries, Northern labor will receive higher real wages than will Southern labor. Northern labor consequently will be "dear" and Southern labor will be "cheap."

In either case, the pattern of trade is determined once the comparative costs are given. In this example, North will have comparative advantage in wheat, and South will have comparative advantage in cotton, *whether real wages are higher in North or in South*. To repeat, trade depends on comparative advantage, on opportunity costs; and comparative advantage has nothing to do with the level of real wages. This fact should always be kept in mind as a secure benchmark when dealing with the obscurities introduced by political orators and by the veil of money and its concomitant artifacts: money wages, money prices, and exchange rates.

THE IRRELEVANCE OF WAGE LEVELS

In order to better understand the importance of opportunity costs and the nature of the money veil that surrounds them, return again to the basic two-nation two-product example first introduced in Chapter 3 and just cited here. The figures shown below represent a set of equilibrium domestic prices under the equilibrium exchange rate assumed to be $1 = 2 pesos.

	Dollar Price per Ton		Peso Price per Ton	
	of North's output	of South's output	of North's output	of South's output
Cotton:	$5	$4.5	10 pesos	9 pesos
Wheat:	$1	$1.5	2 pesos	3 pesos

Next, assume that South has relatively little physical and human capital; South therefore has very cheap labor.

Given all these assumptions, cotton is cheap in South, but *not* because Southern labor is cheap. This should be clear since Southern wheat is dear, and it is produced by the same cheap labor producing Southern cotton. Southern cotton is cheap because its opportunity cost is relatively low, and Northern wheat — produced with dear Northern labor — is cheap because its opportunity cost is relatively low.

In view of the tenacity with which the general public and Secretaries of Labor cling to the idea that cheap foreign labor is a threat, consider yet another example of cheap foreign labor, this time stressing *reductions* in money wages. Retaining the cotton and wheat prices of the North-South table given above, assume that Northern labor averages $10 an hour while Southern labor averages $1 an hour (i.e., Southern labor averages two pesos an hour at $1 = 2 pesos). North has comparative advantage in wheat, South in cotton.

Then South's government, by fiat, lowers *all* wages and *all* prices by 50 percent. Is Southern labor then "cheaper"? Wages are down to one peso per hour; but given unchanged technological conditions, prices are also down by 50 percent. Real wages in South, therefore, are unchanged. But the international effects of these changes in South's money prices and wages are to change the domestic prices to:

	Dollar Price per Ton		Peso Price per Ton	
	of North's output	of South's output	of North's output	of South's output
Cotton:	$5	$2.25	10 pesos	4½ pesos
Wheat:	$1	$0.75	2 pesos	1½ pesos

Both products are now cheaper in South at the existing exchange rate of $1 = 2 pesos.

We have seen this situation before. In Chapter 4, almost exactly the same numbers turned up in the last example presented in the discussion of "sustainable" exchange rates. In the example just given, the exchange rate of $1 = 2 pesos is no longer a "sustainable" rate because, at that rate, and with the new domestic prices, North can no longer pay for its imports from South.

No trade occurs. There is a problem. But the problem is not cheap foreign labor. The problem is the wrong exchange rate. The problem can be cured by changing the exchange rate by 50 percent, from $1 = 2 pesos to $1 = 1 peso, a 50 percent *devaluation* of the dollar, to compensate for the 50 percent Southern deflation. With that change, wheat is again relatively cheap in North, and cotton is again relatively cheap in South. Trade thus resumes between North, with its $10 an hour labor, and South, with its cheap one peso (and still $1) an hour labor.

If you are convinced by these arguments for the irrelevance of wage levels, ask yourself how you would deal with this situation: Suppose you live in North, where wheat producers have a comparative advantage and where cotton producers have a comparative disadvantage. No foreign trade is permitted. Your parents decide to grow cotton. They invest time and money and produce cotton. Then trade barriers are removed, and your parents discover that Southern cotton is priced below their costs of production. They have a terrible problem, and they say "Our problem is cheap Southern labor!" What do you say to them?

FREE TRADE MOVES PRODUCTION TO THE WORLD PPF

To show how real gains flow from comparative advantage specialization and trade, Chapter 5 assumed that, in autarchy, each nation produced *on* its own production possibilities frontier (PPF). This section will demonstrate that in a two-nation world, if the two PPFs of the two countries are combined to form a world PPF, the autarchic production will *not* be on the world PPF. Comparative advantage specialization and trade will be shown to move production to a point *on* the world PPF.

Assume each nation has a straight-line PPF, as in Figure 6-1 where West has comparative advantage in product Y and East has comparative advantage in product X; and each produces at its PPF's midpoint, points E and W. The two nations' PPFs are combined in Figure 6-2, where point E-W represents the two nations' pretrade joint production (which is the sum of East's 30X and 100Y and of West's 20X and 150Y, the outputs of the Figure 6-1 midpoints). Autarchic production at E-W leaves the nations *inside* their combined PPF. Similarly, if every human lived a Robinson Crusoe existence on a separate island, each of us might achieve maximum efficiency within the constraints of our island. But our combined output would fall short of the production possibilities that would become available if we would end our isolation, specialize, and trade.

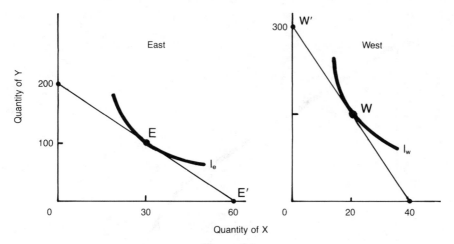

Figure 6-1
Straight-Line Production Possibilities Frontiers
and Pretrade Equilibria for Nations East and West

The two-nation world PPF of Figure 6-2 is derived from the two
straight-line PPFs of Figure 6-1 by means of the following logic: If both
nations produce only X, combined output is 100X, at point A. If, starting
from A, more Y and less X are to be produced efficiently, Y production
should first come only from West. Thus, from A, up to the left, the slope
of the world PPF is the slope of West's PPF. If West produces only Y and
East produces only X, output is 60X and 300Y, at point B. So, from A all
the way to B, the slope of the world PPF is that of West's. If, starting
from B, even more Y and even less X are to be produced efficiently, all
additional Y must come from East; so from output B to the Y axis
intercept, here point C, the world PPF has the transformation-ratio
slope of East.

To summarize, the two nations, in the absence of trade, produce the
total represented by output combination E-W. With *complete* comparative advantage specialization, the two nations' combined output is represented by point B in Figure 6-2 (and by points E' and W' in Figure
6-1). The change in combined output from combination E-W to combination B represents the real gains from comparative advantage
specialization.

Two straight-line PPFs are more easily combined than are two curved
PPFs, but the general principles would be the same for curved as for
straight-line PPFs, and for n nations as for two nations.[6] Autarchic
production *on* individual PPFs can be inefficient for the whole world
because it can be production *inside* the world PPF.

Figures 6-3 and 6-4 present the more general case of nations with
curved PPFs (which, you may recall, reflect increasing cost — as distinct from constant cost — conditions). Pretrade, autarchic production
points, derived by the tangency of PPFs and indifference curves (not
shown) in each country, are indicated by W and E in Figure 6-3. Figure
6-4 shows the two nations' combined output which is increased from
pretrade 66X and 333Y to — roughly — post-trade 72X and 358Y. Note

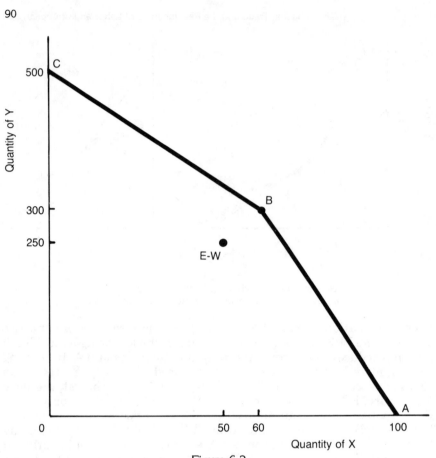

Figure 6-2
Two Nations' Joint Production Possibilities Frontier

that the end points of the combined PPF can be easily derived from the individual PPFs, but the shape of the world PPF is here merely approximated. The shape of the world PPF will be such that comparative advantage production can bring an output, such as at B, yielding more X and more Y than indifference curves, tastes, and PPFs permitted in the absence of trade. Output at B would result from comparative advantage production at points something like E′ and W′ in Figure 6-3.

Notice that the two nations could produce — even in the absence of trade — output combination B on the straight-edged world PPF of Figure 6-2. But that would require *complete* specialization in both countries; the individual national outputs would be at E′ and W′ of Figure 6-1. The welfare consequences of the larger output, B, would surely be inferior to the welfare consequences of the smaller output, E-W; because with output B and no trade, all the X would remain in East, and all the Y would remain in West. Similarly, in the case shown in Figure 6-4, combination B could be produced by nontrading nations producing at points E′ and W′ in Figure 6-3. Without trade, however, these national output combinations would represent a less-than-

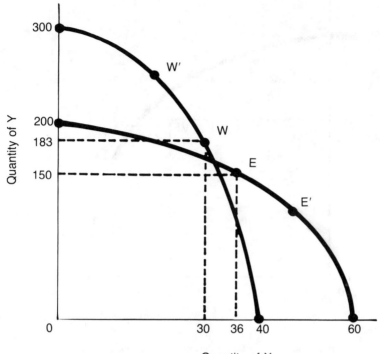

Figure 6-3
Curved Production Possibilities Frontiers and Pretrade and Posttrade Equilibria
for Nations East and West

optimal welfare level in each country. To see this, observe the (taller)
PPF for the West in Figure 6-3. The pretrade production point W is
found by the tangency of the *highest* attainable indifference curve (not
shown) and the PPF. Any other point on West's PPF will be cut by, not
tangent to, a Western indifference curve providing less satisfaction
than the indifference curve tangent at W. Thus the generalization: In
the absence of trade, optimal production is *inside* the world PPF. Trade
is required to put optimal production *on* the world PPF.

FREELY MOBILE LABOR'S EFFECTS ON FACTOR PRICES
AND INCOME SHARES

The foregoing sections of this chapter asserted unreservedly that free
trade would lead to an increase in total world product, or, the same
thing, in total world real income. Both sections permitted the implication that the increases in world income would benefit everyone — or at
least nearly everyone — in every participating nation. That implica-

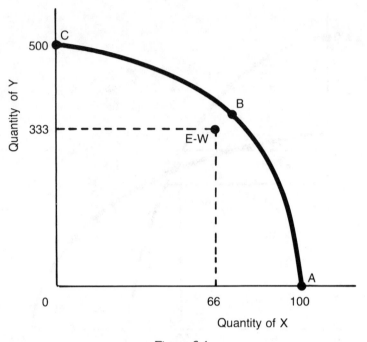

Figure 6.4
Two Nations' Joint Production Possibilities Frontier

tion, if made, would be wrong. Free trade has the same effect on factor incomes that unfettered factor movement has. Some people gain, but some people lose. If all factors are free to move from one area, or one nation, to another, the result must eventually be equality of returns to labor (i.e., wages) in all participating nations (for every particular grade of labor) and equality of returns to capital in all participating nations. The move toward equality will in every case result from a fall in the P_L/P_K ratio in one nation and a rise in that ratio in another nation; real wages will go down in one nation, up in another. Some individuals will gain; some individuals will lose. This section shows the consequences of free mobility of factors.

WHO GETS HURT?

Resource mobility must injure someone. The reason is elementary. In a free market, the price of a resource which is initially relatively scarce will fall when more units are added to its supply. The owners of such a resource, therefore, will suffer. When labor migrates from an area with a lower capital-to-labor ratio to an area with a higher ratio, wages in the latter area fall, and wages in the former area rise. Conversely, returns to capital move down in the area labor is leaving and up in the area to which labor moves.

If, for example, large numbers of Mexicans were to migrate to the United States, the wage of common laborers would fall in the United States and would rise in Mexico. Those engaged in common labor in the United States, before the migration, would become worse off. The migrants into the United States would become better off. Common laborers remaining in Mexico would become better off. Owners of physical and human capital in the United States would become better off as more common labor became available to work with them. Owners of physical and human capital in Mexico would become worse off as less common labor remained to work with them. Gross world product would be up, but some people would be losers. Similar results follow when any other factor of production moves from one nation, or area, to another. The reason these effects follow can be understood more easily after examining a simple model involving the free international mobility of labor.

A SIMPLE MODEL OF THE EFFECTS OF MOBILE LABOR

According to the marginal productivity theory of factor pricing and income distribution with assumptions of perfect competition and constant returns to scale, every input unit is paid the value of its marginal product. This theory will be used here to show the effects of labor mobility upon the division of income between capital and labor. In order to make international comparison possible, the analysis will be couched in *real* terms — that is, total national product equals total national real income, and a factor's equilibrium price is equal to its real (rather than value) marginal product.

Assume that there are only two factors of production: homogeneous labor and homogeneous capital. Figure 6-5 shows the basic relationships. The quantity of labor is measured on the horizontal axis, and the marginal product of labor (MP_L) is measured on the vertical axis. The MP_L line slopes down to the right because of diminishing marginal returns to the variable factor (here labor) used in combination with the fixed factor (here capital). If quantity OL of labor is employed in Nation A, labor's marginal product will be OC = LE which will equal labor's wage. With OL of labor employed at a wage rate of OC per laborer, labor's total income is OLEC. With only the two factors and no government, the nation's total product — or total income — is OLEA. Income distribution is simple: owners of labor receive OLEC, and owners of capital receive the rest, CEA.

Labor will move out of Nation A if, in another Nation, B, labor's marginal product is more than OC. If labor does leave Nation A, the quantity of labor used in Nation A, shown as quantity OL in Figure 6-5, will decline, and the equilibrium marginal product of labor in Nation A will exceed OC. Contrariwise, the additional labor in Nation B will bring equilibrium marginal product there down toward the OC of Nation A. Labor will continue to move from A to B — if travel is costless — until labor's marginal product is the same in both nations — above OC but below the initial level in Nation B.

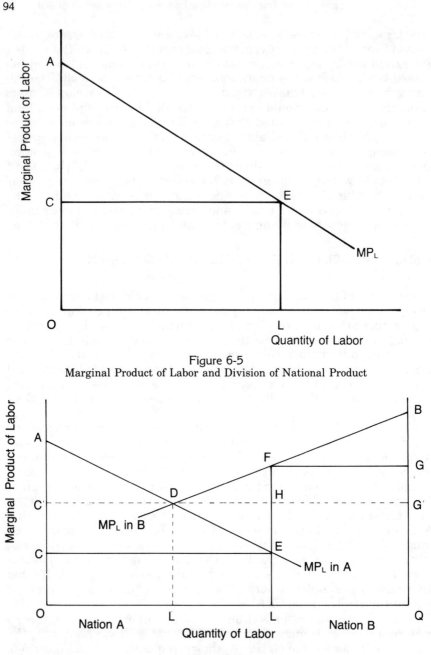

Figure 6-5
Marginal Product of Labor and Division of National Product

Figure 6-6
Marginal Product of Labor and Division of Output in Nations A and B

The immediate objectives here are to identify the effects of this migration upon marginal productivities and upon income distribution within each country. This analysis will be easier if the marginal-product-of-labor curves of the two nations can be shown together in a single sketch.

This is done in Figure 6-6. Nation A's labor quantity is measured from left to right with zero quantity at point O. Nation B's labor quantity is measured from right to left with zero quantity at point Q. Note particularly that the distance OQ is equal to the sum of OL and LQ, the initial quantities of labor employed in Nation A and in Nation B. Total world product is OQBFEA, OLEA from Nation A and LQBF from Nation B.

Initially, Nation B's wage, OG, exceeds Nation A's wage, OC. Labor, therefore, will choose to move from Nation A to Nation B. Given costless and unobstructed movement from Nation A to Nation B, equilibrium will be reached when L'L of labor has moved to Nation B bringing the respective equilibrium marginal products, or real wages, to OC' = OG'. In a sense, this labor migration has the same effect on both nations. The relatively scarce resource in each nation (labor in Nation B, capital in Nation A) becomes less scarce, and its marginal product becomes smaller. The relatively plentiful resource becomes less plentiful, and its marginal product becomes greater.

Nation A's total product is decreased by L'LED, while Nation B's total product is increased by L'LFD. In Nation A, labor's price rises and capital's price falls. Further, labor's share of output rises and capital's share falls. Labor's share of national income increases from OLEC ÷ OLEA to OL'DC' ÷ OL'DA. Conversely, capital's share decreases from CEA ÷ OLEA to C'DA ÷ OL'DA. In the labor importing nation, B, the exact opposite happens: labor's price and share of national income decrease, and capital's price and share of income increase.

AN ASIDE ON THE CONCEPTS OF GNP AND GDP

The preceding section showed the effects upon labor's price and upon capital's price of free mobility of factors. The next section will show the effects upon labor's price and upon capital's price of free trade. But before going on, this aside takes advantage of the irresistible opportunity Figure 6-6 provides to distinguish between the concepts of gross national product and gross domestic product (GNP versus GDP). For the United States, the two measurements are nearly the same; so the distinction is not important. But in many of the small developing countries, GNP and GDP are quite different. One must clearly understand the difference between the two concepts if one is to understand United Nations statistics from small developing nations.

GDP is the less familiar concept. It refers to the market value of total output *within* a nation. In Figure 6-6, Nation A's GDP is OLEA before and OL'DA after labor emigration. Nation B's GDP is QLFB before and QL'DB after labor immigration. GNP is the more familiar concept. It refers to the market value of total output of a nation's resources, regardless of the location of those factors when they produce. Thus in Figure 6-6, Nation A's labor quantity L'L will make the difference between GNP and GDP for each nation. The return to the L'L labor is, after migrating, L'LHD. That output, L'LHD, is produced *in* Nation B, so is part of B's GDP. But, if (and only if) the migrated laborers L'L retain their Nation A citizenship, that output, L'LHD, will derive from the resources of Nation A and will be counted in Nation A's GNP. So, again reading from Figure 6-6, Nation A's GNP is OLEA before and OLHDA after its labor emigrates. Nation B's GNP is QLFB before and QLHDB after foreign labor immigrates into Nation B.

When all of a nation's resources are at home, GNP = GDP. When some of the nation's factors go elsewhere to produce, the nation's GNP will exceed its GDP. This is the case, for example, for South Yemen, many of whose workers are employed near the Persian Gulf. When foreign capital or workers are employed in a nation, that nation's GDP will exceed its GNP. This is the case for most small developing nations, for example, Liberia, in which much foreign capital is at work, as in the Liberian iron ore mines.

Notice that the difference between each nation's GNP, before and after migration, equals the gain to that nation from the move from inefficient to efficient resource allocation. Nation A gains DEH. Nation B gains DFH.

Now for the effects of free trade upon the prices of labor and of capital. Anticipate the final conclusion that free trade between Mexico and the United States, like free resource mobility between Mexico and the United States, will bring equality of wages between Mexico and the United States.

THE EFFECTS OF FREE TRADE ON FACTOR PRICES

In the preceding section, Figure 6-6 depicts a situation in which the marginal product of labor, in pretrade equilibrium, is higher in Nation B than in Nation A. In other words, Nation A is a relatively labor-rich country; and Nation B is relatively rich in capital. Therefore, it follows, as Chapter 7 will show more clearly, that Nation A has comparative advantage in labor-intensive goods, and Nation B has comparative advantage in capital-intensive goods.

When trade opens up between the two nations, Nation A's exports will be relatively labor intensive, and Nation B's exports will be relatively capital intensive. Output of exported goods will increase and output of imported goods will decrease in both countries. Look closely at what happens in Nation B. Output of the capital-intensive good (call it chemicals) increases, while production of the labor-intensive good (radio assembly) decreases. As radio assembly is reduced, capital and labor are laid off. But the capital-to-labor ratio of the laid-off inputs is lower than the capital-to-labor ratio the chemical industry is accustomed to hiring. Therefore, as the export-expanding chemical firms bid for capital and labor, they find, at initial prices, a capital shortage and a labor surplus.

What changes will eliminate this shortage and this surplus? Factor price changes, of course. Labor's price falls; capital's price rises. Both the chemical and the radio assembly industries change their input mix. Both, because labor becomes cheaper and capital becomes dearer, reduce the capital-to-labor ratio in their plants. (Common sense may lead one to doubt that, with a fixed amount of capital and labor in the country, *both* industries can reduce their capital-to-labor ratio. Problem #9 at the end of this chapter provides an opportunity for doubters to convince themselves that both nations can and will reduce their capital-to-labor input ratio.)

The change to a lower K/L ratio follows from the lower price of labor and the higher price of capital. As soon as each industry's K/L ratio goes down, labor's marginal product goes down and capital's marginal product goes up. The result of the movement from autarchy to free trade is that MP_L/MP_K still equals P_L/P_K but labor's price is down and capital's price is up. This conclusion is explained in much more detail in the appendix to this chapter.

Analogously, free trade causes the price of labor to rise and the price of capital to fall in the relatively labor-rich country, A. The general conclusion is that trade based on comparative advantage leads to an increase, in both nations, in the price of the relatively abundant — hence relatively cheap — factor and a decrease in the price of the relatively scarce factor. In other words, factor prices are equalized by trade. This conclusion is identical with the conclusion of the preceding section. Perhaps this pair of conclusions should come as no surprise. In a fundamental sense, free trade is a substitute for free movement of factors. An export of labor-intensive goods, for example, is a surrogate for an export of labor: labor that is embodied in the product — rather than labor itself— is exported.

ARE FACTOR PRICES BEING EQUALIZED?

Given the conclusion that free trade — say between Brazil and the United States — leads to equalization of factor prices in the two countries, the question that is immediately asked is: "Are Brazilian and American wages becoming equal with Brazilian wages rising and American wages falling?" The answer is clearly no — at least as far as the part about American wages falling is concerned. Two points can be made concerning this apparently paradoxical situation. First, as shown in the appendix to this chapter, the conclusion drawn from the factor price equalization theorem is obtained under a set of highly rigid and unrealistic assumptions. The theory is valid only to the extent that these assumptions reflect the reality of international trade. To the extent the assumptions are crude approximations of the real world, the conclusion of the theory remains as a mere prediction of the *tendency* of factor prices to equalize.

Secondly, that tendency may in fact exist, it may even be quite strong, though rendered invisible, swamped beneath the effects of the technological changes and capital accumulation that serve to raise wages in the United States.

This chapter has established two principal generalizations: given initial autarchy and international differences in marginal products of factors, (1) either free trade or free resource mobility will raise total world output and income, and (2) either free trade or free resource mobility will (tend to) lower the incomes per unit of the relatively scarce factor in each nation, while raising the income per unit of the relatively abundant factor in each nation.

The details of the factor price equalization theory are presented in the appendix section which follows. That section may be omitted without loss of continuity. A full appreciation of that section will require a thorough understanding of intermediate price theory.

APPENDIX: FACTOR PRICE EQUALIZATION

To show the effects of free trade on factor prices, another standard tool of intermediate price theory, the Edgeworth box diagram, is needed. For a complete understanding of this device, a brief review of production function isoquants may be in order.

THE PRODUCTION FUNCTION AND ISOQUANTS

A production function is a statement of the technical — or the engineering — relationship between input combinations and output. This relationship is expressed graphically by an isoquant or a series of isoquants, as is shown in Figure 7-2 in Chapter 7, where the concept of the isoquant is reviewed in some detail. In this appendix, assume that the production function is linear and homogeneous — that is, production is subject to constant returns to scale. Output therefore increases in direct proportion to increases in the quantities of inputs.

The slope of an isoquant represents the *marginal rate of substitution* between capital and labor (MRS_{KL}). As we move down along an isoquant, where labor is measured along the X axis, less and less capital is required to substitute for a given quantity of labor, with the level of output remaining constant. Since less capital and more labor is used, the marginal product of capital increases and the marginal product of labor decreases. Given the state of technology, the marginal productivity of factors is determined exclusively by the capital-to-labor ratio used in production.

MRS_{KL} — or the ratio, MP_L/MP_K — is expressed by the slope of an isoquant. One attribute of a linear homogeneous production function is that along a ray (expansion path) such as OR in Figure 7-3, each isoquant has the same MRS_{KL}, or MP_L/MP_K ratio at its point of intersection with that particular expansion path. The ratio is higher to the left of that ray, and lower to the right of that ray.

Drawing upon the marginal productivity theory of income distribution, the preceding section concluded that the equilibrium price of a factor equals its marginal product. This leads to an important conclusion that, as we move down along an isoquant — and as the K/L input ratio decreases — the return paid per unit of capital (P_K) increases and the return per unit of labor, the wage (P_L), decreases if each point considered involves equilibria in the capital and labor markets.

THE EDGEWORTH PRODUCTION BOX DIAGRAM

The Edgeworth production box is named after its originator, Francis Ysidro Edgeworth (1845-1926). Assume that in one particular country two products, X and Y, are produced under conditions of constant returns to scale. There are, therefore, two sets of isoquants, two production functions, one for each product, with both sets linear and homogenous. Like every other nation, this nation has limited (fixed) supplies of the two factors — capital and labor. These limits are shown precisely when the two isoquant series are placed in a constrained box. Figure 6-7 shows one such box.

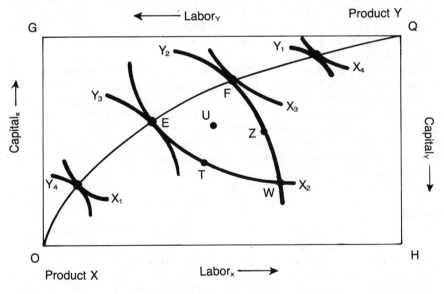

Figure 6-7
The Edgeworth Production Box

The nation's total available supply of labor is expressed by the horizontal distance OH = QG. Since the nation cannot use more factors than are available, the production possibilities are constrained by the edge lines of the diagram forming a box. The production function of X is placed in the box using O as the origin, with the four isoquants (X_1 through X_4) showing increasingly larger levels of output of X. The production function of good Y is placed with its origin at the corner of the box, Q, opposite the other origin, O. The four isoquants (Y_1 through

Y_4) are read from the origin Q along the labor axis (Labor$_Y$ or QG) and the capital axis (Capital$_Y$ or QH). If all inputs were used to produce Y, total output would be that of the Y isoquant passing through point O. (Even though it is not shown in Figure 6-7, there is a Y isoquant passing through point O, just as there is a Y isoquant passing through every other point in Figure 6-7.)

Every point in this box (including each point on the edge line) represents a division (or allocation) of capital and labor to the two products. Although production at every point is technically *possible*, not every point is equally *efficient*. (Here, "efficiency" means a maximum output from the given inputs.) Consider point W within the box. All of the nation's capital and labor are being used. The quantity of output of X is represented by the isoquant X_2. The quantity of output of Y is shown by isoquant Y_2. But this resource allocation is inefficient because the production of X and/or Y could be increased without any increase in input quantities. This could be achieved by dividing inputs, between outputs X and Y, in a way represented by some point northwest of W and between the X_2 and Y_2 isoquants. In contrast with the division of inputs represented by point W, this redivision would devote less labor and more capital to product Y). Then, if inputs are divided as, for example, at point T, the X output is as great as with the point W input division, but Y output is up from Y_2 to the level of the Y isoquant through point T.

Alternatively, if inputs are divided as at point Z, the output of Y is as great as at W, but X output is up from X_2 to the isoquant through Z. Better still is the input division of point U where both X and Y output are greater than at point W. To generalize: Given any input division like that of W where isoquant tangencies are to the northwest, output of both products can be increased by moving to an input division to the northwest. Vice versa, given any input division where isoquant tangencies are to the southeast, output of both products can be increased by moving to an input division to the southeast. To sum: An input division where X and Y isoquants intersect is an inefficient input division.

In contrast, production at a point of isoquant tangencies, such as E or F, is maximally efficient. Take point E, for instance. Here, the isoquants of the two products (X_2 and Y_3) are tangent to each other. This means that an increase in the output of either good is not possible without a reduction in output of the other good. Starting at E, output of X can be increased only by cutting Y output, and vice versa. The same is true of every input division on the line of isoquant tangencies — or *efficiency locus* — OEFQ. To sum once more: Efficient production can be obtained only where X and Y isoquants are tangent to each other; in contrast, if they cross, output of both goods can be increased.

The capital/labor ration used in X production is represented by the slope of a straight line from the origin, O, to the point of production, for example, E. The capital/labor ratio used in Y production is represented by the slope of a straight line from the origin, Q, to the point of production, again, for example, E. Since the slope of OE exceeds the slope of QE, the capital/labor ratio of X production exceeds that of Y production at E.

The "bowing" of the efficiency locus indicates the relative factor intensity (the capital/labor ratio) of the two production functions. In Figure 6-7, the efficiency locus OEFQ is bowed toward the Capital$_X$ axis and toward the Labor$_Y$ axis. This means that equilibrium production of good X requires relatively larger quantities of capital (hence X is capital intensive) and product Y requires relatively larger amounts of labor (Y is labor intensive) than the other product. (Readers ought to try now to guess what this will mean when, in Chapter 7, a theory is presented that will explain which of the two products will become the specialty of the relatively capital-rich nation.)

THE EFFECTS OF TRADE ON FACTOR PRICES

The Edgeworth box diagram can now be used to demonstrate the effects of comparative advantage specialization and trade on factor prices. Suppose the nation's production of X and Y, before trade, is at point E, in Figure 6-8. As trade opens up, this country specializes in one of the two products. Arbitrarily, assume the nation's comparative advantage lies in product X (given this assumption, it must follow that labor is scarce and capital is abundant in this country relative to some other country — more about this in Chapter 7). With specialization and trade, production of X will move alogn the efficiency locus toward Q.

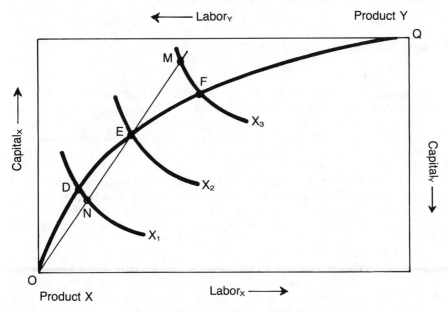

Figure 6-8
The Effects of Trade on Factor Prices

Suppose F is the new production point. Each of the production functions in this appendix is assumed to be characterized by linear homogeneity. Because of this, as a preceding paragraph stressed, the amrginal rate of substitution between capital and labor, MRS_{KL} (measured by an isoquant's slope), is the same at every point along a ray, such as the ray ONEM in Figure 6-8. Further, given the convexity of the isoquants, the MRS_{KL} is lower at all points to the right of any ray and is higher at all points to the left of that ray than it is at points on the ray. Therefore, the MRS_{KL} at point F is smaller than at M, and it is also smaller than at point E. SmallerMRS$_{KL}$ at F than at E means that the marginal product of labor at F is smaller than at E. Consequently, wages are lower, and returns to capital are higher, with trade (at point F) than without trade (at E). When the country specializes in the relatively capital-intensive good X, the country's returns to capital are greater and its returnst to labor are lower.

Conversely, if the nation specializes in the relatively labor-intensive product Y (because labor is relatively abundant and capital relatively scarce compared with the trading partner) and moves along its efficiency locus from the autarchy point E toward point D — thereby raising the K/L production ratio — the nation's returns to capital are lower and its wages are higher than without trade. Comparative advantage specialization and trade inevitably change factor intensities used in production, which in turn raises the returns to the relatively abundant factor and lowers the returns to the relatively scarce factor. Under free trade, some are better off, and others are worse off within an overall framework of rising total output.

FACTOR PRICE EQUALIZATION

If, under free trade, wages rise in relatively labor-rich countries and returns to capital rise in relatively capital-rich nations, will wages and returns to capital be equalized throughout the world? This subsection will show that, under a set of restrictive assumptions, free trade does cause wages to move toward equality in all nations as well as equalizing capital returns throughout the world.

Figure 6-9 presents Edgeworth boxes for two nations, North and South, each producing only two products, X and Y. North is relatively capital rich. Its resource box is therefore tall compared with South's. South is relatively labor rich; so its resource box is wide compared with North's. For both boxes, O is the origin of the production function for X. For South, S is the origin of the production function of Y. For North, N is the origin of the production function of Y. The production functions are assumed to be the same for North and for South. This means that X-isoquants (only one is drawn), based on the single origin O, serve for both North and South. However, the Y-isoquants (not shown), while identical for North and South, must be drawn separately for each

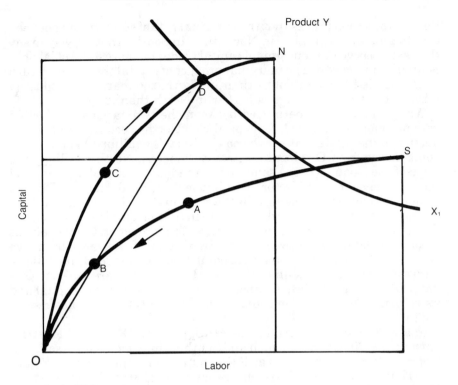

Figure 6-9
Factor Price Equalization

nation, using N and S as origins, respectively. Both efficiency loci are bowed toward the capital axis (when viewed from the origin O). This indicates that X is the relatively capital-intensive good and Y is the relatively labor-intensive product. (If South produced at point A, the K/L ratio for X would be the slope of a line OA; the K/L ratio for Y would be the slope of a line AS; and OA is steeper than AS.)

This model continues to assume constant returns to scale, perfectly competitive markets, no trade barriers, no international factor movements, and free and costless movements of goods internationally. Given these assumptions, free trade leads to factor price equalization.

Suppose that, in the absence of trade, South's equilibrium division of inputs is represented by point A on its efficiency locus, OAS; while North's no-trade equilibrium resource allocation is represented by point C on its efficiency locus, OCN. In relatively capital-rich North, both X and Y are, in autarchy, produced by methods that are more capital intensive than are the methods used in labor-rich South. (To see this, observe that the slope of an imaginary straight line, OC, exceeds the slope of a straight line, OA; while the slope of a straight line, NC, exceeds the slope of a straight line, SA.) This difference in factor intensities in production proves that the marginal rate of substitution between capital and labor is higher in North than in South. Another way to say this is to observe that one unit of capital trades for more units of labor in South than in North. The marginal product of capital (hence the return to capital) is higher in South than in North; the marginal product of labor and, hence, the wage is higher in North than in South.

When free trade is permitted between the two nations, production becomes more specialized. As capital-rich North specializes in the production of the capital-intensive good X, North's equilibrium production point moves from C toward D. As this happens, North's MRS_{KL}, the slope of the isoquants (the same in both industries X and Y because of the free movements of factors within the country) decreases. This development causes an increase in the marginal product of capital (and hence returns to capital) and a decrease in the marginal product of labor (hence wages). One unit of capital trades for more labor. Conversely, as labor-rich South specializes in the production of the labor-intensive good Y and moves its production point from A toward B, its MRS_{KL} increases. Production shifts to where the isoquants are steeper. One unit of capital trades for less labor. The marginal product of capital and its returns fall and the marginal product of labor and wages rise in South.

In a post-trade equilibrium, the MRS_{KL} in both X and Y industries must be the same in both North and South.[7] This conclusion is satisfied by production at such points as B (in South) and D (in North) in Figure 6-9. That points B and D are on the same ray OBD indicates that the MRS_{KL} for X and Y in South (at B) is the same as the MRS_{KL} for both products in North (at D). Identical MRS_{KL}, identical isoquant slopes, for both X and Y in both North and South implies that the marginal product of capital is the same at D and at B, and that the marginal product of labor is the same in the two nations. With capital and labor each paid its marginal product in each nation, the wage rate will be the same in both nations and the rate of returns to capital must also be the same.

STUDY QUESTIONS

1. If, as suggested in the text, your parents have been growing cotton in the North (perhaps protected by a tariff) and Southern cotton suddenly appears in your market (after the tariff is abolished), what can you say to your parents to convince them that their basic problem is not cheap foreign labor?

2. Assume another case. You live in Argentina. Your parents work in a plant manufacturing autos. Argentina then repeals its tariff on auto imports, and cheaper American autos put your parents out of work. The American autos are produced by workers paid five times as much as your parents were paid. How would you explain to your parents the basic cause of their unemployment?

3. How are the values of the endpoints of the Figure 6-4 PPF obtained from the information given in Figure 6-3?

4. In the "East" section of Figure 6-1 and in the "West" section, draw in your estimate of an equilibrium terms-of-trade line. Draw in the Western indifference curve tangent to that equilibrium terms-of-trade line. How much of which product will West export? How much of which product will West import? Next, being careful to provide exact consistency between your Western and your Eastern sketches, draw in the Eastern indifference curve tangent to the equilibrium terms-of-trade line. Finally, check your work to be sure West's export and import quantities match East's import and export quantities.

5. How would Figure 6-2 differ if East's PPF ran from (0X, 300Y) to (90X, 0Y) (i.e., what would be the coordinates of points B and C)? If the pretrade equilibria were at the two nations' PPF midpoints, where would point E-W be located in this new version of Figure 6-2?

6. If capital moves from the United States to Mexico, *ceteris paribus,* what groups of Americans and what groups of Mexicans lose? What groups gain? Try to be exhaustive. In each case, what change is the immediate cause of that group's gain (or loss)? For example, a wage increase might be the "immediate cause" of the gain in welfare of a labor group.

7. If the United States exports capital-intensive goods to Mexico and imports labor-intensive goods from Mexico, *ceteris paribus,* what groups of Americans and what groups of Mexicans gain? What groups lose? Try to be exhaustive. In each case, what change is the immediate cause of that group's gain (or loss)?

The following questions are more difficult than those above.

8. The object here is to identify indifference curves that will — roughly at least — define free trade equilibrium for the two countries in Figure 6-3. In Figure 6-3, draw the terms-of-trade lines tangent to Points E' and W'. Each of the two lines should have exactly the same slope. Next, draw West's no-trade indifference curve tangent to its PPF at W. Then draw West's indifference curve tangent to its terms-of-trade line. Identify the quantities of Western imports and of Western exports.

    Next, draw East's no-trade indifference curve tangent to its PPF at E. Finally, draw East's indifference curve tangent to its terms-of-trade line, but be careful. This tangency must result in Eastern imports equal to Western exports and in Eastern exports equal to Western imports.

9. Assume a nation in autarchy producing two products: chemicals and radio assemblies. The nation is endowed with 100 units of K and 100 units of L. In autarchy, the chemical industry uses 60K and 40L; the radio-assembly industry uses 40K and 60L. When free trade is permitted, the nation exports chemicals and imports assembled radios. Use arithmetic to show that, as radio-assembly is reduced and chemical production is increased, *both* nations will decrease their K/L ratio.

Questions applicable to the Appendix.

10. In Figure 6-7, consider production point T. Draw the other isoquant passing through T. Label that isoquant. Describe the changes that would take place in allocation of uses of labor and of capital if production were to move from T to a point on the efficiency locus (label it "M") where more X *and* more Y would be produced than could be produced at T.

11. In Figure 6-7, let OG = 200 units of capital. Let OH = 11 units of labor. Estimate the numerical values of the coordinates of points E, F, and G. Draw the rays OE and QE. Calculate the K/L ratio for each industry when production occurs at E. Note that the K/L ratio *is* the slope of the ray.

Then draw the rays OF and QF. Calculate the K/L ratio for each industry when production occurs at F. Compare the K/L ratio of industry X at E and at F. Compare the K/L ratio of industry Y at E and at F. If production were to be moved to point G, what would happen to the K/L ratio of industry X? What would happen to the K/L ratio of industry Y?

What generalizations can you formulate about the K/L ratio of *each* industry as production is moved from left to right along the efficiency locus of Figure 6-7?

12. Refer to Figure 6-8. For industry X, how does the MP_L/MP_K ratio at D compare with the MP_L/MP_K ratio at F? How can you be sure? How would the P_L/P_K ratio at D, if D were the equilibrium point, compare with the P_L/P_K ratio at F, if F were the equilibrium point?

13. Given the autarchic equilibria A and C and the free trade equilibria B and D in Figure 6-9, what nation exports what product when free trade is permitted? How can you tell?

14. In Figure 6-9, draw the X isoquants passing through points C and A, the autarchic equilibria. In which country are wages highest? How can you tell this from the slope of the X isoquants through points A and C? As you answer this question, be sure to compare the slopes of these two X isoquants at the points where they intersect the ray, OD.

ENDNOTES

1. This statement was provided in a letter from John W. Leslie, Director of the U.S. Department of Labor's Office of Information. Secretary Marshall asked Mr. Leslie to issue this statement because he was concerned that the following remarks, included in a speech made to the International Ladies Garment Workers Union on June 2, 1977, in Hollywood, Florida, might be misleading when read out of context:

    My philosophy on trade is rather simple. Where foreign imports represent fair and equitable competition, then I believe that American manufacturers must take their chances in the free market. But when foreign goods are produced by workers who are being paid depressed wages... then I believe that the situation is entirely different. In these cases I believe that we must take steps to protect domestic manufacturers from unfair foreign competition....

    There are... serious problems with the rigid "free-trader" philosophy. Free trade assumes that all countries have identical economic systems. Free trade assumes all countries pay the same wages.

    The speech was reproduced in: U.S. Department of Labor, Office of Information, Press Release *News,* 2 June 1977, pp. 8-9.
2. Deborah Sue Yaeger, "Third World Threat: Textile Industry Seeks Curbs on Imports," *Wall Street Journal,* 24 June 1977, p. 28.
3. "Home Truths for Protectionists," *Economist,* 25 November 1978, p. 81.
4. "Notable and Quotable," *Wall Street Journal,* 11 January 1979, p. 22.
5. "U.S. Increased Its 1979 Share of World Markets for Manufactured Goods to 17.4% from 17%," *Wall Street Journal,* 14 July 1980, p. 16.
6. Straight-line PPFs require a rather restrictive set of assumptions; namely, the production functions of both products are identical in their capital-labor ratio and there exist constant returns to scale. For the proof of this generalization, see: Charles P. Kindleberger and Peter H. Lindert, *International Economics,* 6th ed. (Homewood, Ill.: Irwin, 1978), Appendix A.
7. This assertion is made without a proof. For a formal proof of the factor price equalization theorem, see: M.O. Clement, et al., *Theoretical Issues in International Economics* (Boston: Houghton Mifflin, 1967), pp. 20-34.

PART III

THE PATTERN
OF TRADE AND
INTERNATIONAL
COMPETITIVENESS

7

Theories of the Pattern of Trade

International economic analysis is divided into (1) the theory of trade and (2) the theory of payments. The former, often known as the "pure" or "real" theory, is further divided into (a) the theory of the gains from trade and (b) the theory of the pattern (or direction) of trade. In the theory of the gains from trade, the gain from specialization and trade is the *effect,* and international differences in opportunity costs are the *cause.* In the theory of the pattern of trade, international differences in opportunity costs are the *effect;* our task now is to identify the cause of such differences. This chapter will consider theories of the pattern of trade: why does a particular nation export particular products, or, more fundamentally, why does a particular nation have comparative advantage in particular products?

HISTORICAL BACKGROUND

David Ricardo introduced the theory of the gains from trade, but he accepted, with minimal explanation, the pattern of trade as given. Once the labor productivities – or the costs – of the cloth and wine industries in both England and Portugal were known, the pattern (direction) of trade was uniquely established: Portugal exported wine; England exported cloth. Satisfied with being able to demonstrate that gains arose from comparative-advantage specialization and trade, Ricardo did not try to explain how the comparative cost differences arose in the first place. He took for granted the relatively high costs of English wine and of Portugese cloth, bending only so far as to attribute these absolute cost differences to vague "climatic" factors in each country.[1] This theory of the gains from trade was further refined prior to World War I; but no one offered an explicit theory of the pattern of trade beyond the obvious generalization that particular ores and minerals were exported only by nations endowed with deposits of those ores and minerals.

In the two decades after World War I, two Swedish economists – Eli F. Heckscher (1879-1952) and his student, Bertil Ohlin (1899-, who won the 1977 Nobel Prize in economics)– developed an internally consistent theory of the pattern of trade. Specifically, Heckscher and Ohlin ascribed international differences in opportunity (and in money) costs to the interaction of (1) international differences in relative factor endowments and (2) inter-commodity differences in factor ratios in production processes. The theory asserts that if nation A's capital-to-labor endowment ratio exceeds that of nation B, and if product X's least-cost capital-to-labor production ratio exceeds that of product Y, then nation A will have comparative advantage in product X and nation B will have comparative advantage in product Y. This theory of the pattern of trade is known as the Heckscher-Ohlin factor-proportions theory or, for short, the Heckscher-Ohlin theory.

In the mid-1950s, the Heckscher-Ohlin theory suffered a serious setback when, for the first time, sufficient empirical data became available to permit a preliminary test of its predictions. The now famous study by Wassily Leontief found that the actual trade pattern of the United States was the exact opposite of what the theory predicted. The United States, known to have a relatively high capital-to-labor endowment ratio, was found exporting products with relatively low capital-to-labor production ratios. This result, known as the Leontief Paradox, gave rise to a variety of both modified and new theories of the pattern of trade. Most of these modifications and new formulations have helped to reconcile, to a considerable extent, the Heckscher-Ohlin theory and the Leontief Paradox.

REAL COSTS VS. MONEY PRICES

Ricardo's theory of the gain from trade requires comparisons of *real* (opportunity) costs. To demonstrate unequivocally that nations gain from comparative advantage specialization and trade, the no-trade and with-trade "real costs" of production – be they labor time expended or quantities of other products sacrificed – must be compared. Saying that the gain from trade is, say, $1 million is not very meaningful or convincing unless such a monetary value can be translated into tangible "real stuff," e.g., worker-hours saved or tons of wheat and gallons of wine gained. In contrast, theories of the pattern of trade may contain but do not necessitate such a "real" foundation. To explain the trade pattern, one can start with the money costs or the money prices of products expressed in the currency units of each country.

To illustrate this difference, suppose that the pretrade domestic prices of wheat and cotton in North and South are as follows:

	Price per ton of	
	Wheat	Cotton
North:	$1	$5
South:	5 pesos	15 pesos

Under an assumption of perfectly competitive markets, these figures imply opportunity costs (transformation ratios) of $\frac{1}{5}$ ton of cotton per ton of wheat in North and $\frac{1}{3}$ ton of cotton per ton of wheat in South. In other words, domestic price ratios are the reciprocals of the opportunity costs, as shown in Chapter 4.

In Chapters 3 and 5, "costs" had to be expressed as opportunity costs, quantities of other products to be foregone. That treatment of costs was necessary so we could show gains from trade in physical quantities – the possibility of producing and consuming so many more tons of wheat and/or cotton. Although opportunity costs will remain implicit in our analysis of trade patterns, we need not make such explicit use of this rather cumbersome device. In our analysis of trade patterns, instead, the simpler concept of *relative money prices* will be used.

In the above example, relative money prices for wheat/cotton are $\frac{1}{5}$ in North and $\frac{1}{3}$ in South (the same numbers as wheat's opportunity costs but, in this context, representing price ratios between the two products rather than costs of only one product). Wheat is relatively cheap in North, cotton relatively cheap in South; or, reading the same ratios from the opposite perspective, cotton is relatively expensive in North, wheat relatively expensive in South. Therefore, North exports wheat to South, and South exports cotton to North. It is this *difference in pretrade relative prices* that *gives rise to mutually beneficial trade*. Our task, in this and in subsequent chapters, is to identify the causes of these differences, for these differences determine the pattern of trade.

Whether real costs or money prices are used, comparative costs will remain the fundamental determinant of the pattern of trade – unless monopoly business power or government power drives the money price ratios away from the opportunity cost relationships. If, for example, monopoly power or government fiat intrudes into the numerical example just considered, and lowers the Southern wheat price to $2\frac{1}{2}$ pesos or raises the Northern wheat price to $2, North would import wheat and export cotton. Further, governments may intervene to distort exchange rates. Given the original prices of this numerical example, an exchange rate of more than 5 pesos to the dollar would lead North to import both cotton and wheat from South. As theories of the pattern of trade are spelled out in this chapter and the next, the absence of monopoly power and of government intervention will be assumed, unless a contrary case is explicitly noted. Domestic price ratios, therefore, will be assumed to be equal to the reciprocal of opportunity cost ratios.

THE HECKSCHER-OHLIN THEORY

The Heckscher-Ohlin factor-proportions theory constitutes the foundation of the modern theory of the pattern of international trade. This theory, as the introductory paragraphs explained, attributes comparative advantage differences among nations to international differences in *factor proportions*, with two kinds of proportions interacting. These two kinds of proportions – or ratios – are: (1) each nation's ratio of factor endowments (its quantity of capital to its quantity of labor), and (2) the ratio of factor inputs (the quantity of capital relative to the quantity of labor required) in least-cost production of each product. Stripped to its bare essentials, the theory asserts that *each nation has comparative advantage in* (and therefore exports) *those goods whose least-cost production uses a relatively large quantity of the country's relatively abundant factor.* This rather simplistic – and almost tautological – conclusion of Heckscher and Ohlin was nevertheless a very significant contribution to the theory of international trade inasmuch as this first explicit theory of the pattern of trade established a logical linkage between an attribute of trading nations (i.e., the endowed factor ratio of each) and a characteristic of the products being traded (i.e., the factor ratio in the least-cost production of each). The theory, later refined by Paul Samuelson, has a highly elegant and complex construct. Its numerous assumptions are so restrictive that the theory's general applicability to real-world situations is often seriously questioned. Nevertheless, the essentials of the theory will be explored in this text primarily because of the penetrating insight it provides into the basis of the pattern of international trade.

SOME PRELIMINARIES: ISOCOSTS AND INSOQUANTS

The basic framework of the Heckscher-Ohlin theory is built on a simplifying assumption that there are two nations (A and B) producing two goods (X and Y) using two factors of production (capital, K, and labor, L). Nations are characterized by their factor endowments as either "capital rich" (endowed with a relatively large capital-to-labor ratio) or "labor rich" (endowed with a relatively small capital-to-labor ratio). Notice that a nation can be characterized as capital rich or labor rich only by comparison with another nation. Similarly, products are characterized as "capital intensive" – if their least-cost production involves a relatively large capital-to-labor ratio – or as "labor intensive" – if their least-cost production involves a relatively small capital-to-labor ratio. These terms identify the "factor intensity" of a good's production process. Notice, again, that a product can be characterized as capital intensive or labor intensive only by comparison with another product. In order for us to characterize nations and products precisely by their factor proportions, we must develop a few more simple geometric tools.

The Isocost and Relative Factor Prices

Suppose the prices of capital and labor in nations A and B are as follows:

	Capital (per machine-hour)	Labor (per worker-hour)
Nation A:	$2	$10
Nation B:	8 pesos	16 pesos

Can you tell from these figures which nation is capital rich and which nation is labor rich? While a labor unit is 5 times ($10 ÷ $2 = 5) as expensive as capital in nation A, a labor unit is only twice as expensive as capital in nation B. Expensive labor (relative to capital) in A means labor is relatively scarce and capital relatively abundant in A. Similarly, in B, capital is relatively dear because B is relatively short of it; labor is relatively cheap because of its relative abundance. (Remember the assumption excluding monopoly and government power from market price determinations.)

Suppose that we give a budget of $20, per some time period, to a producing firm in nation A. With the $20, it can purchase (hire) 10 machine-hours ($20 ÷ $2 = 10), or 2 worker-hours ($20 ÷ $10 = 2), or some combinations of capital and labor with a total cost of $20. Let us draw this "same-cost" ($20) line in a graph. Figure 7-1 shows the quantity of capital on the vertical axis and the quantity of labor on the horizontal axis. Plot the two extreme points – 10 capital and zero labor *and* zero capital and 2 labor – in the graph and draw a line between the two points. The result is the steeper of the two lines in Figure 7-1. Any point on this line represents a combination of some quantities of capital and labor that can be purchased with $20. Hence the line is called an *isocost* ("iso" means "same").

The $20 isocost for nation A has a slope of (minus) 5, which is the reciprocal of the ratio of the capital price and the labor price ($2 ÷ $10 = 1/5) in that country. The steepness of the slope reflects the scarcity of labor and the abundance of capital. The steeper the slope, the larger the absolute value of the slope, and the smaller the capital-to-labor price ratio; which in turn means that capital is cheaper and more abundant and labor is scarcer and more expensive. The steeper the isocost is, therefore, the more capital rich the country is.

Now, let us do a similar exercise for nation B. A producer in B, with a given budget of, say, 64 pesos per time period, can purchase either 8 capital or 4 labor. The flatter line in Figure 7-1 represents a 64-peso isocost for nation B. The flatness of this line, in comparison with the steeper isocost for A, reflects the relative abundance and cheapness of labor in nation B.

Although an arbitrary pair of "budgets" – $20 for A and 64 pesos for B – is given in the Figure 7-1 illustration, absolute sizes of the budgets are unimportant. What matters is the *slope* of each isocost, and the

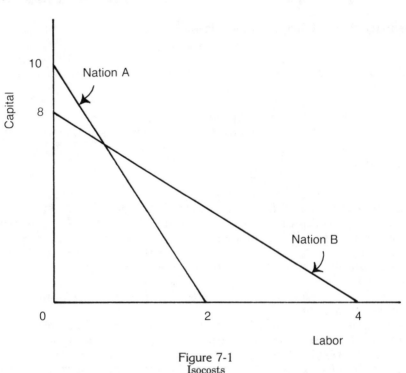

Figure 7-1
Isocosts

slope is determined exclusively by the *relative* factor prices in each country. (Try using different budget figures for each country – e.g., $10 for A and 48 pesos for B – and draw resultant isocosts. You will find that, so long as relative prices hold constant, all isocosts for each country are parallel to each other; that is, they all have the same slope.)

The Isoquant and the Production Function

Now that we have seen how relative factor endowments of nations can be represented by isocosts having different slopes, we must turn to a similar exercise of graphically expressing the relationship between inputs and output. Suppose that a unit of product X can be produced using the combination of OK of capital and OL of labor in Figure 7-2. Point *a* therefore represents an output of one unit of X. Normally, there exist possibilities for substitution between factor inputs. Suppose that the same quantity of X (one unit) can be produced by using a little less capital than OK *and* a little more labor than OL, say, the input combination of point *b*. Similar substitutions of labor for capital will provide the same one-unit output from input combinations represented by points further down and to the right at *c* or at *d*. If all the points representing combinations of capital and labor yielding one unit of X are connected, a convex curve called an *isoquant* – meaning "same quantity" – is traced out. A similar isoquant located further away from the point of origin, e.g., X' in Figure 7-2, represents a larger quantity of X produced, say, 2 units of X. A host of these isoquants, representing various levels of output of a commodity, expresses the *production function* of that commodity. A production function is a statement of a technical relationship between the quantities of inputs and of output.

Figure 7-3 portrays the production function of product X. Five alternative levels of output of good X – X_1 through X_5 – are shown by the five isoquants. The five points a through e represent five possible production points on the ray, OR, from the origin. Along this ray, increases in the quantities of capital and labor are proportional. Between any two points, say, b and d, the percentage difference in capital, K_2 versus K_4, equals the percentage difference in labor, L_2 versus L_4. This is necessarily the case along any ray from the origin.

We now add the assumption, in this case, that between any two points along any ray like OR, the percentage difference in output equals the percent difference in inputs. In other words, a doubling of both inputs – say, from K_2 to K_4 in capital *and* from L_2 to L_4 in labor – would result in a doubling of output – from X_2 to X_4. In such a case, the production function is said to exhibit *constant returns to scale;* if both inputs are increased or decreased by a certain percentage, output is increased or decreased by the same percentage. The basic Heckscher-Ohlin theory assumes that production functions possess this quantity.

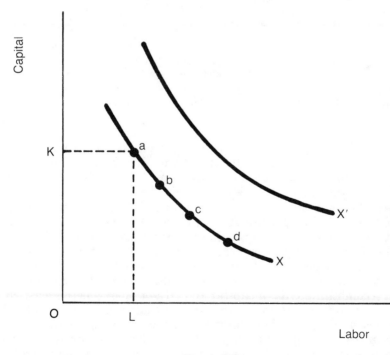

Figure 7-2
Isoquants

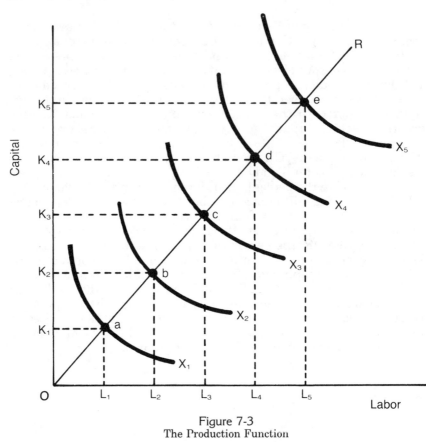

Figure 7-3
The Production Function

Equilibrium in Production

Suppose that the production function of product X in nation A is identical with the production function of product X in nation B. (The Heckscher-Ohlin model assumes this.) Along the isoquant X, exactly where would the least-cost production point be found in each country? In Figure 7-4, representative isocosts of the two countries are shown by the two lines – the steeper line AA′ for nation A and the flatter line BB′ for nation B. Since the steeper line for nation A implies that it is a capital rich country where capital is relatively cheap and labor expensive, it makes sense for it to produce X with relatively high capital intensity – i.e., at a relatively high capital-to-labor ratio. Specifically, point a – combining OK_a of capital and OL_a of labor – is the least-cost production point for nation A. Similarly, the labor rich nation B would find the least-cost production point at b, using a smaller quantity, OK_b, of capital and a larger quantity, OL_b, of labor than nation A. The least-cost production point is found in each case at the tangency of the isoquant and the isocost.[2]

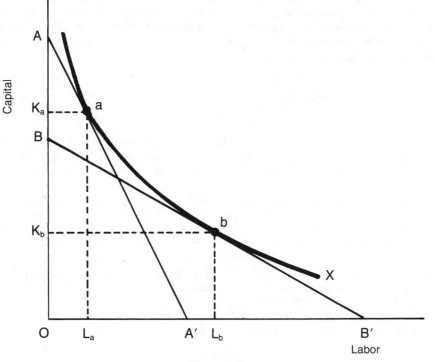

Figure 7-4
Least-Cost Production Points

THE ASSUMPTIONS OF THE MODEL

Two key assumptions of the Heckscher-Ohlin theory have already been identified: the production function of each product is characterized by constant returns to scale and it is the same everywhere in the world. These assumptions enable us to use a single isoquant as representative of the entire production function of a commodity produced in any country. Further, the model requires several additional simplifying assumptions. Perfect competition in both factor and product markets is assumed. A corollary of this assumption is that prices are proportional to costs (in a long-run competitive equilibrium, "cost" will include all costs including normal profits) so that relative money prices of goods in a country reflect their comparative real costs. Factor supplies in each country are assumed fixed and fully employed. Factors of production are immobile across national boundaries, but are perfectly mobile within a country. International movements of goods are completely free and costless. Also, international trade and payments are assumed to be balanced, and the exchange rates assumed to be in equilibrium. This assumption is necessary, as earlier noted, to prevent a bias in the country's exchange rate from distorting the pattern of comparative advantage. Furthermore, the model assumes that international differences in tastes and preferences do not exist, so that international differences in relative prices of goods (and hence comparative advantage) are explained exclusively by supply biases (that is, factor endowment and factor intensity differences).

Factor Intensity Reversals

To be complete, the Heckscher-Ohlin theory requires one additional assumption concerning the nature of the production function: there should be no factor intensity reversals. This concept requires a brief explanation.

Figure 7-5 shows two isoquants, X and Y, representing the production functions of goods X and Y. A pair of steeper isocosts represents the relative factor prices of the capital rich nation, A, and two flatter isocosts are for the labor rich nation, B. Minimum-cost production points for goods X and Y in nations A and B are indicated by the four tangency points, a, b, c, and d. Which good, X or Y, is more capital intensive and which is more labor intensive? Given input prices (and isocost slopes) in A, the capital-to-labor ratio of least-cost production of X, at point a, exceeds the capital-to-labor ratio of least-cost production of Y, at point c. An imaginary line connecting O and a has a steeper slope

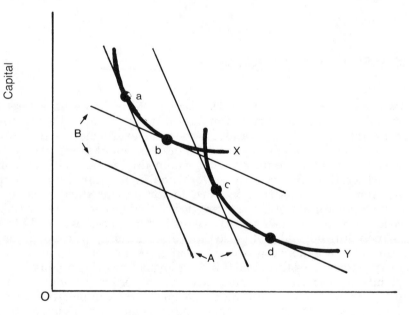

Figure 7-5
Factor Intensities Unequivocally Established

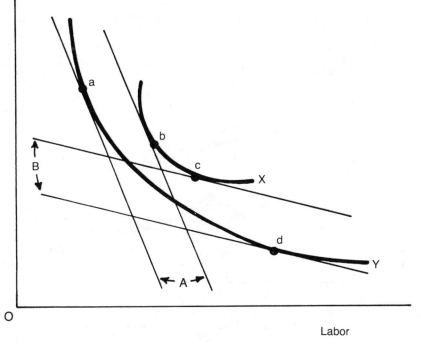

Figure 7-6
Factor Intensities Reversed between Two Nations

(located nearer the capital axis) than an imaginary line linking O and c. We therefore conclude that, in nation A, production of X is more capital intensive than is production of Y. This is also true in nation B. Given input prices in B, the capital-to-labor ratio of least-cost production of X, at point b, exceeds that of Y, at d. An imaginary line connecting O and b has a steeper slope than an imaginary line linking O and d. Thus, X is *always* capital intensive relative to Y, and Y is *always* labor intensive relative to X, in *every* country, independent of the relative prices of factors.[3] This unequivocal classification of products according to their factor intensity is indispensable for the Heckscher-Ohlin conclusion to have any significance.

Now, examine Figure 7-6 where this unequivocal classification of products will not be possible. Here we have two isoquants, X and Y, with Y having a much greater degree of substitutability between capital and labor than X. Under such a circumstance, we have a strange result. Product Y, which is capital intensive in nation A (point a on the isoquant Y has a higher capital-to-labor ratio than point b on the isoquant X) given nation A's isocosts, becomes labor intensive in nation B (point d on the isoquant Y has a lower capital-to-labor ratio than point c on the isoquant X) given nation B's isocosts. In other words, the factor intensity of the two products is reversed as between the two countries. We can no longer definitely classify goods according to their factor intensities; Y is capital intensive in nation A, but is labor intensive in nation B.

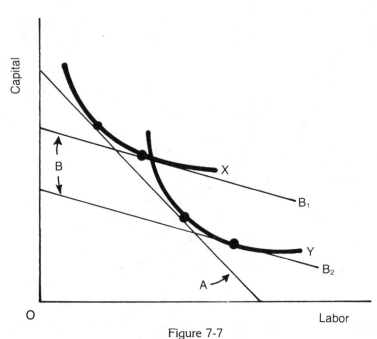

Figure 7-7
The Prediction of the Factor Proportions Theory

When factor intensity reverses itself between countries, the predictive power of the Heckscher-Ohlin theory is lost since the theory presupposes our ability to label a product unambiguously by its factor intensity. To avoid this problem, the model assumes that production functions are not subject to factor reversals.

THE CONCLUSION OF THE MODEL

Figure 7-7 shows two isoquants, X and Y, representing given arbitrary but identical quantities of goods X and Y.[4] Since we assume that the production function of any particular product is the same in every nation, isoquant X is the relevant production function in both A and B, and the isoquant Y applies equally to both A and B. The two isoquants are chosen so both are tangent to the same isocost in nation A. Since we assume that the number of units of X represented by isoquant X is the same as the number of units of Y represented by isoquant Y, the price of X is equal to the price of Y in nation A. For example, if the number of units of X and Y represented by the isoquants X and Y are, say, 17X and 17Y, and if the isocost portrayed represents $1,700 of total cost, then both X and Y would cost $100 a unit in nation A.

In nation B, in contrast, the isoquant X is tangent to the isocost B_1 representing a total cost greater than the total cost represented by the other isocost, B_2, which is tangent to the isoquant Y. In nation B, therefore, the price of X must be higher than the price of Y.

With a little effort, one can look into Figure 7-7 and see the *relative* prices of the two products in the two nations. Since the prices of X and Y are the same in nation A, but the price of Y is lower than the price of X in nation B, the price of X must be *relatively* lower than the price of Y in nation A.

We now have the conclusion of the factor-proportions theory. The relatively capital intensive good, X, is relatively cheaper in the relatively capital rich country, A; product Y, which is relatively labor intensive, is relatively cheaper in the relatively labor rich nation, B. In general, the Heckscher-Ohlin factor-proportions theory states:

A country has comparative advantage in – and exports – those goods that use relatively more of its relatively abundant factor of production, and has comparative disadvantage in – and imports – those goods that require in their production relatively large quantities of that country's relatively scarce factor.

This conclusion has an element of tautology (truism) in it: in essence it says that a country does best what it does best. One would expect that such a plausible hypothesis as this can easily meet an empirical test. Surprisingly, that has not been the case.

THE LEONTIEF PARADOX

Using the 1947 input-output data of the United States economy, Wassily Leontief calculated the capital and labor requirements of an average million dollars' worth of American exports and of an average million dollars' worth of import-competing U.S. goods. His finding is summarized as follows:

	Exports	Import Replacements
Capital (dollars in (1947 prices)	2,550,780	3,091,339
Labor (worker-years)	182.3	170.0

These figures showed that the capital-labor ratio of U.S. exports ($13,991 of capital per worker-year) was considerably lower than that of America's import replacements ($18,184 of capital per worker-year). In other words, while the production of American exports required approximately $14,000 worth of capital per worker-year of labor, the production of American goods competing with imports required about $18,000 worth of capital per worker-year of labor. These figures led Leontief to enunciate his famous conclusion that "America's participation in the international division of labor is based on labor intensive, rather than capital intensive, lines of production."[5] This was a surprising conclusion in view of the generally acknowledged fact that the United States was one of the most capital rich nations in the world.

What, then, are we to assume about the capital intensity of foreign production of the goods America imports? Having no access to the production data of the foreign companies producing the goods America imported, Leontief had to use the input-output figures of the American industries producing competitive (comparable) products. At first sight, this unavoidable substitution may appear to undermine the validity of the test result. One might argue, as did P.T. Ellsworth, that American import-competing industries would naturally use more capital-intensive production methods than the foreign industries producing comparable goods. The capital intensity of American import *replacements,* therefore, is irrelevant; and Ellsworth argued that Leontief should have compared the factor intensity of American exports with that of the American imports in their countries of origin.[6] This argument, however, is not valid since it implies the existence of factor intensity reversals. The reader may recall that the Heckscher-Ohlin theory assumes that production functions are not subject to factor reversals. This assumption means that if American exports are less capital intensive than are America's import substitutes, then the same relative factor intensities must prevail throughout the world. Therefore, there is no need to compare the factor intensities of American exports with those of American imports in their countries of origin. It is only necessary to compare the relative factor intensities of the two categories of products in any one country (e.g., the United States), which was exactly what Leontief did. To have explained the Leontief Paradox in terms of factor intensity reversals would have required rejection of a central assumption of the Heckscher-Ohlin theory.

Since the mid-1950s, many writers have published the results of their studies purporting to explain the Leontief Paradox.[7] Although most of these studies have been able to explain the Paradox on one logical ground or another, none has been successful in unequivocally explaining away the Paradox with the support of totally valid empirical evidence. What is more important for our purposes, however, is the by-product effects of these studies in modifying and extending the basic factor-proportions theory itself. Thanks largely to these modifications and extensions, we now seem to have a fairly good understanding of the causes of the pattern of trade, though we are still without a definitive and general theory of trade patterns.[8]

THE NEW THEORIES OF TRADE PATTERNS

Before venturing into the discussion of the post-Heckscher-Ohlin theories of trade patterns, we must establish one important point: the discussion will primarily be of the pattern of trade in manufactured goods. Problems of empirically supporting the Heckscher-Ohlin hypothesis have centered chiefly on trading in manufactures. That the pattern of trade in primary products is dictated by the availability of essential natural resources in the exporting countries has never been seriously questioned. As Staffan Linder observed:

> It is probable that the factor proportions theorem has gained such wide acceptance only because a pattern of trade in primary products, dictated by differences in natural resource endowments, is so plausible. By a suspect analogy, trade in manufactures has been treated as if governed by differences in capital and labor endowments. Explanations of the factor proportions account always begin with a persuasive assertion that the natural-resource-abundant countries export natural-resource-intensive products.[9]

Differences in natural-resource endowments and natural-resource intensities do not contribute much to the differences in the production costs of manufactured goods because (1) natural resources normally constitute a small portion of total production costs of manufactured products, and (2) primary products are traded among nations so that international differences in their prices are reduced to the differences in transportation costs.[10] It is for this reason that recent developments in the theories of trade patterns have centered primarily on the roles of capital-to-labor ratios and of technology in the production of manufactured goods.

SKILLED LABOR AND HUMAN CAPITAL

One significant modification of the basic factor-proportions model has to do with the problem of the specification of the factors "labor" and "capital." Leontief found that U.S. exports were relatively labor intensive. But specifically what type of labor was embodied in large quantities in U.S. exports? It has generally been recognized that U.S. exports are *skilled-labor* intensive. Donald Keesing confirmed this belief in his study of the labor content of the exports and import replacements of the United States and thirteen foreign countries using the 1962 trade statistics. He found that (1) U.S. exports of manufactured goods were more skilled-labor intensive than its import replacements, and (2) of the exports of the fourteen countries, those of the United States had the highest skilled-labor content.[11]

The creation of skilled labor (that of scientists, engineers, managers, skilled machinists, etc.) requires investment, just as the development of physical capital does. As such, skilled labor may be viewed as a form of capital – *human capital*. Saying that U.S. exports are skilled-labor intensive is therefore tantamount to saying that they are human-capital intensive. Herein may lie an important explanation of the Leontief Paradox. Although the hypothesis has not as yet been definitely supported by an empirical test (primarily because of the conceptual difficulty of adding imputed human capital to the measure of computed capital stock), there is abundant partial evidence suggesting that the United States, which is richly endowed with human capital, has comparative advantage in manufactures with relatively high human-capital-to-other-input intensity.[12]

TECHNOLOGICAL GAPS AND PRODUCT LIFE CYCLES

Capital abundance (both physical and human) and technological sophistication are concomitant with high levels of industrial development. Mature industrial economies that derive comparative advantage from capital abundance are therefore also expected to enjoy the advantages of high technology. This line of thought has led to the development of technology theories of trade. Below we will introduce and briefly discuss three variations on this theme. All of these have been developed with special reference to the United States, the world's undisputed technological leader. Note that each of these arguments assumes that production functions for a particular product will differ from country to country.

The R & D Factor

Closely related to Keesing's labor skill thesis is an attempt to explain U.S. trade performance by attributing it to the intensity of research and development (R & D) activities in the United States. Thus, Gruber, Mehta, and Vernon reported that the export performance of U.S. industries was positively correlated with the industries' R & D expenditures expressed as a percentage of their sales.[13] A similar finding was reported by Keesing. He used the share of 18 U.S. industries' exports in the exports of the comparable industries of the 10 most industrial nations of the West (the "Group of Ten") in 1962 as the indicator of each U.S. industry's export performance. The export share ranged from 59.52 percent (aircraft) to 9.14 percent (primary ferrous metals). As the indicator of each U.S. industry's R & D activities, Keesing used the percentage of scientists and engineers in R & D in total employment as of January 1961. The percentage figures ranged from 7.71 (aircraft) to 0.03 (lumber and wood products). Keesing found that there was a high degree of correlation (the Spearman coefficient of rank correlation being 0.94) between the two rankings.[14]

Technological Gaps

In a 1956 article, Irving Kravis argued that the "availability" of a commodity in a given country confers comparative advantage. Availability was attributed by Kravis to the existence of key natural resources or temporary monopoly created by technical changes and product differentiation. This latter explanation of availability –technical innovation – naturally applies primarily to manufactured goods. An innovating country enjoys comparative advantage in new and differentiated products until its trading partners have learned to imitate.[15]

Michael Posner in his 1961 article refined the concept of the imitation lag by distinguishing between demand lag and reaction lag. The *demand lag* is a lag in consumption; it is the time between the beginning of consumption of a new product in the innovating country and the beginning of consumption in the importing country. The foreign *reaction lag* is the time between initial consumption and initial local production in the importing country. The demand lag and the reaction lag add up to the *imitation lag*. During the demand-lag phase of the imitation lag, the innovating country has no exports because there is no overseas consumption. The innovating country enjoys an export monopoly in the product during the reaction lag since there is no local production in the importing country. The innovating country's comparative advantage during the period, therefore, is solely technology based. After local producers in the imitating country begin producing the product, thereby putting an end to the imitation lag, the exports of the innovating country begin to decrease and eventually cease.[16]

The Product Life Cycle

Building on Posner's two-stage imitation lag, and using the concept of the *product life cycle* which had earlier been developed by marketing theorists, Raymond Vernon expounded a four-stage product life cycle model of U.S. exports of manufactures. He argued that new and differentiated products are likely to be first developed in the United States because of its high per capita income and high wage rates. High incomes are conducive to development of new and sophisticated products, while high wages encourage development of new labor-saving devices. At the first stage of a product's life cycle, the United States enjoys an export monopoly in it. Even though wages are high in the United States, the new product must at first be produced here because close communication between suppliers and customers is essential during the early phase of the product's life cycle if the design is to be improved and the "bugs" are to be removed from the production process. Besides, high costs and prices do not present a very serious problem to producers who enjoy a monopoly situation.

Foreign production begins in the second stage of the product life cycle. By this time a large enough demand in their own markets enables foreign manufacturers to realize sufficient economies of scale. Production technology is sufficiently standardized (i.e., the "bugs" have been eliminated); it therefore becomes easily transferable to technologically sophisticated producers in relatively advanced foreign countries. During this second stage, U.S. exports must compete with locally produced goods. Consequently, the volume of U.S. exports tends to decrease.

In the third stage of the product's life cycle, foreign producers gain competitiveness as they become larger and more experienced. They also benefit from the advantages of their lower wage rates. They thus tend to displace U.S. exports in third-country export markets. Finally, in the last stage of the cycle, foreign manufacturers become sufficiently competitive to export the product to the United States itself. This product life cycle will be repeated as less developed countries with even lower wages begin producing and exporting the product whose production processes are now so standardized that even the technologically least sophisticated producers can readily master them. Thus, the early producers in Western Europe and Japan can anticipate a sequence of events like the sequence observed by the innovating U.S. manufacturers. The manufacturing of the new product moves gradually from the United States to lower-wage, less developed nations as the product matures and its technology becomes more widely diffused.[17]

THE PREFERENCE SIMILARITY HYPOTHESIS

Staffan Linder, Swedish economist and student of Ohlin, expounded a unique theory of trade in a book published in 1961.[18] His main contribution lies in his emphasis on the importance of *internal demand* in a country's ability to produce and export a given manufactured product. He argued that a product must be demanded in large quantities in the home market before it can become a potential export product. He supported this proposition by reference to the producer's lack of familiarity with foreign markets as compared with the domestic market. In the first place, an entrepreneur is most likely to respond to profit opportunities of which he or she is aware, and such opportunities are most likely to arise from clearly discernible domestic needs. If an entrepreneur were to introduce a product demanded only in foreign markets, its production costs would be prohibitively high. In Linder's words:

> [An entrepreneur] would probably be unsuccessful as he would not have easy access to crucial information which must be funnelled back and forth between producers and consumers. The trial-and-error period which a new product must almost inevitably go through on the market will be the more embarrassing costwise, the less intimate knowledge the producer has of the conditions under which his product will have to be used. And, if there is no home demand, the producer will be completely unfamiliar with such conditions.[19]

Linder thus concludes that *"the production functions of goods demanded at home are the relatively most advantageous ones,"* and *"international trade is really nothing but an extension across national frontiers of a country's own web of economic activity."*[20]

If internal demand is necessary for a product to be a potential export product, internal demand is also necessary for the product to be a potential import. (For example, if Japan did not have a large internal demand for automobiles, it would neither import nor export automobiles in any significant quantity.) It follows that the more similar the internal demand structures of a pair of countries, the more intensely competitive is the potential trade in manufactures between them. The actual composition of trade between the two countries will then depend on such factors as product differentiation, technological superiority, and economies of scale.

What forces determine the internal demand structures of a country? Linder asserts that the level of average (or per capita) income is the most important single determinant of a country's structure of demand. In countries with high per capita income, there tend to exist large internal demands for "deluxe" and sophisticated consumer and capital goods, while in poorer countries demands are largely for less sophisticated, more basic products. This observation implies a unique hypothesis of the pattern of international trade: A nation has comparative advantage in those goods whose levels of sophistication are the most compatible with its per capita income level.

In this chapter we have made a survey of the theories of the pattern of trade. Our primary emphasis has been on the Heckscher-Ohlin factor-proportions theory. We have also examined briefly several post-Heckscher-Ohlin theories. With the sole exception of the Linder thesis, all of these post-Heckscher-Ohlin theories have one thing in common with the factor-proportions account: They all try to explain trade patterns by reference to production requirements of a product that are either present or absent in a given nation. In the next chapter, we will make an attempt to synthesize these various alternative theories of trade patterns.

STUDY QUESTIONS

1. What are the two major branches of international trade theory? How do you characterize Ricardian comparative advantage theory?
2. What, in a nutshell, is the Heckscher-Ohlin theory's conclusion?
3. Suppose the prices of capital and of labor in Alegra and in Bianca are as follows:

	Capital	Labor
Alegra:	$4	$20
Bianca	5 pesos	10 pesos

   (a) Which country is relatively capital rich? Why?
   (b) Draw isocosts for the two countries, each with a "budget" of $100. Assume an exchange rate of $1 = 1 peso.
4. Refer to Figure 7-5. Can you tell, by visual inspection alone, which country has comparative advantage in which good? If so, how can you tell?
5. Refer to Figure 7-6. Can you tell, by visual inspection alone, which country has comparative advantage in which good? Which country would be violating the Heckscher-Ohlin prediction?
6. How would *you* resolve the Leontief Paradox?
7. Describe the product life cycle theory of the pattern of trade.
8. Describe Linder's theory of the pattern of trade.
9. All of the post-Heckscher-Ohlin theories discussed in this chapter, with the sole exception of Linder's thesis, have been called neo-Heckscher-

Ohlin theories or neo-factor-proportions accounts. Why is this? In what fundamental sense is Linder's thesis different from all the others?

10. For each of the following cases, identify a factor or factors that may account for comparative (dis)advantage.
    (a) Saudi Arabia exports crude oil.
    (b) The United States is the world's largest exporter of jet airliners.
    (c) Germany exports Volkswagen cars to France; France exports Renaults to Germany.
    (d) Japan's advantage in color TV production is gradually shifting to South Korea and Taiwan.
    (e) Italy exports small-size refrigerators to the United States; America exports large-size refrigerators to Italy.
    (f) Japan does not produce, let alone export, large-size passenger cars in any significant quantities.
    (g) India and Pakistan export low-grade cotton goods.
    (h) France exports fashionable dresses to the United States; the United States exports designer jeans to France.
    (i) The United States exports sophisticated weapons systems.

ENDNOTES

1. Richard E. Caves, *Trade and Economic Structure: Models and Methods* (Cambridge: Harvard University Press, 1963), p. 11.
2. For a proof of this proposition, consult any standard textbook of intermediate microeconomic theory.
3. It is for this reason that we can, within the context of the Heckscher-Ohlin theory, label a product as either relatively capital or labor intensive, despite the fact that the production function may be characterized by a degree of capital-to-labor substitutability (i.e., the isoquant is an arc) permitting the product to be produced with different degrees of input mix. With isoquants like those of Figure 7-5, one product is relatively capital intensive *regardless* of the input price ratio. In contrast, with isoquants like those of Figure 7-6, one product is relatively capital intensive given one range of input price ratios but is relatively labor intensive given another range of input prices.
4. This is not an extreme assumption. "One" X may be a package of, say, 144 units of X, while "one" Y may be a package of 1,000 Y's.
5. Wassily Leontief, "Domestic Production and Foreign Trade: The American Capital Position Re-examined," *Economia Internazionale,* February 1954, p. 25.
6. P.T. Ellsworth, "The Structure of American Foreign Trade: A New View Examined," *Review of Economics and Statistics,* August 1954, pp. 279-285.
7. For a survey of these studies, see: Caves, *Trade and Economic Structure,* pp. 273-82; and Herbert G. Grubel, *International Economics* (Homewood, Ill.: Richard D. Irwin, 1977), pp. 65-87.
8. The following are representative of the post-Leontief developments in the theories of trade patterns. Works that are deemed too technical for our readers are not included. *Books:* Staffan Burenstam Linder, *An Essay on Trade and Transformation* (New York: John Wiley & Sons, 1961); Charles P. Kindleberger, *Foreign Trade and the National Economy* (New Haven: Yale University Press, 1962); G.C. Hufbauer, *Synthetic Materials and the Theory of International Trade* (Cambridge: Harvard University Press, 1966); and Seev Hirsch, *Location of Industry and International Competitiveness* (Oxford: Clarendon Press, 1967). *Articles:* Irving Kravis, "'Availability' and Other Influences on the Commodity Composition of Trade," *Journal of Political Economy,* April 1956, pp.143-155; M.V. Posner, "International Trade and Technical Change," *Oxford Economic Papers,* October 1961, pp. 323-341; Peter B. Kenen, "Nature, Capital, and Trade," *Journal of Political Economy,* October 1965, pp. 437-60; Donald Keesing, "Labor Skills and Comparative Advantage,"

American Economic Review, May 1966, pp. 249-58; Raymond Vernon, "International Investment and International Trade in the Product Cycle," *Quarterly Journal of Economics,* May 1966, pp. 190-207; Donald B. Keesing, "The Impact of Research and Development on United States Trade," *Journal of Political Economy,* February 1967, pp. 38-48; William Gruber, Dileep Mehta, and Raymond Vernon, "The R & D Factor in International Trade and International Investment of United States Industries," *Journal of Political Economy,* February 1961, pp. 20-37; G.C. Hufbauer, "The Impact of National Characteristics and Technology on the Commodity Composition of Trade in Manufactured Goods," in Raymond Vernon, ed., *The Technology Factor in International Trade* (New York: National Bureau of Economic Research, 1970), pp. 145-231; and Robert E. Baldwin, "Determinants of the Commodity Structure of U.S. Trade," *American Economic Review,* March 1971, pp. 126-146.

9. Linder, *An Essay on Trade and Transformation,* pp. 86-87.
10. In 1976, the Japanese steel industry, in spite of Japan's paucity of natural resources, had lower raw material costs in steel production than the U.S. industry. See Chapter 9 for details.
11. Keesing, *American Economic Review.*
12. See Kenen, *Journal of Political Economy;* and Baldwin, *American Economic Review.*
13. Gruber, Mehta, and Vernon, *Journal of Political Economy.*
14. Donald B. Keesing, *Journal of Political Economy,* p. 40.
15. Kravis, *Journal of Political Economy.*
16. Posner, *Oxford Economic Papers.*
17. Vernon, *Quarterly Journal of Economics.*
18. Linder, *An Essay on Trade and Transformation.*
19. *Ibid.,* pp. 89-90.
20. *Ibid.,* pp. 90 and 88, italics his.

8

Theories of Trade Patterns: Syntheses and Elaborations

In the preceding chapter we examined various alternative theories of the pattern of trade, including the factor-proportions account, the technological gap theories, and Linder's preference similarity model. Would it be possible to formulate a general theory of trade patterns by putting together the essential elements of these theories? In this chapter we will first present the general outline of an attempted synthesis. We will then elaborate on some aspects of trade-pattern theories.

THEORIES OF TRADE PATTERNS: A SYNTHESIS

The general outline of a synthesis presented in this section is of necessity speculative and impressionistic. It has not yet been subjected to empirical tests. Nevertheless, we believe that our "general theory" is quite useful for a clear understanding of the pattern of world trade.

We begin by modifying two of the assumptions of the Heckscher-Ohlin model. It is now assumed – realistically – that (1) the production functions – the isoquants – of some products differ from nation to nation, and (2) more than two inputs – capital and labor – are used in the production of some goods. The essential wisdom of the factor-proportions model is its logical linkage between a national attribute (relative factor endowment) and a product property (relative factor intensity). We retain, for most circumstances, Heckscher-Ohlin's concluding generalization:

> A nation has comparative advantage in – and exports – goods using relatively more of its relatively abundant factor of production, while the nation has comparative disadvantage in – and imports – goods using relatively more of its relatively scarce factor of production.

For purposes of teaching and learning, one great advantage of the original Heckscher-Ohlin model is that its production function with one output and only two inputs can be easily represented in a two-dimensional geometric sketch. The great disadvantage of a model involving one output and more than two inputs is that equations are needed for a comprehensive and precise presentation. However, by confining ourselves to one output and only three inputs (with the character of the third changing from case to case), we can continue to use the geometry of standard isocosts and isoquants to present this eclectic model of the modern theory of the pattern of trade.

PRIMARY PRODUCTS

First, to identify comparative advantage in production of primary products, we will use iron ore as an illustrative example. The element iron, Fe, makes up some 6 percent of the crust – the upper 20 kilometers – of the earth's surface. In every place, even those with the highest concentrations of Fe, both capital and labor must be applied in order to obtain marketable iron ore.

Because of the differences from place to place in the concentration of Fe in the earth – and in the depth of deposits below the surface – the yield of marketable ore from any particular combination of capital and labor will differ from place to place. Figures 8-1 and 8-2 portray the resulting contrast between the isoquants of a high Fe-concentration area and the isoquants of a low Fe-concentration area. The axes of these figures show annual inputs of capital and labor; the isoquants show the resulting annual output of marketable ore with a 66-percent Fe content.

Liberia is now one of the world's leading producers of iron ore. Figure 8-1 shows the Liberian isoquant passing through the input combination of 1,000 units of labor and 120 units of capital for the best mine location in Liberia. Denmark has no iron ore mines. Figure 8-2 shows the Danish isoquant passing through the input combination of 1,000L and 120K for the best "mining" location in Denmark. The isoquants in the figures are quite similar in shape, showing the *substitutability* of labor for capital to be about the same in both countries. However, the Liberian isoquant represents an output of 4 million tons of ore a year in contrast with the Danish output of only 0.1 million tons per year from the same input combination of capital and labor. In other words, the Liberian production function is more *efficient* than the Danish production function – forty times more efficient to be exact. (In the basic Heckscher-Ohlin model, both input *substitutability* and input *efficiency* of the production function are assumed to be identical from country to country.)

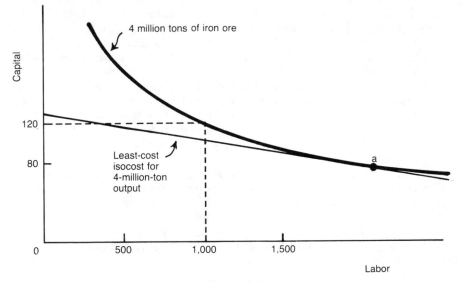

Figure 8-1
Liberian iron-ore production function showing only the isoquant through the input combination 1000L, 120K and the relatively low capital-to-labor isocost tangent to that isoquant

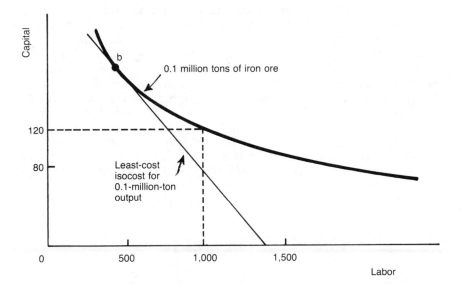

Figure 8-2
Danish iron-ore production function showing only the isoquant through the input combination 1000L, 120K and the relatively high capital-to-labor isocost tangent to that isoquant

Parenthetically, we may note that if Denmark were to produce 0.1 million tons of ore per year, it would not use 1,000L and 120K. Instead, because of Denmark's relatively high capital-to-labor endowment ratio, the least-cost input combination, designated point *b* in Figure 8-2, would comprise about 440L and 180K. Neither would Liberia use 1,000L and 120K to produce 4 million tons of ore. Because of Liberia's relatively low capital-to-labor endowment, the least-cost input combination, designated point *a* in Figure 8-1, would comprise about 2,060L and 76K. But in practice, Liberia will produce iron ore and Denmark will not. If we assume that both Denmark and Liberia have the production functions of equal efficiency for some other products, e.g., batteries, Denmark will have comparative advantage in battery production (the iron ore to be sacrificed per battery will be less in Denmark than in Liberia), and Liberia will have comparative advantage in iron ore production.

Liberia's comparative advantage is due to the difference, shown in Figures 8-1 and 8-2, between Denmark and Liberia in the efficiency of the isoquants – the same combination of capital and labor yielding a much larger quantity of iron ore in Liberia than in Denmark. But this difference is due, in turn, to the difference between the two nations in their relative endowment of the third input, Fe atoms in the soil. The Heckscher-Ohlin generalization applies:

> Liberia has comparative advantage in iron ore which uses relatively more of its relatively abundant factor of production, Fe; while Liberia has comparative disadvantage in batteries which use relatively more of its relatively scarce factors – capital and labor.

In other words, the difference in the two countries' endowment of Fe in the soil is so pronounced that it overshadows the effects of the difference in the capital-to-labor endowment ratio of the two countries.

Figures like 8-1 and 8-2 could be drawn for Guatemala and the United States for bananas (bananas *could* be grown in the United States in greenhouses. See Chapter 3). The Guatemalan isoquant from inputs to 1000L and 120K would represent many more bananas than would the isoquant of the United States from inputs of 1000L and 120K. Guatemala has comparative advantage in banana production because of its relatively great endowment of that third factor, a year-round hot and humid climate. In short, recognition that more than two inputs are involved permits the Heckscher-Ohlin model to explain comparative advantage involving most natural resources.

MANUFACTURED PRODUCTS

The results of recent studies in the patterns of trade in manufactured goods were reported in Chapter 7. Donald Keesing and others found that, in the 1960s, American exports were skilled-labor, or human-capital, intensive. Presumably, this is still true today. Although human capital is both conceptually and empirically difficult to measure, let us assume that we *can* make a clear distinction as among unskilled labor, physical capital (embodied in machines, buildings, and other structures), and human capital (embodied, through education, training, and experience, in managers and workers). Let us treat human capital – or the general level of the technological sophistication of the populace – as the third factor behind the capital-labor isoquant, much as we treated the Fe content of soil as the third factor behind the capital-labor isoquant of iron-ore production. We then distinguish between a manufactured good whose production involves a relatively large amount of human capital (i.e., relatively high technological sophistication), and a different good whose production involves relatively little human capital.

The product that requires little human capital would have nearly the same isoquant in every nation, regardless of the level of technological sophistication of the country. (This is what the basic Heckscher-Ohlin model assumes – that the efficiency of production functions is the same everywhere.) However, and this is the important point, the human-capital intensive good (i.e., technologically sophisticated good) would have an isoquant, through any given combination of physical capital and labor, showing larger output in nations relatively well endowed with technological sophistication than in ill-endowed nations. In other words, the efficiency of the production function of a high-technology good would be higher in technologically advanced nations than in less developed countries. For this human-capital intensive good, the isoquant would be comparable to that of Liberia's Figure 8-1 for the nation well endowed with technological sophistication; while the isoquant would be comparable to that of Denmark's Figure 8-2 for the ill-endowed nation. For production of iron ore, the contrast in the efficiency of the isoquant is explained by contrasting national endowments of the third input, Fe. For this human-capital intensive good, the isoquant efficiency contrast is explained by contrasting national endowments of the third factor, technological sophistication of the populace. In each case, comparative advantage will attach to the product whose least-cost production uses relatively large quantities of the factor with which the particular nation is relatively well endowed.

Paralleling the conclusion reached in the Liberian-Danish iron ore example, we may restate the Heckscher-Ohlin generalization as follows:

A country with superior technological sophistication has comparative advantage in those goods which use relatively more of its relatively abundant factor, technological sophistication; while it has comparative disadvantage in those goods which use relatively more of its relatively scarce factors – physical capital and labor.

What is being recognized here is the potentially overwhelming importance of the third input – technological sophistication of the people – in the production processes of some manufacturing products. To the extent that that factor is important for a product, countries endowed with a high level of technological sophistication have comparative advantage in that product; to the extent this third input is not important, the pattern of comparative advantage tends to be determined by the conventional factor-proportions (i.e., physical capital-to-labor) considerations.

A GENERALIZATION

We now have an overview of our "general theory" of international trade. The trade pattern is determined basically by the juxtaposition of the physical capital-to-labor endowment ratio of a country and the physical capital-to-labor ratios of the least-cost production methods of products, *except* where the third factor – be it a natural resource or technological sophistication – overwhelms the effects on comparative costs of the physical capital and the labor factors. In production of primary products, as we saw in Figures 8-1 and 8-2, the effect of the natural-resource factor overwhelms the effects of capital and labor. Similarly, in the production of technologically highly sophisticated manufactured goods, factor-proportions considerations become relatively insignificant. Technology-intensive goods – whether they are relatively capital- or labor-intensive in their least-cost production – can be produced economically only in a nation heavily endowed with a high level of technological sophistication.

This generalization has a very important implication. Recall that a nation cannot have *comparative* advantage in *all* products. Thus, if a country is heavily endowed with the natural resources needed for the production of some important primary products, then its comparative advantage in other goods tends to be less. Thus, we may expect Saudi Arabia to have a great deal of difficulty developing comparative advantage in anything other than crude oil, natural gas, and some chemicals that use large quantities of cheap oil and gas. By the same token, if a country is heavily endowed with high technological sophistication, it tends to acquire comparative advantage in technology-intensive (or human-capital-intensive) products *and* do relatively poorly in goods that use less sophisticated and more standardized production technology.

Let us apply this generalization to U.S.-Japanese trade relations. The United States is favorably endowed with a variety of important natural resources *and* with an extremely high level of technological sophistication. This unique pattern of factor endowments makes it very difficult for the nation to develop comparative advantage in ordinary manufactured goods such as textiles, steel, bicycles, and television sets. Compare this situation with that of Japan. The nation has few natural resources to speak of, and its level of technological sophistication – though high – is lower than that of the United States. Japan's comparative advantage, therefore, tends to be concentrated in those goods in which the United

States is relatively weak – manufactured goods of intermediate-level technological sophistication. Japan, of course, imports large quantities of primary products (e.g., grain) and technologically-sophisticated goods (e.g., jet airliners and advanced weapon systems) from the United States.

PRIMARY, VERTICAL, AND HORIZONTAL TRADE

Now to a summary description of present world trade wherein we find this trade conveniently falling into three categories: *primary trade,* trade in primary products based on natural resource endowments; *horizontal trade,* between developed nations with high capital-to-labor ratios where variety and innovation are stressed; and *vertical trade* between richer and poorer nations where trade is based on differences in technological sophistication and/or capital-to-labor endowment ratios.

To better understand the nature of the three types of trade, let us briefly examine a few examples of these trade types with reference to the United States and its trading partners. The United States exports agricultural products and imports crude oil – these are examples of primary trade. Its imports of textile and steel products, and its exports of jet airliners and large-capacity computers, are examples of vertical trade. Importing rubber sandals, radios, and bicycles from Mexico, Taiwan, and South Korea, and exporting to them power shovels, machine tools, and helicopters also represent vertical trade. When the United States exports Cadillacs and Fords to Europe and Japan, and imports Jaguars, Mercedes-Benzes and Toyotas from them, the pattern of trade is clearly one of horizontal trade based on product differentiation and innovation. Importing Sony Betamax video recorders from Japan and exporting General Electric refrigerators to it also fall under the same category.

Admittedly it is sometimes difficult to classify particular trade flows, but we believe that by grouping trade patterns into primary, vertical, and horizontal, we highlight the determinants of the present pattern of world trade. Primary trade is attributed to natural-resource endowments, vertical trade is viewed as based on international differences in per capita income levels and the complexity of production technologies, and horizontal trade is explained mainly by reference to product differentiation.

FURTHER ELABORATIONS

The preceding paragraphs have discussed elaborations and modifications of the basic Heckscher-Ohlin model. This section will discuss three further elaborations.

TECHNOLOGICAL INNOVATION

The laws of physics and engineering are the same in every country, but whether a given technology can be effectively applied to actual production processes in a country depends on the complexity of that technology in relation to the technological sophistication of the people of that country.

Most new products or new processes are first introduced in nations that are technologically most advanced. The nations in which the innovations appear tend to retain comparative advantage in the affected products for some time. When a new technology is first developed, the production process is at first known only to the small group of individuals directly involved in the innovation. As a practical matter, the production function — the isoquants — of the new product will exist only in the innovating nation. So this nation will have comparative advantage in this product; for in the innovating nation the opportunity cost of this product will be finite, while in other nations it will be infinite — at least for a time.

As time passes, individuals in other nations will begin to acquire the ability to apply the new technology. But even then the production functions of the prospective imitators will be very inefficient, as Denmark's Figure 8-2 isoquant is inefficient compared to Liberia's Figure 8-1 isoquant. The isoquants of the initially disadvantaged nation may — though they will not in all cases do so — improve and gradually approach those of the original innovating nation. Over time, the knowledge, experience, and skills of the imitating nation's entrepreneurs, managers, engineers, and workers may improve with respect to the particular new technology. The speed at which these improvements can occur, of course, depends on the compatibility of the new technology and the technological sophistication of the imitating nation. In general, we may say that the less complex and sophisticated the particular technology relative to the technological sophistication of the imitating nation, the faster and easier will be the improvement of the imitator's production function.

This improvement in the imitating nation's production function might appear certain to bring this nation comparative advantage in the new product. Presumably, the achievement of this comparative advantage would be based upon the imitating nation's low wage rates which are attributed to its relative abundance of labor (the innovation having been assumed to have appeared in a nation endowed with a high capital-to-labor ratio). But that relative abundance of labor can provide comparative advantage only if the production function allows a considerable degree of labor-for-capital substitution.

In Figure 8-3, the production function of a new product is shown by the L-shaped isoquant, IQ_1. We assume that the production function initially exhibits zero labor-for-capital substitutability (hence the L-shaped isoquant), and that it allows least-cost production only at a high capital-to-labor ratio, reflecting the high capital-to-labor endowment

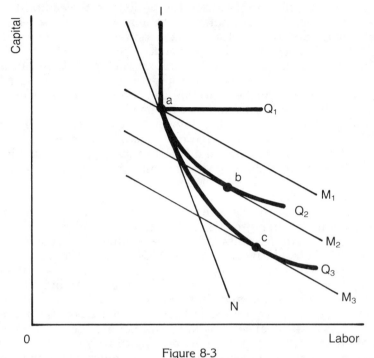

Figure 8-3
Change over time in the shape of a typical isoquant of a new product first introduced
in a nation with relatively high capital-to-labor endowment

ratio of the innovating nation. We also assume that the efficiency of the
production function is the same in both innovating and imitating nations so that the same isoquant, IQ_1, applies to both nations. Initially,
both innovator and imitator produce at point a, where the innovator's
isocost, N, and the imitator's initial isocost, M_1, touch the isoquant IQ_1.
Let us assume that at this point, a, comparative advantage in this
product lies with the innovator.

At first, no one in the imitating country knows how to substitute labor
for capital. As time passes, however, the isoquants may change shape as
engineers and managers work to modify the production process to permit increased substitution of labor for capital. This modification of the
production function is graphically shown in Figure 8-3 as the changes in
the shape of the isoquant from IQ_1 to IQ_2 to IQ_3. Following these
changes, the imitator's least-cost production point shifts from point a to
b to c, where isocosts representing increasingly smaller expenditures,
M_2 and M_3, are tangent to the changing-shape isoquants, IQ_2 and IQ_3.
This development *may* bring comparative advantage to the imitator,
particularly if the innovator, for technical and engineering reasons,
cannot increase the capital-to-labor ratio in the production of this good.

In summary, comparative advantage in a new process may or may not
shift to potential imitators in low capital-to-labor nations. That will
depend on (1) the potential labor-for-capital substitutability of the new

process, (2) the difference between the nations in the capital-to-labor endowment ratio, (3) the complexity of the new technology relative to the technological sophistication of the potential imitating nation, and (4) cost comparisons with other products.

In the 1950s and the early 1960s, Japan grew rapidly in capital-to-labor endowment and technological sophistication. It purchased a large number of new technologies developed in the United States and elsewhere, readily digested them with its newly acquired technological sophistication, and, taking advantage of its relatively low wage rates, developed comparative advantage in a host of new products — ships, synthetic fibers, cameras, consumer electronics, steel, and automobiles, among others. None of these products require *extremely* high technological sophistication or capital-to-labor ratios.

In the last decade, a handful of newly emerging industrial nations — notably South Korea and Taiwan — have made rapid progress reminiscent of Japan's earlier growth (see Chapter 19). With their rapidly expanding domestic markets and rising technological sophistication, coupled with their relatively low wage rates, these semideveloped countries are bound to develop comparative advantage in many of the products in which Japan has had advantage in the 1960s and 1970s. The *Wall Street Journal* reported that Taiwan, in early 1979, started to export small quantities of steel and color television sets to Japan. The price of Taiwanese steel sold in Japan was believed to be considerably lower than prevailing Japanese prices.[1] South Korea is reported to be shifting its exports to "heavy chemicals, electronics, plant, machinery, automobiles, and construction materials."[2] Closely following on the heels of Taiwan and South Korea are some of the more advanced of the LDCs, among which are Mexico and Brazil. India and China, perhaps, will not be too far behind. Against the onslaught of these newly developing industrial nations, the best chances for the industrially advanced nations — including Japan — to maintain and expand their comparative advantage in manufactures lie in their raising the technology intensity and/or capital intensity of their exports. If, and only if, neither is feasible, the affected industries in the advanced nations are destined to lose their comparative advantage to industries in lower-wage nations.

ECONOMIES OF SCALE

The basic factor-proportions model assumes constant returns to scale, so that the production function of every product behaves like that of Figure 7-3. Let us now relax this assumption by recognizing that some production functions offer economies of scale.

With increasing returns to scale, the equally spaced isoquants like the ones depicted in Figure 7-3 would represent proportionally larger quantities of output. For example, instead of the isoquants X_1, X_2, and X_3 representing, say, 50, 100, and 150 units of output (as in the case of constant returns to scale), they may represent 50, 110, and 200 units of output. Conversely, decreasing returns to scale may be expressed by equally spaced isoquants yielding, say, 50, 90, and 125 units of output.

With constant returns to scale in production, the long-run average cost curve of the producer would be perfectly flat. No matter how much output a firm produces, and no matter how large or how small a producer is, average cost is the same. In contrast, when the production function is subject to economies of scale (meaning increasing returns to scale) or diseconomies of scale (meaning decreasing returns to scale), we no longer have a horizontal long-run average cost (LRAC) curve. Figure 8-4 portrays a long-run average cost curve of a firm experiencing varying economies of scale over its output range. At lower levels of output up to A, the firm's LRAC declines, reflecting increasing returns to both inputs capital and labor. In the output range AB, constant returns to scale yield a flat LRAC. Beyond the output level B, the LRAC rises, reflecting diseconomies of scale.

For many primary products and old industrial products, constant returns to scale with a flat cost curve are a good approximation. In the application of new processes, however, increasing returns to scale with a downward sloping LRAC are most relevant. When new technological processes appear, an aspiring imitator must use a production function developed in the country of origin. And at least initially, the imitating firm's output level would be low, and therefore its production cost would be high. Only at larger scales of production can low average cost be reached. But to begin production on a large scale, an entrepreneur must have assured large markets, either domestic or export. The domestic market may be intrinsically too small, or, though large, may be domi-

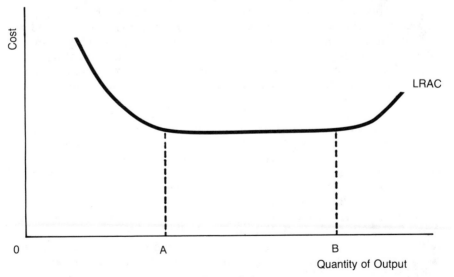

Figure 8-4
The long-run average cost curve of a firm experiencing different scale economies

nated by exports from innovators. (The aspiring imitators may be protected by tariffs until their scales of operation become large enough to yield them lower average costs. This consideration leads to the "infant industry" argument for protection. See Chapter 10.) As for relying on export markets, Staffan Linder already reminded us of the difficulty of developing export competitiveness without having had an experience of catering to the domestic market first. Few new firms can succeed by beginning production based solely or even mostly on foreign sales. Most new firms, therefore, must be able to sell most of their output initially in the domestic market. And, if economies of scale are to be significant, the domestic market must be appropriately large. Only then can the aspiring entrepreneur succeed in adopting a foreign technology.

A large domestic market is associated with a large population and/or a high per capita income. Thus, a successful adoption of new foreign technology would be relatively easier for producers in countries having these attributes. Similarly, countries without these attributes are not likely to develop comparative advantage in products having substantial scale economies, regardless of the factor-proportions considerations. This conclusion constitutes another important exception to the basic Heckscher-Ohlin model.

INCREASING COST INDUSTRIES

The State of Iowa has the best corn farms in the world. It has comparative advantage in corn production over all other areas in the world. Yet it does not produce all the corn for the world. Reunion Island may have the best sugar plantations in the world with comparative advantage over all other land in the world. But the island does not produce all the sugar for all the world. Corn is exported by many U.S. states and by several other nations. Further, some corn is grown profitably in many nations that import corn. Sugar, too, is exported by dozens of nations. Similarly, most primary products and some standardized manufactured products are exported by many nations and are imported, in many cases, by nations in which some of the same products are produced.

These behaviors result from the upward sloping supply curves characterizing the national industries producing these products. Most industries are increasing cost industries. Unlike the economies (or diseconomies) of scale that apply to a *firm,* and lower (or raise) the firm's long-run average costs, increasing cost conditions are applicable to an *industry* as a whole, and are caused by increases in the costs (prices) of inputs. As industrial output increases, the prices of some inputs rise, shifting up each firm's entire long-run average cost curve. The rising costs of each firm result in the upward sloping supply curve for the industry as a whole. Parenthetically, we may note that the increasing cost conditions are implied by the concave-to-the-origin production possibilities frontiers of Chapter 5.

The basic Heckscher-Ohlin model assumes that industries are subject to constant cost conditions. As we saw in Chapter 3, constant cost industries result in straight-line production possibilities frontiers, and comparative advantage specialization under these conditions necessarily results in *complete* specialization. When we have increasing cost conditions, however, PPFs are concave to the origin, and specialization is *incomplete* or *partial*. The Figure 6-3 equilibrium points, W' and E', are examples of such partial specialization.

Exporting countries have lower production costs than importing countries; that is why they *are* exporting countries. As the volume of output of the product in question increases in an exporting country, production costs tend to rise there if the industry is subject to increasing cost conditions. The consequent increases in export prices will enable at least a few firms in an importing country to produce the product and compete with imports in the home market. For example, a few farms in Louisiana may be so efficient as to produce sugar cane with costs lower than those of some sugar plantations on Reunion Island. Some textile and plastic sandal producers in the United States may be lower-cost producers than those in Taiwan. In each of these cases, a few specially favored firms — favored by climate, location, or some other factors — may compete successfully with imports. This result, obtained under conditions of increasing costs, constitutes another exception to the basic Heckscher-Ohlin theory.

Figure 8-5 portrays a situation in which the increasing cost conditions in both exporting and importing nations permit limited production of the traded product in the importing country. The price (or cost) of the traded good is read along the vertical axis which is common to both countries. The demand and supply curves of the product in the importing country, D_m and S_m, are shown in the right-hand side of the diagram. The quantities of the good demanded and supplied are read from left to right, starting with the origin, O. The demand and supply curves

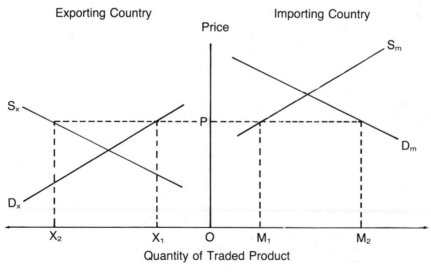

Figure 8-5
Increasing Cost Conditions Resulting in Partial Specialization

of the exporting country, D_x and S_x, shown in the left-hand side of the diagram, are read from right to left, again starting with O. The domestic demand and supply curves intersect at a lower level of price (not labeled) in the exporting country than in the importing country (not labeled), indicating the location of comparative advantage. The rising supply curves in both countries indicate the increasing cost conditions prevailing in this particular industry. Supposing that the two countries are the only nations in the world trading in the product in question, and assuming there are no transportation costs, we can see that equilibrium is established at price P, with exports, X_1X_2, equaling imports, M_1M_2. Production is OX_2 in the exporting country (with consumption being OX_1) and OM_1 in the importing country. OM_1 of this good is produced in the importing country, notwithstanding its comparative disadvantage at all output beyond OM_1, because, at outputs at or below OM_1, the importing nation's most efficient firms have costs equal to or less than the "world" price, P. This result obtains because of the upward sloping supply curves attributable to increasing cost conditions. The reader is invited to draw a similar diagram, but with horizontal supply curves. Specialization, in that case, will be found to be complete.

STUDY QUESTIONS

1. In Chapter 7, we examined the Heckscher-Ohlin theory, the technological gap thesis, the product life cycle model, and Linder's preference similarity hypothesis. Relate these theories to the three types of trade flows discussed in this chapter — primary, vertical, and horizontal trade.
2. Characterize each of the following trade flows as primary, vertical, or horizontal.
   (a) Japan imports low-priced toys made in Hong Kong
   (b) Singapore buys wool from Australia
   (c) Nigeria imports petroleum refining facilities from the United States
   (d) U.S. aircraft manufacturers import jet engines from Rolls Royce of England
   (e) Canada imports passenger cars from the United States
   (f) India imports crude diamonds from South Africa
   (g) Brazil exports coffee beans to Canada
   (h) The United States imports steel from Japan.
3. Refer to Figure 7-7. As the graph is drawn, clearly country A has comparative advantage in good X and country B has comparative advantage in good Y. In this Heckscher-Ohlin formulation, each of the isoquants X and Y is assumed to yield the same quantity of output in both countries. Now, assume that isoquant X yields the same quantity of output in both countries A and B, but isoquant Y yields only 1/3 as much output in country B as in country A.
   (a) What could cause such a sharp discrepancy between the two countries in the efficiency of isoquant Y?
   (b) Demonstrate graphically that the pattern of comparative advantage now reverses itself to: A in Y and B in X.

4. Consider the trade in passenger cars between the United States and Japan. Suppose that the United States has comparative advantage in intermediate and full-sized cars, while Japan has comparative advantage in compact and subcompact cars.
   (a) Is the technology of producing passenger cars highly sophisticated?
   (b) If your answer to (a) above is yes, then how would you explain Japan's ability to compete with America in smaller cars?
   (c) If your answer to (a) above is no, then how would you explain America's ability to compete with Japan in larger cars?
5. How would you account for the apparent *economic* failure of the supersonic jet airliner Concorde developed and marketed jointly by the British and the French?
6. Why is it that the Japanese, who are extremely export-oriented, are not flooding the world markets with Made-in-Japan:
   (a) large-capacity computers
   (b) recreational vehicles
   (c) low-grade cotton shirts?
7. Suppose it is found that the United States lacks comparative advantage in steel production. Does this mean that all the steel mills in the United States should be closed? Why or why not?

ENDNOTES

1. *Wall Street Journal,* 19 March 1979, p. 6.
2. *Business Week,* 30 April 1979, p. 40.

9

International Competitiveness of U.S. Industries

Although comparative advantage is an extremely important and useful concept, its effects must filter through a variety of mediating forces. These include exchange rates, as shown in Chapter 4, and government tariffs, subsidies, and quotas. Netting together these variables, the most proximate cause of trade is not comparative advantage, but *competitive* advantage. Unfortunately, the literature on international trade relations has traditionally paid only scant attention to the concept of competitiveness.[1] In this chapter, we will briefly explain the concept of competitive advantage, and then discuss the changing international competitiveness of U.S. industries in general and of the U.S. steel industry in particular.

COMPARATIVE VS. COMPETITIVE ADVANTAGE

While discussions of trade problems in the economic literature are couched almost exclusively in terms of comparative advantage, the public, in discussing trade issues, do so almost invariably in terms of *competitive advantage*. A *Wall Street Journal* article reported, for example, that many Americans are concerned that the country's international competitive power is declining and foreign competition is strengthening. A middle-aged housewife was reported as saying: "We may still be No. 1, but I don't think we will be much longer. The Common Market, Japan, Russia, all areas of the world are catching up. And I think our own inflation is causing this. It's no longer economical for us to produce anything; it costs too much." Fifty-six percent of those polled in Indianapolis in April 1978 believed that America's ability to compete economically was declining relative to other countries, and only six percent felt it was getting stronger.[2]

COMPETITIVE ADVANTAGE OF A PRODUCT

A nation's comparative advantage in particular products is identified by ranking products according to their opportunity costs. The country has comparative advantage in those goods that are located toward the lower end of the list, and has comparative disadvantage in those goods located toward the higher end of the list. As we saw in Chapter 4, a rate of exchange divides the list into exportables and importables. A rate that equates the monetary values of exports and imports is called the equilibrium rate of exchange. The country is said to have comparative advantage in its exportables, and disadvantage in its importables, defined under an equilibrium rate of exchange.

It is important to note that, if the existing exchange rate is not an equilibrium rate, the actual competitiveness the country has in a product may differ from its comparative advantage. For example, suppose that a country has a very weak comparative advantage in a product; that is, the good is a borderline case, being located very close to the dividing line between exportables and importables, defined under an equilibrium rate of exchange. If the country's currency becomes overvalued for some reason, and the bias in the exchange rate persists, then the country, despite its comparative advantage in the product, may not be able to compete with foreign producers in that product. In other words, the product loses competitive advantage in spite of its basic comparative advantage. A converse of this situation is also conceivable. An undervaluation of the currency makes some of the country's borderline comparative disadvantage products competitive. Goods that would normally (i.e., under an equilibrium rate of exchange) be importables may thus become exportables. An exchange-rate bias can thus distort the basic trade pattern dictated by comparative costs.

The competitive advantage of a product involves an immediate and direct comparison of prices and nonprice considerations in actual trading situations. Any factors that may affect the attractiveness of a product affect its competitiveness. The price factors affecting competitive advantage include, besides the basic comparative production costs and a possible exchange-rate bias, such factors as transportation costs, tariff duties, other taxes and subsidies on production and consumption, and price discrimination (including "dumping") by producers. Nonprice factors include quality differences, product differentiation, delivery, servicing, and the intensity of "export mindedness" of producers and their governments. In sum, whereas comparative advantage is essentially determined by the economic structure of the country and the production functions of products, competitive advantage is affected additionally by many other "surface" phenomena such as an exchange-rate bias, price factors which are not figured in determining comparative costs (e.g., transportation costs and import duties), and a host of nonprice considerations (e.g., product differentiation).

Comparative advantage is a *relative* concept; at least two products must be considered simultaneously. Competitive advantage is simpler; it is an *absolute* concept. A nation's competitive advantage is identified by a direct comparison between the price and nonprice characteristics of a particular good produced in that nation and the price and nonprice characteristics of a competing product imported into that nation. Thus, Japanese steel has competitive advantage over American steel if Japanese steel of a particular grade is offered in America at a lower price than American steel of that grade. And an American computer has competitive advantage over a French computer of the same capacity, speed, and price when maintenance service on the American computer is better than on the French machine. These measures of competitiveness can be made at any point in time.

Another kind of measure of competitive advantage can only be made retrospectively. This is done by calculating a product's export-import ratio in a given country. If, for example, the dollar value of U.S. automobile exports is smaller than the value of automobile imports, then we say that the United States lacks competitive advantage in automobiles. (Competitive advantage, like comparative advantage, is meaningful only to the extent it is used to refer to an individual product or a group of products. We can meaningfully compare the domestic and imported prices of a product, or its export-import ratio, but we cannot do likewise with respect to *all* products with any degree of significance.)

U.S. COMPETITIVENESS IN MANUFACTURES

A large portion of American exports consists of agricultural products, coal, and other raw materials, while public concern about the waning competitiveness of U.S. industries involves concern principally about U.S. manufacturing. Table 9-1 presents a record of changes in the export-import ratio of U.S. trade by product category. Using 100 percent as the borderline between competitive advantage and disadvantage, we can see that the United States in the 1970s had unmistakable competitive advantage in agricultural products, crude materials, chemicals, and machinery in general. Its competitive disadvantage lay in fuels, metals, and motor vehicles. This observation is unavoidably impressionistic. Different impressions may be obtained if different years are chosen or different product categories are used. For example, although the United States had a moderate degree of competitiveness in transport equipment in general, we would expect to find strong advantage in aircraft and strong disadvantage in ships.

TABLE 9-1   EXPORT-IMPORT RATIO OF U.S. TRADE BY CATEGORY,
SELECTED YEARS
(percent)

Product	1965	1970	1972	1974	1976	1978
Merchandise, total	127.0	106.6	88.1	96.9	93.9	82.1
Agricultural products	152.7	125.7	144.6	212.0	205.7	196.6
Crude materials, excl. fuels	93.8	139.0	130.3	180.1	155.4	167.2
Mineral fuel and lubricants	42.8	51.8	32.3	13.5	12.4	9.2
Petroleum and products	20.1	17.8	10.2	3.3	3.1	4.0
Manufactured products, total	142.2	104.9	81.6	104.2	109.8	87.4
Chemicals	311.7	264.1	205.5	219.4	208.8	196.3
Iron and steel	51.2	62.6	28.3	49.7	43.9	23.6
Nonferrous base metals	42.5	53.6	29.5	33.2	31.1	20.5
Machinery, total	382.9	215.1	294.9	204.1	206.1	124.4
Electrical	259.4	132.2	109.5	131.5	125.1	134.8
Transport equipment, total	287.5	110.5	86.2	116.5	124.4	95.8
Motor vehicles and parts	244.4	70.0	60.4	76.8	83.6	64.2
Textiles	66.3	53.1	51.0	111.8	120.9	101.4

Source: U.S. Department of Commerce, *Survey of Current Business*, various issues.

Table 9-1 shows that the competitive advantage the United States had in most manufactured products deteriorated markedly between 1965 and 1972, improved greatly in 1974, and deteriorated somewhat after that. These developments may well be attributed to the progressive overvaluation of the dollar prior to the Smithsonian Agreement of 1971 (see Chapter 16), successive devaluations of the dollar in 1972 and 1973, and the recurrence of overvaluation after imports of petroleum began to surge in 1973. The competitiveness of textiles deteriorated between 1965 and 1972; but, since 1974, the United States has enjoyed a mild degree of advantage in them. This interesting shift in competitiveness may be attributable to, in addition to the exchange-rate changes, the "voluntary" export restraint programs negotiated between the United States and the major textile exporting countries in the early 1970s.

THE IMPORTANCE OF ADVANCED TECHNOLOGY

Table 9-2 lists eleven U.S. corporations that recorded export values of more than $800 million in 1977. Their total exports ($12.9 billion) accounted for 16.7 percent of total U.S. manufactured exports of that year. The main export products of these firms were machinery, equipment, and chemicals with very high technology content. Few items on the list are ordinary consumer (household) products. Table 9-2 paints a picture which is markedly different in tone from the pessimistic observation by the middle-aged housewife quoted at the beginning of the chapter: "It's no longer economical for us to produce anything; it costs too much."

If the United States is to maintain superior competitive advantage in machinery and chemicals so that exports of these products bring home enough dollars to pay for the ever-rising volume of petroleum imports and other raw materials, consumer goods, and whatever overseas commitments the nation has made, it is imperative that the country maintain its lead in technological advances and product innovation. For the high-income, high-wage country like the United States, pressing against the technological frontier is the only way to maintain vitality in its trade relations with other countries without progressive depreciation of its currency. It is understandable, therefore, that the recent reported slowdown in the technological drive of the United States has caused a great deal of concern among international economists and business and government leaders of the country.[3]

TABLE 9-2   THE ELEVEN BIGGEST U.S. INDUSTRIAL EXPORTERS, 1977
(millions of dollars)

Company	Exports	Main Export Products
General Electric	2,100	Gas turbines, aircraft engines, power generating equipment, appliances, motors
Caterpillar Tractor	1,900	Earth-moving and materials-handling equipment
Boeing	1,470	Commercial aircraft
McDonnell Douglas	1,130	Commercial and military aircraft
Lockheed	1,030	Commercial and military aircraft, aerospace items
Du Pont	1,000	Synthetic fibers, plastics, agricultural chemicals, health care products
Dow Chemical	900	Plastic intermediates, caustic soda, magnesium
United Technologies	890	Jet engines, aircraft equipment, telephone and power cables, helicopters, elevators
Eastman Kodak	850	Photographic film, papers, chemicals and equipment
Sperry Rand	850	Computers, farm machinery, hydraulic equipment
Westinghouse Electric	800	Nuclear power plants, electrical generators and equipment, defense equipment

Source: *Business Week*, 10 April 1978, p. 65

THE CAUSES OF SLOWDOWN IN INNOVATION

The causes of the slowdown in innovation in the United States are many and complex. The winding down of the Vietnam War and the space program resulted in a drastic reduction in the amount of basic research supported by the federal government. Between 1963 and 1978, the federal dollar commitment to R & D fell from 3 percent of the nation's gross national product to 2.2 percent.[4] The federal government's role as a source of demand for new products and processes also has diminished. The slowdown in the growth of the world economy starting in the early 1970s, soaring costs and the capital squeeze attributable to the energy crisis, a greater concern for environmental protection and occupational safety which has resulted in an increasingly costlier and lengthier process to obtain new product clearance by the federal regulatory agencies, and the rising tide of consumerism which has made consumers increasingly more conservative and suspicious about what they are buying – all of these factors have combined to make innovation costlier and riskier than it was in the 1950s and 1960s.

With the increased professionalization of U.S. corporate management, a greater emphasis has come to be placed on short-term earnings than on long-term risk taking. The incentive programs for top corporate executives are almost exclusively based on short-term earnings figures. Drastic deterioration in these figures would certainly threaten the job security of the responsible executives. Consequently, they have little choice but to place high management emphasis on short-term business considerations. This has resulted in what has been labeled as the *MBA syndrome*, "a super-cautious, no-risk management less willing to gamble on anything short of a sure thing."[5]

According to one group of management consultants, a totally new product entering a new market has only a one in twenty chance of success, compared to an old product introduced in an old market having slightly less than one chance in one.[6] This fact, coupled with the increasingly harsh regulatory climate, leads most big business bureaucracies to follow the path of least resistance, that is, introducing a new or old product in an old market. In this manner, they can avoid the risks and costs of new technological innovation. The following remark attributed to Du Pont's senior vice-president of research is representative of this no-risk mentality: "Why risk money on new businesses when good, profitable, low-risk opportunities are on every side?"[7] An attitude such as this has an unfortunate implication for the U.S. economy and its international competitiveness, since, as Treasury Secretary W. Michael Blumenthal noted: "Our technological supremacy is not mandated by heaven. Unless we pay close attention to it and invest in it, it *will* disappear."[8]

Generally speaking, it matters little whether the cause of a deterioration in the competitiveness of American products is the slowdown in technological innovation, a higher rate of inflation in the United States than elsewhere, the huge imports of oil, the lack of export-mindedness of

U.S. manufacturers, or the alleged character of American workers who no longer "give a damn."[9] The essential point is that there *is* a rate of exchange between the dollar and foreign currencies that will bring the U.S. balance of payments into equilibrium. Such a rate would necessarily reflect all the economic, social, and political realities which the American public finds difficult to change. The U.S. dollar would buy more abroad, and American wage rates would be relatively higher when translated into foreign currencies, in direct proportion to the extent that technological innovation is pushed vigorously, exports are promoted, workers "give a damn," inflation is controlled, and oil imports are restrained. The U.S. public has a clear choice between promoting these measures and accepting a deterioration in the value of the dollar.

INTERNATIONAL COMPETITIVENESS OF THE U.S. STEEL INDUSTRY

In the preceding section we concluded that the U.S. steel industry lacked competitive advantage in view of the fact that its export-import ratio was substantially less than 100. The industry has persistently lobbied for protection from imports, particularly those from Japan, and in the winter of 1978 the Carter Administration instituted the "reference price" (or "trigger price") system of protection. (See Chapter 11 for details of this system.) In view of the economic and political importance of the industry, as well as the theoretical implications of the industry's costs and prices to our study of competitiveness and comparative advantage, we propose to examine, in this section, the reason for the industry's difficulties in competing with imported steel.[10]

THE U.S. STEEL INDUSTRY IN WORLD MARKETS

In 1950 the United States was the world's largest steel producer, accounting for 46.6 percent of the world's total output of 208 million tons. (Unless otherwise noted, the term "ton" used in this book refers to the *short* (or *net)* ton which equals 2,000 pounds. The British weight – the *long* (or *gross)* ton – equals 2,240 pounds. The Japanese and the Europeans commonly use the *metric ton,* which weighs 1,000 kilograms or 2,204.62 pounds.) In that year, Japan's share was only 2.6 percent, and that of the nine West European nations that now constitute the European Economic Community (EEC) was 26.6 percent. During the quarter of a century that followed, steel output has grown more rapidly in Japan and the EEC so that in 1976 their shares of the total world output of 753 million tons were 15.7 percent and 19.7 percent, respectively, as compared to the United States' share of 17.0 percent. Thus, while world steel output grew by 260 percent between 1950 and 1976 from 208 to 753 million tons, the output of steel in the United States increased by only 32 percent from 97 to 128 million tons.[11]

The rapid growth of the world's steel output has been accompanied by an equally rapid increase in steel exports. Whereas in 1950 only about 11 percent of total production was exported, 22 percent was exported in 1975. The growth of exports by Japan and the EEC has been particularly pronounced. Between 1960 and 1975, exports from Japan increased 53-fold, while those from the EEC increased by 4.5 times. During the same period, the percentage of steel output exported increased from 15 percent to 38 percent in Japan, and from 23 percent to 29 percent in the EEC.[12] The imports' share of total U.S. domestic consumption of steel increased from 4.6 percent in 1960 to 17.9 percent in 1971, dropped to 12 percent in 1975, and rose again to 16 percent in the first half of 1977. In 1976-77, roughly half of U.S. imports came from Japan, one quarter from the EEC, and the remaining quarter from the rest of the world.[13]

The competitive pressures from imports have kept the U.S. steel industry's profits relatively low. The industry's after-tax profits on sales fell from the 1955-57 average of 7.5 percent to 5.3 percent for the 1960s, and to 4.0 percent for the 1970-76 period.[14] In the first half of 1976, the simple average of the nine largest U.S. steelmakers' after-tax profits on sales was 3.3 percent, ranging from Wheeling-Pittsburgh's 0.5 percent to U.S. Steel's 4.9 percent and to Inland Steel's 9.5 percent. Inland Steel's advantage lies in its favorable location and very efficient plants.[15]

COMPARATIVE COSTS OF STEEL PRODUCTION

The difficulty the U.S. steel industry experiences in meeting competition with foreign products on its home ground is fundamentally attributable to the fact that the United States does not have comparative advantage in steel production. Given the 1976 exchange rate between the yen and the dollar, estimates of Japan's steelmaking costs range between 10 percent to 30 percent below the United States'.[16] The estimate by the Council on Wage and Price Stability, shown in Table 9-3, gives the Japanese a 19 percent edge in competitiveness.

We can see from Table 9-3 that Japanese costs are higher in capital, but lower in raw materials and labor. That the Japanese steel producers have lower labor costs and higher capital costs is predictable from the fact that Japan's capital-to-labor endowment ratio is lower than that of the United States and that steel production requires a considerable amount of labor input. Their lower raw material costs, on the other hand, may surprise some readers. In spite of the paucity of natural resources in Japan, the Japanese steelmakers enjoy low costs of raw materials because they are imported cheaply from abroad.

The most significant point, however, is that nine-tenths of the U.S.-Japan cost difference is explainable by the labor cost difference. The result shown in Table 9-3 appears to give evidence to the general theory

TABLE 9-3   TOTAL COSTS OF STEEL PRODUCTION, U.S. VERSUS JAPAN, 1976
(dollars per ton of finished products[a])

Cost	U.S.	Japan
Raw material cost	177.69	159.96
Labor cost	128.08	72.79
Other expenses[b]	4.50	-0.50
Capital costs:		
Depreciation	13.50	17.50
Interest	4.00	17.00
Total costs	327.78	266.75

[a]Weighted average of all steel mill products, including carbon, alloy, and stainless products; costs include finishing of mill products but exclude fabricating process.
[b]Includes scrap credit.
Source: The Council on Wage and Price Stability, *Reports to the President on Prices and Costs in the United States Steel Industry*)Washington, D.C.: Government Printing Office, 1977), pp. 50 and 60.

of comparative advantage and trade patterns we developed in Chapter 8. Steelmaking entails a technology of moderate sophistication, which the Japanese can easily handle. It follows that with the advantage of their lower real wages caused by their lower capital-to-labor endowment ratio, the Japanese can produce steel more cheaply than their U.S. counterparts. Lower real wages do not translate into lower production costs in cases of natural-resource-intensive and high-technology-intensive products because their production functions would be inefficient in Japan. But with respect to manufactured goods of standardized and unsophisticated technology, lower real wages do help, particularly when their least-cost production methods have a low capital-to-labor ratio, as in the case of steel.

Raw Material Costs

The U.S. steel industry enjoys lower costs in coking coal, fuel oil, and electricity, while the Japanese industry has lower costs in iron ore and scrap. With the exception of iron ore ($29.40 in the United States and $18.40 in Japan, per metric ton), the differences in input prices are small, reflecting the worldwide nature of the markets of these materials. Since 1970, the price of ore in the United States has risen more rapidly than world prices.[17] U.S. ore is also more costly to steel producers since it has a relatively low ferrous content. U.S. producers now import about one-third of their ore requirement. Japanese steelmakers enjoy high-quality ore imported from Australia, Brazil, India, Liberia and other sources, and under long-term contracts.[18] Differences in transportation costs make significant differences in the landed prices of raw materials. Land transportation costs seven to ten times as much as water transportation. Thus, while it cost (in 1976) $9.74 to transport a ton of iron ore 900 miles from the upper Great Lakes to Pittsburgh, it cost only \$4.76 to ship the same quantity of ore 5,000 miles from Australia to a Japanese steel mill located at tidewater.[19] This fact helps explain the reason why U.S. steel mills located inland cannot take advantage of low-priced overseas ore.

Labor Costs

It is in labor cost that Japan enjoyed, in 1976, the decisive advantage over the United States. Table 9-4 shows a calculation of U.S. and Japanese labor costs for 1976. Total labor compensation per worker-hour, inclusive of the estimated cost of fringe benefits, was \$12.22 in the United States and \$6.31 in Japan. This almost two-to-one ratio in the wage rate, plus the fact that the Japanese mills had a higher yield of finished product per ton of raw steel, more than offset the fact that the Japanese firms used 17 percent more labor per ton of raw steel produced. The net result was that the Japanese labor cost of a ton of finished product was only about 57 percent of the U.S. cost. By way of comparison, we may note that the West European nations had wage rates (\$8.63 per hour in 1976 for the six EEC nations) somewhere between the U.S. and the Japanese levels, but their labor productivity and production yield were lower than those of either Japan or the United States, so that their labor cost per ton of finished product (\$121.30 in 1976) was only slightly lower than that of the United States.[20]

Rising wage rates that outstrip the gain in labor productivity have been an important contributing factor to the labor-cost increases of the U.S. steel industry. Hourly total employment costs of the industry were only 18 percent above the manufacturing average in 1952. By the mid-1960s, they had risen to a level 30 percent above the manufacturing average, and in 1977 the premium was 64 percent.[21] The 1977 U.S. steel labor agreement raised hourly employment costs by more than 10 percent per year during the three-year contract period through 1980.

TABLE 9-4   LABOR COST CALCULATIONS, U.S. AND JAPANESE
STEEL INDUSTRIES, 1976

	U.S.	Japan
Labor productivity (worker-hours per metric ton of raw steel)	8.21	9.60
× employment cost per worker-hour (dollars)	12.22	6.31
= labor cost per metric ton of raw steel (dollars)	100.24	60.58
÷ 1.1023 to convert metric ton to net ton[a]	1.1023	1.1023
= labor cost per (net) ton of raw steel (dollars)	90.94	54.96
÷ yield (tons of finished steel ÷ tons of raw steel)	0.710	0.755
= labor cost per (net) ton of finished steel (dollars)	128.08	72.79

[a]A metric ton equals 2,204.62 pounds; a net ton equals 2,000 pounds. See text.

Source: The Council on Wage and Price Stability, *Reports to the President on Prices and Costs in the United States Steel Industry* (Washington, D.C.: Government Printing Office, 1977), pp. 52-54

These increases far exceeded the industry's labor productivity growth rate of 1.9 percent (1964-76 average annual rate).[22] The Japanese steel industry also experienced rising wage rates that exceeded the industry's productivity gain, but the disparity between the two was considerably less than that in the U.S. industry. During the 1971-76 period, the average annual rate of increase of the wage rate of the Japanese steel industry was 15.8 percent, as contrasted with the industry's labor productivity growth rate of 8.3 percent.[23]

The high labor cost of steel production in the United States has an interesting theoretical implication. As Chapter 8 showed, a nation with a high capital-to-labor endowment ratio and with high wages will be able to achieve comparative advantage in a product if capital can be easily substituted for labor in production of that product. If steel production were subject to a high degree of capital-for-labor substitution, U.S. steel firms would be able to lower costs by increasing their capital-to-labor input ratio. That they have not been able to achieve a capital-to-labor ratio markedly higher than that of Japanese steel mills implies that, in steelmaking, factor substitutability is rather limited. Since steel production in the United States requires almost as much labor input as its does in Japan, and since real wages are considerably higher in the United States, the labor cost of steel production is inevitably higher in the United States than in Japan. With this important qualification in mind, we concur with the Federal Trade Commission staff report which concluded that:

> The primary differences between U.S. and Japanese unit steelmaking costs is the unit cost for labor. The difference in unit labor cost, in turn, is due primarily to the labor wage rate differential.[24]

Capital Costs

Since the U.S. steel industry has on average older plants than the Japanese industry, it is expected that the former's depreciation allowances would be lower than those of the latter. We see in Table 9-3 that the Japanese steel mills in 1976 had much higher interest costs per ton of finished product than their U.S. counterparts ($17.00 against $4.00). This marked difference in interest costs is attributed to two factors. First, being a less capital-rich nation than the United States, Japan's interest rates would naturally be higher. In 1974, for example, U.S. steel producers paid an average interest rate of 6.9 percent on all debt instruments, while the Japanese steel firms paid an average of 9.4 percent.[25] Secondly, the higher interest rates in Japan may be partly attributable to the greater risk associated with higher leverage. ("Leverage" refers to the use of borrowed money; a firm is more highly leveraged the larger the ratio of borrowed to equity – ownership – investment in the firm. The more highly leveraged the firm, given any particular profit, the more profit per equity dollar.) Japanese steel

producers, like most Japanese manufacturing firms, are highly leveraged. The average debt/equity ratio among Japanese steel firms is
about 5:1 – that is, five parts of debt to one part of equity – as compared
to 1:3 in the United States. Japanese steel firms thus pay higher interest rates on larger amounts of borrowed money than do their U.S.
counterparts.

The estimated 1976 total cost per ton of finished steel product of
$327.78 for the United States and $266.75 for Japan shown in Table 9-3
does not include the "cost" of equity capital. Elementary economics
textbooks tell us that "capital cost" should include, in addition to the
allowances for depreciation and interest payments on debts, a return on
equity, or normal profits, to compensate for the risk taken by the equity
holders. We may calculate the imputed cost of equity capital for U.S.
and Japanese steel industries as follows: We first obtain estimates of
total assets per ton of finished product – $300 for the United States and
$400 for Japan.[26] We then multiply these figures by the equity ratios
(75 percent for the U.S. and 16.7 percent for Japan, derived from their
debt/equity ratios of 1:3 and 5:1). The results are further multiplied by
the arbitrarily chosen "normal" or "expected" rate of return on equity
before tax in each country – 15 percent in the United States and 20
percent in Japan. We use a higher expected rate of return on equity
capital in Japan to compensate in part for the greater risk factor associated with the higher leverage. The results of these calculations show
that the imputed equity costs per ton of finished product in 1976 were
$33.75 for the U.S. steel industry and $13.33 for the Japanese industry.
When these figures are added to the "capital costs" of Table 9-3, we find
that *total* capital costs would be $51.25 per ton in the United States and
$47.83 in Japan. Total 1976 cost of producing a ton of finished product,
including *all* capital costs, would be $361.53 for the U.S. industry and
$280.08 for Japan.

To sum, Japan has an advantage in steel as compared to the United
States because Japan has a lower capital-to-labor endowment ratio
(which implies lower real wages) and steel production requires considerable amounts of labor input. The United States cannot offset its
disadvantage in labor cost because steel's production technology is not
highly sophisticated and its capital-to-labor production ratio cannot be
raised economically. Additionally, Japan has a slight edge on the
United States in raw material costs. America's capital cost advantage
over Japan is very slight.

Full Costs Including Importation Costs

Although comparative advantage considerations require a comparison of only production costs, in order to evaluate competitive advantage
we must consider, additionally, the costs of importing the product. For
even if Japan has comparative advantage in steel, it will not have
competitive advantage in U.S. markets if the cost of importing steel
from Japan exceeds the difference in production costs.

The average cost of importing a ton of steel to U.S. coastal areas was estimated, for 1976, to have been about $60 a ton from Japan and $50 a ton from Western Europe. This cost represents the aggregate cost of all freight, loading, unloading, and insurance, as well as import duties and importers' markups.[27] Adding $60 to the estimated full production cost of Japanese steel ($280), we find that in 1976 the full cost of Japanese steel delivered in U.S. markets by water transportation was about $340. This figure was only 6 percent less than the estimated full production cost of American steel ($362). With such a small cost differential, U.S. producers should have little difficulty in competing with Japanese mills, particularly in inland markets that are not accessible by water transportation, *if* both U.S. and Japanese steel firms charged their full costs.

The report by the Council on Wage and Price Stability concluded as follows:

> The inclusion of transportation costs and duties implies that the Japanese could sell an average mix of products in the U.S. at costs which are approximately five percent below those of U.S. producers. A similar comparison for European producers yields costs which are substantially above those of domestic producers. . . . The Japanese cost advantage would make them competitive in coastal areas, but this does not reflect the value of convenience and customer relations which may favor domestic producers. More inland areas should be highly competitive with imports as a result of additional transportation costs.[28]

Thus, in spite of the lack of comparative advantage, U.S. steelmakers may have competitive advantage over foreign mills in domestic markets. However, foreign producers often offer substantial "discounts" below U.S. list prices. In the middle of the 1960s, imports offered an average discount of about 16-17 percent. In 1976, the discount was about 15 percent.[29] Such a pricing practice implies that the prices of Japanese imports were somewhat below full production cost (inclusive of the imputed cost of equity) and European prices were substantially below full cost. Let us now turn to an examination of foreign steel producers' pricing behavior.

FOREIGN PRODUCERS' PRICING BEHAVIOR

Whereas the theory of comparative advantage generally assumes perfect competition so that prices are equal to long-run average cost, in real-world situations we find firms with monopoly power (in our case, oligopolistic steel firms) pricing their products at above or below long-run average cost (what we have called "full production cost") as market conditions change. In order to evaluate the competitive advantage which nations have in steel products, therefore, it is necessary to examine not only the production costs of steelmakers but also their pricing practices.

Export Prices below Domestic Prices?

Dumping is defined as exporting a product at a price lower than either (1) its domestic price, or (2) its full production cost (see Chapter 11). First, let us ask the question: Do foreign mills export steel at prices below their domestic prices? Table 9-5 records the ratios of export prices to domestic prices of selected steel products of the EEC and Japan over the 1961-76 period. The data show that exporting below domestic prices was a fairly common practice. While European export prices were nearly always below their domestic prices, Japanese prices appear to have fluctuated much more widely relative to their domestic prices, sharply falling relative to domestic prices during a recessionary period (e.g., 1973) but rising markedly during a tight-supply period (e.g., 1975). Over the entire 1961-76 period, the average export prices of the three products were slightly higher than domestic prices in Japan and somewhat lower in the EEC. (It is worth noting that U.S. export prices, although normally above domestic prices, are not always so. For example, the 1968-72 average of the U.S. export/domestic price ratios for cold rolled sheet was 0.93.)[30]

Export Prices below Production Costs?

We have answered the first question: Foreign steel producers do sometimes (or often) export steel at prices below their domestic prices. The second question that must be raised concerning foreign steel producers' pricing behavior is: Do foreign firms export steel at prices below cost? The study by Putnam, Hayes & Bartlett concluded as follows:

> While the evidence is fragmented, it seems clear that the Japanese have used export prices as a principal means for regulating export volume. When additional exports are needed, export prices are cut; when steel is in short supply, export prices are raised. It is also clear that the Japanese are quite willing, when export volume is needed, to price exports below average production costs.[21]

This conclusion that the Japanese priced exports below average production costs was challenged by the authors of the Federal Trade Commission staff report. They pointed out that the cost series and the export-price series used by Putnam, Hayes & Bartlett were not compatible.[32] The report by the Council on Wage and Price Stability implied that foreign steel producers priced exports below average cost, at least occasionally, when it stated:

> The present discounts of as much as 10 to 20 percent below U.S. list prices are indicative of aggressive price competition by European and Japanese exporters. Given their production costs, they cannot sustain such deep cuts for very long.[33]

TABLE 9-5   RATIO OF EXPORT PRICE TO DOMESTIC PRICE BY PRODUCT,
THREE PRODUCTS, EEC AND JAPAN, 1961-1976

	Bars		Cold Rolled Sheets		Plates	
Year	EEC	Japan	EEC	Japan	EEC	Japan
1961	0.96	1.02	1.03	1.03	0.98	0.92
1962	0.91	0.99	0.98	1.03	0.95	0.94
1963	0.86	1.08	0.96	0.97	0.93	0.85
1964	0.87	1.05	0.97	0.98	1.01	1.00
1965	0.88	1.07	0.91	0.98	1.01	1.02
1966	0.87	1.06	0.88	0.97	0.97	0.93
1967	0.87	1.13	0.89	1.05	0.99	0.99
1968	0.89	1.20	0.91	1.05	0.99	1.02
1969	0.82	1.15	0.97	1.10	1.00	1.05
1970	0.87	1.03	0.98	1.28	1.02	1.21
1971	0.86	1.19	0.90	1.46	0.94	1.07
1972	0.88	1.13	0.85	0.89	0.90	0.83
1973	0.94	0.90	0.87	0.83	0.91	0.70
1974		1.04		1.11		1.03
1975		1.21		1.17		1.46
1976[a]		1.06		1.08		0.98
Average for column	0.88	1.08	0.93	1.06	0.97	1.00

[a]Three quarters.
Source: Federal Trade Commission, Bureau of Economics, *Staff Report on the United States Steel Industry and Its International Rivals: Trends and Factors Determining International Competitiveness* (Washington, D.C.: Government Printing Office, 1977), p. 223.

The report, however, admits that "in short, without much better data, it is difficult to compare Japanese export prices with the U.S. and Japanese production costs."[34] With respect to the export pricing of European steel producers, the Council staff report's conclusion was more definitive. It stated that:

Comparing the prices of EEC exports to the U.S. and EEC production costs is similarly difficult, but we can conclude that in 1976 and 1977 the Europeans must have been selling to the U.S. at prices less than the cost of production.[35]

This conclusion is corroborated by occasional admissions by European steelmakers that their export prices do not cover costs of production. For example, a spokesperson for France's second largest steel company, Sacilor-Sollac, was reported as remarking: "We sell at prices which do not correspond to the level of our costs. This situation cannot last. To survive, we must put ourselves on Japan's level of productivity."[36]

GOVERNMENT SUBSIDIES TO STEEL

It has been often argued by the advocates of protection for the U.S. steel industry that foreign steel producers are able to compete "unfairly" in U.S. markets because they are subsidized by their governments. In the EEC, the so-called border tax adjustments amount to an export incentive. The European Value Added Tax, which is assessed on all domestic sales, is exempted on export sales. It is estimated that the average cost of European steel exported to the United States is reduced by no more than $6 per ton of finished product, which is a relatively insignificant incentive considering the fact that European production cost is almost as high as that of the U.S. industry and that the trans-Atlantic importation costs amount to about $50 per ton.[37]

According to one estimate, the cost savings generated by the Japanese Government's various export-promotion programs probably accounted for less than one percent of the cost of steel exported by Japanese firms during the 1965-72 period. Most of these programs, however, have been discontinued since 1972.[38] Another estimate, made by the Federal Trade Commission, places the value of all Japanese export subsidies at $0.43 per metric ton of raw steel produced.[39] The study by Putnam, Hayes & Bartlett concluded as follows:

> In sum, it is difficult to ascribe a significant cost advantage to Japanese producers resulting from incentives or subsidies. The rebate of border taxes, however, amounts to an explicit reduction in the effective cost of European steel. . . .[40]

CONCLUSION

We have seen above that basic production costs, importation costs, and pricing practices all affect competitive advantage of steel products. Japan has a comparative cost advantage in steel production, but U.S. steel firms enjoy the advantage of transportation costs, particularly in inland markets. European steelmakers remain barely competitive in U.S. markets by consistent dumping at prices below costs. During recessionary periods, the Japanese cut export prices sharply – most probably to levels below average costs – to expand their export volume. Government subsidies are insignificant in the cost structure of European and Japanese steel products. These are the basic facts of international competitiveness of steel in U.S. markets.

One factor that must not be overlooked in assessing the price competitiveness of Japanese exports to the United States is the changing valuation of the yen vis-a-vis the dollar. Earlier we noted that the Japanese steel firms' price advantage over U.S. producers in U.S. markets in 1976 was as little as 5 percent (if the Japanese had charged the full cost of production inclusive of normal profits). This differential would be offset many times over by the sharp appreciation of the yen that took place in 1977 and 1978. Of course the actual export prices would not increase in direct proportion to the increased valuation of the yen in part because the Japanese steelmakers' costs of imported raw materials would have become lower under the appreciated yen. Nevertheless, the marked appreciation of the yen in the 1977-78 period, and its subsequent depreciation in 1979-80, must have had a profound effect on the price competitiveness of Japanese steel exports.

Considering the production function of steel products and the nature of the law of comparative advantage, we predict that competitiveness in steel production and export will gradually shift from Europe and Japan to the newly emerging industrial nations such as South Korea, Taiwan, Brazil, and – eventually – China ar.d India. Steel industries in the United States, Europe, and Japan will be forced to make adjustments to the changing structure of world supply of steel. The adjustments,inevitably, will be in the direction of overall reduction in size, higher technology in production, and greater specialization in product mix.

STUDY QUESTIONS

1. Discuss the difference between comparative advantage and competitive advantage.
2. What factors are responsible for the recent slowdown in the technological advances and innovations in the United Sates? What are the implications of this tendency for the international competitiveness of U.S. industries?
3. Many observers have attributed the lack of international competitiveness of the U.S. steel industry to the obsolete plants in the United States as compared to the more up-to-date plants in Europe and Japan. Is this a valid assessment? Why don't more U.S. producers invest in newer plants?
4. Many U.S. steel producers, labor-union leaders, and lobbyists for the industry have attributed the lack of international competitiveness of the U.S. steel industry to the "unfair" competition of foreign steel producers. In view of the analysis presented in this chapter, how would you respond to this charge?
5. How can we account for the lower labor cost per ton of steel produced in Japan as compared to steel produced in the United States?
6. How can we account for the low materials costs of the steel industry in Japan, a nation which has to import most of its raw material needs?
7. Refer to Table 9-3. In order to conclude from this table that in 1976 Japan had comparative advantage in steel production relative to the United States, what key assumption must be made about exchange rates? Making this assumption, explain the results contained in Table 9-3 in terms of the Heckscher-Ohlin theory.
8. Explain Japan's comparative advantage in steel vis-à-vis the United States using the general theory of trade patterns developed in Chapter 8.
9. See if you can obtain the most recent statistics on increases in labor productivity and wage rates in the U.S. steel industry. How do they affect the international competitiveness of the industry? (See, for example, "When Steel Wages Rise Faster than Productivity," *Business Week*, 21 April 1980, pp. 144-148.)

ENDNOTES

1. The following list, although by no means exhaustive, is fairly representative of the limited number of works done on competitiveness over the last two decades: J.M.

Fleming and S.C. Tsiang, "Changing Competitive Strength and Export Shares of Major Industrial Countries," International Monetary Fund, *Staff Papers*, August 1956, pp. 218-248; Richard N. Cooper, "The Competitive Position of the United States," in Seymour E. Harris, ed., *The Dollar in Crisis* (New York: Harcourt, Brace and World, 1961), pp. 137-165; Bela Balassa, "Recent Developments in the Competitiveness of American Industry and Prospects for the Future," U.S. Congress, Joint Economic Committee, *Factors Affecting the United States Balance of Payments*, 87th Cong., 2d Sess., 1962, pp. 27-54; J.M. McGeehan, "Competitiveness: A Survey of Recent Literature," *Economic Journal*, June 1968, pp. 243-62; and Samuel Paul and Vasant L. Mote, "Competitiveness of Exports: A Micro-Level Approach," *Economic Journal*, December 1970, pp. 895-909.

2. "Many Americans Fear the Economy's Ability to Compete Is Waning," *Wall Street Journal*, 17 April 1978, p. 1.

3. See: "Making U.S. Technology More Competitive," *Business Week*, 15 January 1972, pp. 44-50; "The Breakdown of U.S. Innovation," *Business Week*, 16 February 1976, pp. 56-68; and "Vanishing Innovation," *Business Week*, 3 July 1978, pp. 46-54.

4. *Business Week*, 3 July 1978, p. 47.

5. *Business Week*, 16 February 1976, p. 56.

6. *Ibid.*, p. 58.

7. *Ibid.*

8. *Business Week*, 3 July 1978, p. 49; italics original.

9. "The Reluctant Exporter," *Business Week*, 10 April 1978, pp. 54-66; "Too Many U.S. Workers No Longer Give a Damn," *Newsweek*, 24 April 1972, p. 65.

10. The discussion in this section has drawn heavily on three recent studies on the economics of international trade in steel. They are: The Council on Wage and Price Stability, *Reports to the President on Prices and Costs in the United States Steel Industry* (Washington, D.C.: Government Printing Office, 1977) (hereafter CWPS); Federal Trade Commission, Bureau of Economics, *Staff Report on the United States Steel Industry and Its International Rivals: Trends and Factors Determining International Competitiveness* (Washington, D.C.: Government Printing Office, 1977) (hereafter FTC); and Putnam, Hayes & Bartlett, Inc., *Economics of International Steel Trade: Policy Implications for the United States* (Washington, D.C.: American Iron and Steel Institute, 1977) (hereafter PH&B). Also useful are two magazine articles: "Steel's Sea of Troubles," *Business Week*, 19 September 1977, pp. 66-88; and Edmund Faltermayer, "How Made-in-America Steel Can Survive," *Fortune*, 13 February 1978, pp. 122-130.

11. PH&B, Appendix Exhibit A-1.

12. *Ibid.*, Exhibit A-2.

13. CWPS, p. 14.

14. *Ibid.*, p. 39.

15. *Ibid.*, p. 40.

16. *Fortune*, 13 February 1978, p. 124.

17. CWPS. pp. 52-53.

18. PH&B, p. 36.

19. CWPS, p. 71.

20. CWPS, p. 53.

21. *Ibid*, p. 31.

22. *Ibid*, p. xiii.

23. The Japan Iron and Steel Federation, *The Steel Industry of Japan 1977*, p. 27; and The Japan Iron and Steel Federation, *Monthly Report of the Iron & Steel Statistics*, November 1977, p. 23.

24. FTC, p. 108.

25. PH&B, p. 35.

26. CWPS, p. 61.

27. *Ibid.*, pp. 72-74.

28. *Ibid.*, p. xvi.

29. PH&B, p. 42.

30. FTC, p. 223.

31. PH&B, pp. 19-20.

32. FTC, pp. 243-244.

33. CWPS, p. xvi.
34. *Ibid.*, p. 69.
35. *Ibid.*
36. *Business Week*, 19 September 1977, p. 82.
37. CWPS, pp. 92-93.
38. *Ibid.*, p. 93.
39. *Ibid.*
40. PH&B, p. 37.

PART IV

GOVERNMENT INTERVENTION AND OTHER IMPERFECTIONS IN MERCHANDISE TRADE

10

Tariffs, Quotas, Subsidies, and Other Government Barriers to Trade

The logic of the last seven chapters rests firmly upon the concept of comparative advantage specialization. The logic is clear. The general public loses when comparative *dis*advantage production increases at the expense of comparative advantage production. But the logic of public-interest economics is often thrust ruthlessly aside by the narrower self interests of politics. This chapter considers — mostly — the consequences of those narrow self interests. This chapter is about political tools that promote comparative *dis*advantage production.

The evidence of the preceding chapters established one fundamental point about international trade. When exchange rates are in equilibrium, comparative costs determine the international competitiveness of production of each good in each nation; so resources are used most efficiently when international trade is unconstrained by governments.

It follows that in every nation a number of industries cannot be efficient or internationally competitive. Mutually beneficial trade relations require of each nation that some products are exported (for the U.S., wheat, airplanes and diesel pumps) – and some are imported (for the U.S., bananas and many textile, ceramic, and consumer electronic products).

Those are *economic* facts of life. Unfortunately, it is a *political* fact of life that both capital and labor in comparative-disadvantage industries demand — and often get — government protection from foreign imports. Look back now, in Chapter 6, at the special-interest advocacy of Secretary of Labor Marshall. As is usually the case with any parliamentary democracy, the more highly organized and more vocal a special-interest group, the more successful it is in obtaining governmental favors. All special-interest groups, by their very nature, seek to maximize their private interest often at the expense of the welfare of the nation as a whole. Almost always, the costs of such private interest gratification are borne by the general public — the consumer — who must pay in the forms of higher prices, higher taxes,and lower overall living standards. Adding insult to these injuries, demands for protection that inevitably robs the public are often presented as virtuously patriotic proposals designed to appeal to the public's chauvinistic emotions.

However, not all arguments for protection are narrowly self-serving. Some arguments for protection make some sense under certain conditions. Therefore, every educated citizen — or, at least, every student of economics — ought to know the character of each argument for protection and the effects of each type of protection. This chapter describes those effects and those arguments. The chapter closes with a discussion of some "second-best" compromises; reductions in trade barriers like or similar to the reductions of Europe's free trade area and its, quite distinct, common market.

TARIFFS AND QUOTAS

A *tariff* is a *duty,* a tax, levied on an imported commodity. By raising the price of the comparative-advantage import relative to the domestically produced import-competing goods, tariffs accord protection to the comparative-disadvantage domestic producers. A *quota* is a quantitative restriction on comparative-advantage imports; it sets a maximum limit to the quantity of a good that may be imported during a time period. Until recent decades, most quotas were import quotas. But since 1960, a number of nations have been coerced into imposing "voluntary" quotas on specific comparative-advantage exports.

Further, in recent years, as well as over past millenia, states sometimes impose export quotas in order to punish other states. For example, President Carter attempted to punish Russia in January 1980 by restricting grain exports to Russia. We will, therefore, consider both import and export quotas.

At first sight, tariffs and quotas may appear to be quite dissimilar political tools for helping comparative disadvantage producers. But every economics student knows that price and quantity are interrelated. So anticipate seeing that the effects of a tariff and of a quota are nearly the same: price up, imports down, comparative advantage production down, comparative disadvantage production up. Perhaps more surprisingly, anticipate seeing that a domestic subsidy can produce the same effects special-interest groups beg from quotas and tariffs while imposing fewer costs on the general public. Now, the details.

TARIFFS

Customs duties, tariffs, are either ad valorem or specific. An *ad valorem duty* is levied as a fixed percentage of the *value* of the commodity; a *specific duty* is expressed as a fixed sum of money per given *quantity* of the commodity (e.g., so many dollars per ton, per unit, etc.).

Supply as Sum of Domestic Output Plus Imports

Figure 10-1 depicts the demand-and-supply situations of a commodity in the importing country, M, and the exporting country, X. The graphs of the exporting country are in the left half of the figure where the quantity is measured from *right to left*. The quantity axis of the importing country, shown in the right hand side of the figure, is read conventionally from left to right. The demand curves, D_m and D_x, of the two nations are ordinary. The supply curve, S_x, of the exporter and the *domestic* supply curve, S_d, of the importer slope upward either because this is the short run and these are summations of the supplying firms' marginal cost curves or because this is the long run and these are increasing-cost industries.

In the absence of any trade, the equilibrium price in X is OV and the equilibrium price in M is OR. If free trade is permitted and, if we assume —for simplicity —that transportation is costless, the export supply of nation X is measured, at each price, by the horizontal excess of quantity supplied over quantity demanded domestically in X. For example, the

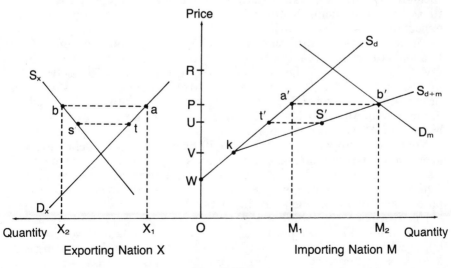

Figure 10-1
Derivation of the Total Supply Curve in the Importing Nation under Free Trade

export supply of nation X at price OU is represented by the excess, ts. This export supply of X is the *import supply* available to nation M. At price OU, the quantity domestically supplied in M is Ut'. Adding the domestic quantity supplied, Ut', and the import quantity supplied, t's', we find that total quantity supplied in M at price OU is Us'.

At price OV, supply and demand intersect in nation X, and no export supply exists. Therefore, in M, total quantity supplied at price OV is only Vk, or the amount shown by the domestic supply curve S_d. Above the price OV, however, supply in M is the sum of both domestic *and* import supplies. Thus, the domestic-*and*-import supply curve, S_{d+m}, in nation M, originates at point W, slopes upward to point k, and at this point kinks away from the S_d curve.

Price OP is special. There, nation X's export supply, ab, becomes nation M's import supply, a'b'. In nation M, this import supply, a'b', is added to its domestic quantity supplied, Pa', to give a total quantity supplied, Pb', which just equals quantity demanded at price OP. Price OP, therefore, is the free-trade equilibrium price at this price; nation M produces OM_1, consumes OM_2, and imports M_1M_2; nation X produces OX_2, consumes OX_1, and exports X_1X_2.

Price Rises by Less Than the Amount of Tariff

Figure 10-2 shows the consequences of imposition of a specific duty. Anticipate that the equilibrium price in the importing nation will rise by less than the amount of the tariff. Recall that imposition of a 10¢ domestic sales tax ordinarily raises price by less than 10¢ as the incidence of the sales tax is divided between buyers and sellers. Similarly here, the incidence of the tariff is divided between importers and exporters.

Figure 10-2 is a duplication of Figure 10-1 except for some omissions to avoid clutter and the addition of a dollar scale on the vertical axis so OV = $1 and OP = $2. Under free trade, equilibrium price is OP = $2; and X exports X_1X_2, the exact amount that M imports, M_1M_2. In M, producers of quantity OM_1 have comparative advantage as do producers in X of quantity OX_2. In M, those who might produce quantities in excess of OM_1 would have comparative *dis*advantage.

Next, we assume a request for a tariff from the small special-interest group comprising laborers, managers, and capitalists of M, who would like to produce beyond OM_1, and those producing OM_1 who would like a higher price. Further, we assume they persuade government to impose a tariff of 50¢ on each unit imported. What follows?

Units are not available for export from X unless exporters are to get to keep above $1 = OV per unit. Since the government of M is to take 50¢ of whatever its residents pay for an imported unit, X exporters can keep over $1 per unit only if M residents pay above $1.50 per unit. So the supply curve of M kinks at k' at price OZ = $1.50. At prices above OZ, import supply is added to domestic supply exactly as in free trade

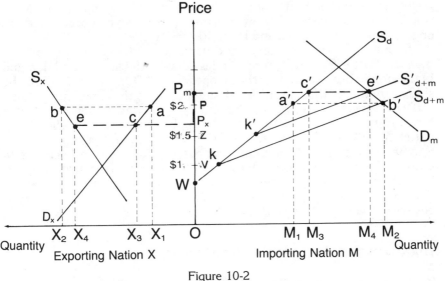

Figure 10-2
The Effects of a Specific Duty of 50 Cents

circumstances. Therefore, S'_{d+m} (shown by the bold, kinked line) kinks
at k' and is parallel to S_{d+m}.

Given S'_{d+m} and D_m, we can easily see the consequences of the 50¢
specific duty. Supply and demand intersect at e' in nation M. Equilibrium price is up to OP_m; consumption is down to OM_4. Domestic comparative disadvantage production is up by M_1M_3 to OM_3. Comparative
advantage imports are down to M_3M_4. The M nation's price of OP_m
minus the government take of 50¢ $= P_xP_m$ gives an equilibrium price
of OP_x in nation X. There, comparative advantage production is down
X_4X_2 to OX_4. Consumption is up to OX_3, and exports are down to X_3X_4.

The duty is 50¢ $= P_xP_m$. Yet equilibrium price in M is up only by
PP_m. So, in the language of public finance, the *incidence on buyers* is
PP_m; the *incidence on sellers* is P_xP. And, necessarily, $P_xP + PP_m =$
50¢. The price in the two nations differs by the amount of the duty, and
the two new prices lie on opposite sides of the old equilibrium price.
The relationship (equality) between nation X's exports, ce, and nation
M's imports, $c'e'$, with a 50¢ differential in price, is shown by the bold,
broken line $ecP_xP_mc'e'$.

Because of the higher price, residents of M consume less. Herein lies
the most visible cost of tariffs to society: a higher price and lower real
incomes. In the exporting country, less is produced and exported; and
though consumption of this product is up, total consumption is down.
We suggest you flip back now to the end of Chapter 3 and review the
consequences that follow for total output when both nations raise comparative disadvantage production at the expense of comparative
advantage production.

We see that 50¢ is divided between an increase in price in M and a
decrease in price in X. In other words, a part of the burden — the

incidence — of the tariff is shifted from the tariff-levying nation, M, to the exporting country, X. How much such shifting can occur depends on the slopes of D_x, S_x, S_d, and D_m in Figure 10-2.

The more elastic the supply and demand in the exporting country (i.e., the flatter S_x and D_x) and the less elastic the supply and demand in the importing nation (i.e., the steeper S_d and D_m), the less will be the shifting of the tariff from the importing nation to the exporting nation.

If the supply curve, S_x, in the exporting nation is horizontal at a certain price level, then the import supply surve, S_m (not shown), to nation M will be a flat line at that price level. The import supply curve, S_m, may also be flat if the importing country is very small relative to total world output of this product. In both cases, changes in the importing nation's demand have no effect on the exporting country's price. So, if a tariff is imposed, the incidence of the tariff will fall entirely upon buyers in the importing country.

TRANSPORTATION COSTS AS A BARRIER TO TRADE

Here, we interrupt this chapter's concentration on government obstruction of trade. We pause to look at the effects of transportation costs. Like tariffs, transportation costs are a barrier — we might call them a "natural" barrier — to trade. Given that analogy, Figure 10-2 can be used to show either the consequences of a 50¢-a-unit tariff or of transportation costs of 50¢ a unit.

Given the initial S_x, D_x, D_m, and S_d curves of Figure 10-2, and given transportation costs of 50¢ a unit between X and M, curve S_{d+m} does not exist. No units are available to M residents unless they pay more than \$1 a unit to X exporters plus 50¢-a-unit transportation costs. Therefore, international trade kinks the supply curve of M at point k', at price OZ = \$1.50. So S'_{d+m} is the supply curve of M when transportation costs are 50¢ per unit. Then, exactly the same as with the 50¢ specific duty, equilibrium in M is determined by the supply and demand intersection at e'; equilibrium price is OP_m in M and OP_x in X.

As with the tariff, the slopes of the initial supply and demand curves determine the way in which the incidence of transportation costs is divided between X sellers and M buyers. The only difference between the two cases is the obvious one: tariff revenues go to government, transportation revenues go to carriers. Those revenues can be portrayed in Figure 10-2 by the area of the rectangle with the quantity traded as base (ce in X or c'e' in M) and height of 50¢.

DOMESTIC EFFECTS OF A TARIFF

We now return to detail the effects of a tariff on residents of the nation imposing the tariff. To simplify our analysis, we assume either the tariff-levying country is small relative to the rest of the world or the world industry has long-run constant costs. Either way, foreign supply is perfectly elastic to the importing nation.

Figure 10-3 shows these conditions for nation M. Domestic supply and demand are shown, as in Figure 10-2, as S_d and D_m. Foreign units become available at price OP (covering production *and* transportation costs). So, with free trade, the supply curve of nation M kinks at point k; and S_{d+m} is a flat line beyond k. In the absence of a tariff, equilibrium is determined by the intersection at e. Domestic production is OQ_1, consumption is OQ_2, and imports total Q_1Q_2.

Figure 10-3 is lettered to show the detailed consequences that follow when M levies a tariff of PP' per unit. The first effect, of course, is to reduce total supply from S_{d+m} to S'_{d+m}. (The supply curve higher *up* in the figure is *less* supply.) The new total supply kinks away from domestically produced supply at point k', at price OP'. The new equilibrium is therefore determined by the intersection at point e'. The price rises from OP to OP' by the full amount of the tariff, PP'; that is, the whole incidence of the tariff falls on domestic buyers.

Domestic consumption is down to OQ_4. The fall in consumption, Q_2Q_4, is called the *consumption effect* of the tariff. Domestic production is up to OQ_3. The Q_1Q_3 rise in domestic production is called the *production effect* of the tariff. The rectangular area, bce'k', represents the tariff revenue of government.

Consumers are definitely worse off under the tariff since they are consuming only OQ_4 instead of OQ_2 and are paying OP' instead of OP.

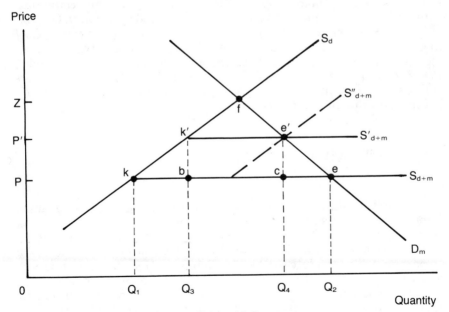

Figure 10-3
Domestic Effects of a Tariff or a Quota

With free trade, this product provides *consumers' surplus* (see Appendix 10A if you are not familiar with this concept) represented in Figure 10-3 by the area above Pe and below the demand curve. The tariff, PP', reduces consumers' surplus by the area Pee'P'.

What are the effects of the tariff on domestic producers? The tariff raises the domestic price from OP to OP' and increases quantity produced from OQ_1 to OQ_3. The producers' total revenue, therefore, increases from the rectangle OQ_1kP to the rectangle $OQ_3k'P'$. The increase in total revenue is represented by the inverted L-shaped area $Q_1Q_3k'P'Pk$. That area divides conceptually into two parts: $Q_1Q_3k'k$ represents added costs to the producers and to society; i.e., the domestic resources used to produce Q_1Q_3 would alternatively have produced output worth $Q_1Q_3k'k$ to society. Area Pkk'P', the remaining portion of the inverted L-shaped additional revenue, is a windfall gain to the domestic producers. Their *net* gain will be Pkk'P' *minus* the costs of organizing and lobbying to obtain the tariff; more on this further along in this chapter.

So much for consumers and producers. What of society as a whole? Area Pkk'P' represents a transfer from consumers to producers with a net effect of zero for the society. Area bce'k' represents a transfer from consumers to their government, again a zero net. Area Q_4Q_2ec represents a nonspending consequence of the tariff. Consumers don't get quantity Q_4Q_2; they don't spend Q_4Q_2ec, but they lose Q_4Q_2ee' in utility. So society suffers a *deadweight loss* represented by the triangle, cee'. And society suffers a second deadweight loss represented by the triangle, kbk'; for with the tariff, consumers give up alternative output worth $Q_1Q_3k'k$ to them to obtain the quantity, Q_1Q_3, they could have obtained from foreigners at a sacrifice represented by the area Q_1Q_3bk.

In sum, the tariff changes total spending on the product from OQ_2eP to $OQ_4e'P'$ with a deadweight loss equalling the sum of the two triangles kbk' and cee'. Deadweight loss equals the loss of consumers' surplus, Pee'P', minus the two transfers: the windfall addition to producers' surplus, Pkk'P' (this concept is also reviewed in Appendix 10A), and the government's tariff revenue, bce'k'.

IMPORT AND EXPORT QUOTAS

As tariff rates have come down successively with each round of multilateral negotiations taking place within the framework of the General Agreements on Tariffs and Trade (GATT, see Chapter 12), the relative importance of quotas and other nontariff trade barriers has increased. Import quotas are widely used in developing nations to restrict imports of all types of goods. In the developed world, import quotas are used largely for the protection of agricultural industries. In addition, the United States has pressured both developed and developing nations into imposing export quotas known euphemistically as "voluntary export restraints" or "orderly marketing arrangements."

Look back at Figure 10-3 to see how the effects of the tariff can be obtained equally well through an import quota. The labor, management, and capitalist lobbyists could request a tariff of PP' to bring them the windfall Pkk'P' for their production of OQ_3. Alternatively, they could lobby for an import quota of a certain size. What quota would raise domestic price from OP to OP'?

Equilibrium price becomes OP' if supply and demand intersect at point e' of Figure 10-3. The demand curve, D_m, is unaffected by the quota, but what does the quota do to the supply curve, S_{d+m}?

What if the quota allowed importation of only *one* unit of the commodity? Where would the new S_{d+m} curve lie? It would be a straight line parallel to S_d and one unit to the right of S_d at all prices above OP (no foreign units are available at or below OP). The equilibrium price under the quota of one unit would be slightly lower than OZ, which is determined by the intersection of D_m and the new supply curve parallel to S_d. As the size of the quota is increased from one unit, the new supply curve—call it S''_{d+m}—shifts to the right, lowering the equilibrium price. So, to get S''_{d+m} to intersect D_m at e', the quota must equal k'e' units. Then S''_{d+m} will be parallel to S_d, and k'e' units to the right at every price above OP, as shown by the broken line in Figure 10-3.

If the lobby gets government to impose a quota of k'e', how will its results compare with those that would follow from a tariff of PP'? The quota of k'e' would raise equilibrium price to OP, it would cut consumption to OQ_4, and it would raise the special-interest group's income from OQ_1kP to $OQ_3k'P'$ — all exactly the same as with the tariff of PP'. So far as the special-interest group is concerned, its members experience exactly the same effects whether government obliges them with a quota of k'e' or a tariff of PP'.

What of the effects on society? The quota, like the tariff, raises total spending on this product from OQ_2eP to $OQ_4e'P'$ with a deadweight loss equalling the sum of the two triangles, kbk' and cee'. But the money represented by the area bce'k' may also be deadweight loss to the society. Actually, bce'k' may go to any one (or combination) of three different groups: (1) government may auction the import rights to the highest bidders, (2) import rights may be assigned to particular domestic persons, or (3) government may assign quota rights to foreign exporters. If import rights are auctioned off, given the world price of OP and the domestic price of OP', bidders can afford to pay government up to bce'k' for import rights. Then, as with the tariff, bce'k' is transferred to government. If import rights are assigned to particular domestic persons — as was done with the U.S. petroleum quotas of 1959-73 — then bce'k' is a windfall transfer to importers. If quota rights are assigned to foreign exporters — as has long been the practice with the U.S. sugar quota — then bce'k' goes as a windfall to foreign exporters and becomes a deadweight loss to the quota-imposing society. There is a fourth — and partly illegal — disposition possible for bce'k'. A bureaucracy may be given the power to sell or assign quota shares; then bce'k' may be divided among government, bribes to bureaucrats, and windfall to those able to buy the licenses assigning quota shares.

In recent years, the United States, through negotiation, has pressured Japan and many developing nations into voluntarily restricting their exports. So far as our sketch is concerned, an export quota of $k'e'$ will have the same consequences as an import quota of $k'e'$. The question "Who will get $bce'k'$?" would remain, however.

In January of 1980, President Carter restricted exports of grain and high technology projects to the Soviet Union. He hoped the restrictions would punish the Russians for their invasion of Afghanistan. The Russian livestock, oil drilling, and computer-dependent industries were threatened with disruption. Australia, Canada, and the Common Market agreed not to provide extra grain to the Russians. Those nations and Japan also agreed to impose some additional restrictions on high-technology exports that might aid Russia's military machine. However, Argentinians provided more grain for Russia; and Europeans boosted sales to Russia of many high-technology products, particularly computers and semiconductors, no longer available from the United States. By the autumn of 1980, the Russians appeared to have minimized the impact of the American embargo.

In April of 1980, the Iranian government's kidnapping and attempts at blackmail entered their sixth month. In exasperation, President Carter then placed an embargo on exports to Iran. Under the embargo, all shipments of U.S. goods except food and medicine were prohibited. In April, Japan and the current and prospective members of the European Economic Community imposed the same restrictions. (Britain exempted shipments of goods for which contracts had been signed before the date of the embargo.) Iran responded by turning to the Communist Block for substitutes.

The limited effectiveness of these attempts to use export controls to punish were reminiscent of the failures of the League of Nations in the 1930s. In September 1931, Japan invaded Manchuria. The "covenant system" of the League called for an economic boycott of Japan. But neither the United States nor Russia was willing to act, and economic sanctions were never seriously considered.

In October 1935, Italy invaded Ethiopia. League members embargoed exports of arms and of some raw materials to Italy and halted all imports from Italy. The latter action was, politically, the most popular. But oil exports, essential for the Italian conquest, were not reduced. In early 1936, France and Britain offered Italy a "compromise" that gave Ethiopia to Italy and gave the League a cosmetic excuse for ending sanctions in July 1936.

The moral seems to be that a government can relatively easily impose import restrictions that reduce the general welfare of its own innocent citizens; but governments are hard put to apply export restrictions that will injure governments guilty of the most flagrant aggression against third parties.

Meaningful choices that can be made have to do with the kind of restrictions to be placed on imports. For example, although the *initial* effects of a tariff and a quota may be identical, their *subsequent* effects are not. Under a tariff PP', in the case of Figure 10-3, the domestic price cannot rise above OP'. Therefore, if demand subsequently increases (D_m shifts to the right), imports will increase while domestic production remains the same. Under the quota Q_3Q_4, in contrast, the absolute maximum amount of imports is fixed; therefore, a demand increase will raise domestic price and increase domestic production while imports remain unchanged.

Again, under the tariff, if domestic costs later rise (i.e., S_d moves to the left), price cannot rise above OP', so domestic production would fall, and imports would rise. Again in contrast, under the Q_3Q_4 quota, a rise in domestic costs would move both S_d and S''_{d+m} to the left. Imports could not rise, price would rise, and domestic production would fall only to the extent that the higher price would reduce the quantity demanded.

These contrasts show that a quota is a more effective barrier to trade than is a tariff. Under a quota, subsequent increases in domestic demand or decreases in domestic supply do not lead to larger imports; whereas under a tariff they do. Thus an import quota, as compared to a tariff, is more certain, inflexible, and attractive to domestic special interests.

SUBSIDIES: ABOVEBOARD PROTECTION

Once again, look back at Figure 10-3 and its initial conditions. Now assume that Congress denies both tariff and quota requests by domestic producers. Look at Figure 10-3 to see the size of subsidy the domestic producers would need in order for them to find their optimum output to be OQ_3 with a total revenue yield of $OQ_3k'P'$. Provision of a subsidy would move S_d to the right. How far to the right must S_d be moved to induce domestic production of OQ_3?

A subsidy to domestic producers cannot change world price from OP. Therefore, the question is: What S_d location would bring domestic production of OQ_3? The answer is: an S_d which passes through point b. Then, the next question is: What size subsidy would move S_d to the right so it would pass through point b? Answer: a per unit subsidy of bk' = PP' = the tariff we have considered.

So what happens if a subsidy of PP' is legislated? The new supply curve of domestic producers, S'_d (not shown), is located to the right of S_d, is parallel to S_d, and passes through point b. Domestic comparative disadvantage production rises to OQ_3. Domestic producers receive OQ_3bP from buyers and Pbk'P' as subsidy from government. Since price holds unchanged at OP, consumption is unchanged at OQ_2. The value of the area bce'k' is not transferred away from consumers to anybody. The deadweight loss of protection is only the area kbk'.

The domestic producers would receive exactly the same total revenue — the area $OQ_3k'P'$ — whether they produce under a tariff of PP' a unit, a quota of k'e', or a subsidy of PP' per unit. Yet, the deadweight social cost of the subsidy would be smaller than the deadweight social cost of the tariff or the quota. Further, tariff, quota, and subsidy all transfer the value of area Pbk'P' from consumers to domestic producers. But the tariff and the quota hide the transfer in higher prices, and few consumers have enough information to realize how much their welfare is diminished. In contrast, under the subsidy, the value of Pbk'P' — the cost to taxpayers of protection — would appear every year in government's budget and would therefore be subject to periodic public scrutiny.

So why don't legislators deny tariffs and quotas and grant subsidies to special-interest groups? Why do legislators prefer the tariff and quota that conceal from the public the value of the Pbk'P' transfer when they could help the special interests just as much with a subsidy that would permit the public to know the true cost of protection? Economists cannot answer these questions; voters, however, may speculate about legislators' motives. One thing, however, is clear. Subsidies "cost" the government some money in the form of increased expenditures, whereas tariffs and quotas do not (they might even bring in some revenues). Public officials and legislators thus seem to opt for "costless" tariffs and quotas, when in fact their true cost to *society as a whole* is greater than that of subsidies. Domestic industry lobbyists help obscure the issue by arguing that they do not seek a government handout, but merely seek protection.

NOMINAL VERSUS EFFECTIVE TARIFF RATES

In recent decades, legislators and bureaucrats in developed nations have been inclined to boast that they have resisted special interests and have reduced most tariffs to negligible levels. Yet the hard-working poor of the developing nations have found themselves unable to sell across those "negligible" tariff barriers — even when helped by the efficient managements of multinational corporations. Why do "negligible barriers" often prove insurmountable?

Here is a sample case. A multinational firm is trying to decide whether to build an instant-coffee manufacturing plant in the Ivory Coast or in the United States. If the plant is located in the United States, the company will have to pay $1.60 per pound for raw materials, plant, machinery, and transportation to the plant and from the plant to retailers. *Value added* in the plant will cost (in wages, salaries, interest, and normal profit) 50¢ a pound. So a U.S. plant could earn a normal profit selling to American retailers at $2.10 a pound.

If the plant is located in Abidjan, the firm will have to pay $1.60 for raw materials, plant, machinery, and transportation (in this case, most transportation cost is associated with the finished product) to the plant and from the plant to American retailers. Value added in the plant will cost only 40¢ a pound. So an Abidjan plant could earn a normal profit selling to American retailers at $2.00 a pound. In this example, the Ivory Coast has comparative advantage in the production of instant coffee.

Next, assume America imposes a ten percent ad valorem tariff on imports of instant coffee. To sell Ivory Coast instant coffee in the United

States, the firm will need to charge $2.00 + 20¢ = $2.20 per pound. If the firm builds the plant in the United States, a price of only $2.10 will provide a normal profit. (For simplicity, assume long-run flat supply curves.)

The *nominal tariff rate* is ten percent. But is it fair to say "this tariff gives ten percent protection?" That is to say, "Does this tariff permit American firms to be competitive when anywhere up to — but not beyond — ten percent less efficient than Ivory Coast firms? Or will this tariff protect inefficiency greater than ten percent?"

To answer the latter pair of questions, "ten percent less efficient" must be defined. The definition of "percent less efficient" is couched entirely in terms of value added. In this example, instant-coffee factories in the United States and those in the Ivory Coast both have to buy, from suppliers, materials costing $1.60 per pound of output. (This equality simplifies the arithmetic of this explanation but is not essential to the argument.) The $1.60 is not for the product of the instant-coffee industry; the $1.60 is for the output of other industries. The instant-coffee industry's production is only that industry's value added: in this example, it is 50¢ in the United States and 40¢ in the Ivory Coast. This industry's "efficiency" can affect only the 50¢ (or the 40¢), not the $1.60.

So, by definition, if the U.S. plants are "ten percent less efficient," they have costs ten percent above the Ivory Coast costs, i.e., 40¢ + 4¢ = 44¢. In this example, the U.S. firm could be ten percent or even 20 percent less efficient (value added of 48¢) and could still undersell, at $1.60 + 48¢ = $2.08, the $2.20 price of imported Ivory Coast coffee.

How much less efficient could the American plant be and still be competitive? The American plant could match the Ivory Coast plant's $2.20 price even if the American value added were 60¢. Since 60¢ is 50 percent more than the Ivory Coast value added of 40¢, the *effective tariff rate* in this case is 50 percent. In every case, a 50 percent effective tariff rate means that the hrotected firm can be as much as 50 percent less efficient than the foreign firm and still be able to match the price of imported units from the foreign firm. More generally, the effective tariff rate measures the extent to which a protected firm can be less efficient than the foreign firm and can still match the domestic price of imports from the foreign firm.

So in this example, it is *not* fair to say "this tariff gives ten percent protection." This tariff permits American firms to be anywhere up to 50 percent less efficient than Ivory Coast firms. So the fair statement is, "this tariff gives 50 percent protection."

One may be convinced that much of the LDCs' criticism of Japan and the developed Western nations is nonsense. But one must understand the concept of effective protection if one is to understand one of the legitimate complaints of Third World critics.

In developed nations, the usual rule is: no tariffs on raw materials, lowest tariffs on partially processed materials, and highest tariffs on finished products (including machinery). The highest tariff may be "only" a nominal five or ten percent on a finished item, but the effective rate of protection may be much higher (as in the instant-coffee example).

The result, for LDC residents, is that they can export raw materials duty-free to developed nations. But if multinational corporations or LDC entrepreneurs consider processing raw materials (e.g., turning logs into plywood or palm nuts into palm oil) in comparative-advantage LDC locations, their products may have to overcome low nominal but highly effective tariffs protecting processors in developed nations' comparative-disadvantage locations. But the situation is even worse — from the point of view of international efficiency and of the aspiring LDC poor — when a multinational firm or an LDC entrepreneur considers producing final products based on LDC raw materials. In many cases, plants in the LDCs would have comparative advantage but not to an extent that would permit such plants to overcome effective tariff rates of 10, 20, or even 40 percent. Faced with the effective barriers kept up by all the developed nations, entrepreneurs are forced to locate new plants within the developed nations. One result is that fewer opportunities exist for LDC residents to learn new skills.

These circumstances are not the result of malicious intent in the developed countries. Rather, the cause is the presence in the developed nations of special-interest groups of labor, management, and entrepreneurs who want protection for themselves when processing LDC raw materials. Few developed nation producers compete with LDC raw-material producers, so few ask for tariffs on LDC raw materials. The few who do are counterlobbied by raw materials *users*. Special-interest petitions for protection of semifinished goods production from tropical raw materials are counterlobbied by users of their products. But petitions for protection of final goods production are not counterlobbied unless consumers organize. The net result: no restrictions on raw material imports from LDCs, moderately effective protection of semifinished processing of LDC raw materials, and highly effective protection of production in developed nations of final products based on LDC raw materials. So, LDC citizens are left with the legitimate complaint that developed nation legislation discourages construction of comparative advantage manufacturing plants in developing nations.

WHY WE HAVE PROTECTION:
SPECIAL INTERESTS AND THEIR ARGUMENTS

If John Q. and Mary Z. Public are injured by protection of comparative disadvantage production, why do we have so much protection? We can — and will below — marshall some public-interest reasons for protection (though in most of these cases, as implied by the argument of a preceding section, subsidies would be more nearly in the public interest than quotas or tariffs). But the realistic answer to our question is that we have extensive protection because Congress and the President are susceptible to special interests' importunities. In this section we will first examine some political theories of special-interest-group behavior, and then will critically evaluate various arguments that special interests use to rationalize their demands for protection.

POLITICAL THEORY OF TRADE RESTRICTION

The economic theories of comparative advantage, of economies of scale, and of competition assure us that international trade delivers many costless benefits to John Q. and Mary Z. Public.

1. International trade expands comparative advantage specialization that raises Gross World Product (GWP).
2. International trade permits fuller utilization of the advantages of large scale production, and so it further raises GWP.
3. International trade thwarts enterprising attempts to acquire monopoly power, and so it extends competitive efficiency and raises GWP still further.
4. Because part of the contribution of international trade to GWP is achieved through increased investment, international trade increases the rate of growth of GWP.
5. Because trade reduces the frictional barriers to dissemination of new skills and technology, it further increases the rate of growth of GWP.
6. Trade restrains cost-push inflation, thereby facilitating less inflationary central bank policy.
7. Finally, trade provides buyers with *both* the cost advantages of economies of scale from long production runs of homogeneous products *and* the advantages of diversity deriving from access to many low cost producers.

Economic theory is clear. For the most part (exceptions are considered below), freer international trade increases public welfare. Yet we know that government restrictions on international trade (hereafter referred to simply as "trade restrictions") have been and continue to be commonplace. We need a political theory to explain the persistent presence of these restrictions.

A Theory of Elections

Our immediate objective is formulation of a theory explaining the decisionmaking process that imposes and maintains — or removes — trade restrictions. We will concentrate on democratic political systems, like America's, where laws are passed by elected representatives.

Our first premise is that candidates act in a manner calculated to ensure their election and that incumbents are candidates for reelection who act in a manner calculated to bring reelection. In America, candidates ordinarily need more than 50 percent of the vote to be elected.

Because each legislator must vote each year on many issues, and because the public comprises many heterogeneous groups, the successful candidate must obtain support from a variety of groups.

To obtain a majority vote, election campaigns require both cash and hours of effort by volunteers. Our second premise is that donors make cost-benefit analyses before deciding to make contributions. Prospective donors estimate the potential benefits to themselves from election of one candidate rather than another. They compare those benefits with the costs they consider bearing to help elect "their" candidates.

On the basis of these cost-benefit comparisons, the public divides into three groups. The first group — the majority — concludes that potential benefits (note these are *not* total benefits from election of some one, but are only differential benefits between the election of competitors) are too small to justify any contribution beyond the effort of voting — if that. The persons in the second group anticipate receipt of "substantial" benefits if a particular candidate is elected, but they also anticipate election of that candidate because of efforts already being made by others. These observers choose to be "free riders." They hope to receive the benefits at no cost to themselves beyond the effort of voting.

A Theory of Special-Interest-Group Organization

Candidates are most influenced by interaction with the third group, those whose cost-benefit analyses show them that their donations will influence the election and that potential benefits exceed the costs of their donations. (We can describe these contributors' behavior most precisely in marginal terms: They will increase donations until the marginal benefit from one more donated dollar or hour just equals the marginal cost of that additional donated dollar or hour.) Candidates, if they are to be elected or reelected, must shape their actions and promises so they will obtain the donations needed to conduct a campaign that, given those actions and promises, will produce a majority vote.

Prospective beneficiaries often recognize that if they operate independently, they will receive no benefits because each acting alone can have no effect on the election or policy outcome while, if many appear likely to act, each individual can anticipate being best off as a free rider. Therefore, the special-interest group must take two steps: First, it must organize all or most potential beneficiaries so all in the organization will assume a portion of the costs. Second, having paid the costs of organizing, the organization must make the donations that will help to elect the candidate who acts and promises to support them.

We are most concerned here with political acts that redistribute income. In particular we are concerned with trade restrictions that take real income from buyers of a product and give additional income to a particular special-interest group of workers, managers, and entrepreneurs. We can make several generalizations about the factors that combine to determine whether potential beneficiaries will or will not organize.

First, the total costs of organizing a group of donors depends on both the number to be organized and their heterogeneity of location and interests. Second, economies of scale bring falling marginal cost of units of organizational effort, but extension of organizing effort to recruit larger numbers may involve rising marginal effort per recruit. Third, organizational costs are less if some existing organization, e.g., a trade group, providing a flow of other benefits can be coopted to bargain with candidates.

The final decision, whether to lobby and whether to organize depend on cost-benefit comparisons. Look back at Figure 10-3 to see what potential benefits beckon a special interest group contemplating organizing and lobbying for protection.

If the group's members begin with free trade and price OP and consider reaching for a specific duty of PP', they can anticipate a revenue increase of $Q_1Q_3k'P'Pk$. As we pointed out above, $Q_1Q_3k'k$ would go to production costs. Therefore, Pkk'P' would be the maximum "benefit" the special-interest producers of OQ_3 could hope to obtain from protection raising price to OP'. They would, we assume "go for it" if they could expect their organizational and lobbying costs to be held below Pkk'P'.

Beyond that simple comparison, they would have to estimate the potential protection level that would yield the highest net of windfall gain less organizational-lobbying costs. The highest price protection could bring them, given the conditions of Figure 10-3, would be OZ. Either a tariff of PZ (or more) or a quota of zero would raise price to OZ, would end imports, and would provide a windfall of PkfZ. A tariff of less than PZ or a quota of more than zero would provide a gross windfall of less then PkfZ but might provide a larger net. Handicapped by lack of complete information, the members of each special-interest group must try to identify their optimal level of organization and lobbying effort and the tariff or quota that will bring them optimal returns.

Using This Theory to Explain the Past

Economic theory predicts that in most cases freer trade raises the general welfare. Our political theory predicts that the general welfare will give way to special-interest trade restrictions if cost-benefit circumstances favor organizational actions that elect legislators who will reduce the general welfare to pay off special-interest supporters. Neither the argument of this chapter nor the historical evidence of Chapter 12 will provide absolutely convincing proof of our hypotheses. But we confidently argue that the evidence of the American past is not inconsistent with our hypotheses. In any case, we owe thanks to Lance E. Davis and Douglass C. North who originated this model in their 1971 book, *Institutional Change and American Economic Growth*.[1]

TRADE RESTRICTIONS FOR THE GENERAL WELFARE

Before reviewing American history in Chapter 12, we must acknowledge, with emphasis, that not all trade restrictions are the result of special-interest lobbying. Many, perhaps most, trade restrictions have been imposed because legislators assumed the restrictions would reward and repay the support provided to the legislators by special interests. But many restrictions have been imposed because legislators believed the restrictions would contribute to the "general welfare" (and, thereby, elicit support for their reelection). Four kinds of arguments have been made by legislators and supported by economists respecting trade restrictions that would promote the general welfare. These four arguments have been: (1) that of the mercantilists, (2) the "need" for a general revenue tariff, (3) the infant industry argument, and (4) the national defense argument. (There is also the change-the-terms-of-trade argument; but it has been too esoteric to have had any practical impact.)

Mercantilism for the Strength of the Nation

After 1400, nation states began to evolve out of European feudalism. The philosophers and political economists we now call "mercantilists" argued that the object of all policies, especially of foreign trade policy, was the strength of the nation. Mercantilism was concerned with "state making."

Under feudalism, observers perceived the economy as mostly static. Feudal kings lived on the revenues of their own estates and raised armies by invoking feudal obligations. Both of these circumstances changed as nations evolved.

First, a nation required a standing army and a navy that had to be paid in coin. Second, the national output was perceived as an essential of national strength *and* as a variable that had to be increased if the nation was to become stronger in war and in peace.

Foreign trade was seen as a source of tax revenue and as a means to increase domestic production. Mercantilists had no conception of comparative advantage or even of the advantages of capital accumulation. They did believe trade restrictions could strengthen their nation.

Before the nineteenth century, almost all European money was metal and traded at its intrinsic value. There were no exchange rates. A quarter ounce of gold had the same value no matter whose profile it bore. Kings, statesmen, writers — and merchants — were convinced their nation had too little money. They wanted more money to expand the domestic market, to raise output, to reduce unemployment, to raise profits, to strengthen the state. And they believed *pecunia nervus belli* (money provides the nerves of war); so they wanted more money to add to tax revenue — to strengthen the state.

But European nations had little precious ore to transform into money. They had not yet invented printed money. They determined to import metal money.

If a nation exported wool and imported timber of equal value, both wool and timber would soon be gone. From the mercantilists' perspective, neither nation would be better off. But if wool were exported and trade restrictions prevented import of any commodity, payment for the wool would arrive in the form of metallic money.

International trade was seen as a zero-sum game. A "favorable" balance of trade meant exported output (sure to be corrupted by moth and rust, or destroyed by mold and digestion) would be balanced by import of durable precious metal. The nation importing those metals would gain what the money exporter would lose.

Mercantilists argued that the national interest would be served by restrictions upon imports and by inducements to export. Therefore: tariffs on imports, bounties (subsidies) on exports, a requirement that goods be carried in the ships of either the importing or exporting nation, rules that colonies buy only from their mother country, and "staples" laws that colonial exports pass through the mother country. The result: a favorable balance on current account, precious metal imports, more output, and more revenue for the crown. Political leaders could believe all of this was in the national interest; and opposition, lacking for centuries any counter theory, was weak. The mercantilists' arguments were well known to America's founders.

The mercantilists were the economists of the sixteenth and seventeenth century. They advocated "mercantilism." Modern economists reject most of the mercantilistic analysis, but the mercantilists' fear of foreign goods persists and influences many modern minds. The moral of this story may be, the evil done by bad economists lives long after them. Young scholars should beware of all the "truths" credited by old economists — today.

The General Revenue Tariff

In the beginning was every government's need to tax. The tax most easily collected was a levy on merchants, and border crossings were the places where merchants were taxed most easily. Fiefdoms, cities, and provinces collected border taxes. Nations, as they evolved and grew, levied taxes at national borders.

Where the principal objective was revenue, this tax was a flat 7 percent (or 2 percent or 20 percent) on every item. Such a *general revenue tariff* has one special efficiency feature. It raises all prices by the same degree. It does not change relative prices among import goods. Therefore, it does not change resource allocation. When the American nation was forming, the conventional wisdom assumed a general revenue tariff would be in the public interest.

The Infant Industry Argument

The plight and promise of infant industries provide a third argument for trade restrictions in the public interest. This argument asserts that laborers, skilled workers, managers, and entrepreneurs are at a disadvantage in one country when they try to imitate a new technology already successfully in use in another country. Until they have accumulated some years of actual practice — of on-the-job training — the aspiring imitators will be inefficient in comparison with the experienced personnel of the technological pioneer. If factor ratios offer convincing evidence that in the long run the imitating nation would be likely to achieve comparative advantage in the new technology, trade restraints may make sense to protect an infant that might otherwise never mature. During much of America's first century, Europe pioneered new technology, and ambitious American entrepreneurs argued for trade restrictions, "in the public interest," to protect — meaning to permit higher prices for — their products. These restrictions can be in the public interest if they raise an infant to comparative advantage maturity and end protection in time to compensate for the costs protection imposes on the public.

As a practical matter, this argument has been discredited through extensive use by lobbyists doomed to remain comparative-*dis*advantaged producers forever. In any case, a genuine potentially comparative-advantage infant industry can obtain as much support from a subsidy as from a tariff of the same size. Lobbyists have rarely concluded that they could afford to pay enough to induce legislators to put a subsidy into the annual budget (the wool subsidy with which President Eisenhower and a Republican Congress rewarded their Rocky Mountain supporters in 1953 is an exception to that rule).

The National Defense Argument

In 1957, President Eisenhower introduced a Voluntary Oil Imports Program requesting American importers to reduce their imports of crude oil by ten percent below their average crude imports for 1954-56.[2] Importers were reluctant to volunteer; so in 1958, the federal government began to boycott all companies that failed to "comply in all respects with the Voluntary Oil Import Program."[3] In 1959, President Eisenhower, acting under authority legislated by Congress in 1955, ordered mandatory quotas on imports of crude oil.[4]

President Eisenhower justified the controls on the grounds of national security. A Defense Department spokesman said the quota was "necessary to maintain a healthy and vigorous domestic industry and specifically to encourage active exploration for further domestic oil reserves."[5] The national defense argument went on to assert that the quotas were needed so the domestic industry would be adequately large in the event that a wartime blockade cut off access to imports.

Critics charged that the quotas had been imposed solely to provide higher prices for domestic oil and for domestic coal, whose producers had been lobbying for a decade for protection.[6] In any event, the national defense argument, in this case, was weakened by the obvious flaw that every barrel of oil excluded by quota would result in one less barrel left in the ground in America in case of future war.

More generally, the national defense argument goes, "Without a tariff (or quota) my industry will wither. Then, if a war is declared, the nation will lack adequate domestic sources of this product." When the special-interest lobbyists make those assertions, legislators listen, and doubters risk charges of "unpatriotic" if they criticize.

But this argument has been soiled by extensive use by special-interest groups of doubtful essentiality for their nation's defense (as well as by the Eisenhower-Kennedy-Johnson-Nixon oil quotas of 1958-74 that led to greater-than-otherwise dependence on foreign oil in the 1980s).

For national defense, as for infant industries, a subsidy can accomplish the same protection a tariff or quota can provide. A special-interest group involved in national defense has a choice. It can go to the Secretary of Defense and ask for a portion of the annual military budget as a deserved subsidy. Or it can go to the legislature and ask for a tariff or quota. In practice, lobbyists rarely even attempt to convince the military that they are important enough to deserve a place in the budget. Exceptions to this are American shipyard and ship owners who continue to obtain annual subsidies from Congress (though not out of the Defense Department appropriation).

THE NONSENSE ARGUMENTS FOR PROTECTION

We know that when government restricts foreign trade, efficiency is cut and world output is cut. That conclusion, though obvious to us, is not — today as in the past — obvious to many intelligent and well-educated people.

Common sense, as Chapter 1 warned, often works in the wrong direction. Most Americans, when they think about it at all, are inclined to see cheap foreign labor as an imminent threat to the jobs of high-productivity, high-paid American workers. The aphorism often erroneously attributed to President Lincoln: "All I know is that if I buy from foreigners, I have their goods and they have my American money; but if I buy from an American, I have the goods, and we still have our money," continues to appeal to good old down-home common sense. An abundance of bumper stickers testify to the ubiquity of these views and fears — "Buy a foreign car, put an American out of work"; "Export goods not jobs"; and the most common of all, simply, "Buy American."

Anyone unfamiliar with such bumper graffiti and doubting these generalizations can easily check on the pervasiveness of the ideas they represent by asking a few friends:

            1.   Would it be fair or reasonable to have tariffs that just make up for the difference between American wage rates and foreign wage rates?

or   2.   (The "scientific tariff" proposal.) Would it be fair or reasonable to have a tariff on every product that just makes up for the difference between American costs of production and foreign costs of production for that product?

or   3.   Should American workers be protected against cheap foreign labor?

If you are curious, address these questions to some biology or political science major you know well.

"Keep American money at home." "Protect American workers from cheap foreign labor." These are among the most appealing of all misconceptions known to common sense. Throughout American history, they have been available to the special interests attempting to organize and obtain protection.

Students of economics may take upon themselves the obligation to explain the truth to misinformed individuals. Chapter 6 provided a basis for responding to the multitude who fear cheap foreign labor, but an economics student may be hard put to convince an engineer or a sociologist who has no idea of the meaning of comparative advantage.

To help people concerned about keeping our money at home, one can try to pierce the veil of money by stressing that only real output is useful to people. Or one can try *reductio ad absurdum* and suggest that if the nation should keep its money at home and be self sufficient then so also should the state or province, the city, the town, and the individual.

Beyond the tyranny of words, the scientific tariff can offer little logical force. If implemented, it would provide work for many accountants (and airlines) to determine *the* cost of production in the United States and *the* cost of production in Taiwan, Brazil, Switzerland, and Russia of every product. Finally, of course, if tariffs were adjusted to make all foreign prices equal to all corresponding domestic prices, international trade would end (convenience assuring only home purchases). Back to Chapter 3 to explain the unwisdom of that.

In recent decades a novel argument has been introduced, a complaint about *dependency* on foreigners. Most citizens of most cities spend much of every day of their lives consuming the products of distant fields and cities. These citizens are truly dependent on those distant cities and fields for their real incomes. Yet in recent years, local special interests have found sympathetic political ears for an argument that purchases from foreign cities and fields are reprehensible. One can respond to this argument by stressing alternatives. Protection reduces alternatives. Can a nation become more independent when its alternatives are reduced?

The answer, to be sure, is not a simple "Yes" or "No," and we will return to the subject in the next chapter. We do offer here the generalization that in most cases, increased protection increases dependence on special interest groups.

Businesspeople often use the argument "They don't follow free trade rules, so we can't." In valid commonsense language, that argument is equivalent to, "Those people are engaged in self-flagellation; therefore, we must do the same."

If one nation reduced protection unilaterally, comparative advantage specialization would increase in that nation and in its trading partners. The increase in GWP would be greater if the partners would also reduce protection. But we gain by moving toward freer trade whether others follow or not.

The concept of reciprocal trade agreements to cut tariffs was raised to an almost mystical position by President Franklin Roosevelt's Secretary of State, Cordell Hull (more of this in Chapter 12). Hull went so far as to assert that that program was a principal means to prevent war. Those agreements have been a principal tool for reducing tariffs, but the fact remains, we gain when we lower protection no matter whether "they" follow or not.

The refusal of others to "play the rules" often goes further. The British government subsidizes Scottish shipbuilding, the French government subsidizes French steel production. The result is that foreign comparative-disadvantage producers achieve competitive advantage over domestic comparative-advantage producers. The latter will object to this scheme, but the people who can benefit from such largesse can argue against protection in such cases. Has not everyone the right to give (and so deter the recipient from purchasing)? Has not everyone the right to receive a gift? In these cases, subsidizing governments tax away from their citizens and offer giveaways (discounted prices) to foreigners who will accept the gifts. Should the governments of the gift recipients object (they can compensate producers displaced by the gifts)?

PROFESSOR FRIEDMAN'S PROPOSAL

To deter the special interests and their representatives in the United States, economist Milton Friedman has proposed a constitutional amendment providing that

Congress shall not lay any imposts or duties on imports or exports, except what may be absolutely necessary for executing its inspection laws.

This is the same language used in Section 10, Article I, of the Constitution to prohibit the imposition of tariffs by the States. The present law is largely responsible for the economic growth of the United States since 1789.

If passed, the proposed amendment (one might anticipate inclusion of a provision "or absolutely necessary to the national defense"), would commit the United States unilaterally to free trade. The general public would gain. A number of special-interests would lose. So this is only an academic curiosity. The general welfare will continue to give way to special-interests' trade restrictions.

Some home-spun wisdom will continue to support the general welfare, e.g., "We must buy from them if we are to sell to them." "Take advantage of foreign competition to keep prices down." Good theory and good common sense — but too long for bumper stickers and too complicated to convince all Congressmen and Congresswomen.

CUSTOMS UNION

Nations may realize that specialization and free trade bring gains to participants, but may not wish, for political or cultural reasons, to abolish tariffs, quotas and other trade barriers vis-a-vis the rest of the world. Nations in close geographic proximity sharing similar historical and cultural backgrounds, however, may identify themselves with one another strongly enough to be persuaded to form a group with few or no internal trade restrictions. Such is the beginning of economic integration among nations. This may be less than ideal, but less protection is better than more. Four stages or degrees of economic integration may be identified.

STAGES OF ECONOMIC INTEGRATION

A *free trade area* exists when a group of countries abolishes tariffs and quotas among them, but each member nation maintains its own restrictive measures on trade with outside nations. The European Free Trade Association (EFTA) consists of seven countries — Austria, Norway, Portugal, Sweden, Switzerland, Finland, and Iceland.

A *customs union* differs from a free trade area in that it has, in addition to free trade among members, a common external tariff against third countries. When a customs union also allows free movement of labor and capital within the community, it is a *common market*. The European Economic Community (EEC), popularly known as the European Common Market, is the best known example of a common market. Established by the Treaty of Rome in 1957, the EEC originally consisted of six nations — West Germany, France, Italy, Belgium, Luxembourg, and the Netherlands. In 1973, Denmark and the United Kingdom joined. In 1978, the EEC committed itself to accept the membership of Greece, Portugal, and Spain. In March 1979, the European Monetary System (EMS, see Chapter 17) came into existence without the membership of the United Kingdom. In June 1979, the first Community-wide direct election to the European Parliament was held. The EEC, thus, is moving steadily toward the ultimate state of economic integration — the *economic union*. In an economic union, economic institutions and policies are united under a single economic and, very likely, political authority. The United States is a good example of an economic *and* political union.

THE ECONOMIC EFFECTS OF A CUSTOMS UNION

Customs union theory attempts to explain the effects of economic integration. The basic question is this: When nations abolish tariffs among themselves and establish a common external tariff, what changes in trade and welfare occur? We know free trade improves participants' economic welfare. But is the formation of a customs union a move toward freer trade, or away from free trade? What can economic theory tell us about the benefits and costs of economic integration?

Suppose both South Korea and Taiwan are producing bicycles, but comparative advantage in bicycle manufacturing rests with Taiwan. The South Korean bicycle industry, therefore, can exist only under the protection of a tariff against imports. Suppose now that the two nations form a customs union. Following the dictate of the law of comparative advantage, Taiwan becomes the sole supplier of bicycles, and Made-in-Taiwan bikes are exported to Korea without duties. Korean resources formerly tied up in its relatively inefficient bicycle industry are reallocated to more efficient uses, say, shipbuilding. The elimination of internal tariffs (between Korea and Taiwan) has stimulated *new* trade hitherto nonexistent. Production of bicycles has been shifted from the high-cost Korean producers to the low-cost Taiwanese manufacturers. The increase in trade brings a higher level of welfare to both nations. This gain in welfare arising from the formation of a customs union (or a free trade area or a common market) is called the "trade creation" effect of economic integration.

Now, suppose that prior to formation of the customs union, Taiwan had no shipbuilding industry and was importing ships, with no tariffs, from low-cost producers in Japan. South Korea had a shipbuilding industry, but its comparative advantage was not as great as that enjoyed by Japan; so the Korean industry could exist only under a highly protective tariff. Now, Taiwan and South Korea form a customs union and impose a common external tariff on ships high enough to make Japanese ships more expensive than Korean ships inside the union. Taiwan must now shift its source of supply of ships from the lower-cost Japanese shipbuilders to the higher-cost Korean shipbuilders. There is obviously a loss in economic welfare, which is called the "trade diversion" effect of economic integration.

Trade creation raises world welfare by shifting production from higher-cost producers to lower-cost producers inside the union. Trade diversion, conversely, lowers world welfare by shifting production from lower-cost producers outside the union to higher-cost producers inside the union. The net effect of a particular economic integration project depends on how large these two opposing effects are. In general, the net trade creation will be greater (1) the lower the common external tariff, (2) the larger the customs union in relation to the outside world, and (3) the higher the pre-union duties of the individual member nations.

APPENDIX 10A: CONSUMERS' SURPLUS AND PRODUCERS' SURPLUS

Most of us pay less for each purchase than we would be willing to pay rather than do without. Also, most of us are paid more for our work than we require to be persuaded to continue in the same job. The difference between what we pay for a purchase and the amount we would pay rather than do without is our *consumers' surplus* on that unit. The difference between what we are paid for our work and the minimum we require to remain at work is our *producers' surplus*. These surpluses are easily seen in standard supply and demand sketches.

In Figure 10A-1, we present a simple market demand curve, AD, for some product. Recall that a demand curve is the horizontal summation of the marginal utility curves of all consumers of this product.

Suppose the equilibrium price is OP = QB, and OQ of the product is bought. What is OQ worth to its buyers? OQ is worth OQBA, the dollar value of the total utilities derived by consumers from OQ of the product. Yet, when consumers buy OQ, they pay only OQBP. The difference, the triangle PBA, represents consumers' surplus, the excess of total value over what is paid for the quantity purchased. The price, OP, is determined by the marginal utility, QB, of the marginal consumer for whom price just equals marginal utility. But on all others among OQ units purchased, marginal utility, indicated by the height of the demand curve (marginal utility curve), AD, is higher than the price paid, which is OP for every unit. The sum total of the excess of marginal utility over price paid on all purchased units is the consumers' surplus. Naturally, consumers' surplus is greater the lower the market price, other things being equal.

Next, producers' surplus, a concept analogous to consumers' surplus. In Figure 10A-2, we present a simple market supply curve, AS, for some product. (The concept may be best grasped if the product envisioned is a service, such as haircuts.) Recall that a supply curve is the

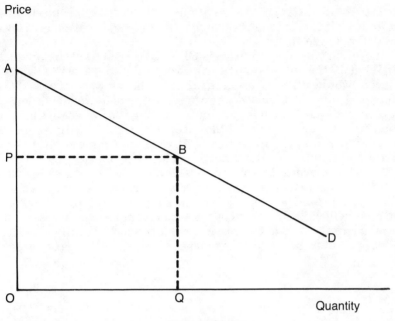

Figure 10A-1
Consumers' Surplus

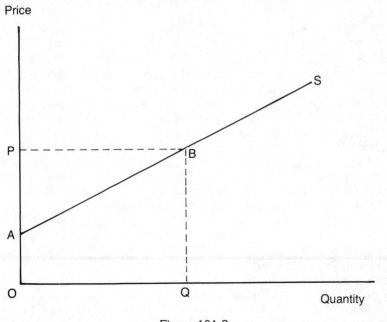

Figure 10A-2
Producers' Surplus

horizontal summation of the marginal cost curves of all producers of this product (if this is long run supply, then the summation is of lowest points on average cost curves).

Suppose the equilibrium price is OP = QB, and OQ of the product is sold. What is the total opportunity cost of OQ to society? OQ, if not produced, would release resources that would be worth OQBA, their total opportunity cost if used elsewhere. Yet, when producers sell OQ, they receive OQBP which is distributed among the owners of the inputs needed to produce OQ. The difference, the triangle ABP, represents producers' surplus, the excess of total revenue over the total the resources could obtain in their next best uses. The price, OP, is determined by the marginal cost, QB, of the marginal producer for whom price just equals marginal cost. But on all other units purchased, marginal cost, indicated by the height of the supply curve, AS, is lower than price paid, which is OP for every unit. The sum total of excess of price over opportunity cost is the producers' surplus. Naturally, producers' surplus is greater the higher the market price, other things being equal.

APPENDIX 10B: THE OPTIMAL TARIFF

There may be an *optimal tariff* in the very best interests of a nation's citizens. The basic idea goes like this: If the foreign supply curve to the importing nation is upward sloping (as in Figure 10-2), the importing nation, by imposing a tariff duty, can force the producers in the exporting nation to accept a price lower than the pre-tariff price. Since the importing nation can acquire the product at a lower price, there is a "gain" or "saving" accruing to that nation. If such a gain exceeds the deadweight loss caused by the tariff, then the tariff brings a net increase in the welfare to the importing nation's citizens. A tariff rate that maximizes such a net gain is the optimal tariff.

Figure 10B-1 shows the logic underlying the optimal tariff. The importing nation, by the assumption of an upward sloping import supply curve, is a monopsonist. By importing less, it reduces the per-unit price paid for units it does import.

With free trade, equilibrium price is $2; quantity M_1M_2 is imported. A 50¢ per unit tariff changes aggregate supply from S_{d+m} to S'_{d+m}. The new domestic price is $2.20, while the price to the exporting nation is cut to $1.70. Imports are cut to M_3M_4. Thus, this nation "saves" 30¢

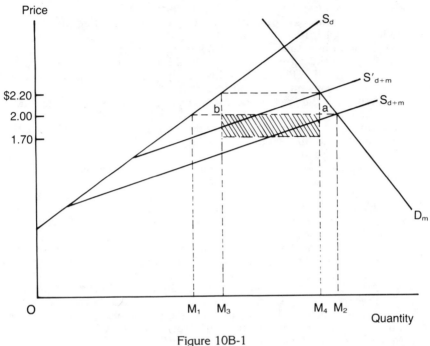

Figure 10B-1
The Optimal Tariff

per imported unit. It "gains" the shaded rectangle (= 30¢ times M_3M_4 units) on the imports, while suffering the deadweight loss of consumers' surplus (the little triangle labeled "a") and of efficiency (the little triangle labeled "b"). Some tariff rate will maximize the net of the savings rectangle of lower price and the two triangles of lost efficiency and consumers' surplus.

The concept of optimum tariff has fascinated many academics and some government officials. But it works only if the victim nations do not retaliate. After an optimum tariff is imposed by one nation, its trading partners may identify an optimum tariff they can then impose. The prospect of successive rounds of retaliation eventually leading to complete cessation of world trade makes the concept of optimum tariff an interesting but impractical academic exercise at best.

STUDY QUESTIONS

1. Refer to Figure 10-1.
    (a) Explain how the S'_{d+m} line, Wkb', is constructed.
    (b) Under free trade, the equilibrium price is OP. Identify the comparative advantage or disadvantage of the following group of producers:
        (I)   Producers of quantity OX_1 in nation X
        (II) Producers of quantity X_1X_2 in nation X

(III) Producers of quantity OM_1 in nation M

(IV) Producers of quantity in excess of OM_1 in nation M

2. Refer to Figure 10-2.
    (a) Explain how the S'_{d+m} line, Wk'e, is constructed.
    (b) Explain the significance of the bold broken line $ecP_xP_mc'e'$.
    (c) Explain the effect of the 50-cent duty on the importing nation's output, consumption, and imports.
    (d) Why does the price in the importing nation not rise by the amount of the duty?
    (e) Under what circumstances would the price in the importing nation rise by the full amount of the duty?

3. Refer to Figure 10-3.
    (a) Explain how the new supply curve, S'_{d+m}, is constructed.
    (b) When domestic producers increased output from OQ_1 to OQ_3, their total revenue increased by the inverted L-shaped area $Q_1Q_3k'P'Pk$. How much of this was the increase in the cost of production? How much, consequently, was the increase in the producers' surplus (or their net revenue)?
    (c) How much of the increase in the producers' cost in 3(b) above was justified from the allocative-efficiency point of view? How much stood for an unnecessary and wasteful use of resources?
    (d) After the tariff was imposed, the consumers' surplus was reduced by the area $Pee'P'$. How much of this loss was transferred to other sectors of the economy? How much was the total deadweight loss to society?

4. Compare and contrast the effects of a tariff and a quota.

5. Compare and contrast the effects of a tariff and a subsidy.

6. Suppose that components of a widget cost $40 in nation Alpha and are imported, at the same price, by the widget assemblers in nation Beta. (Ignore transportation costs.) A widget can be assembled in Alpha at the value-added cost of $10 per unit, whereas it costs more in Beta.
    (a) If the government of Beta imposes a 10-percent tariff on widget imports, what effective rate of protection would the widget assemblers in Beta enjoy?
    (b) What would be the effective rate of protection if the nominal rate on widgets is 10 percent but the cost of widget components, both in Alpha and Beta, is $60?

7. Critically evaluate the arguments that say that tariffs are necessary in order to:
    (a) make up the difference between American production costs and foreign production costs; and
    (b) make up the difference between American wage rates and foreign wage rates.

8. Critically evaluate the argument that imports should be restricted to save American jobs.

9. Does the infant industry argument for protection make sense in each of the following cases? What criteria must be used in evaluating the applicability of this argument?
    (a) the steel industry in the United States
    (b) the automobile industry in South Korea
    (c) the cotton textile industry in India
    (d) the computer industry in Japan
    (e) the aircraft industry in Guatemala
    (f) the bicycle industry in Kenya?

10. Paraphrasing Lance E. Davis and Douglass C. North, the text argues that comparative disadvantage producers make marginal-benefit-marginal-cost comparisons when deciding which candidates to support and what support to give. What is the nature of the costs and what is the nature of the benefits involved in such a comparison?

Alternatively, sketch the marginal cost and the marginal benefit curves of comparative disadvantage producers involved in such a comparison. Then tell what each of the curves measures and explain the shape you have given each curve.

11. Again, paraphrasing Davis and North, the text argues that legislators make marginal-benefit-marginal-cost comparisons when deciding whether or not to arrange for protection for comparative disadvantage producers. What is the nature of the costs and what is the nature of the benefits involved in such a comparison?

ENDNOTES

1. Lance E. Davis and Douglass C. North, *Institutional Change and American Economic Growth* (New York: Cambridge University Press, 1971), pp. 30-35, 178-182, and 258.
2. William H. Peterson, *The Question of Governmental Oil Import Restrictions* (Washington: The American Enterprise Association, 1959), pp. 20-24.
3. *Ibid.*, p. 24.
4. *Ibid.*, pp. 19 and 30.
5. Earl B. Smith, Defense Department Director for Transportation and Petroleum Policy, quoted in *ibid.*, p. 54.
6. This is Peterson's conclusion, *ibid.*

11

More about Special Interests with Market Power

Much of what we have written assumes that the wealth and the incomes of nations will be greater the better the information available to producers and consumers, the greater the freedom of entry for new producers, the more mobile the resources within each country, and the freer trade between countries. Real incomes rise when resources are used more efficiently and when innovations raise the output-to-input ratio. International trade raises the wealth and the incomes of nations by expanding the market area of every traded product in a way that increases the pressure on each producer to be efficient and that expands the opportunities for innovators to raise the output-to-input ratio.

The world's citizens, *as a group,* will gain from freer trade. As our last chapter described, however, special interest groups use a variety of means to co-opt government power to obtain extra income and security for themselves. Similarly, in international trade, special interest groups often develop to obtain and apply international market power to seize extra income for themselves at the expense of most other people. In this chapter we begin our study of international market power with an examination of one such international special interest group — the Organization of Petroleum Exporting Countries (OPEC). We will then study totally different manifestations of international market power — dumping and price discrimination.

EXPORT CARTELS IN GENERAL, OPEC IN PARTICULAR

A *cartel* is a form of collusion among oligopolistic producers through which the benefits of a monopoly are sought by means of such market-restrictive measures as fixing prices, limiting output, and allocating markets. An *international export cartel* exists when producers of the same industry located in different countries, or the governments of those countries, agree to limit the export supply. The effect of a successful cartel — whether domestic or international — is to increase joint profits above the competitive level by limiting output and raising the price above the competitive level.

The most successful export cartel of all time is that of the Organization of Petroleum Exporting Countries. Organized originally in 1960 by five petroleum exporting nations (Iran, Iraq, Kuwait, Saudi Arabia, and Venezuela), the organization remained unsuccessful in raising the price of crude oil throughout the 1960s. But, in 1970 and 1971, a new OPEC member, Libya, challenged the oil producing firms and importing nations. Both those firms and their governments waffled. When Egypt attacked Israel in October 1973, the Arab OPEC nations agreed to use oil as a weapon against Israel and Israel's supporters. Successful in that effort, the OPEC nations then agreed to act henceforward as an export cartel. In this section we will first look at the general theory of cartel behavior. Then we will consider the particular behavior of OPEC.

THEORY OF THE CARTEL

Before studying the behavior of the OPEC cartel, let us briefly review the microeconomic theory of the cartel.

A Competitive Industry Converted into a Monopoly

All the needed considerations appear in Figure 11-1, which portrays the output market circumstances of product X. Demand for X is expressed by the line FG, which also is the marginal utility curve. The area under this marginal utility curve represents total utility to buyers. The supply curve of product X is depicted by the line ES, which is the sum of the individual firms' marginal cost curves. In perfectly competitive equilibrium, price is OC, output is OA, total revenue is OABC, total utility from OA output is OABF, and consumers' surplus is CBF. Producers' surplus is shown by the area EBC. (See Appendix 10A to review the concepts of consumers' surplus and producers' surplus.)

Now assume that in the circumstances of Figure 11-1 either one firm buys all the others to form a monopoly or all the firms in the industry agree to act as a cartel. The cartel-monopoly maximizes its profits by producing at the output level OK at which its marginal cost equals its marginal revenue. The cartel sells quantity OK at price ON = KL. Consumers' surplus *after cartelization* is NLF. Cartelization, therefore, reduces consumers' surplus by CBLN. Of this loss of consumers' surplus of CBLN, the rectangular area CULN is transferred from the consumers to the producers, leaving UBL as a deadweight loss of consumers'

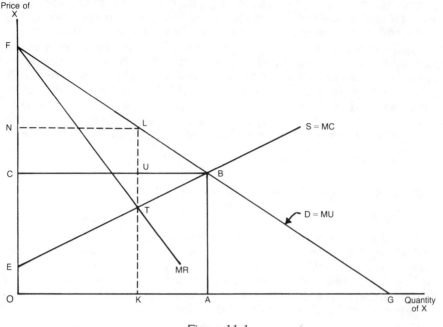

Figure 11-1

A Competitive Industry Converted into A Monopoly-Cartel

surplus. Producers' surplus is reduced by TBU, but is also increased by CULN. Producers, therefore, are made better off by the cartelization. The total deadweight loss to society is represented by the area TBL.

The cartel participants enjoy larger profits (*maximum* profits under the conditions of Figure 11-1) selling quantity OK at price ON than selling quantity OA at price OC. Such extra profits are of course an incentive for new firms to enter the market. The cartel's members, therefore, wish to keep outsiders from entering the market. In addition, the cartel's members must worry, each against the others, about cheating. For the cartel to be effective, the members must, in the first place, agree on the extent to which each member will cut production. Each participant naturally wants to cut less while urging others to cut more. Once agreement is reached on the allocation of quantity cuts, the serpent of temptation instantly appears.

After the production cutback, each firm has excess capacity. In the Figure 11-1 example, each can sell its quota for ON per unit. By lowering its price just a little below ON, one "cheater" could sell all the potential output of its excess capacity. But any sale beyond the agreed production limit is cheating. So, for every cartel member, two questions present themselves: "Can I detect any cheating by a perfidious partner?" and "Can I attain bliss by cheating undetected?"

In sum, cartels are dandy for participants though they always involve three problems: How are production cutbacks to be divided among the membership? How is entry by outsiders to be prevented? How is cheating by insiders to be prevented? Together, these problems are so redoubtable that few cartels are formed, and few endure long. Those that have endured have almost always been protected by government.

On the other hand, what can the buyers of X do to defend themselves against a cartel of X producers? Unfortunately for them, the answer is, "not much," *if* the cartel can prevent cheating and *if* it can prevent X production by outsiders. If the buyers could organize themselves into a monopsony, they could resist, but multiple buyers have, in the past, been unable to do this. Despite the depredations of OPEC in recent years, the oil-importing nations have proved singularly ineffective in this respect.

Demand and Supply Responses to an Export Cartel

An ordinary monopolist or cartel is concerned with the fall in quantity demanded that results when the monopolist-cartel reduces output in order to raise price. An export cartel shares that concern. In addition, if it does not include producers in the importing nations, it will have a second concern affecting sales. As it reduces quantity to raise price, the import-competing producers of the importing nations will raise their output.

Figure 11-2 represents such a situation, one rather like that of OPEC. To simplify, assume the exporting nations consume none of their out-

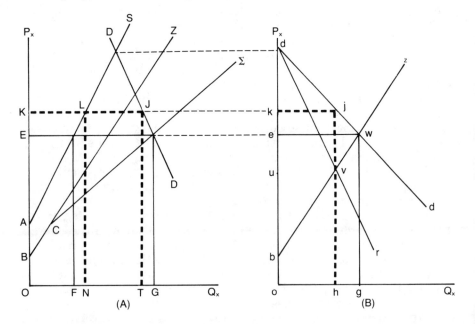

Figure 11-2
Demand and Supply Responses to An Export Cartel

put. However, the importing nations do contain domestic producers providing part of what they use.

Figure 11-2A depicts the circumstances of the importing nations. With free trade, domestic supply is AS. Foreign (or imported) supply is BZ. Total supply is BCΣ, obtained in the sketch by the horizontal summation of AS and BZ. Demand is DD. In equilibrium, price is OE, consumption is OG, domestic production is OF, imports are FG.

Figure 11-2B presents the circumstances of the exporting nations. Domestic supply (or marginal cost) is bz. Demand, dd — and it is all foreign demand — is the horizontal difference between the importing nations' domestic demand, DD, and domestic supply, AS. In free-trade equilibrium, price is oe, and the quantity exported-imported is og (the OE and FG of Figure 11-2A).

Notice the difference in elasticity between DD and dd. For example, if in Figure 11-2A of the importing nations, price is raised from OE to OK, quantity demanded falls by TG. In contrast, in Figure 11-2B of the exporting nations, when price is raised from oe to ok (where ek = EK), quantity demanded falls by hg which is equal to TG plus FN. When the exporting nations raise the price, they lose sales both because the importing nations' buyers buy less *and* because the importing nations' producers produce more. Therefore, at any particular price, demand elasticity along dd is much greater than is demand elasticity along DD.

If all the producers of X were to join a cartel, they would be able to take advantage of DD. If only the exporters of X form a cartel, they will be limited to the much greater elasticity of dd so will be much more constrained in their incentive to raise the price. They will, of course, wish that they did not have to contend with the supply response of the import-competing producers when the export cartel raises prices.

If the export producers do form a cartel and act to maximize profits, they will reduce exports to oh in order to raise price to ok. They will maximize profit by equating their marginal revenue, dr, and their marginal cost, bz. In the importing nations, imports will be reduced to LJ = NT = oh; price will rise to OK; consumption will fall to OT, and domestic production will rise from OF to ON. The importing nations' consumers may complain; but, looking on their bright side, they would be much worse off if their domestic producers had not raised production by FN.

Economic Rent and Monopoly Profits

The supply curve (or the marginal cost curve), bz, in Figure 11-2B represents the opportunity cost of producing various quantities of crude oil in the oil-exporting nations. Suppose the supply curve slopes upward to the right *solely* because of the different degrees of efficiency or "fertility" of oil fields in the exporting nations. Some units of crude oil are supplied at prices near ob from the richest (or the most efficient or "fertile") oil fields, while other units are supplied only at higher prices from less efficient fields. At the competitive equilibrium price, oe, og barrels of crude oil are supplied, but only the last barrel sold has production costs of gw = oe. All the other barrels of crude supplied have production costs lower than oe. This excess of the production cost of the marginal unit over the production cost of other units is called *economic rent.*

Recall, briefly, David Ricardo's identification of this concept in 1817 following his effort to explain the flow of revenue to English landowners like himself. He concluded that economic rent appears when demand for a product induces production from two sources between which there is a cost difference deriving from some advantage given to the one source by nature. In Ricardo's kind of example, two grades of land exist. On the best land, when $100 is spent on labor, tools, seed, and fertilizer, 100 bushels of corn are harvested. At $1 a bushel, farm firms can earn a normal profit on this land. On the inferior land, when $100 is spent on inputs, only 80 bushels of corn are harvested. This land will be used only if the price of corn rises to $1.25 a bushel.

If demand is sufficient, both grades of land will be used. All corn will sell for the same $1.25 a bushel. Owners of the inferior land will receive no economic rent; their revenues will just cover costs. But firms that grow corn on the superior land will have 25¢ per bushel left over after paying all costs. If they own the land, they keep the 25¢. If someone else owns the superior land, the owner will oblige the operating firm to pay the 25¢-per-bushel economic rent to the owner — or go and work on the inferior land where the firm would be no better off than if it stayed and paid.

Ricardo's example contrasted agricultural lands of unequal fertility. But the principle of economic rent applies equally well to oil deposits of unequal productivity. (Figure 11-2B represents not just two grades of oil land but great diversity of oil lands with costs ranging from a low of ob per barrel to hv, gw, and above.) If the least "fertile" oil land requires an input cost of oe per barrel in a case like that of Figure 11-2B, all firms operating on more fertile oil land will have production costs below oe per barrel. Then the owners of the more fertile oil land will, if they are knowledgeable, be able to claim the difference between production costs (including a normal profit) and the price, oe.

In the pre-cartel conditions of Figure 11-2B, the oil-exporting nations, as factor owners, should have enjoyed economic rent of bwe on og of crude oil exported. (This is the same as the exporting nations' producers' surplus. Economic rent and producers' surplus are equal if, and only if, (1) producers and factor owners are identical, and (2) all cost differences between different units of the product supplied are due to differences in the qualities of the resources used.)

After the cartel is formed and the quantity of output is reduced to oh, the price of the last barrel supplied is raised to hj = ok, but its production cost is only hv. Because the production cost of the most expensive barrel (from the least fertile oil land in use) is down to hv, economic rent is down to bvu. Because monopoly behavior has raised price to ok = hj, price exceeds marginal production cost by vj. The cartel, therefore, obtains a monopoly profit of uvjk.[1]

The grievance of the OPEC nations prior to the 1960s was that, with output the equivalent of og in Figure 11-2, they did not collect all the economic rent, bwe. By playing one oil-producing nation's government off against another, the skilled negotiators of oil-producing firms obtained concession agreements that left the firms (mostly Anglo-American) with part of the economic rent even after all royalties and taxes were paid.

The grievance of the oil-importing nations after 1973 is that OPEC's members are now receiving not only the economic rent accruing on their oil resources but also excess profits resulting from their monopolistic pricing and production strategies.

Importers' Countermeasures

Can the importing nations strike back at an export cartel to neutralize the effects of its monopoly pricing? In contrast with the helpless consumers of a domestic cartel's product, importing consumers can strike back at an export cartel. More precisely, they can strike back if their governments have political courage and are able to coordinate with the governments of other victimized nations.

One possible response is a tariff. Consider the possibilities of the case portrayed in Figure 11-2. Suppose the importing governments, in unison, impose a tariff on the imported crude oil. The initial consequence of the tariff would be for the price to rise above OK = ok and the quantity imported to fall below LJ = NT = oh. The final outcome, however, depends on what the exporting cartel does with its quantity supplied.

As the price rises in the importing nations, the imported quantity, LJ, falls, causing an identical decrease in the exported quantity, kj. If the export cartel has committed itself to the perfectly inelastic supply, hj, then the cartel must lower its *export* price below ok = OK in order to sell all of its produced quantity, oh. As a matter of fact, in order to sell all of oh, the *import* price in Figure 11-2A must remain at OK. This means that the cartel's export price must be lower than the consuming nations' import price by the exact amount of the tariff. In other words, the incidence of the tariff would be borne entirely by the exporters, and the importing nations' governments would recover, as tariff revenues, some of the monopolistic profits of the export cartel. In fact, if the tariff rate were high enough, uk in the Figure 11-2 example, the importing nations could collect all of the cartel's monopoly profits.

If, on the other hand, the export cartel chooses to counter the import tariff by reducing its export quantity below oh, the import price would rise above OK = ok. The extent to which the exporters would want to cut back would depend upon the elasticities, in the Figure 11-2 example, of dd and of bz — *and* on the ability of the cartel members to agree as to which among them would bear what portion of the cutbacks. That agreement might be very difficult to obtain if the importers imposed a tariff large enough to take away most of the monopoly profit. Each producer would be eager to have others cut back while it expanded output.

As an alternative response, importing governments could prohibit all imports of the cartel's product, X, except by persons or firms with import "entitlements" purchased at a monthly auction. (These import entitlements should not be confused with the "entitlements to buy cheap U.S. oil" in effect in the U.S. since 1974 and discussed below.) The importing governments could divide the cartel's export total (oh in Figure 11-2B) into "entitlements," each of 10,000X units per month. These entitlements could be sold in a monthly sealed-bid auction requiring a certified check but no identification from the bidders. The importing nations could increase pressure on the cartel by restricting import entitlements to *less* than quantity oh.

The cartel might officially boycott the auction. But its members would have no export sales at all unless they submitted winning — secret — bids. To keep out the producers of output hg in Figure 11-2B, the bidders would have to offer ku per unit. The importing governments might, therefore, hope to collect the whole monopoly-profit area, uvjk, through the auction.

Confronted by tariff or auction, the cartel might threaten to cut exports to zero. The importers would face the loss of imports. The cartel would face loss of revenue. In such a confrontation, who would blink first? Perhaps the one with least political courage.

Given either the tariff or the auction and if unable to accept production cutbacks, the cartel members would be reduced to receipts of ou per unit. Since free markets would bring them oe per unit on a larger output, the cartel members might quickly capitulate and agree to abandon their quantity restriction in exchange for an end to the tariff (or entitlements system).

If an import duty or an auction would benefit the importing nations, why has neither been used against OPEC? We can think of several reasons. If OPEC did respond with production cutbacks, oil prices would rise. Higher oil prices may be feared in the importing nations as inflationary, and they might be politically damaging to those governments. Some importing nations may judge themselves to be unable to risk a sharp reduction in oil imports. We must remember that importing nations differ greatly in their capacity to produce oil domestically and in their access to alternative energy sources. Therefore, vulnerability to import cutoffs differs greatly from country to country. This difference in vulnerability makes it difficult for all the importing nations to agree on a concerted action against the export cartel. In the absence of such a concerted action, the cartel can play one importing nation against another, threatening some with the prospect of sharply higher prices and intimidating others with threats of supply cutoffs. Perhaps what is lacking the most is political wisdom and courage on the part of the importing nations' governments.[2] (See the appendix to this chapter for descriptions of two importer countermeasures that are self-defeating.)

THE ORGANIZATION OF OIL EXPORTING COUNTRIES

This section examines the historical, economic, and institutional aspects of OPEC in its twenty-year development since its formation in 1960. We will also present a few simple models of OPEC's pricing behavior.

HISTORICAL AND ECONOMIC BACKGROUND

After World War II, the demand for all types of energy sources grew rapidly, largely because of the remarkable growth of industrial output of Europe, Japan, and the United States. For the quarter of a century, 1945-70, the world's income elasticity of demand for energy was about one. Each one percent increase in world income brought a one percent increase in energy use at constant prices. Then, because of technological changes and new discoveries of reserves that lowered oil prices, and because of the ease with which oil substituted for coal, petroleum use grew even more rapidly than did the use of other energy sources. Between 1959 and 1974, world consumption of petroleum tripled. This increase represented an annual growth rate of slightly less than 8 percent per year.

So the increase in petroleum use derived partly from growth of demand and partly from the even greater growth of supply that brought the reductions in petroleum prices:

> Between 1947 and early 1970, the "real" or constant-dollar crude oil price at the Persian Gulf decreased by approximately 65 percent. The multi-national companies deserve neither credit nor blame. They competed only as much as the market structure compelled them to, but it compelled a good deal. During these years, billions of dollars flowed into the world [petroleum] industry; rather than a shortage of investment, there was a chronic potential surplus of oil.[3]

The rapid growth of the crude-oil supply and the decline in the price of crude oil were largely the consequences of expanded investment in and output from the Persian Gulf oil fields. This shift to reliance on Middle Eastern oil was caused by the markedly lower cost of discovering oil there, as compared with the other regions of the world, especially North America. In the two decades before 1973, the Middle East's share of the world's total proved reserves increased from 52 percent to 61 percent, while that of North America fell from 30 percent to 9 percent. In the 1970s, moreover, North America's proved reserves declined in absolute terms.[4]

In 1955, the United States produced 43 percent of the world's total output of crude oil, followed by Venezuela which accounted for 15 percent. By the 1970s, the primary source of the world's oil supply had shifted to the Middle East and North Africa. While the United States produced only 19 percent of the world total in 1972, the combined output of the seven Middle Eastern and North African nations (Saudi Arabia, Iran, Kuwait, Libya, Iraq, the United Arab Emirates, and Algeria) amounted to 39 percent. The Soviet Union produced 16 percent, and Venezuela supplied 6 percent.[5]

Governments and Oil Companies

As the center of the world's oil production shifted to the Middle East, the handful of oil-producing nations in this region gradually acquired *potential* monopoly power in the world oil market. To see why this potential power had not become actual monopoly power until the OPEC revolution of 1973, we must first examine the institutional setup of the world petroleum industry.

Before the formation of OPEC in 1960, the world petroleum market outside the United States was dominated by several large multinational oil companies — the so-called *majors* — that had operated in the Middle East before World War II. The eight largest international oil firms include the so-called "seven sisters" — Exxon, Mobil, Standard Oil of California (SoCal), Texaco, Gulf, Royal Dutch/Shell, and British Petroleum (BP) — and the Compagnie Française des Pétroles (CFP).

For years the Middle Eastern crude-oil activities were tightly controlled by the majors. Only they had the organizational, technological, and financial resources needed to prospect for, produce, refine, and market oil and oil products. Neither the host governments nor other lesser firms — known as the *independents* — had the capacities to do all of the highly complex and vertically integrated activities engaged in by the majors. The local governments merely collected royalties and taxes from the majors, while the independents limited their business largely to refining the oil purchased from the majors and distributing it downstream.

In 1951, the majors established a system of "posted prices" (or "tax reference prices") for crude oil, which were used to calculate the royalties and taxes paid to the local governments. Both the royalty and tax rates were negotiable between the host governments and the oil companies. Both governments and firms expected posted prices would be realized prices. But new discoveries of oil and entries of new firms resulted in competitive pressures that forced realized prices below posted prices after 1951. Royalties and taxes, however, continued to be based on the posted prices. Therefore, the reduction in realized price raised the exporting nations' share of total oil revenue. Thus, the oil-exporting nations gained an increasing share of their petroleum's economic rent during the 1950s and 1960s. (The system of posted prices was abolished in December 1974.)

Table 11-1 shows the computation of the total "government take" under the old posted-price system that had existed until December

TABLE 11-1   COMPUTATION OF PER BARREL GOVERNMENT REVENUE,
SAUDI ARABIAN LIGHT CRUDE, 1973 AND 1974
(U.S. dollars per barrel)

	10/1/73	1/1/74
1. Posted price	3.011	11.651
2. Royalty [12.5 percent of (1)]	0.376	1.456
3. Production cost	0.100	0.100
4. Profit for tax purposes = (1) − (2 + 3)	2.535	10.095
5. Tax [55 percent of (4)]	1.394	5.552
6. Government revenue = (2) + (5)	1.770	7.008

Source: Dankwart A. Rustow, and John F. Mugno, *OPEC: Success and Prospects* (New York: New York University Press, 1976), p. 132.

1974. Royalty was expressed as a percent of the posted price. Royalty and production costs were subtracted from the posted price to arrive at per barrel profit, on which a percentage of income tax was levied by the host government. The government's revenue take was the sum of royalties and taxes.

Table 11-1 reveals that per barrel revenue to the Saudi Arabian government as a percent of the posted price was 59 percent in October 1973 and 60 percent in January 1974. The actual government take, however, was larger than these figures suggest because of the *participation agreements*. Under these agreements, the government received a portion of the crude oil output, which was sold by the government to outsiders or back to the oil companies at the negotiated *"buy back price"* which was somewhat lower than the posted price. When these factors were considered, per barrel government take at the end of 1974 exceeded 90 percent of the posted price. (Incidentally, note the extremely low production cost of 10 cents per barrel.)

The Formation of OPEC

Prospecting for and producing oil involves highly complex technology and a great deal of organizational and financial resources. The Middle Eastern countries in the 1950s and early 1960s were not equipped to engage in crude-oil activities themselves. They had, therefore, few alternatives but to rely on the expertise of the major oil companies. Attempts to collect a larger share of their oil resources' economic rent from the oil companies had to be tempered for fear that the majors might threaten to reduce the oil output or even close down operations in a given country.

In 1951, Iran overreached. The Iranian government, under its prime minister, Mohammed Mossadegh (who had overturned the young Shah's government), nationalized the Anglo-Iranian Oil Company. As a counter-measure, the oil companies boycotted Iranian oil. Because the companies controlled tankers and refineries, the government of Iran could not market much oil. Although Iran in 1950 had supplied nearly one-fifth of the world's crude-oil exports, the loss of Iranian oil did not result in a worldwide shortage of oil because the majors rapidly stepped up their production in Saudi Arabia, Iraq, and Kuwait. The Mossadegh government was overthrown in 1953 in a CIA-supported coup d'état, and the Shah was restored to power. The Shah maintained nationalization but accepted a negotiated contract with the oil firms in 1953.

The exporting nations' share of oil revenues rose throughout the 1950s, but their revenue per barrel fell steadily in the late 1950s as the oil companies cut posted prices to match the competition of coal and natural gas and to ward off the inroads of independent oil firms. In 1959, an Arab Petroleum Conference, held in Cairo, resolved that oil companies must not reduce posted prices without consulting the governments of the producing countries. In August 1960, the firms again cut posted prices without consulting the governments. To deal with the immediate problem of the pricing practices of the majors, the representatives of the governments of five oil-producing nations (Iran, Iraq, Kuwait, Saudi Arabia, and Venezuela) met in Bagdad in September 1960 and formed the Organization of Petroleum Exporting Countries.

However, OPEC had little impact over the next decade. Past trends continued. Realized prices edged down, ultimately off by 65 percent in real terms between 1947 and 1970. The exporting nations' share edged up. Throughout the 1960s, the posted price of Saudi Arabian crude remained fixed at $1.80 a barrel while the Saudi government's revenue rose from 78 to 83 cents per barrel.

A major change in the international oil market during the 1950s and 1960s was the increased importance of the independent oil firms. In the early 1950s, independent oil firms had to buy relatively expensive crude produced in the United States or elsewhere, or they had to go to the majors for Middle Eastern crude on which the majors shared in the economic rent. There was therefore a strong incentive for the independents to move into the Middle East and North Africe where crude oil could be obtained at a substantially lower cost than anywhere else in the world. Consequently, the independents were prepared to offer host governments better terms, in price or tax, than the majors were willing to offer. By giving way on economic rent, the independents gradually increased their share of the Middle Eastern and North African crude-oil business. The producing nations thereby gained access to a growing number of experienced and technically competent firms (and personnel) competing for use of their petroleum land. On the other hand, an independent firm with a new source of supply in the Middle East or North Africa was more likely to be dependent on that source than the majors with more widely distributed supply sources.

The Turning Point

For a quarter century, 1945-70, the producing nations struggled to obtain larger shares of the economic rent of their oil resources. In 1970, led by Libya's Colonel Muamer Qadaffi, they began to reach for something more.

In September 1969, Colonel Qadaffi overthrew the somnolent government of King Idris. In 1970, Qadaffi explored the possibility of transferring sales of crude oil to the Soviet Union, and demanded an extra 40 cents a barrel from Occidental Petroleum, an independent with no alternative sources of crude. Occidental's president appealed to Exxon's president for an assured alternative low-cost supply of crude, but the appeal was rejected by Exxon.[6] Occidental capitulated. Then the dominoes fell. Other producing nations threatened cutoffs and got more revenue. Then, leapfrogging, Libya demanded more.[7]

Between 1970 and October 1973, Saudi Arabia won increases of the price of its *marker crude* from $1.80 to $3.01 a barrel. (Marker crude is Saudi Arabian light crude oil. The Persian Gulf region produces more of this grade of oil than of any other. It is a rough average between more-expensive low-sulphur oils and lower-priced, heavier oils.) By October 1973, the Saudi Arabian government was receiving 59 percent of the posted price of the marker crude, as shown in Table 11-1.

In the early 1970s, several oil-producing countries began pressing demands for participation in the oil companies' assets and production operations. The governments' objective was to gain greater control over the production decisions of the crude-oil activities within their borders, and also to get higher revenues per barrel by selling the "equity oil" (or "participation oil") directly to outsiders. (Any oil that the government could not sell was sold back to the oil companies at the "buy back price.") In 1972, Saudi Arabia extracted 20 percent participation from Aramco (the Arabian-American Oil Company, a consortium of four major U.S. companies). By mid-1974, several producing nations, including Saudi Arabia and Kuwait, had achieved 60 percent participation. By the end of the 1970s, most of the key oil-producing nations had either achieved or agreed upon 100 percent participation with companies operating within their territories.

Throughout 1973, because of the rising worldwide demand for petroleum, the market prices of crude oil exceeded posted prices. The governments therefore had little difficulty selling their equity oil at a price well above the posted price, often at $5 a barrel or more.

OPEC's Drive to Maximize Monopoly Profit

The OPEC members' share of non-Communist world production rose from 32 percent in 1951 to 50 percent in 1971.[8] More importantly, in 1971, most internationally traded oil came from OPEC members. They were thus in a position to create an export cartel; but they hesitated, still fearful of effective countermeasures by importing nations.

That fear had been voiced clearly in a 1971 press conference by the Shah of Iran. He spent most of two-and-a-half hours berating the oil companies for attempting to enlist the support of their governments. He threatened to expel the resident producing firms, but he also warned the

OPEC nations: "If the oil producing countries suffer even the smallest defeat, that would be the end of OPEC. And then oil exporting nations will not dare to gather together and to rise against these giants."[9]

But when the Yom Kippur War began between Israel and Egypt on October 6, 1973, OPEC's Arab members decided to use oil as a weapon against the Western countries which supported Israel. They raised the price of marker crude *unilaterally* (for the first time) from $3.01 to $5.12 per barrel. They cut back production by 25 percent immediately with a threat of further reductions of five percent a month. Arab oil-producing nations ordered American oil companies to ship no crude oil to Holland or to America. The rationale was that America and Holland were pro-Israel while France, Britain, Sweden and other nations were not. The export cartel had made its first move. The question of the decade was: Will the importing nations retaliate? The answer was soon clear. The favored French and British and Japanese fawned upon the Arab exporters. The U.S. government scrambled to placate the Arab exporters. No government retaliated; the risk of selective embargo was considered too great by importers.

When Iran, Nigeria, and Libya put their crude oil up for auction (instead of the customary procedure of announcing a sale price), bids were as high as $20 a barrel. The cartel members then knew that their monopoly power would not be challenged. In December 1973, OPEC adopted a new posted price of $11.65 for marker crude. This put Saudi Arabia in the position shown in the second column of Table 11-1. As discussed earlier, per barrel government revenue — when allowance was made for participation agreements — often exceeded 90 percent of posted price at the end of 1974. Thus, by 1974, the oil exporting nations were collecting not only their oil fields' economic rent but also a substantial monopoly profit derived from the cartel's cutbacks in production.

A SIMPLE MODEL OF THE OPEC CARTEL'S MARKET

Figure 11-3 presents a rough model of the importing nations' position in the OPEC cartel's 1973-74 market. No one knows the true location and shape of the actual 1973-74 supply and demand curves, but the estimates shown are consistent with actual events.

With unrestricted trade, domestic supply is AS. Foreign supply (mostly OPEC) is BZ. Total supply is BCΣ, the horizontal summation of AS and BZ. Importers' demand is DD. In equilibrium, price is OE = $3, consumption is OG (= 112 units, chosen to facilitate elasticity calculations), domestic production is OF, and imports are FG.

Figure 11-4 approximates the circumstances of the exporting nations (mostly OPEC) in 1973-74. Domestic supply (or marginal cost) is bz (the foreign supply of Figure 11-3). Demand, dd (again, as in Figure 11-2B, assumed to be all foreign demand), is the horizontal difference between the importers' demand, DD, and the importers' domestic supply, AS, in

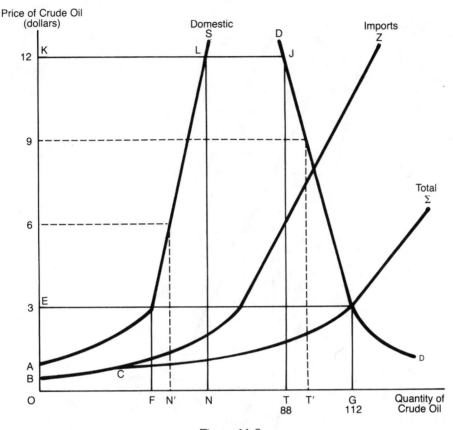

Figure 11-3

Circumstances of Nations Importing
Crude Oil, 1973-74

Figure 11-3. With unrestricted trade, price is oe, and quantity is og (the OE and FG of Figure 11-3).

When OPEC nations launched their cartel, they did not know the location of the relevant supply and demand curves. In the conditions of Figure 11-4, marginal revenue, rr, equals marginal cost, bz, at the quantity oh with a price of ok, a bit above $9. The monopoly had to grope for a price, but we know they ended at about $12 a barrel. Given the approximations of Figures 11-3 and 11-4, did they err? At $12 in Figure 11-3, imports would be only 88 - 60 = 28; and at an output of 28 in Figure 11-4, marginal revenue is far above marginal cost. Therefore, we find that $12 was not the profit-maximizing price. How can we account for this "irrational" choice of price?

Examine Figure 11-4 as a practical example of the more general Figure 11-2B. A cartel is constrained in its incentive to raise prices by sales lost through reductions in quantity demanded and through increases in output from import-competing producers (TG and FN in Figure 11-2A). But the OPEC cartel was spared the full effects of those

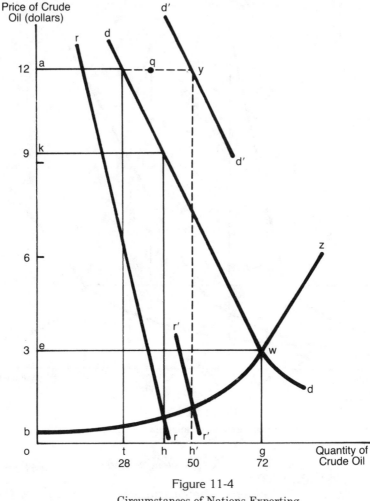

Figure 11-4

Circumstances of Nations Exporting
Crude Oil, 1973-74

increases because the U.S. government's policy (with Canadian following) inhibited those responses. The effect of the policy was to hold down
the price of oil for domestic producers and for domestic consumers.

Once more we simplify the arithmetic to clarify the principles. Before
the cartel, American producers received nearly $3 a barrel for oil. Had
OPEC insisted on a $12 price and had the U.S. government been pas-
sive, import competing oil production would have risen from OF to ON
in the circumstances of Figure 11-3. With price elasticity of demand
equal to 1/5 (= 24/100 ÷ 9/7.5) between $3 and $12, quantity demanded
would have fallen from OG = 112 to OT = 88. But Congressional and
administrative leaders were horrified at the prospect of large windfall
"undeserved" profits for oil-well owners. Consequently, in 1974, Con-

gress set a maximum on the per barrel price of oil from American wells, which, we assume here, was $6 a barrel.

That action kept dollars from "undeserved" oil-well owners, but it raised a problem for petroleum refineries buying $12 OPEC oil and selling in the same market as refineries using $6 American oil. In 1974, the Republican President and the Democratic Congress finessed that problem with a new system of "entitlements." The new law required refineries to pay one "entitlement" along with $6 for every barrel of American oil purchased. The system worked — and works — this way: Assume American refineries import half of their crude oil. The U.S. Department of Energy gives one entitlement to a refinery for each barrel of oil it imports. The refinery pays $12 for the barrel then sells the entitlement for $3 to a refinery buying American oil for $6. Thus, both refineries pay, net, $9 a barrel for oil; American oil-well owners receive only $6, and OPEC exporters receive $12 a barrel. The effect, clearly, is a tax discouraging American production and a subsidy encouraging American imports from OPEC members. These numbers are only approximate, but, for purposes of comparison, the subsidy on imported oil was $2.38 per barrel in 1977.[10] The other result of entitlements was that the average price of petroleum used in America was only $9. The prices of petroleum products have, in consequence, remained below what they would be if government had allowed the average price to rise to $12.

Observe the consequences of the entitlement system in the context of Figure 11-3. In the absence of U.S. government intervention, the price for domestic oil would rise to $12 and domestic production would rise from OF to ON, reducing the exporters' market by FN. (For simplicity, we ignore other importing nations and equate the United States with the "importing nations.") But with price control holding the sales price at $6, American production rises only to ON'. This price control gives the oil exporters the gift of N'N more market, at the $12 OPEC price, than they could otherwise enjoy.

In the absence of government intervention, refiners would pay $12 a barrel for crude oil, and quantity demanded would drop from OG to OT, reducing the exporters' market by TG. But with price control holding the average price at $9, consumption falls only to OT'. This price control gives the oil exporters the gift of TT' more market, at the $12 OPEC price, than they could otherwise enjoy.

Finally observe, within the context of Figure 11-4, the effects of price control and entitlements. From Figure 11-3 we conclude that, in the vicinity of the $12 price, controls make demand greater by N'N plus TT'. Therefore, in Figure 11-4, we show the effective demand as the original dd plus, at prices near $12, (N'N + TT'). The result, d'd', parallel to dd. When we locate r'r', the marginal revenue associated with d'd' near $12, we find that it intersects marginal cost at oh' with the price of $12. Conclusion: given the conditions of Figures 11-3 and 11-4, OPEC would maximize monopoly profit by setting price at $12.

Without American price controls, OPEC would, in Figure 11-4 conditions, have to cut output from 72 to 28 (by 63 percent). With the extra sales given to the monopoly by U.S. controls, OPEC output needs to be cut only from 72 to 50 (by 30 percent). Again, these sketches are only approximations, but they may not be far off. In August 1975, actual OPEC *shut-in capacity* (the percentage of oil that could have been but was not produced from existing wells) was 25.5 percent.[11]

The wonder of the present OPEC cartel has been its durability. As we noted in out introductory review of the cartel theory, cartels tend to dissolve in quarrels over allocation of production cutbacks and in the consequences of irresistible temptations to cheat. This cartel's extraordinary durability may be due in large part to America's decision to assure the cartel a comfortably large export market and to play detective for the cartel.

In the past, cartel dissolution has usually begun when individual members offered secret rebates, discounts, and special credit terms. In the past, cheaters have been able to keep such competition secret. OPEC members might have done so in the late 1970s after the patriotic anti-Israel glue had begun to melt. But in 1977, the U.S. Federal Energy Administration began to require U.S. oil companies to report the details of every purchase of foreign oil "including credit, rebates, and discounts." By that requirement, the Carter Administration made the Federal Energy Agency the enforcement agent for the cartel. Since 1977, American bureaucrats have worked to collect the information that permits OPEC's leaders to see to it that no cartel member cheats.[12]

EVENTS SINCE 1974

By 1973, OPEC's founding five had accepted eight new members: Nigeria, The United Arab Emirates, Libya, Indonesia, Algeria, Ecuador, Qatar, and Gabon. In 1975, the thirteen replaced posted prices with prices set by OPEC governments. The government of each exporting country would sell crude at the official price, but the producing firms could obtain crude, under agreements with the government, at a small discount (1 to 2 percent).

As mentioned earlier, by the late 1970s most major oil-producing nations—including Saudi Arabia, Iran, Kuwait, and Venezuela—had achieved, or reached agreement on, 100 percent participation (nationalization) of the assets and production activities of oil companies operating within their borders. In 1977, for example, Saudi Arabia reached an agreement with the four U.S. majors — Exxon, Mobil, SoCal, and Texaco — on the eventual 100 percent nationalization of Aramco. The reported terms of takeover provided that the Saudi government would compensate the four U.S. companies that had owned Aramco for the net book value of their assets, estimated at $3 billion.[13] Thus the cartel has been able to use its monopoly profits to buy the capital stock the importing countries originally exported to OPEC locations (compare this behavior with the Poga Poga example in Chapter 19).

OPEC's output and pricing policies have been consistent with the model we presented above. The OPEC leaders picked a profit-maximizing output-and-price combination in 1974, then stuck to it while accepting some fluctuations in the real price of crude. Between 1974 and the end of 1978, the price of marker crude rose from $10.09 to $13.35 a barrel, which represented a 32 percent increase in four years, or about 7 percent per year. This rate was lower than the rate of global inflation; so the real price of oil fell during that period. But the Iranian Revolution of early 1979 cut Iranian oil exports and facilitated the cartel's efforts to restrict output. By June 1979, the price of Saudi Arabian marker crude was up to $18 a barrel. Given the world inflation of about 60 percent between 1974 and 1979, that $18 crude put OPEC, in real terms, about where it had been in 1974.

The oil-importing developed nations have continued to intervene in the market to hold down oil prices and, thereby, to encourage imports. A 1980 International Monetary Fund study found that the *real* price of crude oil rose three and one half times between 1970 and August 1979. In contrast, as a result of government intervention, gasoline prices rose, between 1970 and August 1979, only 37 percent in Italy, 35 percent in the United States, 3 percent in Canada and by percentages between 3 and 35 in West Germany, Britain, and France. These small price increases gave consumers little incentive to conserve even though the price elasticity of demand near prices prevailing in the 1970s was about $\frac{1}{2}$ in the short run and unity or a bit higher in the long term.[14]

In contrast, the actions of OPEC members have continued to be rationally self-serving. In a December 1979 meeting, OPEC members for the first time in the history of the organization failed to reach agreement on uniform OPEC prices. The price "doves," Saudi Arabia and Venezuela, pressed for price restraint. The "hawks," Libya and Iran, argued for an increase to at least $30 a barrel. In the end, Saudi Arabia remained at $24 a barrel. Iraq, Kuwait, Indonesia, and Venezuela raised their prices to $26 per barrel. Libya, the leading hawk, raised its price to $34 a barrel. The new OPEC-wide average of $26 a barrel represented a doubling of crude oil price in one year. By the middle of 1980, only six months later, the price of Saudi Arabian marker crude was up to $28 a barrel, and the average price of OPEC oil was near $30 a barrel.

UNCERTAIN PROSPECTS FOR THE 1980s

Short-run disruptions in crude-oil production — such as ones caused by political upheavals, wars, or natural disasters — could put a sudden and sharp upward pressure on the price of oil. The severity of impact of such disruptions on the oil price depends on the capability and willingness of the unaffected oil-exporting nations to increase their output temporarily. In the past, the world oil market has always looked to Saudi Arabia to provide extra output to tide over short-term difficulties. Recent studies have shown, however, that the Saudi's short-term excess capacity is no longer large. Although Saudi Arabia could raise its capacity from the 9.5 million barrels a day it was producing in 1980 to as high as 15 million barrels a day by 1985, such an expansion would require considerable capital outlay and a long lead time. The nation's short-term maximum sustainable capacity in 1979 was estimated to be only about 9.8 million barrels per day, which was not much more than the actual output level.[15] Should these estimates be accurate, then the world petroleum market would be vulnerable to short-run disruptions in crude-oil production, whether the disruptions are spontaneous or deliberate.

Short-term factors may also put a damper on rising oil prices. A global recession, by lowering demand for oil by as much as 5 percent, may cause a temporary glut of oil and lead to, at least temporarily, stable or even declining oil prices. According to OPEC's estimate, world oil stocks had reached 5 billion barrels by 1979.[16] This represents roughly 100 days' consumption at the current consumption rate of about 50 million barrels a day. Consuming nations have accumulated large stocks of crude oil in anticipation of further and continued price increases. Expectation of stable or even lower oil prices is likely to dampen the oil-importing nations' enthusiasm for adding crude oil to their already huge inventories. A slowdown in the rate of increase in world industrial output will thus cause decreases in both consumption and inventory demands for oil.

Slower industrial growth in the importing nations, the end of inventory building, and even the reduction of American and Canadian government controls permitting the movement of domestic prices toward the OPEC price, may have a combined effect of substantially decreasing the world's demand for OPEC's oil. In such an eventuality, OPEC could maintain high and rising oil prices only by curtailing its output substantially.

The OPEC cartel had demonstrated, prior to its December 1979 meeting, that its members could agree on *higher* uniform prices. It has not, however, been able to show that the members can all agree on *lower* uniform prices, or on decisions concerning the *quantity* of crude-oil output in each country. Should demand for oil (or the rate of increase in demand) fall substantially, members may engage in competitive price cutting in order to assure sales of their own oil. Or they may be tempted to refuse to curtail output as mandated by the cartel's output strategy. In either case, such competitive behavior on the part of its members may lead to an eventual breakdown of the OPEC cartel.

Should OPEC leaders succeed in preventing competitive pricing and cheating on output, then the cartel may settle for constant *real* prices for its oil. In the face of shrinking demand for OPEC's oil, the cartel would not be able to survive unless its dominant producer, Saudi Arabia, agreed to curtail its output. This ability of Saudi Arabia to curtail output substantially will no doubt enhance the country's bargaining position within OPEC, enabling it to implement its long-term strategy of tying OPEC's oil prices to the worldwide inflation rate. Under such a strategy, importing nations would continue to be forced to pay monopoly prices, but they would at least be spared the agonies of disruptive price explosions such as the ones that occurred in 1973-74 and 1979-80.

OTHER TYPES OF EXPORT CARTEL

The success of OPEC has stimulated interest in similar commodity cartels by primary-commodity exporting nations. The two best known such associations are the Intergovernmental Council of Copper Exporting Countries and the International Bauxite Producers' Association. The prospects of success in cartels other than oil, however, appear dim. Only oil has all the attributes necessary for a successful cartel. Oil production is concentrated in a handful of nations, some of the principal ones of which share a strong community of interest (i.e., enmity toward Israel). Saudi Arabia, Iraq, and Kuwait have accumulated large foreign exchange reserves so that they could withstand prolonged periods of production shutdown if such an action were necessary to support the cartel price. The supply of nonmember crude oil is price inelastic, so that higher prices result in less-than-proportional increases in output quantity. Most importantly, because of the lack of substitutes, the demand for oil was price inelastic in the vicinity of the original $3-a-barrel 1973 price. Consequently, higher prices do not reduce quantities demanded much but merely increase the sellers' revenues. Other primary commodities lack this critically important attribute of oil. For example, an attempt to raise the cartel price of copper exports sharply would not succeed because some copper users could easily switch to aluminum or other materials.

U.N. Support for Cartels

In the absence of the monopoly, the OPEC nations would receive about two percent of gross world product (GWP). Each year since 1973, however, they have grasped some four percent of GWP. This 100 percent increase in OPEC's share of GWP has been obtained each year by taking away two percent of what would otherwise have been left with Brazilians, Americans, Ethiopians, and other non-OPEC peoples. The extra two percent is represented by the difference, in Figure 11-4, between ogwe and oh'ya.

OPEC's production cutbacks have had a second effect. They have deprived other nations of energy (h'g in Figure 11-4) and have made energy production less efficient (FN' in Figure 11-3), so that they have reduced GWP below what it would otherwise have been. Consequently, Ethiopians, Americans, Brazilians and others have lost both from the transfer *and* from the inefficiency.

Yet poor-nation delegates to the fourth U.N. Conference on Trade and Development (UNCTAD) voted for more production cutbacks and more price increases. In a May 1976 meeting, typical of many others, "The major measures generally favored by the developing countries included an 'integrated program' . . .designed to achieve more stable, equitable, and remunerative prices . . .for a list of commodities exported by developing countries."[17] What those apparently innocuous words meant was: "Bauxite, copper ore, coffee, and cocoa producers should cut output and raise prices." U.N. speakers argue new cartels would take from the rich and give to the poor. But the farmers and traders of Mali, Bangladesh, Haiti, and Rwanda have lost to OPEC, and they would be as certain to lose to any new export cartels. Perhaps the world's poor can hope that unfavorable elasticity conditions will protect them from creation of new cartels.

OGEC: An Organization of Grain Exporting Countries?

OPEC began with exceptional supply and demand conditions: three dominant exporters and inelastic supply and demand. Those conditions are almost — but not quite — unique in world markets. Similar conditions do exist in the world's grain market (other than for rice) where the United States, Canada, and Australia dominate exports and where substitutes are not available to importers.

In world markets in 1960, $1.50 would buy either one bushel of grain or one barrel of crude oil. In early 1972, $1.90 would the same. But in 1980, grain, at about $4 a bushel, is less than one-sixth the price of a barrel of crude oil. The change results from OPEC's output cuts. Other commodity cartels would be hard to organize because so many nations would have to be included. But in 1982 or in 1983, the three dominant grain exporters — the United States, Canada, and Australia — could form an Organization of Grain Exporting Countries (an OGEC) and cut exports enough to raise the international price of a bushel of grain back toward parity with the price of a barrel of crude oil. Inelastic grain demand would assure that OGEC's total grain export revenue would be greater — not forever, but for a long time — on the higher-priced smaller quantity than on the alternatively lower-priced larger quantity.

Supply and demand conditions beckon almost as favorably to grain exporters as to petroleum exporters. Nevertheless, because the *international* grain market is smaller than the *international* petroleum market, OGEC's potential cartel profit is smaller than that which OPEC has already seized. The value of world grain output is much higher than the value of world petroleum output, but most grain is consumed where produced while a larger portion of petroleum production is exported. In 1972, world petroleum exports had four times the value of world grain exports. That ratio suggests the size of OGEC's potential cartel profit. The OPEC cartel wrests two percent of GWP from other nations each year. With a comparable degree of cartel success, OGEC's potential gain might be about one-half of one percent of a somewhat smaller GWP.

The prospect of a successful OGEC joining a successful OPEC raises moral issues. Would it be just for grain producers to join oil producers in restricting exports in order to raise their share of a reduced GWP? LDC delegates to the UNCTAD meetings have already, in effect, said "Yes." But our purpose here is not to present a case for a grain cartel. Rather, our point is that, while grain exporters could form a cartel and would probably be successful, they would be wrong to do so for the same reason that OPEC and every other cartel is wrong. Cartels take away. A particular commodity cartel can benefit particular residents of particular countries, but it does so at the expense of many in other countries. As such, an international export cartel is as undesirable and injurious as any other forms of restrictions on trade. (For more on U.N. proposals for cartels, see the section "Short-Run Fluctuations in Export Prices" in Chapter 19.)

DUMPING AND REFERENCE PRICES

We began this chapter considering governments (or firms) restricting output in order to charge "too much." We turn now to governments (or firms) charging "too little" in order to raise output. So complex — or contrary — is human nature and profit-maximizing behavior that both practices are major problems in the 1980s.

THE THEORY OF THE FIRM AND SPECIAL-INTEREST LEGISLATION

To discuss dumping we must use the newspaper concepts of "unit cost," and "full production cost." Since these concepts are used rather loosely in popular writing, we must, at the outset, identify the equivalent terms in economic theory to make sure we agree on definitions.

Every economics principles textbook tells us that, in the short run, total cost of production is the sum of total fixed cost and total variable cost. If we divide totals by quantity of output, we find that average total cost (ATC) is the sum of average fixed cost (AFC) and average variable cost (AVC). Average total cost is often shortened to average cost (AC). Fixed costs include normal profit, or normal return to the fixed factor, capital. Although the economists' term *average cost* implicitly includes normal profit, the popular meaning of *unit cost* does not, so the popular terms, "unit cost plus fair profit" and "full production cost per unit," are both synonyms for the economist's notion of average cost.

Firms are normally assumed to try to maximize profits. If market price, P, exactly equals AC, the firm "covers costs" and earns a normal profit but no more. If P is higher than AC, the firm earns, in addition to normal profits, *excess* profits. If P is less than AC but greater than AVC, the firm incurs a loss, but remains in operation, in the short run, since it covers some of its fixed costs. The firm must shut down production if P falls below AVC, since revenue would no longer cover variable costs. Please remember, during our later discussion of dumping, that the profit-maximizing rule of competitive market behavior *requires* firms to remain in business and sell below average cost (thereby incurring short-run losses), when price lies below AC but above AVC. This is perfectly acceptable *competitive* behavior, applicable to all business firms, American, European, or Japanese. Sales below average cost during a recession are no more "unfair" than sales above average cost during periods of prosperity. The dynamics of profit-maximizing markets obligate firms to sell sometimes above average cost, and sometimes below average cost. However, firms that sell persistently below cost do not survive in the long run.

Dumping and Antidumping Duties

Article 6 of the General Agreement on Tariffs and Trade (GATT) stipulates that the government of an importing country may impose an antidumping duty equal in value to the difference between the "fair value" and the actual export price, when "material injury" to a domestic industry can be demonstrated. The 1921 Antidumping Act of the United States defined fair value as the foreign market value. This was the traditional definition of *dumping* — exporting products at prices below home market prices. The 1974 Trade Act, however, expanded the definition of dumping to include cases where the export price is less than full production cost (i.e., average cost). The Antidumping Act, as amended, now stipulates that:

> Whenever the Secretary [of the Treasury] has reasonable grounds to believe or suspect that sales in the home market of the country of exportation. . .have been made at prices which represent less than the cost of producing the merchandise in question, . . . , such sales shall be disregarded in the determination of foreign market value. Whenever sales are disregarded by virtue of having been made at less than the cost of production. . . , the Secretary shall determine that no foreign market value exists and employ the constructed value of the merchandise in question.[18]

Sec. 206 of the 1921 Antidumping Act stipulates that the "constructed value" of an imported product shall be the sum of the cost of materials and fabrication or other processing, and an allowance for general expenses and profit. The amount for general expenses shall not be less than 10 percent of the cost, and the amount for profit shall not be less than 8 percent of the sum of cost and general expenses. This method of "constructing" the fair value of an import, which had been applied, prior to the 1974 amendment, only to cases where foreign market value could not be ascertained, is now applicable also to cases in which the home market price is below average cost of production.

Determination of "sales at less than fair value" and "material injury to an industry" takes place in two steps: First, the Treasury Department (prodded by a special interest seeking higher prices) determines whether the export price of an imported product is either below the home price, or, as per the 1974 amendment, below full production cost. If the Treasury finds the price "too low" by either criterion, the case goes to the International Trade Commission (formerly, the Tariff Commission), which determines if the industry is being injured by the imports. If an injury is established by the Commission, the Treasury imposes an antidumping duty equal to the difference between the "fair value" and the actual export price of each shipment.

So, under the 1974 law, when a firm sells at a price below average cost but above AVC, it is dumping. Encouraged by this legislated extention of the dumping definition, U.S. special interests registered so many dumping complaints after 1974 that they threatened to overload the investigative capacity of the Treasury Department. The required procedures are complex and long drawn-out. Foreign producers are sensibly reluctant to furnish production and financial data; and, even when data become available, they are often subject to a wide variety of interpretations. In September 1977, the U.S. Steel Corporation filed an antidumping suit, charging five Japanese steelmakers with below-cost pricing on more than two-thirds of their steel exports to the United States and asking the Treasury to impose a 37 percent antidumping duty on all Japanese steel products.[19]

Japan's Different Division of AC between AVC and AFC

What is regarded as "dumping" by some U.S. producers may be a perfectly normal business practice explained in economics textbooks. For institutional reasons, selling below AC is a much more common practice in Japan than in the United States. Large Japanese firms regard much of their labor cost as fixed costs because of the tradition of tenured employment of regular workers. This leaves AC as it would be for an American firm but raises the AFC and lowers the AVC of Japanese firms. So Japanese firms produce, especially during recessions, at reduced prices where American firms would close down. As profit maximizers, Japanese firms are compelled to sell well below AC when demand is weak and to sell above cost during boom periods, hoping to average satisfactory profits over the years. With much higher AVC, American corporations are led to aim at stable earnings at the expense of the stability of output and employment. With much higher AFC, Japanese firms are led to aim at stable operating rates at the expense of profit stability. Japanese businesses cut prices and sell below cost when demand is weak because of institutional factors unique in Japan. In contrast, U.S. firms maintain prices and lay off workers during recession, and the workers are protected by the strength of the unemployment compensation system. Consequently, Japanese manufacturing supply is much more price inelastic than is American. What constitutes an *unfair* business practice and what is normal *competitive* behavior largely depend on the prevailing institutions and business philosophy of each nation.

PROFIT-MAXIMIZING PRICE DISCRIMINATION

The microeconomic theory of price discrimination explains why many firms price exports below the home market price. Many Japanese manufacturing firms (automobile manufacturers, television set producers, and steelmakers) often price exports to the United States at levels below their home market prices. Many U.S. firms have exported at prices below those charged in the United States. One intuitive, and crude, explanation would be that such firms consider exports as *marginal* business. Instead of seeking maximum profits, they could establish a particular profit goal and seek maximum sales subject to that profit constraint. Then, when they achieve that profit goal from domestic sales, they only charge out-of-pocket cost (AVC) on exports. Even if they make no profit on exports, export sales raise output and employment levels. This explanation may contain an element of truth — in the short run. But in the long run, AVC and AC are the same. A long-run, profit maximizing two-price system must be based on considerations other than the difference between AVC and AC.

The alternative explanation of two-price dumping is based on the economic theory of price discrimination. As explained in every intermediate microeconomics text, a firm facing demand curves of different elasticities can (in fact *must,* if it is to maximize profits) charge higher prices where demand is less elastic and lower prices where demand is more elastic. Japanese firms exporting automobiles, television sets, and steel to the United States face export demand curves more elastic than their home demand curves because of the greater availability of competing substitutes in the export markets. The exporters, therefore, charge lower prices in their export markets than in their domestic markets.

Figure 11-5 portrays the cost and demand situations of an oligopolistic producer whose home demand curve, AA′, is more elastic in the relevant price range than is its foreign demand curve, BB′. (For any given price, BB′ has a higher price elasticity than does AA′.) The corresponding marginal revenue curves are Aa′ for the home market and Bb′ for the foreign market. A horizontal summation of both home and foreign demand curves yields the kinked total demand curve, AGD. Similarly, the kinked marginal revenue curve, ANR, is obtained for the combined market. MM′ is the marginal cost curve of the firm. (For simplicity, the AC curve is omitted.)

To maximize profits, the firm produces OQ where marginal cost equals marginal revenue (at point E). The firm divides sale of OQ between exports Of and home sales Oh, so marginal revenue in each market equals marginal cost, QE. Therefore, it exports Of (with marginal revenue fU) and sells at home, Oh (with marginal revenue, hW). The Oh can be sold at price OH, but the greater elasticity of foreign demand permits only price OF for the Of exported. (We assume there are neither transportation costs nor tariff duties; so export price is equal to foreign market price.) So the domestic price, OH, is higher than the export price, OF. Lucky foreigners! Every profit-maximizing firm must sell at more than one price if it is to equate marginal revenues and marginal cost when facing demand curves with different elasticities.

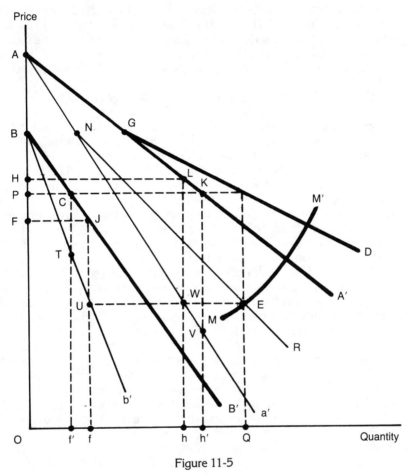

Figure 11-5

Price Discrimination between Home and Export
Markets, and Effects of An Antidumping Duty

The Effects of an Antidumping Duty

We will now assess the effects of antidumping duties in a case where export price is below domestic price and domestic price is above average cost. (We will not consider cases where domestic price is below AC.) Please recall, as we proceed, that the area between the demand curve and price is consumers' surplus, and the area under the marginal revenue curve equals total revenue.

Suppose the government of the importing nation levies an antidumping duty on the product considered in Figure 11-5. Assume the duty is *variable;* that is, its size changes so it always equals the difference between the home price and the export price. At first, the duty will equal the difference between OH and OF. Then the *export market price* will equal OH, or the home market price. (But the *export price* — the receipt on exports — will remain at OF.) This situation cannot be sustained; an excess supply develops in the export market since Of will not sell there at OH.

What to do? The firm cannot increase exports by cutting the price to foreigners because this U.S.-type antidumping duty prevents such a price cut. But the firm *can* move the excess export supply back to the home market and sell it there. This added sale in the home market puts a downward pressure on the home market price, and OH will fall.

The upshot of the above development will be as follows: The U.S.-type antidumping duty provides that final price in both markets must be the same. It certainly makes little sense for the exporting firm to charge a lower export price and allow the importing nation's government to collect the difference as duty revenue. Therefore, when the antidumping duty goes into effect, the firm holds output at OQ, charges OP in both markets, exports only Of', and sells Oh' at home.[20]

Who is better off and who is worse off under this antidumping duty? Consumers in the country that imposes the duty are made worse off. Their consumers' surplus is reduced from BFJ to BPC. Consumers in the exporting country, in contrast, are made better off. Their consumers' surplus increases from AHL to APK. The exporting firm is definitely worse off. While its total output and total cost remain unchanged, its total revenue and profits fall. The revenue reduction can be seen by comparing the gain in total revenue from the added domestic sales (the area hWVh') and the loss of total revenue from the lost export sales (the area f'TUf). The firm's injury is also implied by the circumstance that it is no longer satisfying the profit-maximizing rule, marginal cost equals marginal revenue. Marginal cost, QE, and *overall* marginal revenue, QE, remain equal, but the home market marginal revenue, h'V, is lower and the foreign market marginal revenue, f'T, is higher than QE. The antidumping duty thus injures the importing country's consumers while depriving the exporting firm of an opportunity to maximize profit by means of price discrimination.

STEEL'S TRIGGER PRICES AND THE PUBLIC INTEREST

To deal with the rush of antidumping complaints by U.S. steelmakers, the Treasury Department announced, in December 1977, a program that eliminated the need for U.S. steelmakers to initiate antidumping actions. Under this plan, the Treasury announced reference (trigger) prices for major categories of steel products. If steel was imported at a price below these prices, the Treasury would initiate dumping investigations without waiting for firms to file complaints alleging injury. Investigations were supposed to be completed in as short a time as three months — about one quarter of the time required for a regular antidumping complaint — and importers were required to post bonds at the end of an investigation "proving" dumping. The reference price system thus was designed as a quicker and more effective way of eliminating steel dumping exports to the United States.

In January 1978, the Treasury published a list of reference prices for major steel products for the four geographical areas in the United States. The weighted average of trigger prices plus customs duties of carbon and alloy steel products was $330 a ton, which was $20 — or 5.7 percent — below the weighted average list price of comparable domestic products. (Stainless steel products were not included since they had been covered by quotas under the 1974 Trade Act. In January 1976, the International Trade Commission found that imports of stainless and other specialty steels were causing injury to the U.S. steel industry, and recommended that the President impose import quotas for a five-year period. President Ford imposed three-year tonnage restrictions on imports from the EEC and other countries, and arranged a "voluntary restraint agreement" with Japan. In June 1979, President Carter approved an eight-month extension of the import quotas on stainless and other specialty steels.[21]) The trigger prices were calculated from the production costs of Japanese steelmakers — presumably the most efficient in the world — and included an allowance for overhead costs, profits, and shipping and insurance costs.

The trigger prices were set at levels that eliminated most conspicuous dumping while avoiding a drastic reduction in imports. Most commentators agreed that foreign steel must sell at a discount of at least 10 percent in the United States to overcome the local steel users' preference for domestic suppliers. The 5.7 percent spread between the trigger-plus-duty prices and the domestic list prices would have resulted in a drastic reduction in steel imports, except that U.S. steelmakers took advantage of the situation and quickly withdrew price discounts and raised the list prices by an average of 5.5 percent as of February 1, 1978. In March 1978, the U.S. Steel Corporation tentatively withdrew its antidumping complaints against five Japanese steel firms.

The trigger price system had the same effect as antidumping duties. Both systems could be set up in such a way as to compel exporters to raise export prices and equate them with home market prices or with average cost. Both restricted trade volume and reduced the gains from trade. A 1977 staff report by the Federal Trade Commission estimated that a $332 reference price (including the existing tariff) imposed on steel imports in 1976 would have cost U.S. consumers about $1 billion while bringing U.S. steel producers a gain of about $869 million. Such a reference price would have had an impact equal to that of a 3.5 percent tariff increase, except that the tariff increase would have generated additional tariff revenue of $79 million.[22]

As with any other schemes of price support by government, the steel trigger price system caused higher prices and economic dislocations throughout the domestic economy. Inflation and dislocation, in turn, may have created unemployment of workers. These adverse effects of the trigger price system were noted by an editorial in the *Wall Street Journal* in December 1978. It pointed out that U.S. fabricators of reinforcing rod and structural items were finding their competitiveness deteriorating as their foreign competitors used cheaper steel that was kept out of the U.S. market by the trigger prices. Referring to a Treasury Department study that reportedly had predicted that trigger prices would cost five U.S. jobs for every one saved, the editorial concluded that trigger prices protected some jobs by ending others while adding to inflation.[23]

In March 1980, the U.S. Steel Corporation brought massive anti-dumping complaints against steel producers of seven West European nations, and announced its intent to file similar complaints against Japanese steelmakers. The U.S. government thereupon suspended the trigger price system on the grounds that its investigative staff was too small to deal with both trigger prices and the U.S. Steel charges. This subject will be taken up again in Chapter 12.

APPENDIX: IMPORTERS' COUNTERMEASURES LIKELY TO BE SELF-DEFEATING

The text described two kinds of countermeasures, tariffs and auction of import entitlements, that importing nations can take against an export cartel. The oil-importing nations have been afraid to attempt either against the OPEC cartel.

The United States government has toyed with two other means of retaliation. Both may, in practice, help the cartel.

The first means begins in America with the President lamenting the size of oil imports while exhorting the public to use less oil. Congressional leaders and the Advertising Council may then add their multi-media voices to the appeal. The result, if effective, in the circumstances of Figure 11-4 is to move the demand curve, d'd', to the left.

Lower demand. Lower consumption. Fewer imports. Yes, surely; but fewer dollars for OPEC? A successful program? Probably not.

The petroleum uses that will be foregone because of exhortation are likely the same uses that would be foregone if OPEC's price were moved above $12. With those uses already ended by exhortation, the remaining uses will be those least affected by further price increases. In short, exhortation moves d'd' to the left to a new position, d''d'' (not shown in Figure 11-4), *and* makes the new d''d'' much *less* elastic in the vicinity of the prevailing $12 price. The less elastic d''d'' will have a marginal revenue curve, r''r''. steeper and to the left of r'r'. The new r''r'' will intersect marginal cost, bz, at some quantity below oh'. OPEC would then find that its profit maximizing export quantity is lower and its profit maximizing price is higher than before the Presidential intervention. After OPEC raises price, the cartel may or may not be worse off than before the exhortation campaign. The importing consumers, with lower quantity and higher price, will certainly be worse off.

The second countermeasure toyed with by the Carter Administration was imposition of a quota on imports. For example, given the conditions of Figure 11-4, the cartel chooses to export oh' = ay. To be effective, an import quota would have to be less than ay. If it were, for example, aq, the effect would be a new demand curve for imports, a vertical demand curve, through q. So far as concerns its effect on the market, this is but an extreme form of the Presidential exhortation model just described. The quota moves d'd' left and makes it *perfectly* inelastic.

Given the vertical demand through q, OPEC's profit maximizing price would be the intersection of this vertical line through q and the demand, d'd'. (Above that intersection, demand will be elastic.) So this quota would assure a price increase. OPEC would be worse off than at $12 and oh' sales. But the consumers would also surely be worse off with both higher price and lower quantity. A tariff might also raise price and lower quantity, but the tariff would capture for the importing nation a share of the cartel's monopoly profit. The quota would impose injuries on the importing nation but with no corresponding benefits.

STUDY QUESTIONS

1. Refer to Figure 11-2.
    (a) How is the total supply curve, BCΣ, of the importing nations constructed?
    (b) What are the consequences when the exporters form a cartel?
2. Figure 11-2 shows the consequences that follow when the export cartel cuts exports from og to oh. The text observes that importing consumers would be worse off if domestic producers did not respond to the cartel by raising output from OF to ON. Now assume that domestic producers cannot (or will not) expand production beyond OF. What then will be the consequences for importing consumers when the cartel reduces exports from og to oh? Either draw on Figure 11-2 to show your conclusions or draw a new sketch, letter it, and use it to show your conclusions.
3. Why were the present members of OPEC unable to collect all of their oil land's economic rent before 1973?
4. What was the significance of the revolt against the oil companies started in 1970 by Libya's Colonel Qadaffi? What role did the independent oil firms play in this historic event?
5. Copy the supply curves and the demand curve of Figure 11-3. Copy, in a separate sketch, the curves, dd, rr, and bz of Figure 11-4. Then, in your sketches, show what would happen if the export cartel were to restrict exports to quantity oh and the importing nations' governments were to allow the market to work without further intervention.
6. Compare and contrast the relationships, in the 1960s and at present, between the oil-producing nations' governments and the "major" oil companies.
7. Why is each member of an export cartel tempted to cheat?
8. Why has the OPEC cartel lasted this long? Write a scenario describing possible events leading to the demise of the cartel.
9. Explain how "dumping" is defined.
10. Why would firms want to export at prices below full production costs?
11. Why would firms want to export at prices below their home market prices?

12. Reproduce Figure 11-5 but omit the dashed lines. Add to your sketch an average cost curve cut at its minimum by MM'. Draw your AC curve so that its height, at quantity OQ, is midway between the heights of points F and P. Letter your sketch as needed and identify the area representing the firm's total cost and the areas representing the firm's total revenue when the firm is in profit-maximizing price-discriminating equilibrium.

13. Discuss the similarities and differences between an antidumping duty and the trigger price system.

ENDNOTES

1. Figure 11-2 represents long-run cost conditions where each *firm* has a long-run average cost curve that is a flat line. This case is rarely mentioned in principles, or even in intermediate price theory texts, but it is the necessary consequence of a linear homogeneous production function. So with constant returns to scale for each firm, long-run marginal cost equals long-run average cost for each firm. Therefore, at output oh, with the monopoly in force, hv represents both marginal and average cost for the marginal firm. This is why uvjk can be labelled, unambiguously, "monopoly profit."

2. For details about a tariff on OPEC oil see Hendrick S. Houthakker, *The World Price of Oil: A Medium-Term Analysis* (Washington, D.C., American Enterprise Institute, 1976); for details about entitlements for OPEC oil imports, see M.A. Adelman, "Oil Import Quota Auctions," *Challenge*, January-February 1976; for a summary of both, see Theodore H. Moran, *Oil Prices and the Future of OPEC* (Washington, D.C., Resources for the Future, 1978), pp. 81-85.

3. M.A. Adelman, "The Changing Structure of Big International Oil," in Frank N. Trager, ed., *Oil, Divestiture, and National Security* (New York: Crane Russak & Co., 1977), p. 2.

4. John M. Blair, *The Control of Oil* (New York: Pantheon Books, 1976), p. 15.

5. Nazli Choucri, *International Politics of Energy Interdependence: The Case of Petroleum* (Lexington, Mass.: Lexington Books, 1976), pp. 10-13.

6. Anthony Sampson, *The Seven Sisters* (New York: The Viking Press, 1975), p. 212.

7. The producing firms were concerned that an export cartel was forming. They were also aware, as our theoretical models show, that government action might provide the only defense. They appealed to the European and American governments. The European governments were afraid that the OPEC nations might respond to European resistance by cutting off all exports to selected countries. Fearful of attempting a common stand, they gave way to OPECs growing power. The American stance was even more self-injurious.

> Through several administrations, we have actively helped the cartel of the OPEC nations. "Give them what they want ..." [was the American policy.] I think it was felt we needed friendly regimes at the Persian Gulf. If we made them rich, they could buy arms and defend themselves. Iran shows what a disaster the policy has been ... The only way we can protect ourselves is to take money away from the cartel. Nothing personal, but we can't be friends with the cartel.

> Morris A. Adelman, in an interview, "Ways to Foil the Oil Cartel," In *U.S. News*, April 9, 1979, p. 22. Also, see Adelman's observations in "The Changing Structure," pp. 2, 3, 5-6, and 8. The opinions of Professor Adelman, who is on the M.I.T. faculty, are special because for several decades, he has been America's leading expert on the international petroleum industry.

8. Frank R. Wyant, *The United States, OPEC, and Multinational Oil* (Lexington, Mass.: Lexington Books, 1977), p. 65.

9. Quoted in Sampson, *The Seven Sisters*, p. 224.

10. James L. Sweeney, "Energy Regulation — Solution or Problem," in *Options for U.S. Energy Policy* (San Francisco: Institute for Contemporary Studies, 1977), p. 187.
11. Wyant, *The United States, OPEC, and Multinational Oil*, p. 80.
12. See the letter of outrage from Alan Reynolds and David Henderson, *Wall Street Journal*, 14 November 1977, p. 25.
13. *Encyclopedia Britannica, 1977 Book of the Year*, pp. 609-610.
14. "How the West Helped OPEC," *The Economist*, March 1, 1980, p. 73.
15. "Saudi Oil Production: A Serious Short-Term Problem?" *Business Week*, 10 December 1979, p. 52.
16. "OPEC's Splintered Price Front," *Business Week*, 31 December 1979, p. 30.
17. "Nairobi Conference Launches Programme to Increase Commodity Earnings of Developing Countries," *U.N. Chronicle*, June 1976, p. 39.
18. Sec. 205(b) of the 1921 Antidumping Act, as amended by Sec. 312(d) of the 1974 Trade Act.
19. "Steel Builds Its Dumping Case," *Business Week*, 17 October 1977, pp. 128-130.
20. Should the firm cut output below OQ when it is obliged to charge a single price? The answer may not be obvious; but the fact is that if the firm charges the same price in both markets, the firm's marginal revenue curve remains ANER. Therefore, optimal output remains OQ where MR = MC.
21. *Wall Street Journal*, 13 June 1979, p. 2.
22. Federal Trade Commission, Bureau of Economics, *Staff Report on the United States Steel Industry and Its International Rivals: Trends and Factors Determining International Competitiveness* (Washington, D.C.: Government Printing Office, 1977), pp. 555-571.
23. "Triggering Trouble," *Wall Street Journal*, 7 December 1978, p. 22.

12

Promotion and Obstruction of Comparative Advantage Specialization: American History and Contemporary American Institutions

We have stressed the benefits to society of comparative advantage specialization. We have surveyed the arguments special interests use to raise their prices and their incomes and to reduce comparative advantage specialization. In this chapter, we first review the way in which these competing arguments have worked themselves out in the United States over the past 200 years. Then we concentrate on the character and operation of the contemporary institutions in which special interests and the general welfare compete for favorable legislation and administrative rulings.

Social science hypotheses are not easily proved or disproved. However, we invite you to consider the nonrandom sample of American history presented in the first section of this chapter as support for the hypotheses we developed in Chapter 10, namely: First, that workers, managers, and capital owners weigh the costs and benefits from organizing and lobbying when they decide how much protection to seek. Second, that legislators consider the losses in election support from injuries to the general public and the gains in election support from beneficiaries when they decide how much protection to provide to comparative disadvantage producers.

AMERICAN HISTORY

AS BRITISH COLONIES

Throughout America's colonial period, the ruling English were convinced that the public interest (or at the very least, the national interest) was identical with the precepts of mercantilism. Sir Josiah Child, writing in 1690, described the balance of trade he, and all mercantilists, believed to be in the national interest:

> this *balance* is to be taken by a strict scrutiny of what proportion the value of commodities exported out of this kingdom bear to those imported; and if the exports exceed the imports, it is concluded the *nation* gets by the general course of its trade, it being supposed that the overplus is *bullion,* and so adds to the treasure of the kingdom; *gold and silver being taken for the measure and standard of riches.*[1]

So all British producers were to be encouraged, all were to be protected from import competition. The lobbyists for protection were dominant and unopposed. But gold and silver treasure were not the ultimate objective. British defense — British strength — was seen to depend on *access* to ships, to munitions, to food, cloth, and output in general. Thomas Mun, mercantilism's most eloquent spokesman, was thinking of access to output when he asked:

> For although Treasure is said to be the sinews of War, yet this is so because it doth provide, unite and move the power of men, victuals, and munition where and when the cause doth require, but if these things be wanting in due time, what shall we then do with our money?[2]

The British Navigation Acts therefore severely restricted trade, so that almost all American imports and exports — victuals, munitions, and all else — passed through England and were carried on ships of either England or the British colonies. British law also prohibited most kinds of manufacturing in the colonies. But since the colonies suffered comparative disadvantage in manufacturing, no one minded those sweeping prohibitions. However, before 1765, England imposed little legislation designed to raise revenue from the colonies; and England did even less to enforce those laws. The colonists responded by fully accepting the restrictions confining trade within the empire so long as no attempt was made to raise revenue in America.

But the colonists had long experience with revenue tariffs (as distinct from protective tariffs), for nearly every colonial assembly levied import duties for its own treasury. Further, duties on exports were common; again levied to provide revenue to the individual colonies. Few were designed as protective; many were sumptuary attempts to curb "extravagant" spending on tobacco, wine, "strong water," sugar, and spice; all were widely evaded. Almost all production was comparative advantage production. There was no one interested in protection of comparative disadvantage production.

So the custom was: restrictions keeping trade inside the empire and tariffs for local revenue. After 1763, the crown's efforts to collect stamp taxes and tea and molasses tariffs were attempts to obtain revenue to help cover the military costs of defending the settlers against French and Indian incursions and against piracy. The 1773 tea party and the long war ended such taxation without representation. They also led to comparative disadvantage production and lobbies for protection.

UNDER THE ARTICLES OF CONFEDERATION: 1778-1788

Both the American Declaration of Independence and Adam Smith's *Wealth of Nations* were published in 1776. Smith did not comprehend the concept of comparative advantage. He did cite the advantages of division of labor, of specialization, and of absolute advantage specialization as reasons why nations should move from mercantilism toward free trade. Thereafter, Smith's free-trade rationale provided an intellectual alternative to the mercantilistic argument identifying the national interest with protectionism.

During the Revolutionary War, foreign trade languished and the tariffs of the colonies — now States — were abandoned. Immediately after the war, with "Liberty" the watchword of the age, trade was, initially, largely unrestrained. John Adams, James Madison, Benjamin Franklin, and Thomas Jefferson all espoused free trade. George Washington wrote, "As a citizen of the great republic of humanity, I indulge the idea that the period is not remote when the benefits of free commerce will succeed the devastations and horrors of war."[3]

But two forces brought back tariffs on a broad scale. First, since Americans had decided to be aliens, England treated them as aliens. The formerly large American exports of rice, tobacco, pitch, turpentine, and ships to the West Indies were severely restricted, and high English tariffs were applied to all American goods. Secondly, war had cut off trade with Europe and led Americans into comparative disadvantage production of firearms, gunpowder, nails, salt, paper, and cloth. After the war, comparative advantage British goods returned, cheaper, of course, and of equal or better quality than the American. Buyers welcomed the British products. But American artisans and mechanics, national saviors during the war, now simply in the wrong business, protested the "ruinous excess of British importations."

The Articles of Confederation reserved all taxing powers to the individual States. Protests about British import restrictions and protests about cheap British goods went to State legislators.

Every State imposed property qualifications for the right to vote. In most States, higher property requirements were imposed for office holders than for voters. The lobbyists organized and persuaded (since few people could vote, persuasion costs were less than otherwise), and all the States passed a series of tariff acts ranging from high to very high. The tariffs were needed for revenue. In addition, they were explicitly designed to retaliate against British exclusion and to protect American manufacturing.

England would have lowered tariffs in exchange for a uniform American reduction. But the States would not delegate tariff powers to the national Congress. Smuggling grew rapidly between lower and higher tariff States, and there was a burst of new tariffs against the goods of other States. Massachusetts went so far as to declare more than 50 different commodities contraband if produced anywhere but on Massachusetts soil. Economies of scale were thrust out of reach. The superb *in*efficiency of State self-sufficiency in everything became a realistic possibility.

THE NEW NATION: 1788-1816

In 1788, the American States were separated from one another by protectionist walls like those that divided European nations. Europeans clung to that outrageously inefficient divisive system until the 1957 Treaty of Rome undertook, at last, the abolition of internal European tariffs. But, by 1788, America's comparative disadvantage lobbyists had overreached. The costs of protection became visibly large. Advocates of the public interest prevailed, and in 1778, the ingenious authors of the Constitution of the United States converted the vast reaches of the 13 States — and of the 37 to follow — into a single free-trade area. Article I, Section 10, provides that

> No State shall, without the Consent of the Congress, lay any Imposts or Duties on Imports or Exports, except what may be absolutely necessary for executing its inspection Laws.

That provision has made an incalculably large contribution to American economic growth.

A second change from the Articles of Confederation transferred to Congress the power to levy tariffs on foreign trade. Article I, Section 8, provides, "The Congress shall have Power to lay and collect Taxes, Duties, Imposts and Excises."

George Washington was not inaugurated until 30 April 1789; but on 8 April 1789, Congress began to debate a tariff bill proposed by James Madison. The bill was passed on the fourth of July 1789 with a preamble giving three reasons for its existence: "for the support of the government, for the discharge of the debts of the United States, and the encouragement and protection of manufactures." The first two reasons were the most compelling. As Table 12-1 shows, until the Civil War, most Federal revenue came from tariffs. Even in 1875, over half of Federal revenue came from customs collections! The effective rate of the tariff of 1780 was some 8½ percent, modestly protective in effect, but

TABLE 12-1   REVENUE OF THE FEDERAL GOVERNMENT,
SELECTED YEARS

Year	Total (millions of dollars)	From tariffs (millions of dollars)	Percent from tariffs
1789-91	4.4	4.4	99.5
1800	10.8	9.1	83.7
1825	21.8	20.1	92.0
1850	43.6	39.7	91.0
1875	288.0	157.2	54.6
1900	567.2	233.2	41.1
1925	3,780.1	547.6	14.5
1950	41,310.6	422.7	1.0

Source: U.S. Department of Commerce, *Historical Statistics of the United States, Colonial Times to 1957* (Washington, D.C.: Government Printing Office, 1960), p. 712 and *Historical Statistics of the United States, Colonial Times to 1970* (Washington, D.C.: Government Printing Office, 1975), Part 2, p. 1106.

based on the assumptions that the Federal government required revenue and that customs duties were the most efficient way to obtain revenue.[4]

In January 1791, the House of Representatives asked Alexander Hamilton, Secretary of the Treasury, to prepare a plan, for the "promotion of such manufacturer" as will render the United States independent of others for essentials, particularly for military supplies."[5] He responded with *The Report on Manufactures,* "the strongest presentation of the case for protection which has been made by any American statesman."[6] Hamilton argued for an extensive system of protective tariffs and domestic subsidies to accelerate the growth of American manufactures. Hamilton was thoroughly familiar with *The Wealth of Nations* and incorporated much of Smith's argument in the *Report*. He accepted the proposition that free trade was generally good. However, he argued that America was a special case in which manufacturing potential was very great but was constrained by the lead England, Holland, and France had gained largely through government assistance. His conclusion: American government should assist American manufacturing. Hamilton's facts and logic were as emotionally compelling as are similar facts and the same logic when offered by officials of developing nations in 1980. However, Congress was not persuaded by Hamilton or by the still small number of aspiring comparative disadvantage producers, and the principal objective of tariff legislation remained, for a quarter century, operating revenue for the central government.

INCOME REDISTRIBUTION THROUGH TARIFFS: 1816-1930

Merchandise imports had spurted in 1783-84 following the Revolution's end. Import-competing Americans had protested and obtained protection from the States. Following the War of 1812, merchandise imports spurted again, jumping from $13 million in 1814 to $147 million in 1816. American merchants, shippers, and consumers rejoiced. But war had again attracted many Americans into comparative disadvantage production, and these people cried "Ruin." Which side would Congress take?

The comparative disadvantage producers had become numerous. They had to influence only one Congress; and in 1816, that Congress passed an avowedly protectionist tariff law with rates of 25 to 30 percent on cotton manufactures, iron, leather, cabinetware, carriages, hats, linen, and paper. Thereafter, state societies for the promotion of American manufactures grew in number and size presumably because they provided more benefits than costs to their members (especially through dissemination of technical information). A high point in their lobbying effectiveness followed the July 1827 convention of the Pennsylvania Society for the Promotion of Manufactures. One hundred delegates attended from 13 of the 24 states then in the Union. Concentrating on the "need" for higher tariffs, they issued an "Address" to the people and a memorial to Congress. Their organized effort contributed to passage of the 1828 "Tariff of Abominations" providing the most extreme protection ever to mar American history.[7]

From 1816 to 1860, rates varied with the strength of political coalitions; Southern farmers remained opposed to, and New England manufacturers remained in favor of, protection. Figure 12-1 shows

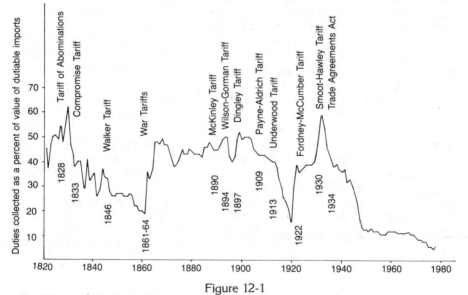

Figure 12-1
Tariff Rates in the United States since 1820 as a Percent of the Value of Dutiable Imports

Source; U.S. Department of Commerce, *Historical Statistics of the United States, Colonial Times to 1970* Washington, D. C.: Government Printing Office, 1975), Part 2, p. 888; and, for 1970-78, U.S. Department of Commerce, *Statistical Abstract of the United States: 100th Edition* (Washington, D. C.: Government Printing Office, 1079), p. 871.

the course of American tariff rates between 1820 and 1978. Note that it shows value of tariff receipts divided by value of dutiable imports (not by value of dutiable *and* free imports). This tends to overstate the degree of protection, but the overstatement is at least partly offset by the omission of the imports of high-duty items that do *not* happen because of the duties.

Between 1860 and 1910, rates were high and rising under a Republican Party supported by comparative disadvantage manufacturers and committed "to encourage the development of the industrial interests of the country."[8] Rates fell between 1910 and 1920 partly because world war slashed imports of high-duty goods. Rates were pushed up through the 1920s to the towering 1930 Smoot-Hawley peak.

The underlying determinant of nineteenth century events was American comparative advantage in agricultural commodities and comparative disadvantage in most manufactured products. Nevertheless, manufacturing lobbies were able to use government power to transfer income from consumers to themselves.

Lance E. Davis and Douglass C. North have argued that the well-financed manufacturing lobby was effective because its own numbers were small, were given other reasons for contributing to their "associations" (the continuing exchange of technical information when there was no technical press), and the costs of influencing legislation were low.[9]

> Because senators were not elected directly, they were particularly responsive to the demands of well-endowed (both financially and in terms of local political power) minority groups. . . the costs of influencing legislation by an elite were lower in the nineteenth century, and when the history books talk about special "ins" with the legislature, they are really talking about this low cost environment.[10]

And potential profits from higher tariffs were immediate and large, especially for firms with a substantial comparative disadvantage.

Davis and North argue further that when the Constitution was amended in 1913 to provide for direct election of Senators, the costs of lobbying income transfers to organized minorities rose, thereby discouraging spending to obtain tariff protection, so contributing to the drop in twentieth-century tariff rates shown in Figure 12-1. In addition, as Davis and North have also carefully described, several other changes occurred in this century to make costs and benefits less favorable to decisions to lobby for high tariffs and more favorable to decisions to lobby for low tariffs.[11]

By 1900, many American manufacturers had achieved comparative advantage. Such manufacturers had nothing at all to gain from tariffs; so they withdrew support from the tariff lobby. Furthermore, potential benefits rose and potential costs fell for comparative advantage producers contemplating lobbying efforts to reduce tariffs. When comparative advantage lay only with primary producers, the export-promotion gains to them from tariff cuts were too obscure and too uncertain to make lobbying attractive, and the farmers were so numerous that the costs of organization were high. The result: no lobbying by exporters for low tariffs before 1900.

But in the twentieth century, the comparative advantage producers were few enough in many industries for the costs of organization to be reduced, and many of those manufacturers learned enough of economic theory to become convinced that potential benefits from lobbying for low tariffs were likely to exceed costs. The pro-tariff lobbies have, therefore, had to face higher persuasion costs because of the now common opposition from organized comparative advantage producers. Figure 12-1 shows the results.

THE SMOOT-HAWLEY PEAK: 1930, IN THE PIT

Since all the low-tariff forces just described have operated throughout the twentieth century, the tariff peak of the early 1930s requires explanation. The immediate cause was America's third encounter with the "hothouse effect" of a war that cut off imports from Europe. During World War I, as during the Revolutionary War and the War of 1812, America became a hothouse for many new producers of goods in which Europeans, when not killing one another, had comparative advantage. After 1918 (as after 1781 and after 1814) Europe's comparative advantage exports wilted the prospects of the new American producers. In the 1920s, the latter were numerous enough to represent many jobs and shareholders yet few enough in number to be able to organize. Finally, they were clear enough as to potential gains to be impelled to finance successful lobbies for the series of tariff increases legislated in 1921, 1922, and 1930.

The peak came with the Smoot-Hawley tariff of 1930. Why did Congress legislate this peak when, as we have argued, understanding of trade theory was spreading, and costs and benefits were changing to discourage comparative disadvantage industry lobbying (even for the War's hothouse infants) and to encourage comparative advantage industry lobbying? The answer, we propose, is that the lobbying incentive passed to comparative advantage industries, *especially* agriculture, before sophisticated theory did and while the particular misconception reigned that "Government measures that have helped them can now help us." As a result, the newly armed good guys went down under self-inflicted wounds.

In supporting that hypothesis, we stress two points. First, Smoot-Hawley was *not* formulated as an anti-depression measure. Second, it was at least as much the result of lobbying by America's comparative advantage industry — agriculture — as by the comparative disadvantage industries.

Why this agricultural perversity? American agriculture enjoyed boom times after 1896. Then, World War I pushed net farm income up further. Buying at wartime price peaks, farm families incurred increased debts for machinery, buildings, and — especially — land.

After 1919, European agricultural output recovered and European governments subsidized agriculture and taxed farm imports. Both market and politics reduced growth of demand for U.S. farm exports.

In America, agricultural supply grew as productivity per worker rose nearly 40 percent between 1910 and 1930.[12] Consumers enjoyed the consequent increases in their living standards as agricultural prices fell by one-third between 1919 and the late 1920s.[13] But as technology changed to permit 72 farm families to produce what 100 had produced only 20 years earlier, rural-urban migration lagged. "Marginal" farm families suffered; all farm families preferred higher prices. Farm organizations grew, turned to government, asked first for subsidies, were rebuffed, then asked for what manufacturers had received — tariffs.

Responding to farm organization importunities, President Hoover called a special session of Congress in June 1929. The Administration proposed *some* tariff increases to aid farm families and but a few manufacturing industries.[14] Hearings dragged on more than a year. At last a coalition of farm-state Senators arose charging government favoritism to manufacturers and demanding "equal treatment," defined as "equal protection." On initial trial votes, industrial-state Senators and agricultural-state Senators each defeated the other's tariff increase proposals. At last, the two groups combined; each supported the other's tariff increases, and farmers obtained "equal treatment" in an unprecedented 195-page bill raising tariffs on hundreds of items.[15] Senators, persuaded by self-serving comparative disadvantage manufacturers, and other Senators, persuaded by self-destructive farmers, combined and produced a bill raising tariffs to the height shown in Figure 12-1.

In the space of one week, over 1,000 American economists petitioned for a Presidential veto.[16] A dozen nations threatened reprisals. But President Hoover signed the Tariff Act of 1930.[17]

Within a year, over a dozen nations — from Britain, France, and Spain to Mexico, Canada, and Argentina — had raised tariffs in retaliation.[18] The tariff increases and the accompanying — and partly consequent — depression cut the value of American exports almost 60 percent between 1930 and 1933.[19]

One other peculiarity, absurd but appealing, of the Tariff Act of 1930 may be noted: The Republican platform of 1904 had declared that the size of the tariff on each product "should always at least equal the difference of cost of production at home and abroad."[20] Woodrow Wilson, for the Democrats, became an advocate of the "competitive tariff." Except that the Republicans understood Alfred Marshall's concept of "normal profit" and President Wilson did not, the two silly concepts were identical.[21]

That principle was incorporated in the Smoot-Hawley tariff law. The first egregious problem in its implementation, for those who acknowledge sloping supply curves, is that in each nation different producers have different costs. But ask yourself: Assuming the government *could* employ enough accountants, engineers, and economists to determine "cost of production at home and abroad" for every product and if the differential tariff *were* then imposed (you decide how to handle transportation costs), how many dark blue 100-percent nylon short-sleeved one-pocketed men's size M sport shirts would we import? How much rolled ¼" sheet steel? How many bananas (which we could grow in New York greenhouses and sell at the price to which the Wilsonian "competitive tariff" would raise Central American bananas)?

The "scientific tariff" is nonsense. Nevertheless, it appeals to uninformed common sense. Happily, no American President, even when authorized to do so, has ever tried to implement it (though trigger prices were a stab in that direction).

RECIPROCAL TRADE AGREEMENT LEGISLATION: 1934

As Figure 12-1 shows clearly, 1934 was a major turning point in American tariff history. Comparative-advantage industry lobbyists appear to have come into the ascendancy. The common sense "can't export unless we import" came to the fore. Yet trade theory sophistication did not grow enough to permit stress on a "general welfare argument" for tariff reduction. Instead, on behalf of the comparative advantage lobbyists, the 1934 amendment justified reciprocal trade-reduction invitations to foreigners as a means for "expanding foreign markets for the products of the United States."

The reciprocal trade agreements program was renewed in 1937, 1940, 1943, 1945, and 1948. Until 1946, tariff reduction agreements were negotiated bilaterally. In November 1946, President Truman announced a new procedure: simultaneous negotiations with 18 other nations. Tradeoffs became thereby easier to arrange, A would grant a reduction B wanted in exchange for C granting a reduction D wanted and obtained by "giving" a reduction to A.

Such tradeoffs were also facilitated because, in 1923, Congress committed the United States to the principle of "unconditional most-favored-nation treatment," and most other nations subscribed to the principle after 1945. This principle provides that if a nation grants a tariff reduction to one other nation (the one thereby "most favored"), the reduction immediately applies to all the granting nation's other trading partners. This principle assures all negotiators that every tariff reduction will apply equally to all. As a result, no nation is "most favored" (but some can be not favored, as is the case for communist nations excluded by America from the benefits of reduction in U.S. tariffs).

CONTEMPORARY AMERICAN INSTITUTIONS: THEIR CHARACTERISTICS AND EFFECTS

The Second World War disrupted ordinary commercial international trade; yet, recovery came swiftly in the late 1940s, greatly helped by American Marshall-Plan gifts to assist the reconstruction of Western

Europe. Traumatized by the effects of the Great Depression, international political leaders worked, in the middle 1940s, to devise means to prevent another Great Depression involving competitive devaluations and attempts to export unemployment.

The International Monetary Fund (IMF)was created in 1944 to permit nations to prevent devaluation of their currencies without increasing import restrictions. The International Bank for Reconstruction and Development (now, simply, World Bank) was also created in 1944, with emphasis on the "Reconstruction," to facilitate financing of imports by the war-weakened European allies. Most important, as a support for the pursuit of mutual gains from comparative advantage specialization, was the formulation, in 1947, of the General Agreement on Tariffs and Trade (hereafter, GATT). The GATT has endured and seems likely to continue to operate, at least through the 1980s, providing an institutional basis for multinational negotiations to reduce trade barriers.

GATT

The United States joined both the IMF and the World Bank in 1944. It joined GATT in 1947. Technically, GATT is not an organization, but an agreement containing rules of conduct in trade relations and schedules of agreed-upon tariff rates. In practice, however, it is an international organization with a permanent staff headquartered in Geneva, Switzerland.

GATT is based on the nondiscrimination principle embodied in its unconditional most-favored-nation (MFN) rule. Therefore, any bilateral tariff concession negotiated within the framework of GATT results in a multilateral reduction of tariff rates. Exceptions to the rule of nondiscrimination are permitted for customs unions, free trade areas, and other traditional trade blocs, as well as for the preferential tariff treatment given by the developed to developing nations. (See the section, "Proposals for a Generalized System of Preferences," in Chapter 19.)

GATT as a rule prohibits quantitative trade restrictions such as export and import quotas. Agricultural products under governmental support programs are exempted from this rule. Exemptions to the rule are also allowed for reasons of balance-of-payments difficulties, economic development, and national security. The MFN rule applies to the permitted quantity restrictions.

Between 1947 and 1967, there were six "rounds" of multilateral tariff negotiations under the sponsorship of GATT, and tariff rates on tens of thousands of products were successively reduced. However, GATT's quota prohibitions have been widely evaded, and quota and other trade barriers have risen as tariffs have fallen.

NEW GUIDING PRINCIPLES

Since the end of World War II in 1945, the American Congress has espoused several new principles to guide American foreign trade policy.

As one might have expected, these principles represent in part the interests of comparative advantage exporters and in part the interests of comparative disadvantage producers determined to minimize imports.

Compensating the Losers: A Nod to Pareto

All of our theory acknowledges that a move toward comparative advantage specialization will force some people to bear the sometimes substantial costs of changing jobs. The concept of *Pareto optimality* provides that a change can make all better off if the immediate winners gain enough to remain better off after fully compensating the losers.

The Trade Expansion Act of 1962 provided for compensation for the bigger losers when tariff reductions or independent growth of imports benefit the general public. Congress authorized assistance for workers, managers, and owners of comparative disadvantage businesses injured by growth of imports.

The Trade Act of 1974 continued compensation to firms and employees and added, for the first time, assistance to communities where resident firms had lost sales because of increased imports. The present law invites groups of workers, who claim import displacement, to apply to the Secretary of Labor for assistance. If the Secretary finds that actual or threatened unemployment of the workers is caused by increased imports, the workers qualify for adjustment assistance consisting of counseling, retraining services, job search allowances, relocation allowances, and supplementary unemployment compensation with a basic benefit of 70 percent of salary to be paid for a period of up to 52 weeks (78 weeks for workers over 60 years of age and those enrolled in training programs).[22]

Compensatory assistance for business firms is administered by the Economic Development Administration of the Department of Commerce. To be eligible, firms must demonstrate that increased imports are an important cause of decreases in the firms' sales and of actual or threatened unemployment of their workers. Adjustment compensation for firms consists of technical assistance and financial assistance. Technical assistance may be obtained from Federal agencies or private sources. In the latter case, the U.S. Government assumes up to 75 percent of costs. Financial assistance may be in the form of direct loans or loan guarantees with terms not exceeding 25 years. The maximum amount of a direct loan is $1 million. A loan guarantee may not exceed 90 percent of the loan balance, and is limited to $3 million. Direct loans or loan guarantees may be used for acquisition, construction, modernization, or expansion of land, plant, buildings, or equipment, or to supply working capital for implementation of a firm's adjustment plan.

The new program explicitly recognizes that tariff reductions benefit most Americans while requiring adaptations that take time and impose costs on many individuals. By acknowledging the need — or obligation — to provide compensation to the injured, society reduces opposition to freer trade and facilitates the reallocation of resources from comparative disadvantage to comparative advantage industries.

There are estimates of the impact on jobs of both an increase in imports and the corresponding consequent increase in exports. In 1977-1978, William Cline led a group that studied the job effects of tariff reductions that seemed possible under the Tokyo Round of multinational trade negotiations (of which much more below). They considered a dozen possible trade liberalization results. The average result (excluding petroleum and textiles) was, for North America, a drop of 42,500 jobs in the import-competing sector and an increase of 39,500 jobs in the export sector.[23]

Notice clearly that our theory predicts that the former number should exceed the latter. When nations move into comparative advantage specialization, they will be able to produce the original output with fewer inputs. The inputs thereby released are the "gains from specialization and trade." Insatiable human wants will put them to new uses.

But let us go one more step to place in perspective the potential effects of an American move to eliminate all tariffs. Cline's group estimated that if all American and Canadian tariffs were eliminated, the *gross* effect (not allowing for *any* increase in exports) would be an end to 361,000 jobs including those of both import-competing firms *and* their suppliers.[24] If spread over eight years (consistent with other tariff cuts of recent decades), 45,000 jobs would be displaced each year.

Surely, 45,000 job cuts is a lot of inconvenience for 45,000 families. But look at this number from the perspective of Table 12-2. Each year between 1963 and 1973, the American and Canadian economies took in, *net*, 1,900,000 additional workers while 450,000 were put out of work by technological change. The latter change sorely inconvenienced 450,000 families bearing the price of progress without assistance from the larger society that received the benefits. Within this context, we can weigh the "problem" of workers displaced by trade liberalization but helped by a society now honoring the principles of movement toward Pareto optimum.

TABLE 12-2   AVERAGE ANNUAL NUMBER OF JOB CHANGES IN THE UNITED STATES AND CANADA DUE TO SELECTED CAUSES FOR THE PERIOD 1963-1973

Causes	Number	Number as Percent of Total Employment
Annual average increase in the civilian labor force	1,900,000	2.3
Estimated annual average number of job changes due to productivity increases	450,000	0.5
Of which: annual average decline in agricultural employment	150,000	0.2

Source: Richard Blackhurst et al., *Adjustment, Trade, and Growth in Developed and Developing Countries* (Geneva: GATT, 1978), p. 59.

The Escape-Clause Defense of the No-Injury Principle

The availability of adjustment assistance has reduced the *net* gains from lobbying by comparative disadvantage industries. However, the latter groups have obtained benefits from a new principle introduced by President Truman in a 1947 executive order. The principle is that tariff concessions should *never* injure domestic producers! President Truman's 1947 executive order added an *escape clause* to all trade agreements to authorize the President to withdraw or modify any tariff concession upon a finding by the U.S. Tariff Commission of injury to domestic producers.

The Trade Expansion Act of 1962 retained the escape clause but with a significantly reduced protective effect. The Tariff Commission had now to find, before it could recommend "relief" to the President, that a tariff concession — not merely import competition — was the "major" cause (i.e., greater than all other causes combined) of a *serious* injury to the domestic industry. The scope for escape clause application, however, was broadened again in the Trade Act of 1974. To determine injury, it is now necessary merely to demonstrate that import competition is a *substantial* — rather than a "major" — cause of injury; and, as before 1962, the injury counts even if unrelated to liberalization of trade restriction laws.

U.S. GOVERNMENT AGENCIES IMPLEMENTING TRADE POLICY

We have devoted many words to laws and to events. We now shift our attention to the agencies of the U.S. government, created by those laws, that are to implement the laws and to shape the events of the 1980s.

The following U.S. Government agencies have major responsibilities in commercial policy matters: the State, Treasury, Agriculture, Labor, and Commerce Departments, the President's Special Representative for Foreign Trade Negotiations, and the International Trade Commission.[25]

Before World War II, the State Department dominated the country's economic relations — particularly those with political implications — with other nations. The Department's Bureau of Economic and Business Affairs continues to deal with economic policy matters. Within the Bureau, trade policy is handled by the Office of the Deputy Assistant Secretary for International Trade Policy.

The Treasury Department's influence and initiative in trade policy matters increased markedly during World War II, gained further during the 1960s; and by the mid-1970s, it had come to overshadow the State Department. The Treasury's activities in international economic matters including commodity agreements, international investment, foreign exchange, and foreign aid are handled by the Office of the Assistant Secretary for International Affairs. The Office of Tariff Administration administers customs laws. It also investigates cases of dumping allegations against foreign producers and charges that foreign governments are giving subsidies to their exporters.

The Agriculture Department deals with export promotion of agricultural products, administers import quotas on agricultural commodities, and helps formulate U.S. trade policy on foreign governments' import barriers against U.S. agricultural products and foreign governments' purchases of the same.

The role of the Deparment of Labor we have already described in our section on "Compensating the Losers."

The Commerce Department's role in trade matters is by custom limited to operational — as compared to policy-making — matters. The Department's main responsibility is the promotion of U.S. nonagricultural exports. It collects data on foreign trade and investment, collects and disseminates information concerning foreign markets and trade opportunities, provides export counseling to U.S. business firms, and promotes U.S. exports abroad by sponsoring overseas trade fairs and missions. The Department also administers U.S. export controls to the Communist-bloc countries, and as described above, administers adjustment assistance to domestic firms injured by import competition under the provisions of the Trade Act of 1974.

The position of the Special Representative for Trade Negotiations was created by the Trade Expansion Act of 1962, and was elevated to cabinet status by the Trade Act of 1974. The Representative's small staff of 20 to 30 professionals is located in the White House. The statutory responsibility of the chief negotiator is to represent the United States in all negotiations dealing with trade agreements (such as GATT negotiations), tariff adjustment, and "orderly marketing agreements" (also known as "voluntary export restraints" or VERs). In practice, the chief negotiator is also responsible for securing congressional support for necessary enabling legislation for trade agreements concluded by the Administration.

The International Trade Commission

The United States International Trade Commission (ITC, formerly the less grandly titled Tariff Commission), unlike all the agencies enumerated above, does not belong to the executive branch, but is rather an independent federal agency created by Congress. The Trade Act of 1974 gave the Commission an expanded authority and importance when it eased the criteria for demonstrating injuries from import competition and made it more difficult for the President to ignore the Commission's recommendation for relief from imports. (In the area of import controls, the ITC handles injury-from-imports cases under the escape clause provisions and the unfair-trade-practice cases, while the Treasury handles the antidumping and countervailing-duty cases.)

The ITC is an independent fact-finding agency with quasi-judicial and quasi-legislative authorities. It has broad powers to study and investigate matters concerning United States foreign trade and its effects on the domestic economy. It investigates complaints filed by parties representing domestic firms, industries, and groups of workers, as well as by government agencies and congressional committees. It also initiates its own inquiries.

The Tariff Act of 1930, as amended, provides that the Commission consists of six Commissioners appointed by the President, and confirmed by the Senate, each serving a staggered nine-year term. Not more than three Commissioners may belong to the same political party, a provision tantamount to requiring that the Commission be half Republican and half Democratic. In September 1978, the ITC had 369 staff members including economists, lawyers, commodity analysts, investigators, and data systems experts. The Commission's fiscal year 1978 budget was $12,213,000. In fiscal 1978, approximately 40 percent of the Commission's work, measured by distribution of employee compensation, was investigations of various sorts. Basic research and furnishing of information and technical assistance to the Congress, other agencies, and the public claimed another 40 percent of the ITC's employee compensation, and the remaining 20 percent was used for executive direction and administration.

The fiscal 1978 *Annual Report* published by the ITC enumerates the following broad responsibilities of the Commission:

Investigating eligibility of and recommending appropriate import relief for domestic industries.

Taking action against unfair practices in import trade, including the importation and sale of items at less than fair value or the importation of items whose production or export was subsidized by a foreign government.

Conducting studies on trade and tariff issues relating to U.S. foreign trade.

Assisting in the development of uniform statistical data to achieve comparability of import, export, and domestic production statistics.

In fiscal year 1978, the ITC completed seventy-one investigations. Commission investigations are conducted under provisions of the three key statutes, which are: the Trade Act of 1974; the Tariff Act of 1930, as amended; and the Antidumping Act of 1921, as amended.

Trade Act of 1974 (Relief from Injury Caused by Imports). Sec. 201 of the 1974 Trade Act provides that the Commission must conduct investigations on its own initiative or upon petition by a firm, a group of workers, or other representatives of an industry to determine whether a product is being imported into the United States in such increased quantities as to constitute a *substantial* cause (which can be less than a *major* cause) of injury, or threat of injury, to the domestic industry.

If the ITC's finding is affirmative (that is, if it finds there is injury), it must recommend a remedy to the President. The recommended import relief measure may take the form of (1) an increase in, or imposition of, a tariff on the product concerned, (2) establishment of a quantitative restriction on imports, (3) negotiation of "orderly marketing agreements" with foreign suppliers or their governments, or (4) provision of adjustment assistance to firms, workers, and communities. Sec. 203 of the 1974 Trade Act stipulates that, if the President does not provide relief in the form recommended by the ITC, then Congress may override the President's action by a concurrent resolution, upon which the President is required to implement the relief recommended by the ITC.

During fiscal 1977, the ITC completed twelve investigations under Sec. 201. Four of the twelve findings were affirmative (sugar, mushrooms, footwear, and television receivers), seven were negative, and on one the Commissioners were equally divided. In the sugar case, the ITC recommended reduced quotas on U.S. sugar imports. President Carter rejected this recommendation, and instead announced that he would attempt to provide a subsidy payment to U.S. sugar growers. The Commission's recommendation for mushroom import restriction was rejected by the President on grounds of national economic interest! In the footwear case, the President rejected the ITC's recommendation for import quotas, and instead expanded adjustment assistance and entered discussions on orderly marketing agreements with principal supplying nations.

On the television import issue, the Commission recommended to the President that the existing 5-percent duty on both black-and-white and color television sets be raised to 25 percent for two years, then lowered to 20 percent in the third and fourth years, and to 15 percent in the fifth year. President Carter rejected this recommendation. Instead, he extracted an orderly marketing agreement from the Japanese. The agreement, reached between the U.S. and Japanese governments in May 1977, called for the Japanese to hold their exports of color television sets to the United States at an annual rate of 1,750,000 sets for three years. This figure represented a reduction of about one-third from the actual import volume of 1976. (The President decided that imports of black-and-white sets were not injurious to domestic producers.)

During fiscal 1978, the Commission completed nine investigations under Sec. 201. Four of the nine findings were affirmative. President Carter rejected three of them on grounds of national economic interest. In the case of high-carbon ferrochromium, the President proclaimed a tariff increase of 4 cents per pound with respect to high-carbon ferrochromium valued less than 38 cents per pound for a period of three years.

Tariff Act of 1930 (Unfair Practices in Import Trade). Under Sec. 337 of the Tariff Act of 1930, the ITC is authorized to make investigations, on its own or after receipt of a complaint from an interested party, to determine whether there exist unfair methods of competition or unfair acts in the importation of articles into the United States. "Unfair trade practices" under Sec. 337 typically involve patent infringement cases or antitrust cases, for example, predatory pricing. If the Commission finds a violation of Sec. 337, it can issue an order excluding the imports or issue a cease and desist order. The President may disapprove such an order within 60 days after its issuance. The ruling of the Commission may be appealed to the U.S. Court of Customs and Patent Appeals.

During fiscal 1977, the ITC concluded nine investigations under Sec. 337. Six of the nine found no violation of Sec. 337. In two cases, the investigations found a violation, and a permanent exclusion order was issued by the Commission. The President allowed those orders to stand. In one case, the investigation resulted in a consent order.

Under a *consent order,* a party consents to refrain from certain actions without admitting past guilt. In July 1977, the ITC for the first time negotiated a consent order with Japanese color television producers. Specifically, Japanese companies agreed not to sell sets in the United States in a "predatory manner." Because there was no formal Commission recommendation, the President was deprived of an opportunity to review the case. The ITC's new activism, manifest in the use of consent orders, was cheered by some U.S. manufacturers, while it irked the White House and some congressional leaders.[26]

During fiscal 1978, the Commission concluded ten investigations under Sec. 337. No violation was found in seven of the cases. In two, the Commission found violations and issued permanent exclusion orders against which the President took no action. In the remaining case, the violation finding resulted in a cease and desist order by the Commission, which was disapproved by the President.

Tariff Act of 1930 (Countervailing Duty). Under Sec. 303 of the Tariff Act of 1930, as amended, the ITC determines the extent of the injury, or threat of injury, to the domestic industry whenever the Secretary of Treasury finds that a duty-free imported article is receiving an export subsidy from the exporter's government. The Trade Act of 1974 expanded the scope of the countervailing-duty law to include both dutiable and duty-free imports. With respect to dutiable imports, the ITC's determination of extent of injury is not required. On dutiable imports and on duty-free imports for which injury size is determined by the ITC, the Treasury imposes an extra duty equal to the amount of the foreign subsidy. During fiscal 1978, the Commission concluded two investigations under Sec. 303. The Commission's finding was affirmative in one case and negative in the other.

Antidumping Act of 1921 (Imports Marketed at Less Than Fair Value). Sec. 201(a) of the Antidumping Act of 1921, as amended, provides that whenever the Secretary of the Treasury advises the ITC that certain imports are sold in the United States at "less than fair value," the Commission must determine within three months whether or not such imports are causing injury to a domestic industry. If the Commission's finding is in the affirmative, the Secretary of the Treasury imposes an antidumping duty on the imports.

During fiscal 1977, the ITC completed eleven dumping investigations under the provisions of the Antidumping Act. The Commission's findings were affirmative in five cases and negative in six. During fiscal

1978, the ITC completed seventeen antidumping investigations. Its determinations were affirmative in nine cases and negative in eight.[27]

The Call for a Comprehensive Export Policy

We have been describing a variety of laws being implemented by a plethora of agencies. In all of these, emphasis is on import controls that serve to transfer a politically-determined slice of American output to comparative disadvantage producers. In contrast, the comparative advantage producers are left to seek their own way in an international market in which information is often expensive to obtain and in which foreign governments often act aggressively to restrict American exports.

The United States is the only major industrial nation without a comprehensive export policy and a trade ministry to promote and administer it. The term "commercial policy" in the United States has traditionally meant "import control policy," whereas in many other nations it has meant policies affecting both imports and exports. However, in recent years in the United States, there has been a surge of interest in establishing a comprehensive export policy. Some business and congressional leaders pressed President Carter for a high-powered federal agency to stimulate U.S. exports. Such a demand reflects the deep concern of some business and public leaders over the declining share of U.S. exports in world markets. The sharp rises in oil prices in recent years have made the problem more critical, for the expected future increases in the oil import bill, if not matched by equally large increases in export earnings, will depress the dollar, retard growth of the U.S. economy, and result in its overall weakening in the decades ahead.

However, a comprehensive export policy for the United States is a long way off. A first step would be creation of a federal agency whose initial task would be to consolidate under one roof the various trade-related functions now scattered throughout the federal bureaucracy. An effective agency would require authority to be able to speak with one voice — vis-à-vis the public, the business community, the Administration, and Congress — calling for an elevated priority for export promotion against other pressing national objectives such as environmental protection or national defense.

In the summer of 1979, President Carter worked for legislation implementing the Tokyo Round agreements (for which, see below). As a byproduct, enthusiasm built up for a regrouping of the federal agencies responsible for trade-related policy-making and administration. Several reorganization schemes were suggested to the President. Congressional leaders preferred creation of a Department of International Trade. The Treasury Department and the State Department jointly proposed consolidation of trade-related policy-making and administration under the Special Representative for Trade Negotiations. The Commerce Department's and Office of Management and Budget's proposal would assign policy-making to the Special Representative's Office, but would assign administration to the Commerce Department, renamed the Commerce and Trade Department. Yet a fourth proposal would establish two smaller-scale agencies — a U.S. Export Corporation for export promotion and a U.S. Trade Policy Administration to administer trade-related laws and regulations.[28]

One of these proposals may become law. The many agencies may become one (or two). Export promotion may obtain its own agency. The new agencies may consolidate or may duplicate. These decisions may be delayed until they fall into the hands of readers of this book.

In the meantime, the principal policy issues involve barriers to imports.

NONTARIFF TRADE BARRIERS: ESPECIALLY "VOLUNTARY" QUOTAS

Neither compensation nor no-injury protection has kept comparative disadvantage firms and workers from organizing and obtaining new forms of protection. As tariff levels have fallen, quotas and other trade barriers have become more confining. The net effect, as shown by Figure 12-1, has been lower tariffs, but the new nontariff barriers are worth billions of dollars to their instigators.

In America, the simple quota has been introduced and continues to serve several industries. America's sugar quota was begun in the 1930s. Its primary purpose was to raise price for Louisiana cane growers and Ohio and Idaho beet growers. A secondary purpose was to raise the incomes of Hawaiian, Puerto Rican, Filipino, and Cuban cane growers. The quota raised the domestic price some 80 percent above the world price in 1936.[29] The law has been revised often, with a major reallocation when Castro's Cuba was excluded from the American market on grounds that it had jailed thousands of political prisoners.

The Less Developed Countries (LDCs) have clear comparative advantage in sugar production. The living standards of tens of thousands of LDC poor depend on the price of sugar. In 1978, only 20,000 farms produced sugar in the United States. Yet the issue in America was whether quotas would raise the domestic price to 18¢ a pound as advocated by the sugar lobby's principal spokesman, Idaho's Senator Church, or to 14¢ a pound as advocated by the Administration.[30] Either way, LDC farmers, with a depressed price of 7¢ and American consumers had to lose.[31]

American petroleum producers also obtained quota protection from all American Presidents between 1955 and 1973. In 1955, President Eisenhower first announced the wondrous concept of "voluntary" oil-import quotas. Later, he gave assurances that the limits would remain voluntary; but he warned that if they were exceeded, he would employ compulsion. In 1959, he issued a proclamation ordering mandatory import limits on all petroleum imports.[32]

By 1969, the oil import quota added $5 billion a year to the cost of petroleum bought by Americans.[33] The effective actions of the Organization of Oil Exporting Countries (OPEC) during the November 1973 Yom Kippur War created an entirely new situation for America. But the Eisenhower-Kennedy-Johnson-Nixon petroleum quota had had one certain and one possible relevant consequence. Restricted imports, 1957-73, resulted in larger consumption of domestic oil so reduced the oil still underground in America in 1973. Perhaps more importantly, the Eisenhower restrictions *lowered* the price of oil outside the United States and injured oil exporting nations. That shock was one incentive inducing leaders in oil exporting nations to seek ways to form a cartel that could restrict production and raise export prices. Had American leaders not been the first to obstruct the international oil trade, OPEC might never have followed that lead to its own spectacular successes.

"Voluntary" import quotas were followed by "voluntary" export quotas. Textiles is one large manufacturing industry in which developing nations have in recent decades shown clear-cut comparative advantage. So, America's comparative disadvantage producers persuaded President Eisenhower to threaten import quotas unless Japan "voluntarily" restricted exports. Japan complied in 1956. Campaigning for the presidency, John F. Kennedy promised further controls. In 1962, 33 nations signed an agreement in which comparative advantage exporters agreed to restrict cotton textile exports to the United States. In 1970 and 1971, exporters agreed to restrict shipments of woolen and synthetic fiber products.[34] Extended in 1973, those restrictions remain in force inhibiting the rise of the world's poor.

Other American comparative disadvantage firms and unions have been able to obtain government support to obtain other "voluntary" restrictions on exports, including Formosan mushrooms, Mexican tomatoes and strawberries, Japanese color television sets, and European and Japanese steel. Also U.S. import quotas have been extended to cotton, peanuts, meat, and some dairy products. All of these recent quantitative restrictions damage efficiency more than would roughly equivalent tariffs, for tariffs always invite cost cutting by exporters. Quotas offer no incentive to anyone to cut costs — as Chapter 10 stressed.

Whether trade restrictions are to rise or fall in future depends in part on the readers of this book. The welfare of American consumers and the aspirations of the LDC poor clearly call for free trade in sugar and in textiles. Yet the comparative disadvantage producers will continue to press for protection. California's Governor Brown opened his 1979 presidential campaign with a New Hampshire speech complaining that, "even our allies are stealing our jobs" and calling for stiffer controls on cheap foreign imports.[35] The world's poor have much to fear from Americans who, with good intentions, obstruct expansion of the comparative advantage industries of the LDCs.

THE TOKYO ROUND

BACKGROUND TO THE TOKYO ROUND

In 1945, tariffs were the principal barrier to free trade. Multinational negotiations brought down the levels of American and of most developed nations' tariffs over the years 1945-57. In 1957, a new element was introduced into international trade prospects.

In 1957, six European nations signed the Treaty of Rome and established the European Economic Community. After 169 years, Belgium, France, Germany, Italy, Luxembourg, and the Netherlands imitated America's Constitutional common market.

American exporters were alarmed. Trade theory promised rapid expansion of the European economy, but the new common tariff threatened to keep America out. Reacting to this prospect of trade diversion (to review trade diversion, refer to Chapter 10), Congress passed the Trade Expansion Act of 1962 giving the President authority to negotiate multilateral tariff reductions of up to 50 percent. The subsequent "Kennedy Round" of GATT negotiations resulted in a 1967 agreement calling for an average tariff reduction of 36 percent (e.g., from 25 to 16 percent) on some 60,000 products. These reductions were effected over the years 1967-72. American tariffs had been cut about 4 percent in 1956; they were cut another 5 percent in 1962. By the time the Kennedy Round was completed in 1967, the tariff rates in major trading nations had been reduced to such low levels that their trade-restricting effects became minimal. The U.S. average tariff rates, for example, dropped from a high of about 47 percent in 1934 to about 7 percent in 1972. In that year, tariffs averaged 10 percent for the industrial countries.[36]

After 1967, the world's comparative disadvantage producers shifted to lobbying for nontariff trade barriers. They were successful, and those barriers proliferated in all the developed nations. In response, a new round of GATT negotiations began in 1973. Its focus was on the establishment of a code governing the use of nontariff barriers.

Not all Americans welcomed the effort. Between 1967 and 1974, the U.S. President had had no blanket authority to negotiate multilateral tariff reductions. In the meantime, the protariff lobbyists had enjoyed a resurgence led by labor unions. Two Democrats introduced highly protectionist legislation, the Burke-Hartke Bill, promising Draconian restrictions on imports. Quotas were proposed for *all* imports not already quantitatively restricted. The quotas were to be set at the average of 1965-69 imports and were to be calculated and applied on a country-by-country basis. The bill was clearly contrary to the public interest, but it was defeated only following a determined campaign by the Nixon Administration which had to promise concessions to the comparative disadvantage lobbyists.

The Trade Act of 1974

The Trade Act of 1974 provided protectionist measures as the price of defeat of Burke-Hartke. It also empowered the President to join GATT's Tokyo Round.

To permit more restrictions on trade, the escape clause was liberalized as described above. The President was given an expanded authority to place restrictions upon imports and to negotiate voluntary export restraint arrangements. The Act provided for a closer policing by Congress of the actions of the President to make sure that the President takes authorized steps to protect American business. The Act also gave the President authority to retaliate against "unfair trade practices" by withdrawing tariff concessions or by imposing import quotas. Finally, the Act strengthened the provisions of the antidumping and countervailing-duty laws by insuring speedy consideration of complaints by affected parties.

In the public interest, the Act gave the President extensive new authority to negotiate bilateral and multilateral reductions in tariff rates — as much as 60 percent of all tariff rates (Sec. 101). The Act also authorized the President to negotiate bilateral or multilateral agreements for reduction, elimination, or harmonization of nontariff barriers to trade (Sec. 101). Both of these negotiation authorizations were to expire in five years; without those authorizations, the United States could not have participated in the Tokyo Round.

RESULTS OF THE TOKYO ROUND

The new round of multilateral trade negotiations began with a 1973 ministerial (i.e., high level) meeting in Tokyo, thereby earning the title "the Tokyo Round" though negotiators later moved to Geneva. The United States formally participated after January 1975 under the authority of the Trade Act of 1974. The two principal objectives of the Tokyo Round were: (1) general reduction, by formula, of tariff rates on manufactured products, and (2) reduction or elimination of nontariff barriers to trade.

Tariff Reductions

In April 1979, the Tokyo Round negotiations were concluded. In all, 99 nations had participated in negotiations at one time or another, but only one developing country — Argentina — initialed all the accords. Other LDCs were unwilling to sign, charging that the agreement did not contain enough concessions to their interests.

Tariff rates are to fall by 52 percent for raw materials, 30 percent for semifinished goods, and 33 percent for finished products. The reduction of rates on finished industrial products is to average 31 percent for the United States, 27 percent for the European Community, 28 percent for Japan, and 34 percent for Canada. Most of these rates will be put into effect over an eight-year period that began in January 1980. By the time all scheduled reductions have been completed in 1988, the average tariff rate will be 4.3 percent in the United States, 2.5 percent in Japan, and 4.2 percent for all industrial countries.

The U.S. tariff reduction of 31 percent on industrial products will have little effect on the U.S. economy since existing rates are already low. U.S. rates on some industrial goods, such as automobiles, became zero in January 1980 (followed immediately by company and union appeals for quotas). Textiles and apparel, however, are to remain highly protected by tariffs. They constitute 95 percent of the remaining imports still sheltered by duties over 30 percent.[37]

Codes to Curb Nontariff Barriers

More important than the reduction of tariff rates, however, are this round's agreements covering various types of nontariff barriers that had proliferated over the years partly as ways of substituting for past tariff cuts. The Tokyo Round produced agreements in four major areas, each covered in a separate "code." [38]

Subsidies and Countervailing Duties. The code on export subsidies and countervailing duties covers the most controversial of the nontariff barriers. Many governments subsidize domestic producers. Some subsidies are *direct export subsidies* specifically designed to improve the price competitiveness of the industry in world markets. Other subsidies are given for domestic reasons — for example, maintaining employment or developing certain regions — but may have an unintended side effect of enhancing the recipient industries' export competitiveness. The code prohibits direct export subsidies, except in agriculture, and contains a statement that specifically recognizes that indirect (or "domestic") subsidies, as well as direct agricultural subsidies, may injure trading partners. An exact definition of indirect subsidies is to be worked out under the provisions of this code.

The code also prohibits use of countervailing, or retaliatory, duties, except where subsidized imports can be proved to be causing "material injury" to a domestic industry. (Under U.S. law in effect before July 1979, countervailing duties could be applied to any subsidized imports.) Disputes under this and other codes are to be resolved by a panel of experts selected by GATT.

Government Procurement. The code on government procurement policies bans, with exemptions, laws and regulations requiring government offices and agencies to purchase only domestic products. The U.S. federal "Buy American" law, therefore, had to be repealed to conform with this code. The code lists, for each nation, government agencies that will accept supply bids from foreign countries. The code requires that bidding on government contracts must be open, and announcements must be made with ample lead time. This new code may increase the U.S. government's procurements from foreign suppliers by $300 million a year, while U.S. producers could win $1.3 to $2.3 billion of additional foreign government business (in 1979 prices).

Customs Valuation. The code establishes invoice price as the basis for valuing imported goods for tariff duty purposes. In the past, several nations used various methods to inflate customs valuations in order to give domestic industries greater protection. The "American Selling Price" method used by the United States for customs valuation of benzenoid chemicals and some other products was a classic example. (Under this method, selling price within the United States, instead of invoiced price, was used.) The United States agreed to abandon this practice.

Technical Standards. Governments in the past used unreasonable standards and specifications for products to arbitrarily exclude some imports. The code does not specify standards, but instead establishes rules for setting standards and settling disputes. It requires open procedures and encourages uniformity in setting standards.

In addition to the four codes enumerated above, the accords included agreements on the elimination of tariffs on trade in civilian aircraft among major industrial nations, and several agreements covering trade in agricultural products among industrial nations. Two other codes — to curb counterfeiting of merchandise and to permit temporary safeguard measures against sudden surges of imports — could not be completed prior to the initialing of the accords.

Under the provisions of the Trade Act of 1974, no Congressional approval of the tariff cuts was required. In June 1979, President Carter submitted to Congress a bill to bring various U.S. laws into conformity with the Geneva accords on nontariff trade barriers. In July 1979, the bill was approved overwhelmingly by Congress, and was signed into law by President Carter. After all participating governments pass enabling legislation, the final agreements will be signed.

The true significance of the Tokyo Round's results lies in its success in reaching an international agreement to work toward dismantling protectionist nontariff trade barriers, in setting up procedures for the task, and in providing mechanics for dispute settlement. America's comparative advantage exporters stand to gain more from the accords than do those of any other nation, because America's market has been relatively open compared to its trading partners'. While U.S. policies and practices — some of which were admittedly protectionist — were public, nontariff barriers in many foreign countries were often shrouded in secrecy. By requiring increased "transparency" in international trade policies, the new codes will produce greater equality of opportunities among producers of all nations and lower prices for consumers of all nations. An international monitoring and appeals mechanism provided in each of the codes will help minimize the chances that the new open rules will be violated.

What next? Tariff and nontariff barriers are down. But the American press reports a new pervasive climate of protectionism in the world. As the price of petroleum rises, many political leaders solicit support (readily and mendaciously at hand from comparative disadvantage producers) for restrictions on imports of everything else *and* subsidies on exports — taxing everyone to "help" everyone. Ingenious interventions result, as with provision of cheap government loans to import-competing and to exporting firms. The new freer-trade rules can be breached. But comparative advantage producers and the public have been gaining. If Davis and North are correct about the new cost and benefit conditions, the public may stay ahead.

One prediction, recently firmly made, is that the complexities of the remaining trade barriers (e.g., government subsidized loans) are too great to permit any more multinational wide-ranging negotiations. Instead, negotiators expect a new bilateralism of one-on-one meetings.[39] We shall see.

THE FREE-TRADE ENGINE OF GROWTH

From the experience of the past 60 years, we may have a clearcut test of the proposition that trade restrictions inhibit domestic growth while freer trade stimulates domestic growth. Between the two World Wars, national policies looked inward. Foreign trade was severely restricted by every industrial nation. Uncertainty discouraged aggressive efforts to export. Neither Gross World Product nor merchandise exports grew very fast. In contrast, as Table 12-3 shows, over the quarter century, 1948-73, international trade was freed to serve as an engine of growth, and Gross World Product rose an average of 5 percent a year. In the ongoing battle between comparative disadvantage producers and the public, Table 12-3 shows what is "in it" for the public. Chapter 19 will provide much more information regarding the relationships between foreign trade growth and domestic growth in output per person.

TABLE 12-3   AVERAGE ANNUAL GROWTH OF GROSS WORLD PRODUCT AND OF MERCHANDISE EXPORTS, 1913-48 AND 1948-73
(percent)

Quarter century	Gross World Product	Merchandise Exports
1913-48	2	0.5
1948-73	5	7

Source: Richard Blackhurst et al., *Trade Liberalization, Protectionism, and Interdependence* (Geneva: GATT, 1977), pp. 7-8.

STUDY QUESTIONS

1. The text uses the term "greenhouse effect" when describing one of the consequences of the Revolutionary War, the War of 1812, and World War I. What, in this context, is the meaning of the term and what were its consequences?
2. No one can provide a definitive answer to this question. You are merely being asked to speculate. What would have been the likely consequences if Hamilton's tariff proposals had been implemented?
3. In what products did America have comparative advantage in the eighteenth century? In terms of the Heckscher-Ohlin theory, explain why America had comparative advantage in those products.
4. Apply the questions of #3 to the twentieth century and answer them. What changes occurred between 1790 and 1980 in America's relative resource endowment? Be explicit as to the countries with which you compare America.
5. Among American exports in 1790, what items represented primary trade, what items represented vertical trade, what items represented horizontal trade (if any)?
6. Describe the main features of the General Agreement on Tariffs and Trade (GATT).
7. Identify the antitrade and the protrade features that have been incorporated into U.S. trade legislation since the end of World War II.
8. Explain the principle of adjustment assistance. How does it differ basically from the safeguard provisions (or the escape-clause provisions)?
9. Explain the role played by the International Trade Commission in the U.S. government's commercial policy.
10. Critically evaluate the export promotion policy of the U.S. government. What progress, if any, has been made in this area during the last few years?
11. Describe the operation of some of the more commonly used forms of nontariff trade barriers (NTBs).
12. What were the major achievements of the Tokyo Round of GATT's multilateral trade negotiations?

ENDNOTES

1. Josiah Child, *Discourse of Trade* (London, 1690), p. 152, quoted in Lewis Haney, *History of Economic Thought*, 4th ed. (New York: Macmillan, 1949), p. 122.
2. Thomas Mun, *England's Treasure by Forraign Trade* (London, 1664), chap. 2, quoted in Alexander Gray, *The Development of Economic Doctrine* (London: Longmans Green, 1931), p. 90.
3. Cited in George Bancroft, *History of the United States of America* (New York: D. Appleton & Co., 1890), vol. VI, p. 181.
4. Asher Isaacs, *International Trade: Tariff and Commercial Policies* (Chicago: Richard D. Irwin, 1948), p. 173.
5. William Macdonald, ed., *Select Documents Illustrative of the History of the United States, 1776-1861* (New York: Macmillan, 1901), p. 98. An illuminating economic interpretation of the *Report* is presented in Charles H. Hession and Hymann Sardy, *Ascent to Affluence* (Boston: Allyn and Bacon, 1969), pp. 102-108.
6. Isaacs, *International Trade*, p. 149ff.

262

7. *Ibid.*, pp. 181-182; also Lance E. Davis and Douglass C. North, *Institutional Change and American Economic Growth* (New York: Cambridge University Press, 1971), pp. 179-180.
8. Isaacs, *International Trade*, p. 194.
9. Davis and North, *Institutional Change*, p. 180.
10. *Ibid.*, p. 258.
11. *Ibid.*, pp. 181-182.
12. U.S. Department of Commerce, *Historical Statistics of the United States: Colonial Times to 1970* (Washington, D.C.: Government Printing Office, 1975), Part 1, p. 498.
13. *Ibid.*, p. 489.
14. Frank W. Taussig, *The Tariff History of the United States*, 8th ed. (New York: G.P. Putnam's Sons, 1931), p. 491.
15. E. E. Schattschneider, *Politics, Pressures and the Tariff: A Study of Free Private Enterprise in Pressure Politics, as Shown in the 1929-1930 Revision of the Tariff* (New York: Prentice-Hall, 1935), pp. 31-36.
16. This petition is reproduced in full in Isaacs, *International Trade*, pp. 232-234.
17. Readers may be interested in reading Jude Wanniski, *The Way the World Works* (New York: Basic Books, 1978), chap. 7, where the author argues that the Smoot-Hawley tariff was the *principal* cause of the Great Depression.
18. Isaacs, *International Trade*, pp. 235-237.
19. Department of Commerce, *Historical Statistics*, Part 2, p. 884.
20. Schattschneider, *Politics*, p. 8.
21. Taussig, *The Tariff History*, pp. 418-419.
22. For the period April 1975 through September 1976, the average benefit period was for 30 weeks. This was "modest" in the midst of the worst recession in 40 years. P. Henle, *Trade Adjustment Assistance for Workers* (Washington, D.C.: Library of Congress, Congressional Research Service, 1976), p. 10. (mimeograph)
23. W. Cline et al., *Trade Negotiations in the Tokyo Round: A Quantitative Assessment* (Washington, D.C.: The Brookings Institution, 1978), pp. 125-126.
24. *Ibid.*
25. For more detail about all these agencies, see Steven Cohen, "Washington's Policy-Making Machinery," *The Making of United States International Economic Policy* (New York: Praeger, 1977), pp. 41-62, reprinted in John Adams, ed., *The Contemporary International Economy: A Reader* (New York: St. Martin's Press, 1979), pp. 76-96.
26. "Once Obscure Agency Takes Prominent Role in Monitoring Imports," *Wall Street Journal*, 25 November 1977, p. 1.
27. The discussion in this subsection is based largely on U.S. International Trade Commission, *Annual Report*, for fiscal year 1977 and fiscal year 1978.
28. "Wanted: A Stronger Policy to Stimulate U.S. Exports," *Business Week*, 16 July 1979, pp. 88-89.
29. Jack T. Turner, *Marketing of Sugar* (Homewood, Ill.: Irwin, 1955), p. 84.
30. *Wall Street Journal*, 19 June 1978, p. 24.
31. Over the years 1966-70, American sugar buyers paid an extra $20,000 per year per sugar-growing farm because of the quota, according to Andrew F. Brimmer, "Imports and Economic Welfare in the United States," remarks before the Foreign Policy Association, New York, 16 February 1972, cited in C. Fred Bergsten, *The Cost of Import Restrictions to American Consumers* (New York: American Importers Association, 1972), p. 15.
32. William H. Peterson, *The Question of Government Oil Import Restrictions* (Washington, D.C.: American Enterprise Association, 1959), pp. 18-19 and 30.
33. Bergsten, *The Cost of Import Restrictions*, p. 3.
34. Details of the agreements and of the relevant debate are given in Gerald M. Meier, *Problems of Trade Policy* (New York: Oxford University Press, 1973), pp. 92-179.
35. *The Economist*, 15 September 1979, p. 39.
36. Cline et al., *Trade Negotiations*, p. 2.
37. "Carter Discloses Highlights of Tariff Reductions that U.S., Main Trading Partners Sct in Geneva," *Wall Street Journal*, 22 June 1979, p. 4.
38. The following discussion of the four codes draws upon: "Industrial Lands Initial an Accord on Tariffs, Trade," *Wall Street Journal*, 13 April 1979, p. 3; and Peter Nulty, "Why the 'Tokyo Round' Was a U.S. Victory," *Fortune*, 21 May 1979, pp. 130-134.
39. Greg Conderacci, "The Tokyo Round Could Be Last of Its Kind," *Wall Street Journal*, 15 June 1979, p. 18.

PART V

FOREIGN EXCHANGE AND THE BALANCE OF PAYMENTS

13

The Foreign Exchange Market

As children, we grew accustomed to using money to buy goods and services. This chapter (and subsequent chapters) is special because it describes the foreign exchange market where money is used to buy money. Until we travel outside the country, most Americans have no reason to use dollars to buy some other money. Rarer still is the need to use one foreign money, such as German marks, to buy another foreign money, such as Ghanaian cedis.

But almost everyone involved in international trade — whether in goods, or services, or securities — is obliged to buy or sell foreign exchange. As a rule, exporters want to end up with the domestic money they must have to pay their employees and suppliers. Therefore, importers often buy the currency of the exporter's country and use the purchased foreign currency to pay for their import purchases (in large part, this is what tourists do). Alternatively, an importer pays the exporter in the importer's currency. Then the exporter must sell the importer's currency for the exporter's home currency (this is what the Parisian George V Hotel must do when paid with $50 bills or with $50 in travelers' checks). The term *foreign exchange* refers to the money (coins, paper notes, checking accounts) and the near-money (savings accounts, certificates of deposit, bills of exchange, and Treasury bills) of one nation owned by residents of another nation. Technically, foreign exchange is liquid claims, in foreign currencies, held by residents of one nation against foreign residents. *Foreign exchange transactions* refer to all sales of one currency for another wherever the transactions occur and whoever the buyers and sellers may be.

In economics principles textbooks and in U.S. banking statistics, "currency" refers only to coins and paper money and distinguishes between them and demand deposits, the other component of M_1. In the statistics and literature of international economics, a nation's "currency" means that nation's monetary unit, whether in the form of coins, paper notes, demand deposits, time deposits or other near-money; and the *foreign exchange rate* is the price (or range of prices, see below in this chapter) in the domestic currency of a foreign currency.

Dollars can be sold for yen in New York or in Tokyó, or in Cleveland, or Bombay, or Rio de Janeiro. The buyer and seller of yen may be American and Japanese, respectively, or both may be Japanese, or both may be Mexican. Buyer and seller may meet face to face or may negotiate by telephone, or telex, or by mail. The currency traded may be in the form of coins (though rarely so), or of paper notes, or checking accounts, or travelers' checks, or bills of exchange. Wherever, whoever, however one nation's money is bought with another nation's money, it is a foreign exchange transaction.

Newspapers, bankers, and even some economists sometimes write or speak of "the New York foreign exchange market" or "the Tokyo market for pounds sterling." Such terms can be useful in identifying transactions taking place in a particular city. But most pound, and yen, and dollar transactions in the foreign exchange market involve people in two cities. Thus, the geography is usually not significant. So the more useful concept is that of the dollar-yen market, the pound-franc market, and the mark-dollar market. Each of these markets is distinct, and each is unconditionally *worldwide*.

THE PARTICIPANTS IN THE FOREIGN EXCHANGE MARKET

The foreign exchange market involves four layers of participants —

1. Exporters and importers of goods and services (including all tourists who set off to import souvenirs, other foreign goods, and the services of foreign hotels, airlines, restaurants, and tour guides) and exporters and importers of stock shares, bonds, and other IOUs. These are, of course, the most numerous among the market's participants.
2. Foreign exchange *dealers,* most of which, in the United States, are large commercial banks.
3. Foreign exchange *brokers,* specialists concentrated in large port cities. There are only a few dozen in America.
4. Central banks, only one per nation.

As in wheat markets, there are so many buyers and sellers in foreign exchange markets and entry to the market is so easy that, in the absence of government intervention designed to influence prices, foreign exchange markets are bona fide examples of textbook perfect competition. However, as we will stress below, the decade of the 1980s — like that of the 1970s — is likely to be characterized by persistent and ubiquitous government intervention. In markets for the major currencies, this intervention has not, in general, involved restrictions on what private traders might do. Instead, government intervention has involved purchases and sales, sometimes enormous purchases and sales, by monetary authorities. Thus, in the contemporary world, actual exchange rates are the result of the buy and sell orders of a multitude of private participants and of a small number of government leviathans.

Foreign exchange *dealers* buy and maintain an inventory of foreign exchange from which they make sales at a profit (or loss). Most U.S. foreign exchange dealers are large commercial banks with international banking departments. In New York City, there are approximately one dozen such banks. Together with the branches of some large foreign banks, they account for the bulk of foreign exchange transactions there. But scattered across the country in such remote places as Ohio, Mississippi, and Idaho, smaller banks act as dealers for some of their clients who may be nearby firms with large export sales and executives who often travel abroad. Nearly all of the smaller among America's 14,000-odd banks have correspondent relations with larger banks that are dealers in foreign exchange. So one can buy and sell pounds, marks, yen, and francs and even the more exotic cedis, gourdes, and ringgits in most of the cities of America and of the world.

When dealers cannot match the supply of and demand for a given currency among their own customers, they turn to foreign exchange *brokers*. Brokers do not "take positions" in foreign exchange as do dealers; that is, brokers do not themselves buy or sell foreign exchange for their own inventories. Instead, brokers — usually specializing in particular currencies — earn commissions by arranging sales between dealers.[1]

Dealers and brokers are in close communication with each other by telephone and telex, both within a country and across national boundaries. As a result, the rate of exchange for any given currency tends to be the same everywhere in the world at any given moment. Any divergency is corrected almost instantaneously by *arbitrage* activities; that is, by the activities of dealers who buy and sell the same currency at two different rates in two different markets making a profit until their initiatives have brought the rates together.

Central banks may act neutrally in the foreign exchange market; they may participate only to facilitate their Treasury's foreign exchange transactions or to assist in check clearing. Alternatively, and commonly in recent years, they may enter the foreign exchange market determined to prevent a change — or to moderate a change — in the value of their currency.

In the United States, the Federal Reserve Bank of New York acts as agent for the entire Federal Reserve System and for the U.S. Treasury Department in dealing with exchange dealers and brokers. When the Fed enters the market to support the dollar, it ordinarily tries to conceal its intervention. To the extent possible, it tries to create the impression that there is a natural increase in the quantities of dollars demanded. The Fed may use the tactic of asking an obscure bank in an outlying region (the Midwest, for example) to serve confidentially as its "front" in placing dollar buying or selling orders in the New York market. Alternatively, the Fed official may ask the trusted managers of large New York banks to blend in the Fed's buy order with their regular business, so that the Fed's buying remains undetected. At other times when the Fed wants its buying intent to be publicized, its officials openly telephone dealers and brokers with offers to buy dollars. Central banks throughout the world use more or less similar tactics to camouflage or to publicize their intervention. Correspondingly, foreign exchange dealers and brokers everywhere have developed various tactics to detect when central banks are intervening.[2]

While central banks try to keep intervention secret, individuals try to pierce the veil of secrecy because windfall profits can be made by outsiders who learn in advance of forthcoming government intervention. For example, suppose the current rate — the "spot rate" — to be $1 = 200 yen. Suppose, further, the Federal Reserve decides to sell enough yen (adding to the yen's supply in the dollar-yen market) so the exchange rate will change to $1 = 210 yen. Anyone holding yen before the Federal Reserve intervention can profit from that intervention. An owner of 200,000 yen could buy $1,000 before the intervention and could sell the $1,000 for 210,000 yen after the intervention, for a windfall of 10,000 yen — less transactions costs.

VARIOUS RATES OF EXCHANGE

With privileged information, that is an easy way to make money. We will soon be considering other ways to earn a living in foreign exchange dealings. First, however, we need to consider the variety of exchange rates that can exist between two currencies at a single point in time. Usually, a foreign exchange transaction involves a trade of purchasing power between two parties separated by thousands of miles and at least one international border. Both parties want assurance that they will get what they pay for (how, for example, would you find a reliable lawyer if you were cheated by someone in Turkey?). Reliable legal documentation is therefore demanded by all parties.

A variety of documents are available to assure secure trading. The transactions costs for each kind of transfer document differ from the transactions costs associated with every other kind of transfer document. Anticipate, therefore, that "the" exchange rate between dollars and yen (or between any other pair of currencies) will depend upon the kind of documents used in the particular process used to effect a currency trade. Expect also that other factors such as size of transaction will affect transactions costs and, thereby, will affect "the" exchange rate.

Among the different rates are, for example, rates for bank transfers (cable or telephone) for large transactions, rates for sight drafts, for travelers' checks, and for bank notes. The bank transfer rate is generally accepted as the *basic rate* to be cited in newspapers and in textbooks. Funds transferred by this method become available for payment after two working days. The rate for bank sight drafts (drafts payable on demand) may be the same as for cable transfers, or may be slightly higher. In New York and London, the *selling rate* (i.e., the rate at which large customers can buy the currency from the dealer) is normally about one-tenth of a percent above the dealer's *buying rate*. The rates for bank notes may be substantially higher *or* lower than the rates for bank transfers, depending on the demand and supply conditions of bank notes in a given market on a given day. The reasons for this variation are straightforward. For example, every May and June, European-bound tourists want to buy more British, Danish and German bank notes than are brought to New York by returning tourists. Therefore, the dollar price of European bank notes rises. Autumn brings a reversal, and the dollar price of European bank notes falls. Because transactions costs are especially high for dealers handling bank notes (they are bulky, counting is laborious, theft is more likely), the spread between the selling and the buying rates is larger for bank notes than for bank transfers; in some cases it exceeds ten percent.

The following is an excerpt from the foreign exchange quotations for June 27, 1980, from the *Wall Street Journal*.[3]

	U.S. Dollar Equivalent	Currency for U.S. Dollar
Britain (Pound)	2.3555	0.4245
Canada (Dollar)	0.8704	1.1489
France (Franc)	0.2446	4.0885
Japan (Yen)	0.004601	217.35
Switzerland (Franc)	0.6175	1.6195
West Germany (Mark)	0.5688	1.7580

The explanation given below the caption "Foreign Exchange" reads as follows: "The New York foreign exchange selling rates below apply to trading among banks in amounts of $1 million and more, as quoted at 3 P.M. Eastern time by Bankers Trust Co. Retail transactions provide fewer units of foreign currency per dollar." The quotation for West Germany (Mark) for this day being 0.5688 means that it took $0.5688 to buy one German mark; similarly, the figure in the last column 1.7580 means that it took DM1.7580 to buy one U.S. dollar. Note that the first column of quotations (U.S. Dollar Equivalent) expresses the value of a currency in terms of the number of domestic currency units. This method of stating the foreign exchange rate is used in nearly all nations. In Britain, however, it has been customary to express the value of the pound sterling in terms of the number of units of a foreign currency. In the United States, both methods are used: the news media normally report the value of the dollar in terms of foreign currency units, while in professional financial reporting it is customary to quote foreign currencies in terms of U.S. dollars.

The various exchange rates discussed so far are called *spot* rates of exchange, the rates that apply to exchange transactions requiring immediate delivery (meaning within two working days). Foreign exchange dealers also make a market in what is known as *forward exchange*, a promise to deliver or take delivery of foreign currencies at a later date. Forward exchange and the forward exchange market will be discussed later in the chapter.

THE SPOT EXCHANGE MARKET

The foreign exchange market proper is the market for spot exchange. Sales and purchases of spot exchange must be consummated within two working days. Unless otherwise noted in this book, the terms "foreign exchange" and "foreign exchange market" refer to spot exchange.

In Chapter 4 we observed that the demand for foreign exchange is the same as the supply of the national currency, that the supply of foreign exchange is the demand for the national currency, and that the equilibrium rate of exchange is determined by the interaction of the supply of and demand for foreign exchange, or else is controlled by government intervention in the foreign exchange market. We have also noted that for every pair of national currencies, there is one foreign exchange market, that it should not be identified with any specific geographic location, and that the residents of both countries can be either suppliers or demanders. The determinants of supply of and demand for foreign exchange and the causes and effects of their changes will be discussed in subsequent chapters. This section will examine the institutional aspects of foreign exchange markets.

INTERNATIONAL TRANSFER OF PAYMENTS

International transfers of funds are effected by either transfers or drafts. We will examine these two methods in turn.

Payments by a Transfer

A *transfer* is an order sent by cable, telex, telephone, or mail by a domestic bank to a foreign bank instructing the foreign bank to transfer a sum of funds from the domestic bank's account to the account of a specified party. To illustrate, let us assume that an American importing firm trades with a German exporter on an open-account basis, settling the balance (the importer's Accounts Payable, which are the exporter's Accounts Receivable) from time to time by bank transfers. Suppose that the American firm must pay 200,000 Deutsche marks to the German firm. The American firm pays the required amount in dollars (say $100,000, assuming the rate of exchange is $0.5/mark) to a large New York Bank by drawing a check against its demand deposit (d.d.) balance at the bank. The American bank then sends a cable to its correspondent bank in Germany, instructing it to transfer DM200,000 from the American bank's account to the German firm's account. Two days after the American firm's purchase of the transfer, the German firm can draw mark checks against its newly acquired mark balance in the German bank. The results of this financial transaction are shown in these balance sheets:

The American Import Co.

d.d. in American Bank −$100,000	Accounts Payable −$100,000

The American Bank

d.d. in German Bank −DM200,000	d.d. of American Import Co. −$100,000

The German Bank

	d.d. of American Bank −DM200,000 d.d. of German Exporter +DM200,000

The German Exporter

d.d in German Bank +DM200,000 Accounts Receivable −DM200,000	

A T-account lists *assets* on the left side and *liabilities* and *net worth* on the right side. For example, suppose an automobile worth $5,000 is your entire earthly possession, and you still owe $3,000 on it to your bank. Your *equity* in the car (or your *net worth)* is then $2,000. Your balance sheet looks like this:

Assets		Liabilities & Net Worth	
Automobile	$5,000	Loan from Bank Net Worth	$3,000 $2,000

As is always the case with double-entry bookkeeping, the left and the right sides must always balance. Often, in order to show the effects of a transaction, we enter only the changes in a T-account. In that case, the changes within an account also must balance out.

Now, let us go back to the transaction between the American importer and the German exporter taking place through their respective banks. The American Importing Company's assets decrease by $100,000 as it draws a check against its demand deposit balance in the American Bank, but the company's liabilities (Accounts Payable to the German Exporter) also decrease by $100,000. Since both sides of the importer's T-account are down by $100,000, the account balances out. The counterpart of these changes occurs in the exporter's T-account. The exporter gains assets (demand deposits in the German Bank) and loses assets

(Accounts Receivable from the American Importing Co.), each worth DM200,000. So the exporter's T-account is in balance. Neither do the two intermediary banks gain or lose any net worth. (For the sake of simplicity of exposition, we ignore the service fees charged by the banks. This omission does not change the analysis materially.) The American Bank loses assets (DM200,000) but also loses liabilities ($100,000) so its account is in balance. The German Bank's liabilities decrease and increase by the same amount (DM200,000) so its balance is unaffected. The net effect of the whole process is that the American importer discharges its Accounts Payable obligations in dollars, and the German exporter gets paid in marks. This simple illustration clearly demonstrates a fundamental fact of international payments: an international payment is almost always effected by a transfer of debt between banks. In our illustration, the demand deposit debt of the American bank to the American importer is eliminated and is replaced by a demand deposit debt of the German bank to the German exporter.

As we have already noted, foreign exchange rates differ from transaction to transaction depending on the size of transactions costs. Since transactions costs per dollar involved are lower on very large transactions, dealers give both buyers and sellers better prices on very large transactions (involving millions of dollars) than on those of moderate size (involving tens to hundreds of thousands of dollars). And dealers give better prices on transactions of moderate size than on small transactions. The least favorable prices are those encountered by tourists in hotels and restaurants; these prices are common yet atypical, for most foreign exchange moves in the large transactions of businesses and governments.

Conventions of the Market

The foreign exchange market functions more smoothly because of a number of conventions observed by all participants in the market. Connected by telephone and telex to other market participants, each money trader (each one an employee of a dealer bank) learns instantly of rate changes. Because prices change so often in foreign exchange markets, one convention holds that a quoted price is good for only one minute. In a telephone conversation, a dealer may tell a prospective yen buyer "The price is $0.005085 per yen." The prospective buyer may reply, "I don't know if I'll buy at that price; I must make another phone call first." When calling back 70 seconds later to place a buy order at $0.005085, the prospective buyer may be told, "The price is now $0.005091." Had the callback been made within 59 seconds the buyer could have obtained the yen at $0.005085 *even* though the price had by then moved to $0.005091.

More favorable to importers and exporters is the market convention that once a money trader quotes a price, the trader's firm is obliged to sell or buy *all* the foreign exchange the customer wants at the quoted price. This is so even if the amount to be sold is so large that in the process of obtaining the total, the dealer forces the price up. It is so even if the amount the dealer must buy is so large that, to dispose of it, the dealer will have to accept a fall in price. Clearly, the dealers are able to assume that most of the time they *are* in a perfectly competitive market.

Because dealers prefer to avoid inventory gains and losses, most try to hold minimal amounts of foreign exchange in inventory. Each dealer goes often to other dealers, frequently through brokers, to obtain or to dispose of the foreign exchange quantities that are the differences between what the customers of an individual dealer request or tender on a particular day.

A good-sportsmanship convention protects the foreign exchange dealers. If a dealer's (bank's) money trader makes an obvious error when quoting a price, for example, by inverting two numbers, as with $0.00519 instead of $0.00591, customers would be considered unethical if they would place a large order at that price. There are no legal sanctions for such unethical behavior, but a culprit would be ostracized by all dealers and brokers.

Payments by a Bank Draft

Small- and medium-size funds are transferred usually by means of a draft. A *draft* (or a *bill of exchange*) is an unconditional order in writing addressed by one person to another, requiring the latter to pay on demand at a fixed or determinable future time a certain sum in money to order or to bearer. There are three parties to a draft. The person who writes the draft is the *drawer* (or the *maker*), the person ordered to pay is the *drawee*, and the person to whom the draft is payable is the *payee*. (In contrast, a bond or a promissory note has only two parties — the maker and the payee.) The drawee is obligated to honor the draft because of some previously made contractual arrangement between the drawer and the drawee. The drawer admits his or her liability to the payee by the fact of signing his or her name to the instrument. The draft is a negotiable instrument in that it may be transferred from one holder to another by endorsement. Because of the implicit liability of the drawer to the payee, the drawer must pay the amount of the draft to the payee or to any subsequent endorsee in the event the drawee fails to honor the instrument.

It may be noted that the *check* that is commonly used for effecting domestic payments is a variant of the draft. In this case, the drawee is a bank, which is ordered by the drawer to transfer the bank's demand deposit debt from the drawer to the payee.

When both the drawer and the drawee of a draft are banks, the instrument is called a *bank draft* (or a *banker's draft* or a *banker's bill*). (A *bank bill*, in contrast, is a bill drawn by an exporter on the importer's bank or its correspondent bank. The term is used to differentiate from a *trade bill* — or *commercial bill* — which is a bill drawn by the exporter on the importer.) Unlike a transfer, the use of a bank draft does not require the beneficiary (the payee) to first acquire a bank balance. To illustrate, let us assume that an American resident wants to send 80,000 lire to her relative in Italy. She can buy an 80,000-lira bank draft from an American bank, paying it $100 (assuming an exchange rate of 800 lire/dollar) and a small fee. She then mails the draft to her relative in Italy, who can cash it at an Italian bank. As in the case of a transfer, the international payment is effected by changes in the debt positions of the banks involved. The difference is that the transfer goes from payer to payer's bank to payee's bank to payee. The bank draft goes from payer to payee to payee's bank to payer's bank.

PAYMENTS AND FINANCING OF MERCHANDISE TRADE

Bank drafts are commonly used by individuals and small business firms in payment for overseas purchases of goods, services, and securities, and for remittance of gifts. Bank drafts are also used, along with checks and transfers, in the settlement of trade balances that arise from open account arrangements. While the use of open accounts has become increasingly common in recent years, the bulk of merchandise trade is still conducted under different, more traditional, payment arrangements.

Under the traditional method of payment for imports, bills of exchange drawn by the exporter on the importer or the importer's bank are used. The former is called a *trade* (or *commercial) bill,* while the latter is known as a *bank bill.* When the drawee of the bill is obligated to pay on demand (i.e., on presentation to the drawee), the bill is a *sight bill* or a *sight draft.* If a bill is payable at some later date (e.g., ninety days after sight), it is a *time bill* or a *time draft.*

Most importers are either unwilling or unable to pay cash for the merchandise they import; they often need time to liquidate the purchased goods to raise funds with which to make the payment. In other words, importers need short-term financing. Many exporters, on the other hand, are not eager to extend credit, even if they are capable of doing so, to the importers who conduct business in a different political and legal environment. Exporters thus tend to want to be paid for their merchandise as soon as it is shipped. The question, then, is: How can an exporter receive payment as soon as the merchandise is shipped, while the importer is allowed a certain length of time before the payment is made? In other words, how can the import be financed? Who would provide the credit? The conventional means of paying for imports by bills of exchange solves this problem, as well as providing an efficient means of effecting a payment transfer.

The Use of a Trade Bill and Trade Acceptance

To facilitate our understanding of the use of bills of exchange in international trade, let us examine the payment for, and financing of, an American export of merchandise under different payment arrangements. A British importer, I, is to pay $2,000 (£1,000) to an American exporter, E, for merchandise. Importer I does not wish to pay for 30 days;

E wants to be paid at once. Someone else must finance the 30 day loan to I. Exporter E ships goods for which importer I is to pay $2,000 in 30 days. We will consider, first, financing through a "trade acceptance," and, second, financing through a "bank acceptance."

A "trade acceptance" begins as a "bill of exchange." Exporter E obtains the shipping documents (at a minimum, the bill of lading and an insurance certificate) from the shipping company. The *bill of lading* gives the holder legal title to the merchandise. In accord with a previous agreement made with importer I, exporter E draws a bill of exchange on I for $2,000, payable to a London bank, ILB, thirty days after sight. That is to say, the bill of exchange asserts that I is to pay ILB 30 days after getting the bill. The London bank is designated the payee because it is a correspondent bank of the New York bank, ENB, with which exporter E deals. Exporter E then attaches the shipping documents to the bill, and sells ("discounts") it to its bank, ENB. In discounting, the exporter is paid perhaps $1,980, equal to the face value of the draft ($2,000) *minus* a discount. In this way, exporter E is paid immediately after the shipment of merchandise. The discount of $20 represents the interest charge for the use of the bank's funds, and constitutes part of the exporter's cost of doing business.

Bank ENB then airmails the documents to its correspondent, bank ILB, in London, which presents the draft to importer I for "acceptance." To indicate its acceptance of the obligation to pay the bill in thirty days, the importer I writes "accepted" on the face of the draft, dates, and signs it. In return, Importer I receives from ILB the shipping documents which entitle I to claim the merchandise when it arrives in Britain. The bill, signed by the drawee (importer I), is now an *acceptance,* or a *trade acceptance* since it is an IOU of a trading firm. The London bank ILB keeps the acceptance for 30 days, and presents it upon maturity to importer I and collects $2,000. Bank ILB then adds $2,000 to ENB's account with ILB. (We ignore any service fee ILB may charge against ENB.) In this way, the New York bank ENB earns an interest (discount) of $20 for tying up its funds ($1,980) for 30 days.

In the above example, the New York bank ENB was the financier for the export-import trade. If ENB chooses not to finance the trade, it may sell the bill as soon as it is accepted, either in the New York or in the London money market. An insurance company, another bank, or an individual may be the buyer, paying $1,980 now in anticipation of a $2,000 payment in 30 days. (If the buyer is British, the $2,000 acceptance becomes part of Britain's foreign exchange.) Whoever buys the acceptance becomes the financier for the trade.

If the bank ENB chooses to finance the bill, the initial discount is a low-risk short-term investment well secured by collateral. This collateral (the bill of lading, etc.) is surrendered to importer I only when I accepts the bill. If importer I fails to accept the bill, bank ENB usually has recourse to exporter E for reimbursement. At worst, bank ENB can take charge of the merchandise, sell it, and recover part or all of its funds — less disposal transactions costs.

If bank ENB is dissatisfied with the documentation or questions the credit worthiness of exporter E, ENB may choose merely to provide a bill collection service by acting as an agent. In this case bank ENB does not take title to the bill, and expects a fee from the drawer E. Bank ENB may make a partial or total *advance* against the bill, the advance being a short-term loan to exporter E based on a promissory note. The bank will later recover the advance out of the proceeds of the bill. If importer I fails to honor ther draft, exporter E must reimburse the advance to bank ENB.

The Use of a Bank Bill and Bank Acceptance

What if the British importer I is a small firm, located far from London, whose credit worthiness is not known to the American exporter E and its bank ENB? In such a case, E may agree to draw a draft on the importer's home bank, IB, on the strength of a *letter of credit* issued by bank IB. First, importer I obtains a line of credit from IB, which is an authorization to borrow up to some specified maximum. Bank IB then issues a letter of credit to I, naming a beneficiary, exporter E, and specifying the time limit of the credit and the shipment of merchandise to be covered. Upon receipt of a copy of the letter of credit from IB, exporter E draws up a document called a *bank bill*, a draft on bank IB. Exporter E then discounts the bank bill, together with the shipping documents, at its New York bank ENB. Thus E is paid and satisfied. Bank ENB mails the bank bill to its correspondent London bank ELB, which presents it to the importer's home bank IB for acceptance. Bank IB accepts the bill, and obtains the shipping documents. Bank IB delivers documents to importer I in exchange for a promissory note. The bank bill accepted by IB is now called a *bank acceptance* or *banker's acceptance*. The disposition of the bank acceptance by bank ELB is the same as in the case of the trade bill. Again, whoever buys the acceptance is the financier for the export-import trade. Thirty days later, the financier collects the face value of the acceptance from bank IB. How the bank loan based on the promissory note is paid back is up to the terms of agreement between the borrower I and the lending bank IB.

In the above illustration, the instrument need not be a time bill and acceptance. The letter of credit may authorize exporter E to draw a *sight* bill on bank IB. In that case, banks ENB and ELB merely provide collection services charging fees. The draft drawn by E is presented to IB through ENB and ELB. Bank IB pays bank ELB the face value of the bill upon presentation; the proceeds are transferred back to exporter E through bank ENB. In this case, bank IB is the financier of the trade since importer I is to pay back the loan to bank IB over time.

THE FORWARD EXCHANGE MARKET

If you buy £1,000 today at $2 = £1 and then hold the pounds for six months, you will earn $100 if the rate of exchange changes to $2.10 =

£1. Of course, if the rate changed to $1.96 = £1, you would lose $40. Some people try to anticipate and profit from changes in foreign exchange rates. These people are called "speculators."

Most importers and exporters specialize in some activity other than foreign exchange speculation. They are experts in manufacturing, or insurance, or wholesaling, or transportation. In speculating, many of them would be gullible novices. Therefore, they are willing to sacrifice the chances of windfall gains from exchange-rate changes if they can be assured of protection against losses from exchange-rate changes. The *forward exchange market* provides that protection at the cost of that sacrifice.

FORWARD EXCHANGE

The forward exchange market is a market for forward contracts. A *forward contract* is a written agreement to buy or sell foreign exchange, to be delivered at a specified time in the future, at a rate agreed to on the date of the contract, regardless of how the spot rate changes in the meantime. No foreign exchange changes hands at the time of the agreement; only promises are made to deliver or take delivery of foreign exchange at a later date. Foreign exchange dealers offer such contracts, normally requiring a margin in the form of a cash deposit of ten percent of the face value of the forward contract. In a well developed foreign exchange market there is usually a deep and broad market in the futures of major currencies. For instance, the *Wall Street Journal* dated July 1, 1980, reported the following forward (futures) rates for June 30, 1980.[4]

(In U.S. dollars per unit of national currency)

	British pound	Canadian dollar	French franc
Spot rate	2.3600	0.8691	0.2442
30-day forward rate	2.3422	0.8661	0.2436
90-day forward rate	2.3190	0.8648	0.2426
180-day forward rate	2.2990	0.8640	0.2414

	Japanese yen	Swiss franc	W. German mark
Spot rate	0.004556	0.6148	0.5673
30-day forward rate	0.004541	0.6170	0.5675
90-day forward rate	0.004528	0.6211	0.5676
180-day forward rate	0.004529	0.6287	0.5713

Note that the forward rates of the British pound, the Canadian dollar, the French franc, and the Japanese yen were lower than their respective spot prices, while the forward rates of the Swiss franc and the German mark were higher. Currencies whose forward rates are higher than the spot rates are said to be *at a premium* with respect to the spot rate. Those whose forward rates are lower than the spot rates are quoted *at a discount* compared to the spot rate.

The forward exchange market provides a convenient means for hedging against foreign exchange risks, as well as for speculating in exchange rate fluctuations.

HEDGING

Suppose that an American importing firm has just accepted a 90-day time bill of exchange that calls for a payment of DM20,000 90 days hence to a correspondent bank of the German exporter. If the spot rate of exchange is $0.5/mark, the American importer knows that it must pay $10,000 in 90 days, provided the spot rate 90 days hence will remain at $0.5/mark. But there is no such assurance; exchange rates are known to fluctuate. Suppose in 90 days the mark appreciates so that the spot rate rises to $0.6/mark. Then, in 90 days, the American importer must come up with $12,000 (DM20,000 × 0.6) instead of $10,000. The contingency of having to pay the additional $2,000 is the *exchange risk* of the importer. How can the importer be protected from such a risk?

Hedging in the Spot Market

One method of hedging — a rather cumbersome one — is for the American importer to borrow $10,000 in America now, convert them into DM20,000 at the current spot rate of $0.5/mark, and hold the mark funds in a German bank until the draft falls due. (We assume that the importer has no idle cash.) In 90 days time, the importer can use the mark funds to pay the draft. Since it must pay interest on its dollar loan in America but can also earn interest on its mark deposit in Germany, the American importing firm may gain or lose on interest depending on the respective interest rates in the two countries. Suppose that they are 10 percent in America and 6 percent in Germany per year, or 2.5 percent in America and 1.5 percent in Germany for 90 days. The importer in that case pays $250 interest on its dollar loan and earns DM300 or $150 on its mark deposit in Germany. The difference, $200, is the cost of hedge against the exchange risk. If, on the other hand, the interest rate is higher in Germany than in America, the American importer will of course earn a profit by hedging. Note that this type of hedging involves only the spot market, and the cost of hedge depends on the interest-rate differential between the two financial centers.

Hedging through the Forward Market

There is a simpler, and more common, way of hedging against an exchange risk — one that involves the forward exchange market. The importing firm can buy forward marks from an American bank; that is, it can enter into a forward contract for purchase of DM20,000 to be delivered 90 days hence. Suppose the 90-day forward rate currently is $0.51/mark, or at a premium of $0.01 (or 2 percent) compared to the spot rate. The importing firm buying DM20,000 on a 90-day forward contract is assured of a delivery of DM20,000 90 days hence, provided it pays the bank $10,200   (DM20,000 × 0.51) at the time of delivery. The extra $200   ($10,000 × 0.02) is the cost of *forward cover* to the importer.

The relative desirability of these two alternative methods of hedging — one using the spot market and the other using the forward market — depends on how the two countries' interest-rate differential compares with the percentage difference between the forward and spot rates. In our foregoing two illustrations, the (90-day) interest-rate differential is 2 percent (2.5 percent in Germany vs. 1.5 percent in America) in Germany's favor, while the 90-day forward mark is selling at a 2 percent premium in the mark's favor. The hedging cost to the American importer consequently is $200   ($10,000 × 0.02) under either method. If the 90-day interest-rate differential is only 1 percent and the 90-day forward mark rate is at a 3 percent premium, then hedging by spot costs only $100 while a forward cover costs $300. An astute reader may have already suspected a logical link between the interest-rate differential and the forward premium (or discount). This relationship will be analyzed later in the chapter in conjunction with the discussion on interest arbitrage.

SPECULATION

Some individuals and firms do specialize in speculation. Exchange-rate fluctuations present many with opportunities to speculate for quick profits. For an understanding of the difference between hedging and speculation, the concept of a *position* in foreign exchange is crucial. When people incur an obligation to pay (deliver) foreign currency which they do not have, they are said to take a "short" position (or to "go short"). Persons in that position are taking a net liability position in foreign exchange; they will be hurt by an appreciation of the foreign currency, and will benefit from its depreciation. To illustrate, suppose that an American resident has an obligation to pay DM2,000 six months hence and the current spot rate is $0.50/mark. In terms of the U.S. dollar, her obligation is to pay $1,000 six months later. If the mark appreciates to

$0.60/mark in six months, her dollar obligation will be $1,200. This, of course, is an exchange risk of having a net (*open*) short position in the mark. If the mark depreciates to $0.40/mark, on the other hand, the American stands to gain $200. To take a "long" position (or to "go long"), conversely, means acquiring foreign currency without a need for it or incurring an obligation to dispose of it. A long position is thus synonymous with a net asset position. When a person takes a long and a short position of a given currency simultaneously, as in the case of selling a foreign currency forward and buying the same amount in the spot market, that person is said to have a *covered* position.

A hedger (as well as an arbitrager) always takes a covered position; in fact, it is this position that provides a hedge (or a cover). In our previous example of an American importing firm hedging in the forward market, its long position in the forward mark was covered by its short position arising from its obligation to pay marks when the accepted bill fell due.

Speculators Take Open Positions

A speculator is one who deliberately takes an open position, either short or long, in the hope of making profits from exchange-rate fluctuations. Just as hedging can be accomplished in either the spot or the forward market, speculation can be tried in either market. As in hedging, the comparison of the interest-rate differential in the two countries and the premium or discount on forward exchange is crucial in determining the relative profitability of the two methods of speculation. Suppose an American woman is convinced that the value of the Swiss franc will rise sharply in six months. The current spot rate is $0.60/franc, and the 180-day forward franc rate is $0.62/franc. If the woman believes that the spot rate in six months will be as high as $0.70/franc, how would she go about speculating in the franc?

One way to speculate in the franc is to borrow dollars in America, buy spot francs, and hold them for six months. Suppose the woman borrows $42,000 from her bank, buys 70,000 francs ($42,000 ÷ $0.60) in the spot market, and deposits them in a Swiss bank. If the interest rates in America and in Switzerland are 10 percent and 8 percent per year, respectively (5 percent and 4 percent per half year), then her net interest cost would be one percent of $42,000 per half year, or $420. Suppose the spot rate of the Swiss franc in fact rises to $0.70/franc in six months. She can then withdraw the 70,000 francs deposited in the Swiss bank, sell them for $49,000 (70,000 francs × $0.70) in the spot market, and realize a gross profit of $7,000 ($49,000 – $42,000). Subtracting the interest cost of $420, she obtains $6,580 as a net gain from the speculation.

Speculating in the Forward Market

Alternatively, the woman can speculate using the forward market. In this case, she does not even need to borrow dollars in America (assuming she does not have to put up a margin for a forward contract). She can buy 70,000 francs in the forward market, contracting to deliver $43,400 (70,000 francs × $0.62) in exchange for 70,000 francs six months hence. If the spot rate indeed rises to $0.70/franc during the six-month period, she can settle the account with the foreign exchange dealer by simultaneously selling 70,000 francs for $49,000 (at the spot rate of $0.70/franc) and delivering to the franc seller $43,400. This will leave her $5,600, the gain from speculation.

Whereas speculation in the spot market requires having sizable working capital or being able to borrow money in the domestic money market, speculation in the forward market normally requires about 10 percent of the forward contract as a margin. Speculators in the forward market can therefore leverage their assets on borrowed funds substantially.

INTEREST ARBITRAGE AND INTEREST PARITY

Whenever there exists a difference in the short-term interest rates between two financial centers, investors will be motivated to shift funds from one market to another to earn the differential. For example, if the rate of interest is higher in London than in New York, American investors can convert their dollar funds into pounds and invest them in interest-bearing assets in London. Such a flow of short-term funds simultaneously increases the quantities of spot pounds demanded and spot dollars supplied in the dollar-pound market, exerting an upward pressure on the spot rate of the sterling (expressed as the number of dollars per pound). As the American investors take an open position in the sterling, they expose themselves to an exchange risk. If the pound subsequently depreciates vis-à-vis the dollar, their sterling investments will lose value in terms of the dollar. And this exchange loss may even be greater than the gain in interest income. The American investors must therefore hedge against the exchange loss by selling forward sterling in an amount equal to the sterling value of their investments. In other words, they buy spot sterling and sell forward sterling at the same time, thereby providing themselves a forward cover. Such an investment is called *covered investment,* or *interest arbitrage.* Realizing that the net gain from interest arbitrage is the difference in interest rates minus the discount (if any) on forward exchange, we can see that such an investment will take place only when the interest-rate differential exceeds the discount on forward exchange.

Going back to our previous example, we note that the interest-rate differential (between relatively high London and relatively low New York rates) will tend to raise the spot sterling rate (as spot pounds are demanded) and lower the forward sterling rate (as forward pounds are sold). As the spot rate rises and the forward rate falls, the discount on forward sterling widens, raising the cost of forward cover. Concurrently, as investment funds move from New York to London, the interest-rate differential tends to narrow, reducing the potential gain in interest income. Interest arbitrage is thus self-limiting; the flows of funds themselves tend to limit the opportunity for further investments. When the interest income is just equal to the cost of forward cover, we have a situation which is termed *interest parity:* there is no incentive for covered investment.

The Interest Parity Line

The relationship among interest-rate differential, forward premium (or discount), and interest parity is expressed graphically in Figure 13-1. The vertical axis measures the interest-rate differential, the i.d., between New York and London. Positive values of the i.d. indicate a rate higher in London than in New York. The horizontal axis measures the forward-rate differential, the f.d., of the pound sterling *expressed as an annual rate.* Positive values of the f.d. indicate that the forward pound is at a premium compared to the spot pound; negative values represent discounts on the forward pound. Note that the f.d. values are converted to annual equivalents so they can be compared directly with the i.d.'s, which are per annum figures. For example, if the 90-day forward sterling rate is $1.99/£ and the spot sterling rate is $2.00/£, the premium on forward sterling is minus $0.01/$2.00, or − 0.5 percent. When converted to an annual rate, this discount on forward sterling is − 2.0 percent (− 0.5 × 4, since 90 days is approximately ¼ of one year). The f.d. value, in this case, is − 2, which means that the cost of forward cover is 2 percent of the invested amount. If the f.d. value is positive, it means that interest arbitragers realize a capital gain, in addition to the interest gain, because the forward sterling is at a premium.

Any point on this graph shows a combination of (1) an annual percentage interest-rate gain (the i.d.) and (2) an annual percentage forward gain or loss (the f.d.), of interest arbitrage between New York and London. Take point A, for instance. Shifting funds from New York to London results in an interest-rate gain of 5 percent (i.d. = 5) at the forward coverage cost of 3 percent (f.d. = − 3). The arbitrager's net gain is 2 percent. This percentage figure is known as the *covered (interest) differential.* The covered differential, the c.d., is equal to the algebraic sum of the interest-rate differential and the forward-rate differential, or: c.d. = i.d. + f.d. At point A in Figure 13-1, c.d. = 5 + (− 3) = 2.

In Figure 13-1, the interest parity line, I, is drawn equidistant to both axes; it is the locus of investment points at which the algebraic sum of

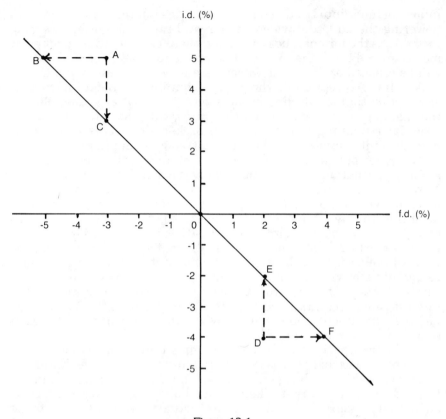

Figure 13-1
The Interest Parity Line

the i.d. and the f.d. is zero. Since the c.d. is zero along line I, there exists no incentive for investors to move funds. Take point B, for example. Since the interest income (5 percent per year) is just offset by the cost of forward cover (5 percent per year), there is no flow of covered investments between New York and London. Along line I there exists interest parity.

The area to the right (northeast) of the interest parity line contains investment points that result in flows of covered investment funds from New York to London. There, c.d. values are positive. In financial circles, this situation is described as the case where the covered differential is "in favor of London." Conversely, the area to the left (southwest) of line I has negative c.d. values; arbitragers shift funds from London to New York. The covered differential is now "in favor of New York."

Equilibrium

Investment points with the c.d. values other than zero indicate disequilibrium situations. Let us look at point A again. As we noted earlier, inflows of funds into London tend to reduce the interest-rate differential (lowering the i.d.), and widen the forward-rate differential (lowering the f.d.). As the flow of funds continues, therefore, the investment point moves toward the I line. An equilibrium (a no-flow-of-funds situation) will be reached on the I line somewhere between points B and C. The broken line AB represents the path to equilibrium under an extreme assumption that the decline in the arbitrage activities is due solely to the changes in the forward and spot rates, with the interest-rate differential remaining unchanged. The broken line AC represents the path to equilibrium under the other extreme assumption.

To further our understanding of the interest parity line, let us examine the situation involving inflows of arbitrage funds from London to New York. At point D, the interest-rate differential between New York and London is negative, meaning that the differential is in New York's favor (i.e., the New York interest rate exceeds the London rate, in this case, by 4 percentage points). The positive f.d. value indicates that forward sterling is at a premium, and, what is the same thing, the forward dollar is at a discount. This discount on the forward dollar represents a forward-cover cost for interest arbitragers who buy dollars spot and sell them forward. As the arbitrage activities narrow the interest-rate differential and increase the discount on the forward dollar, the investment point moves toward the line I and settles on it somewhere between E and F.

The interest parity hypothesis may imply that the demand and supply of forward exchange arise solely from interest arbitrage. In reality, however, traders (as hedgers) and speculators also participate in the forward exchange market. Their demand and supply, therefore, exert additional pressures on the formation of actual forward rates. If interest arbitrage fails to achieve interest parity in a real-world situation, the disequilibrium must be attributed to the activities of traders and speculators.

Thus far we have assumed that banks offer checking and savings accounts in only the currency of the nation in which each bank is located. We have recognized that banks act as foreign exchange dealers that buy and sell foreign currencies. But we have assumed that banks accept deposits and make loans only in the currency of the country in which they are located. This assumption has been made increasingly unrealistic, since the 1950s, by the phenomenal growth of the supranational money market called, now somewhat inaccurately, the Eurocurrency market.

THE EUROCURRENCY MARKET

A *Eurocurrency* or *Euromoney* is a checking or savings account deposit in a bank but denominated in the currency of a nation other than that of the nation in which the bank is located.[5] An ordinary German bank checking account is denominated in marks, but one denominated in dollars is a *Eurodollar* account. Similarly, a Swiss bank checking account denominated in German marks is a *Euromark* account. The bulk of Euromoney is Eurodollars, or dollar-denominated liabilities of banks outside of the United States, located mainly in Europe. Some of these banks are branches of American banks. Other Eurocurrencies now include Eurosterling, Euro-Swiss francs, Euroyen, and so on. Note that the location of the deposit bank is not important as long as it is located outside the country of issue of the currency. Yen deposited in a Singapore bank, for example, are Euroyen. (Some people use the term *Asiacurrency* for currencies deposited in banks in Asia. The more common practice, however, is to use the term *Euro*currency for all deposits outside the nation of issue, wherever the bank of deposit may be located.)

THE MECHANICS OF EURODOLLAR CREATION

Until the 1960s, European banks, including American branch banks, offered only accounts denominated in the currency of the country where the particular bank was located. When someone deposited a $1,000 check to a checking account in a bank, say, Germany, the changes were these:

A Bank in Germany

Dollar denominated checking account in a U.S. bank:	Mark checking account of the depositor:
+$1,000	+DM2,000

The bank took title to a dollar checking account balance in a bank in America. The depositor received a mark checking account balance (we assume an exchange rate of $1 = DM2). Many such transactions still occur.

In contrast, Eurodollars come into existence when someone with a $1,000 check, drawn against a bank in America, deposits that check in a bank in Europe (or elsewhere outside of the United States) and obtains a dollar denominated checking (or savings) account balance:

A Bank in Germany

Dollar denominated checking account in a U.S. bank:	Dollar checking account of the depositor:
+$1,000	+$1,000

As before, the bank in Europe obtains a dollar asset. Unlike anything that went before, that bank accepts a liability denominated in dollars rather than in the local currency. Something new under the sun.

Eurodollars first came into being through deposits of checks drawn against banks in America. But Eurodollars also come into being when a borrower gives a bank, located outside America, an IOU denominated in dollars and receives, in exchange, a checking account balance denominated in dollars; for example:

A Bank in Germany

Borrower's IOU:	Dollar checking account
+ $1,000	of the borrower: + $1,000

Banks which create Eurodollars by lending earn interest on the loans. The more and larger the Eurodollar loans, the larger the earnings.

However, Eurodollar banks must have enough dollar assets to cover all checks drawn against them. More precisely, Eurodollar banks must have dollar cover for the *net* of dollar withdrawals and dollar deposits. This is the standard situation described in the banks-must-have-reserves portion of every elementary economics textbook's money-and-banking chapter.

Federal Reserve requirements specify the character and amounts of reserves each member bank must have. State laws specify reserve requirements for non-member state-chartered banks. In contrast, most Eurocurrency deposits are *not* subject to governmental reserve requirements. Each bank is therefore on its own when determining "prudent" lending practice.

This system *could* be abused. Recall the post-Jackson era of American unregulated banking that earned the pejorative, "wildcat banking." International commentators have written volumes of concern about the dangers of the unregulated supranational banks. But twenty years of experience have accumulated. Eurodollar banks have, so far, not destroyed themselves by imprudent overlending.

THE GROWTH OF EUROCURRENCY VOLUME

Eurocurrency banks give prospective regulators no basis for arguing that regulation is needed to protect the public from insolvencies. But the Eurocurrency banks give regulators fits because the relative independence of the multinational-currency banks weakens the central banks' ability to control the growth of the money stock.

The size of the Eurocurrency market, measured by the foreign currency liabilities of banks in Europe and other parts of the world, has increased from less that $10 billion in the early 1960s, to over $110 billion in 1972, and to over $660 billion by January of 1980. In the early 1960s, more than 90 percent of Eurocurrencies were Eurodollars. In 1977, Eurodollars constituted nearly 80 percent of Euromoney. Throughout the late 1970s, Euromark, Eurosterling, Euro-French franc, Euro-Swiss franc, and Euroyen deposits all grew faster than did Eurodollar deposits. By 1979, Eurodollars constituted only 66 percent of Euromoney.

The primary suppliers of Eurocurrencies are multinational corporations that place their idle cash balances for short-term investment, and, in recent years, the Arab oil exporting countries. Residents of Western Europe are the largest depositors and borrowers in the Eurocurrency market. They accounted for $370 billion of gross Eurocurrency deposits and $358 billion of Eurocurrency loans in 1979. Residents of Middle East oil exporting countries are the largest net providers of funds. Their net positions in the Eurocurrency market was $62.2 billion in December 1979.[6] Governments and large business firms throughout the world have been the chief borrowers. A few dozen large banks operate in the market which is truly global in character and scope. Billions of dollars of loanable funds flow through the integrated global network linked by major financial centers located in New York, London, Bahrain, Singapore, and other places. Because of the strategic location of these centers, time differences between regions of the world present no problem; at a given moment in time a pair of financial centers (e.g., London and New York, or Bahrain and Singapore) has overlapping business hours.

REGULATION Q AND THE RUSSIANS

Two factors can be identified as having been primarily responsible for the development of the Eurodollar market. One was the Federal Reserve System's Regulation Q. By placing a ceiling on the rate of interest American banks could pay on time deposits, Regulation Q encouraged depositors to move money from America to Britain. During tight money periods, well-established British banks of high standing offered higher interest rates than those permitted by Regulation Q. Thus, Federal Reserve policy encouraged the movement of large amounts of dollars from the United States to London. That dollar outflow created a shortage of loanable funds in the United States, and prospective American borrowers then turned to the London money market for loan. So the market grew from transfers of existing dollars and from the creation of new dollars.

The other factor contributing to the development of the Eurodollar market was the desire of the Soviet Union and of some others to hold dollars not subject to the controls and regulations of U.S. authorities. The Russians are said to have been concerned that in the event of international conflict, the U.S. government would confiscate or at least freeze any Soviet dollar assets in banks in America. Eurodollar accounts permit the Soviets to hold dollars not subject to such risks. Further, the Soviets may find West Europeans more agreeable ideologically than Americans.

The special significance of the Eurocurrency market lies in its supranational character. Eurocurrencies are truly "stateless money." Depositors enjoy a minimum of regulations in the Euromoney markets. Banks that may be tightly regulated in their home markets are almost completely free of governmental control in their overseas operations. There is no supranational central bank in this supranational money market. The development of such a global market has naturally presented difficulties for national monetary authorities in implementing their monetary policies. During periods of tight money, for instance, borrowers can raise needed funds in the Eurocurrency market with relative ease, thus circumventing the restrictive effects of the tight money policy of their governments. Thus, the Eurocurrency market symbolizes a gradual erosion of national economic sovereignty and a step toward a fully integrated world economy.

A FAILED ATTEMPT TO CONTROL

According to one estimate, the size of the Euromarket in the middle of 1979 was $900 billion, or $560 billion if the duplication in interbank deposits was removed. The net size of the market had grown by 25 percent a year for the preceding several years. This sharp rise in the size of the market, and the fear that it was feeding global inflation, generated, in mid-1979, discussions among the world's central bankers about the means of controlling the market. The United States proposed a plan for cooperatively establishing formal controls over the Eurocurrency market by means of a worldwide reserve requirement. Each central bank was to impose upon its commercial banks the same reserve requirement no matter where they operated in the world. With a reserve posted on overseas deposits, their cost advantage over domestic deposits would disappear; consequently, interest-rate differentials between domestic and overseas (Euromarket) lending would also disappear. Without a sizable difference in interest rate, the need for the Euromarket itself would greatly diminish. The plan was supported strongly by Germany, but other nations were cool to it. Britain and Switzerland vehemently opposed it, out of concern for the diminishing importance of London and Switzerland in the international financial system. The opponents argued that if too much liquidity was generating inflationary pressures, tighter domestic monetary policies were the answer. The U.S.-German counterargument was that tighter domestic money and higher interest rates would result in a severe worldwide recession.[7]

STUDY QUESTIONS

1. In economics we make a distinction between a flow variable and a stock variable; for example, income is a flow and wealth is a stock. Is foreign exchange a flow or a stock? How can you be sure?
2. You read in the newspaper that the "dollar has declined in the London foreign exchange market." What exactly does this mean? What is likely to have happened in the New York, or Paris, foreign exchange market? Why do discrepancies not develop on a given exchange rate at different locations? Who does what to prevent them?

3. Explain the differences between a foreign exchange dealer and a foreign exchange broker.
4. International payments are affected almost always by transfers of debts between banks. Explain.
5. What is a draft (or a bill of exchange)? Who are the three parties to a draft? How does a draft differ from a promissory note? What is a bank draft?
6. Explain the difference between a trade bill and a bank bill, and between a time bill and a sight bill.
7. Why is it often necessary to use a time bill to settle a merchandise trade transaction?
8. What is a trade acceptance? What is a banker's acceptance?
9. Briefly explain how the payment and financing is made in the following transaction: A Cleveland, Ohio, firm imports merchandise worth $100,000 from its trading partner located in Hamburg, West Germany. Three banks are involved in the transaction: the importer's Cleveland bank, the Cleveland bank's correspondent bank in New York City, and the New York bank's correspondent bank in Hamburg. The shipment is authorized by the letter of credit issued by the Cleveland bank. A 90-day time bill is used. The dollar acceptance is discounted by the Hamburg bank in the Eurodollar market.
10. A French importing firm has accepted a time bill that requires a payment of $10,000 90 days later. The firm fears, however, that in 90 days the dollar will appreciate substantially. Explain how it can hedge against the exchange risk by using the forward exchange market. Assume that both the spot and the forward rates are at 4 francs/dollar.
11. John Smith, a U.S. resident, is convinced that the Japanese yen will appreciate dramatically over the next six months. He has $10,000 at his disposal, which he wants to use to speculate on the yen. The spot rate is now ¥250/dollar, and the 6-month forward rate is ¥240/dollar. The short-term interest rate is 10 percent in Japan and 12 percent in the United States. A margin of 10 percent is required on a forward contract. Assume there are no fees for spot transactions. How much money can John Smith make if the spot rate in six months indeed reaches ¥200/dollar,
    (a) if he uses the spot market only?
    (b) if he uses both spot and forward markets?
12. What essentially is the difference between the hedger and the speculator in the foreign exchange market?
13. Suppose short-term interest rates are 12 percent per annum in New York and 8 percent in West Germany. The spot rate between the German mark and the dollar is DM2/dollar, and the 6-month forward rate is DM1.995/dollar. Assume the spot rate 6 months hence will remain at DM2/dollar.
    (a) How much will a German interest arbitrager with a capital of DM200,000 earn in six months?
    (b) For this arbitrager to break even, how large must the discount on the forward dollar be?
14. In 1980, the estimated gross size of the Eurocurrency was roughly $1,000 billion, of which about 75 percent was Eurodollars. (The *net* size of the Euromarket, exclusive of interbank deposits, was roughly six-tenths of the gross size.) These figures compared with the U.S. money supply figures as follows: M_1 money, including domestic bank checking-account balances (minus government and bank-owned deposits) *plus* paper currency and coins, was about $350 billion. M_4 money, including M_1 *plus* time deposits in commercial banks and nonbank thrift institutions *plus* negotiable time certificates of deposit issued in denominations of $100,000 or more, amounted to nearly $1,000 billion. Since Eurocurrency deposits are

mainly in the form of time deposits, their size can better be compared to the M_4 — rather than the more commonly used M_1 — definition of the U.S. money supply.

See if you can find the most recent statistics on the sizes of the Eurocurrency market, and of the amounts of M_1 money and M_4 money in the United States.

ENDNOTES

1. For an interesting description of a day in the life of a London exchange trader, see: "Money Trader's Role Is Vital, but Don't Believe What Novels Tell You," *Wall Street Journal,* 5 September 1978, p. 1.
2. See "How Fed Intervenes in Currency Market to Defend the Dollar," *Wall Street Journal,* 14 November 1978, p. 1; and "Dealers Devise Special Tactics to Detect When Central Banks Are Propping Dollar," *Wall Street Journal,* 20 November 1978, p. 1.
3. *Wall Street Journal,* 1 July 1980, p. 28.
4. *Ibid.*
5. For an excellent introduction to the Eurodollar market, see: U.S. Congress, Joint Economic Committee, *Some Questions and Brief Answers about the Eurodollar Market,* 95th Cong., 1st Sess. 1977; and Carl H. Stem et al., *Eurocurrencies and the International Monetary System* (Washington, D.C.: American Enterprise Institute for Public Policy Research, 1976).
6. "Stateless Money: A New Force on World Economies," *Business Week,* 21 August 1978, pp. 76-85; and Federal Reserve Bank of Chicago, "The Eurocurrency Market," *International Letter,* 4 July 1980, pp. 1-2.
7. See: "A Gathering Storm over Euromarket Controls," *Business Week,* 4 June 1979, p. 118; and "Eurocurrency Market Is under Scrutiny by Central Banks for Possible Regulation," *Wall Street Journal,* 12 June 1979, p. 12.

14

The Balance of Payments: Accounting

We often hear the news media report that the United States has a problem because its balance of payments is in "deficit." This chapter answers questions about the balance of payments (hereafter, BOP): What is the balance of payments? What is a BOP "deficit"? Why is such a deficit a problem? Why should a "surplus" be a problem?

THE MEANING OF A DEFICIT OR A SURPLUS

The news media give even more attention to the "balance of *trade*.' But the balance of trade compares only total value of a nation's mer chandise exports with total value of that nation's merchandise import₅ during a particular year (or month). Merchandise is only a portion o: the items traded internationally. The term "foreign trade" may make one think first of merchandise trade, but many services (e.g., transportation, insurance, legal advice, use of capital), money (currency, checking account balances), and other financial assets (stocks, bonds, and other IOUs) are also exported and imported. The BOP catalogs *all* the imports and *all* the exports of a nation: merchandise, services, money, other financial assets, and even gifts, during some particular time period.

A nation's BOP reports all of the economic transactions between that nation's residents and the residents of the rest of the world during some particular time period. Because the BOP is comprehensive, it is of major importance for forecasting, for economic analysis, and for policy making. In contrast, the balance of trade and the balance of goods and services are of less importance because they represent only particular items among the many the nation imports and exports.

BOP DEFICIT, FOREIGN EXCHANGE SHORTAGE

Because preparation of a BOP is an exercise in double-entry book-keeping, every BOP must balance. What, then, is a BOP deficit (or surplus)? A deficit (or surplus) exists when, in the foreign exchange market, the quantity of foreign currency demanded exceeds the quantity of foreign currency supplied. In other words, more home currency is being offered for foreign exchange than there is foreign exchange offered for home currency. There is then a deficit in the amount of foreign currency available. Conversely, a surplus means less home currency is offered for foreign exchange than there is foreign exchange offered for home currency. Then, there is a surplus of foreign currency, and the BOP is in surplus. Deficits and surpluses in the foreign exchange market and in the BOP are thus synonymous. Note especially that if one nation has a deficit of size x, other nations must have a surplus of size x. Turn back to Figure 4-2 where this relationship is shown. North's currency is the dollar, so the peso is North's foreign exchange; and the dollar is South's foreign exchange. Panel 4-2(B) shows that at the exchange rate OB', North has a deficit of GJ of foreign currency available to it. This GJ is North's balance-of-payments deficit. In the two-nation world of Figure 4-2, North's deficit of GJ *is* South's surplus.

If this Northern deficit, and Southern surplus, of GJ pesos is multiplied by the exchange rate of OB' dollars per peso, the product is the dollar value of the dollar surplus of foreign exchange available to South. Assuming that the exchange rate OA' of Panel 4-2(A) equals 1/OB', the dollar surplus of South appears in Panel 4-2(A) as CF (which is equal to GJ times OB'). Repeating, South's dollar surplus, CF, is the dollar value of North's peso deficit, GJ.

So the reverse of the principle is also true. Whenever any one nation has a balance-of-payments surplus of y, other nations, collectively, must have a balance-of-payments deficit of y.

Chapter 4 stressed that, under a freely fluctuating rate, quantities of foreign exchange demanded and supplied are equated by market forces. Under a freely fluctuating rate, a nation cannot experience a balance-of-payments surplus or deficit.

Balance-of-payments surpluses and deficits arise only when, in the foreign exchange market: (1) supply and demand tend to change the nation's existing exchange rate, and (2) some government intervenes to resist that change. In Figure 4-2, North's deficit may exist because the Northern government is intervening in the market. Alternatively, the Northern government may refrain from any intervention in the foreign exchange market while intervention by the Southern government produces the peso shortage, the BOP deficit of North, and the dollar surplus, the BOP surplus of South.

Later we will give other reasons why BOP deficits and surpluses are "problems." For the moment, only recognize that a BOP deficit means that the country's currency is overvalued. As shown in earlier chapters, an overvalued currency distorts the pattern of trade of a country by reducing the international competitiveness of some of that country's comparative advantage industries. A BOP surplus means that that country's currency is undervalued. The surplus is also a problem because the undervalued currency generates allocative inefficiency by according too much competitiveness to that nation's comparative disadvantage industries.

INTERVENTION WHEN GOVERNMENTS BUY OR SELL FOREIGN EXCHANGE

In the absence of government intervention in the foreign exchange market — or "management" of exchange rates by monetary authorities — the exchange rate is free to vary in response to market forces, and therefore there can be neither a surplus or deficit. This does not mean, however, that a nation running a surplus or deficit is necessarily intervening. As the Figure 4-2 example showed, an individual nation may experience a surplus or deficit even when it abstains from all intervention in foreign exchange markets. Every foreign exchange market exists between two nations' currencies. If one of the two nations abstains from intervention while the other does intervene, the exchange rate will be kept in disequilibrium. Both nations will then have a BOP problem. One will suffer a surplus; the other will suffer a deficit.

The existence of an equilibrium rate of exchange does not necessarily mean that neither government is intervening. Suppose both the U.S. dollar and the Japanese yen are "floating," and the Bank of Japan intervenes in the yen-dollar market by buying dollars so the dollar becomes overvalued and the yen undervalued. Consequently, Japan will develop a surplus, while the United States suffers a deficit without intervening. In such a case, equilibrium could be restored through counterintervention by the American monetary authorities. If the Federal Reserve intervenes in the yen-dollar market by buying yen, the dollar's overvaluation will diminish and America's deficit will be reduced. Our conclusion here is that government intervention in foreign exchange markets can both *cause* surpluses and deficits and, used judiciously, can *correct* imbalances caused by other governments' intervention.

Observe the means by which governments were assumed to intervene in these markets to keep the exchange rate away from the equilibrium that would end all surpluses and deficits. In each case, some government was assumed to be either buying or selling foreign exchange with the purpose of influencing the exchange rate. This is the means currently most used by developed nations to influence exchange rates. There are other means. All will be described at length in this and subsequent chapters.

Before 1973, most nations refused to let their exchange rates change at all when market supply or demand changed. Exchange rates were *fixed.* The purported merits and demerits of that system, which had been in effect for a quarter century, were widely debated. Some politicians, some business managers, some traders, and some economists argued in volumes that fixed rates were essential for smooth flows of international trade and investment. Other politicians, managers, traders, and economists argued, also in volumes, that freely fluctuating rates would be far superior to fixed rates.

In 1973, there was a quantum jump in general acceptance of the proposition that exchange rates were best set by the market. Almost everywhere, fixed exchange rates were abandoned. The free marketers appeared to have won. But they didn't. Fixed exchange rates are no more among major currencies. Yet, most governments have chosen to intervene continuously in the market for their currency; so nations continue to experience BOP surpluses and deficits. The reasons for this situation will be discussed in subsequent chapters.

DOUBLE-ENTRY BOOKKEEPING IN THE BALANCE OF PAYMENTS

The American balance of payments attempts to record every American import and every American export. We know that many Florida imports are not recorded. Other imports and exports also escape surveillance; but the omitted total may never approach five percent of the whole.

THE TWO SIDES OF THE BALANCE: EXPORTS AND IMPORTS

What may seem strange at first is that the total value of imports always equals the total value of exports. Every import (or export) involves an exchange of two items of equal value; there is a quid pro quo in every transaction. Whether the import (export) initiator is an individual, a corporation, or a government agency, the trade agreement always involves an exchange of some import for some export of exactly equal value. For example, a $20,000 automobile imported from Germany may be matched by $20,000 in cash exported from the United States to Germany. Even if an American resident makes a gift by sending $1,000 in cash to an uncle in Greece, America's BOP records export of $1,000 cash to Greece and import of $1,000 worth of (the Greek uncle's) "good will" from Greece. (This particular convention may seem odd at first. After a while, one gets used to it.) Thus, no international transaction can be one-sided; every transaction must have an export side and an import side of equal value. Consequently, the total value of exports must always equal the total value of imports in the balance of payments. (This is true even when the state of a BOP justifies the term "surplus" or "deficit" in that balance. As we shall see shortly, there is no paradox here. A "surplus" or "deficit" may exist because of the unique way these terms are defined.)

The BOP statement consists of two sides — exports and imports. Each side is divided into a number of account categories. Whenever an amount is entered in some category on one side, an equal amount must be entered — in every case, without exception — in a category (generally some different category) on the other side. It is this double-entry bookkeeping that assures the equality of the sum of one side to the sum of the other side.

The export side of the American (or any other country's) BOP is often labeled "credits" (or "+"), since every export entitles Americans to some reward, i.e., "credits" Americans. Conversely, the import side is often called the "debit" (or "−") side, since every import "indebts" Americans to the foreigners who send the goods, services, IOUs, or some other items of economic value to America.

CAPITAL FLOWS: EXPORTS AND IMPORTS OF CLAIMS

If an American imports $30,000 worth of cacao and pays the Malaysian exporter with a Boston bank checking account (c.a.) balance, the pair of BOP entries for America are:

Exports	Imports
$30,000 c.a.	$30,000 cacao

America imports $30,000 worth of cacao, and exports $30,000 checking account money (a kind of claim) to Malaysia. The "export of claims" needs a few words of explanation, for an export of claims can take either of two forms. If the American importer sends to Malaysia a check written against the American's Boston bank account, the transaction causes an *increase in foreigners' claims on Americans*. (The Boston bank's demand deposit liabilities to the Malaysian exporter are increased.) If, on the other hand, the checking account the American importer uses is not with a Boston bank, but with a London (or Malaysian) bank, then the drawing of a check against it and sending it to Malaysia results in a *decrease in America's claims on foreigners*. ($30,000 worth of formerly American-owned financial assets — or claims — in the form of checking account money in a London, or Malaysian, bank has now been transferred to the Malaysian exporter.) More on this below.

To test your understanding of imports and exports of claims, consider the case of an American importing $10,000 worth of British corporate bonds and paying the British firm with a check drawn against a Boston bank. The two BOP entries for America are:

Exports	Imports
$10,000 c.a.	$10,000 bonds

In this case, the export of a claim (checking account balance) of $10,000 involves an increase in foreigners' claims on Americans, and the import of $10,000 in bonds results in an increase in America's claims on foreigners. Now suppose, instead, the corporate bonds imported into America are *American* bonds (issued originally by an American firm and later purchased by the British firm), and the check drawn by the American importer is against the importer's London bank checking account. In this case, the effect on American-British debtor-creditor relationships would be different, though the two BOP entries would be the same as those above. Exporting American-owned checking account balances in a London bank involves a decrease in America's claims on foreigners. Importing American bonds results in a decrease in foreigners' claims on Americans. Such changes in claims are called *capital flows.*

THE BALANCE OF INTERNATIONAL ASSETS AND LIABILITIES

These differences show up more vividly in the context of the *balance of international assets and liabilities* (hereafter, BIAL). The BIAL is the balance sheet of a nation vis-à-vis the rest of the world. Its assets side shows all claims on foreigners. The liabilities side shows all obligations to foreigners (foreigners' claims on us). The net of the two sides (shown on the liabilities side) is the nation's net international investment position. America's BIAL as of December 31, 1978, is shown in Table 14-1. The table introduces some technical terms. *Direct investment* refers to ownership involving control as distinct from *portfolio investment* which embraces loans and minority ownership. *Short term* refers to loans (as distinct from ownership) maturing in one year or less.

All imports and all exports merit mention in the nation's balance of payments (observe that it is a statement about *flows*). Imports or exports merit mention in the BIAL (the nation's statement about *stocks*

TABLE 14-1   AMERICA'S BALANCE OF INTERNATIONAL
ASSETS AND LIABILITIES AS OF
DECEMBER 31, 1978
(in billions of dollars)

Assets			Liabilities and Net Position		
Claims upon foreigners			Claims by foreigners		
U.S. Government		73	To governments		175
Official reserves	19		U.S. Gov't Securities	131	
Other	54		Other	44	
Private		377	Private		198
Direct Investments	168		Direct Investments	41	
Other long term	73		Other long term	61	
Short term	136		Short term	96	
Total		450	Total		373
			Net Claims on foreigners		77

Source: U.S. Department of Commerce, "The International Investment Position of the United States: Developments in 1978," *Survey of Current Business,* August, 1979, p. 56.

of claims) only if they affect ownership or debtor-creditor relationships vis-à-vis foreigners.

Consider again the examples just described. An American imports $10,000 in British corporate bonds and pays with a check on a Boston bank. The resulting changes in America's BIAL are:

Assets	Liabilities
Private	Private
Other long term +$10,000	Short term +$10,000

Contrast that example with the one in which an American imports a $10,000 AT&T bond and pays the British seller with a check on a London bank. The changes in the BIAL are then:

Assets	Liabilities
Private	Private
Short term −$10,000	Other long term −$10,000

Both cases involve the same pair of BOP entries:

Exports	*Imports*
$10,000 c.a.	$10,000 bond

but the BIAL entries are quite different.

One more example, the one where an American writes a $30,000 check drawn on a Boston bank to pay for imports of cacao. The movement of the $30,000 checking account balance is entered in both the BOP *and* the BIAL. In contrast, the cacao import is entered in the BOP but *not* in the BIAL. It is not entered in the BIAL because it is not, as is the checking account balance, a claim on anyone. The BIAL entries for this transaction are:

Assets	Liabilities
	Private
	Short term +$30,000
	Net claims −$30,000

The first entry (Private: Short term, +$30,000) arises because the Boston bank (a private U.S. resident) owes the Malaysian exporter $30,000 more than before. The second entry (Net claims: −$30,000) requires a few words of explanation. Since the BIAL involves double-entry bookkeeping, there must be two entries for each transaction. If America's assets increase by x dollars, its net claims on foreigners increase by x dollars. Conversely, when the nation's liabilities to foreigners increase by y dollars, its net claims on foreigners decrease by y dollars; and this is what happens in our present example.

To recapitulate: an American export of a claim means either a decrease in U.S. assets or an increase in U.S. liabilities, and an American import of a claim means either an increase in U.S. assets or a decrease in U.S. liabilities. Whether an American import or export of a claim involves a change in U.S. assets *or* liabilities depends on who originally issued the instrument of claim (e.g., a bond).

SHORT-TERM vs. LONG-TERM CAPITAL FLOWS

Conventionally, exports and imports of claims are divided into two account categories — short-term capital and long-term capital — depending on the length of maturity of the claims involved. Entries in the short-term capital account take place whenever the claim (debt instrument) matures in one year or less. Included in this category are cash, checking and savings account balances, bills of exchange, Treasury bills, and so forth. Long-term capital involves claims of maturity of longer than one year. Exports and imports of "minority" stocks and bonds, as well as direct investments, are included in this category. Thus, the transaction in the foregoing example involving an American import of a $10,000 bond (long-term capital) in exchange for an export of a $10,000 checking account (short-term capital) is made in two BOP entries, one in the long-term capital account and the other in the short-term capital account:

	Exports	*Imports*
Long-term capital		$10,000 bond
Short-term capital	$10,000 c.a.	

Contrast this distinction with the distinctions made, and described above, in the BIAL. Incidentally, the BOP entries for Britain are the mirror image of America's.

	Exports	*Imports*
Long-term capital	$10,000 bond	
Short-term capital		$10,000 c.a.

Notice that for *every* entry in the U.S. BOP, there is a mirror-image entry in the BOP of another nation; notice further that this mirror imagery in entries applies also to the BIAL.

MAJOR ACCOUNT CATEGORIES

The complete balance of payments may be divided into the following five major categories of account:
  A. Merchandise
  B. Services
  C. Unilateral transfers
  D. Long-term capital
  E. Short-term capital

Merchandise

Merchandise refers to traded goods. The net balance of this account is commonly known as the Balance of Trade. (The United States BOP published by the Department of Commerce excludes transfers of goods under U.S. military-agency sales contracts from the merchandise account, and lists them as a separate category.)

Services

Entries in this account include traded activities such as the use of a hotel room, an airplane or boat ride, the use of loan or equity capital, and insurance protection. When a French tourist traveling in the United States spends $1,000 for hotel accommodations, meals, entertainment, transportation, and gifts, the entire amount is considered an American export of (tourism) "service" even if part of the money spent by the tourist is on goods. The two entries for America are:

	Exports	*Imports*
Services	$1,000	
Short-term capital		$1,000

The import of short-term claims involves some combination of BIAL increases in American financial assets and BIAL decreases in American liabilities to foreigners, depending on whether the French tourist writes a check on a foreign bank or on an American bank.

One important subcategory of the services account requires a few words of explanation. When a resident of America holds foreign stocks, bonds, or any other types of interest or profit-earning financial assets, the American is in fact letting foreigners use the services of America's money, or capital. In other words, America is exporting the "use-of-money" (or "use-of-capital") service. The reward for such an export, of course, is an import of money (itself, short-term capital) called "interest and dividends." Thus, $2,000 of dividends received by an American holder of foreign company stocks is recorded in America's BOP as follows:

	Exports	*Imports*
Services	$2,000	
Short-term capital		$2,000

In the published BOP statistics, this subcategory of the services account is often labeled "interest and dividends" or "income on foreign investments." It is important to see here that the purchase or sale of the debt instruments themselves should not be confused with periodic (usually annual) payments of interest and dividends. The sales of bonds and stocks, when they take place, are recorded in the long-term capital account, not as a service item.

Do not underestimate the importance of services. As Table 14-2 shows, the value of America's service exports is over half the value of America's merchandise exports.

Unilateral Transfers

Unilateral transfers are synonymous with "gifts and grants." One unique characteristic of this type of transaction is that there appears, at first sight, to be no quid pro quo. If Mexican immigrants in America (U.S. residents) send a $3,000 check to their relatives in Mexico as a gift, the immigrants receive nothing tangible in return from Mexico. But as we pointed out earlier, BOP recording is double-entry book-keeping; if something is exported from America, something else must come into America as a counterflow. And indeed we find such a counter-flow; it is an import of "good will" from Mexico. Send a gift and receive, one may assume, "good will" in exchange. Each entry in the unilateral transfers account can be viewed as a "good will" export or import. The Mexican immigrants' transaction is recorded thus:

	Exports	*Imports*
Unilateral transfers		$3,000
Short-term capital	$3,000	

Gifts and grants need not be in money, of course. If, for example, American residents receive a free gift of an automobile from their relatives in Sweden, then the two entries for the American BOP will be exports of good will (unilateral transfers) and imports of merchandise. So, just as the dividend payment is *not* entered on the "interest and dividends" row of the balance of payments, the gift is *not* entered on the "unilateral transfer" row. The payment is entered in the money row. The gift is entered in the row appropriate to the character of the gift: merchandise, money, or a bond.

Current Account and Capital Account

The three categories — merchandise, services, and unilateral transfers — are grouped together in most statistical tables as the *current account* of the balance of payments. All items entered in these three subaccounts are "current" as distinct from all items entered in the two capital subaccounts. The two subaccounts, long-term capital and short-term capital, are grouped together in the *capital account*. All items entered in either of the two capital subaccounts represent claims against the future and are distinct from current account items in that each capital item is a claim on the future.

The five subaccounts, merchandise through short-term capital, are shown separately in every detailed balance-of-payments statement. However, for many purposes, the only distinction needed is between the current account and the capital account.

Capital

Entries in the capital accounts result from exports or imports of claims. Claims consist of money, bonds, and all kinds of IOUs; and shares of stock, and all other forms of title to property. Every entry in the capital account of the BOP requires an entry, a change, in the nation's BIAL. In contrast, an entry in the merchandise, services, or unilateral transfers section of the BOP does not involve any entry in the BIAL.

The reason for the above contrast is important in understanding the concepts of BOP capital entries, of BIAL changes, and of international capital movements. That reason has to do with the concepts of *capital stock* and of *investment*.

Recall the equation, $Y = C + G + I$, or, simpler and more useful in our present context, $Y = C + I$, where Y is national income (or output), C is consumption, and I is investment. (We assume that both depreciation — or capital consumption allowance — and indirect business taxes are zero, so that Y = gross national product = net national product = national income.) The relevant definitions recognize that the total output, Y, of a particular time period is either *consumed* — used up by private persons or by government — as C, during that period, or is carried over to the next time period. That portion of output carried over is *investment*, I, and is added to the nation's capital stock, the accumulation of not-yet-used-up output of all past years.

Domestic Investment. So far this explanation has been a review of concepts from elementary economics. In the introductory principles course, "investment" is regarded primarily as *domestic investment*. But a nation can invest in two ways — domestically and in foreign countries. The portion of a nation's output which is not consumed may be added to the nation's stock of capital such as factories, stores, homes, airplanes, farm equipment, sewers, and inventories of all sorts of goods. This portion is the domestic investment. Naturally, domestic investment does not involve foreigners; there is no change in the country's claims against foreigners or foreigners' claims against the nation's residents. Hence domestic investment does not appear in the nation's BIAL (or in its BOP statement).

Foreign Investment. Output that is not consumed during a time period can be shipped abroad as exports. These exports are "investments" in the sense that the residents of the nation acquire claims on foreigners for the goods shipped. This acquisition of claims is recorded in the BOP as imports of claims in the short-term capital account. In the BIAL, the nation's claims on foreigners increase (or foreigners' claims on the nation decrease) by the same amount. As the nation acquires a net claim on foreigners, it is making an investment — a *foreign investment*. There is very little difference between this type of investment and domestic investment. In both cases, the nation sets aside a portion of its current output, so that it can consume more in the future. The only difference is *where* it is set aside — at home *or* abroad in the hands of foreigners.

NFI. An export of merchandise results in foreign investment as evidenced by a counterflow of an import of claims. Conversely, an import of merchandise results in foreign "disinvestment" (a negative investment) and is accompanied by an export of claims. If exports of merchandise, services, and gifts exceed imports of merchandise, services, and gifts during a time period (i.e., if imports of claims *exceed* exports of claims resulting in an increase in the nation's *net* claims on foreigners), then the nation has made a *net* foreign investment.

The national income equation given above must now be rewritten as $Y = C + I + NFI$ where I is domestic investment and NFI is net foreign investment. Using X for exports and M for imports, we can further rewrite the equation as $Y = C + I + X - M$ since $NFI = X - M$. We will return to this equation in the next chapter.

As an illustration of transactions involving NFI, consider the following case. Assume that America and Brazil are the only two nations in the world, and, during a year, only the following two transactions take place between the two countries —

1. A Brazilian firm imports $4,000 worth of corn from America, paying for it by a check drawn against a dollar bank account in São Paulo.
2. An American firm imports $3,000 worth of coffee beans from Brazil, paying for it by drawing a check against its New York bank account.

The four BOP entries for America are:

	Exports	*Imports*
Merchandise	$4,000 corn	
Short-term capital		$4,000 c.a.

	Exports	*Imports*
Merchandise		$3,000 coffee
Short-term capital	$3,000 c.a.	

America's NFI equals exports minus imports, or $4,000 - $3,000 = $1,000. America has *invested* $1,000 of its output in Brazil; it can expect to recover $1,000 worth of output from Brazil in a subsequent year — plus interest or dividends.

NFI and the BIAL. How would these transactions affect America's BIAL? The $4,000 check drawn by the Brazilian firm against its São Paulo bank account increases America's assets (claims on foreigners: short term, private) by $4,000, while the $3,000 check drawn by the

American firm against its New York bank account increases America's liabilities to foreigners (foreigners' claims on America: short term, private) by $3,000. The difference, $1,000, is the increase in America's net claim position vis-à-vis Brazil (or the rest of the world). The changes in America's BIAL are as follows:

Assets	Liabilities	
Private	Private	
Short term +$4,000	Short term +$3,000	
	Net Claims +$1,000	

This increase in America's net claims of $1,000 is, of course, the other side of the coin of America's NFI of $1,000.

We must now warn the reader against the very confusing uses of terminology respecting *capital flows*. In the foregoing corn/coffee bean illustration, America had a net foreign *investment* of $1,000. Output-not-consumed moved, net, from America to Brazil. In other words, America *exported* capital; there was a capital *outflow* from America to Brazil. Confusion threatens because America's capital *export* (outflow) involves an *import* (inflow) of claims. America exported a $3,000 claim and imported a $4,000 claim (here claims are private short-term claims, or checking account money). America's net *import* of claims of $1,000 was involved in its net *export* of capital of $1,000. In short, an import of claims accompanies an export of capital; vice versa, an export of claims accompanies an import of capital.

BALANCE OF PAYMENTS BOOKKEEPING: AN EXERCISE

To see how a nation's balance-of-payments statement is prepared, we will develop in this section a hypothetical BOP for America assuming a few simple transactions. For each transaction, we will identify two entries in appropriate accounts. We then post all the entries in a single worksheet, in which a summary BOP is prepared. All transactions involving money payments are assumed to have been made by drawing checks against commercial banks. (Figures are in millions of dollars.)

a. Exports of merchandise, $30 million.

	Exports	*Imports*
Merchandise	30	
Short-term capital		30

b. Imports of merchandise, $27 million.

	Exports	*Imports*
Merchandise		27
Short-term capital	27	

c. U.S residents receive interest and dividends on previous investments, $7 million. This transaction involves exports of "use-of-capital" service and imports of checking account money (a short-term claim). Beginners tend to make mistakes when working with interest and dividends. To avoid confusion, always identify the direction of the money movement and make that entry first.

	Exports	Imports
Services	7	
Short-term capital		7

d. U.S. tourists spend $2 million abroad. This transaction involves imports of tourism (or travel) service:

	Exports	Imports
Services		2
Short-term capital	2	

e. U.S. residents remit $1 million to their relatives abroad. This involves imports of good will. To avoid confusion with unilateral transfers, always enter first, in its appropriate line and column, the thing given. Second, make the unilateral transfer entry.

	Exports	Imports
Unilateral transfers		1
Short-term capital	1	

f. The U.S. Government ships $3 million worth of grain to a developing nation under the foreign aid program. This transaction involves no money payments. A merchandise export is offset by a good-will import of equal value.

	Exports	Imports
Merchandise	3	
Unilateral transfers		3

g. U.S. residents purchase $5 million worth of foreign bonds and stocks from abroad. This long-term capital *outflow* involves *imports* of long-term claims. The offsetting short-term capital *inflow* involves the *exported* short-term claims (money).

	Exports	Imports
Long-term capital		5
Short-term capital	5	

h. A European firm ships $4 million worth of machinery to its U.S. subsidiary as payment for its majority share in the U.S. firm. No money changes hands. A U.S. export of long-term claims (ownership shares in the U.S. firm, a direct investment) is exchanged for a U.S. import of machinery. This is a long-term capital *inflow*.

	Exports	Imports
Merchandise		4
Long-term capital	4	

i.   U.S. Government bonds worth $6 million become due, and proceeds
     (the principal only) are paid to foreigners. This transaction entails
     imports of long-term claims (imports of U.S. Government bonds
     back to America) and exports of checking account money (short-
     term claims).

	Exports	Imports
Long-term capital		6
Short-term capital	6	

The foregoing transactions have been posted in a worksheet, and
appropriate balances have been computed. You should have no difficulty in identifying each transaction since no two transactions involve
the same amount.

<u>Balance of Payments Worksheet</u>
(in millions)

	Exports (+)	Imports (−)	Balance
Merchandise	$30 and 3	$27 and 4	$+2
Services	7	2	+5
Unilateral transfers		1 and 3	−4
Long-term capital	4	5 and 6	−7
Short-term capital	27, 2, 1, 5 and 6	30 and 7	+4
Total	$85	$85	$0

Note that the two sides of the balance of payments balance at $85
million each; so total net balance is zero. This equality, as we discussed
earlier, is assured by the double-entry bookkeeping method used in
preparing the statement.

VARIOUS CONCEPTS OF DEFICIT
OR SURPLUS IN THE BOP

We have said that BOP deficits and surpluses often result from government intervention to prevent or to modify otherwise free-market
movements of exchange rates. We have also said that surpluses and
deficits are "problems" because they injure some groups and because
they cannot be continued indefinitely. Now we must be more precise.
Exactly how is the BOP deficit or surplus measured?

First, we must explain the apparent paradox of our report that a
surplus (or deficit) can exist in a balance of payments in which double-
entry bookkeeping requires equality between the two columns. The
paradox is resolved when we recognize that when we look only at any

single line in the BOP, the two sides are not necessarily equal. "Deficit" or "surplus" can, therefore, appear on any one line or for any subset of line items of the BOP.

CURRENT ACCOUNT BALANCES

For example, in the worksheet presented in the preceding section, the merchandise account shows a "surplus" of $2 million. This is America's *Balance of Trade*. In popular usage, America is said to have here a "favorable balance of trade" of $2 million.[1]

If we look only at the merchandise *and* the services components, the American transactions shown in the preceding section sum algebraically to a *Balance on Goods and Services* of +$7 million. Again a "surplus."

If we look only at the merchandise and the services *and* the unilateral transfer components, the American transactions of our example sum algebraically to a *Current Account Balance* of +$3 million ($2 + $5 − $4 million). Another surplus. This balance is especially interesting because it is the net value of current output (of goods, services, and good will) exported in exchange for claims. The Current Account Balance in BOP accounting is synonymous with Net Foreign Investment (NFI) in national income accounting. The net claims position of the nation's BIAL is changed by the value of its Current Account Balance for any particular time period.

If we look back at the entire right hand column of our worksheet, we see that the individual balances of the five lines add vertically to zero. (In our illustration, $2 + 5 − 4 − 7 + 4 = 0$.) This means that if a horizontal line is drawn *anywhere* across this worksheet, the numerical value of the sum of the line balances *above* the drawn line must equal the numerical value of the sum of the line balances *below* the line. However, the sign — plus or minus — is different between the summed balances above and below the line.

For example, draw a line across the worksheet below unilateral transfers and above the long-term capital account. Above the line is the Current Account Balance of $3 million = NFI. Below the line, the balances sum to −$3 million (−$7 + $4 million), the net value of capital imports and exports. More precisely, the −$3 million represents the net value of claims imported and added to the nation's BIAL. The negative sign shows that the nation had to give up domestic use of $3 million in output in order to export that output to pay for the imported claims. Looked at differently, the negative sign shows that the nation is being "charged" or "debited" for acquiring $3 million worth of claims from foreigners, the claims that arose from investing (or exporting, net) $3 million of current output abroad, for which the nation is "credited" above the line.

THE BALANCE OF PAYMENTS DISEQUILIBRIUM

The term, "balance of payments," is used here sometimes to mean the balance sheet in which all imports and exports are recorded. The same term is also used here, as in all foreign trade literature, to mean the deficit or surplus involved in government purchase and sale interventions in foreign exchange markets.

The *Official Reserve Transactions Balance* (hereafter, ORTB) results when a horizontal line is drawn across a nation's BOP so that the only transactions below the line are those involving official short-term capital flows. The ORTB shows the size of a nation's BOP disequilibrium better than any other type of balance.

The net official short-term capital flow of the United States for 1978 was $31.7 billion, which was the sum of the following two changes:[2]

Change in U.S. official reserve assets:
+$0.7 billion
Change in foreign official assets in the United States: +$31.0 billion

The first figure (the positive $0.7 billion) indicates that in 1978 the United States Government *exported* (hence the positive number) $0.7 billion worth of its official reserves (mostly foreign currencies). Therefore, in America's BIAL, the asset, "Claims upon foreigners: U.S. Government, Official reserves," decreased by this amount.

The second figure (the positive $31.0 billion) shows that the United States *exported* (hence the positive number) official short-term claims (in this case, mostly U.S. Treasury bills) worth $31.0 billion to foreign official agencies. Therefore, in America's BIAL, the liability, "Claims by foreigners: to government," increased by that amount. The sum of the two figures, plus $31.7 billion, indicates that America had a *deficit* in the ORTB of $31.7 billion in 1978. (Remember, a positive number 'below the line" indicates a BOP deficit; a negative number indicates a surplus.)

The United States "financed" its "above the line" deficit of $31.7 billion by exporting, net, $31.7 billion in official short-term claims to foreigners. In other words, the foreigners gave America $31.7 billion more in the "above the line" items (goods, services, good will, long-term claims, and private short-term claims) than they received from America, in exchange for the increase in net government short-term liabilities to them of the same amount.

In 1979, the ORTB was $15.5 billion in surplus. U.S. Government official reserves rose by $1.1 billion, and claims by foreign governments fell by $14.4 billion.[3] The U.S. government imported $1.1 billion in claims upon foreigners. U.S. individuals and institutions imported $14.4 billion in U.S. Treasury bills and other claims on Americans formerly held by foreigners. An above-the-line surplus was financed by a net reduction of \$15.5 billion in short-term claims of foreign governments on the United States. The U.S. BIAL rose by \$15.5 billion.

In the ORTB, the short-term capital movements placed "below the line" are assumed to take place to "finance" or "accommodate" *autonomous* movements of all the items placed "above the line." Autonomous movements are those movements (exports and imports) that take place for their own sake. In contrast, *accommodating* flows of official short-term capital take place to fill the gap between the quantities of foreign exchange demanded and supplied at prevailing exchange rates.

There are several other measures of BOP surplus or deficit. We will mention only one. When the balance of the long-term capital account is added to the Current Account Balance (i.e., the line is drawn between long- and short-term capital), we obtain the *Basic Balance*. In the hypothetical example we were using for America's BOP, the Basic Balance shows a \$4 billion deficit.

SOME BOP STATISTICS

Actual balance-of-payments statements published by governments and international agencies are usually much more detailed and complex than the various examples shown above. Unilateral transfers and capital accounts are often divided into private and government. The "exports" and "imports" figures of many accounts are netted out. Often, sizable "errors and omissions" (or "statistical discrepancy") appear, acknowledging the inability of statistics collectors to identify all international transactions. The process of collecting statistics does not provide simultaneous reporting of credits and debits for individual transactions, and thus is apt to lead to errors and omissions. Errors and omissions are frequently combined with private short-term capital, under the assumption that it is in this type of transaction that errors and omissions are most likely to occur.

Table 14-2 presents the BOP figures for the United States for 1979 as reported by the Department of Commerce. Table 14-3 shows the BOP of Canada, Japan, and the United States for the same year as reported by the International Monetary Fund. Note that the figures for the United States are significantly different in some accounts and balances between the two tables. These discrepancies reflect in part the lack of consistency in the definition of some terms and the differences in methods of statistics collection and presentation.

The composition of the official short-term capital flows of the three countries reported in Table 14-3 reveals the important difference in the ways in which the accommodating official reserve transactions take place in these countries. The official short-term capital flows of the United States are almost exclusively in the forms of changes in liabilities to foreign official agencies (i.e., changes in "Claims by foreigners: *to* governments" in the BIAL), while the official short-term capital

TABLE 14-2   BALANCE OF PAYMENTS OF THE UNITED STATES, 1979
(in billions of dollars)

Merchandise		−29.45 (= Balance of Trade)
Exports	182.07	
Imports	−211.52	
Services		34.79
Travel and transportation, net	−2.74	
Investment income, net	32.31	
Other services, net[a]	5.21	
Unilateral transfers, net		−5.65
Private	−0.99	
Government	−4.66	
BALANCE ON CURRENT ACCOUNT		−0.32
Capital flows:		
Net changes in U.S. government assets other than official reserve assets		−3.78
Net changes in U.S. private assets		−58.53
Direct investment	−24.76	
Portfolio investment	−4.97	
Other claims (largely short-term)	−28.81	
Net changes in foreign private assets in the U.S.		48.34
Direct investment	7.67	
Portfolio investment	7.60	
Other claims (largely short-term)	33.07	
BALANCE ON CAPITAL ACCOUNT		−13.97
Allocations of special drawing rights		1.14
Statistical discrepancy		28.70
OFFICIAL RESERVE TRANSACTIONS BALANCE		15.55
Official short-term capital, net		−15.55
Net changes in U.S. reserve assets	−1.11	
Net changes in foreign official assets in the U.S.	−14.44	
TOTAL BALANCE		0

[a]Includes military transactions.
Source: U.S. Department of Commerce, *Survey of Current Business,* March 1980, p. 54.

flows of the other two nations are exclusively in changes of their reserve assets (i.e., changes in "Claims *upon* foreigners: of government" in their BIAL). This difference is attributed to the fact that the U.S. dollar is the *key reserve currency* in that most other nations hold their reserves in U.S. dollars. This difference in the method of financing BOP deficits and surpluses will be explained in the next section.

BOP, BIAL, AND THE FOREIGN EXCHANGE MARKET

Assume a country called Aruba, whose national currency is the peso, conducts all international transactions using a currency called the dollar. Aruba's relevant foreign exchange market is therefore the peso-

TABLE 14-3   BALANCE OF PAYMENTS OF CANADA, JAPAN, AND THE UNITED
STATES, 1979
(in billions of U.S. dollars)

	Canada	Japan	U.S.
Merchandise	3.84	1.93	−29.45
Exports	57.29	101.10	182.05
Imports	−53.45	−99.17	−211.50
Services	−8.65	−9.14	35.35
Exports	7.96	25.28	104.37
Imports	−16.61	−34.42	−69.02
Unilateral transfers, net	0.53	−1.11	−6.07
BALANCE ON CURRENT ACCOUNT	−4.28	−8.32	−0.17
Long-term capital, net	2.15	−13.05	−21.86
BASIC BALANCE	−2.13	−21.37	−22.03
Private short-term capital, net	5.13	6.07	5.51
Errors and omissions	−3.73	2.43	28.54
OFFICIAL RESERVE TRANSACTIONS BALANCE	−0.73	−12.87	12.02
Official short-term capital, net	0.73	12.87	−12.02
Changes in reserve assets	0.73	12.87	2.47
Changes in liabilities to foreign official agencies	0	0	−14.49

Source: International Monetary Fund, *International Financial Statistics*, July 1980.

dollar market. Aruba's foreign exchange rate is expressed as so many pesos per dollar. Figure 14-1 portrays Aruba's foreign exchange market. The demand-for-dollar curve, D, represents the demands of Aruba's residents to import merchandise, services, good will, stocks, bonds, and short-term financial claims. This demand curve for dollars slopes down to the right because the lower the peso price of a dollar, the cheaper foreign imports are in pesos, and hence the more imports and the more dollars Arubans want.

The supply-of-dollar curve, S, reports the supply of dollars in the peso-dollar market, arising from foreigners wanting to import Aruban merchandise, services, good will, stocks, bonds, and short-term IOUs. The curve S slopes up to the right because the cheaper the peso (i.e., the more pesos per dollar), the cheaper the Aruban exports are in dollars, and the more of Aruba's exports foreigners want to buy, hence more dollars are supplied to the market. (We seem to be stating the obvious, but the supply and the demand curves will have these usual shapes only if certain elasticity-of-demand-for-imports conditions are met. More of this in Chapter 15.)

These decisions to import (of the Arubans and of foreigners) are all assumed to be *autonomous*; that is, they are undertaken by businesses, individuals, and governments for reasons *other* than an intent to influence the exchange rate. Autonomous entries on the imports (or debit) side of Aruba's BOP give rise to Aruba's demand for foreign exchange (here dollars); autonomous entries on the exports (or credit) side of Aruba's BOP generate the supply of dollars in Aruba's foreign exchange market. This is the all-important linkage between Aruba's (or any country's) balance of payments *and* its foreign exchange market.

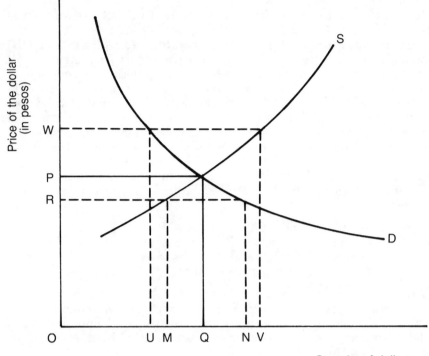

Figure 14-1
Autonomous Supply and Autonomous Demand in the
Foreign Exchange Market of Aruba

Given the conditions shown in Figure 14-1, the foreign exchange market would be in equilibrium at the exchange rate of OP pesos per dollar. OQ dollars would be demanded and supplied. In Aruba's BOP, the total dollar value of autonomous exports would equal the total dollar value of autonomous imports. The ORTB would equal zero. Aruba's BOP would show neither surplus nor deficit.

FOREIGN EXCHANGE RESERVES

But what if the exchange rate were OR pesos per dollar? Such a situation could exist temporarily at the start of an adjustment period following sudden shifts in S and/or D. However, if such a situation lasts for any length of time, one can be sure that MN, the difference between OM (the quantity of dollars autonomously supplied at exchange rate OR) and ON (the quantity of dollars autonomously demanded), is being supplied from outside the autonomous decision-makers. The most likely source of the extra non-autonomous (i.e., accommodating) supply of dollars is the government of Aruba. To be this source, the Aruban government must possess dollars. These dollars would be called Aruba's *foreign exchange reserves*.

In Figure 14-1, the disequilibrium exchange rate, OR, overvalues the peso and undervalues the dollar (see Chapter 4). At this rate, autonomous decisions to demand dollars (to import from abroad) will total ON. Autonomous decisions to supply dollars (to import *from* Aruba) will total OM. There is a foreign exchange, or a balance-of-payments (ORTB), deficit of MN. In a free market, the peso price of dollars would rise to OP. But if the Aruban government "draws down" its dollar reserves and sells MN dollars (to buy pesos) during each time period, the exchange rate will stay at OR, preserving the overvaluation of the peso. Since no nation ever possesses infinite reserves (with the exception of a key-currency nation), the limited reserves it does possess (or can borrow) will be the limit to the intervention it can accomplish.

To sum, at the disequilibrium exchange rate, OR (overvaluing the peso);

> foreign exchange and ORTB deficit (MN)
> = autonomous imports (ON) − autonomous exports (OM)
> = decrease of foreign exchange reserves
> = official short-term capital inflow.

Aruba's loss of dollar reserves means that America's official liabilities to Aruba are reduced by that much. In terms of BIAL changes, both Aruba's "Claims upon foreigners: by government" and America's "Claims by foreigners: to government" are reduced by the amount of Aruba's deficit, MN.

If Aruba and America were the only nations in the world, then MN would be America's foreign exchange and BOP surplus. Note that America's foreign exchange market and its BOP are in surplus disequilibrium without an active intervention by the American government. At the disequilibrium exchange rate, OR (undervaluing the dollar), America experiences:

> foreign exchange and ORTB surplus (MN)
> = autonomous exports (ON) − autonomous imports (OM)
> = decrease in claims by foreign government
> = official short-term capital outflow.

Alternatively, the rate OR could be maintained through the exclusive intervention of the American government. In that case, the American government must enter its foreign exchange market and buy pesos. The effects of this intervention, on the dollar-peso market and the two nations' BOP, are identical as in the case of the Aruban intervention. The only difference is in the BIAL. This time, America gains foreign exchange (peso) reserves, and Aruba's official liabilities to foreign government increase by the same amount.

Next, much more briefly, what would happen if the Aruban government's accommodating intervention were to hold the exchange rate at OW in the Figure 14-1 situation? The artificially maintained exchange rate, OW, means that Aruba is undervaluing the peso (making the peso cheaper in dollars as compared to its free market value). At the exchange rate of OW, autonomous import decisions, in Aruba and abroad, will supply UV dollars more than will be demanded. If the Aruban government chooses to intervene to hold the rate at OW, it must buy dollars. In its BOP, Aruba will show an ORTB surplus, "above the line," of UV. Below the line, the government will be importing dollar denominated short-term claims. Those imported dollar claims will be added, in Aruba's BIAL, to the asset account, "Claims upon foreigners: by government." (In America's BIAL, the change will be to increase its liabilities account, "Claims by foreigners: to government.") This surplus will be a problem to Aruba because the pesos the Aruban government issues to mop up dollars will increase Aruba's money supply and add to inflationary pressures there.

If the intervention were to be done exclusively by the American government, then it must sell pesos for dollars. America's reserves of pesos decrease, and Aruba's liabilities to the American government increase, by the amount of the official short-term capital flow from Aruba to America.

SUMMARY OF INTERVENTIONS' EFFECTS

In order to facilitate the readers' understanding of this rather complicated matter, we present below a summary chart of the two types of intervention—at OR and at OW—done by the two governments.

Intervention to Keep Rate at OR
(peso overvalued, dollar undervalued)

	Aruba (deficit)	**America (surplus)**
ORTB, below the line:	official short-term capital inflow (export of claims)	official short-term capital outflow (import of claims)

Initiative:
1. By Aruba.............Sell dollars.
   BIAL changes: Decrease in claims on   Decrease in claims by
                    foreign government   foreign government
2. By America ....Buy pesos.
   BIAL changes: Increase in claims by   Increase in claims on
                    foreign government   foreign government

Intervention to Keep Rate at OW
(peso undervalued, dollar overvalued)

	Aruba (surplus)	**America (deficit)**
ORTB, below the line:	official short-term capital outflow (import of claims)	official short-term capital inflow (export of claims)

Initiative:
1. By Aruba.............Buy dollars.
   BIAL changes: Increase in claims on   Increase in claims by
                    foreign government   foreign government
2. By America ....Sell pesos.
   BIAL changes: Decrease in claims by   Decrease in claims on
                    foreign government   foreign government

If the Aruban government intervenes, it buys or sells dollars, and, as a result, America's liabilities to the Aruban government increase or decrease. The American government intervenes by buying or selling pesos, and the size of Aruba's liabilities to the American government increases or decreases. Note that the balance-of-payments (ORTB) below-the-line entries are unaffected whether the initiative for intervention comes from the Aruban government or the American government. Aruba's deficit (America's surplus) is always accompanied by a flow of official short-term capital from America to Aruba, whether that flow is realized through the American government gaining peso reserves or through the Aruban government losing dollar reserves. Vice versa, Aruba's surplus (America's deficit) is always accompanied by a flow of official short-term capital from Aruba to America.

Intervention can of course come simultaneously from both governments. For example, Aruba's surplus (official short-term capital exports from Aruba to America) of $100 million may be accomplished by the combination of a $70 million increase in the Aruban government's dollar reserves (America owes Aruba $70 million more than before) *and* a $30 million decrease in the American government's peso reserves (Aruba owes America $30 million less than before).

In today's real world, most interventions in foreign exchange markets are conducted by governments other than the U.S. government. As subsequent chapters will show, the U.S. dollar continues to play the role of the *key currency*, which means it is held as reserves by governments of other nations and is used for intervention purposes by them. The present international monetary system of "generalized managed floats" (see Chapter 17) has lessened the world's dependency on the dollar somewhat, but traditions die hard. As Table 14-3 showed, other nations' accommodating transactions are almost exclusively in U.S. dollars, and America's BOP deficits or surpluses are almost totally financed by changes in U.S. short-term liabilities to foreign official agencies.

Because America is the "key currency country," it could, technically, run deficits indefinitely by ever increasing its liabilities. More about this later. Because other nations can possess only finite quantities of foreign exchange reserves, their deficits must be reduced sooner or later—before their reserves run out.

Whereas deficits cannot be supported forever because of the limited availability of foreign exchange reserves, surpluses — so far as technical constraints are concerned — could continue indefinitely. But, as with central bank open-market purchases of treasury bonds, so with central bank purchases of a foreign exchange surplus — every purchase adds to the domestic money stock (unless, of course, such purchases are offset by open market sales of government securities). Further, given a fractional reserve system, every dollar of the central bank purchase (of treasury bonds or of foreign exchange) permits the domestic money supply to expand by a multiple of that one dollar. Large and protracted BOP surpluses thus inevitably generate inflationary pressures within the domestic economy. More on this subject near the end of Chapter 15.

STUDY QUESTIONS

1. The mercantilists assumed that a favorable balance of trade in 1710 would bring gold and silver into the country. We would not expect such a result from a 1985 balance of trade. Why the difference?
2. Refer to endnote 1 of this chapter. First, describe a "*more* favorable balance of trade," and, secondly, describe the "*most* favorable balance of trade a nation could possibly achieve." Your conclusion may surprise you.
3. It is easy to see why a balance-of-payments deficit is a problem. Explain why a payments surplus is also a problem.
4. Suppose an American firm *exports* $200 million worth of bonds, and is paid for by checking account balances.
   (a) Does this constitute America's long-term capital *inflow* or *outflow?*
   (b) Make a pair of entries in America's balance of payments.
   (c) The exported bonds may have been initially issued by American residents or by foreign residents. Depending upon who initially issued the bonds, two different pairs of BIAL entries can be made. Make these entries in America's BIAL.
5. Set up a worksheet for America's balance of payments with the following five account categories: merchandise, services, unilateral transfers, long-term capital, and short-term capital. Record each of the following transactions in the worksheet, and compute the balance for each account category. Assume all transactions involving money payments are made by drawing checks against some commercial banks. (Figures are in millions of dollars.)
   (1) Exports of merchandise, $86
   (2) Imports of merchandise, $90
   (3) Foreign tourists spend $6 in the United States
   (4) U.S. residents receive interest on foreign savings accounts, $12
   (5) U.S. firms remit $7 in dividend checks to foreign residents
   (6) U.S. residents remit $3 to relatives abroad as gifts
   (7) After an earthquake in San Francisco, the city receives $2 worth of medicine from Canada
   (8) U.S. residents purchase $8 worth of foreign bonds and stocks
   (9) Volkswagen Co. ships $9 worth of machine tools to its plant in Pennsylvania as part of the company's direct investment in the United States
   (10) Foreign banks purchase $4 worth of banker's acceptances from U.S. banks
   (11) The City of New York floats $10 in bonds in Saudi Arabia
   (12) U.S. firms acquire ownership interests in foreign firms, $13.
   (a) Find the sizes of: the balance of trade, the balance on goods and services, the current-account balance, and the basic balance.
   (b) During the year, the U.S. government's official reserve assets decreased by $1 million, while America's liabilities to foreign official agencies increased by $4 million. Find the size of America's official reserve transactions balance. Given that balance, how large was the balance of the *private* short-term capital account?
6. Suppose America's national income figures for a given year consisted only of the following (in billions): consumption of goods and services, $800; domestic investment, $200; exports of goods and services, $100; and imports of goods and services, $80. Assume both net unilateral transfers and net long-term capital flows were zero. Compute the following:
   (a) the (gross or net) national product

(b)   the net foreign investment
(c)   the total investment
(d)   the change in the net claims on foreigners in the BIAL
(e)   the current-account balance in the BOP

7. Suppose the Indian government maintains an overvalued rate for the country's currency rupee. Explain what would be happening to India's:
(a)   official reserve transactions balance
(b)   relationship between autonomous imports and autonomous exports
(c)   official short-term capital flow
(d)   foreign exchange reserves (or official claims on foreigners)
(e)   official liabilities to foreign governments

8. Set up a worksheet for America's balance of payments. Assume all transactions involving money payments are made by drawing checks against commercial banks. Record each of the following transactions in the worksheet:
(a)   American firms export $500 million in equipment to Saudi Arabia as part of their direct investment there.
(b)   The Saudi Arabian government exports $600 million in oil.
(c)   The Saudi Arabian government nationalizes a particular oil facility in Saudi Arabia and pays the owner, an American firm, $300 million.

ENDNOTES

1. The use of the term "favorable" (for a surplus) and "unfavorable" (for a deficit) balance of trade dates back to the days of mercantilism when net imports of precious metals, achieved by means of net exports of merchandise, were regarded as favorable. It must be noted that a "favorable" balance of trade means the nation is giving foreigners more goods than it is receiving from them. Whether such a state is truly favorable or unfavorable to the nation depends on the circumstances of the particular time and place.
2. Department of Commerce, *Survey of Current Business,* March 1980, p. 54.
3. *Ibid.*

15

The Balance of Payments: Adjustment

In the preceding chapter we observed that a nation's balance of payments is in equilibrium when total autonomous exports (credits) and total autonomous imports (debits) are equal. When there exists a sizable difference between the two sides for some length of time (say several months or longer), the nation's balance of payments is in disequilibrium. In that case, the nation's foreign exchange market is also in disequilibrium, and its currency is either undervalued or overvalued. At that disequilibrium rate of exchange, autonomous credits and autonomous debits are not equal, and the difference between the quantities of foreign exchange demanded and supplied is accommodated by a movement of official short-term capital.

The imbalance in the nation's international payments and foreign exchange market can be eliminated in several ways. First, the exchange rate may move toward the equilibrium rate, either by the working of market forces or by government intervention in foreign exchange markets. Second, the sizes of autonomous credits and debits in the balance of payments — hence the supply of and the demand for foreign exchange — may change, again either autonomously or by government policy measures. In this second case, the necessary changes in the payments and foreign-exchange variables are likely to work through changes in the levels of output, and/or changes in domestic prices. The process, whether automatic or discretionary, through which a balance-of-payments and foreign exchange disequilibrium is corrected is called the international payments *adjustment* process.

ADJUSTMENT THROUGH CHANGES IN EXCHANGE RATES

As in most other types of market disequilibrium, certain forces are at work in the foreign exchange market to restore equilibrium. In the absence of government intervention, these forces *will* restore and maintain equilibrium, or at least near-equilibrium, given enough time. Given a disequilibrium situation, the size of changes that are required in the quantities of foreign exchange supplied and demanded depends on the elasticities of the supply and demand curves. In extreme cases, certain elasticity values *may* prevent the market from moving toward equilibrium. In this section, we will examine the determinants and the likely size of foreign exchange elasticities. We will then discuss the implications of different elasticity values on the adjustment process. But first, a brief review of the concept of price elasticity of supply and demand.

THE ELASTICITY CONCEPT

The price elasticity of demand (or supply) indicates the degree of responsiveness of quantity to a price change. It is measured by the ratio of the percentage change in the quantity demanded (supplied) to the percentage change in the price; or $\triangle Q/Q \div \triangle P/P$ where $\triangle Q$ and $\triangle P$ are the changes in quantity and price, and where Q is the average of the initial and final quantities, and P is the average of the initial and final prices. When this ratio (to be easily remembered as the Kewpie — the Q-P — Doll Ratio, the KDR, of $\%\triangle Q$ over $\%\triangle P$) is greater than one, the demand (or supply, for the formula is the same for both) is said to be "elastic." Notice why this is a sensible adjective; the issue is: how responsive — how "elastic" — is quantity when price changes? If the KDR is more than one, $\%\triangle Q$ is more than $\%\triangle P$; the demand (or supply) quantity response is elastic. If the KDR is less than one, $\%\triangle Q$ is less than $\%\triangle P$; and the supply (or demand) quantity response is said to be "inelastic." And if the KDR equals one, $\%\triangle Q = \%\triangle P$, and the elasticity is said to be "unitary."

When demand is elastic, a change in price produces a change in sellers' total revenue (which, like buyers' total expenditure on the product, equals P times Q) in the *opposite* direction. For example, if the KDR for demand is two, a decrease in price will result in an increase in revenue. This result occurs because the revenue loss caused by the price cut is more than offset by the revenue gain from the elastic — here twice as large — quantity increase. Conversely, when demand is inelastic, a change in price produces a change in sellers' total revenue (buyers' total expenditure) in the *same* direction. Finally, when demand is unit elastic, a change in price results in no change in total revenue.

Avoid the error of beginners and remember that slope of a demand curve is (except for vertical and horizontal demand curves) *not* a measure of the degree of elasticity. The best way to remember this is to understand clearly how elasticity differs from section to section along a straight-line demand curve sloping down to the right.

Consider such a straight-line demand curve, sloping down from a y-axis beginning to an x-axis intercept. This demand curve and the two axes form a triangle. Total revenue from any particular P-Q combination is the area of the rectangle, inscribed within the triangle, with its upper right corner at that P-Q point. Construct the total-revenue rectangle for a P-Q point near the upper left end of the demand line. Compare that with the total revenue from a price a bit lower. Compare that with the total revenue at a price another bit lower. Clearly, the lower the price, the greater the total revenue. Price down, total revenue up; demand is elastic.

Next, construct the total revenue rectangle for a price below the midpoint of this demand line. Compare that area with the total-revenue rectangle of a lower price and with the total-revenue rectangle of an even lower price. As price goes down, total revenue goes down (and vice versa); so demand is inelastic. The same slope all along the line; but the left half is elastic, the right is inelastic. Further, if one does the precise arithmetic, one finds that the elasticity value (the Kewpie Doll Ratio) decreases as one moves down along the demand line from left to right.

THE DEMAND FOR FOREIGN EXCHANGE

Let us now return to the foreign exchange market between the Northern dollar and the Southern peso which we first encountered in Chapter 4. The foreign exchange market of South, the peso-dollar market, is depicted in Figure 15-1. We have adopted the convention that the "peso-dollar market" means the dollar is foreign exchange with its price denominated in pesos. Let us assume that trade is only in merchandise. We now ask the question: What determines the elasticity of this demand for dollars?

In Figure 15-1, dollar demand slopes down to the right. The lower the exchange rate (peso price of the dollar), the greater the quantity of foreign exchange (dollars) demanded. You expect that for goods and services. Why is it also true for foreign exchange?

Perhaps an obvious reason: the demand for dollars *is* the demand for imported goods and services. The relationship can be easily seen by an examination of Figure 15-1. Assume that we are back with the two-nation two-product model so all of the demand for dollars derives from Southerners' demand for wheat. Assume further that Northern wheat's price is $4 a ton and comes from a constant-cost industry. The last assumption insures that wheat's dollar price holds constant regardless of the amount Southerners buy.

Now convert the dollar-demand aspect of Figure 15-1, with values read along the inner scales, into a wheat-demand function with values read along the outer scales. Because we already know the dollar price of

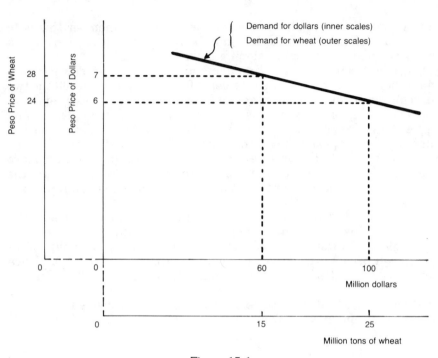

Figure 15-1
Demand for Dollars and South's Demand for Wheat

wheat ($4 per ton) and two values on the quantity-of-dollars scale ($60 million and $100 million), we can easily calculate numbers appropriate to the new wheat-quantity scale. Thus, $60 million buys 15 million tons of wheat, and $100 million buys 25 million tons of wheat, at $4 a ton. We now have numbers for the two scales of the horizontal axis as a measure of foreign exchange demand *and* as a measure of Southern wheat demand.

But the demand line cannot yet serve as a demand-for-wheat line because the vertical axis does not (yet) show the price of wheat. The wheat demand curve appears as soon as we add a peso-price-of-wheat scale (the outer scale) on the vertical axis. Its numerical values derive easily because, in this context, the peso price of wheat is the peso price of the dollar times the wheat price of $4. If, for example, the peso price of dollars is 7 pesos/dollar, then the peso price of wheat is 28 pesos per ton since one ton costs $4. At this price, Southerners demand 15 million tons of wheat. Alternatively, if the peso price of dollars is 6 pesos/dollar, the peso price of wheat is 24 pesos per ton at which price the Southerners demand 25 million tons of wheat.

To summarize, we began with the demand curve for foreign exchange and a fixed foreign-exchange price for imports. We then divided foreign exchange quantities demanded by the import foreign exchange price of $4. This gave quantities of wheat demanded by Southerners. Next, we multiplied peso price of foreign exchange by the $4 foreign exchange price of imports (but, dropping the dollar sign). This gave peso prices for wheat. In brief, given $4 wheat, we divided the horizontal axis dollar figures by 4 and multiplied the vertical axis peso-price-of-dollar figures by 4. Had wheat cost $7 or $½ per ton, the multiplications and divisions would have been by the 7 or by the ½.

The result is to show that the demand-for-imports line becomes, by calculating additional scales, the line that is demand for foreign exchange. We can say the demand curve for foreign exchange looks like the demand curve for imports, because it *is*. And the elasticity of demand for foreign exchange will be the same as the elasticity of demand for imports.

This exercise is important as a means to show the relationship between commodity import and foreign exchange markets. But reasoning from foreign exchange to import markets is the reverse of most practical work. The mechanics are the same but reversed if one reasons *from* the commodity import *to* the foreign exchange market.

A reminder: We have been careful to say "Southerners' demand for wheat" but "the demand for foreign exchange," and *not* "the Southern demand for foreign exchange." The reason for this, as we stressed in Chapter 4, is that the demand of peso owners for foreign-exchange dollars comes from Southern importers *and* from Northern exporters who have accepted payment in pesos.

THE SUPPLY OF FOREIGN EXCHANGE

Derivation of foreign exchange demand is easy.[1] Derivation of foreign exchange supply is not.

In the peso-dollar market, the supply of foreign exchange arises from the demand for South's exports. North's importers may offer dollars to buy pesos to pay Southern exporters. Or Southern exporters, paid in dollars, will tender those dollars to buy pesos to pay their workers, suppliers, and creditors. In either case, the proffered dollars derive from South's exports.

In the last subsection, we obtained Southern import demand from foreign exchange demand by merely revising axes. Foreign exchange supply does derive from Northerners' demand for South's exports. But the derivation cannot be accomplished by mere revision of axes. The derivation is more complex. Yet the process will prove familiar because it is the one used to derive total revenue numbers from ordinary demand curves. We used it earlier in this chapter when reviewing elasticity concepts.

As usual, an example helps. First, we assume South's export supply is perfectly elastic (cotton is a constant cost industry). Therefore, the peso price of exports is the same no matter how much Northerners buy. Next, we assume that when Northerners' sloping straight-line demand for Southern exports is converted into demand for pesos, the result is the straight-line foreign-exchange demand curve of Figure 15-2A. Here, for the first time, we show demand in the dollar-peso foreign exchange market. *Dollar* price of pesos is on the y axis, and pesos are the foreign exchange.

The equation of this demand-for-pesos curve, is

$$P = 0.8 - \frac{0.8}{25}Q_d \text{ or } Q_d = 25 - \frac{25}{0.8} \text{ P.}$$

We use it to calculate the quantities demanded (column 2) for each of the prices (column 1) in Table 15-1.

Now the trick is to convert the peso demand curve of Figure 15-2A and the peso demand numbers (column 2) of Table 15-1 into a dollar supply curve and a dollar supply table. The first step requires the conversion of dollar price of pesos (the vertical axis of Figure 15-2A and column 1 of Table 15-1) into peso price of dollars. This is an exercise in calculation of reciprocals. For example, if 1 peso costs $0.1, then $1 costs 10 pesos. If 1 peso costs $0.2, then $1 costs 5 pesos. We have made these calculations and show them in column 3 of Table 15-1. We have entered some of these values on the vertical axis of Figure 15-2B, where we are to show the derived supply curve of dollars. Note the inversion of order of rates: the $0.8 dollar price of pesos corresponds with the 1.25 peso price of dollars. The $0.4 dollar price (*below* $0.8) corresponds with the 2.5 peso price (*above* 1.25 pesos).

To complete the conversion of peso demand into dollar supply, the key concept is that at any dollar price in Figure 15-2A, dollar *supply* is the area of the rectangle that can be inscribed within the demand-curve-two-axis triangle at that price. Begin at $0.4 times 12.5 million = 5 million dollars. This is the area of the rectangle that fits between the origin and point U in Figure 15-2A. That area, the quantity of dollars supplied (or the quantity of pesos demanded), is plotted against the 2.5 peso price in Figure 15-2B, yielding point U'. The dollar supply figure, 5 million dollars, is entered in column 4 of Table 15-1 corresponding to the 2.5 peso price of dollars. From the demand curve for pesos, we have derived one point on the supply curve of dollars.

We began at point U because it is the midpoint of the peso demand line. As we reported earlier in this chapter, above such a midpoint, demand is elastic; below, it is inelastic.

The other supply points of dollars (also reported in column 4 of Table 15-1) are calculated in the same way, dollar price times peso quantity demanded on the peso demand curve of Figure 15-2A. If we begin at V in Figure 15-2A (which corresponds with V' in Figure 15-2B) and consider the lower dollar prices of pesos — $0.7 per peso, $0.6 per peso, and $0.5 per peso — the inscribed dollar-supply rectangle gets larger and larger — $2.187 million, $3.749 million, and $4.688 million. In Figure 15-2B, these dollar supply quantities are shown with their corresponding peso prices of dollars — 1.429 pesos, 1.667 pesos, and 2 pesos. The higher the peso price of dollars, the larger the quantity of dollars supplied. The same information is shown in Table 15-1. Figures in column 3 are, row by row, the reciprocals of the figures in column 1; column 1 times column 2 gives column 4.

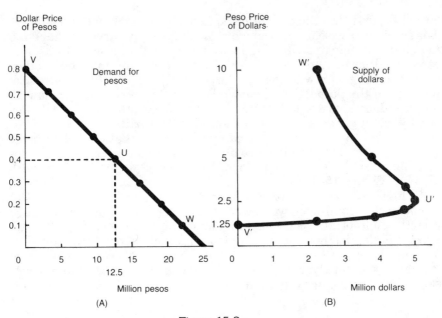

Figure 15-2
Demand for Pesos and Supply of Dollars

TABLE 15-1   DERIVATION OF SUPPLY OF DOLLARS
FROM DEMAND FOR PESOS

Demand for Pesos		Supply of Dollars	
(1) Dollar price of pesos	(2) Millions pesos demanded	(3) Peso price of dollars	(4) Million dollars supplied
0.1	21.875	10	2.188
0.2	18.75	5	3.75
0.3	15.625	3.333	4.688
0.4	12.5	2.5	5
0.5	9.375	2	4.688
0.6	6.25	1.667	3.749
0.7	3.125	1.429	2.187
0.8	0	1.25	0

So far, this derivation of dollar supply from the elastic (upper half) portion of the peso demand curve is a bit complicated but brings no surprises. The surprises (which you may already have noticed in Figure 15-2B) come when we derive dollar supply from the inelastic portion of the peso demand curve.

Compare the dollar prices of pesos for the bottom half, UW, of the Figure 15-2A demand curve with the corresponding peso prices of the dollar for the U'W' section of the Figure 15-2B supply curve. Two surprises, first that the peso prices spread out so much in Figure 15-2B. The second surprise is the backward sloping supply curve. Perhaps you may have anticipated this. When we began at V in Figure 15-2A and considered lower and lower prices for the peso, the inscribed dollar-supply rectangle grew larger and larger until the price $0.4 per peso of point U on the peso demand curve. We should know that if, below U, lower and lower prices for the peso are considered, the inscribed dollar-supply rectangle gets smaller and smaller. The arithmetic can be verified in Table 15-1. From this we can generalize: if the demand for pesos is elastic, dollar supply will slope up to the right; if the demand for pesos is inelastic, dollar supply will slope "backwards," up to the left, as with U'W' in Figure 15-2B.

We have been using the terms "peso demand" and " dollar supply." To complete this discussion, we now repeat its generalizations in language directly appropriate to the peso-dollar market. If demand for South's exports is elastic, then the supply of foreign exchange in the peso-dollar market slopes up to the right. But if demand for South's exports is inelastic, the supply of foreign exchange in the peso-dollar market slopes backwards, up to the left.

THE SUPPLY-DEMAND INTERSECTION

We have now shown that the foreign-exchange demand curve will slope *down* to the right. We have also shown that inelastic demand for exports will produce a foreign exchange supply curve that slopes *down* to the right. So we confront another of the exasperating complexities of international trade.

In almost all other cases in economic analysis, supply-demand intersections produce both equilibrium and stability. This means that if price is either above or below the intersection, market forces push it back toward equilibrium. But if demand for exports is inelastic so the foreign exchange supply curve slopes down to the right, the supply-demand intersection *may* be a stable equilibrium. Or, it may be *unstable*. In that case, once price is above *or* below the equilibrium level, market forces will push it farther away from equilibrium. Since that situation brings nightmares to central bankers, we need to look closely first to see what circumstances result in an unstable equilibrium in the foreign exchange market, and, second, to see how likely those circumstances are in the real world.

Figure 15-3 portrays four foreign exchange demand curves intersecting a supply curve, S, part of which slopes up to the right, part of which slopes up to the left. Demand curve D_1 is elastic where it intersects the well-behaved portion of the supply curve at point A. Demand curve D_2 is inelastic where it intersects the well-behaved portion of the supply curve at B. Both equilibria are stable. In either case, if price is moved away from equilibrium, market forces send the price back toward equilibrium.

Rate of Exchange

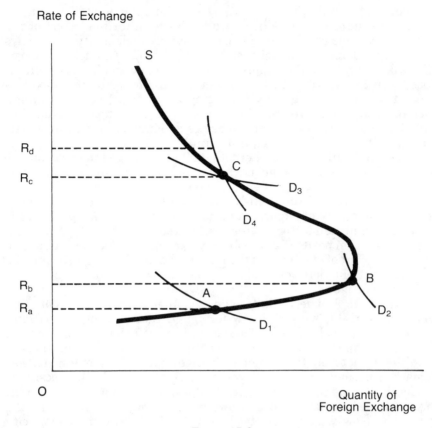

Figure 15-3
Stable and Unstable Equilibria

A portion of foreign demand for this country's exports is inelastic. Therefore, at point C, the foreign exchange supply curve is backward sloping. If demand is elastic enough to be flatter than supply at point C — as is demand curve D_3 — the equilibrium is stable. If, given D_3, the exchange rate is moved away from OR_c, market forces will send it back toward OR_c.

In contrast, if demand is sufficiently less elastic, as with D_4, so that the demand curve is steeper than the supply curve at the point of intersection, C, then we have an unstable equilibrium. If some temporary factor moves the rate of exchange upward from OR_c to, say, OR_d, quantity demanded will exceed quantity supplied. Market forces will push the rate higher. So equilibrium at C is unstable in the sense that any small displacement, either up or down, from the equilibrium rate will generate further movement away from the equilibrium. Such an unstable equilibrium, call it "exchange market perversity," appears whenever the foreign exchange supply curve is negatively sloped and flatter than the demand curve where the two curves cross.

From the foregoing, we see that, by itself, supply inelasticity is not a sufficient condition to produce an unstable equilibrium. Short of the unlikely extreme of a flat supply curve, supply inelasticity can always be offset by demand elasticity sufficiently high so the demand curve slopes down and cuts the supply curve from below and from the left, as does D_3 in Figure 15-3. Inelasticity of demand for a country's exports opens the door to trouble by producing a backward bending foreign exchange supply curve. But if that nation's own import demand is sufficiently elastic, its foreign exchange demand curve will be elastic enough to provide a stable equilibrium.

Alfred Marshall and Abba Lerner (1903-   ) described the prerequisite for a stable foreign exchange market in terms of the sum of two Kewpie Doll Ratios or in more dignified language, the sum of two coefficients of elasticity. First, the "Marshall-Lerner condition" assumes that in each country the supply of exports is perfectly elastic; this keeps domestic prices constant no matter how much is exported. Then the Marshall-Lerner condition posits that the foreign exchange market will be stable if the coefficient of elasticity of the nation's demand for imports plus the coefficient of elasticity of foreigners' demand for the nation's exports add to one or more.

In Figure 15-3, where the foreign exchange supply curve slopes up from left to right, we now know foreigners' demand for the nation's exports is relatively elastic. Therefore, the coefficient of elasticity of foreigners' import demand is more than one, and the Marshall-Lerner condition is met from the foreign exchange supply side alone. So long a demand is normal and slopes down to the right (so the KDR is positive), the foreign exchange market is in stable equilibrium at A or at B or at any point in between. Of course, we have already seen that from the geometry. Now we are able to determine this if we know elasticity values even if we never see geometric representations.

Where the foreign exchange supply slopes backward, we now know that the coefficient of elasticity of foreigners' import demand is less than one. Given our knowledge of the Marshall-Lerner condition, we can tell that, at C, the coefficient of elasticity of D_3 exceeds one minus foreigners' elasticity of demand for imports. We also know that at C, the coefficient of elasticity of D_4 must be less than one minus the coefficient of elasticity of foreigners' demand for imports.[2]

ELASTICITIES IN THE REAL WORLD

What are the elasticity values in the real-world situations? Is the Marshall-Lerner condition usually met so that currency depreciation produces an increase in the nation's trade balance? Or are relevant elasticities such that changes in exchange rates tend to produce the perverse effect of driving the exchange rate farther away from the equilibrium level?

Studies made during the 1930s and 1940s often produced results showing low elasticities and led to the so-called elasticity pessimism. Studies undertaken since the 1950s, however, have demonstrated that the earlier results had some serious theoretical flaws, and that the real-life elasticities are probably high enough for most countries so that exchange-rate changes tend to restore equilibrium.[3]

The studies of elasticities undertaken in the 1960s produced largely estimates of *short-run* elasticities based on correlations between the price variable and the same-year quantity variable. These studies neglected the fact that the coefficient of elasticity is greater the longer the period of time considered. In 1972, in review of the evidence of 16 years, Helen Junz and Rudolph Rhomberg concluded that the current-account response to exchange-rate changes requires four to five years — not the eighteen months to two years then being widely cited. They showed that less than 50 percent of the full effect occurs during the first three years following the price change, while another two years must pass before the next 40 percent of the full effect can come into force.[4] In a separate study made by the Federal Reserve Bank of New York examining the U.S. export record between 1973 and 1978, it was found that "adjustment lags extending two or three years after a major change in price competitiveness appear to be characteristic of United States exports."[5]

What would cause such long lags in the response of trade volumes to changes in relative prices? As an illustration, let us use an example of U.S. imports of television sets from Japan. Suppose that production costs of television receivers are rising at the same rate in both nations, that there is no difference between Japanese and American made sets as far as nonprice factors are concerned, and that imports are invoiced in dollars. Why would an appreciation of the yen, under such circumstances, result in a decrease in U.S. imports of television sets from Japan only after a lag of two or three years or longer?

First, there may be a *pricing lag*. The Japanese exporters would realize that each TV set exported brings in fewer yen per dollar as the yen appreciates. Since their profits per unit of television exported decline, they would naturally be tempted to raise their dollar export prices to preserve their profit margins. They may not do so, however, at least in the short run, for several reasons. The exporters and importers may have a long-term contract, in which case changing the price would be difficult. The exporters may believe that the yen appreciation is transitory; that is, they may anticipate a yen depreciation in the near future. In that case, they are likely to maintain the existing (dollar) export price and absorb the loss rather than changing the export price which would have to be raised soon afterwards. Or, the Japanese manufacturers may be willing to take a considerable reduction in profits, especially if the export price covers the marginal cost of producing exported units, in order to maintain their market shares or keep their work force employed. If the yen appreciation lasts long, and if its magnitude is substantial, the Japanese producers would eventually be compelled to raise their (dollar) export prices.

Suppose that U.S. importers of Japanese TV sets are now informed of the new, higher list prices of Japanese sets. Would they immediately raise their prices to wholesalers? Perhaps not, if they believe that exchange-rate change is transitory, if they do not like frequent price changes, and if they are concerned about their customer relations and market shares. The similar lag of pricing decisions may extend all the way down to the final retailer.

Secondly, there may exist a *switching lag*. The U.S. importers, wholesalers, and retailers all have inventories of TV sets purchased earlier at lower prices. Until these inventories are cleared away, new orders would not be placed. Even after their inventories are depleted, some buyers may not switch their sources of supply immediately to domestic producers. Shifting the source of supply is not costless. An electric appliance store that has been handling a Japanese-brand television set for years would have to incur substantial costs in advertising, customer relations, and servicing if it must switch to an American brand. Buyers in general, for similar reasons, may accept the new, higher prices and either pass them on down the line to final users, or absorb the loss, particularly if they believe the exchange-rate change will be short-lived.

It is because of these time lags between exchange-rate changes and changes in trade volumes that elasticity values found in the past studies, measured over relatively short periods of time, were often low. Most economists now believe that import and export elasticities are much greater than the early estimates, especially if the time period under consideration is lengthened from one year to several years. The elasticity pessimism of the early decades has now been replaced by guarded optimism.

THE TERMS-OF-TRADE AND THE J-CURVE EFFECTS

In the short run, import and export elasticity values may be very low because of the switching lag, so that trade balances may exhibit perverse movements (deteriorates with a currency depreciation and improves with an appreciation) even if the long-run elasticity values are high enough to satisfy the Marshall-Lerner condition.

To see how this could happen, assume that all of America's imports and exports are invoiced in dollars, the pricing lag is nonexistent, and the switching lag is substantial (a few years or longer). Now, suppose that the U.S. dollar depreciates sharply against the German mark. In America, import prices in dollars rise sharply, while export prices in dollars remain unchanged. Vice versa in Germany: import prices in marks fall, while export prices in marks remain unchanged. America's terms of trade (the ratio of export prices to import prices) deteriorate, while those of Germany improve.

Because of the assumption of a switching lag of several years, the response of import and export volumes to changes in prices will be minimal in the short run in both America and Germany. Let us assume, for simplicity, that quantity changes are zero. What would be the effects of these developments on the balances of trade of America and Germany? In America, the dollar *value* of exports remains unchanged (both the export *volume* and dollar export prices are unchanged), while the dollar *value* of imports rises (the import *volume* remains unchanged but the dollar import prices rise). So, America's trade balance deteriorates. Conversely, in Germany, the trade balance improves immediately following the appreciation of the mark.

These perverse movements of trade balances occur because, in the short run, the switching lag in trade-volume adjustment is substantial. Since the traded quantities remain unchanged, the trade balance moves in the same direction as the change in the terms of trade. A currency depreciation causes a deterioration in both the terms of trade and the trade balance; an appreciation causes their improvement. This perverse movement of the trade balance following an exchange-rate change is known as the *terms-of-trade effect.*[6]

Given a few years' time, however, trade volume begins to respond to changed prices. The longer the time allowed, the greater the change in quantities. Higher import prices in America decrease the quantity of imports. Lower prices (in marks) of American goods in Germany increase the quantity of U.S. exports there. Both import and export elasticity values go up. Given high long-run elasticity values, these quantity changes will more than offset the terms-of-trade effect, so that the balance of trade will improve in America and deteriorate in Germany.

In the United States, the phenomenon of a dollar depreciation causing an initial deterioration in the trade balance followed by a sharp improvement has come to be called the *J-curve effect.* Think of trade deficits as measured down and trade surpluses as measured up, and you will see why that appellation is picturesquely appropriate.

Table 15-2 shows that the J-curve pattern was observed in the U.S. trade balances in the 1976-78 period. Between the end of 1976 and the end of 1978, the value of the dollar fell by nearly 15 percent in terms of the effective rate computed by the IMF and by 33 percent against the Japanese yen. The U.S. trade deficit, however, increased from $3 billion in the fourth quarter of 1976 to $11 billion in the first quarter of 1978. It then fell to $6 billion in the fourth quarter of 1978. The volume and value of U.S. exports, as well as its trade balance, did not show a sign of significant improvement until the second quarter of 1978.

Table 15-2 also shows the changes in the exchange rate and the volume and value of Japan's exports and imports over the 1976-78 period. Between the end of 1975 and the end of 1978, the yen appreciated by over 50 percent. The turnaround in the volume of exports did not come, however, until the first quarter of 1978. Reflecting the continued surge in Japan's trade balance during 1978, the yen continued to appreciate rapidly in that year. This caused the *dollar value* of Japan's exports to continue to rise in spite of the decline in the *volume.* The trade surplus finally showed a significant decline in the last quarter of 1978. If we assume that the appreciation of the yen started in the first quarter of 1976, we see that its impact was not felt until two years (in terms of export volume) or two and a half years (in terms of trade balance) afterwards.

TABLE 15-2 EXCHANGE RATES AND TRADE BALANCES, UNITED STATES AND JAPAN, 1976-1978

	1976				1977				1978			
	I	II	III	IV	I	II	III	IV	I	II	III	IV
United States												
Effective exchange rate[a]	100.0	101.4	100.9	101.3	101.3	100.6	99.9	97.5	94.2	92.9	88.1	86.5
Yen per U.S. dollar[b]	100.0	99.0	96.4	97.4	94.7	91.1	88.1	81.8	78.8	73.1	63.9	63.2
Volume of exports[b]	100.0	107.5	97.6	106.9	102.0	107.8	98.5	103.0	101.5	118.6	109.1	119.4
Volume of imports[b]	100.0	106.1	111.2	114.1	118.7	125.8	120.4	120.4	127.4	131.9	130.6	133.7
Value of exports[c]	27.3	29.4	27.4	30.6	29.4	31.9	29.0	30.3	30.8	36.6	34.5	40.0
Value of imports[c]	28.1	30.4	31.9	33.6	36.4	38.2	37.7	39.4	41.9	43.9	44.1	46.1
Exports minus imports[c]	-0.8	-1.0	-4.5	-3.0	-7.0	-6.3	-8.7	-9.1	-11.1	-7.3	-9.6	-6.1
Japan												
Effective exchange rate[a]	100.0	102.2	105.3	104.0	107.0	111.1	114.8	122.9	125.4	135.2	152.6	152.3
U.S. dollar per yen[b]	100.0	100.9	103.9	102.7	105.7	110.0	113.6	122.4	126.9	136.6	156.5	158.3
Volume of exports[b]	100.0	113.2	117.2	123.4	115.0	123.5	126.0	131.6	123.9	120.1	121.2	125.6
Volume of imports[b]	100.0	107.0	111.0	113.5	111.2	111.1	109.5	113.1	112.2	116.9	117.6	126.4
Value of exports[c]	14.2	16.1	17.1	18.7	17.5	19.4	20.2	22.2	21.6	23.3	24.7	26.0
Value of imports[c]	12.7	13.7	14.4	15.4	14.8	15.5	15.5	16.2	15.8	16.7	17.4	20.9
Exports minus imports[c]	1.5	2.4	2.7	3.3	2.7	3.9	4.7	6.0	5.8	6.6	7.3	5.1

[a] IMF MERM weights, 1976(I) = 100.
[b] 1976(I) = 100.
[c] Billions of U.S. dollars, fob.

Source: International Monetary Fund, International Financial Statistics, May 1979.

ADJUSTMENT THROUGH CHANGES IN OUTPUT

The analysis of BOP adjustment through exchange-rate changes presented in the first section of this chapter assumed that national macroeconomic variables such as total output, total income, money supply, and average prices neither affected, nor were affected by, changes in exchange rates. In reality, however, changes in exchange rates are bound to have effects on these variables, and vice versa. Consequently, the effectiveness of an exchange-rate change as a cure for exchange-market disequilibrium may be reinforced or compromised by changes in domestic macroeconomic variables. The balance of payments may even be moved from disequilibrium to equilibrium through changes in domestic macroeconomic variables while exchange rates are left unchanged (that *was* the way the old "gold standard" worked).

Balance-of-payments disequilibrium can be corrected through two different sorts of changes in internal variables. The first is through output changes, possibly accompanied by some price changes. This will be the topic of this section. The second, to be discussed in the next section, is through changes in money supply necessarily accompanied by changes in prices, interest rates, and at least nominal — and possibly also in real — income. (For the sake of simplicity of exposition, our analysis will thus be divided largely into (1) the *real* changes in output and income and (2) their *nominal* changes attributed primarily to monetary factors. It must be clearly understood, however, that this dichotomy is unrealistic. As Figure 15-12 will show, real and nominal changes are closely intertwined in reality.)

Throughout this second section, we will assume that domestic prices hold constant. When real output changes, either money supply or money velocity is assumed to change to accommodate those output changes. Therefore, the familiar national-income accounting concept of "national income" will be synonymous with real output, and every change in national income will represent an equal change in real output.

National income and foreign trade are connected primarily through the positive relationship that exists between income level and the public's decisions about amounts to import. In the simple Keynesian national-income determination model, consumption is larger and imports are larger, the larger the national income. As income rises, more is consumed and more, necessarily, is imported as consumers choose more of some goods produced abroad and more of other goods domestically produced but using imported materials. Using this positive income-import relationship as our basic building bloc, we will develop the simple Keynesian model of national-income determination in an *open* (i.e., having international trade) economy. We assume our readers are familiar with the most basic concepts of national income accounting and income determination found in elementary economics textbooks. Nevertheless, we begin with a review of the simplest *closed* economy.

A SIMPLE MODEL OF A CLOSED ECONOMY

We begin with a national income model with no government sector and no foreign trade. Total national income, Y, viewed from the disposition-of-output side, is the sum of revenues from consumption, C, and investment, I. (This Y is a synonym for gross national product, the market value — in current prices — of all final goods and services produced domestically during some time interval.)

This is, of course, a circular flow model in which Y as total value of final output equals Y as total value of income from disposition of output. Looked at from the use-of-income side, Y is either consumed, C, or saved, S. In equations, these definitional relationships are expressed as follows:

disposition of output: $Y = C + I$, and

use of income: $\qquad Y = C + S$.

These are truisms. They describe *actual* outcomes for every time period. With government and international trade included, they would describe the disposition of total output and the use of total income in every time period for every country in the world.

These definitional relationships are useful as a framework of national-income determination analysis; but to explain how equilibrium output and income levels are determined, it is necessary to refer to *intended* or *planned* values of the variables.

National income is in equilibrium when total *planned* expenditures, $C + I$, just equal total *planned* use of income, $C + S$; or

$$\text{planned } C + I = \text{planned } C + S, \text{ or}$$
$$\text{planned } I = \text{planned } S.$$

In other words, income is in equilibrium when planned nonconsumption use of output, I, just equals planned nonconsumption use of income, S. If consumption is viewed as the main stream of the circular flow from income back, via purchases, to income; then old income not spent on consumption, i.e., S, is a leakage from the circle and nonconsumption purchases, I, is an injection. When planned $I = $ planned S, planned injection equals planned leakage, and the macroeconomy is in equilibrium.

Hereafter, we will often need to distinguish between *planned* and *actual* values of S and I (and later, of imports, M, and exports, X). To save space, we will follow the standard convention and always mean planned S, I, M, and X when those concepts are used without a modifier. When we need to distinguish planned from actual, we will use the two modifiers.

Investment spending is considered autonomous; i.e., determined from outside the model and is not affected by changes in Y. Accordingly, as we begin to portray the model in geometric form, the investment curve is drawn, as in Figure 15-4, as a horizontal line. Saving, on the other hand, is assumed to be a positive function of income. In Figure 15-4, the S line is drawn with a positive slope. The ratio of a change in savings, $\triangle S$, to its causal change in income, $\triangle Y$ — or $\triangle S/\triangle Y$ — is known as the *marginal propensity to save,* MPS. It is represented by the numerical value of the slope of the S-curve in Figure 15-4.

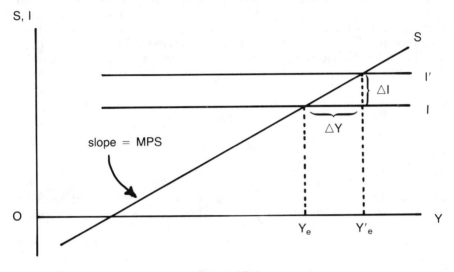

Figure 15-4
Equilibrium Income of a Closed Economy

Given the initial circumstances of S and of I in Figure 15-4, the nation is in domestic equilibrium if and only if income equals Y_e so S will equal I. A change in the level of investment will bring an income change that is a multiple of the investment change. If investment rises from I to I' in Figure 15-4, the new equilibrium Y will be Y'_e, where S has risen enough to equal the higher I. The change in income, $\triangle Y$, is a multiple of the change in investment, $\triangle I$. The ratio of that income change to the investment change, $\triangle Y/\triangle I$, is known as the *multiplier.* The size of the multiplier is equal to the reciprocal of the marginal propensity to save, or 1/MPS. If the sizes of the investment change and the MPS are known, the size of the income change needed to restore equilibrium can be calculated. That needed income change always equals investment change times the multiplier; thus, $\triangle Y = \triangle I \times 1/MPS$.

A SIMPLE MODEL OF AN OPEN ECONOMY

Still assuming there is no government, we now add foreign trade to our model. The disposition of national income remains either consumption or saving; that is, $Y = C + S$. But total income now derives from three sources: domestic C, domestic I, and exports, X. That may appear to imply that $Y = C + I + X$, but it does not. This Y measures gross *national* product, the value of production by this nation's people only. But domestic C will include French champagne and Costa Rican bananas. Domestic I will include Korean steel and Japanese machinery. Even Fords, shipped out as part of X, include Zimbabwean chrome and Canadian bauxite. To get *national* product, the import components must be subtracted from C, from I, and from X. To simplify the matter, we subtract all the imports out in a lump. So we have the equation $Y = C + I + X - M$; total income derives from three sources with part of the flow from each leaking off for imports. Henceforward, I represents domestic investment only, and $(X - M) = NFI$ represents foreign investment.

The national income identities of an open economy are:

$$Y = C + I + X - M,$$

and

$$Y = C + S;$$

and, therefore,

$$C + S = C + I + X - M.$$

These are truisms and, in the absence of government, would describe the situation in every area for every time period whether national-income equilibrium or disequilibrium prevails.

Equilibrium is, as always, special in that all the plans are then mutually consistent. Manipulating our last equation by dropping C from both sides and moving other elements about, we get these two descriptions of equilibrium conditions where all the variables are interpreted in the planned sense.

$$S + M = I + X,$$

and

$$S - I = X - M$$

All the "plans" are domestic except for X. There, the plans are by foreign importers. Both equations state conditions for national income equilibrium; each gives precisely the same information but with differences in organization and emphasis. We shall examine the meaning and implications of each.

The $(S + M) = (I + X)$ Model

This approach is an extension of the leakage-injection $(S = I)$ model of a closed economy. In an open economy, leakage from the circular flow's income stream consists of saving *and* imports. Injections come from domestic investment *and* from exports.

We have already noted that imports are positively related to the level of income. The import function, shown in Figure 15-5, therefore, is drawn as an upward sloping curve. The slope of this curve, expressed by the ratio $\Delta M/\Delta Y$, is the ratio of a change in imports to a change in income, and is called the *marginal propensity to import*, MPM.

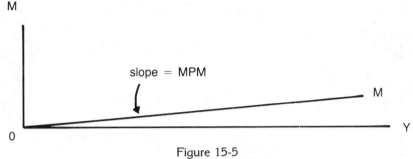

Figure 15-5
Imports as a Function of Income

To obtain a leakage function, we add the saving and import functions. Geometrically, the leakage function is represented by an upward sloping curve $(S+M)$ in Figure 15-6 which is constructed by vertically summing the height of the saving curve and the import curve at each level of income. The slope of this curve is equal to the sum of the slopes of the saving curve and of the import curve, or MPS + MPM. If, for example, $MPS = 0.2$ and $MPM = 0.05$, the slope of the $(S+M)$ curve is 0.25.

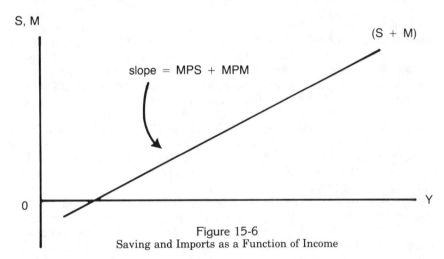

Figure 15-6
Saving and Imports as a Function of Income

We assumed earlier that investment is autonomous and drew the investment function as a horizontal line. Similarly, we assume exports are exogenously determined and draw the export function as a horizontal line. To obtain an injection curve, we add vertically the investment line and the export line. The $(I+X)$ function is therefore represented as a horizontal line, as in Figure 15-7.

Equilibrium in an open economy is found at the income level where $(S+M) = (I+X)$, or where the $(S+M)$ curve intersects the $(I+X)$ curve. In Figure 15-7, this occurs at the level of income Y_e. How does the multiplier work in this situation? To find this, let us assume that there

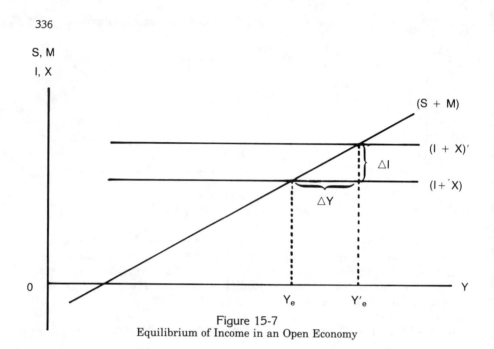

Figure 15-7
Equilibrium of Income in an Open Economy

is an initial increase in investment of $\triangle I$. The $(I+X)$ function is now raised by $\triangle I$, so that a new $(I+X)$ curve — $(I+X)'$ — intersects the $(S + M)$ curve at the new equilibrium level of income Y'_e. The change in income, $\triangle Y$, is again larger than the initial change in investment, $\triangle I$. Specifically, the change in income is equal to the initial change in investment times the multiplier, where the multiplier is the reciprocal of the sum of MPS and MPM. Or, $\triangle Y = \triangle I \times 1/(MPS + MPM)$. If the initial increase in investment is $10 million, and MPS = 0.2 and MPM = 0.05, then the ultimate increase in income caused by the initial change in investment will be $40 million. The multiplier is 4, or equal to $1/(0.2 + 0.05)$. What happens here is much like what happens in a closed economy.

The multiplier working in an open economy is often called the "foreign trade multiplier." This phrase is somewhat misleading. It does not mean that the multiplier applies only to change in foreign trade variables X and M. Instead, it refers to the multiplier that is at work *in an open economy,* that is, an economy that has trading relations with the outside world. A better title would be the "open-economy multiplier," for its paradigm applies to any initial change in spending, be it in exports or in consumption, government, or domestic investment.

The (S − I) = (X − M) Model

To obtain a different perspective, the above general truths can be restated in an alternative form. When national income equilibrium is achieved, (S − I) (the excess of planned domestic saving over planned domestic investment) is equal to (X − M) (the excess of planned exports over planned imports). Assuming net unilateral transfers are zero, (X − M) represents both the balance of goods and services *and* the current account balance (defined in Chapter 14 as Net Foreign Investment).

The advantage of the (S + M) = (I + X) formulation of national income equilibrium is its placement of both leakage variables on one (left) side and of both injection variables on the other (right) side. Its disadvantage is its admixture, on each side, of internal and external variables. The advantage of the (S − I) = (X − M) formulation is that it links internal balance (domestic income equilibrium) with external balance (the current-account balance). As we shall see shortly, when the (S − I) = (X − M) formulation is graphed, we can read visually both internal and external balances.

The formula (S − I) = (X − M) also tells us an interesting fact about the equilibrium level of national income. (S − I) means the excess of domestic saving over domestic investment. Households and businesses save part of their income. Domestic investors direct unconsumed output into such domestic investment uses as buildings, equipment, and inventories. But some of the net output not consumed domestically may be "borrowed" by foreigners in the form of an excess of our exports over our imports. In this case, we have invested abroad; Net Foreign Investment is positive. Or an excess of domestic (C + I) over domestic Y may be offset by an excess of imports over exports. In that case, our NFI is negative.

If we substitute NFI (Net Foreign Investment) for (X − M) and rewrite the equation (S − I) = (X − M) as (S − I) = NFI, and further transform the last equation to S = (I + NFI), we can see the relationship clearly. If national income is to be in equilibrium, saving must equal the sum of domestic investment, I, and foreign investment, NFI.

Suppose we observe that (S − I) = (X − M) = \$5 billion. This is a surplus in the current account. It may or may not be accompanied by a surplus in the balance of payments. In general, there are three possibilities: two extremes and the range between them.

At one extreme, the central banks may have decided unreservedly to support the initial exchange rate. Then, in the simplest version of the case, i.e., with net autonomous capital (long-term and private short-term) movement zero, the balance of payments will also be \$5 billion in surplus. Either the domestic central bank will have added \$5 billion to its foreign exchange reserves or foreign central banks will have reduced their reserves by \$5 billion, or some combination of these two kinds of changes with the two totalling \$5 billion. In the messier version of this case, the net autonomous capital movement will be neither zero nor \$5 billion. Then the payments balance will be the algebraic sum of \$5 billion and the net autonomous capital movement. That sum will be equal to the change in foreign exchange reserves. But the benchmark criterion here — the foreign exchange rate — will be unchanged.

At the other extreme, the central banks may have decided they will not intervene in foreign exchange markets. In that case the $5 billion current-account surplus will derive from a multitude of private decisions responding to market determination of flexible commodity prices, security prices, interest rates, and exchange rates. Central bank reserves will be unchanged. The balance of payments will then, necessarily, be in equilibrium with the $5 billion current-account surplus offset by $5 billion in net imports of stocks, bonds, and other IOUs in the capital (long-term and private short-term) accounts.

Between these extremes is an infinitude of possible combinations of central bank reserve changes *and* of changes in exchange rates. In such in-between situations, the central bank(s) will have decided to intervene to moderate but not to prevent changes in the exchange rate. Given the $5 billion current-account surplus, the payments balance will then be the algebraic sum of that $5 billion and the net private capital movement.

In the remainder of this section, our attention will be focused on the relationship between the level of national income and the current-account balance. The relationship between the current-account balance and the balance of payments will not be specified. Since the current account is ordinarily the largest component of a nation's balance of payments, it is safe to assume that the changes in the balance of payments tend to follow the changes in the current-account balance. Under this assumption, then, the term "external balance" used here refers explicitly to the current-account balance, but also, more generally (but less accurately) to the balance of payments. (Chapter 18 will present a model that incorporates autonomous capital flows and thereby explicitly recognizes the difference between the current-account balance and the balance of payments. See Figure 18-1.)

Figure 15-8 shows a geometric derivation of the $(S - I)$ function and the $(X - M)$ function. The upper half of Panel A presents S and I curves. The value of I subtracted from the value of S vertically at each level of income gives us the value $(S - I)$, which is plotted in the lower half of Panel A. The slope of the $(S - I)$ curve is the same as that of the S curve, or equal to the marginal propensity to save. S and I are equal at income level Y_a; therefore, in the lower half, we find $(S - I) = 0$ at Y_a. The upward sloping $(S - I)$ curve implies that, as the level of income rises, an increasing amount of saving will become available for foreign investment in the form of trade (current-account) surplus.

Panel B of Figure 15-8 shows a similar derivation of the $(X - M)$ curve from the X curve and the M curve. When M is subtracted from X, $(X - M)$ is positive below income Y_b. At Y_b, $(X - M) = 0$. Above Y_b, M exceeds X so that the $(X - M)$ values are negative. The $(X - M)$ curve is negatively sloped, with its slope being equal to the negative of the marginal propensity to import, or $-MPM$. This negative slope of the $(X - M)$ curve implies that the current-account balance is negatively related to the level of income. As income rises, less domestic saving can go into foreign investment, and the external balance changes from surplus (investment abroad) to deficit (borrowing from foreigners).

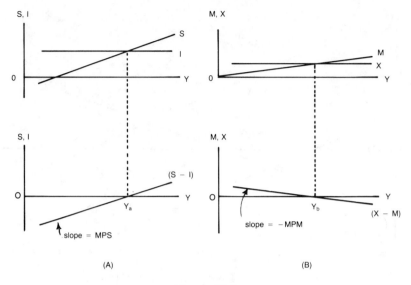

Figure 15-8
Derivation of $(S - I)$ and $(X - M)$ Curves

If $(S - I)$ rises with income and $(X - M)$ falls with it, they must become equal at one level of income, which, of course, is the equilibrium level of income. In Figure 15-9, three different levels of equilibrium income — Y_1, Y_2, and Y_3 — are shown to correspond to three alternative levels of $(X - M)$, intersecting with a single $(S - I)$ curve. With $(X - M)_2$, $(S - I) = (X - M) = 0$ at Y_2. In this case, there exist both an internal balance (income equilibrium) and an external balance (zero current-account balance). Internal and external balances, however, need not coincide. With $(X - M)_1$, income is in equilibrium at Y_1, but with a current-account deficit of Y_1A. Conversely, with $(X - M)_3$, income is in equilibrium at Y_3, and there is a current-account surplus of Y_3B.

When Domestic Investment Changes

Let us now use geometry to show the multiplier process at work, with injection and leakages in the $(S - I) = (X - M)$ framework. We use two numerical illustrations; in each, we assume MPS = 0.2 and MPM = 0.05 so the multiplier is $1/(0.2 + 0.05) = 4$. In our first example, assume that both income and the current account are initially in equilibrium at Y_1 in Figure 15-10. Suppose now the level of investment spending rises by $100 million per year. As soon as this increase in I injection is planned (and before Y changes), the downward shift of the $(S - I)$ function shows a negative net domestic saving plan of −$100 million ($= Y_1A$). (Note that the $(S - I)$ shifts *downward* as

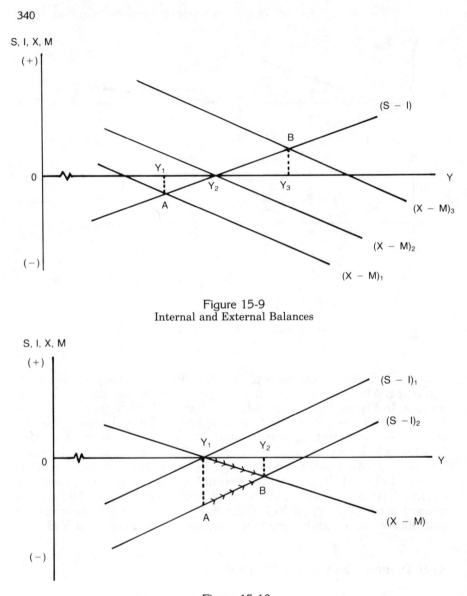

Figure 15-9
Internal and External Balances

Figure 15-10
The Effect of a Rise in Investment Spending on Internal and External Balances

the planned investment function shifts *upward.*) With no change, yet, in Y, net foreign investment $(X - M)$ remains zero. Income is in disequilibrium. The increase in actual investment, however, will trigger a multiplier process, pushing the income level upward. Income will reach a new equilibrium at Y_2, which is \$400 million higher than Y_1, since:

$$\Delta Y = \Delta I \times \frac{1}{MPS + MPM} = \$100 \text{ million} \times \frac{1}{0.2 + 0.05} = \$400 \text{ million}$$

As the income level rises from Y_1 to Y_2 through the working of the multiplier mechanism, two things happen. First, along the $(S - I)_2$ line, the amount of $(S - I)$ gradually increases. This is because saving is a positive function of income. Secondly, along the $(X - M)$ line, the amount of $(X - M)$ gradually decreases. This is because imports are a positive function of income. The two will become equal at income level Y_2, with both the net domestic saving $(S - I)$ and the net foreign investment $(X - M)$ being negative and equal to Y_2B. Income is in equilibrium again at Y_2 with a current-account deficit of Y_2B. What is the numerical value of this deficit?

We know the external balance was zero initially at Y_1. As income rose by \$400 million, a deficit developed because imports increased with rising income. The change in the size of imports can be easily calculated by multiplying the change in income by the marginal propensity to import, or:

$$\Delta M = \Delta Y \times MPM = \$400 \text{ million} \times 0.05 = \$20 \text{ million.}$$

The current-account deficit at Y_2, or Y_2B, is therefore equal to \$20 million.

When Exports Change

For our second illustration, let us assume an initial increase by \$100 million in the level of exports. The effects of this change on national income and the current account are shown in Figure 15-11. As before, both income and the current account are initially in equilibrium at Y_1. The autonomous upward shift in the export function raises the $(X - M)$ curve to $(X - M)_2$, resulting in a planned net foreign investment of \$100 million ($= Y_1A$). Net domestic saving ($= 0$) and net foreign investment ($= \$100$ million) are now unequal, and the income level is in disequilibrium. The multiplier process pushes income to a new equilibrium at Y_2, \$400 million higher than Y_1, since:

$$\Delta Y = \Delta X \times \frac{1}{MPS + MPM} = \$100 \text{ million} \times 4 = \$400 \text{ million.}$$

At Y_2, which is \$400 million higher than Y_1, the current account shows a surplus of BY_2. How large is this surplus?

We know the external balance was zero initially at Y_1. After the increased export injection of \$100 million, the multiplier process pushes the income level up by \$400 million. With the new equilibrium level of income up \$400 million and an MPM of 0.05, imports increase by \$20 million. Since exports initially increase by \$100 million and imports subsequently increase by \$20 million, and since the current account was

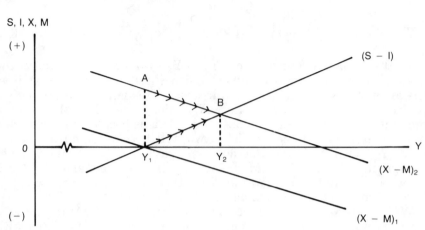

Figure 15-11
The Effect of a Rise in Exports on Internal and External Balances

zero initially, the new current account at Y_2 must show a surplus of $80 million.

This result can be computed as follows:

$\triangle(X - M) = \triangle X - \triangle M.$
Since $\triangle M = \triangle Y \times MPM$, we can substitute for $\triangle M$ to get:
$\triangle(X - M) = \triangle X - (\triangle Y \times MPM) = \$100 \text{ million} -$
($400 million $\times 0.05$) $= \$80$ million.

In this second illustration, we find the initial $100 million increase in the surplus caused by the export increase is automatically reduced by $20 million as the multiplier process raises income and imports. But the surplus is not eliminated because the $400 million income increase raises domestic saving by $80 million. With domestic investment unchanged, this increased domestic saving serves to finance the $80 million net foreign investment, so the current-account surplus of $80 million remains.

If the initial change were a $100 million *decrease* in exports, there would be an initial $100 million deficit in the current account. But falling income of $400 million would lower imports, and reduce the external deficit by $20 million while at the same time lowering domestic saving until negative net foreign investment of $20 million (the net investment of foreigners in this country) would just fill the gap between domestic investment and saving plans.

Referring back to Figure 15-11, we see that the smaller the MPS — hence the flatter the $(S - I)$ curve — the greater the effect of a change in exports on income and the closer $\triangle M$ will be to the initial $\triangle X$. (Using Y_1 as a pivot, make the $(S - I)$ curve flatter. You will see that Y_2 will be higher and $(X - M) = BY_2$ will be smaller.) Only in the extremely unlikely case of zero MPS, or a flat $(S - I)$ curve, will a change in exports induce an income change big enough to make $\triangle M = \triangle X$. Only under such a circumstance would the current-account adjustment by changes in income be *complete,* so that equilibrium income would necessarily be accompanied by a current-account balance of zero.

FULL EMPLOYMENT AND INCOME ADJUSTMENT

Payments adjustment through income changes works through changes in *real* income (output). The description in the last subsection assumed no constraints on increases in real output. But real income, by definition, cannot rise above the full employment level. Thus, the process of international adjustment through income changes breaks down if income levels above the full employment level are required for restoration of external equilibrium. This point is succinctly brought to focus in the so-called *absorption approach* to the analysis of an exchange-rate devaluation.

Assume, for the sake of simplicity, that an economy's production, consumption, and trading are limited to goods. The nation's balance of trade, $(X - M)$, is then synonymous with its balance on current account. As noted earlier, the country's national income is expressed by an equation:

$$Y = C + I + X - M.$$

The nation's income (output) can be divided into two parts. The sum of C and I may be called "absorption" in the sense that it represents that part of national output "absorbed" (or "utilized") by domestic households and business firms. The second part of Y represents that part of output that is "utilized" by foreigners — that is, the trade balance $(X - M)$. If we use A for absorption — meaning always *domestic* absorption — the income equation can be rewritten as :

$$Y = A + (X - M), \text{ or}$$
$$Y - A = X - M.$$

Output less domestic absorption is what is made available to foreigners as a trade balance. The term $(Y - A)$, of course, is equivalent to the $(S - I)$ used earlier in this section. The excess of output over absorption is the same as the excess of domestic saving over domestic investment. The equation $(Y - A) = (X - M)$, however, tells us something that is only implicit in the equation $(S - I) = (X - M)$.

Assume a case where $(Y - A) = (X - M)$ so that national income is in equilibrium. (The equation $(Y - A) = (X - M)$ can, as can the equation $(S - I) = (X - M)$, be interpreted either in an *actual* or *planned* sense. Used in a *planned* sense, $(Y - A) = (X - M)$ is a condition for national income equilibrium.) Next, assume that exogenous factors raise M *or* lower X, leading to a deterioration in the nation's external balance $(X - M)$. One way to correct the imbalance is to devalue the nation's currency. Assuming the elasticity conditions are met, we can expect the devaluation to increase the $(X - M)$ balance. For $(X - M)$ to increase, however, the left side of the equation $(Y - A)$ must also increase by the same amount. If Y represents a full employment level of output, the trade balance $(X - M)$ can be increased only by reducing the absorption, A. Thus, for a devaluation to be successful in improving the nation's external balance under conditions of full employment, domestic absorption must be reduced. The policy implication of this conclusion is that if devaluation is to work under full employment conditions without causing inflation, the government must, by contractionary monetary and fiscal policies, reduce domestic consumption and/or investment.

ADJUSTMENT THROUGH CHANGES IN MONEY, PRICES, AND INTEREST RATES

The two primary types of international payments adjustment discussed thus far — adjustments through changes in exchange rates and through changes in income — exclude any consideration of the monetary factors, i.e., the money supply, domestic prices, and interest rates. In this section we will present a simple model that incorporates monetary factors. Such a model, by necessity, has to be less clearcut and definitive than the simple exchange-rate or income model. To assist the reader in sorting out the interactions among different variables, a diagram sketching the maze of relationships leading from an initial deficit to an eventual reduction of the deficit is presented in Figure 15-12. Each box in the diagram is labeled by a letter to facilitate the tracing of the sequence of events leading to equilibrium restoration. For example, the sequence ZECBZ represents the process of adjustment through changes in exchange rates. A deficit, given a degree of flexibility in exchange-rate movements, causes the nation's currency to depreciate. Provided the elasticity conditions are met, the depreciation improves the country's trade competitiveness, which, by improving its trade balance, leads to a decrease in the deficit. Similarly, the sequence ZDYBZ indicates the adjustment mechanism through income changes discussed in the preceding section. (The arrow in each box represents the direction of change in each variable in the case of a deficit disequilibrium. For a surplus disequilibrium, all the *boxed* arrows should be reversed.)

HUME'S PRICE-SPECIE-FLOW MECHANISM

The earliest model of international payments adjustment was credited to the 18th-century English philosopher-historian David Hume (1711-1776). Under the gold standard, a country running a balance-of-payments deficit experiences an outflow of gold (the measure of the size of the deficit), which reduces the country's money supply. Hume assumed

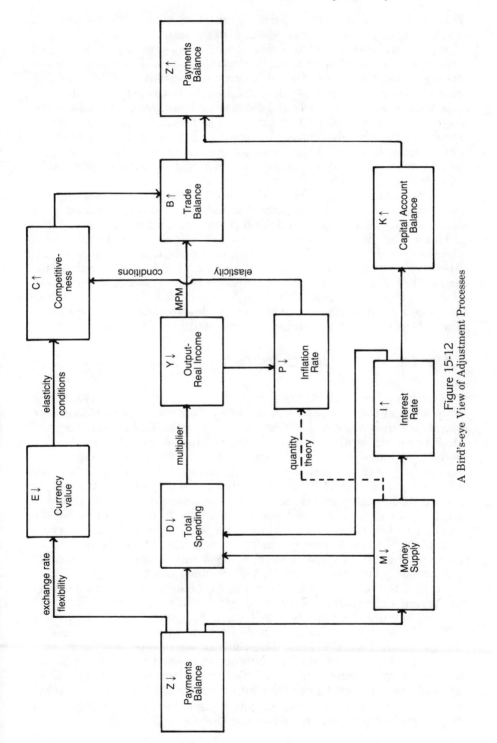

Figure 15-12
A Bird's-eye View of Adjustment Processes

neither the velocity of money nor the quantity of output could change. These extreme assumptions yielded his classical *quantity theory of money* which states that the price level in a country is directly and proportionally related to the quantity of money. Therefore, any decrease in the nation's supply of money necessarily results in falling prices. Lower prices improve the country's competitive position in world trade, increasing its exports and decreasing its imports. The balance-of-payments deficit (which in this model was measured by net exports of specie) is thereby eliminated. In terms of Figure 15-12, this so-called *price-specie-flow mechanism* traces the sequence ZMPCBZ. The same process works in reverse in a surplus country; the inflow of gold results in rising prices which help reduce the surplus.

The classical quantity theory of money on which the price-specie-flow mechanism was based is no longer accepted as valid by contemporary economists. Of course, it would not have looked so simple-mindedly silly if Hume had only recognized the roles of velocity and of real output changes. In Hume's defense, we should note that in Hume's day literate Europeans, rather like contemporary Club of Rome adherents, had little faith in growth. They premised a nearly static output level. Given that premise, Hume's conclusions followed. Today, most economists assume that changes in money stock affect, first, total spending and interest rates; then, prices *and* real output.

ADJUSTMENT THROUGH CHANGES IN MONEY SUPPLY

If exchange rates fluctuate freely, the quantity of foreign exchange supplied and the quantity demanded remain equal, even though the quantities may vary widely from week to week. The money stocks of trading countries are then unaffected by their foreign trade.

But if a central bank intervenes to influence foreign exchange rates, it must buy or sell foreign exchange. When a central bank buys or sells anything, it pays or is paid with a change in its liability, the *reserve account* of the commercial banks. In a fractional reserve banking system, every change of $1 (or 1 yen or 1 franc) results in a change in the nation's money stock by a multiple of the $1. So central bank intervention to buy or sell foreign exchange has exactly the same multiplied effect on the nation's money stock as has central bank intervention to buy or sell government securities in the open market.

Thus, if the central bank intervenes in the foreign exchange market to prevent *depreciation* of its currency, it will support a deficit in the nation's balance of payments. It will sell its foreign exchange reserves and will be "paid" with reductions in its liabilities, the "reserve assets" of domestic commercial banks. The central bank's net sales of foreign exchange will equal the nation's balance-of-payments deficit (assuming no other central banks intervene). So the nation's money stock will be pressed down by a multiple of the deficit, unless the central bank makes equal open market purchases of government securities or undertakes some equivalent initiative to support the original money stock.

If the central bank, instead, intervenes to prevent *appreciation* of its own currency, it will buy foreign exchange, equal in domestic-currency value to its balance-of-payments surplus, thereby increasing the reserve account balances of commercial banks. The nation's money supply will then expand by a multiple of that surplus — unless offsetting open market sales or other initiatives are effected.

The tight money situation caused by a BOP deficit and the accompanying rise in the interest rates tends to discourage spending in general, which tends to reduce output and income (sequences ZMDY and ZMIDY). The monetary effect of a deficit is thus to reinforce the income effect. The change in the interest rate may also affect the balance of payments through its effect on international capital flows. As the contraction in the money supply causes interest rates to rise in a deficit country, and conversely interest rates fall in surplus countries, a substantial interest-rate differential may develop between financial centers. As we saw in Chapter 13, such interest-rate differentials may induce interest arbitrage activities. Exports of bonds and other IOUs from the deficit country to surplus countries increase. This increase in exports of debt paper is a short-term capital flow into the country tending toward a deficit. This capital inflow helps reduce the deficit (sequence ZMIKZ).

ADJUSTMENT THROUGH CHANGES IN PRICES
CAUSED BY CHANGES IN INCOME

In the discussion of the simple adjustment process through income changes presented earlier in this chapter, we assumed that prices remained constant. We know, however, that in reality prices tend to rise (or more precisely, the rate of inflation, already present, tends to become higher) with rising income, especially under full employment conditions. During a business-cycle downswing, in contrast, prices tend to fall (or the inflation rate tends to be lower).

Let us assume that a country's rate of inflation becomes higher than other countries' whenever the country's national income level rises, and becomes lower whenever income falls. Now, suppose a drop in foreign demand reduces this country's exports. The foreign exchange rate would begin to rise, but if the government is determined to prevent this, it will intervene, sell foreign exchange, and support a deficit in the nation's balance of payments. The drop in exports will reduce national income by an equal amount, and the working of the multiplier will reduce national income even more. As we showed earlier, this fall in income will help eliminate the balance-of-payments deficit by decreasing imports (sequence ZDYBZ).

Additionally, given our newest assumption, the income decline will cause the nation's inflation rate to fall below other countries'. Provided the elasticity conditions are met, the nation experiences an improvement in its international competitiveness, which leads to a reduction in the deficit (sequence ZDYPCBZ).

THE THREE TYPES OF ADJUSTMENT COMBINED

Under a system of fixed exchange rates, if exports fall, government must either sell foreign exchange or force reductions in imports. The balance-of-payments deficit will then persist until domestic incomes and prices fall enough to restore internal and external equilibria (vice versa where the initial change is an increase in exports).

This arrangement subordinates domestic production and prices to the principle that the exchange rate must not change no matter how large the domestic price and production changes required to keep the exchange rate constant. As we shall see in subsequent chapters, this necessity for accepting fluctuations in the domestic variables was one of the principal reasons why most nations have now abandoned fixed exchange rates.

In contrast, under a regime of freely floating exhange rates, a change in exports has relatively little effect on domestic output and prices. The exchange rate changes to restore equilibrium. The same is true, also, under the system of "fixed" exchange rates when a government responds to disequilibrium by unfixing the rates and devaluing its currency or revaluing it upward.

Under the present system of "managed floats," all three types of adjustment — changes in domestic incomes and domestic prices *and* changes in foreign exchange rates — come into play and reinforce each other. To see the combined effects of these processes at work, consider first a country whose exports have leaped upward to produce a balance-of-payments surplus. Assume also that its government will not permit completely free movement of the exchange rate and/or assume inelasticity of demand so trade volume responds minimally to price changes. Then, much of the cure for a BOP disequilibrium must come through changes in domestic income and domestic prices.

Any increase in exports will bring a multiplied expansion in domestic income. The income expansion will bring increased imports (and possibly some exports cut, if domestic producers lose "export eagerness") that will trim the surplus.

The rising income level may also cause a higher rate of inflation in this country, especially if the economy is at or near full employment. Further, the surplus may be accommodated by the central bank's purchases of foreign exchange. Those purchases will add to the domestic bank's legal reserves; the domestic money stock will rise, and domestic inflation may be accelerated. Increased domestic prices will raise imports, lower exports, and trim the balance-of-payments surplus.

Finally, to the extent that government commitment to a stable exchange rate is incomplete, the effects of the original jump in exports will be to lower the exchange rate (an appreciation of the domestic currency). This change will also reduce exports, raise imports and — if the Marshall-Lerner condition is satisfied — reduce the surplus. All three adjustment effects work in harmony toward restoration of equilibrium. If government permits only modest change in the exchange rate, the burden of the adjustment will fall on domestic income and price changes.

Alternatively, consider a case of a nation favoring a highly flexible exchange rate and experiencing an exogenous drop in exports. Limited government intervention will produce a balance-of-payments deficit, but the bulk of the adjustment in this case will be in the foreign exchange rate. The depreciation of the country's currency will reduce the deficit by improving the country's competitiveness, but an unavoidable time lag will separate those trade effects from the currency appreciation that causes them. During that interval, domestic income and domestic price effects will be at work.

The original drop in exports will depress domestic income which, in turn, will reduce imports of goods and services. The central bank's sale of foreign exchange reserves will reduce the money stock and, with output down, the rate of inflation will be cut. This change in relative prices will — again with the inevitable lag — reduce imports and raise exports.

The reduction in commercial bank reserves and in money stock may raise domestic interest rates (and so lower bond prices). Foreigners, attracted by the lower bond prices (higher interest rates), will demand a larger quantity of this nation's bonds, and its exports of IOUs of all kinds will increase.

The domestic recession and dampened inflation will make domestic goods and services relatively cheaper to residents and foreigners. The currency depreciation will make domestic goods and services cheaper for foreigners and will make foreign goods and services more expensive for residents. When importers in all countries begin to make large long-run adjustments to these price changes, the nation's exports will rise, its imports will fall, and the multiplier's income and price effects will be turned about. If the nation's currency depreciation is relatively large, its expansive effect on the domestic economy will be large. That effect, netted against the recessionary consequences of the original drop in exports, may result in only a small drop in domestic income and the inflation rate. The burden of the adjustment to the export decline will, as we premised in the case, take the form of change in the foreign exchange rate.

APPENDIX: ESTIMATION OF ELASTICITY VALUES

Our task is to make a crude estimate of the elasticities of U.S. demand for foreign imports and of foreign demand for U.S. exports for 1978. Although the method used below to estimate elasticity values is admittedly too crude to warrant attaching any degree of significance to the result, the reader nevertheless may, by going through the exercise, learn something of the complexity of the basic relationships.

For changes in the exchange and trade volumes, data in Table 15-2 are used. Additionally, the following assumptions are made: (1) real gross national product of the United States increased by 4 percent, and that of the rest of the world by 3 percent, during the year, (2) the inflation rate in the United States and in the rest of the world was the same, and (3) the income elasticity of U.S. demand for imports is 1.5, and that of the world demand for U.S. exports is 1. (The income elasticity of demand for imports is the ratio of the percentage change in the quantity of imports demanded to the percentage change in income.)

Percentage changes are calculated by using, as the base, the arithmetic mean of the first and the last values, which are the values of the first and the last quarters of 1978. For all the other variables not mentioned above, *ceteris paribus* assumptions will apply.

First, we must find the percentage changes in the prices the foreigners paid for U.S. exports and in those which the U.S. residents paid for foreign imports. Since the inflation rate throughout the world is assumed to be the same, the only changes in export and import prices come from changes in the exchange rate. Table 15-2 shows that during the period the effective rate of exchange of the dollar decreased from 94.2 to 86.5. Thus, the price foreigners paid for U.S. exports decreased by:

$$\frac{94.22 - 86.5}{\frac{1}{2}(94.2 + 86.5)} = 0.085, \text{ or by 8.5 percent.}$$

Similarly, the prices the U.S. residents paid for foreign imports increased by 8.5 percent.

Next, we must find percentage changes in the quantities exported and imported. Table 15-2 shows that the volume of U.S. exports, with the first quarter of 1976 used as the base, increased from 101.5 to 119.4 during 1978. Similarly, the volume of U.S. imports increased from 127.4 to 133.7. These trade volume data, however, must be adjusted for the increase in gross national product of the United States and the rest of the world. The logic behind this adjustment is that increases in trade volumes are a natural concomitant of increases in output and income. Specifically, we must adjust the trade volume figures by the growth rates of the economies and their income elasticities of demand for imports.

Since gross national product of the rest of the world increased by 3 percent during the period, and since the income elasticity of the world demand for U.S. goods is 1, we can expect that increases in world output and income alone would have caused a 3 percent increase in U.S. exports. Thus, the index of the volume of U.S. exports for the last quarter of 1978 must be adjusted downward from 119.4 to 115.9 (= 119.4 ÷ 1.03) in order to eliminate the effect of the increase in world income on the volume of U.S. exports. The percentage increase in the volume of U.S. exports attributable to changes in exchange rate alone would then be:

$$\frac{115.9 - 101.5}{\frac{1}{2}(115.9 + 101.5)} = 0.132, \text{ or 13.2 percent.}$$

The index of U.S. import volume can be similarly adjusted for the change in U.S. income. Since the U.S. economy grew by 4 percent during 1978, and since the income elasticity of U.S. demand for imports is 1.5, we could expect the volume of U.S. imports to grow by 6 percent (4 percent × 1.5) merely from the increase in U.S. income and output. The index of U.S. import volume of the last quarter of 1978 — 133.7 —must therefore be adjusted downward by 6 percent to 126.1 (= 133.7 ÷ 1.06).

The percentage decrease in the volume of U.S. imports attributable solely to change in the exchange rate would then be:

$$\frac{127.4 - 126.1}{\frac{1}{2}(127.4 + 126.1)} = 0.010, \text{ or } 1.0 \text{ percent.}$$

We are now in a position to compute the elasticity values. The price elasticity of foreign demand for U.S. exports is equal to 13.2 percent (percentage change in quantity) divided by 8.5 percent (percentage change in price), or 1.55. The price elasticity of U.S. demand for foreign imports is equal to 1.0 percent (percentage change in quantity) divided by 8.5 percent (percentage change in price), or 0.12.

STUDY QUESTIONS

1. Suppose that Saudi Arabia's foreign exchange consists solely of U.S. dollars, and that the world's demand for Saudi crude oil is inelastic. What shape would you expect the supply curve of the dollars in the riyal-dollar market to take — normal or backward bending? (Hint: Refer to Figure 15-2. Substitute Saudi Arabia for South, crude oil for cotton, and riyals for pesos.)

2. From the hypothetical demand schedule for Saudi Arabian riyals shown below:
   (a) Derive the supply-of-dollars schedule in the riyal-dollar market (see Table 15-1).
   (b) Draw the demand-for-riyals curve and the supply-of-dollars curve (see Figure 15-2).

Demand for Riyals

Dollar price of riyals	Billion riyals demanded
0.1	100
0.2	90
0.3	84
0.4	80
0.5	78

3. Suppose Saudi Arabia's demand for dollars is as shown below.
   (a) Draw in the demand-for-dollars curve over the supply-of-dollars curve you drew in question 2(b) above.
   (b) What factors, do you think, account for the inelasticity of the country's demand for dollars?
   (c) Is the equilibrium you find in (a) above stable or unstable?

Demand for Dollars

Riyal price of dollars	Billion dollars demanded
10	16
5	18
3.333	20
2.5	21.5
2	22.5

4. Explain why the depreciation of a currency is likely to cause an immediate deterioration of the country's terms of trade and balance of trade.

5. Explain why the depreciation of a currency is likely to cause an improvement in the country's balance of trade over a period of several years following the depreciation.

6. Suppose national income is initially in equilibrium at $1,000 billion. Saving is $250 billion, domestic investment is $200 billion, exports are $150 billion, and imports are $100 billion. Marginal propensity to save is 0.1; marginal propensity to import is also 0.1
   (a) Draw the (S + M) curve and the (I + X) curve in a graph (see Figure 15-7).
   (b) How large is the country's net foreign investment (or balance of trade)? Can its value be read directly in the graph?
   (c) Suppose exports increase to $170 billion. How large is the new equilibrium level of income? Show the result by drawing the new (I + X) curve in the graph you drew in (a) above.
   (d) Find the new numerical value for each of the variables in the equation (S + M) = (I + X). How large is the new net foreign investment?

7. Return to the initial circumstances of Question 6 above.
   (a) Draw the (S − I) curve and the (X − M) curve (see Figure 15-9).
   (b) How large is the country's net foreign investment (or balance of trade)? Can its value be read directly in the graph?
   (c) Explain why the country's net foreign investment must equal the value of (S − I).
   (d) Suppose exports have increased to $170 billion. How large are the new equilibrium level of income and the new external balance? Show the results in the graph.
   (e) Find the new numerical values for each of the variables in the equation (S − I) = (X − M).

8. Suppose a country which is currently suffering a serious balance-of-payments deficit disequilibrium under a fixed exchange-rate system tries to restore the external balance by devaluing its currency. Under what two circumstances would the devaluation fail to achieve the desired effect?

9. Explain how the price-specie-flow mechanism would have worked. Why would it not work under modern conditions?

10. The text asserts, "Where the foreign exchange supply slopes backward, we now know that the coefficient of elasticity of foreigners' import demand is less than one." Refer to Figure 15-2 and explain how this is known.

ENDNOTES

1. The text reasons from demand for dollars in a one-import world to demand for that product. Of course, cause and effect runs the other way. Demand for dollars derives from demand for wheat.

2. For the mathematical derivation of the Marshall-Lerner condition, see: Herbert Grubel, *International Economics* (Homewood, Ill.: Irwin, 1977), Appendix to Chapter 14; and Charles P. Kindleberger and Peter H. Lindert, *International Economics,* 6th ed. (Homewood, Ill.: Irwin, 1978), Appendix H.

3. For a representative study of price elasticities based on trade of the 1950s and 1960s, see: Hendrik S. Houthakker and Stephen P. Magee, "Income and Price Elasticities in World Trade," *Review of Economics and Statistics,* May 1969, pp. 111-125.

4. Helen B. Junz and Rudolph R. Rhomberg, "Price Competitiveness in Export Trade among Industrial Countries," *American Economic Review,* May 1973, pp. 412-418.

5. "United States Export Performance," Federal Reserve of New York, *Quarterly Review*, Winter 1978-79, pp. 49-56.

6. For selected countries over the period, January 1973-April 1978, the evidence "implies that if the reaction of trade volume to the exchange rate is sluggish, as assumed here, the response of the trade account to an exchange rate change is in most instances likely to aggravate existing imbalances in international trade during the first year." Erich Spitaller, "Short-Run Effects of Exchange Rate Changes on Terms of Trade and Trade Balances," *International Monetary Fund Staff Papers*, June 1980, p. 343.

PART VI
THE EVOLVING
INTERNATIONAL
MONETARY SYSTEM

16

The International Monetary Systems Before March 1973

The *international monetary system* consists of the sum total of the institutions — i.e., laws, rules, customs, procedures, organizations, instruments, facilities, etc. — for effecting international payments. Over the past century, three major types of such system have existed, one evolving into another.

For forty years or so before 1914, there existed a full-fledged gold-standard system. World War I, the Great Depression, and changing assumptions about the role of government put an end to that system.

At a conference held at Bretton Woods, New Hampshire, in 1944, the industrial nations agreed on a blueprint for a new international monetary order. That plan was, in large part, put into effect in the years immediately following the end of World War II in 1945. The Bretton Woods agreement brought into being a new institution, the International Monetary Fund (IMF), charged with responsibility for supervising the new regime. Variously called the dollar-exchange system, the adjustable-peg system, or — most commonly — the Bretton Woods system, the new regime worked fairly well for twenty years or so. But in the mid-1960s, the Bretton Woods system began to experience serious difficulties, and it broke down completely in the early 1970s. By March 1973, a substantially different system, commonly known as the system of managed floating, had emerged.

In this chapter, we trace the evolutionary process leading from the gold standard to the breakdown of the Bretton Woods system.[1] In the next chapter, we describe the operation of the present system of managed floating. In Chapter 18, our attention will focus on the issues and problems in the present system.

THE GOLD STANDARD

A country is on the gold standard when its currency unit is defined in terms of a specified quantity of gold, and its monetary authorities stand ready to buy and sell unlimited quantities of gold at the price defined in the ratio of gold quantity to the currency unit. When two or more countries are on the gold standard, and allow the unrestricted export and import of gold, an international gold standard exists.

BEFORE 1914

In the 1930s, the British pound sterling was defined as containing 113.0015 grains of fine gold, and the U.S. dollar had a gold content of 23.22 grains of fine gold. (There are 480 grains in a troy ounce.) Thus, in terms of gold content, the pound was worth 4.8665 times as much as the dollar (113.0015 ÷ 23.22 = 4.8665.) The pound consequently was worth $4.8665. This rate of exchange was referred to as the *mint par* of exchange.

Under the international gold standard, the market exchange rate between two currencies fluctuated around the mint par within a small range determined by the cost of shipping gold between the countries. Assume, for simplicity, a dollar/pound mint par of $4.87/pound and shipping costs of 2 cents per 113.0015 grains of gold (one pound's worth) between New York and London. In that case, the actual exchange rate between the dollar and the pound could fluctuate within $4.87 ± $0.02, i.e., between $4.85 and $4.89. Then suppose, given these conditions, a sudden boom in the United States raised the market exchange rate to $4.92/pound. An arbitrager could then buy 113.0015 grains of gold from the American monetary authority by paying the official price of $4.87, ship the gold to London at an expense of 2 cents (total cost: $4.89), sell it to the British authority for one pound sterling, and sell that pound at the assumed rate of $4.92/pound for a profit of 3 cents. If done on a large enough scale (and quickly, to minimize interest expense), the arbitrager could make a profit without assuming any risk.

Such arbitrage activities were undertaken by individuals pursuing self-interest in response to market signals. But these self-serving private initiatives served both to move a nation from BOP disequilibrium (defined, then, as the value of the gold flow) to BOP equilibrium and to move the market exchange rate back within the price range where gold movement would be profitable. In the case just described, arbitrage — the export of gold from America to Britain — increased the supply of pounds in the dollar/pound market and put downward pressure on the dollar/pound exchange rate. Arbitrage stopped as soon as the rate fell to the $4.89/pound level.

Conversely, if the rate temporarily fell below $4.85, arbitrage activities caused a flow of gold from London to New York to push the rate back to $4.85/pound. (The reader is encouraged to work through the process by which the arbitrager could make a profit in the latter situation.)

The "limit" rates — $4.89/pound and $4.85/pound — were known as the *gold export point* and the *gold import point* for America (or the gold import and export points for Britain). Under the international gold standard, the exchange rate was held by gold arbitrage within the gold export and import points established by the mint par and the cost of shipping gold.

That the exchange rate did not normally lie outside the gold points did not mean that foreign exchange markets were always in equilibrium. When a country's payments situation deteriorated (meaning that autonomous debits — or imports — in its balance of payments exceeded autonomous credits — or exports), the exchange rate rose (depreciating the country's currency) and passed across the gold export point, resulting in an outflow of gold. Had the outflow continued, the nation's supply of gold might eventually have been exhausted. But the gold standard was kept viable by the adjustment mechanism operating continuously to restore each deviant nation to a BOP and foreign exchange equilibrium. How did the adjustment process work under the international gold standard?

ADJUSTMENT UNDER THE GOLD STANDARD

The previous chapter reported that David Hume answered the question of adjustment under the gold standard by formulating the price-specie-flow mechanism and the quantity theory of money. The process was simple. Loss of gold in the deficit country resulted in falling domestic prices. Gain of gold in the surplus country led to rising domestic prices. The change in relative prices restored equilibrium to both the deficit and surplus countries.

A more modern explanation of the adjustment mechanism under the gold standard sees it as working through both the price, interest rate, and income effects explained in the preceding chapter. This explanation argues as follows: the deficit nation's gold outflow reduced the nation's money stock so that market forces pressed interest rates up. Further, the nation's monetary authority (though in the late nineteenth century, the United States and some other gold standard nations managed quite well without a central monetary authority) raised the rediscount rate either responding to the market or trying to hurry it along. The surplus nation's growing monetary stock pressed its interest rate down.

The deficit nation's rising interest rate induced a short-term capital inflow (i.e., encouraged the surplus nation's residents to import interest-bearing paper from the deficit nation). That addition to the deficit nation's exports contributed to the restoration of BOP equilibrium.

In addition, this explanation identifies two forces acting on incomes to help restore equilibrium. First, the movement into deficit usually involved a fall in exports. That fall set in train a multiplied decline in national income that reduced import demand. Second, the investment drop (due to higher interest rates) reduced national income to a multiplied extent that also reduced import demand. As usual, vice versa in the surplus nation.

In this explanation, the interest rate would rise in the deficit nation and fall in the surplus nation. But prices, income, output, and employment would fall in the deficit nation and rise in the surplus nation. Thus the return to equilibrium would follow from a general contraction in the deficit nation (likely involving growing unemployment) and a boom (likely involving accelerated inflation) in the surplus nation.

Now you can see why the gold standard cannot be a realistic alternative in the 1980s. Before 1914, central banks were primarily interested in protecting their countries' gold reserves so their currency would continue to be convertible into gold at a fixed rate. But since 1945, monetary authorities have made two other objectives — full employment and price stability — their principal goals. If the gold standard is to function properly, each government must sacrifice internal stability — i.e., stability of domestic employment and price levels — for the sake of maintaining a fixed external equilibrium. This few modern governments are willing to do.

Since World War II, government leaders have been reluctant to expand their nation's economies and to accept additional inflation "merely" to curb BOP surpluses. They have been even more reluctant to depress their nation's economies and swell their unemployment rates "merely" to end BOP deficits.

Under the gold standard "rules of the game," each participating nation surrenders a degree of economic sovereignty by agreeing to perform passively the obligatory responses to wrong-headed initiatives in other nations. To see this in worst-possible scenarios, consider two cases. First, nation A initiates a substantial domestic inflation. A develops a BOP deficit. Gold flows from A to B. Playing the rules of the game, B accepts the gold inflow, the increase in its money stock, the fall in its interest rates, and the consequent boom and inflation no matter how large they become.

Second, the opposite case, with A again the initiator. Nation A drives unemployment up and prices down (of course, this case is not likely in our era). Gold flows from B to A. Again, playing the rules of this game, B is passive and accepts the gold outflow, the decline in its money stock, the rise in its interest rate, and the consequent rise in domestic unemployment.

Playing the rules means foregoing an independent domestic economic policy. Contemporary governments refuse to do this. Instead, they strive to insulate domestic monetary and fiscal programs from international pressures.

This contemporary insistence on sovereignty over domestic macroeconomic policy might conceivably be reconciled with the gold-standard fixed exchange rates. For example, if a nation A inflates, B could respond to the gold inflow by open market sales that would fully offset the effects of that gold inflow. Or if nation A were to deflate (unlikely as that would be), nation B could respond to the gold outflow by central bank open market purchases that would fully offset the effects of the gold outflow. In both of these cases, the adjustment burden would then fall entirely (except for changes in B's gold reserves) upon the initiating nation — but only if it cared about its reserve position. As will be seen below, this was close to the practice of much of the world much of the time under the Bretton Woods system of 1950-1970.

AFTER 1914

The classical gold standard prevailed only through the years from about 1875 until the outbreak of World War I. Over the next several decades, the system gradually broke down.

It has never been restored. Between 1919 and 1933, the key industrial nations returned to — and left — a modified gold standard, the *gold-exchange standard*. Britain, the United States, and France "returned to gold" in the 1920s. But most nations (and at that time there were only about 65) held their international reserves not as gold but as checking or savings accounts or as government bonds in Britain, France, or the United States. These other nations pegged their currencies to the dollar, franc, or pound. They held little gold but could exchange their reserves for gold; thus a "gold-exchange" system or standard.

For a variety of reasons, the modified system did not approximate the effects of the old gold standard. Britain chose a par value that greatly overvalued the pound and condemned the nation to a decade of deflationary pressure.[2] Other nations also set par values above or below equilibrium values and so chose years of deflationary or inflationary pressures from international transactions.

Further, the adjustment system no longer worked smoothly, partly because wages and prices became increasingly rigid downward. Britain, for example, suffered its post-1925 decade of stagnation largely because domestic prices were too high relative to world prices and because British prices, and wages, were slow to fall.

Finally, the adjustment mechanism ceased to work at all because central banks deliberately acted to offset the effects of gold flows. Policy embraced chronic BOP imbalances, and these led, in the early 1930s, to the disintegration of even the modified residual of the gold standard.

During the decade of the 1930s, international monetary relations were characterized by instability, mismanagement, and a consequent chaos. At first, many nations tried to defend unrealistic above-equilibrium par values. Then, many devalued their currencies, competing to reduce export prices below the world average to stimulate exports and reduce domestic unemployment. That was, at best, a zero-sum game of beggar thy neighbor with the objective of gain at the expense of others. Consequently, world trade shrank, and all lost.

Several nations, Germany and Austria in particular, controlled foreign exchange strictly and even reverted to barter. Then political threats gave rise to massive flows of gold from Europe to the United States. America's monetary gold stock leaped from $4 billion in 1929 to $10 billion in 1935. By 1941, the American gold stock of $22.7 billion embraced nearly four-fifths of the world's monetary gold. An observer must still be surprised that President Roosevelt's Federal Reserve was able to prevent the prosperity that ought to have followed from that gold influx.

When governments began to construct a new international monetary order in 1944 (the next-to-last year of World War II), decisionmakers were greatly influenced by their perceptions of the events of the 1920s and 1930s. The Bretton Woods architects agreed that two particular "evils" of the past were to be avoided: (1) No more fluctuating exchange rates; these they associated with destabilizing currency speculation and with competitive beggar-thy-neighbor devaluation. (2) And no more gold-standard exchange rate rigidity requiring deflation and unemployment to end a BOP deficit. They therefore groped for a compromise between the reassuring stability of fixed rates and the potentially alleviating flexibility of agreed-upon rules for infrequent change in the fixed rate. From that search came the "adjustable peg," fixed rates with rules for occasional adjustments of the peg.

THE BRETTON WOODS SYSTEM

The Bretton Woods conference agreed on an international monetary system based on fixed rates, the adjustable peg, and provisions for international cooperation to determine when adjustments should be allowed. The conference also brought forth a new institution, the International Monetary Fund (IMF), through whose facilities individual currencies were tied to the new "key" reserve currency, the U.S. dollar.

THE IMF AND THE ADJUSTABLE PEG

The IMF began operations in 1946 with 44 initial members. The Soviet Union had signed the Agreement (constitution) but never ratified it. By 1980, 138 nations — including Romania, Laos, and mainland China, but not the Soviet Union or Taiwan (thrown out when mainland China was admitted in 1980) — were members.

The IMF's original Articles of Agreement obligated each member nation to declare a *par value* of its currency in terms of gold or the U.S. dollar and to maintain the actual exchange rate within 1 percent (changed to 2¼ percent in 1972) of the par value by selling or buying dollars in its foreign exchange market. The Articles allowed a member to change its currency's par value only when it experienced a "fundamental disequilibrium," a concept never clearly defined. Combining exchange rate stability with flexibility, the new scheme earned the title, the "adjustable peg system." And it did provide exchange rates that were stable but that could be adjusted within reason and in an atmosphere of international cooperation, thereby avoiding competitive depreciation, a fact of the 1930s, a bogey of the 1940s.

Another Bretton Woods innovation was the prohibition against exchange controls. Article VIII of the Agreement prohibited exchange controls over current-account transactions. However, Article VI author-ized exchange controls over capital-account transactions. This meant a nation should not restrict purchase or sale of foreign exchange used for current-account transactions. But the nation could restrict purchase and sale of foreign exchange used to import or export stocks, bonds, other long-term IOUs, or — especially — Treasury bills or other short-term IOUs. Such controls were deemed necessary in case cur-rencies became subject to a massive speculative attack.

The Agreement could prohibit particular foreign exchange actions by member nations. But the Agreement could not prevent governments (and, occasionally, natural catastrophies) from behaving in ways likely to cause temporary or even chronic BOP disequilibria. In the latter case, of a fundamental disequilibrium, the solution was to be consultation within the IMF then adjustment of the peg to a new value. (In practice, "consultation within the IMF" usually came *after* a nation had made its devaluation decisions.)

But what to do during a temporary BOP disequilibrium, one that reasonably objective observers would agree would soon be ended by forces already visibly under way? A primary purpose of the system was to isolate domestic policies from the influence of BOP disequilibrium; so the solution was not to be change in domestic monetary-fiscal policy. The Agreement sought a stable peg, so the solution could not be jump to a new peg — temporarily — then jump back to the status quo ante. Finally, exchange controls over current-account transactions were pro-hibited; and all agreed that exchange controls over capital-account transactions were "bad form" to be avoided if possible. What could be done for "temporary" disequilibria?

The authorized solution looked much like Hume's price-specie-flow mechanism but both gold and *hard currencies* (i.e., those with the unchallenged pegged values) were to enter the flow. A member's first line of defense against a temporary deficit was to involve protection of the pegged value of its currency by covering the shortage of foreign currency by selling its own *reserves* of gold and hard currencies. If its owned reserves proved inadequate, it could borrow more from the IMF. Such borrowing is called exercising a nation's *drawing rights* in the Fund.

Upon joining the Fund, each member was assigned a *quota* according to which it was required to deposit a sum of gold and domestic currency to the Fund. These funds were loaned to members that experienced temporary disequilibrium. Such loans were to be repaid when the deficits turned to surplus.

Every IMF member agreed to strive to maintain long-term equilib-rium in its balance of payments under the declared par value. When a disequilibrium situation persisted, the member was to pursue monetary and fiscal policies with care so the external disequilibrium would not be exacerbated. However, the member nation was *not* required to sacrifice internal full employment and price stability objectives "merely" for the sake of restoring external equilibrium. Whenever the existing par value became clearly incompatible with underlying economic conditions, the member was permitted to "repeg" its currency to a level consistent with those conditions (so legitimizing any changes in internal economics conditions).

These were the essential features of the Bretton Woods's international payments system. It was an ingenious innovation and a bold experiment. It provided an *adjustment* mechanism. It provided *liquidity*. And the system worked for almost 25 years, at first quite adequately but later less and less so. What brought about the demise of the Bretton Woods system? The answer to this question lies in the critical role the U.S. dollar played in the system.

THE ROLE OF THE U.S. DOLLAR

We noted earlier that by the eve of World War II, nearly four-fifths of the world's monetary gold was owned by the United States. For this reason alone, a return to a broad-based gold standard was unthinkable. Nations did want to base their currencies on something solid, such as gold, but they simply could not. They did not possess enough gold to support such a system. Further, war had severely damaged the manufacturing and distribution systems of most European nations. In the immediate postwar years, their leaders hoped for very unfavorable balances of trade that would bring them American materials and equipment that would accelerate European recovery. America had the gold, and America had the goods. Finally, the United States had been able, since 1935, to hold the gold price at $35 per ounce of gold. In the language of that time, the world suffered "a dollar shortage" while the dollar "was as good as gold." Under these circumstances, the dollar became the world's leading *key currency,* the one used by most other nations to settle accounts with yet other nations.

When the IMF was created, the United States, still possessing some 80 percent of the world's monetary gold, reconfirmed its commitment to its ten-year old peg of $35 = 1 ounce of gold. Other nations, lacking gold, pegged their currencies to the dollar, thus, indirectly tying them to gold; e.g., 10 pesos = $1, implying 350 pesos = 1 ounce of gold. These other nations then sought dollar reserves to provide the liquidity needed to tide them over temporary BOP deficits.

Their central banks saw little reason to hold gold. Reserves of gold earned no interest. Dollar reserves, held usually as Treasury bills or other short-term IOUs, did. Thus evolved the dollar-gold system (the gold-exchange system) of the 1950s and 1960s. Private business decisions made the U.S. dollar the world's principal *transaction currency* as the bulk of world trade was transacted in dollars. Government decisions made the U.S. dollar the world's principal *intervention currency* as central banks accumulated dollar reserves and drew down or added to those reserves when intervening in currency markets to maintain the peg.

What were the advantages and disadvantages of this dollar-gold system? For the rest of the world, during the 1950s, the advantages were (1) the availability of ample liquidity as nations did obtain dollar reserves growing as rapidly as their trade and (2) interest earned on reserves. Disadvantages for the rest of the world were the risks that the United States might (1) reduce the gold content of the dollar, i.e., devalue by changing the peg to more than $35 per ounce of gold or (2) simply stop redeeming dollars in gold. A nation switching from dollars to gold the day before a dollar devaluation would score a windfall gain. A nation staying with dollars over that night would earn only one more day's interest. Thus nations would continue to hold reserves as dollars only as long as they had confidence in the ability of the United States to maintain the $35 peg and convertibility. (This "convertibility" was only between the central banks. Some nations did permit their citizens to hold gold, but from 1933 until 1975 the American government made possession of gold — other than jewelry — a federal crime for American citizens.)

The system provided the United States with the advantage of paying for net imports of goods, services, stocks, bonds, and property titles with IOUs that contemporary America did not have to think about repaying. The practice could go on so long as foreign central banks were eager — or at least willing — to add to their dollar reserves.

But the United States paid for this ability to run deficits indefinitely (1) by effectively relinquishing its ability to change its foreign exchange rate and (2) by reaching the 1970s with foreign central banks threatening to turn in those accumulated dollar reserves for — something. Any other nation could change the value of its currency vis-à-vis *all* others by changing its peg to the dollar. But the United States could only change its gold peg, and even if it were to have done so, the dollar would have remained unchanged in value in terms of all the currencies pegged to it. Other nations could change the dollar value of their individual currencies, but the United States could not change the other-currency value of the dollar. The United States therefore could not utilize the Bretton Woods prescription for curing fundamental disequilibrium. Then, during the 1960s, the evolving world economy brought a growing conviction that the United States was in fact moving into fundamental disequilibrium. The holders of dollar reserves began to lose confidence in the U.S. dollar.

LIQUIDITY, GOLD, AND SPECIAL DRAWING RIGHTS

As we stressed in Chapter 14, no reserves are needed or even usable and no BOP deficits or surpluses can occur where exchange rates are left entirely to market forces. But the Bretton Woods system of fixed rates permitted BOP surpluses and deficits; and reserves were required if nations were to weather their temporary deficits. Secular growth of trade volume swells the potential size of deficits; so central bankers assume that national reserves should grow in line with growth in national trade.

Through the 1950s and 1960s, international trade burgeoned; merchandise trade grew at a compound rate of 7 percent between 1948 and 1973. "Between 1948 and 1973 the volume of world trade increased nearly sixfold."[3] Central banks "needed" growing reserves. Between 1960 and 1969, however, total international reserves (defined as the sum of gold and foreign exchange holdings, and reserve positions in the IMF) grew from $61 billion to $79 billion, or at an annual rate of only about 2.8 percent.

The additional reserves could have been provided by continued American exports of Treasury bills and other short-term IOUs. But during the early 1960s, the international community became increasingly uneasy about the ability of the United States to redeem in gold its mounting liquid liabilities. Those liabilities had grown larger each year, but America's monetary gold stock (valued still at $35 an ounce) fell from $24.56 billion in 1949 to $10.9 billion in 1968.[4] The suspicion grew that the dollar was no longer as good as gold. In order to restore the international community's confidence in the dollar, the U.S. monetary authorities tried to reduce U.S. payments deficits. But the elimination of U.S. deficits would mean that the world would be deprived of its most important source of liquidity. This dilemma came to be known in the 1960s as the *liquidity problem.*

The Barbarous Relic

Gold itself did not appear to be an alternative source of much reserve growth. World trade grew at a much faster pace than did gold production. That was of course not surprising. Mining costs rose with the general inflation. Between 1935 and 1968, U.S. prices rose 150 percent[5] while the gold price stayed fixed. No wonder gold mines closed down. Further, the fixed price of gold held constant the value of extant gold reserves even as the prices of traded wheat, sugar, and cloth rose.

The monetary gold that existed in 1935 would have been worth 150 percent more than it was worth in 1968 (over $27 billion) had the gold price risen as much as other prices. More gold would have been mined between 1935 and 1968 had the gold price risen as much as other prices. But the American government (supported by most others — except France) wanted to hold the gold price constant because the immediate benefits from a gold price increase would have been unevenly distributed among various nations. In particular, policymakers did not want to bestow benefits upon white South Africans or upon Russians, and those two nations were, and are, the world's leading gold producers. That bit of policymaking may, in retrospect, have been the century's outstanding example of cutting off the nose to spite the face.

But there was another obstacle. A consensus had begun to grow during the 1930s that an international monetary system based on a yellow metal must be irrational. There was said to be no inherent or logical reason why that particular commodity should be treated as money par excellence. That view was summarized in John M. Keynes's pejorative description of the monetary use of gold as a "barbarous relic." Into the 1960s, the anti-gold argument grew in conviction: Gold remained entrenched only because of the emotion, the passion, gold evoked in people's minds for historical and traditional reasons. Resources were wasted when used to mine gold that would only be reburied in bank vaults.

But the most compelling argument may have been this: a monetary system does not need a commodity base. Gold had long been *demonetized* in domestic monetary systems. Time therefore to *demonetize* gold out of the international monetary system.

Special Drawing Rights

So dollars had become suspect, and gold was scorned. Still, pegged rates required growing reserves; and ingenuity brought forth a new reserve asset, Special Drawing Rights (SDRs).

In 1967, the Articles of Agreement were amended to authorize the creation of SDRs. Between January 1970 and January 1972, SDR 9.4 billion were created and distributed among the member nations. In September 1978, the IMF Board of Directors agreed to make a new allocation of SDR $4 billion in January 1979, SDR 4 billion in January 1980, and SDR 4 billion in January 1981. As of the end of May 1979, the total SDR allocation amounted to 12.2 percent of total reserves of all the member nations.

The value of one SDR was originally set to equal the gold content of one 1970 U.S. dollar. However, the devaluations of the dollar in terms of gold in 1971-73 changed the dollar/gold ratio so that by the end of 1973 one SDR had become worth about $1.21. In 1974, the IMF members agreed to use a new valuation system for the SDR, measuring it in terms of the weighted average value of a "basket" of 16 major currencies. In April 1980, the size of the basket was reduced to only five: the dollar, West German mark, Japanese yen, French franc, and British pound. In June 1980, one SDR was worth about $1.32.

SDRs are assets of national central banks. They can be exchanged only between central banks. The central bank of a nation in need of foreign currencies to defend an exchange rate may use SDRs to buy those foreign currencies from other central banks.

Given the limitations on their use, SDRs are most directly comparable with the reserve liabilities (RLs) of the U.S. Federal Reserve. These RLs are assets of commercial banks. They come into existence (for the most part) when the Federal Reserve buys Treasury securities. Then, with the stroke of a pen (or the punch in a computer) the Federal Reserve pays for the purchase (whether from Chase Manhattan or from Aetna Insurance or from Jane Doe) by creating RLs equal in value to the purchase. Once in existence, RLs are inaccessible to the public but are used to pay for transactions between commercial banks.

Similarly, SDRs are created by the stroke of a pen (or the punch in a computer). However, they are not created to pay for IMF purchases. They are created and distributed to members whenever the IMF Board of Directors decides to do so (which is comparable to the Federal Reserve Open Market Committee's complete freedom to choose when and how many RLs it will create to pay for open market purchases). Once created, the SDRs are accessible only to central banks that are free to use them to pay for transactions between themselves.

SDR's Possibilities

Regular drawing rights involve a mere pooling of members' reserves and a loan of pooled reserves to a member (as a savings and loan association pools its depositors' money then makes loans from the pool). A regular drawing causes no change in total reserves. But an IMF issue of SDRs adds to international reserves. New reserves come into being where none existed before, and they do so without the real costs of mining and refining a metal and without burdening a nation by adding to its key currency role. The SDR is a new reserve form based on international trust. Like the dollar, it depends for its scarcity value upon a board's willingness to restrict the growth of its volume. In contrast, gold's scarcity value depends on market forces. However, despite intellectual arguments to the contrary, the world financial community continues to have more faith in the gold market than in discretionary bodies of humans.

If more and more SDRs are created and accepted by all IMF members (the willingness to accept might fall sharply for all members if only one or a few important members were to decide to boycott SDRs), the relative importance of the dollar as an international reserve currency will diminish. The United States, accordingly, will be gradually relieved of the burden of being the world's primary supplier of liquidity. The dollar, over the long haul, might even become "just another currency," enabling the United States to pursue an independent exchange rate policy. As a by-product of such a process, the IMF might even emerge as a genuine central bank for national central banks.[6]

From the 1960s into the 1970s, enthusiasm for SDRs grew, and the demonetization of gold proceeded. Up until 1968, a consortium of central banks participated in the London gold market to maintain equality between the official gold price and the free market price. In 1968, the consortium withdrew from the gold market. The result was a two-tier price system. The official price remained fixed; the free market price moved away from it and fluctuated daily.

In 1971, the United States ended free convertibility of dollars into gold for foreign central banks (more on this in the following section). In January 1975, the ban on U.S. residents' private holding of gold was lifted and was followed by a public auction of a small amount of the Treasury's monetary gold. The IMF also started to auction portions of its gold in 1976, and by March 1979 the Fund's gold holdings had decreased by 24 percent. Although the IMF still lists its gold holdings on the books at 35 SDRs per fine ounce, that is merely an accounting price since gold is no longer used to define the par value of SDRs or of a currency, nor is gold exchanged between the Fund and member nations.

What will be the future role of gold? In 1977, Robert Solomon of the Brookings Institution predicted that gold would continue to be "at the bottom of the pile" of nations' international reserves, but would gradually "seep out of official reserves and into the market" as it is occasionally sold in the market by central banks whose reserves in other forms have become depleted.[7] Nevertheless, the events of 1979 and 1980 suggest that all reports of the demise of gold as a monetary base are premature.

THE COLLAPSE OF THE BRETTON WOODS SYSTEM

The instability of the Bretton Woods system became increasingly serious in the 1960s. That instability was due to America's inability to eliminate its BOP deficit and to the attendant problems of erosion of confidence in the dollar and of massive speculative capital flights from it.

BEFORE AUGUST 1971

The Japanese and Western European economic recoveries were completed by the end of the 1950s. Their competitive strength in world trade improved markedly in the 1960s and put downward pressure on the value of the dollar. The United States sold gold, and foreign central banks bought dollars to maintain the pegged dollar values of other currencies. (The principal concern of foreign governments was that appreciation of their currencies would reduce sales and employment in their export industries.) The artificially protected dollar became increasingly overvalued throughout the 1960s.

The overvaluation, of course, raised imports and reduced exports of goods and services. Further, the overvalued dollar reduced the dollar cost to U.S. firms of foreign materials and wages. The Europeans were finally imitating the 180-year-old example of the U.S. Constitution's free trade area. Expected rates of return in Europe and elsewhere were higher than otherwise since the overvalued dollar gave foreign production a competitive advantage on sales to America. For all these reasons, Americans initiated large capital outflows for direct investments abroad and for loans to foreign borrowers, and each of these transactions involved an American import of a property title, a share of stock, or an IOU paid for with dollar exports.

The U.S. government, with extensive political and military commitments abroad, increased, each year, its overseas grants, loans, and military assistance; and each of these transactions involved an American import of good will, IOUs, or goods or services (though the latter might be produced abroad *and* consumed abroad by the U.S. State Department, army, or foreign assistance agency) paid for with dollar exports. Toward the end of the 1960s, the American government sharply increased the inflation rate as the war on poverty and the war in Vietnam were both financed through Treasury borrowing supported by Federal Reserve open market purchases.

These were the factors that contributed to large U.S. BOP deficits and the attendant weakening of the dollar. During the 1958-1970 period, the cumulative BOP deficits of the United States exceeded $50 billion. These deficits were the principal reason for the $13-billion reduction in U.S. gold reserves and the increase of about $47 billion in U.S. liabilities to foreign central banks.

The large increase in America's official liquid liabilities raised serious doubts in the minds of foreigners about the ability of the United States to maintain the gold parity of the dollar. The dollar thus came under a series of speculative attacks in early 1971. Many Americans used their dollars to import short-term IOUs denominated in yen or in European currencies. Foreign holders of dollars sold them for more of those short-term IOUs denominated in yen or European currencies. Since few individuals or businesses bought dollars except for immediate use in buying something, the foreign-currency pegs were maintained only through Federal Reserve sales of American reserves or through foreign central bank additions to their dollar reserves.

Between January and August 1971, $20 billion in assets fled from the dollar. Fed by growth of a conviction the dollar would be devalued, the tempo of the flight from the dollar accelerated in the summer of 1971. The supply of dollars pressed against the capacity of foreign central banks to buy them, and the dollar did begin to fall. In early August 1971, dollar sales (and purchases) rose to enormous proportions in foreign exchange markets. On Thursday, August 12, *and* again on Friday, August 13, foreign central banks bought some $1 billion to buttress the rapidly declining value of the dollar. Within this context, President Nixon announced the emergency measures of August 15, 1971.

The Asymmetrical Exchange Rate Fixing

As stressed earlier, the main cause of the dollar crisis of 1971 was the persistent change in the relative prices and prospects of the United

States vis-à-vis Western Europe and Japan. The result was a fundamental disequilibrium. But the United States had pegged the dollar to gold. Europe and Japan had pegged their currencies to the dollar. The cure for the fundamental disequilibrium — had America had the power— would have been devaluation of the dollar in terms of the European currencies and the yen. But America did not. Europe and Japan had the power; so the cure *should* have been appreciation of their currencies. That upward revaluation would have raised the real incomes of most Europeans and Japanese by reducing the prices to them of imports from America. But the change would have reduced European and Japanese exports. Those governments feared that step; so, between 1945 and 1971, few countries revalued their currencies upward.

The extreme case was Japan. In spite of the enormous increases in productivity, output, and international competitiveness of the Japanese economy over the entire period, the value of the yen was kept unchanged, from 1949 to 1970, at 360 yen to the dollar. The undervaluation of the yen became particularly conspicuous toward the end of the 1960s as evidenced by sharp rises in Japan's international reserves. The total reserves of the nation, which had remained about $2 billion throughout the early and mid-1960s, rose to $2.9 billion in 1968, $3.7 billion in 1969, $4.8 billion in 1970, and $15.4 billion in December 1971. Japan's trade surplus also increased by leaps and bounds in the latter half of the 1960s; it rose from $375 million in 1964 to $4 billion in 1970, and then to $7.8 billion in 1971.

West Germany showed similar, but less drastic, signs of currency undervaluation. The nation's trade surplus more than doubled between 1964 and 1970. Its total international reserves, which had stayed between $7 and $8 billion during 1961-65 and somewhat above $8 billion during 1966-67, rose to nearly $10 billion in 1968. Following the exchange-market crises of 1969, the Deutsche mark was upvalued 9.3 percent, and German reserves fell to $7.1 billion by year's end. However, by the end of 1970, German reserves had risen to $13.6 billion. Germany then accepted the inevitable, and the mark was set afloat in May 1971.

For years, Japan, West Germany, and other surplus nations refused to upvalue their currencies to restore equilibrium in their balances of payments. Instead they blamed the United States for failure to control its BOP deficits. They argued that the deficits of the United States were attributable primarily to the rampant inflation in the United States caused by the war on poverty and the Vietnam war, and admonished the United States to "put its own house in order" before complaining about other nations' surpluses. The Germans were reluctant, and the Japanese adamantly refused, to raise the value of their currencies since that course of action would have reduced sales, output, and employment in most exporting industries.

Implicit in the surplus nations' argument was the belief that the burden of adjustment ought to fall on the deficit country. What was not fully appreciated by those who blamed the United States for inaction was that the Bretton Woods pegging system placed all the burden of exchange rate adjustment upon the nations that had pegged their currencies to the dollar.

Those rules left the United States only one option, the gold standard solution for which the Bretton Woods conference was to have found an alternative. The surplus nations, by refusing upvaluation, called on the United States to initiate a sharp contraction in its economic activities. Sufficiently deflationary price-and-income policies in America would have restored BOP equilibrium to Europe, Japan, and America, but the IMF charter had originally seemed to promise that that course would never be urged on any member nation.

Speculative Movements of Short-Term Capital

A second fatal flaw of the Bretton Woods system was the adjustable peg, for it proved an irresistible inducement to speculative movements of short-term funds when nations postponed devaluation until after private market participants had become convinced that the nation was in fundamental disequilibrium at the existing exchange rate. Smart money then used the overvalued currency to buy undervalued currencies. There was no risk that the overvalued currency would be repegged to an even more overvalued rate; the IMF would never have permitted that. With patience, the buyers of the undervalued currencies would awaken one day to newspaper headlines announcing upvaluation of those currencies. The result for the speculators, windfall gains.

During the 1950s and 1960s, most of the exchange controls imposed "temporarily" during World War II were removed. Short-term capital movements became largely unconstrained. When deficit nations postponed devaluations, the direction of future exchange-rate changes became known; only the timing and magnitude of the changes were left to speculation. So speculators could win big; they could not lose (unless interest rate comparisons showed opportunity cost losses).

The adjustable peg system was, therefore, an invitation to destabilizing speculation, for speculative capital movements aggravated the BOP deficits that caused them (e.g. if the dollar was judged overvalued, dollars owners would supply more to the foreign exchange market, speculating on mark and yen appreciation and adding to the downward pressure on the dollar). This vicious circle of deficit, speculation, greater deficit and greater speculation, in combination with the inability of the United States to cure its deficit, finally destroyed the Bretton Woods system.

AUGUST 1971 THROUGH MARCH 1973

August 15, 1971, was the beginning of the end of the Bretton Woods system. On that day, President Nixon made a historical announcement, suspending gold convertibility of the dollar and imposing a temporary 10 percent tax on all imports. He invited foreign governments to revalue their currencies against the dollar, promising that the import surtax would be removed when a currency realignment was effected.

Most major trading nations, except Japan, responded to the U.S. measures by closing their foreign exchange markets for a few days. When they were reopened on August 23, pegs were abandoned, and most currencies were allowed to float against the dollar. Japan alone kept the market open and supported the old yen-dollar rate until August 28 when the yen, too, was floated. The officials of the Japanese government and the Bank of Japan resisted closing the exchange market as long as possible hoping the crisis might blow away. But the speculative attack on the yen — the only major currency left after 23 August with the pre-August 15 parity — was massive. During the eleven days before the yen was floated, the Bank of Japan absorbed well over $4 billion in a futile effort to defend the old yen-dollar parity. On August 27, dollar sales reached crisis proportions — on that day alone, the Bank of Japan bought $1.2 billion in dollars. The decision to float the yen was finally reached that day.

Where did that $4 billion come from? Would there have been more to come? Some of the dollars originated in Japanese commercial bank borrowing in the Eurodollar market. Consider how that worked. A Japanese bank would borrow $100,000 in Europe then would sell the dollars to the Bank of Japan (at the pegged 360 yen = $1) for 36,000,000 yen. Then the bank would wait. If the yen's upvaluation were delayed, the bank could lend the yen so would lose daily the difference between the interest earned on its loan and the (higher) interest accruing to its European creditor. When the upvaluation finally came, the bank immediately bought back the $100,000 plus accrued interest at the new rate (e.g., 300 yen = $1); $100,000 for 30,000,000 yen. The gain in this for-example would have been 6,000,000 yen, about 16%, less loss on net interest costs. So long as the Japanese government was willing to lose, there was *no* limit to the billions of dollars that would have been offered.

But a large portion of the dollars sold to the Japanese government may have had a more mundane source. The great bulk of the increase in dollar supply (and of the decrease in dollar demand) was attributed to a form of speculation practiced by traders of goods and known as "leads and lags." Most of Japan's exports and imports were invoiced in dollars. Japanese exporters, realizing the yen value of their dollar sales receipts would decrease if the yen were to float upward, accelerated collection of their export proceeds from foreign importers. This increased the supply of dollars in the Tokyo Foreign Exchange Market. Japanese importers, on the other hand, postponed payments for their imports as long as possible. This decreased demand for dollars. The net effect of exporters leading and importers lagging in payments was a few billion dollars of excess supply at the pegged rate. The Bank of Japan, which had a tight exchange control over capital-account transactions, could not control speculative behavior in current-account transactions. Similar practices appeared in August 1971 in all the nations with undervalued currencies.

Between August and December of 1971, most major currencies were permitted a *dirty float,* no pegged rate but government support at rates representing appreciation of 5 to 8 percent against the dollar. The United States expressed dissatisfaction with those rates and demanded larger upvaluations. The European and Japanese governments strongly resisted the U.S. pressures, arguing that further upvaluations would have excessively adverse effects on their export industries. Instead, they tried to persuade the U.S. government to devalue the dollar unilaterally by raising the price of gold. The speculation against the dollar persisted, while government officials and central bankers exchanged demands and suggestions, and foreign central banks continued to buy dollars.

The Smithsonian Agreement

Negotiations among the finance ministers of the ten major trading nations (the Group of Ten) began in December 1971 with a view toward re-establishing and realigning exchange rate parities. An agreement was reached at the meeting held on December 17-18 at the Smithsonian Institution in Washington, D.C. The U.S. dollar was devalued by 7.89 percent in terms of gold, with the price of gold increased from $35 to $38 an ounce. Against the dollar, the yen was raised by 17 percent, and the mark by 13.57 percent. Other European currencies were also revalued but to a lesser extent. The participants further agreed to support the new rates within a band of central rate plus-or-minus 2¼ percent, instead of the previous band of plus-or-minus 1 percent. This Smithsonian Agreement was intended as an interim agreement until a more permanent reform of the international monetary system could be undertaken.

Events Leading to March 1973

The Smithsonian Agreement indeed proved to be an interim arrangement. Several major nations could not maintain the agreed-upon rates and allowed their currencies to float either upward or downward. The dollar continued to depreciate vis-à-vis other currencies. The $6.4 billion deficit in 1972 in the U.S. balance of trade created an expectation of further devaluation of the dollar. A massive flight of funds from the dollar to the mark in early February 1973 led to a further ten percent devaluation of the dollar against the other major currencies. That measure, however, was insufficient to stem the tide. The Japanese foreign exchange market was closed on February 9 after the Bank of Japan had absorbed another $1.1 billion. During the first seven days of February, the German central bank had to purchase $6 billion to prevent the mark from exceeding the Smithsonian rate ceiling. European exchange markets were closed on February 12, 1973, reopened on February 14, and were closed again on March 1. During the next two weeks, deliberations were held in an effort to work out the shape of an alternative exchange rate system. When the exchange markets reopened on March 19, 1973, all major currencies were floating, independently or jointly, against the dollar. (Eight European currencies, including the mark, were pegged to each other but floated jointly vis-à-vis the dollar.) Now that no major currencies were tied to the dollar, it also became a floating currency, though as with all the other major currencies, the float was a dirty one in which central banks continued to intervene in the interests of stability — or of domestic exporters. The emergence of this system of managed floats marked the final end of the Bretton Woods system following the collapse of August 1971 and the brief resuscitation under the Smithsonian Agreement.[8]

STUDY QUESTIONS

1. What are the gold standard "rules of the game"? Explain why the international gold standard would not work under contemporary conditions.
2. Explain how the "adjustable peg" worked under the Bretton Woods system.
3. How was liquidity provided by the International Monetary Fund to member countries suffering from balance-of-payments deficits?
4. Explain the role the U.S. dollar played in the Bretton Woods system. What were the advantages and disadvantages of this role to the United States? Which outweighed the other?
5. What is the SDR? What are the similarities and differences between regular drawing rights and special drawing rights?
6. What brought about the demise of the Bretton Woods system? Discuss both the basic (or underlying) causes and the immediate cause.
7. What was the significance of the U.S. measures of August 15, 1971?
8. What are "leads and lags"? Is this a form of speculation or hedging?
9. What did the Smithsonian Agreement accomplish? Was the effect of the Agreement long-lasting? When did the current system of generalized managed floats begin?
10. When governments intervene in foreign exchange markets to obtain BOP surpluses, which industries are they helping, their comparative advantage industries or their comparative disadvantage industries? Which of their industries are thereby injured? In what ways are particular industries helped or injured? What bearing do these overvaluations of the 1960s and 1970s have on the Davis-North political theory of trade restrictions presented in Chapter 10?
11. How might events in foreign exchange markets have differed if Federal Reserve policy had been more restrictive and if taxes had been raised during the war-on-poverty and the Vietnamese-war period 1963-73? Why those differences?

ENDNOTES

1. For a detailed account of the history of the international monetary system from the classical gold standard to the formation of the International Monetary Fund, see

Leland B. Yaeger, *International Monetary Relations: Theory, History, and Policy* (New York: Harper & Row, 1975), 2nd ed., chapters 15-19.

2. See "The Economic Consequence of Mr. Churchill" in John Maynard Keynes, *Essays in Persuasion* (New York: W.W. Norton, 1963), pp. 244-270. Writing immediately after Britain's return to gold in 1925, Keynes warned that international equilibrium would not be restored until Britain suffered a ten percent deflation: "Mr. Churchill's [then Chancellor of the Exchequer] policy of improving the exchange by 10 percent was, sooner or later, a policy of reducing every one's wages by 2s. in the £. He who wills the end will the means," p. 245.

3. Richard Blackhurst et al., *Trade Liberalization, Protectionism, and Interdependence* (Geneva: GATT, 1977), p. 8.

4. U.S. Department of Commerce, *Historical Statistics of the United States: Colonial Times to 1970* (Washington, D.C.: Government Printing Office, 1975), Part 2, p.995.

5. *Ibid.*, p. 210.

6. For an article that argues that the IMF is indeed emerging as a world central bank, see Anthony Scaperlanda, "The IMF: An Emerging Central Bank," *Kyklos*, 1978, pp. 679-690; reprinted in John Adams, ed., *The Contemporary International Economy: A Reader* (New York: St. Martin's Press, 1979), pp. 248-256.

7. Robert Solomon, *The International Monetary System, 1945-1976: An Insider's View* (New York: Harper & Row, 1977), pp. 334-335. A detailed discussion, with many interesting episodes, of the changes in the international monetary system from 1945 to 1976 is found in Solomon.

8. For a lively history of the period 1945-1979, see Martin Mayer, *The Fate of the Dollar* (New York: Times Books, 1980).

17

The Present International Monetary System

THE CHARACTERISTICS OF THE SYSTEM

The contemporary international monetary system – often referred to as the *system of generalized managed floats* – is a hybrid system, a cross between the two extreme systems of freely fluctuating rates and rigidly fixed rates. We argue here that the present system is not a distinctly different system. We argue, instead, that it, like many other possible systems, is a variant within the spectrum that ranges from freely fluctuating to rigidly fixed rates. The Bretton Woods system was a variant lying closer to the fixed rate system. Present arrangements lie closer to the fluctuating rate system. As hybrids, monetary systems may be regarded as variants within a spectrum, rather than totally different systems. At one extreme of the spectrum is a rigidly fixed system, and at the other is a freely fluctuating system. As hybrids, both the Bretton Woods system and the contemporary system of managed floats share most of the characteristics of the two pure (extreme) systems in varying degrees.

THE PURE MODELS

Just like the models of perfect competition and pure monopoly in price theory, the two extreme forms of international monetary systems are not often found in reality. Nevertheless, systematic thinking requires a clear understanding of the characteristics of the extreme benchmark cases. The essential characteristics of the two theoretical models are as follows.

The Freely Fluctuating System

The *freely fluctuating* (or perfectly flexible) *exchange rate system* is characterized by: (1) absence of government intervention in exchange markets, (2) volatility of exchange rates, (3) no role for government foreign exchange reserves, and (4) the absence of balance-of-payments constraints on domestic economic policies. Exchange rates are determined solely by the forces of demand and supply in foreign exchange markets; therefore, rates fluctuate — sometimes widely — as short-run shifts in demand and supply occur. Since quantities demanded and supplied in foreign exchange markets are equated automatically by market forces, deficits and surpluses cannot exist. Consequently, a nation's foreign exchange market and balance of payments are always in equilibrium, no accommodating flows of official short-term funds take place, and governments have no occasion to use foreign exchange reserves to influence rates. Since the balance of payments is always in equilibrium, governments can pursue domestic economic policies without being constrained by BOP considerations.

For the system to work as described above, two important assumptions must be met. First, as demonstrated in Chapter 15, the (price) elasticity conditions must be met. Otherwise, a temporary dislocation of the exchange rate from the equilibrium value will generate a cumulative move away from equilibrium. Secondly, if there exists destabilizing speculation, it must be more than offset by stabilizing speculation. When the rate of exchange temporarily deviates from the fundamental equilibrium level, speculation normally works to push the rate back to equilibrium. This is called *stabilizing speculation*. In contrast, *destabilizing speculation* drives the rate further away from the fundamental equilibrium level. (By "fundamental equilibrium rate" we mean the rate that would obtain if government did not intervene to influence the rate and if all other market participants were fully informed about relevant variables. See the next chapter.)

When, for example, the value of a currency begins to fall away from equilibrium, stabilizing speculators will buy the currency, believing the value of the currency will rise toward their (accurate) perception of equilibrium. Destabilizing speculators will sell the currency thinking the value will continue to fall toward their (misinformed) perception of the equilibrium. Similarly, when the fundamental equilibrium rate begins to fall away from the current rate, stabilizing speculators will sell the currency believing the market rate will move toward their (accurate) perception of the falling fundamental equilibrium. Destabilizing speculators will buy the currency, thinking the fall will be arrested and the rate will rise to their (misinformed) perception of the fundamental equilibrium. The return toward fundamental equilibrium will be delayed until the better informed stabilizing speculators begin to outweigh the misinformed destabilizing speculators.

The Fixed Exchange Rate System

The *fixed exchange rate system* is characterized by: (1) stable exchange rates, (2) direct government exchange-market intervention using accommodating financing of deficits and surpluses, (3) the need for sizable foreign exchange reserves, and (4) an obligation to subject domestic policy choices to balance-of-payments considerations if BOP deficits and surpluses are to be avoided. In the case of a quasi-fixed rate system like the adjustable peg, periodic attacks of pro-equilibrium-rate speculation will occur when policy choices have changed the fundamentals and left the peg at a clearly visible disequilibrium.

The fixed exchange rate system that lingered into the 1930s was abandoned after World War II because national leaders claimed that they could attain superior domestic policy objectives if freed from BOP constraints. The Bretton Woods system of quasi-fixed rates broke down, as we showed in the preceding chapter, because so many policy leaders so often accepted changes in the domestic fundamentals while procrastinating on decisions to change their pegs to the new equilibrium levels.

THE HYBRID SYSTEM

The present system emerged in March 1973. It is not fundamentally different from the Bretton Woods system it replaced. Both are hybrid systems. Both share many characteristics of the two "pure" systems. Specifically, both hybrids are characterized, in varying degrees, by: (1) variability in exchange rates, (2) the need for accommodating financing of deficits and surpluses by governments, (3) the need for international reserves, (4) a linkage between exchange rates and domestic policy variables, and (5) the absence of freedom from destabilizing flows of short-term capital.

The major differences between the systems before and after March 1973 are as follows: First, under the present system, exchange rate changes are freer and more frequent; therefore, the chance of any currency, including the dollar, remaining grossly over- or undervalued for a considerable length of time is much smaller now than under the previous arrangements. Second, because exchange rate changes under the present system are more frequent, smaller in magnitude, and not unidirectional, speculative capital flows in anticipation of exchange rate changes are less frequent and less disruptive. Third, the pivotal role of the U.S. dollar is considerably lessened. Instead of other currencies circling around the gold-anchored dollar, all major currencies, including the dollar, circle round each other.

FOREIGN EXCHANGE ARRANGEMENTS

Under the present system, most major currencies are floating, either independently or jointly with others. As of April 30, 1980, the following types of foreign exchange arrangements were observed. Ninety-four currencies were pegged to other currencies — 41 to the U.S. dollar, 3 to the pound sterling, 14 to the French franc, 3 to the other currencies, 15 to SDRs, and 20 to other "baskets" of currencies. (Note, the value of SDRs is determined by reference to a "basket" of 5 major currencies.) The exchange rates of 4 currencies were adjusted according to a set of domestic indicators, while 8 European currencies (of Belgium, Denmark, France, Germany, Ireland, Italy, Luxembourg, and the Netherlands) were floating jointly under the European Monetary System (see below). Mostly floating independently were 33 other currencies, including those of Australia, Canada, Japan, the United Kingdom, and the United States.[1]

Thus, there now exist several important groups of currencies with a considerable degree of exchange rate stability within them. Notable among these currency groups are those which revolve around the U.S. dollar, the pound sterling, SDRs, and the European Currency Unit (the currency unit of the European Monetary System). The last group encompasses the currencies of 22 nations — 8 European currencies, as well as 14 tied to the French franc.

MEASURES OF EXCHANGE RATE MANAGEMENT

In a nation with a floating currency, the monetary authorities' management of exchange rates constitutes the nation's *exchange rate policy*. The most commonly used means of exchange rate management is intervention in the spot foreign exchange market. For most countries, intervention is effected by purchases or sales of U.S. dollars. For example, the Bank of France sells dollars for francs to support the value of the franc. (The dollar then depreciates in the franc-dollar market.) The U.S. authorities (the Treasury and Federal Reserve) traditionally hold only a limited amount of foreign currencies. Therefore, if they are to buy dollars, they must first borrow foreign currencies from their counterparts in other nations.

Intervention in the forward market, although it is as effective as trading in the spot market, is used relatively infrequently by central banks as a means of intervention. Nevertheless, the Bank of England is reported to have engaged in significant forward intervention in 1976. In addition to direct intervention in exchange markets, governments and monetary authorities can indirectly influence the exchange rate by controlling flows of capital or of merchandise. Changing interest rates to encourage or discourage capital flows, and introducing or dismantling controls over capital flows, are thus regarded as alternative measures of exchange rate management. Similarly, tariffs, quotas, and import licensing are often used — particularly by LDCs — as means to restrict demand for foreign exchange and to support an overvalued domestic currency.

THE NEW IMF CHARTER

Floating of currencies that had been forbidden under the Bretton Woods system was tentatively adopted in March 1973 as a temporary arrangement to be replaced later by a more fundamental reform of the international monetary system. The managed floating system, however, has now been fairly firmly established as the only realistic arrangement. Two developments were responsible for the general acceptance of floating rates. They were: (1) the continued growth of world trade without excessive fluctuations in exchange rates, and (2) the relative ease with which the floating-rate system coped with the oil crisis of 1973-74.

The IMF's New Article IV

Acceptance of the floating-rate system has now been codified by an amendment to the IMF's Articles of Agreement. After extensive deliberations and negotiations between Fund officials and representatives of key member nations, a new Article IV of Agreement was approved by the IMF Board of Governors in April 1976 and was ratified by two-thirds of the member nations in 1978. The three key provisions of this second amendment to the Fund's charter (the first permitted creation of SDRs) were: (1) legitimatizing floating rates, (2) downgrading the monetary role of gold, and (3) designating the SDR as the principal reserve asset in the international monetary system.

Of special importance was the amendment to provisions concerning exchange arrangements. Under the amended Article IV, countries are free to choose their own exchange rate system from among alternatives including a free float; a managed float; or a rate pegged to one currency, a group of currencies, or SDRs (but not to gold). Member nations undertake an obligation to "collaborate with the Fund and other members to assure orderly exchange arrangements" and to "avoid manipulating exchange rates or the international monetary system in order to prevent effective balance of payments adjustment or to gain an unfair competitive advantage over other members." Regardless of the type of exchange arrangement adopted by a member, the Fund is to "exercise firm surveillance over the exchange-rate policies of members" and to "adopt specific principles for the guidance of members with respect to those policies."[2]

By an 85-percent majority, the Fund may reintroduce "a system of exchange arrangements based on a stable but adjustable par value." Any proposal to restore a fixed exchange rate system could be vetoed by the United States which has more than 15 percent of the Fund's voting power. Even if the Fund should decide to return to an adjustable-peg system; under a separate provision, a member could remain without a par value, provided it ensure that its exchange arrangements are consistent with the purpose of the Fund. This provision for a possible return to an adjustable-peg system and the separate provision that permits countries to maintain a float is a result of the compromise between the French who demanded a staged return to par values and the Americans who insisted on floating rates. According to Robert

Solomon, the United States, in order to obtain the concession from the French, had to agree to intervene more actively in exchange markets to preserve stability of exchange rates.[3]

The central point of the amended Article IV is not the legalization of floating rates per se, but the broad requirement that members must ensure *orderly exchange arrangements*. The heart of the new IMF charter is its recognition that a member's exchange rate system and policy must not become a source of harmful destabilizing influence on the international economic community — a lesson learned from the Bretton Woods experience.

Three Basic Ground Rules

The revised charter acknowledges that most of its members have a domestic obligation to achieve a "satisfactory" level of employment with "reasonable" price stability, but members are enjoined from trying to achieve these goals by use of exchange policies harmful to other members. The need to protect the international community from harmful and inconsistent exchange policies by individual nations leads to general agreement that exchange rate policies must be subject to collective surveillance.

Developing a set of specific rules that guide members' exchange rate policies is extremely difficult. Setting up internationally acceptable "norms" for exchange rates would be next to impossible because of the existence of divergent underlying economic conditions in each country and the absence of effective harmonization of domestic economic policies. Large and sharp changes in exchange rates may not necessarily call for intervention; if underlying economic conditions are changing rapidly and drastically in one direction, exchange market intervention to suppress or reverse the attendant change in the exchange rate may in itself constitute a disruptive action. Conversely, not intervening in the market which is producing a stable rate over a long period of time in spite of substantial changes in underlying economic conditions may also constitute a disruptive market behavior. Using the size of a member's changing balance-of-payments surplus or deficit, or changes in its official reserves, as a guide for intervention is also unlikely to be appropriate in all cases because exchange rates could be managed indirectly, without affecting the sizes of these variables, by such measures as changes in interest rates and capital controls.

Accordingly, the IMF in April 1977 adopted a set of broad principles for the guidance of members' exchange rate policies, and a set of criteria and procedures to accompany them. The three basic ground rules are:

A. A member shall avoid manipulating exchange rates or the international monetary system in order to prevent effective balance of payments adjustment or to gain an unfair competitive advantage over other members.

B. A member should intervene in the exchange market if necessary to counter disorderly conditions which may be characterized *inter alia* by disruptive short-term movements in the exchange value of its currency.

C. Members should take into account in their intervention policies the interests of other members, including those of the countries in whose currencies they intervene.[4]

Rule A prohibits manipulative practices with respect to exchange rates. The phrase "manipulating exchange rates" must be interpreted broadly. A nation that has an adjustable-peg system and that leaves the exchange rate unchanged when a surplus is mounting and when underlying conditions clearly indicate that equilibrium could be achieved with a lower (ie., upvalued) exchange rate is in fact manipulating its exchange rate. Similarly, when a nation with a floating currency intervenes to suppress or reverse long-run movements of the rate, it is manipulating the exchange system.

Rule B specifically recognizes that the free play of market forces do not always result in exchange rates that are consistent with underlying economic and financial conditions. (*Underlying conditions* refer to all the relevant factors — both domestic and foreign — that affect a nation's balance of payments; they include, among others, the level of income and output, the level of prices, interest rates, and governments' economic policies.) Speculative forces may generate disruptive short-term movements in rates that are clearly excessive given the underlying conditions. "Disorderly conditions" in the exchange markets produced by destabilizing speculation are counterproductive for international trade and investment, and a judicious use of "intervention" is called for to iron out the short-run gyrations in exchange rates. (This point will be discussed further in the next chapter.)

Rule C explicitly recognizes the reciprocal nature of exchange rate arrangements, as well as implicitly recognizing the problems of key-currency countries in whose currencies exchange market intervention is conducted. A slight degree of exchange rate bias that has few economic consequences for each intervening nation may have a serious cumulative effect on the economy of the nation whose currency is used for intervention purposes. Rule C would prevent this.

Criteria for Consultation

What criteria are to be used by the IMF in determining if consultation with a member may be in order? The April 1977 guidelines list the following—

1. "protracted large-scale intervention in one direction in the exchange market;"
2. "behavior of the exchange rate that appears to be unrelated to underlying economic and financial conditions including factors affecting competitiveness and long-term capital movements;" or

3. the existence of any of the following actions when undertaken for balance-of-payments purposes: an unsustainable level of official borrowing or official short-term lending; restrictions on, or incentives for, current transactions or payments; restrictions on, or incentives for, the inflow or outflow of capital; or the pursuit of monetary policies that "provide abnormal encouragement or discouragement to capital flows."

These factors will trigger a Fund inquiry into the exchange rate policies of members. Once a decision is made to consult a member, the Fund's appraisal of the member's exchange rate policy is to take into account "the developments in the member's balance of payments against the background of its reserve position and its external indebtedness," as well as its "general economic situation and economic policy strategy."[5] These criteria are rather vague and general. In other words, the Fund has no specific rules for the members to follow; rather, it lists some basic principles and tries to evaluate each member's exchange rate policy on a case-by-case basis.

THE ROLE OF THE U.S. DOLLAR

The U.S. dollar under the present international currency arrangement is, at least technically, just another currency floating against other currencies. It is no longer the anchor of international money as it once was under the Bretton Woods system. Nevertheless, the dollar still plays several important roles. First, it is still by far the most important *transaction currency*; private traders, investors, and speculators conduct their business largely in dollars. Secondly, it is still the most important *reserve asset* for most countries. Thirdly, being an important reserve currency, it is also an important *intervention currency*. National monetary authorities use U.S. dollars for intervention in foreign exchange markets to support or to depress exchange values of their own currencies.

Autonomous Entries in the ORTB

The special role of the U.S. dollar as the principal means of international payment complicates and confuses U.S. balance-of-payments accounting. Because foreign governments use dollars as foreign reserves, it is often very difficult to determine whether a given movement of dollars is autonomous or accommodating. For example, foreign governments sometimes use their currency to buy dollars *not* to support the dollar but simply to add to their own stock of foreign exchange reserves. Such purchases show up "below the line" in calculations of the Official Reserve Transactions Balance (ORTB). These purchases of dollars are made by governments that want to build up their foreign reserves —

their liquidity — so they *can* intervene, if needed, *in the future* to support the value of their currencies. Such purchases are made for the future, but they show up *now* as a deficit in America's ORTB. They are autonomous (to accommodate future deficits of the buying nations) but their negative recording in the "changes in reserve assets" BOP line is presumptive evidence that they are accommodating a current American deficit.

When interpreting America's ORTB, one must always allow for the possibility the figure is smaller than otherwise because of autonomous purchases of dollars being added to contingency reserves. Most nations now preside over a dirty float. Officials presiding over dirty floats want more dollar reserves, the larger the value of their foreign trade; for the larger the trade, the bigger the possible short-run fluctuations Therefore, as long as the dollar remains the principal intervention currency, and as long as world trade expands, foreign governments will continue to add to their contingency dollar reserves. Interpreters of the American ORTB will have to continue to guess at the true division of the ORTB between autonomous and accommodating flows.

Foreign Central Bank Manipulation of the Dollar

Because the dollar is the most important intervention currency, one very important consequence follows. Other nations' interventions in exchange markets affect the exchange rate of the dollar. The United States therefore still suffers the problem that determination of the exchange value of the dollar is largely in the hands of foreign monetary authorities. This legacy of the Bretton Woods system is one of the most serious weaknesses of the contemporary international monetary system.

The relative smoothness of changes in the exchange values of major floating currencies has been achieved by frequent, and often massive, intervention by central banks in foreign exchange markets. In 1978 alone, total intervention by the world's central banks amounted to some $50 billion. During January-June 1980, gross market intervention by major central banks was at an annual rate above $120 billion.[6]

The U.S. Federal Reserve maintained a passive role in determination of dollar exchange rates until the end of 1977. In early 1978, however, it started to sell marks to support the dollar. Foreign currencies used by the Federal Reserve Bank of New York — as agent of the Federal Reserve System and the U.S. Treasury — are supplied to it through the *reciprocal currency agreement* (known as the "swap network") between major central banks. Under this arrangement, central banks agree to extend, simultaneously, predetermined amounts of credit to each other to be used for intervention in foreign exchange markets. This arrangement is particularly useful for the United States agencies that traditionally carry only small reserves of foreign currencies. The total credit facility available to the Federal Reserve in June 1980 was a little over $30 billion. Table 17-1 shows details of the swap network in 1978.

TABLE 17-1   FEDERAL RESERVE SWAP NETWORK FACILITY
(millions of dollars)

Institution	As of October 31, 1978	Increases effective Nov. 1, 1978	Total Facility Nov. 1, 1978
Austrian National Bank	250		250
National Bank of Belgium	1,000		1,000
Bank of Canada	2,000		2,000
National Bank of Denmark	250		250
Bank of England	3,000		3,000
Bank of France	2,000		2,000
German Federal Bank	4,000	2,000	6,000
Bank of Italy	3,000		3,000
Bank of Japan	2,000	3,000	5,000
Bank of Mexico	360		360
Netherlands Bank	500		500
Bank of Norway	250		250
Bank of Sweden	300		300
Swiss National Bank	1,400	2,600	4,000
Bank for International Settlements	1,850		1,850
Total	22,160	7,600	29,760

Source: Federal Reserve Bank of New York, *Quarterly Review,* Winter 1978-79, p. 64.

THE EUROPEAN MONETARY SYSTEM

Since March 1979, eight European nations — Belgium, Denmark, France, West Germany, Ireland, Italy, Luxembourg, and the Netherlands — have participated in the European Monetary System (EMS). (All the members of the European Community, except the United Kingdom, are members of the EMS.) The EMS has several features akin to the Bretton Woods system, and is therefore nicknamed the "mini-IMF." The participating nations' currencies are tied to each other in a "parity grid" that relates each currency to a central rate that is a weighted average of the eight currencies. A currency's value must be maintained by intervention within 2.25 percent above or below the central rate. (The Italian lira is allowed to fluctuate within a band of 6 percent above or below the central rate.) The members are issued European Currency Units (ECUs) against their deposits — part required quota, part discretionary — with the European Monetary Cooperation Fund (EMCF) of U.S. dollars and gold. Gold constitutes 20 percent of the quota, and is valued at the market price. The value of the ECU is determined by a weighted average of all the currencies in the European Community (including the pound sterling). Presently the ECU is merely a unit of account, much as the SDR is. The amount of ECUs is expected to grow as members convert more dollars and gold into ECUs. EMS planners hope the ECU will someday become an important reserve asset and intervention currency, much as the U.S. dollar is today. Since the growth of the ECU into a full-fledged intervention currency is expected to take years, an interim arrangement was made to provide short- and medium-term credit to member nations for intervention purposes. The credit, totaling

$32.5 billion, is to be used in a manner similar to that of the current swap network.[7]

Reasons for European Support

The system was born out of the West Europeans' — primarily German and French — desire to dethrone the U.S. dollar from the position of key reserve and intervention currency. They hoped that by creating a new reserve asset based on the strong German mark, the dollar's stronghold on the international monetary system could be weakened. For Germany, tying the mark with other European currencies has an advantage of protecting its dollar export competitiveness in the event of dollar depriciation. If the dollar weakens and the mark appreciates, as often happened in the past, but other European currencies do not appreciate, Germany's export competitiveness will suffer both in Europe and in dollar areas. If, on the other hand, other European currencies appreciate with the mark, Germany's competitive position in Europe — which absorbs half of Germany's exports — would be protected.

The weaker-currency members of the EMS like France and Italy regard it as insurance against Europe-wide inflation. If the mark alone appreciates, those countries' imports from Germany will become more expensive in terms of local currencies, adding to inflationary pressures. Tying their currencies to a strong currency like the mark, therefore, is one way to fight inflation.[8]

One major concern of the weaker-currency countries was the eventuality of a stronger currency such as the mark pulling up their exchange rates to unacceptably high levels, thus reducing their competitiveness in areas outside the EMS. Another concern was that weak-currency member nations with overvalued currencies would be forced to intervene massively in exchange markets with consequent heavy losses in reserve assets. Worse yet, they were afraid that Germany might pressure them to adopt contractionary monetary and fiscal policies in order to reduce their deficits, with the inevitable result of rising unemployment and economic slowdown. Italy agreed to join the system only after it was allowed to keep the lira rate within 6 percent above or below the central rate — an exception to the 2.25 percent rule. Although the United Kingdom had worked closely with Germany and France in the development of the plan, it decided at the last moment not to participate in the system. The United Kingdom, however, is expected to join eventually.

Experience with the System

The new system was working fairly well in mid-1980, partly because, it was believed, the crucial mark-dollar rate had been relatively stable. Intervention, however, was being conducted primarily through the dollar, contrary to the original understanding that it be made in member currencies.

A second strain surfaced early within the system. Germany began selling dollars for marks to support the value of the mark; it was concerned that depreciation of the mark would add to inflationary pressures in Germany by raising import prices. (Americans are hard put to empathize with citizens of nations where imports are a large percentage of GNP.) The high value of the mark, however, acted to pull up the values of other currencies in the EMS, creating a tendency to overvalue some of them. Specifically, the Belgian franc and the Danish krone had difficulties keeping pace with the strong mark, and some realignment of the parities within the system was deemed likely. That development, only three months after the start of the system under a relatively stable mark-dollar rate, points to the fundamental weakness of the system. The weakness is characteristic of any scheme of fixed exchange rates; it exists because a regime of fixed exchange rates works only when underlying economic and financial conditions in the participating nations are similar and their domestic economic policies are closely harmonized. If not, the system easily collapses when different currencies exhibit substantially different rates of change in values. Just as the Bretton Woods system broke down under the pressure of the declining dollar, the EMS could collapse under the pressure of the rapidly rising value of the German mark, or by a sharp decline in one or two of its major currencies. The future of the EMS, therefore, is by no means certain. How long a system that contains the basic flaw of a fixed exchange rate system can stay viable remains to be seen.

What Future for ECU and Dollar?

What would be the effect of the development of the EMS on the American dollar? There are both short-run and long-run considerations. In the short-run, the EMS would have a destabilizing effect on the dollar as its members move out of the dollar into the ECU. Demand for the dollar would fall, putting downward pressure on the value of the dollar in exchange markets. In the long run, however, the development of other reserve assets – be they the ECU, the SDR, or other currencies – is bound to help the dollar by removing the strait jacket of the current status of the dollar as the world's key reserve and intervention currency. As the dollar genuinely becomes "just another currency," it will be freed from the unwelcome role of the world's only generally acceptable medium of international exchange. The U.S. monetary authorities in such an eventuality will become able to determine independently the exchange value of the dollar and pursue their own monetary and exchange rate policies without being constrained by the behavior and policy objectives of other nations.[9]

In September 1979, the Deutsche mark was revalued upward by 2 percent and the Danish krone was devalued by 3 percent against the other EMS currencies. The Danish krone was devalued further by 5 percent in November 1979. Notwithstanding these minor changes in exchange rates, the intracommunity exchange rates were much more stable in 1979 than during the preceding years. Exchange rate instability among the member currencies in 1979 was reduced by almost two-thirds from the 1973-78 average.[10]

A BRIEF HISTORY SINCE 1973

In this section we will briefly examine how the present international monetary system has worked since the first oil crisis of 1973.

THE OIL CRISIS AND ITS AFTERMATH

The new international monetary system was put to a severe test in late 1973 and early 1974 when the Organization of Petroleum Exporting Countries (OPEC) engineered a sharp cutback in the supply of oil and a consequently huge increase in the price of oil. Between October 1973 and January 1974, the OPEC cartel raised the price of crude oil from $3 per barrel to approximately $12 per barrel (see Chapter 11). This four-fold increase in the price of oil produced a massive transfer of purchasing power from the oil consuming countries to the oil producing nations. Total oil revenues of the OPEC nations amounted to roughly $22 billion in 1973 but rose to some $105 billion in 1974. This addition to OPEC purchasing power represented nearly 1.5 percent of Gross World Product. A little less than half of the $105 billion was spent on OPEC nation imports of goods and services. But because OPEC nations did not increase current-account imports as rapidly as their oil revenue increased in 1974, the OPEC nations increased their imports of diverse IOUs and other securities. Most of this massive outflow of OPEC capital went to the United States and to some West European nations. Of OPEC's $55 billion in net oil revenues (net of $50 billion in imported goods and services), $20.5 billion went to Eurocurrency deposits (largely dollars-denominated), $10.5 billion went to bank deposits and government securities of the United States, and $6 billion went to sterling deposits and government securities of the United Kingdom.[11]

The oil price increases altered the structure of the balance of payments of the oil importing nations. The oil price increases reduced the current-account surpluses and reduced, equally, the capital-account deficits of the developed nations. That is to say, the developed nations began to receive more valuable oil and fewer IOUs and other securities in payment for their exports; developed nations' net foreign investment was reduced.

Most developing oil importing nations experienced current-account deficits in 1972 and 1973. The November 1973 oil price increases raised the value of oil importing LDC merchandise imports — but only because they found optimistic lenders willing to accept LDC IOUs in exchange for cash used to pay for the more expensive oil. So the debt of the oil importing LDCs ratcheted up with no visible matching increase in their prospective ability to repay such additional debts. (More on this subject in the next chapter.)

Oil's Effect on Other Prices

Since oil is an input in production of a wide range of products, the November 1973 oil price jump led inevitably to widespread sharp adjustments in patterns of production and consumption. (College instructors and textbook authors often exaggerate when showing price changes in their diagrams, but even these people rarely change isocosts enough to reflect a quadrupling of one input price.) The developed nations' BOPs, in the years after 1973, showed extensive adjustments resulting from that initial change in relative prices.

The quadrupled oil price gave a once-for-all push to cost-push inflation. But it arrived immediately after several years of extraordinary increases in the money stocks of Japan, the United States, and Western European nations. The ongoing inflation permitted the losers — briefly — to harbor the illusion they were escaping the real loss. But that illusion was dispelled when central bank attempts to control the inflation resulted, in many nations in 1974 and 1975, in the deepest contraction since the Great Depression of the 1930s. Yet general price increases remained large in 1975, and recovery from the recession did not come until 1976.

The balances of payments of individual nations were less affected by the general increase in inflation rate and reduction in growth rate than by differences among nations in those rates. Those differences were due in important part to differences among nations in degree of vulnerability to the lower supply and higher price of oil. At first, Japan was considered the most vulnerable, and the United States the least vulnerable, to the oil and energy crisis. The Japanese yen and several European currencies — particularly the pound sterling — floated downward relative to the dollar in 1974 and 1975. The annual rate of increase in the consumer price index was 23 percent in Japan in 1974 and 24 percent in the United Kingdom in 1975; these figures were much higher than the comparable rates in the United States — 11 percent in 1974 and 9 percent in 1975. During the 1973-75 period, West Germany was the only major industrial nation which managed to contain the consumer price increases to a single digit (6.9 percent in 1973, 7.0 percent in 1974, and 6.0 percent in 1975). Consequently, the Deutsche mark remained stronger than all other major currencies throughout this period (see Figure 17-1).

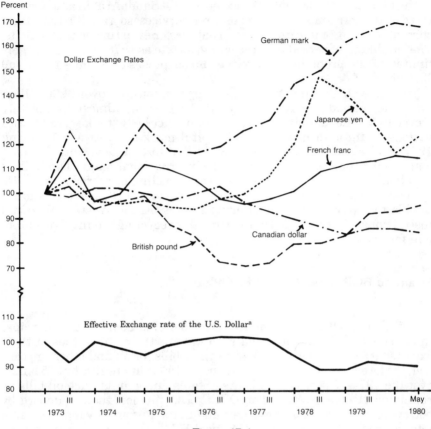

Figure 17-1

Exchange Rates of Selected Currencies, 1973-1980, 1973(I) = 100

[a]An index showing the average exchange rates between the U.S. dollar and 20 other major currencies with weights derived from the IMF's Multilateral Exchange Rate Model (MERM).

Source: International Monetary Fund, *International Financial Statistics*, various issues.

Recycling

In 1974, some commentators feared that OPEC nations would continually run huge current-account surpluses that would result in massive accumulation of financial assets — called "petrodollars" regardless of their actual currency denomination — that would undermine the viability of the international financial system and lead to a catastrophe. Thus far, nothing like this catastrophe has materialized. The worriers feared the OPEC nations would receive higher incomes, would choose not to spend all of the increase on current-account imports, and would refuse to lend the difference to others who *would* spend it. In fact, OPEC nations raised current-account imports and cheerfully loaned to earn interest. Between 1974 and 1978, the OPEC members showed, like nouveau-riche households, quickly increased purchases, so their current-account surplus sharply decreased from nearly $55 billion in 1974 to roughly $10 billion in 1978.

Most OPEC nations, with the exceptions of Saudi Arabia and Kuwait, increased their imports of goods and services so rapidly that their current accounts came quickly into balance or even turned into deficits. The "problem" of petrodollar recycling, as late as 1978, was thus largely limited to the problem of recycling the surpluses of Saudi Arabia and Kuwait.

The huge OPEC current-account surplus, totaling over $200 billion over the period of 1972 through 1978, was almost completely recycled to the deficit countries — particularly to key industrial nations — through international capital markets. Between 1974 and 1977, capital markets provided $90 billion in long-term international loans and $105 billion in short-term international loans. The bulk of this lending undoubtedly involved the recycling of petrodollars.[12] No "problem" was apparent at the time. However, if LDC borrowers prove unable to repay many loans during the 1980s, the Western financial institutions will conclude that petrodollar recycling did involve a problem for them.

Financing BOP Debts Caused by OPEC

Not all non-OPEC nations ran BOP deficits. Some of the principal industrial nations experienced greater growth in the values of their exported goods and services than in their bills for oil and other imports. Net, the foreign exchange reserves of non-OPEC nations rose by $75 billion over the 1974-77 period. The United States financed its huge oil bills by running BOP deficits. Many non-OPEC LDCs financed their oil imports by borrowing in world capital markets and in the Euromoney market a sum totaling $44 billion between 1974 and 1977.[13]

Many developing members of the International Monetary Fund also received relief from the Fund. In August 1975, the IMF members agreed to liquidate by auction one sixth of its gold holdings — or 25 million ounces — for the benefit of its LDC members over a period of four years. (An additional 25 million ounces were sold back directly to all the members at a price equivalent to SDR 35 per ounce.) The four-year gold sales program was completed in May 1980. The program yielded the IMF a net profit (after deducting the capital value of gold at SDR 35 per ounce) of $4.6 billion. Of this amount, $1.3 billion was transferred to 104 LDC members in proportion to their quota as of August 31, 1975. A trust fund was set up with the remainder of the gold proceeds, from which loans are made to eligible developing members that are willing to accept IMF surveillance over their policies to improve their balance-of-payments positions.[14]

EXCHANGE RATE RECORDS

Figure 17-1 shows the record of flexibility of the world's six major currencies between January 1973 and May 1980. The upper part of the graph shows movements of the U.S. dollar exchange rates of five major currencies. The lower part of the graph shows movement of the *effective* (or trade-weighted) exchange rate of the U.S. dollar. (The effective exchange rate used here is the index of exchange rate of the currency in question in relation to 20 other major currencies as calculated by the IMF using weights derived from the IMF's Multilateral Exchange Rate Model, or MERM.)

After a short-lived recovery in 1976, the economies of Europe and Japan experienced a protracted, mild recession through 1977 and 1978 with their real GNP growth rates considerably below their average annual growth rates for the 1960-73 period. These economies were sluggish throughout the 1977-78 period because European and Japanese policymakers feared renewed inflation. Mindful of their peoples' concern about inflation, the European and Japanese governments pursued restrictive monetary and fiscal policies. The United States alone pursued expansionary domestic policies, and the growth rate of the U.S. economy in the 1977-78 period was higher than that of its 1960-73 annual average. As a consequence, the inflation rate in the United States accelerated throughout the 1976-78 period, while in Europe and Japan it decelerated. Higher rates of economic growth and inflation in the United States than in Europe and Japan, enormous trade and payments deficits in the United States, accompanied by surpluses elsewhere, especially large in Germany and Japan. As a consequence, the U.S. dollar depreciated considerably against the mark and the yen over the 1976-78 period, as seen in Figure 17-1, despite massive intervention by the Bundesbank and the Bank of Japan to support the dollar. Fueled by speculation, the pace of the depreciation of the dollar quickened in the fall of 1978, until it was reversed by the dollar defense program announced by President Carter on November 1, 1978.

The U.S. dollar-defense measures of November 1978 included the following features: (1) a tightening of U.S. monetary policy, including a 1 percent increase in the Federal Reserve discount rate to a historic high of 9½ percent; (2) a $7.6 billion increase in the total swap network facility to about $30 billion (see Table 17-1) to finance U.S. intervention in foreign exchange markets to support the dollar; (3) drawing by the U.S. Treasury of $5 billion equivalent of ordinary and special drawing rights in the IMF to obtain additional German marks, Japanese yen, and Swiss francs; (4) the Treasury's issuance of foreign-currency denominated securities up to $10 billion equivalent; and (5) a substantial increase in the amounts of monthly gold sales by the Treasury.

The announcement of the program was followed by massive intervention by the Federal Reserve Bank of New York in the foreign exchange markets of the German mark, the Swiss franc, and the Japanese yen. These operations were coordinated with other central banks' intervention in their own markets. The immediate effect of the coordinated effort was a sharp rebound of the dollar. By December 1978, the doller's appreciation relative to the late-October lows had reached 11¾ percent against the German mark, 15½ percent against the Swiss franc, and 11½ percent against the Japanese yen.[15]

During the first quarter of 1979, the dollar rose 10 percent against the yen and 1 percent against the German mark and the Swiss franc. This increasing strength of the dollar enabled the U.S. authorities to buy back foreign currencies. As a result, the Federal Reserve and the Treasury had, by May 1979, repaid all their swap debts to foreign central banks and, in addition, had accumulated $6 billion equivalent of marks, yen, and Swiss francs.[16]

Sharp rises in international oil prices that took place in the second half of 1979 changed the picture somewhat. The higher oil prices added massively to America's oil bill, slowed down the process of improvement in U.S. current-account balance, and exacerbated the inflation in the United States. The dollar softened somewhat against the European currencies. The U.S. dollar, however, appreciated sharply against the Japanese yen, rising from about ¥195/dollar in January to about ¥240/dollar in December 1979. This sharp depreciation of the yen was attributed to the fact that (1) the previous efforts by the Japanese government to expand the domestic economy and reduce large trade and current-account surpluses finally took hold, and (2) Japan was more vulnerable than any other industrial countries to the oil crisis.

Accelerating inflation rates in the United States in late 1979 and early 1980 pushed U.S. interest rates to unprecedented high levels. These high U.S. rates markedly increased the demand for dollar-denominated liquid assets, causing an appreciation of the dollar against other currencies. With the declining U.S. interest rates in mid-1980, however, the dollar's rally came to an end.

HOW WELL HAS THE SYSTEM WORKED?

What can we conclude about the performance of the system of generalized managed floats during its brief existence since March 1973? Most commentators believe the regime has worked well — far better than expected. The often-feared disruption of world trade and investment did not take place. Table 17-2 shows the growth of world trade adjusted for price changes for the 1972-79 period. In real terms, world trade averaged 6.8 percent annual growth between 1972 and 1979. This compares favorably with the average annual growth rate of approximately 8 percent when the world economy experienced a decade of sustained growth between 1960 and 1970. Table 17-2 shows that the world trade volume decreased by 5 percent in 1975, but 1975 was an exceptional year. Trade volume responds sensitively to changes in output and income; and the 5 percent decline in trade volume in 1975 can be attributed to the deep recession of 1974-75. (In a similar six-year period 1955-61 with the recession of 1957-58 sandwiched in the middle, the total volume of world trade increased at an annual average rate of 6 percent, with a decline in 1958 of 1.3 percent.)[17]

Especially noteworthy is the fact that the new monetary system weathered the oil crises of 1973-74 and 1979, and the Iranian and

Afghanistan crises of 1979-80, without difficulty. Had the world had a fixed exchange rate system when these crises flared, the system would certainly have collapsed under the weight of massive flows of speculative funds. In the years since the floating system was introduced, there have been no sudden money panics, and the world's foreign exchange markets have not had to be closed one single day.

However, we should not leap to the cavalier conclusion that the floating rate system has met all possible tests with flying colors. Peter Kenen warns that payments for oil have been made almost exclusively with dollars and sterling, and that the OPEC surpluses remain held in those two currencies. A crisis of major proportions will no doubt develop if huge sums of petrodollars ever begin to cross the world's foreign exchange markets.[18] (It may be noted, however, that a massive conversion of dollars and pounds into other currencies will not be in the best interest of the OPEC nations. If they make an attempt to unload substantial amounts of dollars and pounds, the values of these currencies will fall sharply, causing substantial capital losses to their owners.)

Outside the remote possibility of petrodollar withdrawals causing a worldwide financial panic, the most serious single problem remaining in the present international monetary system is that of the U.S. dollar — its status as the key transaction-reserve-intervention currency and the threat posed by the Damoclean sword representing the huge dollar overhang. These problems will continue to generate a measure of instability in the present international monetary system. These and other problems and issues will be discussed in the next chapter.

TABLE 17-2   CHANGES IN WORLD TRADE VOLUME, 1972-1979

Year	Trade Volume[a]	Percentage Increase over Preceding Year
1972	1,430	—
1973	1,605	12.2
1974	1,693	5.5
1975	1,610	−5.0
1976	1,804	12.0
1977	1,878	4.1
1978	1,992	6.1
1979	2,263	13.6

[a]Total world exports plus total world imports, in billions of 1975 U.S. dollars.

Source: International Monetary Fund, *International Financial Statistics*, various issues.

STUDY QUESTIONS

1. Explain the difference between stabilizing speculation and destabilizing speculation.

2. Compare and contrast the main features of the freely fluctuating exchange rate system and the rigidly fixed exchange rate system. Between the two extremes, where do the Bretton Woods adjustable peg system and the contemporary system of managed floats fit in?

3. Explain the similarities and differences between the Bretton Woods system and the present system of managed floats.

4. Explain both the narrower and the broader meaning of a nation's "exchange-rate policy."

5. Identify the significant features of the amended Article IV of the IMF Agreement.

6. Discuss the three basic rules for members' exchange rate policies adopted by the IMF in April 1977.

7. Discuss the role of the U.S. dollar under the contemporary international monetary system. How does it differ from the currency's role under the Bretton Woods system?

8. What is the "swap arrangement"? Why is it particularly useful to the United States?

9. Discuss the main features of the European Monetary System. Why is it nicknamed the "mini-IMF"?

10. Which special-interest groups in Germany have reason to lobby for an arrangement that links the mark to other European currencies in the ECU? What can these particular groups gain from such an arrangement?

11. What are the balance-of-payments entries when:
   (a) OPEC members sell $200 billion in oil, import $160 billion in goods and services, and settle the difference in New York and London bank accounts?
   (b) OPEC members use bank accounts to buy $40 billion in certificates of deposit from London and New York banks?
   (c) New York and London banks buy $30 billion in bonds from oil importing LDCs?
   (d) The LDCs use the bond proceeds to buy OPEC oil?

ENDNOTES

1. International Monetary Fund, *International Financial Statistics,* July 1980, p. 11.
2. "Article IV: The Proposed Exchange Arrangements," *IMF Survey,* 19 January 1976, p. 20.
3. For a detailed account of international negotiations leading to the amended Article IV, see Robert Solomon, *The International Monetary System, 1945-1976: An Insider's View* (New York: Harper and Row, 1977), Chapter XVII.
4. International Monetary Fund, *Annual Report 1977,* Appendix II, pp. 107-109; reprinted in Jacques R. Artus and Andrew D. Crockett, "Floating Exchange Rates and the Need for Surveillance," Princeton University, *Essays in International Finance,* No. 127, May 1978, p. 36.
5. *Ibid.*
6. Federal Reserve Bank of Chicago, *International Letter,* 6 June 1980, p. 1.
7. "European Monetary Plan Seen Complex, Perhaps Unworkable, Set of Compromises," *Wall Street Journal,* 7 December 1978, p. 4.
8. Bruce Nussbaum, "How Europe's New Currency Union Will Hurt the Dollar," *Business Week,* 31 July 1978, p. 82.
9. For excellent discussions on the workings and future prospects of the EMS, see Philip H. Trezise, ed., *The European Monetary System: Its Promise and Prospects* (Washington, D.C.: The Brookings Institution, 1979).

10. "European Monetary System Working Fine But Hasn't Faced Major Assault on Dollar," *Wall Street Journal,* 10 March 1980, p. 16.
11. Charles N. Henning et al., *International Financial Management* (New York: McGraw Hill, 1978), p. 152.
12. Tilford Gaines, "Petrodollars Revisited," Manufacturers Hanover Trust, *Economic Report,* September 1978.
13. *Ibid.*
14. *IMF Survey,* 19 May 1980, p. 145.
15. "Treasury and Federal Reserve Foreign Exchange Operations," Federal Reserve Bank of New York, *Quarterly Review,* Winter 1978-79, pp. 63-67 and Spring 1979, pp. 67-70.
16. "U.S. Paid Off 'Swap' Debt, Built Reserves of Foreign Currencies as Dollar Climbed," *Wall Street Journal,* 5 June 1979, p. 7.
17. International Monetary Fund, *International Financial Statistics,* various issues.
18. K. Brunner and A. Meltzer, eds., *Institutional Arrangements and the Inflation Problem* (Amsterdam: North-Holland, 1976), pp. 115-121; reprinted in John Adams, *The Contemporary International Economy: A Reader* (New York: St. Martin's Press, 1979), p. 306.

18

Issues and Problems
in the Present System

The contemporary international monetary system is a hybrid system, a cross between a fixed exchange rate system and a freely fluctuating rate system. As such, it is characterized by the strengths and weaknesses of both systems. Nevertheless, since the present system leans more heavily toward the floating than toward the fixed rate system, and since the world has had experience with generalized floating for less than a decade, most of the theoretical and policy issues and problems encountered today are related to floating rates. In this chapter we examine some of the more important of these issues and problems.

THE ISSUES OF EXCHANGE RATE VOLATILITY

We can imagine an extreme case where most market participants have perfect knowledge of market conditions and where exchange rates are determined by free market forces. In that case, exchange rates would change in response to changes in underlying economic conditions (income and output levels, price levels, interest rates, monetary and fiscal policies, and so on). Barring externalities, trade and investment flows would be optimal if they were to take place guided by rates of exchange consistent with underlying economic conditions.

SPECULATION AND THE FUNDAMENTAL EQUILIBRIUM RATE

Since 1973, when most currencies were allowed to float, several exchange rates have fluctuated more widely than can be explained (at least, in retrospect) by changes in underlying economic conditions. That bald assertion begs support from empirical evidence.

First, how to measure changes in underlying economic conditions? Change in domestic price levels is a crude proxy variable approximating the net effects of changes in all underlying economic conditions.

Artus and Crockett compared price movements and exchange rate movements in seven major industrial nations over the years 1973-76 inclusive. First, they calculated deviations of each nation's dollar exchange rate from a thirteen-month centered moving average. The deviation range was as low as plus-or-minus 2 percent for Canada and as high as plus-or-minus 10 percent for Germany, France, and Switzerland.

Second, they calculated deviations of each nation's consumer price index from a thirteen-month centered average of the U.S. consumer price index. That second deviation range was as low as plus-or-minus 1 percent for Canada and France but was no higher than the plus-or-minus 3 percent of Japan and the United Kingdom.[1] Clearly, *price-relatives* varied much less than exchange rates varied.

In some cases, major currencies depreciated by some 20 percent in six months then appreciated by roughly 20 percent in the next six-month period (and vice versa). Between January and October of 1978, the Japanese yen appreciated by 36 percent against the dollar (See Figure 17-1). Such wide variations in exchange rates are hardly explainable by changes in underlying conditions which are by their very nature much less volatile.

Since changes in underlying economic conditions cannot — ordinarily — produce exchange rate fluctuations of so great a magnitude, the observed variations in exchange rates must be attributed in part to the presence of misinformation and inefficiency (as well as continued government interventions as was the case with the yen in 1978) in exchange markets. Inefficiency appears in exchange rate results when market participants are unable to digest all available true information, discount it, and incorporate it in the exchange rate. Misinformation is introduced from many sources including the statements, or purported statements, of influential government officials. Finally, central bank interventions, and rumors of interventions, in a dirty float can move the rate away from equilibrium and can press it up, then down, then up.

In an exchange market that is less than fully efficient, some participants fail to allow for and discount all available information and consequently "misbehave." Misinformation will also produce market misbehavior. Actual exchange rates are thus at times influenced by destabilizing speculation and, so, diverge from equilibrium values that correspond to underlying economic conditions.

The Role of Speculators

In Chapter 13 we observed that speculators in foreign exchange markets are those who deliberately take, for a profit, a net (long or short) position in a currency. Speculators provide an important function

in a foreign exchange market. They specialize in gathering and processing all relevant information about present and future conditions
underlying the market. When both efficient and well informed, their
buying and selling activities push the market rate toward equilibrium;
that is, their actions cause it to incorporate all relevant economic
information.

Importers and exporters of goods, services, stocks, bonds, and property
titles (the ultimate demanders and suppliers of foreign exchange) also
speculate through the leads and lags described in Chapter 16. But lead
and lag behavior is secondary to the primary import-export interests of
these people. Only speculators specialize in processing market information (and, not infrequently, misinformation) and in buying and selling
currencies for the sole reason that they believe current market values
are temporarily out of tune with underlying economic conditions. The
function of speculation is thus one of stabilizing (or equilibrating) the
market; without speculators' activities, the equilibrating function of
the market would be greatly lessened. An efficient foreign exchange
market implies the existence of ample *stabilizing speculation* preventing lengthy dislocations of the actual rate from the long-run equilibrium rate.

The point is not that the absence of speculators would keep foreign
exchange markets from equilibrium. Ordinary importers and exporters
would operate in daily, in hourly, equilibrium even if no speculators
breathed or moved. But as everywhere in the world, information is
expensive to obtain. Ordinary importers and exporters are specialists in
activities other than foreign exchange markets. Few can afford to spend
much time or money to acquire information about changes in current
conditions affecting those markets; much less can they afford to pay to
obtain information about likely future changes affecting foreign exchange markets.

Since speculators have always been there participating in free exchange markets, one cannot report from history the consequences of
their absence. But we can speculate that without speculators, foreign
exchange rates would alternate between slow changes, lagging behind
changes in fundamentals, followed by sharp sudden changes brought on
by ultimate recognition of those fundamental changes. This sequence
would be a softened version of the adjustable peg system. Its irregular-
ity would result principally from the inability of ordinary traders
to learn quickly about prospects for future changes in underlying
conditions.

Destabilizing Speculation

When underlying economic and financial conditions of a country
deteriorate, the rate of exchange of the nation's currency should fall.
Stabilizing speculation works to prevent the rate from over- or under-
reacting to the change in underlying conditions. Yet in the real world of

considerable misinformation, another type of speculation — *destabilizing speculation* — may develop. Once the exchange rate begins to fall, a conviction may develop that the new equilibrium is quite far from the old. That conviction may be supported by knowledge that governments had artificially supported the former rate. The result, once the rate starts down, is that every decline encourages many speculators to expect further depreciation. When the convinced are sufficiently numerous, their behavior produces cumulative, temporarily self-fulfilling disequilibrating exchange rate movements. Importers and exporters may be induced to join; then one nation's exporters ask to be paid as late as possible while its importers strive to pay sooner. Vice versa within that nation's trading partners. This kind of speculation by professional speculators and ordinary importers and exporters results in and from self-fulfilling prophecies. In consequence, exchange rates sometimes vary more than can be explained by changes in underlying determinants of exchange rate equilibrium.

Up to this point in this book, we have assumed that foreign exchange markets are well informed and fully efficient; so actual rates, barring government intervention, accurately reflect underlying economic conditions. We now modify this assumption. We recognize that, in the short run, under attacks of destabilizing speculation, the actual rate of exchange — even though freely determined without government intervention — may not be equal to the equilibrium rate that is compatible with the trend in underlying economic conditions. We thus recognize explicitly that absence of government intervention in foreign exchange markets is not a sufficient condition for equilibrium; actual rates, even though freely determined without government intervention, can be disequilibrium rates if there exists destabilizing speculation caused by market inefficiency and misinformation.

The Fundamental Equilibrium Rate

Just as the concept of "fundamental disequilibrium" was fuzzy but crucial to the Bretton Woods system, the concept of "fundamental equilibrium rate" is crucial — and also difficult to define operationally — under the present system of managed floats. Conceptually, the definition is simple: it is the rate of exchange that equates the demand for and the supply of foreign exchange, in the absence of government intervention *and* destabilizing speculation. It is the perfectly competitive equilibrium of perfect knowledge and mobility. The operational problem arises because of the difficulty of accurately estimating the size of destabilizing speculation, let alone ascertaining the existence and extent of government intervention. Nevertheless, the literature on floating exchange rates is replete with reference, either explicit or implicit, to the fundamental equilibrium rate, reflecting its conceptual significance.

Benign Government Intervention in 1975 and in 1978

The realization that an actual free rate may deviate from the fundamental rate reveals an interesting fact about the role of government intervention in foreign exchange markets. Heretofore we have stated or implied that government intervention is necessarily undesirable in that it tends to move the exchange rate away from equilibrium. We now recognize, however, that central bank intervention in foreign exchange markets may be desirable, if the following conditions are met: (1) the actual rate is deviant from the fundamental rate, and (2) government officials are more capable than private participants in the market in accurately estimating the level of the fundamental rate. To fully understand this proposition, consider what happened to the U.S. dollar in the late 1970s.

Since generalized floating began in 1973, cumulative, self-fulfilling movements of the exchange rate of the dollar were observed at least twice. The first occurred in the autumn of 1974 and early winter of 1975. The deepening recession in the United States, the decline in U.S. interest rates, and concern over a new outbreak of hostilities in the Middle East combined to cause a sharp decline in the exchange rate of the U.S. dollar. By late January 1975, the dollar had fallen to a level patently inconsistent (at least in retrospect) with the basic strength of the U.S. economy and its trade and payments situations. The Federal Reserve sale of $600 million of foreign currencies drawn under the swap arrangements reversed the decline of the dollar, and the value of the dollar climbed steadily afterwards in 1976. The swap debts were repaid within several months after the use of the funds. A similar sequence of events took place in 1978. As described in the preceding chapter, the dollar became increasingly undervalued throughout 1978 until reversed by massive Federal Reserve intervention in November and December of 1978. All of the swap debts were repaid by the end of April 1979.

These two events had several things in common. They both involved U.S. intervention at the end of a dollar slide that had lasted several months. The deterioration of the exchange rate of the dollar was cumulative, feeding upon itself; and it went too far in relation to the long-run equilibrium value. That the dollar exchange rates prevailing in January 1975 and October 1978 were clearly out of line with the fundamental rates can be seen, in retrospect, by the fact that the dollar climbed steadily after each intervention and that swap debts were paid back each time within several months. If the U.S. intervention had been against the fundamental market forces, it would have required ever-increasing sales of foreign currencies. But, instead, central bank intervention broke the psychological backbone of the cumulative dollar downslide; the market recovered quickly and the rate then moved on its own volition toward the fundamental equilibrium rate.

Causes of Destabilizing Speculation

The dollar's slide had developed not because of a cabal of speculators conspiring to "take the dollar for a ride" but primarily because too many large banks and multinational corporations, imperfectly informed, became too cautious and uncertain about the immediate future prospect of the dollar. They therefore became increasingly hesitant about assuming net positions in dollars, and began to hedge in growing volume against foreign exchange risks. Leads and lags in export and import payments exacerbated the situation. Had the Federal Reserve been more knowledgeable *and* more aggressive, it might have intervened early enough, before the market mood's cumulative deterioration began. This slide could then have been prevented. But Federal Reserve diffidence was countenanced, at least in part, by uncertainties in the central bank about fundamentals. Everyone, even Arthur Burns, lacked perfect knowledge. Therefore, the destabilizing speculation against the dollar that occurred in 1975 and 1978 was not the result of an aggressive conspiracy to "gang up on the dollar" to force depreciation. Instead, it resulted from speculators' uncertainty regarding the long-run equilibrium value of the dollar.

The degree of market inefficiency that existed could be explained by the lack of information available to the market participants concerning fundamental market conditions and concerning the attitude of U.S. monetary authorities. If enough speculators had known, before November 1978, the true fundamentals, more would have acted to counter the incipient destabilizing trend. Alternatively, had speculators known that U.S. monetary authorities were (1) convinced the market was moving away from equilibrium and (2) preparing to abandon their traditional "benign neglect" to intervene against the trend, the private traders would quickly have reversed that destabilizing trend.

The Federal Reserve intervention of 1978 was a milestone in establishing the U.S. dollar as "just one of the currencies." That intervention convinced most of the world's foreign exchange market participants that the U.S. central bank will intervene when its staff believes the exchange rate is moving away from fundamental equilibrium. Private traders have henceforth the need to anticipate future developments in the fundamentals *and* future interpretations and interventions of the Federal Reserve. This may make the market more stable — especially so if the Federal Reserve staff prove more accurate in prediction than individuals who risk their own assets in the market.

EXCHANGE RATE FLUCTUATIONS AND INTERNATIONAL TRADE

Before the practice of floating became widespread, many economists argued eloquently that widely fluctuating rates would have a disastrously restrictive effect on flows of international trade. This prediction, as we saw in the preceding chapter, did not materialize. Since 1973 the volume of world trade has been expanding nearly as fast as before, and the modest reduction in growth seems due entirely to recessions and chaotic government energy policies.

Exchange Rate Fluctuations and the Volume of Trade

The first question now is why anyone should have thought that fluctuating exchange rates would lead private buyers of goods and services to buy less than otherwise. Simple rate changes are surely no threat to trade volume.

Exporters whose currencies appreciate *will* lose sales when the foreign-currency values of their prices rise. But currency appreciation will lower those same exporters' production costs to the extent that they use imported materials which, after the appreciation, will cost less in domestic currency. Therefore, domestic costs will fall, domestic prices of such products may fall, and export prices, in foreign currencies, may not be raised by the full extent of the appreciation.

We noted in Chapter 9 that the appreciation of the yen in recent years has not raised the export prices of Japanese steel products in proportion to the appreciation because the costs of imported raw materials have been reduced by the appreciation. Similarly, the West German central bank reported in its 1974 annual report that appreciation of the mark since floating began "was very largely, though not fully, offset for West German foreign trade by lower cost and price rises in the Federal Republic of Germany."[2]

Of course, most important in this regard is the obvious symmetry in the changes. To the extent that one currency appreciates and so inhibits exports, other currencies depreciate and stimulate exports. There is no *a priori* reason to expect either of these changes to exceed the other.

However, uncertainty, ever the foe of trade, is introduced by the change from fixed to variable exchange rates. That risk threatens every trader with the possibility that the exchange rate at the time a contract is executed will be unfavorably different than at the time the contract was signed. (Of course, every trader faces the possibility that domestic prices — reflecting underlying fundamentals — will change between contract signing and execution. But as we stressed earlier, foreign exchange prices vary more than do fundamentals.)

But even this risk can be eliminated because importers and exporters can protect themselves from exchange risks by using a forward cover. Forward markets for all major currencies up to maturities of one year are now well developed. The costs of forward cover — the differences between the spot and forward rates — do raise the costs of international trade. But even these costs involve symmetrical benefits since only half of the participants in the forward market incur these costs. An exporter who sells a foreign currency forward reaps a *gain* if the currency is quoted at a premium. Similarly, an importer who buys forward exchange at a discount makes a profit. Thus, for international trade as a whole, and excepting bookkeeping transactions costs, the costs of and gains from forward coverage cancel out. The gains and costs even tend to cancel out in the long run for a single exporter or importer if the forward quotation fluctuates between premium and discount.

Further, traders can obtain protection from exchange risks through means other than use of forward markets. If a firm both imports and exports, exchange risks are largely neutralized within itself. In Chapter 13, we noted that hedging can also be accomplished in spot markets. An exporter, for example, borrows foreign currency equal in value to expected foreign currency receivables, and immediately exchanges it for domestic currency in the spot market. The loan is repaid later with the export proceeds. In other cases, export contracts with an exchange rate guarantee may be arranged. For long-term deals, some governments provide exchange-risk guarantees to their exporters.

In sum, exporters and importers have ample opportunities to protect themselves against risks of exchange fluctuations. The steady expansion of the world's trade volume since floating started in 1973 is in part the result of traders taking advantage of these opportunities.

Exchange Rate Fluctuations and the Pattern of Trade

Some prognosticators argued that a free exchange market would result in fluctuations so excessive that they would distort the *pattern* of world trade, shifting resources alternately toward and away from export industries. As we observed in Chapter 9, an industry's international *competitiveness* is determined by the comparative advantage the nation has in the industry's product *and* by the bias (i.e., the deviation from the fundamental equilibrium rate) in the existing rate of exchange. Thus, industries enjoying comparative advantage but located at or near the bottom of the comparative advantage ranking may alternately acquire and lose competitiveness as the actual rate of exchange fluctuates around its long-run equilibrium value. Such shifts would involve unnecessary adjustments on the part of capital and labor, and would be wasteful.

This claim of welfare costs of exchange fluctuations, however, has not been convincingly supported by empirical evidence. Rather, casual empiricism seems to suggest that when exchange rates move adversely, international traders often keep prices at an unprofitable level to protect their market shares. To the extent that the traders enjoy any degree of market power (including less-than-perfect immediate freedom of entry to an otherwise perfectly competitive industry), losses suffered while the exchange rate is unfavorable to them can be offset by extra profits earned while the rate is in their favor. Thus, if the traders price their products in agreement with the fundamental equilibrium rate of exchange, their short-run losses and their short-run extra profits cancel out over an exchange rate cycle, provided, of course, such a cycle is symmetrical.

In this area, we should remember that fixed exchange rates have not guaranteed an undistorted trade pattern. When the fixed rate is not an equilibrium rate (which was often the case before 1973), the competitive advantage of an industry does not necessarily reflect its comparative advantage alone. Worse, such a distortion is likely to persist under a fixed exchange rate system since rate changes under such a system are infrequent as a rule. Thus, when the imperfection of the freely floating rate system (i.e., "excessive" rate fluctuations) is compared with the imperfection of the fixed exchange rate system, we find that there is no *a priori* reason to conclude that the trade-pattern distorting effect of one system is any greater than that of the other.

FLOATING RATES AND INFLATION

Many people have argued that a floating rate system is inflationary. A simple version of the argument runs as follows: If a country tends toward a BOP deficit, the depreciation of its currency immediately raises the price of imports, generating an inflationary pressure. (The depreciation lowers export prices only in foreign currencies.) Before the depreciation has time to effect an improvement in the trade balance, the inflation caused by the depreciation *raises* export prices enough to wipe out the benefits of the depreciation, and the deficit grows instead of disappearing. So the currency depreciates further, creating additional inflationary pressures. Thus, this argument asserts that floating throws a deficit nation into a vicious circle of inflation and depreciation.

But this argument has three serious flaws. First, it does not relate inflation to floating per se; rather, it merely explains the process of inflation in a deficit (depreciating) country. Second, it presumes that the additional domestic inflation will be "enough to wipe out the benefits of the depreciation." But the assumptions are not strong enough to compel that result, while the consequences are not very interesting if they involve only wiping out *some* of the "benefits" of the depreciation.

Third, the argument fails to acknowledge that floating does not create inflationary pressures, but merely confines inflation's consequences within the nation in which they originate, in contrast with a system of fixed exchange rates. When exchange rates are rigid, a nation with a higher rate of inflation than elsewhere runs a BOP deficit and loses its foreign exchange reserves to surplus nations that experience increased inflationary pressures.

Part of the inflationary pressure generated in the deficit country is thus exported to surplus nations. As Professor Gottfried Haberler (1900-) put it: "under fixed exchanges a country can export some of its inflation, while under floating it has to swallow the inflation which it generates."[3]

A more sophisticated argument relating inflation to floating involves the now well-known *ratchet effect* of domestic price changes. Because of the downward rigidity of prices and wages in industrial nations, particularly in the manufacturing sector dominated by big business and big labor, prices tend to rise with an increase in demand but do not fall much with a decrease in demand. Thus, business cycles tend to push prices upward with a ratchet effect, without offsetting declines. The changes in exchange rates, therefore, tend to have asymmetrical effects on prices; depreciation raises domestic prices, but appreciation leaves prices largely unchanged. Although this argument seems to make a lot of common sense, empirical tests thus far have failed to produce an unambiguous conclusion.[4] On an *a priori* ground the ratchet effect is hard to refute; what is in question is its magnitude — whether floating through the ratchet makes a *significant* difference in inflation rates, or affects them only *marginally*.

ISSUES IN EXCHANGE RATE MANAGEMENT

JUSTIFICATION FOR INTERVENTION

The desirability of active official intervention in exchange markets as a matter of policy must be evaluated in the light of the discussion in the preceding section. If the market forces work in such a way as to produce rates that are at or near fundamental equilibrium most of the time, and if deviations of actual rates from the equilibrium level are minor and harmless, then the best policy would be one of *laissez faire* in the foreign exchange market. The preceding discussion, however, led to a conclusion that exchange markets are at times ill-informed and less than fully efficient so that actual exchange rates may deviate substantially from the fundamental rates. We also found that exchange rate fluctuations have recognizable costs in the forms of transactions costs, temporary distortion of trade patterns, and possibly greater inflationary pressures.

What must be stressed at the outset is the basic premise of exchange rate management: official intervention in the foreign exchange markets should not, and cannot, be aimed at influencing long-run equilibrium rates. Equilibrium rates must be compatible with the underlying economic and financial conditions, and only appropriate macroeconomic policies can secure stability in these conditions. If speculators believe a central bank is supporting an exchange rate inconsistent with the fundamental equilibrium value, they can profit surely and handsomely by buying all the currency the central bank sells from its reserves in anticipation of an eventual rise in the undervalued currency's value. Any central bank's reserves, or its swap network credit, however large, will be exhausted by sensible risk-avoiding speculators if the rate the central bank tries to impose on the market is grossly out of line with the long-run equilibrium rate.

What, then, are justifications for exchange rate management by governments? There are two broad categories of justification. First, there is ample justification for smoothing out short-run and erratic fluctuations in the exchange rate which are unrelated to underlying conditions of equilibrium but are caused by transitory or nonrecurring events such as bunching of exchange orders; political, economic, or natural "shocks"; or seasonal variations in trade balances. Intervention of this type will not necessarily produce a fundamental rate change, but will rather limit short-run deviations from it. If the direction of intervention showed no systematic bias, the country's reserves would show no net change in either direction over some meaningful length of time.

The second type of justifiable intervention concerns cumulative movements of exchange rates caused by destabilizing speculation. When, for whatever reasons, a nation's currency value moves markedly in one direction, there often develops an expectation the change will continue. Ordinarily, stabilizing speculation will occur, taking positions in the currency in anticipation of an eventual reversal of the direction of the change.

However, as stressed earlier in this chapter, stabilizing speculation may be weak and insufficient. In 1978, for example, after a continuous decline in the value of the dollar for over a year, participants in foreign exchange markets anticipated a substantial improvement in America's trade balance, the natural consequence of the much cheaper dollar. When the trade balance did not improve — we now know that the J-curve effect was to blame for the delay — the market psychology deteriorated quickly, and the value of the dollar continued to fall. In such an event, monetary authorities should intervene strongly and offer a measure of resistance to the trend away from fundamental equilibrium. Such a policy would offset destabilizing speculation and would reduce divergence between actual and fundamental equilibrium rates. Such intervention would clearly be in harmony with the amended IMF charter that obligates each member nation to "counter disorderly conditions" in the foreign exchange market.

PROBLEMS OF ESTIMATING EQUILIBRIUM RATES

Recognizing the need for intervention is one thing; knowing when and how much to intervene is another. The foregoing discussion implicitly assumed that officials know what the appropriate, long-run equilibrium rate of a currency is at a given moment in time, or at least know when an actual value is "excessively divergent" from the fundamental equilibrium value. In practice, however, estimating the fundamental equilibrium rate is quite difficult. It is difficult for government officials. It is equally difficult for speculators whose livelihoods depend on the accuracy of their decisions.

This difficulty has often accounted for official procrastination in exchange market intervention. If one is not sure as to what the appropriate rate is, then it would be natural to leave the rate movements to market forces and hope for the best. This is the reason why the U.S. officials did not intervene, in early 1975 or late 1978, until it became abundantly clear that a crisis was brewing. Are there not better ways of knowing when intervention is in order? Are there any formulae, criteria, or guidelines for estimating the equilibrium rate of exchange?

Under pure floating with efficient and fully informed exchange markets and no time lag in adjustment, the existing rate at any given moment in time *is* the fundamental equilibrium rate. This definition of exchange market equilibrium is of no use for our present purposes because the need for intervention arises from the very reason that floating is not pure, exchange markets are not fully efficient, there exist time lags in adjustment, and government officials and private speculators must each guess what the other group believes and is about to do. On the other end of the spectrum is a rigidly fixed exchange rate system, under which an equilibrium rate is said to exist when a nation's balance of payments shows no surplus or deficit on an official-reserves-transactions-balance basis over the long run. This definition, too, is of limited use for defining an equilibrium rate under managed floating. Intervention under a system of managed float is a short-run event; intervention should dampen week-to-week and sometimes day-to-day fluctuations, as well as seasonal and cyclical fluctuations in exchange rates. There consequently is no time to wait for the long run (meaning at least several months) to establish an equilibrium rate in reference to payments surplus or deficit.

THE PURCHASING POWER PARITY DOCTRINE

Since a rate of exchange is the ratio of the values — or purchasing power — of two currencies, an equilibrium rate of exchange could presumably be determined by comparison of price levels in the two countries. This method was originally developed in the 1920s and has been known as the *purchasing-power parity* (PPP) *doctrine.* Although the doctrine itself has some serious technical flaws, the concept is often implicit in popular (and sometimes professional) discussions of exchange rate matters. For example, a statement that exchange rate changes do (or should) reflect differences in inflation rates among nations implicitly recognizes a direct relationship between changes in exchange rates and changes in the domestic purchasing power of currencies.

The most sensible version of the PPP doctrine, or the so-called *relative* version, relates *change* in the equilibrium rate of exchange between two currencies to *change* in the price levels in the two countries during the same time period. If, for example, prices in Germany doubled after a base period when the mark-franc exchange rate was in long-run equilibrium, and prices in France did not change during the same time period, then the equilibrium mark-franc rate would be twice as high at the end of the period as in the base period. This apparently straightforward and logical method of estimating equilibrium nonetheless raises many troublesome questions.

Problems with Applications of PPP Theory

How, especially if the government has been intervening persistently, do we find a recent base period when the exchange rate was known to be in fundamental equilibrium? Which type of price index should we use? (Wholesale prices? Consumer prices? Prices of *all* goods and services? Or only prices of *internationally traded* goods and services?) How do we handle the problems of capital flows? (They affect the BOP, yet they are not reflected by price levels.) How do we account for the foreign-trade effects of differences between nations in rates of change in income and output levels? (Income levels as well as price levels affect BOP balances.) Finally, how do we estimate the BOP effects of differences between nations in changes in interest rates? When we examine these questions, we realize that relative changes in prices of goods and services are but *one* — albeit an important one — of the many determinants of the equilibrium rate of exchange.

Should we, then, abandon the PPP comparison as a guide for estimating an equilibrium rate of exchange? Prior to 1973, most international economists would have given a qualified yes to this question. Under an adjustable peg system, exchange rate changes are normally infrequent in most nations, and consequently a considerable length of time usually elapses between them. Often, too, need for adjusting a pegged rate arises because of changes in underlying conditions other than price changes. For this reason, sole reliance on price changes as a guide for making exchange rate changes was considered ill advised.[5]

In recent years, however, there has occurred a resurgence of interest in the PPP method. With floating of major currencies, changes in exchange rates are more frequent, smaller in magnitude, and more spontaneous than under the Bretton Woods system. Studies have shown, too, that changes in national price levels are correlated with long-run changes in exchange rates. A recent study by Henry Goldstein, for example, found that "even under dirty floating, large changes in relative domestic price-levels have substantial and significant impact on the exchange rate." His test covered data for seven major industrial nations over the 15-quarter period, 1973(II) through 1976(IV). (Goldstein also tried to find a correlation between PPP and two other variables — real economic activity and interest rates. But he found no consistent correlation in either case.)[6]

Most commentators now agree that *large* changes in prices — like those during periods of substantial inflation — are the single most important determinant of changes in exchange rates. So *changes* in price-levels can fairly well explain *changes* in exchange rates, particularly over the long run. But, for the reasons enumerated above, PPP is a poor guide for estimating an equilibrium rate of exchange for a given moment in time.

The object of the *absolute* version of the PPP doctrine was determination of such a moment-in-time equilibrium rate in circumstances in which the foreign exchange market had been subject to lengthy government intervention. PPP calculations can cover both goods and services currently traded internationally and goods and services not currently traded. But PPP calculations are not — while equilibrium exchange rates are—affected by changes in interest rates, in capital transactions, in real aggregate incomes, and in expectations of future changes in prices and in all the other variables. For these reasons, PPP is almost totally useless for estimating an equilibrium rate of exchange. At best, PPP provides a rough guide for estimating the direction and magnitude of changes in equilibrium rates of exchange over some length of time.

PPP and Purchasing Power of Currencies

We must point out one useful corollary of the above discussion. Since PPP and exchange rates are determined by different — albeit overlapping — factors, they yield two distinctly separate indexes. In the past, unfortunately, rejection of PPP as a determinant of exchange rates resulted in rejection of the concept of PPP. That was unfortunate because PPP is superior to exchange rates as a measure of several comparative international developments. For example, PPP based on consumer prices provides the best international comparison of living standards; the use of exchange rates — equilibrium rates or not — often gives highly misleading living-standards results for the same reasons that PPP cannot be used to estimate exchange rates. Professor Irving Kravis of the University of Pennsylvania contrasted the 1978 results of the two methods. A mark-dollar PPP rate for 1978, computed by comparing prices of 110 consumer goods and services, was DM3.12/dollar as compared to the average exchange rate for the year of DM2.08/dollar.[7] Thus, a U.S.-German comparison of GNP or of living standards, when made by using the exchange rate, would have grossly overstated the German and understated the American levels.

Today, most international comparisons of domestic economic variables use exchange rates. Table 18-1 shows that such comparisons are misleading. The figures are estimates of per capita consumption of goods and services in 1978 expressed as a percentage of the U.S. level. The first column's figures were compiled by the IMF using the year's average exchange rates. The second column shows estimates of living standards gauged by Kravis using PPP rates.[8] A comparison of the two columns reveals that the use of exchange rates grossly overstates relative consumption levels in Japan, West Germany, and France. For example, per capita consumption in Japan in 1978 was about 56 percent of the U.S. level according to Kravis's estimate, while exchange rate conversion shows a much higher level of 80 percent. These discrepancies point to an important fact students of international economics must bear in mind: the equilibrium rate of exchange equilibrates the balance of payments and the foreign exchange markets; it may not be suited for other purposes, and its careless use in international comparisons may lead to a highly distorted picture of reality.[9]

TABLE 18-1   COMPARISON OF CONSUMPTION LEVELS OF SIX MAJOR
NATIONS USING EXCHANGE RATES AND PPP RATES, 1978
(Percent)

	Using Exchange rate[a]	Using PPP rate[b]
West Germany	94	66
France	88	68
Japan	80	56
United Kingdom	54	57
Italy	47	46
United States	100	100

Source: [a]International Monetary Fund, *International Financial Statistics;* [b]*Wall Street Journal,* 1 May 1979, p. 40.

THE "DIRTY" FLOAT

Because central banks frequently and effectively intervene in foreign exchange markets, the present floating currency system is often re-ferred to as a system of managed or "dirty" floats, to be contrasted with free or "clean" floats. Two important points must be made concerning this distinction. First, as we pointed out in a previous chapter, un-der a system of generalized floats, no currency can float freely or "cleanly" unless every other major currency floats freely. If even one major currency remains fixed or managed, every other currency be-comes a managed currency. Second, an important distinction can be made between merely managed floating and "dirty" floating. Pro-fessor Gottfried Haberler proposes that "dirty floating" refer only to intervention aimed at suppressing or reversing exchange rate move-ments consistent with changes in underlying economic conditions. He would then limit "managed floating" to intervention intended to prevent or moderate sharp and disruptive short-run (i.e., daily and weekly) fluctuations or to moderate (but not suppress or reverse) long-run movements.[10] In this book, we subscribe to this distinction between dirty and managed floating.

Why do policy makers choose "dirty" floating? The most often men-tioned purpose is to gain competitive advantage in trade through com-petitive undervaluation. In 1976, Japan was accused of engaging in competitive undervaluation of the yen, not through depreciation, but through restraining the yen's appreciation while its BOP surplus mounted. C. Fred Bergsten, Senior Fellow of the Bookings Institution, offered this interpretation to the Subcommittee on International Eco-nomics of the U.S. Congress Joint Economic Committee:

> Since early July of 1976, the yen has appreciated by about 5 percent. This is clearly a move in the right direction. There was intervention by the Japanese authorities to keep the rate from rising faster during the appre-ciation, however — published reserves rose by a further $543 million in July and $350 million in August — so the market seemed to want to carry the move further.... The Japanese effort, first to avoid and subsequently to

retard, appreciation of the yen in 1976 was readily understandable. The recovery of the Japanese economy has been sluggish. Unemployment has remained high by Japanese standards. The growth of both consumption and investment has been disappointing. . . .[11]

Japanese government sources, according to Bergsten, denied there was "dirty" floating, and offered a variety of defenses for the Japanese behavior. They avowed the intervention was simply to smooth out the market; the sharp increase in the BOP surplus was wholly cyclical; and Japan's large trade surplus was temporary. Bergsten rejected all these arguments on various technical grounds,[12] and Japan's dollar reserves continued to grow.

Whether the Bank of Japan actually intended to suppress the exchange rate of the yen in the summer of 1976 is hard to prove. Everything considered, however, retrospect appears to show the Bank did suppress a sharp appreciation of the yen that would have hurt Japan's chances of using export-led growth to escape its recession. One thing certain, though, is the fact that Japanese officials did not prevent further appreciation of the yen. Between July 1976 and October 1978, the yen appreciated by 52 percent against the dollar.

Some monetary authorities intervene to *under*value their currencies to encourage exports. Other monetary authorities intervene to *over*value their currencies to make imports cheap. Some nations do the latter to avoid the inflationary effect of rising import prices. Other nations overvalue simply to keep cheap the imports which incumbent governments especially value.

By intervening, monetary authorities can restrain a depreciation of their currency that would raise import prices and generate inflationary pressures. We noted earlier that in the spring of 1979 West Germany tried to slow depreciation of the mark against the dollar out of concern over rising import prices. This concern about rising import prices serves as a benign check against competitive depreciation of currencies. Without this concern about inflation, the temptation to intervene to keep the currency undervalued would be greater. Under the Bretton Woods system, countries could have the cake and eat it too inasmuch as they could keep their currencies undervalued without immediately experiencing inflationary pressures. (Excessive undervaluation would eventually lead to inflation through the tendency of the surplus to effect an increase in money supplies.) Under a floating system, depreciation immediately raises import prices through the terms-of-trade effect. The United States dollar defense program of November 1978 was largely motivated by concern that high import prices were contributing to the high domestic inflation rate.

Many less developed nations utilize both elaborate controls and reserves to maintain overvalued currencies and — to the extent reserve use permits — BOP deficits. Most of these LDC governments then control allocation of foreign exchange and sell it only to nationals importing "approved" goods and services: e.g., pumps, plows, machinery (to substitute cheaply for domestic labor!), and quite often, Mercedes and Scotch.

It goes almost without saying that a "dirty" float need not involve active intervention in foreign exchange markets or even any conspicuous movement of the exchange rate. Any attempt by monetary authorities to keep a rate stable while underlying economic conditions are changing appreciably, constitutes a "dirty" float. Conversely, pressing the rate to change to a degree inconsistent with underlying conditions also constitutes "dirty" management.

The dollar exchange rate has in recent years changed — sometimes — to a degree inconsistent with underlying conditions *not* because of U.S. intervention but because of the U.S. tradition of "benign neglect" derived from the special position of the dollar as the key reserve and intervention currency. Some commentators have called this "dirty float by default."

MONETARY POLICY AND EXCHANGE RATES

A nation's monetary policy is closely related to its exchange rate policy in that when monetary policy generates international differentials in interest rates, short-term capital movements follow and lead to changes in exchange rates. Thus, exchange rates can be influenced directly by intervention in exchange markets, or indirectly by monetary policy that changes interest-rate differentials.

Since monetary policy's effects touch domestic income and prices, and, through changes in interest rates, the exchange rate and the balance of payments, monetary policy measures must be applied with caution so as not to cause adverse effects on the nation's external balances. How much independence has a nation's monetary authority when pursuing monetary policy?

Given one — rather unrealistic — set of assumptions (free floating, free movements of capital, high price elasticities of import demands, the absence of the J-curve effect, and the absence of destabilizing speculation), it can be shown that monetary policy can be pursued without disturbing external balances. Suppose the monetary authorities of a nation currently experiencing a BOP equilibrium adopt an expansionary monetary policy and lower interest rates. This move tends to generate a deficit on both current and capital accounts — on the current account because of rising domestic income and price, and on the capital account because of capital outflow induced by interest arbitrage. But as quickly as goods, services, and securities import demands rise, demand for foreign exchange rises. The domestic currency depreciates, and the quantity supplied (though *not* the supply) of foreign exchange rises as foreigners find this nation's merchandise, services, and — perhaps — shares more attractive. Both imports and exports rise through continuous foreign exchange equilibrium to a new plateau consistent with the initiating nation's new monetary policy. The end result will be a higher level of economic activity and equilibrium in international payments, with a depreciated currency and a current-account surplus offsetting the capital-account deficit caused by interest arbitrage. Conversely, a contractionary monetary policy and higher interest rates will result in a lower level of economic activity, currency appreciation, a payments equilibrium, a current-account deficit, and a capital-account surplus. In general, a change in the autonomous capital-account balance caused by the interest-rate differential will be offset by an opposite change in the current-account balance, so the BOP will remain in equilibrium.

The foregoing analysis is shown graphically in Figure 18-1. The graph is similar to those used in Chapter 15, except that the $(X - M)$ curve is modified to incorporate capital flows. Assume that $(X - M)$ represents the current-account balance, K is the autonomous capital-account balance, and $(X - M + K)$ is therefore the balance of payments. Suppose, in Figure 18-1, both income and international payments are initially in equilibrium at Y_1, where $(S - I) = (X - M + K)$ and $(X - M) = K = 0$. Income is in equilibrium since $(S - I) = (X - M)$, and the balance of payments is in equilibrium because $(X - M + K) = 0$.

An expansionary monetary policy with lower interest rates shifts the $(S - I)$ curve to $(S - I)'$. Externally, the lower interest rate will induce interest arbitrage which will result in capital outflow, turning the value of K negative. Meanwhile, the incipient payments deficit causes the flexible rate to rise (i.e., the currency of the nation depreciates), shifting the $(X - M)$ curve upward to $(X - M)'$. New internal and external equilibria are obtained at income level Y_2, where $(S - I)' = (X - M)'$ — for income equilibrium — and $(X - M + K)' = 0$ for external equilibrium. A current-account surplus of aY_2 just offsets the autonomous capital-account deficit of aY_2, which is equal to the negative of the value of K.

The foregoing analysis implies that there exists a direct, one-to-one relationship between interest-rate differentials and the exchange rates. This relationship holds, of course, only if *all* the assumptions listed above are indeed valid. Any one (or more) of the assumptions may be easily violated, invalidating the direct relationship between interest-rate differentials and the exchange rates. In such a case, of course, the induced changes in autonomous capital flows need not completely offset the changes in the current-account balance caused by the monetary policy measures.

Empirical evidence concerning the relationship between interest-rate differentials and exchange rates is inconclusive. For example, note the peculiar relationship that was observed between the mark-dollar exchange rate and the short-term interest-rate differential between Germany and the United States between 1974 and 1978. The mark-dollar rate and the interest-rate differential expressed as a premium of U.S. certificate-of-deposit (CD) rate over the German interbank rate moved up and down together, almost paralleling each other, during the 1974-76 period. Beginning in early 1977 and until the end of 1978, however, they moved in exactly opposite directions; the mark-dollar

S,I,X,M,K

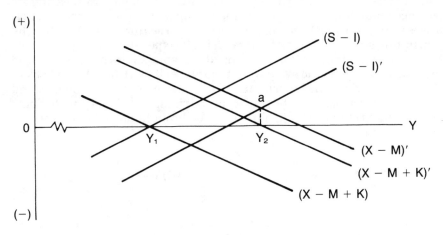

Figure 18-1
Effects of Expansionary Monetary Policy with a Freely Floating Exchange Rate

rate declined sharply while the U.S. interest-rate premium over the German rate rose continuously.

THE PROBLEM OF RISING OIL PRICES

The price of oil rose from about $12 a barrel in 1974 to about $14 in 1978, but the real price of oil fell during the period because the world inflation rate was even higher. As noted in the preceding chapter, the current-account surplus of the OPEC nations fell sharply between 1974 and 1978 as their imports of goods and services rose much faster than expected. The international money and capital markets, thanks in part to the flexible exchange rates, managed to weather the storm of rising oil prices and succeeded in recycling the huge surpluses of the oil exporting nations. Thus, the earlier pessimism concerning the viability of the international monetary and financial systems had largely evaporated by 1978.

The situation, however, turned drastically for the worse in 1979. The continued expansion of world industrial output, coupled with the Iranian crisis in the spring of 1979, created a condition of tight oil supply for the first time since 1973-74, enabling OPEC to raise the price of oil in several steps in 1979. Between the end of 1978 and the end of 1979, the average price of oil almost doubled, rising from about $14 to about $28 a barrel. (The average price in the summer of 1980 was about $30 a barrel.) Such sharp increases in the oil price might be repeated in the 1980s. Whether the international economy is capable of repeating its past accomplishments and absorbing the impact of such increases in oil prices is an open question. Some observers are beginning to fear that the continuing strain of paying for increasingly expensive oil may sooner or later topple the international financial system. Others believe that the international economic system that managed to withstand the shock of the quadrupling of the oil price in 1973-74 will continue to find new and better ways of absorbing the impact of the rising OPEC surpluses. Some even predict that OPEC surpluses will be brought down before the end of the decade.

THE SPECTER OF CHRONIC GLOBAL STAGFLATION

The most immediate impact of the soaring oil price on the world economy is its impact on the general price level. According to one econometric study, the oil price increases of 1979 were estimated to add about 2 percent in 1979 and 1.3 percent in 1980 to the U.S. inflation rates.[13] The rising oil price has also had a contractionary effect on the oil importing nations as governments have tried to control inflation by imposing tight monetary and fiscal policies. According to the same study, the 1979 oil price increases reduced the real gross national product of the United States by 1.1 percent in 1979 and 2.8 percent in 1980.[14] Thus, oil importing nations are threatened by the specter of chronic stagflation (i.e., stagnation-cum-inflation) for years to come.

We do assume that the OPEC monopoly's price increases contribute to general price inflation. We assume that the institutions created during the Great Depression assure this result. But it was not always so. Once upon a time when a monopoly raised price and took a larger portion of buyers' spending, economists would have predicted a drop in buyers' demand for other items. The consequent price declines on those items would add to *relative* price changes but would have left the *general* price index *unchanged*. Once upon a time. Now, we assume business and labor institutions and central banks will not permit the prices of those other items to fall very much.

The soaring oil price also has an ominous implication for world trade. Concerned about the costs of ever more expensive imported oil, the leaders of industrial nations consider restrictions on other imports and devious devices to expand their exports. Simultaneous attempts by all the industrial nations to trim imports and expand exports artificially may result in the resurgence of beggar-thy-neighbor protectionism and worldwide trade wars. During the 1980s, in contrast with the 1974-79 period, the OPEC nations may not increase their imports of goods and services as rapidly as their oil revenue. Leaders of some OPEC nations (particularly Arab nations) fear that an attempt to modernize their society too rapidly may bring about political unrest as it did in Iran. In a different direction, the oil importing LDCs are not in a position to absorb expanding exports from the industrial nations because the only way they can repay their rising debts to the oil exporting nations is by expanding their own net exports. The cheering generalization remains, of course, that every increase in exports tends to generate a matching increase in imports on the part of the exporter or on the part of nations borrowing from the exporter.

THE THREAT OF DEFAULT ON LDC LOANS

For the oil importing LDCs, higher prices of oil mean fewer oil imports, more exports, currency depreciation, or increased debts. The oil importing LDCs' current-account deficits totaled less than $10 billion in 1973 but increased sharply through the 1970s, matched by an increase in their combined capital-account surpluses (i.e., net borrowing). The LDC borrowing to finance oil, development-related, and frivolous imports took the form of direct loans from some OPEC nations, loans from the special IMF oil facility, loans from the World Bank, floating of long-term bonds in the world's capital markets, and borrowing in the Eurocurrency market. Eurocurrency loans took the form of revolving credits, typically for a period of three to eight years but for as long as fifteen years in some cases, with interest rates readjusted every six months to changes in the six-month Eurodollar time-deposit rate of London banks, known as the London interbank offering rate, or LIBOR.

In 1979-80, the LDCs were caught in a two-way squeeze between sharply higher oil prices and the industrialized economies' recession that reduced the demand for LDC exports. The LDC current-account deficit totaled $45 billion in 1979 and was expected to rise to $55 billion or above in 1980. LDC debt increased at an annual rate of 15 to 16 percent. It rose from $100 billion in 1974 to $300 billion in 1980. Their combined debt-service obligations rose from $15 billion in 1974 to some $50 billion in 1980.[15]

Most developed industrial nations have managed to pay for increased oil bills by exporting more goods and services. In contrast, the non-oil LDCs have borrowed more. Private lenders have been convinced they would be repaid. But if many LDCs are one day forced to declare default on all private debts, the world's financial and economic system will be hit by a crisis of enormous proportions. If that day comes, the OPEC monopoly may stand revealed as a most cruel monster.

The foregoing analysis leads us to conclude that the best way to keep sharply rising oil prices from cruelly distorting the structure of world trade and finance is to restrain the growth of petrodollars and to find better and more effective means of recycling the growing volume of petrodollars. Such a means will have to involve increased oil prices in the United States and Canada to reduce oil imports, and recycling practices in which oil exporters receive secure IOUs.

The OPEC nations' surplus of oil revenues over their import bills was expected to be about $110 billion in 1980, or roughly twice as much as the 1979 figure. The non-oil LDCs' payments deficit for 1980, in contrast, was expected to reach $70 billion. These developments generated much interest, in the spring of 1980, in the idea of having the IMF set up a new facility called the "substitution account" whereby the OPEC's surplus dollars were to be absorbed by the IMF and loaned out to developing nations experiencing serious BOP difficulties. The OPEC surplus nations were to deposit their petrodollars in this account in exchange for special, interest-bearing IMF liabilities denominated in SDRs. To make such assets attractive to the OPEC nations, it was proposed that the new IMF account could be backed by some of the IMF's gold holdings.

Although the proposal of a gold backed substitution account received strong support from most of the developed nations, neither the OPEC nations nor the non-oil LDCs were enthusiastic about the plan. The OPEC nations were concerned about the IMF's ability to pay attractive interest rates on the deposits, and the developing nations were fearful that the plan, if implemented, would substantially diminish the amount of IMF gold that could be sold to the public. (As discussed in the preceding chapter, the auctioning of IMF gold provided billions of dollars of loanable funds for developing nations.) Because of these and other political and technical problems, the proposal of the gold backed substitution account was shelved indefinitely at the April 1980 meeting of the Fund's policy group.[16]

STUDY QUESTIONS

1. What are the "underlying economic conditions" that affect the exchange rate of a currrncy?
2. What causes a foreign exchange market to "misbehave"? (Assume there is no government intervention.)
3. Is the absence of government intervention a sufficient condition for exchange market equilibrium? Why or why not?
4. Under what circumstances would government intervention in foreign exchange markets be clearly desirable? What type of intervention should governments avoid?
5. Does the system of floating exchange rates tend to contribute to global inflation? Critically evaluate.
6. What is wrong with trying to estimate a change, over time, in the fundamental equilibrium rate between two currencies from changes in the price levels in the two countries during the same time period?
7. How is "dirty floating" defined in this book? Does the IMF condone (or encourage) dirty floating? clean floating?
8. What considerations would motivate governments to engage in dirty floating?
9. In general, what is the relationship between the interest-rate differential and the exchange rate? Briefly explain why a given monetary policy measure, say a lower interest rate, need not disturb the external balance.
10. Reproduce lines $(S - I)$ and $(X - M + K)$ of Figure 18-1. In your sketch show the consequences of a shift to a restrictive monetary policy. Then, write an explanation of the effects shown in your graph.

11.   Why might OPEC's price increases lead to the imposition of foreign exchange controls by the governments of oil importing LDCs? How might such controls work?

ENDNOTES

1. Jacques R. Artus and Andrew D. Crockett, "Floating Exchange Rates and the Need for Surveillance," Princeton University, *Essays in International Finance*, No. 127, May 1978, p. 4.
2. *Report of the Deutsche Bundesbank for the Year 1974*, p. 58; cited in Jacob S. Dreyer et al., eds., *Exchange Rate Flexibility* (Washington, D.C.: American Enterprise Institute, 1978), pp. 35-36.
3. Gottfried Haberler, "The International Monetary System after Jamaica and Manila," *Weltwirtschaftliches Archiv*, 1977, pp. 1-27; reprinted in John Adams, ed., *The Contemporary International Economy: A Reader* (New York: St. Martin's Press, 1979), p. 223.
4. Andrew D. Crockett and Morris Goldstein, "Inflation under Fixed and Flexible Exchange Rates," *IMF Staff Papers*, March 1976, pp. 226-271.
5. For an excellent survey of studies on the PPP theory, see: Lawrence H. Officer, "The Purchasing-Power-Parity Theory of Exchange Rates: A Review Article," *IMF Staff Papers*, March 1976, pp. 1-60.
6   Henry N. Goldstein, "Floating Exchange Rates and Modified Purchasing Power Parity: Evidence from Recent Experience Using an Index of Effective Exchange Rates," *Proceedings of 1978 West Coast Academic/Federal Reserve Economic Research Seminar*, pp. 166-183.
7. "Despite the Dollar's Decline, U.S. Retains Top Living Standard among Major Nations," *Wall Street Journal*, 1 May 1979, p. 40.
8. *Ibid.*
9. See P.A. David, "Just How Misleading Are Official Exchange Rate Conversions?" *Economic Journal*, September 1972, pp. 979-990.
10. Haberler, "International Monetary System," p. 227.
11. U.S. Congress, *Guidelines for Exchange Market Intervention*, Hearing before the Subcommittee on International Economics of the Joint Economic Committee, 94th Cong., 2nd sess., 18 October 1976 (Washington, D.C.: Government Printing Office, 1977), p. 12.
12. *Ibid.*, pp. 13-14.
13. "The Price That Costly Oil Exacts from the Economy," *Business Week*, 24 December 1979, p. 11.
14. *Ibid.*
15. "The Petro-Crash of the '80s," *Business Week*, 19 November 1979, pp. 178-79.
16. "IMF Interim Committee Keeps Its Focus on Inflation and Recycling of Oil Dollars," *Wall Street Journal*, 28 April 1980, p. 10.

PART VII
ECONOMIC DEVELOPMENT, MNCs, AND STATE TRADING

19

Economic Development and International Trade

By *economic development,* we mean a persistent increase in the real income of the typical families in an area. Such economic development means change, and a principal developmental change is the growth of trade. When an area begins to develop, it begins to produce more of particular products. It therefore exports more of those products and imports more of others. If the developing area is only a small part of a nation, the increased trade may be mostly internal. But if the developing area comprises all or most of a nation, much of the increased trade will be international.

If the world's developing nations, initially poor, are to rise out of poverty, they must be able to export to — and import from — the developed nations. But vested interests in the developed nations often resist the changes required if the poor are to increase their exports. The increased exports from comparative advantage producers in developing nations always inconvenience developed-nation producers who resent their fall to comparative disadvantage inferiority. The comparative disadvantage producers usually resist; and, if they can afford to obtain political clout, they can restrict trade and inhibit the economic development of the aspiring poor. In Chapter 12, we reported briefly on the efforts of America's comparative disadvantage sugar and steel producers to prevent their displacement by comparative advantage producers in the developing poor nations.

Despite the obstacles thrown up by the sugar and steel lobbies and by numerous other lobbies in developed nations, many poor nations have achieved significant economic development during the past century. This chapter concentrates upon the growth experience and the foreign trade experience of developing nations in recent decades.

A COMMON PATTERN

Many successful developing nations follow much the same pattern as they become more productive and move away from their initial circumstances of subsistence agriculture. First, subsistence farm families add to the size of their farms. They continue to grow food on the same areas as before. But they use all of the additional land to produce export crops.

Second, import substitution begins. That is to say, small domestic firms expand to produce manufactures initially imported in exchange for the farmers' new exports. The new firms are protected by distance and the shipping costs of imports. As the little manufacturers grow, they bid workers away from agriculture.

Third, some of the now larger manufacturers acquire comparative advantage in world markets and begin to export. These firms must pay wages that attract more workers out of agriculture. In the twentieth century, health has improved so rapidly in the poor nations that population growth has provided additional urban workers at wages well below those that would have been required if nineteenth century death rates had persisted.

Fourth, the narrow concentration of manufactured exports in a few industries gives way to a spreading comparative advantage. The developing area exports an increasing, and a changing, variety of manufactures.

Finally, growth of the service sector accelerates both absolutely and relatively. The relative importance of manufacturing declines. In 1980, in Africa, Latin America, and Asia, only Japan was in this final phase.

Each of these phases of economic development requires changes in production methods and growth of trade. For comparison, observe the nineteenth century experience of Europe's great powers as evidence of the importance of the growth of foreign trade during economic development. Between the Napoleonic Wars and World War I, European foreign trade grew rapidly. Most arresting, the foreign trade of each large European nation grew as a percent of that nation's GNP.

Over the years 1827-35, United Kingdom commodity exports were 9 percent of the kingdom's GNP. Over the years 1909-13, commodity exports were 19 percent of GNP.[1]

Between 1825 and 1834, French commodity exports averaged only 7 percent of National Income. Over the years 1905-13, commodity exports averaged 26 percent of French National Income.[2]

In 1840, German commodity exports were estimated to have been 7 percent of National Income. Over the immediate prewar years, 1910-13, commodity exports were 18 percent of German National Income.[3]

This is not, we must caution, a theory of cause and effect. A nation's government cannot simply decide to export in order to grow. But the historical evidence is clear. In most cases in which the real incomes of a nation's typical families have grown rapidly, that nation's exports and imports have grown even more rapidly. Observing this phenomenon, the Norwegian economist, Ragnar Nurkse, argued that exports were the "engine of growth" for many nations, especially Argentina, Australia, Canada, New Zealand, South Africa, the United States, and Uruguay.[4] An American economist, Irving Kravis, reviewed the data for these countries and others and concluded that "engine of growth" was misleading, for that metaphor made exports the driving force required to lead growth. Instead, Kravis suggested foreign trade deserves the title, the "handmaiden of growth."[5] We offer that as a term that vividly portrays the association, not necessarily causal, that persists between growth of trade and growth of family real income.

THE FIRST STEP AWAY FROM SUBSISTENCE AGRICULTURE

We have argued that for most nations, economic development involves a pattern with five phases. Between 1880 and 1914, the first step in that pattern was taken by most of the tropical nations in the world.

In 1850, most of the people in the world made their livings in subsistence agriculture. They worked with little physical capital and with primitive, but decidedly ingenious, technologies. Per capita outputs were small, and death rates were so high that population growth was quite modest. Subsistence families, as the name implies, got by on their own production. They had little to trade. There were few traders.

But after 1880, that condition changed throughout the tropics. European traders arrived with offers that farm families accepted. Trade expanded, output per family rose, and death rates fell.

The subsistence farm family, dependent for survival on its own crops, continued to produce its own food. But each family increased its workload by increasing the area it cultivated. On this added area, families planted rubber, cacao, palm oil, coconut, and mulberry trees, tea and coffee bushes, rice, peanuts, and cotton. Their additional products were sold. Millions of farm families, mostly in the tropics, moved in a few decades from subsistence to commercial agriculture.

Nobel laureate W. Arthur Lewis has explored that change most thoroughly.[6] He stresses the universality of the change.

> The response did not depend on race, religion, or culture. [There was] rapid growth in all tropical areas, whether the participants were Catholic, Buddhist, Pagan, white, black, or yellow, aggressive, as the Columbians are said to be, happy-go-lucky like the Brazilians, or "mystical" like the Burmese. Wherever fresh lands existed that could be profitably used, the people responded abundantly.[7]

A few countries, India, Java, and Egypt in particular, had little unused land in 1880. Their farm families were unable to expand their little farms and join the transformation. But in tropical countries other than India, tropical exports increased an average of three percent per year between 1883 and 1913.[8]

The character of the transformation is shown in the subsistence-family production possibility frontier of Figure 19-1. Subsistence crops are shown on the x axis. Commercial crops are shown on the y axis. In isolation, the family produced well inside their possibility frontier. With little or no opportunities for trade, families have no reason to produce rubber, cacao, or cotton beyond the small amounts they use themselves. Further, they produce less food than they could produce working full time because they are able to produce all the food they can eat by working less than full time.

Nevertheless, each year, most subsistence families suffer some months with little food and some weeks of near starvation. This suffering results from the tropical combination of climate, insects, rodents, and bacterial spoilage. Throughout the tropics, a dry season, with little or no rain for three to six months, permits harvests during only a portion of the year. Subsistence families must store food for use during the dry season and during the initial months of the rainy season. But irresistibly aggressive insects, rodents, and bacteria limit the amounts of food that can be kept into the last weeks before the next harvest. In West Africa in the 1970s, a rule of thumb was that one half of stored food would be lost in just three months of storage. Choosing an optimal allocation of time among crop growing, crafts, religious duties, social exchanges, and leisure; subsistence families choose a production combination like that of Point A in Figure 19-1.

During the transformation of the tropics after 1880, subsistence farmers moved to a production combination like that of Point E, in Figure 19-1, *on* the production possibilities frontier. They continued to produce — roughly — the same amount of food. They added production of a commercial crop.

Adam Smith, ignorant of the concept of comparative advantage, had argued that foreign trade benefited a country by enabling it to use land and labor that would otherwise be unused. The classical economists, stressing gains from comparative advantage, criticized Smith for this assertion. But given the assumptions of the model in Figure 19-1, Smith was right.

Of course comparative advantage is also "right." Yet the family producing at E might continue to do so even though comparative advantage would identify an "optimal" production point to the left of E. The constraint felt by the family followed from the unreliability of foreign traders in the tropics. If the family produced at E, and war, bankruptcy, death, or negligence kept the foreign trader from buying the family's commercial crop, the family members would find themselves greatly inconvenienced; but they would still have their own food production. If the family moved production well to the left of E, it would become dependent on trade for food. If the traders then failed to appear with food, some of the family might die.

Between 1880 and 1913, the farm families of Ghana (then the Gold Coast) created the world's largest cacao industry. Lacking transportation facilities, they moved most of each year's millions of tons of product on their heads. They were willing to work hard and to trade, but decades

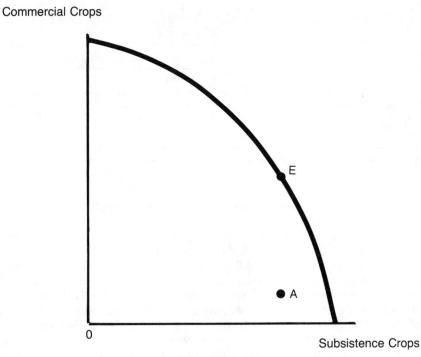

Commercial Crops

Subsistence Crops

Figure 19-1
Production Possibility Frontier for a Subsistence Farm Family Producing First
in Isolation Then When Trading with Outsiders

passed before they were able to feel secure enough to begin comparative
advantage specialization and move to production to the left of E.[9]

DEPRESSED INTERLUDE BEFORE THE
RESUMPTION OF WORLD DEVELOPMENT

A peak was reached in 1913, the culmination of a century of economic
development touching, eventually, most of the earth's people. Then the
guns of August 1914 introduced nearly forty years of depression, war,
and labored recovery from the effects of war. General development was
not resumed until after 1948.

Table 19-1 contrasts the quarter century, 1948-73, with the 35 years,
1913-48, for the entire world (excepting Russia, China and nations
dominated by them). Between 1913 and 1948, the world's real output
grew little faster than population, and world trade grew less rapidly
than population. Comparative advantage specialization among nations
was reduced as international trade per person fell; and output per
person rose only one percent a year on average. In the quarter century
after 1948, world population growth doubled, but output rose more than
twice as fast; international trade grew even more rapidly; and per capita

TABLE 19-1 CONTRAST BETWEEN 1913-48 AND 1948-73 IN PERCENTAGE GROWTH OF GROSS WORLD PRODUCT AND OF WORLD TRADE: TOTALS AND PER CAPITA

	Average annual change	
	1913-48	1948-73
Gross world product	+2%	+5%
Per capita GWP	+1%	+3%
World trade	+½%	+7%
Per capita world trade	−½%	+4.5%

Source: Richard Blackhurst, et al., *Trade Liberalization, Protectionism, and Interdependence* (Geneva: GATT, 1977), pp. 7-8.

output grew at triple the rate of the war-and-depression interlude. Economic development again reached — in different degrees — most of the world's people.

The families of the tropics shared in the post-1914 fall in the growth rates of output and of trade. Between 1883 and 1913, the quantity of the tropics' foreign trade grew 3.6 percent per year. From 1953 to 1967, it grew 4.5 percent a year. But between 1913 and 1950, tropical trade grew only 2.2 percent per year,[10] and between 1929 and 1937, the volume of tropical trade grew only 1.6 percent a year. Further, because the prices of tropical exports fell more than did the prices of tropical imports, the tropics exported 1.6 percent more per year during the thirties but were each year able to buy *fewer* imports than the year before. Tropical development came almost "to a standstill" during this 37 years of depression.[11]

MANUFACTURING: IMPORT SUBSTITUTION, THEN COMPARATIVE ADVANTAGE SPECIALIZATION

When the depression and the world wars finally ended, economic development became once more widespread, though far from universal. Table 19-2 compares growth in the already developed countries (Western Europe, Japan, Canada, and the United States) with growth in the developing nations (most in the tropics). For lack of data, China, Russia and nations dominated by them are omitted from the calculations.

Between 1953 and 1973, real output grew more rapidly in the developing countries (LDCs) than in the developed countries (DCs). But because population grew more rapidly in the LDCs than in the DCs, real output per person grew more rapidly in the DCs, 4 percent, than in the LDCs, 3 percent.

An important caution: the statistics of Table 19-2 are rough averages for a large number of dissimilar countries. Some countries, included in the averages, experienced very little economic development (e.g., Britain, Upper Volta, Burma, Argentina). Some experienced very rapid development (e.g., Spain, Japan, Taiwan, South Korea). When concerned with any particular country, one must look at its particular

TABLE 19-2   CONTRAST BETWEEN LESS DEVELOPED COUNTRIES
AND DEVELOPED COUNTRIES IN GROWTH OF NATIONAL PRODUCT:
TOTAL AND PER CAPITA, 1953-73
(Average Annual Change)

	LDCs	DCs
Gross national product	+6%	+5%
Per capita GNP	+3%	+4%

Source: Richard Blackhurst et al., *Adjustment, Trade, and Growth in Developed and Developing Countries* (Geneva: GATT, 1978), p.7.

statistics. In almost every instance, they will be quite different from the averages reported here.

As economic development has progressed in the LDCs in recent decades, manufacturing has grown and has bid workers away from agriculture. Table 19-3 shows that manufacturing grew some 25 percent faster in the LDCs than in the DCs between 1963 and 1973. Despite the meanness of the OPEC monopoly that slowed growth for both rich and poor, the LDCs maintained a 6 percent growth rate between 1973 and 1976. As Table 19-3 shows, the LDC growth rate became twice that of the DCs.

TABLE 19-3   CONTRAST BETWEEN LESS DEVELOPED
AND DEVELOPING COUNTRIES IN GROWTH OF
MANUFACTURES 1963-73 AND 1973-76
(Average Annual Change)

	LDCs	DCs
1963-73	+7.5%	+6%
1973-76	+6%	+3%

Source: Blackhurst et al., *Adjustments, Trade, and Growth*, p.8.

However, as we earlier reported in Chapter 12 and in the opening paragraphs of this chapter, labor, management, and owners in developed-country manufacturing have successfully erected barriers, especially quotas, to LDC manufacturing exports. As a result, LDC exports as a share of world manufacturing exports are down. More on this shortly.

Despite DC opposition, the common pattern of economic development has continued to unfold in many countries. The expansion of commercial agriculture has been followed by the growth of manufacturing, the growth of manufacturing exports, and the diversification of manufacturing exports.

In the tropics, many farm families have, in the circumstances of the Figure 19-1 example, begun to specialize in comparative advantage crops, have cut back on food growing, moved to the left *along* their PPFs, and have approached the conditions of the Figure 5-14 Southern equilibrium. They specialize in a cash crop and import food. Simultaneously with such moves to specialization, national PPFs move out as capital accumulates, literacy spreads, and economies diversify.

Table 19-4 shows the dramatic changes that occurred between 1963 and 1976 in the list of "Most Important LDC Exporters of Manufactures." Hong Kong nearly maintained its position at the top of the list, but India, Mexico, Israel, Pakistan and Argentina suffered sharp drops in relative importance. In contrast, Singapore, Brazil, Thailand, the Philippines and — most impressively — South Korea catapulted upward in importance.

Finally, among the leading developing countries, manufacturing exports have become more diversified. We can measure product concentration in manufacturing exports by identifying products according to the Standard International Trade Classification. We can then look at a nation's ten most important export products to see the share of manufacturing exports made up of those ten.

In 1965, ten products made up 70 percent of all South Korean manufacturing exports. But as comparative advantage spread to other products in the developing economy, the leading ten products made up only 53 percent of manufacturing exports in 1976. In Brazil, the fall in importance of the top ten, between 1965 and 1976, was from 55 to 39 percent. Even in laggard India, the top ten manufactured exports fell from 79 percent of all manufactured exports in 1965 to 53 percent in 1976.[12]

EXPORTS AS AN ENGINE OF GROWTH

We have stressed the historical association of economic development and growth of foreign trade. We have also stressed our view that that relationship is not always one of cause and effect. However, there are important cases in which the relationship *is* one of cause and effect.

For many of today's industrial nations, international trade did serve, and still serves, as a powerful engine of growth (for which term, here, read "development").

Consider the many ways in which the growth of a nation's foreign trade can serve to raise the real incomes of that nation's families. First,

TABLE 19-4 PORTION OF LDC MANUFACTURING EXPORTS ORIGINATING IN PARTICULAR COUNTRIES: 1963 CONTRASTED WITH 1976
(Percent)

	1963	1976
Hong Kong	20	16
India	20	7
Mexico, Israel, Pakistan, and Argentina together	17	11
Singapore	1	4
Brazil	1	6
South Korea	1	16
Thailand	Under 1	4
The Philippines	Under 1	4

Source: Blackhurst et al., *Adjustment, Trade, and Growth*, pp. 19-20.

of course, trade permits comparative advantage specialization. Resources are, therefore, used more efficiently, and real incomes rise. This involves comparative statics. With restrictions on trade, resources are used less efficiently. As restrictions are removed, resources are used more efficiently. This kind of change moves production out from inside the world's production possibility frontier to a point nearer to that frontier. But freer trade does not itself move the possibility frontier. Yet each expansion of trade has a secondary effect that does move the production possibility frontier out. As trade grows, technological information moves from the DCs to the LDCs. This information flow adds to the human capital stock of LDC manufacturers, farmers, financiers, and traders. To get products in the form they want, DC importers must contribute to this information flow. To get products in the form they want, LDC exporters must pass on this information to their local suppliers. Some of this information flow is mundane, e.g., how to arrange machines and workers to shape a particular piece of plastic. Much is more esoteric, e.g., how to arrange, whom to see, for loans; how to cope with DC government regulations; how to design, package, and finance for DC markets.

Further, the growth of LDC trade brings DC investors information regarding production possibilities in the LDCs. There then follow, where the information is favorable, capital movements from the DCs to the LDCs. For the LDCs, this has the happy result of raising the average and marginal products of labor without the need for labor to forego consumption in order to permit domestic investment.

JAPAN, TAIWAN, AND SOUTH KOREA

Japan was an LDC at the turn of the century. By the eve of World War II, Japan had become a semideveloped country. The most rapid growth of the Japanese economy took place in the 1950s and 1960s, so that by the end of the 1960s the nation had overtaken the West in technological sophistication in most areas.

Throughout the 1950s and 1960s, exports served as a powerful engine of growth for the Japanese economy. Not that the growth was "led" by exports; exports accounted for only about 10 or 11 percent of the nation's GNP. Japan's experience can be better described as one of export-*supported* growth. Exports enabled Japan to acquire the foreign exchange necessary for imported raw materials, fuels, foodstuffs, and sophisticated capital equipment. Japan's entrepreneurs seized the "advantages of backwardness."[13] They purchased the more advanced nations' latest technology, made it (more so in the earlier years) labor intensive, and built it into new plants, many of them producing a sizable portion of their output for export.

During the 1970s, a handful of semideveloped countries (SDCs) — notably Taiwan and South Korea — have displayed rapid export-led growth. Table 19-5 compares gross national product per capita of Japan, South Korea, and Taiwan over the 1953-1978 period expressed as a

TABLE 19-5   GNP PER CAPITA OF JAPAN, SOUTH KOREA, AND TAIWAN,
1953-1978, AS PERCENT OF U.S. GNP PER CAPITA

	Japan	South Korea	Taiwan
1953	9.8	5.6	6.5
1958	13.5	6.9	5.1
1963	22.3	4.5	5.9
1968	32.4	4.3	7.2
1969	34.8	5.1	7.1
1970	39.3	5.4	8.1
1971	41.8	5.3	8.5
1972	50.9	5.4	9.0
1973	61.6	6.2	10.5
1974	63.1	7.8	13.1
1975	62.8	7.9	12.7
1976	63.3	9.5	12.2
1977	70.0	10.8	13.6
1978	88.4	12.9	14.7

Source: International Monetary Fund, *International Financial Statistics*, various issues.

percent of U.S. gross national product per capita. Taiwan and South Korea are following Japan's lead with a lag of 15 to 20 years. For example, as Table 19-5 shows, Japan's GNP per capita reached 10 percent of the U.S. GNP per capita about 1953. Taiwan reached the same level in 1972-73, and South Korea did so in about 1977-78.

While Japan's wages (reflected by GNP per capita) are rapidly approaching the U.S. level, those in Taiwan and Korea are still considerably below the U.S. level. Thus, Taiwan and South Korea can be expected to show continued rapid growth in the years to come, taking advantage of their relatively low wage rates combined with rising technological sophistication. We noted earlier (Chapter 8) that the commodity composition of these two nations' exports is becoming more like that of Japan in the 1960s. In the early 1980s, the industrial nations will encounter a flood of low-price, high-quality Made-in-Korea and Made-in-Taiwan motorcycles, steel, cameras, ships, television sets, and automobiles.

Figure 19-2 shows that the export growth of Taiwan and Korea over the 1968-78 period was more rapid than that of Japan. The growth of the two SDCs' exports during the 1975-78 period was especially impressive. Volume nearly doubled in just three years.

The association between trade growth and economic development is clear-cut. During the 1975-78 period, the Japanese worker's real monthly earnings (i.e., nominal earnings adjusted for the rise in consumer prices) rose nine percent. In South Korea, the comparable figure was a 67 percent increase.

We want to make two points about the rapid rise in wages in SDCs. First, the growth of trade has been followed by the growth of real wages, i.e., by economic development. Second, the growth of real wages has been followed by the growth of exports.

Initially low wages resulted from relatively abundant labor. That abundance gave the SDCs (then, LDCs) comparative advantage in

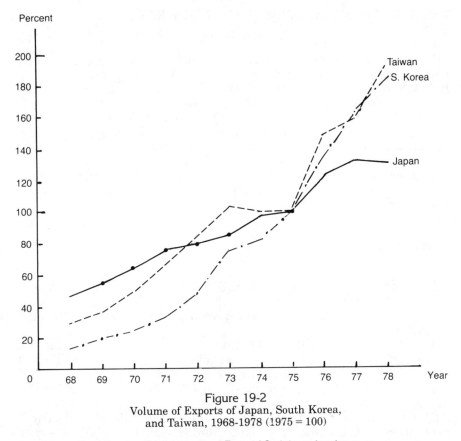

Figure 19-2
Volume of Exports of Japan, South Korea,
and Taiwan, 1968-1978 (1975 = 100)

Source: International Monetary Fund, *International Financial Statistics*, various issues.

export goods — textiles, apparel, footwear, and electric and electronic products — characterized by relatively unsophisticated technology and relatively high labor intensity.

As the SDCs moved into comparative advantage manufacturing, labor productivity and real incomes rose. Concurrently, entrepreneurial, managerial, and labor experience and sophistication changed in ways that brought comparative advantage in new areas. Human and physical capital accumulated; the variety of manufacturing exports increased; and real wages grew further. Economic development appeared to feed upon itself; but, as we shall stress below, government "reforms" can easily halt economic development.

As the per capita incomes of the SDCs continue to rise following Japan's lead, many more new "Japans" will undoubtedly appear in the international trade scene of the 1980s. Singapore is already doing as well as — if not better than — Taiwan and South Korea. Mexico, Malaysia, and Brazil are often mentioned as the next-generation SDCs. The underdeveloped parts of Europe — Spain, Portugal, Greece, and Turkey — may also be ripe for an economic "take-off."

THE SOUTH KOREAN – ARGENTINEAN CONTRAST

We turn now to a comparison, or — more precisely — a contrast, between two countries: one, we have already briefly considered, the Republic of Korea, is representative of nations that have joined the world's market economy and have grown; the other, Argentina, is representative of nations that have opted out of the world economy by concentrating on comparative disadvantage import substitution. In South Korea, foreign trade has grown — both exports and imports — and economic development has been rapid. In Argentina, foreign trade stagnated for decades, and economic development has been very slow. The contrast is in large part the result of deliberate government policies.

South Korea

First, about Korea. From 1910 to 1945, Korea was a Japanese colony. In 1945, the country was divided at the 38th parallel. Russia occupied the North. An American military government ruled the South until August 1948.

The South is smaller in area than the state of Virginia, but its population is more than seven times Virginia's. Much of the land is mountainous. Only one-fifth is arable.

The North invaded the South in June 1950. An armistice ended the war in July 1953.

The division of the country had left the South with little electrical generating capacity. Manufacturing was disrupted by the political split and by war. In 1953, manufacturing production was only one-third of the 1940 level.[14] Calculated in 1976 prices, per capita income was only $196.[15]

During the next ten years, the Korean government concentrated on maximizing receipts of U.S. government aid and on tariff and quota protection of import-substituting nondurable consumer goods. Between 1953 and 1962, economic development proceeded slowly and without much of an increase in exports. In 1960, per capita GNP reached $244 (in 1977 prices).[16]

During the 1945-60 period, two institutional changes laid a base for accelerated development. Large landholdings (many taken from the Japanese) were divided among farm families. In 1958, the average farm size was 2.2 acres; and no one was permitted to own more than seven acres.[17] Therefore, since most South Koreans farmed, and since most owned their land, most South Koreans were given an incentive to maximize output per acre.

Second, both the American Military Government and the successor Korean government stressed education. Nearly 80 percent of South Koreans were illiterate in 1945. Fewer than 30 percent were illiterate in 1960.[18] Most South Koreans became ready to apply more sophisticated production techniques.

A new government took office in 1961. It adopted policies encouraging more savings, more imports, more exports, and more direct foreign investment. It allowed interest rates to rise into the teens (partly to offset inflation), and domestic saving rose from 4 percent of GNP in 1963 to almost 17 percent in 1969.[19]

It reduced quotas and eliminated tariffs on raw materials imported for use in exports; it devalued the won. It changed tax laws to favor production efficiently earning a profit on exports. In 1962, it gave foreign investors a three-year tax holiday, a 50 percent tax cut for the five years following the holiday, and other favorable terms.[20]

Finally, the labor market was very much like that in Taiwan; no minimum wage laws, no obstructing unions.[21]

I have explained the boom as largely accounted for by Taiwan's taking advantage of her one cheap resource — labor... manufacturers were not inhibited from employing more labor by any wage regulation, industrial disorder, or restriction on sacking workers; in short, labor really was cheap.[22]

Between 1963 and 1975, manufacturing employment in South Korea grew 10.7 percent per year. Exports also grew. In 1960, exports comprised 3.3 percent of Korea's GNP; in 1977, the figure was 36 percent of GNP.

Import substitution accounted for [approximately] 21 percent of Korea's growth... during 1955-63 and none during subsequent periods. Export growth accounted for an estimated 10 percent in 1955-63, 22 percent in 1963-70, and 56 percent in 1970-73.... Thus, Korea is an extreme example of export-led growth.[23]

Between 1960 and 1977, the per capita GNP of Korea increased an average of 7.4 percent a year, rising from $244 in 1960 to $820 in 1977 (both figures in 1977 prices). Over the same 17-year period and in the absence of unions and minimum-wage laws, real wages rose an average of 7 percent a year.[24]

This export surge and economic development occurred while Korea maintained one of the world's most equal income distributions with nearly proportional taxes and almost no government efforts to redistribute income.[25] Finally, readers should note that Korea's leap into sustained development did not result from either the Vietnamese War or a surge of foreign aid. "Only a tiny fraction of South Korea's exports" was related to the Vietnamese War, and "the period of accelerated growth" was a "period of decreasing ... foreign aid."[26]

Argentina

In contrast with South Korea, Argentina is the eighth largest nation in the world. It is four times the size of Texas, is richly endowed with fertile land, ores, minerals, oil, and gas, but has only seven-tenths the population of South Korea. Nevertheless, over the past half century,

Argentina provides the classic model of how to inhibit economic development and foreign trade.

In 1929, Argentina was already semideveloped. In 1977 prices, per capita GNP was $1,365, seven times the 1953 figure for South Korea. Seventy-five percent of the population was literate.[27] During the early decades of this century, real urban and rural wages in Argentina were as high as or higher than in Western Europe.[28]

Argentina's income distribution has, for decades, been more equal than that of most nations. Yet, over the past half century, the Argentine government has concentrated on income redistribution. Programs transferring real income from urban workers to rural entrepreneurs and rentiers have alternated with programs transferring real income from rural entrepreneurs and rentiers to urban workers. The results are peculiar. For example, from 1957 to 1958, the real incomes of urban workers rose some 29 percent; from 1958 to 1959, they fell 39 percent![29]

In this persistent scuffle over division of the pie, government "reforms" have obstructed growth of the pie. Since 1929, import substitution has been protected by tariffs, quotas, and multiple exchange rates (the peso price of the dollar is higher to prospective importers the greater the protection government chooses to give to producers of a particular product). Further, something very close to xenophobia has led Argentineans to discourage foreign investment ever since 1929.[30] The greatest protection was provided to the oldest manufacturing industries, the lowest protection to the newest industries, an odd version of infant industry protection.

Protection was finally reduced in 1976. By 1977 the nominal rate of protection on manufacturing was *down* to 37 percent.

As a result of the government constraints, manufacturing exports have been kept tiny. In 1960, Argentina's manufacturing exports totaled $44 million worth, only 4 percent of the nation's total exports.[31]

As a further result of the government's constraints, economic development has been slow since 1929. In 1977 prices, per capita GNP was only $1,700 in 1977 compared with the $1,365 in 1929. The Argentinean per capita GNP was 40 percent of that of the U.S. in 1929. By 1977, it was down to 20 percent, cut in half through the effects of minimum wages, unions, tariffs, and quotas.[32]

HONG KONG: IN ORDER TO DEVELOP, A NATION NEEDS...

What *does* a nation need in order to develop? Political commentators and the conventional wisdom have stressed a number of factors which, we suggest, are not essential. Consider Hong Kong. It is known as a "city state," but it is in fact one of the world's *middle*sized nations in population and in output. Of the 125 members of the World Bank in 1979, 36 had populations smaller than Hong Kong's, and 75 had GNPs smaller than Hong Kong's.

What is essential for development? Is a temperate climate essential? Hong Kong is south of Havana, south of Calcutta, and south of almost all of Egypt and of Bangladesh.

Is rich agricultural land essential? Hong Kong embraces 400 square miles, part on the mainland, part on rocky islands, one of which is Hong Kong Island. Only 50 square miles are farmed. Some 50 square miles are built up. The other 300 are useless or nearly so.

Are rich natural resources essential — coal, gas, ores, minerals? Hong Kong has none. Yet, because Hong Kong has no trade restrictions, her residents have had access to all the world's resources at international prices.

Is foreign aid essential? Hong Kong was very poor in the 1950s. It took in millions of mostly poor refugees. Yet it received almost no foreign aid.

Is extensive government planning essential? The Hong Kong government has planned only its own narrow public service activities. Hong Kong has no central bank. Until the 1970s, it declined even to estimate GNP statistics.[33] The government does not direct production. It imposes few regulations on business. "Even in 19th-century terms, Hong Kong can be said to be the freest economic system on the planet."[34]

Is free trade essential? No. But Hong Kong, lacking many of the conventional "essentials," does have free trade in goods *and* in capital; and over the period 1960-77, real GNP per capita grew an average 6.5 percent a year.[35]

Finally, is stable government essential? Probably. Hong Kong does have that too.

PROBLEMS AND PROPOSALS
OF THE DEVELOPING NATIONS

We have briefly surveyed the successful economic development of several nations. We have shown, as in Tables 19-2 and 19-3, that on average LDCs have begun to change as rapidly as DCs. Yet many LDCs still show no signs of getting on paths clearly leading away from poverty.

OBSTACLES TO EXPORT GROWTH

Some of the constraints are internal. Many LDC governments are unstable, being rocked by frequent coups and countercoups. Few African heads of state are permitted to retire gracefully. Southern Africa and Central America host rural and urban guerillas. Such instability may discourage saving, investment, and development.

Some of the constraints are deliberate government policy. We have already described Argentina as a case in point. Many LDC governments promote economic inefficiency through elaborate subsidies, price controls, and regulations on domestic and foreign trade.

But LDC political leaders and some less biased observers cite external factors as important obstacles to the growth of LDC exports. We will now examine these factors.

Table 19-6 shows current-account imports and exports of non-oil-exporting LDCs over the years 1970-78. Imports persistently exceeded exports by 25-30 percent, reflecting capital imports. That capital movement can be encouraging but only to the extent that the capital imports contribute to expansion of efficient production.

TABLE 19-6 EXPORTS OF NON-OIL-EXPORTING
DEVELOPING NATIONS 1970-78

Year	Exports[a]	Imports[a]	Trade Balance[b]	Exports as Percent of World Exports[c]
1970	37.0	47.2	− 10.2	13.1
1971	38.6	53.0	− 14.4	12.2
1972	46.3	58.1	− 11.8	12.3
1973	67.4	79.7	− 12.3	12.9
1974	98.1	130.9	− 32.8	12.7
1975	94.0	138.4	− 44.4	11.8
1976	115.3	144.9	− 29.6	12.8
1977	135.2	163.6	− 28.4	13.2
1978	152.3	195.4	− 43.1	12.8

[a]Billions of U.S. dollars.
[b]Exports minus imports, billions of U.S. dollars.
[c]Not including exports of Centrally Planned Economies.
Source: International Monetary Fund, *International Financial Statistics*, various issues.

The non-oil-exporting LDCs' share of world trade remained roughly between 12 and 13 percent during the 1970s. But that represented a sizable decline from the 1953-55 average of about 21 percent. The industrialized nations increased their share of world exports from about 64 percent in 1953-55 to about 73 percent before the 1973-74 oil crisis. Since then, their share has dropped back to 66-69 percent. In contrast, the oil exporting nations' share of world exports has increased from the 1970-73 average of about 7 percent to a post-1973 average of about 14 percent. (The shares of total world exports — not including exports of Centrally Planned Economies — in 1978 were as follows: industrialized countries, 68.5 percent; nonindustrialized Europe, 4.1 percent; Oceania and South Africa, 2.6 percent; oil exporting countries, 11.9 percent; and non-oil LDCs, 12.9 percent.)[36]

What factors account for the slow growth of exports of the developing countries? First and foremost, their exports consist largely of primary products. With a few exceptions (notably petroleum), the world's demands for primary products have not increased as fast as have demands for manufactured goods. We are here of course talking about the low income elasticity of demand for primary products. That low income elasticity has been reinforced by the rapid development of numerous synthetic materials (e.g., synthetic rubber, rayon, and nylon). More and more natural raw materials have been replaced by the products of chemical industries using gas and oil as feedstocks. As for agricultural products, they are in general notoriously low in income elasticities of demand. Furthermore, agricultural industries in the developed nations are heavily subsidized and protected for political reasons. Agricultural exports from LDCs, therefore, face high tariff and quota walls.

In most LDCs, the most abundant factor of production is unskilled labor. The LDCs' comparative advantage, therefore, lies in unskilled-labor-intensive products using relatively little capital and requiring relatively unsophisticated technology. Low-grade cotton textile goods, pottery and ceramics, toys, footwear, and many other types of sundry goods typically found in five-and-ten-cents stores are often the only types of manufactured goods in which particular LDCs have comparative advantage. Unfortunately for these poor LDCs, the developed industrial nations have declining industries producing these same products. Therefore, imports of these goods from LDCs often become objects of protectionist measures.

DETERIORATION IN THEIR TERMS OF TRADE?

In the late 1950s, some economists — notably the Argentinean, Raul Prebisch — advanced a hypothesis that the terms of trade (i.e., the index of export prices divided by the index of import prices) of developing nations showed a persistent, long-run tendency to deteriorate. The Prebisch argument was based on the observed higher income elasticity of demand for manufactured than for primary goods. Therefore, given constant supplies, any increase in income raises the demand for and the price of manufactured goods (DC exports) more than the demand for and the price of primary products (LDC exports). Such price changes would move the terms of trade in favor of the DCs.

This argument was used to justify LDC withdrawal from the world market in favor of protection of import-substitution inefficiency. It has also been used to explain why not all LDCs develop, and it serves as one basis for LDC demands for special preferential treatment in trade relations with the developed world.

However, the Prebisch-type hypothesis of secularly deteriorating terms of trade of developing nations has not been supported by historical records. The non-oil-exporting LDCs' terms of trade improved in the late 1940s, declined sharply in the 1950s, and improved again in the 1960s. Figure 19-3 shows the movements of the terms of trade of both developing and industrial nations between 1961 and 1978. The LDCs' terms of trade generally improved throughout the 1960s and into the 1970s until they dropped sharply in 1974 and 1975 reflecting rising oil prices. They then recovered markedly in 1976 and 1977. Throughout the period shown, the change in the terms of trade was more favorable to developing than to industrial nations. With a greater degree of industrialization in the semi-industrial countries like South Korea and Taiwan, and with continued economic expansion of the industrial na-

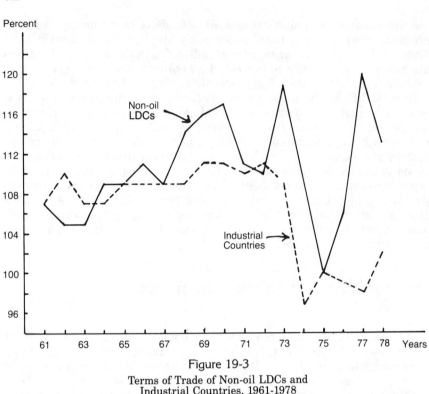

Figure 19-3

Terms of Trade of Non-oil LDCs and
Industrial Countries, 1961-1978

Source: International Monetary Fund, *International Financial Statistics*, various issues.

tions, world demands for industrial raw materials and foodstuffs will increase steadily and substantially in the decades to come. The current oil crunch may be a harbinger of an age of rising prices of raw materials of all sorts. If this prediction is correct, then we will witness secularly improving terms of trade for primary-product producing nations.

In 1974, inspired by the Prebisch hypothesis of secularly deteriorating LDC terms of trade, some 70 developing nations established a permanent agency of the United Nations known as the United Nations Conference on Trade and Development (UNCTAD) with Prebisch as the first Secretary-General. UNCTAD has been vocal in presenting to the developed world the LDCs' demands for a new deal in economic relations between rich and poor nations. In 1974, the United Nations General Assembly adopted, over some objections from industrial countries, a resolution entitled the *Declaration and Action Programme on the Establishment of a New International Economic Order*. The program called for actions, on the part of both LDCs and developed nations, concerning: (1) measures to improve the terms of trade for LDCs, (2) a new scheme to stabilize primary-product prices, (3) preferential access to the markets of the developed nations for LDC manufactured products, (4) the formation of raw-material producers' associations (export cartels), (5) fuller participation of LDCs in decision-making in the international monetary system, and (6) increased transfers of financial resources from the developed to the developing nations.[37]

SHORT-RUN FLUCTUATIONS IN EXPORT PRICES

Because both supply of and demand for primary commodities are in general price inelastic, short-run shifts in demand (such as those caused by business cycles in industrial nations) or short-run shifts in supply (such as those caused by weather variations) tend to generate sharp fluctuations in prices. Such price fluctuations cause wide year-to-year fluctuations in the export earnings of many developing nations that produce and export only a few primary products. Instability in export earnings, in turn, injects an element of instability and uncertainty into their overall development programs (planners are almost all reluctant to take responsibility for investing surpluses).

To deal with the "problem" of unstable primary-product prices. UNCTAD members voted in 1976 for an "integrated commodity program." It would involve creation of a common fund of about $6 billion to finance buffer stock operations for each of ten commodities including coffee, copper, cotton, rubber, and sugar. By international agreement involving both producing and consuming nations, an upper and a lower support level would be established for each commodity If, for example, the coffee price were to decline to its lower support level, funds borrowed from the common fund would be used to purchase coffee to be added to a buffer stock. If the price were to rise to the upper limit, coffee from the stock would be sold to reduce the price, and the proceeds would be returned to the common fund. Proponents assume that as prices of some commodities rise, those of others would fall. Thus, there would be substantial economy in the use of resources in the common fund. The total financial resources needed to stabilize the prices of the ten commodities would be much less than if each commodity price were to be stabilized from a separate fund.

Past experiences with commodity agreements cast doubt on the assumptions underlying the UNCTAD proposal. Since the end of World War II, there have been five major commodity agreements involving coffee, sugar, tin, wheat, and cocoa. Most used export quotas as the primary means to regulate prices. Most collapsed because of acute shortages or surpluses caused by weather variations or short-run shifts in demand. Only the tin agreement has utilized a buffer stock. Studies show the tin buffer stock has had little effect on the stability of the price of tin. The main problem is the smallness of the size of the buffer stock (i.e., due to the small size of the stabilization fund). The same studies show that, for an effective stabilization of the price of tin, a buffer stock six times larger than the present stock would be needed.[38]

Behind the demand for price stabilization is an implicit assumption that equates stable prices with stable revenue and rising welfare. A recent study criticizes that assumption. This study showed that if supply shifts were the cause of price instability, then price stabilization would raise total revenue and welfare of the commodity exporting country. But the study also showed that if demand shifts were the cause of price instability, then price stabilization would reduce the exporter's total revenue and welfare. The study concluded that, as producers, LDCs would benefit from stabilization of prices of only 5 commodities — sugar, coffee, cocoa, cotton, and jute — out of the 17 commodities examined.[39]

In view of discouraging experience with previous commodity agreements and given the inconclusive results of recent studies, industrial nations — which would be asked to contribute to the common fund — have been lukewarm toward the buffer stock proposal. They fear that much more than the proposed $6 billion would be ultimately required for successful operation of the buffer stocks. (Studies show that adequate stabilization of the copper price alone would require $6 billion.[40]) Developed-nation policy makers feel that such a large sum of capital could be used much more effectively if invested in developing nations' economies instead of being tied up in warehoused sugar or in piles of copper ore.

They also fear that a price stabilization program would degenerate into a price *support* program whose purpose would be to keep prices above equilibrium levels. Therefore, developed nations have accepted the idea of a $750 million common price-stabilization fund "in principle" largely to avoid antagonizing developing nations, but there has been little progress in negotiations that would bring cash to implement the proposal.

PROPOSALS FOR A GENERALIZED SYSTEM OF PREFERENCES (GSP)

Because of difficulties associated with primary exports, many developing nations have sought to increase their output and exports of manufactured goods as a source of stable and increasing foreign exchange earnings. But they have found their exports to developed nations impeded by protectionist walls. The structure of protection in industrial nations is particularly biased against these very labor-intensive goods in which LDCs enjoy comparative advantage. There are several reasons for this.

First, developing nations have been passive participants in negotiations for the tariff reductions taking place under the auspices of the General Agreement on Tariffs and Trade (GATT). A cardinal principle of GATT negotiations is the most-favored-nation (MFN) rule, under which bilateral tariff concessions are automatically extended to all GATT members without reciprocity. Since most LDCs have few concessions to offer, they have chosen in the past to settle for participation in the concessions exchanged among industrial nations. Since past tariff reductions have centered upon products which developed nations are interested in exporting, the unsophisticated products — in which LDCs have comparative advantage — have been left with relatively high effective tariff rates (review Chapter 10).

A more important reason why the industrial nations' tariff structure discriminates against LDCs lies in DC efforts to protect declining labor-intensive industries. For domestic political reasons, industrialized nations' governments protect their labor-intensive, low-technology industries — such as textile, apparel, and footwear industries — against competition from lower-priced imports. DC tariff rates on these products therefore tend to be much higher than the rates on unprocessed raw materials. In general, tariffs in industrial nations are higher the more comparative disadvantage they have in the products; this is because there is no need to protect industries that enjoy comparative advantage — they would develop export competitiveness without protection. In contrast, DC industries that once enjoyed comparative advantage but have lost it because of changes in relative factor supplies can exist only with protection. The structure of DC protection militates against optimum resource allocation throughout the world — by preserving inefficiency in developed nations and by impeding the development of light manufacturing industries in LDCs according to their comparative advantage.

To correct this anomaly, the LDCs demanded that developed nations levy lower tariff rates on manufactured exports from LDCs than on exports from developed nations. The idea is known as the Generalized System of Preferences (GSP); "general" in the sense that *all* industrial nations would accord the *same* preferential treatment to *all* manufactured exports of *all* developing nations. The LDCs, through UNCTAD, pushed the idea vigorously and persistently, until in 1970 the industrialized nations agreed to establish a version of the GSP.

In 1971, GATT waived the most-favored-nation rule for a period of ten years so DCs could grant preferential treatment to LDCs. Western Europe and Japan adopted their versions of the GSP in 1971-72, and the United States and Canada established theirs in 1976.

Unlike the "generalized" system originally envisioned, the systems actually established are narrow in coverage and differ greatly from one version to another. The European and Japanese versions use import ceilings to limit the quantity of duty-free entry. The U.S. GSP excludes such important products as textiles, footwear, steel, glassware, and watches from coverage. The U.S. GSP has no quantitative limitations, but preferences can be removed where the International Trade Commission finds a domestic industry being injured by increases in imports. These GSP schemes have had minimal effects on LDC exports. Studies show that LDC exports have been increased much more by GATT's multilateral negotiations than by the limited preferences accorded under the GSP.[41] This conclusion has led some economists to argue that the best chances for the LDCs to expand their exports lie not in seeking non-reciprocal, preferential treatment from developed nations but in searching out mutually beneficial tariff-reduction agreements with both developed and developing nations on the reciprocal, most-favored-nation principle.[42]

Within DCs, many leaders still argue for protection of comparative disadvantage domestic industry. The LDC advocates of the GSP are opting to join the world economy. Developed nation citizens can help the latter group by supporting GSP legislation.

CONCLUSION

What are the prospects for the LDCs in the 1980s? Many LDC citizens are still not participants in economic development. Some have no hope of significant change where they are. For example, those who eke out a living on the southern margin of the Sahara Desert will have to move if they are to escape recurrent starvation.

But most of the people in the world are now caught up in the development process. Not always, not everywhere, but in most places an association persists between economic development and international trade.

Many LDC politicians complain about commodity price fluctuations and about DC barriers to LDC exports of manufactures. But many LDCs are developing rapidly despite these problems.

Clearly, what happens within an LDC is mostly a function of the actions of its government and the behaviors of its residents. We have provided only a sample of the kinds of actions that LDC governments take that inhibit growth. Beyond some modest degree, import-substitution policies are anti-growth. So are indigenization programs. So in general are all government programs that restrain international movements of goods, services, and capital. During the 1980s, some of the 100 odd LDCs are sure to be much more effective than others in promoting development, but outsiders will have little influence on any of those governments.

Yet citizens of the industrial countries can influence LDC development. DC trade barriers do inhibit LDC growth. Though DC tariffs have been sharply reduced in recent decades, quotas — especially "voluntary" export quotas — are increasingly restrictive. An entirely new anti-LDC concept, "the reindustrialization of America," became prominent at both the Democratic and Republican 1980 presidential nominating conventions. For many, that concept calls for policies that will maintain old-line blue-collar manufacturing with semi-skilled workers making textiles, steel, autos, and toys. Lobbyists now speak of "the right to jobs" in what we know to be comparative disadvantage industries. How successful those lobbies will be we do not know. We do know that each success of those lobbies will be a failure for the aspiring LDC poor.

Among the LDCs' two-thirds of the world's population, half the people are under age twenty. If these children and youths are to lead lives slightly better than their parents', many must take jobs in manufacturing. If the DCs do not permit LDC manufacturing exports to expand, the LDCs will continue their misbegotten North-South alliance with OPEC countries that charge them heavily for the resource they will increasingly need, instead of lining up with the countries that have the technology and institutions they want. Commercial bankers in rich countries will have to write off debts to poor countries whose only hope of servicing the debt is to export the goods produced with the assets procured with those loans.[43]

The London *Economist* printed that warning in 1977. The issue is not yet resolved. In cannot be resolved by anyone's single decision. Rather, each month during the 1980s, DC governments will make decisions affecting LDC trade. In each case, special DC interests and the public's mercantilistic biases will be pitted against the welfare of the average American and of those aspiring LDC poor. Students who have read this book can expect to encounter many opportunities to explain the issues to other people.

STUDY QUESTIONS

1. Use a replica of Figure 19-1 to show the consequences if a subsistence farm family moves directly from autarchy to full comparative advantage specialization and trade. For a fancy bit of review, draw in the equilibrium terms-of-trade line and the family's indifference curve that will identify precisely the quantity the family will sell and the quantity it will buy.
2. What happened, between 1929 and 1937, to the tropical countries' terms of trade? The change must have been at least how big?
3. In the section headed "Exports as an Engine of Growth," the third paragraph begins, "Consider the many ways..." Which of the changes described in that paragraph and in the next paragraph will affect the *location* of the nation's production possibility frontier? Why, in each case, the effect you cite?
4. Would you attribute most of the recent growth in per capita output in South Korea to movements within the nation's production possibility frontier, along the frontier, or associated with movements of the frontier? The text does not provide proof for an unambiguous answer; so make the best case you can to support your answer.
5. Why, in a single world market, should Argentinean output per person fall while Hong Kong's output per person rises relative to American output per person? Give specifics, go beyond the text — and argue with the text — if you can.
6. Presumably, you have used the concept "marginal efficiency of capital" in other courses. What is the effect of the instability of LDC governments on the marginal efficiency of capital in LDCs? How does the cause-and-effect relationship operate so that change in the marginal efficiency of capital in LDCs will affect international investment flows?
7. Sketch supply and demand curves and Engel curves (plot income on the y axis, quantity on the x axis) and demonstrate the text's assertion, "given constant supplies, any increase in income raises the demand for and the price of manufactured goods...more than the demand for and the price of primary products."
8. Explain how productivity change could make one better off even while one's terms of trade deteriorated.

9. If you produced and sold a product whose price fluctuated widely from year to year, how might you handle your cash flow so you would not be cash short during years of low prices?
10. Suppose you are in charge of a buffer stock operation. How would your actions change if you were to shift from a price stabilization program to a price support program?
11. Why do developed nations pass laws to protect comparative disadvantage labor-intensive industries?
12. What groups would benefit from universal adoption of the proposed Generalized System of Preferences? Be specific, why would each group benefit? What groups would lose? Why?

ENDNOTES

1. Simon Kuznets, "Quantitative Aspects of Economic Growth of Nations: X. Level and Structure of Foreign Trade: Long Term Trends," *Economic Development and Cultural Change,* Part II, January 1967, p. 96.
2. *Ibid.,* pp. 98-99.
3. *Ibid.,* p. 102.
4. Ragnar Nurkse, *Equilibrium and Growth in the World Economy* (Cambridge, Mass.: Harvard University Press, 1961).
5. Irving Kravis, "Trade as a Handmaiden of Growth: Similarities between the Nineteenth and Twentieth Centuries," *Economic Journal,* December 1970, pp. 850-72 and "A Reply to Mr. Crafts' Note," *Economic Journal,* September 1973, pp. 885-88.
6. W. Arthur Lewis, *Tropical Development 1880-1913: Studies in Economic Progress* (Evanston, Ill.: Northwestern University Press, 1970).
7. W. Arthur Lewis, *Aspects of Tropical Trade 1883-1965,* the 1969 Wicksell Lectures, the University of Stockholm (Stockholm: Almquist & Wicksell, 1969), p. 11.
8. *Ibid.*
9. Lewis, *Tropical Development,* p. 23.
10. Lewis, *Aspects,* p. 8.
11. *Ibid.,* p. 12.
12. Richard Blackhurst et al., *Adjustment, Trade and Growth in Developed and Developing Countries* (Geneva: GATT, 1978), p. 17.
13. Alexander Gerschenkron, *Economic Backwardness in Historical Perspective* (Cambridge, Mass.: Harvard University Press, 1962), pp. 362-363, 151, 157 and 169-170.
14. Charles R. Frank, Jr. et al., *Foreign Trade Regimes and Economic Development: South Korea* (New York: Columbia University Press, 1975), p. 9.
15. Joel Bergsman, "Growth: A Tale of Two Nations, Korea and Argentina," *Report: News & Views from the World Bank,* May-June, 1980, p. 2.
16. *Ibid.*
17. Paul W. Kuznets, *Economic Growth and Structure in the Republic of Korea* (New Haven: Yale University Press, 1977), p. 130.
18. *Ibid.,* p. 92.
19. Frank et al., *Foreign Trade Regimes,* p. 17.
20. *Ibid.,* pp. 102-104.
21. Bergsman, "Growth" draws the parallel.
22. Ian Little, "Taiwan's Growth in an International Context," Chapter 7 in Walter Galenson, ed., *Economic Growth and Structural Change in Taiwan* (Ithaca: Cornell University Press, 1979), pp. 481-482.
23. Bergsman, "Growth," where he cites a World Bank draft by Yuji Kubo and J. Lewis.
24. *Ibid.*
25. *Ibid.,* p. 6.
26. Frank et al., *Foreign Trade Regimes,* p. 2.
27. Bergsman, "Growth," p. 1.

28. Carlos F. Diaz-Alejandro, *Essays on the Economic History of the Argentine Republic* (New Haven: Yale University Press, 1970), pp. 41-43.
29. Bergsman, "Growth," p. 3.
30. Laura Randall, *An Economic History of Argentina in the Twentieth Century* (New York: Columbia University Press, 1978), Chapter 8.
31. Bergsman, "Growth," p. 3.
32. *Ibid.,* p. 1.
33. Alvin Rabushka, *The Changing Face of Hong Kong* (Washington: American Enterprise Institute, 1973), pp. 23-28.
34. Theodore Geiger, *Tales of Two City-States: The Development Progress of Hong Kong and Singapore* (Washington: National Planning Association, 1973), p. 145.
35. The World Bank, *World Development Report, 1979* (Washington, D.C.: The World Bank, 1979), p. 127.
36. International Monetary Fund, *International Financial Statistics,* September 1979, p. 46.
37. United Nations General Assembly Resolution 3201 (S-VI) and 3202 (S-VI), 1 May 1974, reprinted in John Adams, ed., *The Contemporary International Economy: A Reader* (New York: St. Martin's Press, 1979), pp. 414-423. For a sympathetic interpretation of the New International Economic Order, see Carlos F. Diaz-Alejandro, "International Markets for LDCs — The Old and the New," *American Economic Review,* May 1978, pp. 264-269, reprinted in Adams, *Contemporary,* pp. 474-481.
38. Mordechai E. Kreinin and J.M. Finger, "A Critical Survey of the New International Economic Order," *Journal of World Trade Law,* November-December 1976, pp. 493-513, reprinted in Bela Balassa, ed., *Changing Patterns in Foreign Trade and Payments,* 3rd ed. (New York: W.W. Norton, 1978), pp. 126-149.
39. Ezriel M. Brook and Enzo R. Grilli, "Commodity Price Stabilization and the Developing World," *Finance and Development,* March 1977, pp. 8-11; reprinted in Adams, *Contemporary International Economy,* pp. 440-448.
40. Kreinin and Finger, "Critical Survey," in Balassa, *Changing Patterns,* pp. 140-141.
41. *Ibid.,* p. 133.
42. *Ibid.;* see also: Isaiah Frank, "Reciprocity and Trade Policy of Developing Countries," *Finance and Development,* March 1978, pp. 20-23, reprinted in Adams, *Contemporary International Economy,* pp. 433-439.
43. *Economist,* 16 July 1977, p. 84.

20

Two Other Subjects: Multinational Corporations and Communist State Trading

Two subjects remain to be covered. One, multinational corporations, represents behavior usually associated with responses to market forces. The other, state trading by agencies of communist governments, represents behavior largely insulated from markets. Each has advocates who believe the behavior of the one tends to optimize individual satisfactions and who believe the behavior of the other is generally injurious to individuals. Each reader must decide such normative issues for her- or himself.

MULTINATIONAL CORPORATIONS AND ECONOMIC DEVELOPMENT

A multinational corporation (MNC) is loosely defined as an enterprise operating in more than one nation. MNCs contribute to economic development in LDCs by bringing physical capital, improved technology, and managerial expertise to the LDCs. By doing so, they raise the average and marginal products of LDC labor.

There are many reasons why a business may choose to extend its operations across national boundaries. Some of the reasons have to do with sale of output: when IBM manufactures in Paris and when Honda manufactures in Marysville, Ohio, they are inside the tariff walls that might otherwise exclude them. Some of the reasons have to do with access to inputs: when a Japanese plant located in America in 1979, it gained access to subsidized energy; when American plants locate in Malaysia, they gain access to cheap labor. In all cases, of course, the basic motivation is the desire to earn a higher rate of return on capital. The effects of the multinationals' foreign investments may be seen more clearly through examination of a simplified example.

POGA POGA

Assume an island republic called Poga Poga, with some 50,000 people who make their living by fishing and farming. Output is low; per capita income is about $300 per year.

A foreign company then floats in a plywood-and-paper factory at a total cost of $10 million and with an expected life of 10 years. (Such a factory was actually built in Japan. It was towed round the Cape of Good Hope, and is now in operation well up the Amazon River.)

By this MNC action, capital flows — or, more precisely, in this case, floats — into Poga Poga. The Poganese balance of payments would show this capital inflow in this way:

	Imports	*Exports*
Current account:		
Merchandise	$10 million factory	
Capital account:		
Long Term		$10 million factory

In this case, as in most cases in which MNCs expand overseas operation, the firm makes a *direct investment,* i.e., it acquires a controlling share (in this example, 100 percent) of ownership in a foreign business. Once the MNC acquires the foreign business, the MNC may be impelled to provide managerial skills, appropriate technology, and training of local citizens, all in order to maximize its profits.

Assume that the new Poganese factory hires 1,000 Poganese then shows these figures for its first year of operation (in millions):

Total revenue from sales		$5.0
Total expenses		
Wages to Poganese	$0.5	
Logs, delivered from Africa	0.3	
Depreciation	1.0	
Fuel and foreign management salaries	0.2	
Sum		2.0
Return on capital (= 30%, pretax, on capital)		3.0

If Poga Poga taxes away one-third of the profit, the firm will clear 20 percent on its capital.

The new factory will contribute $5 million to the Poganese GDP. But only wages to the Poganese and taxes collected by Poga Poga will represent output of that nation's resources. Therefore, of the $5 million, only $1.5 million will count in Poga Poga's GNP, and $3.5 million will count in the GNP of other nations (see Chapter 6 for GNP and GDP definitions).

The Poganese balance of payments would show (in millions):

	Imports	*Exports*
Current account:		
Merchandise	$0.3 logs	$3.0 plywood
	0.1 fuel	2.0 paper
Services	0.1 management	
	2.0 use of capital	
Capital account:		
Long Term	1.0 repatriation	
Short Term	5.0 checking account	3.5 checking account

Most of the entries are straightforward except that the dividends are a service import, and the depreciation payment to the parent company involves an entry in short-term capital exports (the checking account payment) and an entry in long-term capital imports (a capital outflow, the reduction in value of the floating factory).

Direct investment takes place in search of higher rates of return for capital. Capital moves from a nation where it is relatively abundant to a nation where it is relatively scarce. Imported capital should raise the real output of the receiving nation more than it reduces the real output of the investing nation. As shown in Chapter 6, the net effect of free factor mobility is to equalize factor prices and raise real gross world product.

The plywood-paper plant could have been built to operate somewhere else where the company would have cleared about 20 percent on capital. But because the firm decided to locate the plant in Poga Poga, the Poganese receive $500,000 in wages. Since they volunteer to work in the plant, they indicate that they are better off there than in fishing or farming.

The benefits of direct investment in the host country often far exceed the immediate benefit of increases in real wages for the MNCs' employees. Direct foreign investments are almost always accompanied by inflows of technology and managerial and marketing skills. Output and income in the rest of the economy rise through linkage effects; other industries such as those supplying materials or providing transportation experience increased demand. Higher output and income may generate larger savings, which can contribute to the growth of the entire economy. Larger exports by the affected industries, as well as the capital inflow, help improve the host nation's balance of payments. There are also external benefits such as MNC training of laborers and managers.

THE OBSOLESCING BARGAIN AND INDIGENIZATION

Before the parent firm decided where to locate the factory, the Poga Poga government might have been eager to attract the firm, its $500,000 payroll, and its other potential benefits to Poga Poga. The firm, at that stage, would see Poga Poga as only one among dozens of possible locations for the new plant. If Poga Poga's representatives could convince company officials that Poga Poga would be likely to be the best choice, the company representatives would sit down with Poga Poga officials (perhaps from the Ministries of Planning, Treasury, Agriculture, Commerce, and Foreign Trade) to discuss the terms that would apply to this plant if it were to be located in Poga Poga. The company might be conducting similar talks in several other countries. The negotiations would, at a minimum, cover taxes, import duty exemptions, and labor practices. During this bargaining preceding the firm's selection of the Poga Poga site, the government might be glad to grant the firm privileges; and the 33⅓ percent tax rate might look very good to that government. But later, after the plant is established, the government perspective may change.

The company is exporting a $5 million output each year. The Poganese receive $500,000 in wages and $1 million in taxes. The company collects $1 million in depreciation and $2 million in profit.

Government officials and Poganese academics may begin to covet the firm's revenue. Proposals may be made to obtain more of the firm's profit. The phenomenon of the *obsolescing bargain* will have appeared.[1] The bargain, which the host government accepted to obtain the plant, will have begun to obsolesce in the eyes of that government. With the plant in hand, the Poganese will begin to want more than that original bargain will give them. Commentators may even complain that the company is "taking $3 million out of the country each year," that it is "taking out more money than is being put into the country" and that it is "taking out capital and failing to reinvest in the country." These commentators seldom mention the benefits accruing to the host nation in the forms of improvements in its balance of payments, increased tax revenues, wages earned by local workers, and all the external benefits derived from the venture.

Were the plant fastened in the ground, the government might throw out the old bargain and impose new taxes and obligations on the firm. If the plant is on pontoons and the Poganese navy is small, the company may escape new demands. In most LDCs, the obsolescing bargain appears, and the outcome depends upon the mobility of the firm.

The Poga Poga government might take another tack. Local academics and journalists might complain about "foreign dominance" by the plywood plant. The government might then raise enough money, say $10 million, to buy the local plant *or* to bring in a second plant and, in the latter case, to double manufacturing employment in the country. The usual meaning of "indigenization" in recent decades has been to buy out the foreign owners of an existing plant rather than to add to employment, output, and growth by building a new plant. Indigenization is now commonplace and goes by such mellifluous local names as Malaysianization and Nigerianization. Unfortunately, for the LDC poor, indigenization means that the LDCs export capital *to* the DCs (the LDCs must export goods and services in exchange for imported title to the foreign plant). The LDC poor workers necessarily suffer when government deliberately holds down manufacturing employment and output in order to gain indigenous title to the existing plant.

EXPANSION AND DIVERSIFICATION OF MNC INVESTMENT

Between 1971 and 1975, direct overseas investments outstanding by U.S. corporations rose from $83.0 billion to $133.2 billion in terms of yearend book values. During the same period, the yearend book values of foreign MNCs' direct investments in the United States increased from $13.9 billion to $26.7 billion. Of the $133.2 billion U.S. direct investment, $31.2 billion were in Canada, $49.6 billion were in Western Europe, and $3.3 billion were in Japan. Thus, roughly two-thirds of America's direct foreign investments were in the developed industrial areas.[2]

America's direct investment activities were in high gear during the 1960s. Corporations found overseas costs — both materials and labor — substantially lower than in the United States, largely due to overvaluation of the dollar under the fixed exchange-rate system. The situation changed markedly in the early 1970s with the floating of major currencies. The overvaluation of the dollar and the counterpart undervaluation of some major currencies were corrected more or less; and, as a consequence, the outflow of direct investment from the United States slowed down considerably. Between 1965 and 1973, America's direct investment measured as a percentage of the same year's export value averaged 14 percent. Between 1974 and 1978, the comparable figure was 7.3 percent.[3]

Not only the *size* of direct investment, but also its *direction,* has changed appreciably in recent years. The substantial appreciation of the West European currencies vis-à-vis the U.S. dollar has made U.S. labor and materials relatively less expensive than in the 1960s. The United States also offers cheaper energy than Europe and Japan. With the slowing down of European and Japanese growth rates, the United States has become relatively more attractive for foreign MNC investments. Some semideveloped countries such as Taiwan, South Korea, Spain, and Brazil have also become attractive investment targets for American, European, and Japanese capital.

Thus, the U.S.-based MNCs are retreating from Europe and expanding operations elsewhere. In 1977, America's direct investment in Europe and direct disinvestment from Europe roughly equaled, while in the same year America's direct investment in the world other than Europe exceeded direct disinvestment from those areas by nearly $5 billion dollars. Direct investment in the United States by foreign MNCs, on the other hand, increased threefold (from about $2 billion to nearly $6 billion) between 1972 and 1978.[4]

In 1979, direct foreign investments in the United States were estimated to total at least $40 billion, while American companies' direct investments abroad were estimated at $155 billion. Each was increasing at an annual rate of about $6 billion. Foreign direct investments in the United States were therefore increasing at a faster rate than was American direct investment abroad. Two primary motives for foreign companies' investments in the United States are the depreciated dollar and the growing protectionist sentiments in the United States. These developments have made producing in the United States both more economical and more secure than continuing to produce at home to export to America.[5]

Many foreign companies' American operations have been successful. For example, the American subsidiary of France's Pechney Ugine Kuhlmann — producer of steel and nonferrous metals — in 1978 contributed 98 percent of the company's worldwide profits while providing less than one-fifth of sales. Japan's Sony produced 40 percent of the company's $800 million 1978 sales in the United States at its San Diego plant. It also successfully exported color television sets to Latin America and magnetic tape to both Europe and Japan.[6] With greater flexibility of exchange rates and diminished growth potential in Europe and Japan, direct investments by foreign MNCs in the United States are expected to grow. More important, perhaps, are the expected increases in the flows of direct investment from the United States, Europe, Japan, and some OPEC nations to some of the developing nations that hold great promise of high growth and profitability. Factors that make a nation attractive as a prospective area of direct investment include: large and expanding domestic markets, an educated and disciplined labor force, low wage rates, cheap energy and other raw materials, and political stability.

Nations that exhibit these characteristics are able to attract MNC direct investments. Malaysia is one such nation that demonstrates the growing diversification of MNCs by nation of origin. By the summer of 1978, 10 MNCs based in Italy, 60 based in India, and 220 based in Japan were operating in Malaysia, a country of 13 million people.[7] That diversification will continue as more LDCs succeed in attracting MNCs and as semideveloped countries send forth more and more of their own MNCs.

STATE TRADING

From about 1890 until 1914, European Russia was the most rapidly developing of the then LDCs.[8] That development took place largely in response to market forces. After the October Revolution of 1917, Russia opted out of the world's market system. Since 1917, Russian economic development and that of other Centrally Planned Economies (CPEs) have had to manage without the pricing signals provided by markets.

This book deals primarily with trade and payments within the market-oriented (or capitalist) world. Because of the fundamental differences that exist between the economic systems of capitalist nations and

the Centrally Planned Economies, trade (and payments) relations between a capitalist nation and a CPE, or those between CPEs, cannot be
subjected to the tools of analysis developed in this book (e.g., the principles of comparative costs, and the demand-and-supply analysis of foreign exchange markets). Discussions of the ideology, economics, and
institutions of CPEs are beyond the scope of this book. This section
limits itself to very brief descriptions of (1) international trade practices
of the Soviet Union, and (2) the trade relations between CPEs.

INTERNATIONAL TRADE PRACTICES OF THE SOVIET UNION[9]

In the Soviet Union, foreign trade is conducted exclusively by a state
trade monopoly. The Ministry of Foreign Trade manages this monopoly
through its 60 or so foreign trade corporations. Each of these corporations is a legal entity capable of signing a contract with a foreign firm.
Each foreign trade corporation specializes in exports and imports of a
given product category (e.g., *Traktoroexport* deals in farming and road
building equipment). An import contract signed by a Soviet foreign
trade corporation with a foreign firm may specify a settlement in a hard
currency, an in-kind (barter) payment, or an extension of credit by the
exporting firm, its bank, or its government. One form of the barter-
payment method may involve the exporter in a "counter purchase" of
Soviet products. An increasingly common practice is for the foreign
exporter to be paid in the goods produced in the joint-production or
joint-exploration venture.

What motivates a Soviet planner to want to export or import? To
answer this question, one must first understand the peculiarities of the
Soviet planning system. First, Soviet prices do not accurately reflect the
scarcity values (or opportunity costs) of different goods. This is because
Soviet prices are determined on the basis of the labor theory of value
which has long been discarded in the West as archaic and incomplete.
According to this theory, prices should reflect only the quantity of labor
embodied in each product; the "productivity" of capital is not recognized. Moreover, the theory does not allow demand (or use value) conditions to affect prices. Since prices do not represent opportunity costs,
prices cannot be used to calculate comparative costs. This makes it
difficult for Soviet planners to ascertain which goods they can most
advantageously export or import.

The second peculiarity of the Soviet system is the method of supply
planning based primarily on the physical quantity of goods, with prices
serving no resource-allocation function. For each product, planners
seek balance between "sources" (largely production) and "uses" (largely
consumption and investment). Whenever there develop planned or un-
planned shortages in a product category, planners try to close the gap by
importing. Contrarily, planned "sources" may exceed planned "uses" in
some product categories. The planners then want to dispose of the
surplus by exporting.

Basically, the Soviet planner prefers autarchy to international trade. Trade is used as a convenient means to close the gap in the "materials balance" method of planning, but it is regarded as a necessary evil. (Like weather, foreign trade can inject an element of uncertainty into the planning process, disrupting hard-to-achieve balances.) This is why Soviet planners prefer bilateral barter — needed imports paid for by exports of "surplus" goods. Payments of hard currencies for imports — earned by the Soviets by exports of surplus goods or of gold — are made only when the foreign exporters are not willing to accept payments in kind.

In Soviet foreign trade practices, the domestic (official) ruble prices of the traded goods and services are irrelevant. In the first place, as pointed out earlier, Soviet prices are arbitrary and irrational, reflecting neither relative costs nor relative use values. Secondly, meaningful comparison of domestic and world prices is impossible because the ruble exchange rates are arbitrarily and politically set with little economic significance. (Since there is no international trading in rubles, the value of the ruble in terms of foreign currencies cannot be determined.) Soviet foreign trade is conducted in terms of prevailing world prices, and the Soviet foreign trade corporations are subsidized or taxed according as they incur losses or earn profits due to the discrepancy between the domestic and world prices.

COMECON AND INTRA-BLOC TRADE

What is the nature of the trade relations between CPEs? Here we briefly examine the economic relations between the Soviet Union and its East European trading partners.[10]

In January 1949, the Council for Mutual Economic Assistance (COMECON) was formed under Soviet leadership. The stated objective of the new organization was to promote coordination and integration of economic activities among East European socialist nations. In fact, the Soviet Union intended to use the organization as a vehicle for coordinating the supply planning of CPE nations on the basis of a "socialist division of labor." This division of labor turned out to mean a scheme of specialization between the more and the less developed nations within the bloc. Specifically, the more industrially developed nations (the Soviet Union, East Germany, and Czechoslovakia) would supply industrial goods to the less developed countries (Romania and Bulgaria) in exchange for the latters' supply of agricultural products. This strategy met with strong resistance from the less developed bloc countries which felt that their chances of rapid industrial development would be hampered by such a division of labor.

Intra-COMECON trade in a given year is conducted on the basis of the average of the world prices of the five preceding years. Bookkeeping is done using a unit of account called the transferable ruble (or COMECON ruble), the purpose of which is to facilitate intra-bloc multilateral clearance of trade balances. In actual practice, however, trade among COMECON members remains largely bilateral. Bilateralism is necessary to minimize uncertainty in each nation's supply planning. If, for example, the transferable rubles earned by nation A in exports to nation B were spent by nation A on imports from a third nation C, then C's supply planning would face an unexpected and unforeseen disruption. There is thus a tendency for every member of COMECON to spend transferable rubles bilaterally. In recent years, 'more than 90 percent of all intra-COMECON trade has been settled bilaterally.[11]

The use of world prices for intra-bloc trade does not mean that such trade takes place according to the principles of comparative costs. In order to take advantage of specialization and to gain from trade, each nation must adapt its trading and production patterns to relative prices prevailing in the world. Specifically, each nation must find in which goods it has relatively low opportunity costs. This would be very difficult for a centrally planned economy since its domestic prices and exchange rate do not accurately reflect cost and demand factors. Even if such calculations were feasible, the economic planners would probably not let comparative-cost considerations dictate their production and investment decisions because that would mean abandoning planning autonomy. As mentioned earlier, the worst enemies of central planning are said to be weather and free foreign trade.

The sharp rises in the price of oil since 1974 have generated a strain in the trade relations within COMECON. Since intra-bloc prices are adjusted to world prices with a lag of several years, the Soviet Union — the major supplier of oil to the bloc nations — finds it is selling oil to COMECON members at a price substantially lower than the price it can get in the world market. Since the Soviet Union needs hard currencies for importing goods and technology from the West, it has set a limit on the amount of oil it provides to the COMECON members. This has compelled the East European nations to seek additional supplies of oil in the world market, which has meant they need more hard currency. To earn hard currencies, the East European nations must now sell more goods to the West. This increase in the volume of trade between the East European nations and the rest of the world has resulted in a lessening of economic integration within the COMECON bloc.

OPEC's impact on COMECON appeared to be growing during 1980. Russia raised its oil prices to the Eastern European states as OPEC lifted its prices. The Eastern countries were therefore obliged to send more units of their output to Russia per barrel of oil imported. Greater exports to the east promised fewer exports to the west for the machinery and technological advice the Eastern Bloc countries were seeking to accelerate growth. Presumably, no matter how great the strains within COMECON, caused by this deterioration in the terms of trade of Russia's partners, COMECON will survive.

STUDY QUESTIONS

1. Show the balance of payments entries for Poga Poga when the government implements Poganization and buys the plant from the MNC. Show Poga Poga making real payment, perhaps in fish and copra (payment with Poganese money would leave the MNC with the same dollar-valued claim on Poga Poga as when the MNC held title to the plant).
2. Show the balance-of-payments entries for Poga Poga if its government, instead of Poganizing the MNC's plant, buys and imports a second $10 million plant.

    Following this action, how would Poganese wages compare with wages given your answer to question 1? Why the difference?
3. The text reports $5 billion in American direct investment outside Europe and about $5 billion in foreign direct investment in the United States during 1977. Show how these transactions appear in the American balance of payments.
4. Consider the case of a Japanese firm involved in a joint venture to produce oil in Russia. Assume the Japanese firm earns a $1 million-a-year return on the project. Show the Japanese balance-of-payments entries when the Russians pay the Japanese MNC with "goods produced in the joint-production venture."
5. Why can "the value of the ruble in terms of foreign currencies" *not* be determined? There *is* a ruble black market. Our hint: What portion of trade goes through the black market?
6. What are the "accomplishments" of COMECON?

ENDNOTES

1. For a brief analysis of the factors affecting the obsolescing bargain, see Raymond Vernon, "The Future of Multinational Enterprise in Developing Countries," in Stephen Guisinger, *Private Enterprise and the New Global Economic Challenge* (Indianapolis: Bobbs-Merrill Educational Publishing, 1979), pp. 4-9.
2. *International Economic Report of the President, 1977* (Washington, D.C.: Government Printing Office, 1977), pp. 161 and 163.
3. International Monetary Fund, *International Financial Statistics,* various issues.
4. "Neo-Mercantilism in the 80's: The Worldwide Scramble to Shift Capital," *Business Week,* 9 July 1979, pp. 50-54.
5. Hugh D. Menzies, "It Pays to Brave the New World," *Fortune,* 30 July 1979, pp. 86-91.
6. *Ibid.*
7. *Malaysia: Your Profit Centre in Asia* (Kuala Lumpur: Federal Industrial Development Authority, 1978), pp. 22-23.
8. Raymond Goldsmith, "The Rate of Growth in Tsarist Russia, 1860-1913," *Economic Development and Cultural Change,* April 1961, pp. 462-463.
9. For a general survey of the characteristics of Soviet foreign trade, see: Franklyn D. Holzman, "Foreign Trade Behavior of Centrally Planned Economies," in Henry Rosovsky, ed., *Industrialization in Two Systems: Essays in Honor of Alexander Gerschenkron* (New York: John Wiley & Sons, 1966); Howard J. Sherman, *The Soviet Economy* (Boston: Little, Brown and Co., 1969), chap. 8; U.S. Congress, *Soviet Economy in a New Perspective,* Joint Economic Committee, 94th Cong., 2nd sess., 14 October 1976 (Washington, D.C.: Government Printing Office, 1976), pp. 81-96 and 677-738; and Paul R. Gregory and Robert C. Stuart, *Soviet Economic Structure and Performance* (New York: Harper & Row, 1974), chap. 8.

10. For discussions of trade relations between the Soviet Union and East European nations, see: Franklyn D. Holzman, *International Trade under Communism: Politics and Economics* (New York: Basic Books, 1976); and U.S. Congress, *East European Economies Post-Helsinki,* Joint Economic Committee, 95th Cong., 1st sess., 25 August 1977 (Washington, D.C.: Government Printing Office, 1977), pp. 135-173.

11. U.S. Congress, *East European Economies Post-Helsinki,* pp. 136-137 and 168.

INDEX